Freud and His Patients

DOWNSTATE PSYCHOANALYTIC INSTITUTE
TWENTY-FIFTH ANNIVERSARY
SERIES

Mark Kanzer, M.D., General Editor

Volume   I. Mark Kanzer, M.D. and Jules Glenn, M.D., Editors
Volume II. Mark Kanzer, M.D. and Jules Glenn, M.D., Editors
Volume III. Shelley Orgel, M.D. and Bernard D. Fine, M.D., Editors
Volume IV. Joseph T. Coltrera, M.D., Editor

Freud and His Patients

Volume II
Downstate Psychoanalytic Institute
Twenty-Fifth Anniversary
Series

edited by
Mark Kanzer, M.D., and Jules Glenn, M.D.

New York • Jason Aronson • London

PREFACE TO THE SERIES

Freud's royal road to the unconscious was the dream. However, as the father of psychoanalysis, his legacy to all included a far broader royal road, psychoanalysis itself, which pointed the way to the understanding of the psychology of man. Could even Freud himself have envisioned the complex routes taken by the discipline he fathered, its influences upon the arts and social sciences as well as practically every form of psychotherapy? Could he have foreseen the many tasks required of psychoanalytic institutes and psychoanalytic educators?

Psychoanalytic education with its many demands could well be a full-time job, yet it has so far been able to enjoy the wise luxury of requiring that its educators also have a firm footing in clinical psychoanalysis; that its teachers also be, often full time, clinical practitioners. The benefits of this somewhat anachronistic tradition have been considerable, but the price has been high. Psychoanalytic teachers must attend to their patients and then search for precious hours with which to plan, organize, and accomplish their teaching mission. Is it a mission in the full sense? Perhaps not, but it can be a most compelling and fulfilling aspect of one's career, as it has been for those of us who have been part of the Downstate Psychoanalytic Institute.

The Institute, founded by Drs. Howard Potter and Sandor Lorand, and itself parent to, and later in some respects child of, the Psychoanalytic Association of New York, has been shameless in its demands on the time and energy of its members. And yet it has become a part of us, a structuring part of our professional identity, of our self systems, and, by extension, an important and loved foundation of our professional family ties.

Absorbed in this demanding relationship, we were surprised to discover that this parent-child to us all, so warmly and ambivalently loved, in the sense that all such love is ambivalent, would in 1974 celebrate its twenty-fifth birthday.

We had a new task: to determine how a twenty-fifth anniversary of a psychoanalytic institute should most appropriately be acknowledged. There were to be, of course, the usual celebrations and testimonials. But these excellent occasions, relatively private gatherings, occur and become memories.

Perhaps more important are the desirable group self-observations and developmental evaluations. A psychoanalytic institute should, first and foremost, educate graduates who are able practitioners of psychoanalysis. But while this may be a necessary and wholesome criterion of adequate accomplishment, by itself it scarcely represents excellence. For it is always a hope that among the graduates will be some with the creative spark enabling them to make original scientific contributions. Even this is not enough: a healthy institute must also provide the systems and structures which enable its teaching programs to continue and develop, constantly supplementing courses and faculty with new ideas and new people. Ultimately, older faculty members will retire, and new teachers must be available. Finally, the institute must be able to take its place, as well as should its members individually, within the scientific and professional community.

Evaluating these steps according to a rough timetable, one could say that by age ten a psychoanalytic institute should be able to point to a growing body of graduates beginning to participate scientifically and organizationally on local levels and beyond. From years ten to twenty the institute's own graduates should be able to form the core first of the teaching faculty and then of the training analysts of the institute. Eventually, the administrative positions of the institute should be filled by its own graduates, who by this time have had the the chance to gain experience at these tasks. At twenty-five, Downstate has completed these steps, though happily without the parochial rigidity which might otherwise have precluded a welcome to talented and congenial colleagues from other programs who wished to join and enrich us.

We of the Downstate Psychoanalytic Institute are pleased with the quality of our programs and our graduates. We believe that we have accomplished these goals while creating a cohesive psychoanalytic group with a shared commitment to ideals which in no way detracts from the individual styles of its members. We hope that we are not complacent in our judgment that the goals for the first twenty-five years have been achieved well.

After all the anniversary celebrations, there was still the feeling that something more should be done. For this we have turned, through these volumes, to our colleagues, that we might share with them through their work an affirmation of our ideals as analysts—as observers, seekers of knowledge, enlighteners, and helpers. We hope that these four Anniversary Volumes will, through the work of the members of Downstate Psychoanalytic Institute, provide a glimpse of what we all treasure so much about our Institute: an atmosphere where we can work together pursuing our common goals individually and collectively, inspiring one another and enriching the creative capacity of all. The Downstate Institute has offered such an atmosphere. In return we offer these volumes as an expression of our gratitude for its existence and its excellence.

There are many people to whom we are indebted for their work on these volumes; only a few can be singled out for their contributions. Dr. Mark

Kanzer, General Editor, comes first. He has been not only a wise editor but a stimulator of new ideas and contributions. The only problem was to limit his efforts, for his quest for excellence and his productivity know no bounds. Dr. Jules Glenn was his able assistant overall and co-editor with him for Volumes I and II. Drs. Shelley Orgel and Bernard Fine were co-editors for Volume III, Dr. Joseph Coltrara editor for Volume IV. Each of them gave many hours of enlightened editorial advice to authors and fellow editors alike. It was a pleasure to work with all of them

We are grateful to the Department of Psychiatry of the Downstate Medical Center for providing our Institute its home, and to Drs. Howard Potter and those after him who chaired the Department of Psychiatry during these twenty-five years.

Special thanks are due to Drs. Robert Savitt, Merl Jackel, and Samuel Lanes, Presidents of the Psychoanalytic Association of New York during the years that these volumes were in preparation. It was the understanding sponsorship of the Psychoanalytic Association of New York that allowed this project to get under way. More than special thanks are due also to Drs. Howard Potter and Sandor Lorand for their instrumental role in the formation of the Downstate Institute, and to Drs. Sylvan Keiser, Mark Kanzer, Sidney Tarachow, William Console, Maurice Friend, Leonard Shengold, and Roy Lilleskov, and to Miss Vera Krassin and all those others who have worked so hard to help the Institute grow and prosper. Finally, we are indebted to all of the candidates and to all of the faculty members who, collectively, made the Downstate Institute such a wonderful place to work, to teach, and to learn.

Alan J. Eisnitz, M.D.
Director, Downstate Psychoanalytic Institute 1972–1975
Chairman, Editorial Board, 25th Anniversary Series

Postscript: After these volumes were completed and the above preface written, an important change occurred to our Institute. As conditions in Brooklyn, and more specifically at the Downstate Medical Center, no longer favored the continued development of psychoanalytic education there, it was decided to move.

On July 1, 1979 The Psychoanalytic Institute transferred its affiliation to the New York University Medical Center. This entailed moving the offices and classes to Bellevue Psychiatric Hospital in Manhattan. While we now have a new name—The Psychoanalytic Institute at New York University

Medical Center—and a new home, the candidates, faculty, and administra
tion remain the same. We are still the same psychoanalytic institute.

To extend Dr. Eisnitz's developmental analogy further, we can say that the
Institute had achieved the degree of independence and autonomy which
permitted it to leave home when that departure was indicated. We now look
forward to our new affiliation with New York University in hopeful
anticipation that our spirit and our accomplishments will continue as before.

In a sense, therefore, these volumes not only celebrate the anniversary
which occasioned their preparation, but are also a tribute to our thirty years at
the Downstate Medical Center.

Roy K. Lilleskov, M.D.
Director, Downstate Psychoanalytic Institute 1978–1979
Director, The Psychoanalytic Institute
at New York University Medical Center

CONTENTS

PART I
INTRODUCTION

PART II
DORA

PART III
LITTLE HANS

PART IV
THE RAT MAN

PART V
THE SCHREBER CASE

PREFACE

Freud's case histories constitute a major part of the analytic tradition. "Dora," "Little Hans," "The Rat Man," "The Wolf Man," and Judge Schreber" transcend the boundaries of the clinical and assume legendary proportions as part of the human heritage. The techniques Freud used and the conclusions he drew were often superseded before he reported his findings. What remains is the stamp of his genius as he found his way into territories of the human mind that none had explored before. We hope to set forth some of the significance of these explorations in a form that will be useful to teachers and students not only of psychoanalysis but of the broadest aspects of human relationships as well.

Although articles and books on each of these cases have previously been published individually, the present volume is the first to include studies of all the case histories. We have attempted this re-evaluation of Freud's work within an integrated frame work.

As the preceding volume of the Downstate Anniversary Series, *Freud and His Self-Analysis,* has shown, Sigmund Freud possessed even in adolescence the remarkable ability to "mercilessly dissect" his own feelings. At the same time he was capable of turning an equally critical and understanding eye upon other human beings, contemporary as well as historic or fictional. These tendencies, combined with his literary talents, gave him an affinity and often an identification with great literary figures (Kanzer 1976). The circumstances of his life drew him, however, to science, medicine and ultimately to the treatment of nervous disorders and the establishment of the science of the operations of the unconscious mind. His recognition of the accidental in his career (what others might have called fate) was stated in the indirectly autobiographical appraisal of another genius, Leonardo da Vinci. The closing lines of the da Vinci manuscript bear the stamp of Freud's own thinking and style: "The apportioning of the determining factors of our life between the 'necessities' of our constitution and the 'chances' of our childhood may still be uncertain in detail; but in general it is no longer possible to doubt the importance precisely of the first years of our childhood. We all still show too little respect for Nature which (in the obscure words of Leonardo which recall Hamlet's lines) 'is full of countless causes—*ragioni*—that never enter exprience! Every one of us human beings corresponds to one of the countless experiments in which these *ragioni* of nature force their way into experience" (Freud 1910, p. 137).

As Freud sought to clarify the *ragioni* within the mind, his laboratory—though always universal—increasingly came to be the "analytic situation" that he devised to follow the interchanges between his patients and himself as he sought simultaneously to understand and to cure their mental ailments. A new type of scientific report came into being, one which brought into focus the personality of the investigator as well as that of his subject. The essentials of drama were inherent in these interchanges and we find that empathy as well as merciless dissection were the necessary equipment of the investigator. When a patient described a dream, Freud thought back to his spontaneous and scientific interest in his own dreams before he became a therapist and was prepared to see in these communications important data that were to be taken with the utmost seriousness. He would think of similar dreams of his own, so that these "uncanny" phenomena were resolved into meaningful manifestations of unconscious thought that were both self-analytic and remarkably informative about his patients. Scientific laws about dreaming and mental processes resulted and ultimately the most daring and universal of all formulations about the mind—the principle of psychic determinism—was formulated. The principle of psychic determinism holds that no idea is accidental or meaningless but belongs in a context determined by the experiences that anteceded it. The mind was no longer a haven of free will, as it might subjectively seem, but part of the workings of Nature which must be fully respected. On such a basis the origin and cure of symptoms could be formulated; beyond that, child rearing, education and all aspects of thought were opened to possibilities that were more than reward for the loss of the illusory freedom of the will.

Freud's case reports record the exchanges with his patients on which a new view of mankind—comparable to those of Copernicus or Darwin—was founded. Freud noted without apology that they were comparable to the work of novelists, but maintained that he could find no more scientific way of rendering available the complexity of the mind. At the same time he recognized that great novelists and playwrights were keen psychologists and self-analysts and that their affinities were comparable to differing routes taken by travelers as they pressed toward the same goal.

Our volume, in discussing the case histories of Freud, attempts no systematic or comprehensive review. As part of the Downstate Anniversary series, its pragmatic point of departure lies in the random studies made over the past twenty-five years by individual members of the faculty in pursuing the aims of updating or commenting on the original cases in relation to newer developments in clinical and theoretical psychoanalysis. New studies have been written especially for the present volume. Problems in teaching students were also a factor in our selections as was the uncovering of new material relating to the cases. We have underlined the basic organization of these papers by including integrative summaries at the end of the sections on each of the cases. A final summary of the entire volume provides a synthesis of the historical, technical and conceptual aspects of all the case histories.

Another aim has been strengthened by our preceding volume: to trace in the case histories material relevant to Freud's own personality both for biographical reasons and to remark its influence on the course of the treatment. This last aim is the most speculative—but speculative, it is hoped, in the tradition of psychoanalysis and to be validated by its usefulness to the reader.

In the case histories Freud himself sometimes takes the lead in commenting on his own reactions and pointing to analogies in his personal life. His metaphors are a source of information whose potentialities have scarcely been touched. Extensive biographical studies on Freud have illuminated his relationships to his patients. All these avenues to insight have been explored in the present volume in special articles that seek to elucidate the portions of the case histories stamped with the unique features of Freud's own personality so that we will be better able to understand the patients as well as the investigator who created psychoanalysis.

Our acknowledgments and gratitude are also due in the highest degree to Dr. Alan Eisnitz, Director of the Downstate Psychoanalytic Institute in 1974, who conceived the idea of the anniversary volumes and has promoted them on every level, including the editorial, where his insistence on anonymity must reluctantly be accepted. Downstate takes pride in the fact that Dr. Eisnitz was the first (and Drs. Leonard Shengold, Roy Lilleskov the second and third) director to date who was wholly trained within its own facilities.

Dr. Shengold's article in our earlier volume struck an appropriate note for the celebration to which these works are dedicated—the university and medical settings as traditional backgrounds for the broad viewpoints inherent in the historical development of psychoanalysis and of Freud himself.

We wish to thank Doris Main, Deborah Tax, Gerri Bevaro and Jeanine Simonelli for their valuable secretarial services.

Dr. Glenn especially appreciates the help and encouragement of his wife, Sylvia Glenn, during the years that *Freud and His Self-Analysis* and *Freud and His Patients* were in preparation.

Mark Kanzer, M.D.
Jules Glenn, M.D.

References

Freud, S. (1910). Leonardo da Vinci and a memory of his childhood. *Standard Edition* 11:63–137.

Kanzer, M. (1976). Freud and his literary doubles, *American Imago* 33:236-243. Also in *Freud and His Self-Analysis, Vol. 1 of the Downstate Twenty-fifth Anniversary Series*. Edited by M. Kanzer and J. Glenn. New York: Jason Aronson.

ACKNOWLEDGMENTS

We wish to thank those authors and publishers that have granted permission to reprint the following articles that appear in this volume:

Langs, Robert (1976). The misalliance dimension in Freud's case histories. Dora. *International Journal of Psychoanalytic Psychotherapy*. Edited by Robert Langs 5:301–318. New York: Jason Aronson.

Kanzer, Mark (1952). The transference neuroses of the Rat Man. *Psychoanalytic Quarterly* 21:181–189.

Shengold, Leonard (1971). More about rats and rat people. *International Journal of Psycho-Analysis* 52:277–288.

Niederland, William G. (1959). Schreber: father and son. Psychoanalytic Quarterly. 28:151–169.

Niederland, William G. (1959). The "miracled-up" world of of Schreber's childhood. *Psychoanalytic Study of the Child* 14:383–413.

Niederland, William G. (1963). Further data and memorabilia pertaining to the Schreber case. *International Journal of Psycho-Analysis* 44:201—207.

Blum, Harold P. (1974). The borderline childhood of the Wolf Man. *Journal of the American Psychoanalytic Association* 22:721–742.

Halport. E. (1975) Lermontou and the Wolf Man. *American Imago* 33:315-328

The *Journal of the American Psychoanalytic Association* and the *Psychoanalytic Study of the Child,* Volume 14, were published by the International Universities Press.

The *American Imago* is published by Wayne State University Press.

Part I

Introduction

We have underlined the basic organization of these papers by including integrative summaries at the end of the sections on each of the cases. A final summary of the entire volume provides a synthesis of the historical, technical and conceptual aspects of all the case histories.

Another aim has been strengthened by our preceding volume: to trace in the case histories material relevant to Freud's own personality both for biographical reasons and to remark its influence on the course of the reatment. This last aim is the most speculative—but speculative, it is hoped, in the tradition of psychoanalysis and to be validated by its usefulness to the reader.

Chapter 1

NOTES ON PSYCHOANALYTIC
CONCEPTS AND STYLE
IN FREUD'S CASE HISTORIES

JULES GLENN, M.D.

Freud wrote his major case histories in the heroic era of psychoanalytic discovery. In this chapter I will describe some of the general problems that Freud coped with in these works and place them in historical perspective, juxtaposing his conception of each case against his other theoretical and technical accomplishments. In part this chapter will serve as a guide to those readers who are not fully familiar with the development of psychoanalysis so that they may place the histories in proper perspective as they read them. A section on Freud's countertransference will carry forward the theme of *Freud and His Self-Analysis* into this volume as a basic frame of reference for understanding Freud's theory and technique.

Freud composed the first major history, the Dora case, in 1900 and published it in 1905. Prior to that he had written several pre-analytic case reports for *Studies on Hysteria* (Breuer and Freud 1893–1895). The last major clinical study, that of the Wolf Man, appeared in 1918. Following that, a minor clinical description of the analysis of a "homosexual woman" was printed in 1920.

Freud faced many dilemmas concerning tact and tactics in these publications. He had to devise a means of presentation which would reveal the social and family background essential to the understanding of his patients while concealing their identities. He had to describe the intimate details of his patients' strange fantasies without antagonizing and repelling his Victorian readers. He had to present revolutionary ideas and data never before observed (except in the protective disguise of fiction) in a convincing manner and introduce a new vocabulary with appropriate metaphors. He had to bridge the apparent gap between the psychological and the biological in describing the clinical reality he brought to light.

Fortunately Freud's extraordinary literary capacity enabled him to achieve these aims. He did not avoid the immediate wrath of many of his readers who were horrified by his revelations, but his artistic presentation enabled his ideas to prevail despite opposition. Even when anti-analytic forces are powerful, Freud's writings retain their appeal, and many of his ideas have become a part of the intellectual milieu shared by Freudians, anti-Freudians and even those who have never heard of him.

Marcus (1975), examining Freud's paper on Dora from the point of view of literary criticism, noted that Freud used the techniques of certain writers like Ibsen and Nabokov in conveying the complexities of his patients' conflicts and his theoretical explanations. Certainly these observations apply to the other histories as well. Freud observed that his papers read like stories, and realized that this was the only way to present the labyrinths of his patients' lives and minds. Comparing modern case histories with Freud's, the reader cannot but regret the lackluster writing we find today in all but a few psychoanalysts' articles.

Freud's literary style reflected his way of viewing the patient as a complex individual raised in a complicated social milieu which influenced his biological dispositions. The latter was in turn subject to the individual's particular history. Those who attack Freud for a primarily biological orientation or malign him for an excessive concentration on familial influences have failed to recognize Freud's insistence on the interweaving of numerous forces.

Reading the case histories, one is impressed by the fact that Freud's descriptions start from the surface, a basic technical procedure as well. He describes Dora's family's intrigues and concealments with remarkable clarity (Freud 1905a). Her mother is described in less detail than her father and Herr K., but the brief bold sketch of her personality gives one a striking impression of the woman. Freud also describes Dora's symptoms, another surface manifestation, before introducing us to her more private thoughts and eventually to the unconscious fantasies which explain her symptoms in the social context already revealed. As one set of symptoms is explained—for instance, the cough and aphonia which express Dora's unconscious love for Herr K.—Freud returns to the surface and then gradually solves another clinical puzzle through a slow revelation of unconscious sources. Eventually most of Dora's disturbance lies bare before us. But even then Freud points to unsolved mysteries, to his failures in fully understanding many other facets of the case. Since the analysis ended prematurely, solutions to these mysteries were suggested by Freud and later by his readers.

Freud discovers why Dora refused Herr K.'s advances at the lake and recognizes her desire for vengeance against her analyst as a transference. Always eager to learn more, he realizes after the analysis that he had failed to appreciate the homosexual current. But it remains for the modern reader to apply the newer knowledge of adolescence and hence clarify Dora's transferences and Freud's reaction to her.

In the cases of Little Hans (Freud 1909a), the Rat Man (Freud 1909b) and the Wolf Man (Freud 1918) Freud also starts from the surface and gradually plumbs the depths. At times he ignores the surface—as in his failure to appreciate the impact of Hans's tonsillectomy—but his approach remains the same. First the careful and detailed observation of the family setting, the present social setting, the symptoms. Then, as the patient reveals more of his inner life, the unconscious explanations will emerge or be constructed. The setting in which the Rat Man's obsessions regarding the payment for his glasses appeared is described. So too are the confusing details of his obsessions, which Freud's insistent questioning clarified. The patient's early relationships with his parents, his identification with his father and his conflicts over choosing a mate come under scrutiny. Then the unconscious wishes and fantasies can be reconstructed and the patient cured.

Despite Freud's remarkable writing ability, the observant reader will find certain obscurities in his prose. These stem from inevitable early deficiences in a new and complex field. Freud later altered and improved his conceptualizations and his followers have furthered the work of clarification.

All of the case histories were written during the dominance of the topographical point of view, prior to the establishment of the structural point of view (Freud 1923a). The modern reader may become confused by Freud's terminology since he used words that continued to acquire different meanings. It is often necessary to "translate" Freud's pre–1923 language into that of today.

According to the topographical point of view, the personality comprises the *system conscious*, the *system preconscious* and the *system unconscious*. Repression causes thoughts to remain in the unconscious part of the mind. There they are governed by the primary processes: there is a tendency to immediate discharge of impulses and to ready displacement of energy. The conscious and preconscious parts of the mind, on the other hand, follow secondary processes: impulses were bound and inhibited or were discharged in an orderly, organized way. Inconsistencies between these concepts and clinical observation led Freud to adopt the structural point of view in which ego, id and superego supplemented and conflicted with each other (Freud 1923a). In the new view, consistent with observed data, the ego and superego are each partly conscious and partly unconscious. Freud's use of the term *system conscious* and especially the *system preconscious* prior to 1923 referred to a great extent to the psychic organization which was later called the *ego,* and the term *system unconscious* was applied to the configurations which were later designated as the *id.* This theoretical change gave rise to a change in the theory of technique. Whereas Freud previously believed the essence of treatment was to make the unconscious conscious, he now arrived at a new dictum: "where id was, there ego shall be" (1933, p. 80).

In later developments further clarification of concepts led to the differentiation between the terms *ego* and *self,* which are used interchangeably in the case histories to the reader's confusion. The concepts of *self-representation* and *object-representation* added to further understanding. Today the *ego* refers to those functions of the personality which serve to mediate between the outside world, the drives and superego. It utilizes defense mechanisms against drives and affects and utilizes them adaptively. It establishes compromise formations which minimize anxiety. The *self* refers to the entire organism, both the physical and psychic aspects. The *self-representation* is the individual's concept of himself which is different from the actual *self;* the *object-representation* is the individual's concept of his objects (the people about him whom he loves or hates) which differs from the objects themselves (Jacobson 1964, Hartmann 1964).

The term *defense,* which Freud originally used in 1894, was replaced by *repression* as an omnibus term for all defenses. Thus Freud referred to reaction formation, isolation, projection, etc., as forms of repression. Later the term *defense* was reinstituted and *repression* was relegated to the status of a single form of defense, albeit a major one.

Let us review the appearance of some of the defense mechanisms in Freud's cases. Freud identified important defenses like repression, projection, displacement, isolation, reaction formation and regression prior to the publication of the case histories and discussed their clinical appearance as he wrote about Dora, Little Hans and his other famous patients. Some defenses—undoing, for instance—were described, but not named.

Freud used the term *repressed* to describe the discrete defense that we now call *repression* as early as 1893 in *Studies on Hysteria* (1893–1895). He stated that "it was a question of things the patient wished to forget and therefore intentionally repressed from conscious thought . . ." (p. 10). He refers to the basic mechanism of making ideas unconscious throughout the case histories.

It is not certain that Freud would label as projection (which it is) Dora's utilization of a string of reproaches against others to hide her own similar self-reproaches; he compares these to children's *tu quoque* arguments (they may say "you're another" if accused of a vice) and then mentions the projection in paranoia (Freud 1905a). In discussing Hans in *Inhibitions, Symptoms and Anxiety* (1926) he states that phobics *project* an inner fear onto the outer world, making it possible to avoid the seemingly external danger. Many analysts would now call this *externalization* rather than projection. Freud states that although projection occurs in anxiety hysteria, it is absent in obsessive compulsive neuroses where the conflict is completely internalized. The modern clinician may be skeptical of this formulation and note that the Rat Man did indeed use projection.

Projection is mentioned in a footnote to the Wolf Man history in which Freud indicated that his patient used this defense frequently. Referring to the Wolf Man's attributing a new insight to his analyst, Freud stated, "In his *usual way* he passed it off on me, and by this projection tried to make it seem more trustworthy" (Freud 1918, p. 37; italics mine). In the Schreber case Freud (1913a) demonstrated in detail the importance of projection in paranoid states, a fact that he had recognized as early as 1895.

Displacement (and, associated with it, condensation) was considered a manifestation of unbound energy and primary processes prior to and throughout the case histories (Freud 1895, 1900). Displacement resulted from the free mobility of energy characteristic of the unconscious. In 1936 Anna Freud noted that the ego used the primary processes, i.e., displacement, for defensive purposes. In *The Interpretation of Dreams* (1900) and in *Fragment of an Analysis of a Case of Hysteria* (1905a), displacement disguised the wish that the dream conveyed. Many of the manifest elements of Dora's dreams resulted from displacement: the jewel case symbolized her genitals and referred to jewelry which stood for the male genitals as well as the drops of fluid which appear during sexual excitement. Displacement also played a significant role in Dora's symptom formation. Through displacement upward from her genitals to her chest or throat, for example, she developed a sensation of chest pressure on the one hand and a chronic cough as well.

Although he describes displacement in the Little Hans history (1909a), Freud did not apply the term to Hans's case until *Inhibition, Symptoms and Anxiety* (1926). Hans's fear of horses rather than his father is a prominent part of his pathology. Similarly, although displacement runs rampant in Schreber's "basic language", i.e., the primary process, Freud does not mention displacement per se, not even in his description of the defensive shifting of affection from men to women in the formation of erotomania (Freud 1913a).

The obvious use of this device by the Rat Man is forthrightly brought to the reader's attention in that paper. Freud states that ". . . it is an inherent characteristic in the psychology of an obsessional neurotic to make the fullest possible use of the mechanism of *displacement*" (1909b, p. 241). This mechanism is also described in the dreams and symptom formation of the Wolf Man (Freud 1918).

The Rat Man affords ample opportunity for studying the defense mechanisms that characterize obsessive-compulsive neurosis: displacement, regression, isolation, reaction formation and undoing. Freud emphasized that repression is less significant in obsessional patients than in hysterics. The former often recall early pathogenic events but fail to recognize connections: utilizing the mechanism of *isolation "an interval of time is inserted* between the pathogenic situation and the obsessional thought that arises from it, so as to lead astray any conscious investigation of its causal connections" (Freud 1909b, p. 246).

Today the term *isolation* has taken on other meanings as well. Not only does it indicate a separation of ideas; it also refers to the related clinical fact that affect ordinarily associated with a particular thought is absent (*Inhibition, Symptoms and Anxiety* 1926). In addition to its defensive function isolation can act as an adaptive mechanism, as in concentration.

Isolation was described as early as the 1895 Project and again in *The Interpretation of Dreams* (1900). It was not until *Notes upon a Case of Obsessional Neurosis* (1909b) that Freud demarcated the mechanism which he later, in *Inhibitions. Symptoms and Anxiety* (1926), called *undoing*. The Rat Man first removed a stone from the road to prevent injury to his lady and then replaced the stone so that she might be hurt. Freud stated that "Compulsive acts like this, in two successive stages, of which the second neutralizes the first, are a typical occurrence in obsessional neurosis" (Freud 1909b, p. 192). Borrowing a term from Jones (1908), he added that the patient *rationalized* his bizarre behavior.

Freud called attention to *reaction formations* in *Three Essays on the Theory of Sexuality* (1905b) and in *Character and Anal Erotism* (1908) where he stated that they are counter forces to unstructured urges, and include shame, disgust and morality. Strangely enough, the term does not appear in the Rat Man study. The meaning and appearance of *reaction formation* was clarified in *Inhibitions, Symptoms and Anxiety* (1926) where Freud maintains that they occur normally during latency as well as in obsessive compulsive neuroses and hysteria. In that paper he specifically noted Little Hans's reaction formations. Review of Dora, the Rat Man and the Wolf Man reveals that each uses that particular defense. Dora became disgusted rather than sexually excited by fellatio fantasies; the Rat Man hid his hatred for his lady behind a wall of love;

and the Wolf Man developed religious rituals in his childhood to combat his sadism.

Freud's insistence that reaction formations result in normal character traits was confirmed by Hartmann (1964) who suggested that defenses that arise out of conflict may later continue their existence in the conflict-free sphere as secondary autonomous ego functions. Hence a child whose reaction formations originally prevented the anxiety involved in anal conflicts may later utilize this mechanism adaptively; he may become orderly and efficient.

The multiple usages of the term *regression* make it impossible to cover this area well. Regression can be temporal in its direction, i.e., to an earlier stage of development, or formal, i.e., to a less complex psychic organization. Further, regression can involve the drive, the ego or the superego. Freud also used the term to refer to another type of regression, topographical regression, in which the libido does not "force its way through to action" (Freud 1897, p. 270), but, as in dreams, produces images. This concept was enlarged upon in the *Interpretation of Dreams* (1900).

By 1905, in *Three Essays on the Theory of Sexuality*, Freud developed the libido theory and outlined the normal progression from the oral stage to the anal stage to the phallic stage and then into latency, puberty and adulthood. Oral eroticism and genitality had been described in Dora's case, but not anal eroticism, latency and puberty which were discussed in the *Three Essays*. In that paper Freud introduced the idea of libidinal regression and then explicitly applied the term *regression* in a footnote added in 1915 (p. 232). This concept found clinical verification in the Wolf Man's history. Referring to his patient's suppression of masturbation after his Nanya threatened castration, Freud states: "His sexual life, therefore, which was beginning to come under the sway of the genital zone, gave way before an external obstacle, and was thrown back by its influence to an earlier phase of pregenital development . . . the boy's sexual life took on a sadistic-anal character" (1918, pp. 25–26).

Regression was not mentioned in the case histories of Dora and Little Hans. But Freud did state that Dora "summoned up her infantile affection for her father so as to keep her repressed love for Herr K. in its state of repression" (Freud 1905a, p. 86), clearly a defensive use of regression. Regression from acting to thinking and from adult affects to infantile affects are described in the Rat Man's case (1909b, p. 244). Schreber's libidinal regression under the influence of frustration to "somewhere between the stages of auto-eroticism, narcissism and homsexuality" (Freud 1913a, p. 62) was described in that paper.

Another significant confusion originates in Freud's grappling with the phenomenon of *anxiety*. The knowledgeable reader is aware that eventually Freud recognized anxiety as the ego's reaction to real or fantasied danger. (Real anxiety is equivalent to fear.) Thus in 1926, reassessing the case of Little Hans, he states that Little Hans's anxiety was due to the ego's reaction to the danger of emerging id impulses and the fantasy of his father's opposition. Defenses as displacement and repression appeared in reaction to the danger as a way of controlling the anxiety. When Freud wrote the case histories his position was that anxiety resulted from repression of the libido; the repressed libido was transformed into anxiety. Freud applied this theory to Hans and concluded that his anxiety resulted from an increase in libido which had been repressed. (Similar formulations appeared in other major case histories as well.) At the same time that this was Freud's official explanation, he made observations and offered explanations which heralded his later theory. Hence he told Hans in their single therapeutic session: "Long before he was in the world . . . I had known that a little Hans would come who would be so fond of his mother that he would be bound to feel afraid of his father because of it" (1909a, p. 42). The fear of his father, Freud added, "was derived from his hostility toward whimE" (p. 126). He feared his father "who was going to punish him for the evil wishes he was nourishing against him" (p. 44). These formulations, which adumbrated the second theory of anxiety, had already been stated in his description of the Oedipus complex in *The Interpretation of Dreams* (1900). At the same time the transformation theory of anxiety prevailed. Freud quoted the following statement of Hans's father with approval: "This suppressed hostile wish is turned into anxiety about his father" (1909a, p. 44). Here aggression, considered a form of libido, becomes anxiety.

The reader may be at a loss to understand Freud's 1909 position. We must realize that Freud was an excellent observer whose early attempts at organizing his data fell short and required revision; that indeed, along with his conscious theory, bits and pieces of alternate explanations were background and counterpoint. We may note parenthetically that Freud never surrendered the theory that anxiety was dammed-up libido. Finding it difficult to give up previous positions, Freud retained this idea despite its demonstrated lack of value.

Although the *superego* was first recognized as a structure within the personality in the *Ego and the Id* (1923a), Freud's earlier scientific writings contain many references to guilt, morality and ideals (Freud 1895, 1896). He mentions the *unconscious* sense of guilt in 1907 but had laid the ground for this concept as early as 1894 in the *Neuro-Psychoses of Defense*. The ego-ideal, later incorporated into the concept of the superego, was introduced in *On Narcissism: An Introduction* (1914a).

In the case histories themselves Freud mentions Dora's "sexual guilt" in a footnote; he refers to Hans's lack of sense of guilt when he was not yet three, implying that he would later acquire this; he discussed the sense of guilt in both the Rat Man and the Wolf Man at greater length, demonstrating its pathological influence. He mentions Schreber's "high ethical standing" as a laudable trait. The reader can see how, in addition, moral influences led to disavowal of homosexuality and consequent paranoid ideation in Schreber's case.

Freud reviewed Little Hans and the Wolf Man in relation to the structural theory and the second theory of anxiety. He observed that Hans had a positive Oedipus complex which included fear of his father castrating him for his desires to kill him and possess mother. He stated that the ego's fear of castration, "[its] attitude of anxiety is the primary thing and which sets repression going" (1926, p. 109). The additional use of displacement, regression and projection as defenses resulted in Hans's fear of the horse. The Wolf Man's fear of wolves biting him also involved displacement from the father and also resulted from regression, an oral anxiety replacing the phallic fear of castration. But the Wolf Man's negative Oedipus complex made for a different configuration. "The little Russian . . . [wished] to be loved by his father . . . [and] thought that a relation of that sort presupposed a sacrifice of his genitals—of the organ which distinguished him from a female" (1918, p. 106).

Freud focused primarily on the infantile, conflictual unconscious aspects of the personality. Conscious and rational aspects of the mind had been known before Freud. The revolutionary contribution of psychoanalysis is the discovery of the unconscious and irrational parts of the mind. Nevertheless Freud recognized the significance of contrasting the rational and the irrational, a task later taken up by Hartmann when further understanding of the ego made it necessary to formulate the adaptive point of view more specifically.

In discussing the Wolf Man's conflicts over money Freud makes this differentiation clear. "We are accustomed to trace back interest in money insofar as it is of a libidinal and not of a rational character, to excretory pleasure, and we expect normal people to keep their relations to money entirely free from libidinal influences and regulate them according to the demands of reality" (1918, p. 72). In modern terms we would say that realistic dealing with money is an *autonomous ego function* which exists in the *conflict free sphere* (Hartmann 1964). Conflicting and irrational forces derived from libido, aggression and other sources may invade this area, giving it heightened interest or causing it to become enmeshed in conflict, interfering with realistic aims.

Freud called attention to the adaptive use of drives transformed through sublimation. He made specific references to sublimation in many of the case studies. At that time he emphasized the importance of the altered aim of the drive. Later, recognition of the changed character of the drives, their desexualization, clarified the processes alluded to in the Wolf Man quotation above.

It remained for Hartmann to use the term *neutralization* to include both desexualization and the alteration and taming of the aggressive drive. He also suggested that adaptive sublimated activity utilizes a primary neutral ego energy as well as neutralized energy.

Confusion may also arise in the reader who is not aware that Freud's case histories were written prior to the *dual instinct theory* (Freud 1920a). At the time of the case histories Freud considered the libidinal and the self-preservation drives basic: aggression was merely a part of the libidinal instinct. It is interesting that even in the histories he described the manifestations of aggression as if it were an independent instinct. His statements, for instance, that Little Hans desired his mother sexually and wanting, as a result, to get rid of his father and feared his father's retaliation, seems more congruent with the second than the first instinct theory.

In Freud's 1920 theory of instincts, the basic drives were libido and the death instinct, the latter being turned toward others as aggression after an initial fundamental self-direction. Most analysts today consider libido and aggression the essential drives, dropping the death instinct (Fenichel 1945).

Theories of development were also modified throughout the time of the case histories. The *Three Essays on the Theory of Sexuality* (1905b) presented the essentials of the libido theory and the progression from oral to anal to phallic stages and the Oedipus complex. These were elaborated throughout Freud's work.

Although libidinal development was generally portrayed accurately, Freud's attempt in the Schreber Case to provide a schema to explain the origin of homosexuality and paranoia was sadly lacking. He proposed a progression from auto-erotism to narcissism (which led to love of similar persons, i.e., homosexual loves) to object love. His attempt at correcting this primitive plan in *On Narcissism* (1914a) was heuristically successful. Not only did he detail narcissistic object relations but he also suggested that primary narcissism (in which cathexis is completely directed toward the self) gave rise to outward direction of libido which in secondary narcissism is redirected inward. Today we have detailed direct observations strongly arguing that the matter is still more complicated (see A. Freud 1965, Mahler, Pine and Bergman 1975, and Part V, chapter 4 of the present volume).

A complex development also occurred in regard to Freud's observations and conceptualizations on the patient's relationship with his analyst. Breuer's original panicky reaction to his patient's falling in love with him foreshadowed the problem. Freud came to realize that the patient's emotional response to the doctor was a transference, a displacement from earlier reactions to parents, siblings or other significant persons. At first the transferences were resistances to be dispensed with, not interpretable elements (Freud 1905a). Then the transferences became analyzable so that their function as resistance could be overcome. They also fostered the patients' conviction as to the actuality of repressed memories that were being recovered (Muslin 1977). They provided further clues to the patient's pathology and his earlier relationship with his parents. As Freud made these discoveries, his explanations were relatively simple: individual transferences were described.

In *Remembering, Repeating and Working Through* (1914b) Freud stated that when the analysis is carried out properly, the patient develops a "transference neurosis," an intense relationship with the analyst, which contains the essence of the neurotic conflicts previously expressed in symptomatology. Freud described transferences in each of his cases but never, not even in the case of the Wolf Man, first written in 1914 but published in 1918, did he discuss a transference neurosis. The reader nevertheless may be able to recognize this complex configuration in Freud's cases, as Kanzer does in the case of the Rat Man (1952; Part IV, chapter 1 of the present volume).

Nor did Freud fully appreciate the impact of his behavior on his patient. He noted that Dora responded to certain phrases of his, like "Where there's smoke there's fire," but he did not recognize how his providing a reality basis for certain of his reactions rendered the transference difficult to analyze. A large number of examples of Freud's impeding behavior are presented in this volume, especially in the papers of Langs (Part II, chapter 3; Part IV, chapter 5; Part VI, chapter 4) and myself (Part II, chapter 1; Part III, chapter 2). Freud introduced the concept of countertransference in 1910. Strachey (1958) attributes the scantiness of Freud's writings on countertransference to a reluctance to reveal himself to those many patients who would read his work and thus impede their analyses. This certainly must have been a factor but it cannot be the total explanation. The reader will recall that Freud, whose self-analysis before his colleagues was unusually and perhaps unwisely frank, nevertheless reserved the right to keep secrets to himself. He refused to reveal to Jung certain associations to a dream, as it would undermine his authority. And in the "dream book," he consciously withheld certain associations and interpretations as well as the fact that many of the dreams were his own.

Aside from Freud's conscious restraints, designed to protect himself, his family and friends as well as his patients from the impact of the inevitable human foibles that confession would bring to light, there were unconscious forces at work. Schur has described Freud's intense defense against recognizing Fliess's error after his friend, mentor and "analyst" caused a serious and dangerous nasal infection in Irma (1966; chapter 6 in *Freud and His Self-Analysis*). Unknowingly, Freud protected himself against recognition of Fliess's failing. Freud denied the organic basis for his patient's illness and offered a psychological explanation of her symptoms instead.

There is reason to believe that Freud did not recognize countertransferences to Dora, as I have indicated in Part II, chapter 1. This thesis is stronger, as I have pointed out (1975), when we recall that Freud named Dora after a maid (Freud 1901) and thus reacted to Dora as if she were a maid, complementing her self-image as a servant. This fact should be juxtaposed with Freud's special relationship with his seductive and punitive Nannie, an incestuous figure who, he proclaimed, was the "prime originator" of his neurosis (Freud 1954, p. 219). It has been suggested that Freud's travel inhibition which kept him from Rome resulted from his unconsciously equating Rome, his mother and his Catholic nursemaid whom he accompanied to church and who introduced him to Christian theology at an early age (see Jones 1953, Schur 1972, Grigg 1973, Swan 1974). In 1900, at the time that he analyzed Dora, an incestuous object identified with his Nannie, Freud's self-analysis had not proceed d sufficiently for him to be able to travel to Rome; this was an accomplished on September 2, 1901. Remnants of this inhibition remained, for he turned Dora away in 1902 and was not able to travel to Athens until 1904.

Freud's reactions to the Rat Man and the Wolf Man were quite different from those toward Dora and the "homosexual woman." Compare his retreat from analyzing the two eighteen-year-old girls with his patience with these men. He complimented the Rat Man, reassured him of his clearheadedness and his capability at analysis. He fed him, sent him a post card. Freud allowed his latent sadistic impulses to reveal themselves as he supplied the words that completed the Rat Man's description of his torture. He supplemented his patient's needs to be pressured by urging him to bring his girlfriend's picture and tell him her name (see Kanzer, Part IV, chapters 1, 6).

In 1910 Freud wrote Jung that he was beginning to see that one had to "surmount countertransference" (McGuire ed. 1974, p. 291). In that same year Freud wrote, "we have become aware of the 'counter-transference,' which arises in him [the analyst] as a result of the patient's influence on his unconscious feelings" (p. 144). As "no psychoanalyst goes further than his own complexes and internal resistances permit" (p. 145), continued self-analysis is necessary. The analyst must "recognize this counter-transference in himself and overcome it" (p. 145). Nevertheless, in 1914 Freud's countertransference to the Wolf Man expressed itself in his suggestion that the patient give him a gift at the end of the analysis, supposedly to relieve his feelings of dependence and gratitude. Freud had told the Wolf Man that he had "first class intelligence," that "it would be good if all his pupils could grasp the nature of analysis as soundly as [he]." He even told the patient of his own family and of his literary tastes (Gardiner 1971). Analysts are understandably reluctant to reveal their own primitive drives in writing, and training analysts are restrained by the confidentiality demanded by professional ethics from revealing their candidate analysands' foibles when they may be identified by colleagues.

Freud's chief technical papers appeared between 1912 and 1914, after he had written most of his major case histories, but prior to articles on the Wolf Man and the "homosexual woman." Although Freud specifically states that he is omitting descriptions of technique in his case histories and Anna Freud (1971) warns against drawing conclusions from the limited data presented, the reader cannot help but note Freud's therapeutic procedures and their development. Reading his histories and descriptions of analyses by patients, he will observe that Freud at times behaved contrary to the principles that he laid down, even *after* espousing them.

As stated above, Freud adhered to the principle that one should start from the surface and proceed to the depths. He often interpreted unconscious material more rapidly than is done today and at times missed salient surface determinants (as Hans's tonsillectomy), but the principle remained. He warned against giving "a patient the solution of a symptom or the translation of a wish until he is already so close to it that he has only one short step more to make in order to get hold of the explanation for himself" and then added, "In former years I often had occasion to find that the premature communication of a solution brought the treatment to an untimely end . . ." (1913b, p. 140). Freud must have learned this caution from his analysis of Dora as well as other patients.

A related principle involved early confrontation of resistances. Freud recommended that the patient be told the "basic rule," a procedure he had followed in the cases of Dora and the Rat Man, as well as previously. (He did not suggest to Hans's father that his child should be asked to free associate, indicating awareness that the child's developmental stage would not permit successful adherence to this tenet, thus anticipating the procedures of child analysts.) He suggested that when resistances follow, the analyst "must take up the challenge then and there and come to grips with it" (1913b, p. 137).

Freud did not use the terms *therapeutic alliance* (Zetzel 1956) or *working alliance* (Greenson 1967) in his technical or other papers, but he recognized this had to be established and took steps to facilitate this development: "If one exhibits a serious interest in him [the analysand] carefully clears away the resistances that crop up at the beginning and avoids making certain mistakes," then transferences from persons "by whom he was accustomed to be treated with affection" will occur (1913b, pp. 139–140). The analyst should not analyze the transference until it has become a resistance. In the case of the Rat Man, Freud went beyond these suggestions. He attempted to further the patient's confidence in and commitment to treatment by assuring him that he, the patient, was an intelligent and stable man who would benefit from analysis. And he told Dora his estimate of the duration of treatment. Many would frown upon these attempts to strengthen the positive transference or establish a therapeutic alliance (as we would phrase it today) because they create expectations that might influence the course of the analysis adversely and because they violate another of Freud's principles, that the treatment must be carried out in a state of abstinence (Freud 1919). The degree of gratification that Freud provided the Rat Man by his assurances was beyond what we would believe optimum for most neurotic patients, although the possibility that the Rat Man's disturbance was more severe, borderline, and warranted such an approach is supported by clinical data and by the extremely successful outcome. When the analyst behaves as if he were ominscient, the patient may obtain gratification from feelings of union with such a powerful person.

We know from Freud's original notes on the Rat Man's treatment that Freud went further in gratifying his patient. He sent him a postcard, lent him a book, and he fed him. Langs has described complications that these acts created. Presumably Freud established and adhered more strictly to the rules of abstinence after observing the consequences. We cannot be certain. When he analyzed Hilda Doolittle in 1933 and 1934, he took her to the alcove in which he housed much of his collection of antiquities and showed her certain pieces, an act that was extremely gratifying to the patient (Doolittle 1956). As with the Rat Man, we may wonder whether this procedure was appropriate to her ego structure.

Eissler (1953) states that deviation from the essential analytic procedure, interpretation, is appropriate when the patient's ego deviations make them necessary. Eissler points to certain parameters that Freud knowingly used—the suggestion that a phobic patient enter the feared situation and, in the case of the Wolf Man, the establishment of a termination date in a stalemated analysis—in order to provide a strong motive for analytic work.

Freud's case histories were not written simply as illustrations of the psychoanalytic theory or process. Several had more specific aims. Dora was written to demonstrate "how dream interpretation is woven into the history of a treatment and how it can become the means of filling in amnesias and elucidating symptoms" (1905a, p. 10). Along with demonstrating the technique of dream analysis Freud attempted "to demonstrate the intimate structure of a neurotic disorder and the determination of its symptoms" (p. 13). In the discussion of Little Hans, Freud considered how far the analysis of the child supported the assertion of the *Three Essays on the Theory of Sexuality* and contributed to the understanding of phobias; he wondered "whether it can be made to shed any light on the mental life of children or to afford any criticism of our educational aims" (Freud 1909a, p. 101).

The Wolf Man provided analytic material contradicting Adler's assertion that the will to power was of greater importance than the sexual drive, and Freud further rebutted his "opponents," Jung and Adler, for their contentions that early childhood experiences did not determine later fantasies. After presenting his clinical findings, Freud asserted that, "As things stand, it seems to me more probable that the fantasy of rebirth [to which Jung has recently drawn attention and to which he has assigned such a dominant position in the imaginative life of neurotics] was a derivative of the primal scene than that, conversely, the primal scene was a reflection of the fantasy of rebirth" (pp. 102–103).

Despite a tendentious quality, Freud does not restrict his clinical observations. He repeatedly broadens his vistas, critically allowing himself to reach new and surprising conclusions, tempting the reader to join him in independent discovery. Hence while insisting that dreams are primarily unconscious disguised wish fulfillments, a cherished belief, Freud also revealed the clinical significance of the dream as an expression of intent. As such he adumbrated Kanzer's (1955) study of the communicative function of the dream.

Freud provided vivid descriptions of clinical data which permit us to continue his work, to reevaluate and reconstruct. As he did, so can we benefit from his errors. Like him we can utilize his data and additional information (as the Wolf Man's own reports, Felix Deutsch's [1957] follow-up of Dora, and Freud's original notes of his analysis of the Rat Man) to confirm, correct and elaborate on his brilliant revolutionary insights. The articles in this book attempt these difficult tasks.

References

Breuer, J. and Freud, S. (1893–1895). Studies on hysteria. *Standard Edition* 2:1–305.

Deutsch, F. (1957). A footnote to Freud's "Fragment of an analysis of a case of hysteria." *Psychoanatytic Quartery*, 26:159–167.

Doolittle, H. (1956). *Tribute to Freud*. New York: Pantheon Books.

Eissler, K. R. (1953). The effect of the structure of the ego on psychoanalytic technique. *Journal of the American Psychoanalytic Association* 1:104–143.

Fenichel, O. (1945). *The Psychoanalytic Theory of Neurosis*. New York: Norton.

Freud, A. (1965). *Normality and Pathology in Childhood*. New York: International Universities Press.

——— (1971). Introduction, *The Wolf Man by the Wolf Man*, ed. M. Gardiner. New York: Basic Books.

Freud, S. (1894). The neuro-psychoses of defence. *Standard Edition* 3:43–61.

——— (1950/1895). Project for a scientific psychology. *Standard Edition* 1:295–397.

——— (1896). Draft, K., Extract from the Fliess papers. *Standard Edition* 1:220–229.

———— (1897). Letter 75, Nov. 14, 1897, Extracts from the Fliess papers. *Standard Edition* 1:228–271.

———— (1900). The interpretation of dreams. *Standard Edition* 4/5.

———— (1901). The psychopathology of everyday life. *Standard Edition* 6.

———— (1905a). Fragment of the analysis of a case of hysteria. *Standard Edition* 7:7–122.

———— (1905b). Three essays on the theory of sexuality. *Standard Edition* 7:130–243.

———— (1907). Obsessive actions and religious practices. *Standard Edition* 9:117–127.

———— (1908). Character and anal erotism. *Standard Edition* 9:169–175.

———— (1909a). Analysis of a phobia in a five-year-old boy. *Standard Edition* 10:5–149.

———— (1909b). Notes on a case of obsessional neurosis. *Standard Edition* 10:155–318.

————(1910). The future prospects of psychoanalytic therapy. *Standard Edition* 11:141–151

———— (1913a). Psycho-analytic notes on an autobiographical account of a case of paranoia (dementia paranoides). *Standard Edition* 12:9–82.

———— (1913b). On the beginning of treatment. *Standard Edition* 12:123–144.

———— (1914a). On narcissism: an introduction. *Standard Edition* 14:73–102.

———— (1914b);. Remembering, repeating and working through. *Standard Edition* 12:147–156.

———— (1918). From the history of an infantile neurosis. *Standard Edition* 17:7–122.

———— (191). Lines of advance in psychoanalytic therapy. *Standard Edition* 17:159–168.

———— (1920a). Beyond the pleasure principle. *Standard Edition* 18:7–64.

———— (1920b). The psychogenesis of a case of homosexuality in a woman. *Standard Edition* 18:147–172.

———— (1923a). The ego and the id. *Standard Edition* 19:12–59.

———— (1923b). The infantile genital organization: an interpolation into the theory of sexuality. *Standard Edition* 19:141–145.

————(1926).Inhibitions,symptoms and anxiety.*Standard Edition* 20:87–172.

———— (1933). New introductory lectures on psycho-analysis. *Standard Edition* 22:5–182.

———— (1954). *The Origins of Psychoanalysis*, ed. M. Bonaparte, A. Freud and E. Kris. New York: Basic Books.

Gardiner, M. (1971). *The Wolf Man by the Wolf Man*. New York: Basic Books.

Glenn, J. (1975), Unpublished discussion of Freud's Adolescent Cases I: Dora, at the American Psychoanalytic Association, December 1975.

Greenson, R. R. (1967). *The Technique and Practice of Psychoanalysis*. Vol. I. New York: International Universities Press.

Grigg, K. A. (1973). "All roads lead to Rome": the role of the nursemaid in Freud's dreams. *Journal of the American Psychoanalytic Association* 21:108–126.

Hartmann, H. (1964). *Essays on Ego Psychology*. New York: International Universities Press.

Jacobson, E. (1964). *The Self and the Object World*. New York: International Universities Press.

Jones, E. (1908). Rationalization in everyday life. *Journal of Abnormal Psychology* 3:161–169.

———— (1953). *The Life and Work of Signmund Freud*. Vol. 1. New York: Basic Books.

Kanzer, M. (1952). The transference neurosis of the Rat Man. *Psychoanalytic Quarterly*, 21:181—189. Also Part 4, Chapter 3 of this volume.

———— (1955). The communicating function of the dream. *International J. Psycho-Analysis* 36:260–266.

Mahler, M. S., Pine, F. and Bergman, A. (1975). *The Psychological Birth of the Human Infant*. New York: Basic Books.

Marcus, S. (1975). *Representations: Essays on Literature and Society*. New York: Random House.

McGuire, W., ed. (1974). *The Freud/Jung Letters*. Princeton N.J.: Princeton University Press.

Muslin, H. L. (1977) Transference in the Rat Man case: the transference in transistion. Presented at the April, 1977 meeting of the American Psychoanalytic Association.

Schur, M. (1966). Some additional "day residues" of the specimen dream of psychoanalysis. In *Psychoanalysis—A General Psychology*, ed. R. M. Loewenstein et al. New York, International Universities Press. Also in *Freud and His Self-Analysis*, vol. 1 of the Downstate Twenty-fifth Anniversary Series. New York: Jason Aronson, 1979.

———— (1972). *Freud: Living and Dying*. New York: International Universities Press.

Strachey, J. (1958). Papers on technique. Editor's introduction. *Standard Edition* 12:85–88.

Swan, J. (1974). *Mater* and nannie: Freud's two mothers and the discovery of the Oedipus Complex. *American Imago* 1:1–64.

Zetzel, E. R. (1965). Current concepts of transference. *International Journal of Psycho-Analysis* 37:369–376.

PART II

Dora

Chapter 1

FREUD'S ADOLESCENT PATIENTS:

KATHARINA, DORA AND THE

"HOMOSEXUAL WOMAN"

JULES GLENN, M.D.

With the exceptions of Erikson (1961, 1964) and Schlesinger 1969) psychoanalytic studies of adolescence fail to include an analysis of Freud's excellent clinical descriptions of three eighteen-year-old girls. (See, for instance, Blos 1962, Lorand and Schneer 1961, Caplan and Lebovici 1967, H. Deutsch 1944, 1967, A. Freud 1958, Friend 1972, Pearson 1968, Harley 1974.) Adatto (1966), Blos (1962, 1972), Friend (1972), Lewin (1973) and Marcus (1976) are aware that Dora was an adolescent. Blos (1962) lists Freud (1950a) in his Chronological Bibliography of the Psychoanalytic Literature on Adolescence and refers to Freud (1920) in his discussion of homosexuality. Friend (1972) refers to Freud (1905a) in his paper. Neither Friend nor Blos discusses Freud's three eighteen-year-old patients, however. Rogow (1978), whose paper appeared after this chapter was drafted, also recognizes Dora's adolescent status, and in fact has ascertained that her birth date was November

I want to thank Drs. Isidor Bernstein, Harold P. Blum, Bernard D. Fine, Milton E. Jucovy, Mark Kanzer, Eugene Kaplan, Shelley Orgel, Jay Shorr, and Herbert J. Urbach for their helpful suggestions. I also am indebted to Mrs. Albert Sax for her editorial help.

1, 1882. She was thus, he states, "not quite eighteen when she began her analysis in October, 1900" (p. 342 footnote). In addition, Rogow has identified Dora as Ida Bauer, the sister of Otto Bauer, "an influential Marxist theoretician and leader of the Austrian Socialist Party from 1918 to 1934" (p. 355).

Lewin (1973) attempts a reanalysis of Dora, but does not discuss her adolescence as such. Similarly, Muslin and Gill (1978), whose article also appeared after this chapter was drafted, discuss technical and theoretical considerations in the analysis of Dora without going into the significance of her adolescence. Marcus (1976), while emphasizing the literary characteristics of Freud's case report, also makes some telling comments on her adolescence.

Indeed, Freud himself does not appear to have realized that Katharina (Breuer and Freud, 1895–1897), Dora (Freud 1905a), and the unnamed "homosexual woman" (Freud 1920) were adolescents. Although his calling them "girls" indicates that he was aware that they had not achieved full maturity at eighteen, he was not explicit regarding this point and did not discuss the influence of their developmental level (see Marcus 1976). Erikson (1964) has clearly demonstrated that the applications of insights from our present knowledge of adolescence can be fruitful in adding to our understanding of Dora. In this paper I will attempt to cast more light on Dora as a teenager, and to discuss the other two eighteen-year-olds as well. This study encompasses the developmental point of view (Settlage et al. 1974). The patients are seen to have been in a state of flux, struggling to advance from one level of integration to another.

In 1905 Freud published his monumental work on the transformations of puberty in the *Three Essays on the Theory of Sexuality*. This paper, an essential building block on which further understanding of adolescence was later constructed, is also a cornerstone of the libido theory. The incorporation of these findings into the structural theory was yet to come. It is not surprising then that the analytic picture of adolescence was far from complete when Freud studied the three adolescent cases. Analytic theory did not spring forth at once, but, like all scientific knowledge, resulted from repeated obervations, from insight followed by insight. It would be worthwhile to apply present knowledge and theory to the exquisite clinical observations of a time of less sophisticated knowledge.

Current psychoanalytic understanding can elucidate the lack of therapeutic success in two of the patients, Dora and the "homosexual woman." In each case lack of adequate knowledge of adolescent drive and defense organization and the appearance of typical but unrecognized transference and countertransference configurations made it impossible to institute the required technical measures.

For the purposes of this paper I would define adolescence in girls as the period from menarche to the consolidation of the personality. Both physiological and psychological aspects of this phase would be taken into account. In this definition, preadolescence, the period from the start of the psychological changes resulting from the increased hormonal secretions to the menarche, would not be considered part of adolescence proper. The term *prepuberty* refers to the physiological and physical changes associated with preadolescence.

In evaluating the physiological and psychological developmental status of the three patients to be discussed, we must keep in mind that when they lived, the age at which prepuberty started was about the same as at present, but that adolescence generally started much later. When Katharina and Dora were teenagers the average age of menarche for European girls was approximately sixteen and three-quarters years, three or more years later than is the case now. (I am indebted to Mrs. Erna Furman (1975) for alerting me to this data and suggesting that psychological consequences must occur.) In the second decade of the twentieth century, when the "homosexual woman" attained menarche, the average age at which the first period occurred was fourteen and three-quarters. According to the data collected by Tanner (1962), whereas the average age of menarche was thirteen in 1955, the average age of the first period of a German girl of 1895 was sixteen and a quarter years. He offers no statistics for Austrian girls.

Tanner's data regarding the age of prepuberty at the time of Freud's three patients are limited and not clear-cut. Of course there is no information as to the levels of hormone production at that time. There is some information about one indication of prepuberty: the age at which more rapid acceleration of height occurs. Statistics are available for Swedish girls only, and these are limited to 1883 and 1938. The peak of the Swedish girls' growth spurt in 1883 occurred at the age of twelve on average, three and a half years prior to menarche. This peak appears to occur somewhat earlier for Swedish girls of 1938. In 1938 the average age of the start of the growth spurt was eleven, while the height of the growth spurt occurred at twelve, a year before menarche.

Juggling these figures, it would appear that in Katharina's and Dora's day preadolescence lasted longer than it does now; it started at the same age as now (or perhaps slightly later), but adolescence proper started about three years later. One must remember that the scene by the lake, which happened when Dora was sixteen, may well have occurred at about the time she had her first period. We may assume with confidence that each of these eighteen-year-old patients had entered adolescence.

Freud may have failed to consider them adolescents because he had no clear concept of the criteria for the end of this development stage. Consolidation (Blos 1962), commitment (Pumpian-Midlin 1965) and the establishment of a firm sense of adult identity (Erikson 1959) were yet to be part of psychoanalytic theory. In addition, perhaps Freud's blind spot regarding his teenage patients stemmed from a societal expectation that at eighteen adolescence would be over. Although it is possible that in the period of 1890–1920, when Freud wrote about these patients, many young women of their age had achieved sufficient stability so that even now we would consider them past the age of adolescence, it is likely that even the "stable" young women of Dora's time were quite infantile. Marriage occurred at an earlier age than now. Young women, however, were often treated like children by their parents until they were married and then were treated like children by their husbands. The social setting at that time made prolongation of adolescence difficult to perceive.

There is insufficient evidence to determine the level of development of Katharina at the time Freud saw her. Close examination of Dora and the "homosexual woman," however, makes it clear that neither had progressed to adulthood; both were still enmeshed in attempts to overcome their attachments to their parents. Dora was still attempting to achieve a firm heterosexual position and the "homosexual woman" was bound more to homosexual than heterosexual pursuits.

Summary of Dora's Case History with an Emphasis on the Adolescent Process

Dora was brought to Freud by her father, a former patient whose luetic infection had been diagnosed and cured. She had suffered from dyspnea, migraine, a nervous cough, and aphonia for years, but these were not sufficiently disturbing to impel Dora to enter treatment when she first consulted Freud at the age of sixteen. Even when she was eighteen she agreed to psychoanalysis only because of her father's influence.

Several events led to the decision that she be analyzed. Shortly before a consultation with Freud at eighteen her parents found a suicide note that she had written. This and her fainting after insisting that her father break up with the K.'s led her father to ask Freud to "try to bring her to reason," to "talk Dora out of her belief that there was . . . more than friendship between himself and Frau K."

Indeed, in the course of the analysis Dora complained vehemently about the affair between Frau K. and her father, an affair which her keen eye clearly perceived. The K.'s and Dora's family had developed intimate relations when Frau K. nursed Dora's father who had been stricken with tuberculosis when Dora was six. Since the two families were extremely close, Dora developed strong attachments to Frau K., with whom she shared secrets, and to Herr K., who took her for walks and bought her presents. Herr K. tried to seduce the young girl when she was fourteen. He proposed to her at sixteen, shortly after her first visit to Freud. Herr K.'s denial that he had proposed infuriated Dora and made her urge her father to terminate his relations with the K.'s.

The analysis demonstrated that Dora was not aware of her love for Herr K., but that many of her symptoms were derivatives of her unconscious affection. She developed aphonia and the nervous cough as an expression of distress at his absence. Speech, for instance, lost its value when she could not speak to Herr K. In addition, the oral symptomatology derived from repressed wishes for fellatio.

The analysis, which lasted three months, centered around two dreams which cast much light on Dora's personality and symptomatology. The first dream occurred when "we were engaged upon a line of enquiry which led straight towards an admission that she had masturbated in childhood." After Dora blamed her father both for her illness and for her genital discharge which she connected with his syphilis, Freud told her that leukorrhea was due to masturbation. In the sessions after that she played with a small reticule, placing her finger into it, opening and closing it, a symptomatic act indicating a symbolic masturbation, a fact which Freud emphasized with marked frankness. On the day that Dora reported the first dream she played "secrets" with Freud by hiding a letter from him. She told Freud the dream a few days after it occurred.

A house was on fire. My father was standing beside my bed and woke me up. I dressed quickly. Mother wanted to stop and save her jewel-case; but father said: "I refuse to let myself and my two children be burnt for the sake of your jewel-case." We hurried downstairs, and as soon as I was outside I woke up. [Freud 1905a, p. 64]

The dream had been a recurrent one which she had first dreamed at L. when she was sixteen. At that time, while on a walk around the lake, Herr K. tried to propose to Dora, but she, offended, rebuffed him. She felt that she was being dishonorably seduced. Later that day she awoke from a nap to find Herr K. standing beside her bed. Soon thereafter, feeling in danger of further seduction when the key to her room disappeared, she decided to leave L. with her father. She expressed this resolve in the dream which repeated itself nightly until they actually left.

Freud further interpreted the dream as a demonstration that Dora summoned her old love for her father to protect her against her present unconscious love for Herr K. Later he connected this event with the realization that Dora wished her analyst would kiss her and that this forbidden desire made her decide to leave treatment.

I regret having to omit the details of the web of associations that led to these interpretations and to other insights that emerged from the dream, in particular the linking of sexual wetness, enuresis, and Dora's early use of bedwetting in childhood to put out the sexual fires.

The second dream appeared a few weeks after the first. It occurred while Dora and Freud were trying to understand why she had said nothing about the proposal by the lake for several days before suddenly telling her parents. Freud also wondered why Dora felt injured by K.'s proposal.

I was walking about in a town which I did not know. I saw streets and squares which were strange to me. Then I came into a house where I lived, went to my room, and found a letter from Mother lying there. She wrote saying that as I had left home without my parents' knowledge she had not wished to write to me to say that Father was ill. "Now he is dead, and if you like? you can come." I then went to the station and asked about a hundred times: "Where is the station?" I always got the answer: "Five minutes." I then saw a thick wood before me which I went into, and there I asked a man whom I met. He said to me: "Two and a half hours more." He offered to accompany me. But I refused and went alone. I saw the station in front of me and could not reach it. At the same time I had the usual feeling of anxiety that one has in dreams when one cannot move forward. Then I was at home. I must have been travelling in the meantime, but I know nothing about that. I walked into the porter's lodge, and enquired for our flat. The maid-servant opened the door to me and replied that Mother and the others were already at the cemetery. [p. 94]

On the third of the three days that were spent analyzing this dream, Dora announced that two weeks previously she had decided to terminate the analysis on that very day. The associations to the dream clarified a great deal about the complex feelings Dora had toward Herr K. and her parents.

On the day that Herr K. proposed to Dora at the lake at L. he had said, "You know I get nothing from my wife." These words were offensive to Dora because she had learned that Herr K. had used those very words when trying to seduce a maid. Her pride and common sense were offended and she slapped his face out of jealousy and a desire for revenge. She identified with the maid who had written to her parents of having been seduced, waited to ascertain Herr K.'s intentions and then left after giving notice. A maid's notice being two weeks, Dora repeated the act of leaving after that period of time when she terminated the analysis.

Dora became aware of her love and tenderness for Herr K. The appearance of hysterical symptoms imitating appendicitis nine months after the episode at L. derived from her wish to become pregnant. Dora wanted to marry Herr K. and hoped that he would propose sincerely. Instead he accused her of fabricating the story of the scene by the lake. Sadly, this accusation was supported by Dora's other love object, Frau K. No wonder Dora was furious.

The second dream expressed Dora's craving for revenge against Herr K. and her father as did Dora's suicide note: her father was dead. Her anger was transferred to Freud, whom she left.

When Dora returned fifteen months later, Freud determined after "one glance at her face" that she was not in earnest over her request for further help. At the end of the single session Freud "promised to forgive her for having deprived me of the satisfaction of affording her a far more radical cure for her troubles" (p. 122).

During that session Dora told Freud that she had confronted Frau K. with the fact that she and her father had an affair and had gotten Herr K. to admit what happened at the lake. Dora told her father of her vindication. She also reported that a facial neuralgia had appeared two weeks previously when she had read of Freud's becoming a professor. This pain was a self-punishment for having slapped Herr K., and for her transferring her vengeful wishes to Freud.

Discussion

Although Dora's age, eighteen, indicates to us that she was an adolescent, other characteristics made it clear that she had not left that developmental stage at the time of her analysis. She was still attempting to disentangle herself from her parental ties. Indeed, the fact that her father brought her to the analyst, as do the parents of many teenagers, is a reflection of her adolescent dependence on them. This common mode of entrance into treatment can create difficulties, as it did in Dora's case. The teenager's wish for autonomy leads to a struggle against the analyst, who is foisted on her and who, in addition, is felt to be an agent of the parents from whom she is trying to break away. In Dora's case Freud discovered a peculiar type of pathological family interaction which made it especially difficult for the teenager to progress past adolescence.

Typically the adolescent, under the pressure of the phase-appropriate increase of drives, finds himself struggling against renewed libidinal and aggressive cathexis of his parents. In Dora's case the family's providing her with Herr K., a man much older than she was, led to a secondary struggle against an intense love for an unacceptable oedipal substitute. Finding a non-incestuous object was difficult when she was thrown together with an older man married to a woman who was a mother-substitute. As we will see, the intimacy of the analytic situation is a threatening one for a young woman who is trying to avoid attachment to older men. As Freud suggested, oedipal rivalry, jealousy and desire for revenge spurred Dora's wish to break up her father's affair with Frau K. But, in addition, her antagonism toward her father and Herr K. must also have reflected a defensive need to avoid sexual urges toward them. Typically, adolescents make liberal use of the mechanism of reversal, changing love for their parents to hatred. This defense serves an adaptive function when it leads to independence and a new adult sense of identity. Freud did not fully appreciate the complexities involved, since at the time he was still struggling to recognize simpler forms of transference.

Nor did Freud fully appreciate Dora's adolescent seductiveness, possibly because her antagonism masked it, possibly because a teenage ingenuousness made the patient appear less openly sexual than she was. Her playing with the reticule, which Freud correctly interpreted as a derivative of masturbatory wishes, appears to have been a seductive gesture as well, an unconscious invitation to penetration.

Dora's marked bisexuality, another typical and unresolved adolescent problem, was clearly manifest. Not only was she still attracted to both Herr K. and Frau K.; Freud had reason to believe that the transference to him contained both heterosexual and homosexual elements.

Freud was impressed by Dora's intellectual acuity. She could ferret out the evidence of her father's intimacies with Frau K. and draw correct conclusions about them. She could observe adult hypocrisies and lies with accuracy. Yet at the same time, she could ignore significant aspects of the family situation that failed to serve her purposes. This is a common picture in adolescence: a typically increased cognitive capacity juxtaposed to certain defects of reality testing. This failure to appreciate reality is often a result of increased drives which make action imperative even before their possible results can be evaluated.

Piaget and Inhelder (1969) have described teenagers' achieving the stage of formal operations in which they can make deductions from hypotheses regardless of reality. They emphasize how this can lead to the search for ideals so typical of this time of life and so obvious in Dora's case. Adolescent narcissism joins with cognitive ability to enhance wishes for perfection and truth, for idealism. A primary determinant of the increase of narcissism at this age is the defensive shift of cathexis from object-representation to the self and self-representation (A. Freud 1958, Blos 1962). Certain types of planned adaptive and non-adaptive actions of adolescence are results of the advanced cognitive state of the adolescent (Glenn and Urbach 1979); Blos (1966) considers acting out a phase-specific characteristic of adolescence. (Blos uses the term broadly and does not restrict it to acting out in the transference.)

Freud's careful observation of Dora provides us with the opportunity to evaluate the complex motives for some of her behavior, specifically Dora's breaking off of treatment and her return to Freud for a single visit after one year. In the interim, she dramatically achieved a tacit admission from Frau K. that the latter had had an affair with Dora's father, and from Herr K. that he had indeed attempted to seduce her. She then "brought the news of her vindication home to her father."

The reader will recall that Dora's father "handed her over to [Freud] for psychoanalytic treatment" when she was eighteen in order to have him "try to bring her to reason," to " 'talk' Dora out of her belief that there was something more than a friendship between him and Frau K." This primary motivation of Dora's father overshadowed his wish that she be relieved of her symptoms.

Freud uncovered a fascinating social interaction. Dora's mother was a compulsive housewife and a frigid woman; her father found sexual gratification in an affair with Frau K. The family encouraged Dora's friendship with Frau K., with whom she spent many intimate hours, while Herr K., who spent much time with her, gave her gifts and at least twice attempted to seduce her. A type of conspiracy occurred. "She was right in thinking that her father did not wish to look too closely into Herr K.'s behavior to his daughter, for fear of being disturbed in his own love-affair with Frau K." For a long time Dora "made herself an accomplice in the affair" by dismissing "from her mind every sign which tended to show its true character." Erikson correctly characterizes this as "a classic example of fatefully perverted fidelity" (1964, p. 172) in which each of the adults burdened her "with truths and half-truths which were clearly unmanageable for an adolescent." In this complex situation Dora fell in love with Herr K. and developed symptoms which were expressions of conflicts over her unconscious libidinal desires.

Freud became only partially aware of the transference while the treatment was in progress. During the analysis he observed that Dora was suspicious of him as she was of her father; she feared he might not be straightforward. Later he noted that Dora felt towards him as she did to Herr K. He postulated that she must have wished him to kiss her as she had wanted Herr K. to, and stated: "This would have been the exciting cause which led her to . . . form the intention of stopping the treatment" (p. 74).

Freud certainly demonstrated the displacement from father and Herr K. to himself. But he did not definitely prove that transference occurred; to do so, he would have had to demonstrate oedipal wishes from early childhood either through the patient's recall or through confirmation of reconstructions. Freud did offer a reconstruction which the patient confirmed in part. Today we would have more stringent requirements for proof that the reconstruction was true. An incomplete analysis of but three months cannot be expected to clearly demonstrate as much as a longer treatment would. Knowledge from other patients, however, convinces us of the transference involved in these displacements.

Freud failed to observe that his own behavior reinforced Dora's conviction that he was like her father and Herr K. Without being aware of this, he could not make the interpretations necessary to allow Dora to continue her analysis. Simply accepting Dora as a patient must have convinced the young woman that he intended to do just what her father wished, that is, to bring her to her senses and get her to ignore the affair. Freud's refusal to put the truth aside was not so potent as Dora's unanalyzed transference expectation that he would do just that. Hence Freud was viewed as one of the conspirators.

Freud's premature interpretations of Dora's symptomatic acts and their masturbatory significance must have convinced her that he was a dangerous sexual adult trying to seduce her. Freud's determination not to submit to Victorian taboos kept him from hesitating to discuss sexual subjects frankly with such a young woman very early in the analysis, even when his lack of caution served to accentuate the transference and frighten the patient. Following his explanations about autoerotic activity she had the first dream which contained a determination to leave a dangerous house; she must have been terrified that her wishes would come true. The analyst's failure to interpret her fear and its reality reinforcement led to Dora's flight.

Freud interpreted the second dream, which occurred soon after the first, as an expression of revenge. She would leave Freud after a period equivalent to a maid's notice just as she wished to leave Herr K. after a similar time. Because Herr K. had toyed with her as he had with a maid, because he did not seriously propose a permanent union, she would leave him. And so she would part from her analyst.

The development of ego psychology impels us to supplement Freud's description of Dora's dynamics. I suggest that Dora, fearing betrayal and desertion, turned a passive situation to one in which she was active: she became the deserter and perhaps betrayed Freud by ending treatment. When Freud wrote Dora's case history, he conceptualized anxiety as a manifestation of repressed libido. Clinical facts later convinced him that anxiety led to repression. Dora's separation anxiety was defended against by her choice of activity.

Let us summarize the determinants of Dora's leaving analysis that we have arrived at thus far.

1. Distrust of Freud, who reminded her of her wily and lying father. The transference was intensified by the reality of Freud's accepting the adolescent as a patient, and thus tacitly, in her view, joining the family conspiracy.

2. Fear of Freud as a seducer who discussed sexual matters frankly but

prematurely. Again, reality reinforced the displacement from Herr K., who in turn represented her father.

3. Fear of her own sexual wishes toward Freud which involved transference feelings.

4. A need to turn from passive to active when threatened with desertion or betrayal.

5. Revenge against Freud, which was again transferred from her desire to get even with other adults, including Herr K.

Another probable determinant of the patient's flight from analysis is the diminution of parental support to which Freud alluded in his postscript. Once the girl's father realized that the analyst would not attempt to convince Dora that he and Frau K. were not engaging in an affair, his enthusiasm for the treatment waned. Dora's need to please her father was one of the chief influences that brought her into treatment; with this motivation diminished or even reversed, Dora was less likely to continue. The analysis of an adolescent is a difficult enough undertaking; without parental backing it often fails. If the parent is unconsciously opposed to the truth it exposes, he may sabotage it.

Erikson (1964) and, following him, Schlesinger (1969) emphasized Dora's adolescent ideal of searching for the truth, yet we have noted that she was selective about what aspects of truth she would recognize. According to Erikson, her view of the truth differed from Freud's: she sought the "historical truth" while Freud was interested in the "psychic truth." Erikson suggested that this clash and Freud's failure to appreciate fully her idealism led her to return to her analyst a year after the termination for but a single visit.

Although many teenagers consciously seek the truth, unconscious wishes and defenses usually prevent their searching for the entire truth in undistorted form. Dora perceived only aspects of the external, historical truth. Knowledge of Herr K.'s wishes was avoided in part because she had to repress her own sexual response. By emphasizing parts of the truth, for instance immoral or dishonest behavior by his parents, while ignoring other admirable characteristics, the adolescent is able to maintain a disapproving distance from figures whom he finds threatening incestuous objects. As we will see, stating the truth can be a hostile act in itself. There are other vicissitudes of distortion as well. If the adolescent's need for idealization of parents, their surrogates or of himself predominates, he may ignore ignoble aspects and see only admired traits. This may defensively act to prevent the depression that results from decathexis of parental representation and devaluation of adults. Low self-esteem resulting from failure of parent or child to achieve ideals, to live up to the impossible narcissistically tinged standards typical of teenagers, may also be combatted in this way. Although Dora's depression and her idealism may well have followed such patterns, there is insufficient evidence to make definite statements along these lines. In addition, distortions under the illusion of seeking the entire truth may serve as rationalizations.

Dora returned to Freud after she learned that he had achieved the rank of professor. She told him of her confrontation with the grown-ups who had dishonestly conspired to use her as a pawn to facilitate their affair. Of the many features of her last session, Freud emphasized two: that Dora was insincere in stating that she wished help, and that she was bent on revenge.

In my opinion, his conclusion that Dora was insincere, based on her initial appearance, was rash. He must certainly have seen signs of hostility. However, not only is ambivalence a frequent configuration in our patients; it is especially so in teenagers. They typically defend themselves from attachments to adults, especially parents and their surrogates, by a sneering opposition. I suspect that Freud did not properly evaluate Dora's teenage hostility and that he responded too intensely to it. Her reaction to feeling deserted first by Herr K. and then by Freud, who decided to "forgive" Dora rather than analyze her, was built on an affectionate tie to men. Her therapeutic alliance rested in part on her positive transference. It was also built on a hope of finding a neutral, non-incestuous, non-corrupt object with whom to establish a new type of relationship with what Erikson calls a mentor. Dora's failure to continue the analysis was in part due to Freud's failure to encourage her to do so. It is not simply that Freud would not become her mentor; he declined to continue to be her analyst. The reader will recall that when Dora announced that she was there for her last session, Freud accepted it as a fait accompli. He did not offer appropriate advice to continue in conjunction with analyzing her resistances and conflicts. He did not attempt, as we would now, to discover the basis for her statement. Although ostensibly continuing the analysis to the end, he in fact ignored the main issue before Dora and him.

There was also a narcissistic element in Dora's return to Freud after a year's absence. She had learned that her analyst had become a professor. She must have been proud to have been connected with such an esteemed person and decided to resume contact with him. But, narcissistically wounded as she had been by those loved adults who had deceived, used, and dropped her, she was always ready to attack those she admired.

Teenage idealism, the typical search for the truth, has a narcissistic core, incorporating fantasies of union with a perfect object. Dora, yearning for this ideal, must have appreciated Freud's remarkable integrity and his single-minded search for truth in his work. After all, he had not actually submitted to her father's will; rather, he had encouraged Dora to face the reality of the conspiracy surrounding her. She must have described her confrontations of Herr K., Frau

K., and her father with the truth about their relationships with the expectation that Freud would approve. Despite Erikson's contention that Freud frowned on this as "acting out," I can find no statement of disapproval in the case study. Freud's concept of the truth, however, did reach beyond Dora's; his included the internal wishes and conflicts as well as the external setting and environmental influence. He also recognized that the cathexis of the external truth could be used as a defense against recognizing the internal conflicts.

In summary, Dora returned to Freud not only to underline her revenge. She also returned because he was a narcissistic object with whom she wished contact, because he was a man of integrity who shared her adolescent love of truth, and because he might prove to be a non-incestuous object that she could use as a mentor or an analyst to achieve a cure of her difficulties.

After Dora stopped her analysis, she told Frau K. that she knew of the affair with her father, got Herr K. to admit that the scene at the lake had in fact occurred, and reported her vindication to her father. This remarkable activity grew out of her analysis, but Freud did not attempt to understand its meaning.

We have already discussed Dora's adolescent love for the truth, but this alone does not explain her need to *tell* the truth to the adults. I would suspect that despite her insistence during her analysis that the affair did occur and her reporting the scene at L., she was not completely sure of the reality of these events; she did not have sufficient confidence in herself to know with certainty that her perceptions were correct when the adults denied them. Hence, she had to get the grown-ups to confirm her observations. Schlesinger (1969), who emphasizes the family interaction, states that the adult denial of the truth was "a threat to her ego-cognitive powers."

The confrontation was, in addition, an act of revenge against those who tried to hide the truth. She invoked what can be called honesty in the service of sadism as she attacked Frau K., Herr K. and her father.

Dora also was reversing the childhood situation in which adults insist that the children tell the truth no matter how painful it is. She became the aggressor who forced honesty on her cowering victims. Such an act of defiance ordinarily serves to make the teenager feel equal or superior to his parents and hence more independent of these adults. As such it is a sign of the transition from adolescence to adulthood. But Dora remained fixated at this stage and failed to achieve an adaptive autonomy.

I have mentioned that Erikson (1964) believed Freud had frowned on the confrontation described as "acting out." Although Freud did not mention this possibility, I believe that the telling did contain an element of defense against the impact of the analysis. Dora seemed to be trying to prove that the internal determinants of her behavior were less important than the external events—or not significant at all. Although ostensibly complying with the shared analytic ideal of the truth, Dora may have been dissipating its effectiveness through her actions.

A number of factors led her to walk out a second time and never return. The pull of the transference deprived her of the relatively neutralized attachment to the analyst that is needed for the therapeutic alliance. The unanalyzed wish for him as an incestuous object, her reactive adolescent antagonism, and her vengeful displaced feelings became dominant once again. In the course of a successful analysis the relatively rational and neutralized therapeutic alliance is balanced against the intense drive-dominated transferences; the two may coexist and alternate. Freud's failure to analyze the irrational aspects of Dora's relationship to him led her to become narcissistically wounded once more, this time by the doctor who would not encourage a resumption of treatment. Probably, too, she was fearful of continuing the search for the truth in the caverns of her inner psyche as well as in the external world. We have already mentioned her paradoxical compliance with her father's wish that she stop treatment. Sadly, we must add that Freud himself prevented Dora from returning to treatment by not offering to continue the analysis.

The term *acting out* does not adequately characterize Dora's behavior. She did act out insofar as she substituted action for words and thoughts, thus repeating past experiences. Freud never determined what the early childhood experiences were; in this sense, the action was defensively effective. Deutsch's (1957) description of the middle-aged Dora clearly and sadly demonstrates that satisfactory adaptation was never achieved, either in the short term or in the long run. Dora grew into a disgruntled hypochondriacal woman, still accusing those about her of infidelity and corruption. Her bungling attempts at adaptation through contact with Freud, through seeking the truth, through breaking ties with her parents and parental surrogates, through attempting to find decent replacements, did not succeed. As an adolescent she had used her keen cognitive capacity to expose the deficiences of the adults. She continued to do this, but was not able to channel her abilities so as to rid herself of her symptoms and find a reasonable degree of gratification.

Freud's inactivity when Dora decided to leave analysis and his hasty and premature judgment that Dora was insincere in her request to resume treatment suggest the existence of countertransference. Although he does not spell out his conscious reasons for not resuming treatment, it would appear that he felt analysis had not been and could not be successful due to several factors: Dora had transferred her wish for revenge against Herr K. and her father to him, and deprived and would continue to deprive Freud "of the satisfaction of affording her a far more radical cure for her troubles."

Freud made a similar formulation in the case of the "homosexual woman." We will compare Dora and that patient after discussing Katharina.

Katharina

Another adolescent patient in whom Freud discovered a fierce commitment to the truth was Katharina. His session with her was more a consultation than a treatment. This second adolescent girl is actually the first that Freud reported (Breuer and Freud, 1895–1897). Since he saw her only once and did not have detailed information about the transference, her reliability or her general character, we are on shaky ground in trying to evaluate Freud's conclusions and draw our own. Katharina was one of the patients that Freud thought was seduced by a parent. Later he recognized that oedipal fantasies often lay behind a patient's conviction of an incestuous encounter (Freud 1954). Although I am inclined to believe Katharina's tale, we cannot be certain about the accuracy of an account given in a single interview. Nevertheless, let us attempt to evaluate Freud's observations and conclusions. He did learn a great deal about Katharina, then "perhaps eighteen," in a single informal session.

Again we find adolescent ambivalence. At first this young woman appeared depressed and antagonistic—"sulky-looking," Freud says. But nevertheless she was very cooperative, willing to reveal extremely personal experiences to Freud in the hope of attaining relief from certain symptoms.

While Freud was on vacation, Katharina, the daughter of his landlady, asked him for help with her hysterical symptoms: dyspnea, anxiety, feelings of pressure on her eyes and chest, and a hallucination of an angry man. Through skillful, sympathetic and tactful questioning and interpretation, Freud learned of the following sequence of events.

Katharina's father (in the original paper Freud identified this man as her uncle but later corrected this disguise) was an alcoholic and had made unsuccessful attempts to seduce his daughter when she was fourteen and again later. At an early unspecified age she had also seen him attempt to enter the room of another girl, her cousin; when Katharina was sixteen she caught her father in bed with this cousin. Mild symptoms of anxiety, dyspnea, and pressure had appeared previously, but after this primal scene observation they became severe. Although Katharina kept this discovery to herself for a while, she finally told the truth to her mother, who had indeed noticed that something was wrong. The subsequent fights between her parents led to their divorce. Father, in a furious state, blamed Katharina for causing the separation and threatened her. As the young woman talked of these events, she realized that her hallucnation was of her father's angry face. Eventually Katharina also told her mother of her father's attempt to seduce her.

Although he did not psychoanalyze Katharina, Freud was able to reach certain conclusions. He reconstructed the girl's disgust at remembering the discovery of her father and cousin together with the feelings she had experienced when her father had tried to seduce her when she was fourteen. These feelings to which Freud directs our attention were of disgust and the pressure against her of her father's body, probably his penis, but we should also suspect the sensations of her own inner excitement.

According to Freud, Katharina was unaware of the meaning of the attempt at seduction at fourteen, but it attained a traumatic impact at a later date when she acquired an understanding of sexual life. The discovery at sixteen was both an ''auxiliary moment'' (i.e., a moment in which the previous potential trauma became converted to an actual trauma) and an actual traumatic moment producing the hysterical symptoms. In 1895 Breuer and Freud contended that a psychic trauma, occurring while the patient was in a hypnoid state, led to the appearance of hysterical symptoms which were memories of the disturbing event. Freud used Katharina to demonstrate the sexual nature of the pathogenic trauma. We will put aside the 1895 theory of the psychopathology of hysteria in this account since Freud later disowned it and concentrate instead on Freud's concepts of and observations on adolescence.

Interestingly enough, Freud did not seem to consider Katharina an adolescent. In his only comment about adolescence during the clinical discussion of this patient, he referred to her lack of knowledge about sex at fourteen as typical of adolescence; by implication, her conscious knowledge of the sexual act at eighteen indicated a later stage of development. Nevertheless, Freud's careful observations supply us with information that enables us to see indications of a number of adolescent characteristics: the increase of drives at that age; her struggle against dependence and reliance on her parents; her reactions to incestuous temptations; her ambivalence; her teenage idealism; her capacity for planned action.

I would like to underline Katharina's idealism, her interests in the truth, an adolescent trait that Dora also possessed. It took courage to ferret out her father's secret rendezvous, even though the truth taxed her psychic equilibrium and caused her great anxiety so that she had to repress inner feelings and deny important segments of reality. But she nevertheless steadfastly exposed her father to her mother. We can certainly agree with Freud's hint that Katharina was jealous and add that she sought revenge against her unfaithful father, as Dora had done. We suspect in addition, however, that by exposing her father's acts she sought to protect herself from future incestuous temptations and paternally inflicted traumata. We should not, moreover, ignore the idealism of adolescence, the insistence that child and adult live up to standards of perfection, that the truth be upheld. The developing ego-ideal of the teenager which is based, as we have noted, on narcissism and increased cognitive capacity, also impelled Katharina to discover and announce the truth. But of course the libidinal aspects should not be ignored; as Freud suspected, both adolescents and younger children react with intense bodily sensations to sexual stimulation.

Freud specifically commented on the possibility that adolescents possessed greater sexual knowledge than was generally believed in his day. In what would appear now to be a naive view, he attributed Katharina's lack of awareness of sexuality at fourteen to simple ignorance. Then, in a daring speculation for 1895, he astutely suspected that the lack of awareness and "splitting off of elements" were in truth due to "conscious rejection" of sexual knowledge already acquired at that age. He thought that perhaps even adolescents possessed "sexual knowledge far oftener than is supposed or than they themselves believe." As a result of Freud's discoveries, we would not agree with this and add that not only did "conscious rejection" of such knowledge occur, but unconscious repression also.

Summary: The Psychogenesis of a Case
of Female Homosexuality

The unnamed woman that Freud studied was a "beautiful and clever girl of eighteen" who had distressed her parents, especially her father, by pursuing a society lady ten years her senior. This lady, known to be heterosexually promiscuous, also engaged in homosexual relations, but not with Freud's patient. In fact, despite the patient's adoration, the lady repeatedly and coldly rejected her, advising her to give up her homosexual interests. The patient for her part was quite open in her friendship; but at the same time she lied and was deceptive to her father regarding her meeting with the lady. After her father angrily discovered her with her friend, she attempted suicide by jumping over a wall onto a railway line. After that her parents sought help and eventually brought her to Freud. She had no urgent desire to be freed of her homosexuality, which was latent and had not been gratified except through a few kisses and embraces. Nevertheless, she agreed to undertake analysis for her parents' sake, since she had caused them grief.

In childhood, the "homosexual woman" experienced the usual Oedipus complex and later she started to become interested in her older brother as a substitute for her father. Her mother preferred her three brothers to her. The penis envy which she developed after seeing her brother's genitals at five or before persisted with intensity to the time of the start of treatment. She was a feminist who felt it unjust that boys had more freedom than girls and who bemoaned the status of women. From an early age she was an active, aggressive girl, "spirited," Freud said. During prepuberty she acquired sexual information with normally mixed feelings. As a schoolgirl she had fallen in love with a strict mistress, a mother substitute.

At the age of thirteen or fourteen she developed an exaggerated affection for a two-year-old boy and soon replaced this with an interest in "mature, but still youthful women." Freud suggests that her homosexual interest "was probably a direct and unchanged continuation of an infantile fixation on her mother." With her mother's pregnancy and the birth of her third brother when she was sixteen her interest in women became fixed.

As Freud portrayed her, she manifested in the few months that he treated her many of the characteristics of an excellent analytic patient. She described dreams which shed considerable light on her pathology. The analysis moved forward almost without any signs of resistance, the patient participating actively with her intellect, although remaining absolutely tranquil emotionally. As we will see, this isolation and the patient's hostility led Freud to terminate the treatment.

With the help of a series of dreams, Freud was able to understand the intensity of his patient's homosexual desires. Puberty, he noted, revives the Oedipus complex; hence she desired at that time to have a child by her father. But instead "her unconsciously hated rival, her mother," bore the baby. Furious at her father, she turned away from him and other men; she repudiated the feminine role. Identifying with the lost libidinal object, her father, she became "a man and took her mother in place of her father as an object of her love." She then sought substitutes for her mother who was in fact sexually unattainable.

At the same time, by losing her interest in men she "retired in favour of her mother" and took revenge on her father who was distressed by her homosexuality. In addition, at the same time that the "homosexual woman" tried to achieve homosexual gratification from the older woman, she attempted to satisfy *heterosexual* desires, for the woman reminded her of her older brother.

The complexity of the patient's motivation is seen in Freud's analysis of her attempted suicide. This at once represented despair over fear of losing the woman she loved; self-punishment for her fury at her mother, her father and the woman who, like her father, wanted the affair stopped; symbolic expression of the wish to "fall" and thus have a child by her father; and an attack on her rival, her mother, with whom she identified.

Freud discussed another series of dreams which he believed were false or hypocritical. These dreams, which were easily interpreted, "anticipated the cure of the inversion through the treatment, expressed joy over the prospects in life that would then be opened before her, confessed a longing for a man's love and for children.'' The latent content of these dreams, however, contradicted the patient's conscious desires to continue with her bisexual propensities. Freud believed that in addition to trying to mislead and disappoint him, his patient was communicating a desire for his favor, but that this motivation was insufficient to permit a successful therapeutic result. He attributed his patient's use of isolation and doubt to displaced antagonism from her father to himself.

Freud decided to terminate the treatment after he determined that the girl's hatred for her father was so intense that she would make the treatment a failure in order to get revenge against the analyst, a father surrogate. He therefore suggested to the parents that the treatment be continued with a woman analyst rather than with himself.

Discussion

Our summary fails to do justice to the complex psychoanalytic insights that so beautifully organize the remarkable clinical observations. So rich is this paper that it seems ungrateful to tease out the characteristics that Freud did not study here, to emphasize what Freud ignored but hinted at. His unstated awareness that his patient was indeed an adolescent is revealed in his calling her a girl as well as a woman.

Twice during this paper he mentions adolescence, but each time he refers to an age younger than the patient's. First, he notes that she had experienced ''a revival of her infantile Oedipus complex at puberty'' when her mother became pregnant. Here he refers to an observation already made in the *Three Essays* (1905b), of the heightening of the libido that occurs at puberty. Freud again comments on adolescence when he states that ''even in a normal person it takes a certain time before the decision in regard to the sex of the love object is finally made. Homosexual enthusiasms, exaggeratedly strong friendships tinged with sensuality, are common enough . . . during the first years of puberty'' (1920, p. 168).

We can certainly see both the increased sexual interest of the adolescent and the bisexual conflict in the ''homosexual woman.'' She was so preoccupied with her infatuation that other interests were subordinated. Freud apparently did not realize that even the older adolescent can be undecided regarding object choice and then, with proper treatment or favorable circumstances, become heterosexual.

Another feature of adolescence, the dependency on and affection for the parents, is clearly seen in the way the treatment was initiated. As with Dora and most other adolescents, the parents brought her for treatment and she started analysis in part to please them. But, as is so often true, her struggle against parental attachment was characterized by an increase in hostility. We now recognize that her anger toward her father and mother were not simply drive-determined but had defensive and adaptive functions as well. Although Freud was thrown off by his failure to recognize the defensive aspects of the patient's adolescent ambivalence, he was nevertheless trying to cope with a problem of adolescent analysis, the difficulty in dealing with the transference manifestations. Female adolescents, drive-dominated as they are, often develop a sexual interest in the male analyst which is very difficult to deal with, and at times is unmanageable. Adolescence is characterized by lapses of reality testing which make it difficult for the analyst to show his patient that the infatuation with the analyst is based on past emotions and experience. Furthermore, adolescence is also characterized by an intense narcissism which often makes the analyst's attempts at analysis rather than gratification represent an insulting and humiliating rejection.

The patient will probably avoid such complications by the same devices with which she evades her intense attachment to her parents. She will turn away from the parent-like analyst and become intensely antagonistic. These mechanisms have adaptive functions in that they encourage the discovery of new, non-incestuous objects and foster phase-appropriate independence, separation, and individuation; it is also true that they frequently seem to work against analysis.

One technical means of attempting to avoid the defensive withdrawal from a threatening heterosexual attachment to the therapist is having the patient see an analyst of the same sex. This technique, however, does not always succeed since a person of the same sex can be a libidinal threat and since, as we have seen, factors other than sexual ones are at work. Freud thought that in the case of the "homosexual woman," treatment by a woman would bypass the transference of her wish to achieve revenge against her father. This seems an unlikely outcome to me, however, since it is possible to have a paternal transference to a woman as well as to a man. And certainly there is antagonism toward mother as well as father in this case.

Freud's paper was written sixteen years before Anna Freud described the defenses typical of adolescence in *The Ego and the Mechanisms of Defense*. Freud's description of the patient's "participating actively with her intellect though absolutely tranquil emotionally" (1920, p. 163) suggests the use not only of isolation but also of intellectualization, a defensive and adaptive mechanism typical of adolescence. It is true that those defenses can be used for resistance, but the teenager's enthusiastic use of his recently improved cognitive capacities to figure things out can also be of great value in analysis. Certainly Freud found it so; he learned a great deal about the psychogenesis of his patient's disorder. Those aspects of intellectualization that lead to resistance can often be analyzed. Although I do think that many adolescents are analyzable, I do not wish to be over-optimistic about the outcome of all analyses of adolescents. Which teenagers are analyzable is still subject to our scrutiny. (In 1971 a Panel on the Indications and Contraindications for the Psychoanalysis of the Adolescent probed this question at the May Meetings of the American Psychoanalytic Association—see Sklansky 1972.) I trust that it is valuable to raise the issues that analysts are attempting to clarify in the years following Freud's descriptions of Katharina, Dora and the "homosexual woman."

Countertransference to Adolescents

We may now attempt to reconstruct the interaction between Freud and two of his adolescent girl patients, Dora and the "homosexual woman," which led him in each case to a similar dynamic formulation of the resistances. In both instances Freud attributed the ending of analysis to the negative transference. In Dora's case he felt she left because of a wish to get revenge on her father and Herr K., now represented in the transference by Freud. Hence, he refused to continue the analysis when she returned after more than a year. In the "homosexual woman's" case, he anticipated the treatment's failure due to similar motives: the patient would take revenge on Freud, who was a substitute for her father, by making the analysis unsuccessful. Jones (1955) attributes the decision to terminate the treatment of the homosexual girl to Freud's greater experience, but perhaps it would be more accurate analytically to say that Freud, because he anticipated that he would become the deserted victim again, utilized reversal in order to become the active rejector instead. At any rate, in each case Freud did not entertain the possibility that a typically adolescent means of dealing with fears of the positive transference played a major role in interfering with the analytic process.

Each of these young women manifested the ambivalence typical of teenagers. In each, the affectionate, seductive interest in the analyst gave rise to a compliant attitude. Dora and the "homosexual woman" each provided Freud with fascinating dreams and useful associations which, especially in the former, were of tremendous value in the formulations of psychoanalysis. But each also reacted to this libidinal stream with the defensive reversal that Anna Freud has described: antagonism and resistance served as defenses against affection. The need for revenge against the father who failed to protect or turned away from the patient were additional sources of the patient's transferred antagonism to the analyst.

In most instances the libidinal component of this complex adolescent configuration is threatening to the analyst, and it is unlikely that this would not have been true of Freud. I suggest that, utilizing denial and repression, Freud under-estimated his patients' affection and desire for help, while overestimating their aggressive desires for revenge. The patients' vengeful wishes were used as a justification for terminating treatment and thus avoiding seeing patients who might evoke erotic responses in the therapist. Erotic responses in the analyst, especially when unrecognized, often come into conflict with the superego, since the patient is experienced as a tabooed oedipal object.

When Dora announced the ending of her treatment, she acted in such a way as to encourage the analyst to urge her to continue. By this subtle and disguised seduction she was attempting to get Freud to behave as she wished Herr K. to do. Such action on the part of a patient would ideally result in analysis of her motives and defenses. Freud, perhaps responding defensively to Dora's prov-ocation, remained passive; he neither analyzed nor advised.

The reaction that I am suggesting that Freud underwent is similar to that seen typically in parents who, trying to stem their attraction to their adolescent chil-dren, react instead to their children's sneering rebellious behavior by engaging in battles with them. Both adults and teenagers frequently try to push each other away.

That Freud did indeed treat Dora as if she were a child is seen in a certain paternalistic and even patronizing attitude:

> I opened the discussion of the subject with a little experiment, which was, as usual, successful. There happened to be a large match-stand on the table. I asked Dora to look round and see whether she noticed anything special on the table, something that was not there as a rule. She noticed nothing. I then asked if she knew why children were forbidden to play with matches.
>
> "Yes; on account of the risk of fire .. .."
>
> "Not only on that account. They are warned not to 'play with fire,' and a particular belief is associated with the warning." [1905a, p. 71]

When Dora does not come up with a full and correct answer, Freud author-itatively explains the connection between water, fire, enuresis and sexuality. In this approach he was reinforcing Dora's picture of him as a parent—and a seductive but prohibiting one at that.

In the cases of both Dora and the "homosexual woman" Freud expected respect. He objected to the manifestations of the negative transference as un-alterably dangerous to their treatments. Kanzer (personal communication) has noted that Freud's patient tolerance of the extreme hostility displayed by the Rat Man stands in marked contrast to his decisions to abandon the analyses of the two eighteen-year-olds. In a similar vein, Kanzer has observed that Freud patiently endured the Wolf Man's apathy but could not permit the "homosexual woman's" supposed lack of emotional involvement.

It is striking that Freud describes telling the "homosexual woman's" parents of his decision to end her therapy. In his text, if not in his actual action, he writes as if she were a dependent child whose opinions and reactions regarding termination or transfer need not be considered.

In addition to these considerations there is a more specific suggestion that Freud had erotic interests in female patients who were considered forbidden oedipal substitutes. In his discussion of the Irma dream, Grinstein suggests that the injection given to Irma was a derivative of Freud's unconscious wish to inject Irma sexually as part of the treatment. He states: "We may conjecture whether and to what extent Freud projected upon Otto his own feelings of a libidinal countertransference nature" (1968, p. 44).

Summary

Three eighteen-year-old girls—Katharina, Dora and the "homosexual woman"—were described by Freud before the development of ego psychology and the conceptualization of a comprehensive psychoanalytic theory of adolescence. Although he did not state that they were adolescents, Freud described many of the characteristic problems of that period of development in his case histories of these three young women.

Neither Dora nor the "homosexual woman" had achieved personality consolidation or a stable identity as an adult heterosexual woman; whether Katharina had is not clear from the material presented.

In addition we note in these cases the increased drive that is typical of puberty, the struggle against the intense attachment to parents and to certain adults who are perceived as parent surrogates, adolescent ambivalence, marked narcissism, adolescent idealism, and increased cognitive capacity.

It would appear that the termination of the analyses of Dora and the "homosexual woman" were in part due to Freud's failure to recognize their adolescent status, the defense mechanisms typical of the period, or his own countertransference reactions to them. Psychoanalytic knowledge had not yet reached the point that would enable him to realize that adolescent drive, defense, and adaptive organization require special technical measures.

References

Adatto, C.P. (1966). On the metamorphosis from adolescence into adulthood. *Journal of the American Psychoanalytic Association* 14:485–509.

Blos, P. (1962). *On Adolescence.* New York: Free Press of Glencoe.

———— (1966) Acting out in relation to the adolescent process. In *A Developmental Approach to Problems of Acting out,* ed. E. N. Rexford. New York: International Universities Press.

———— (1972). The epigenesis of the adult neurosis. *Psychoanalytic Study of the Child* 27:106–135.

Breuer, J., and Freud, S. (1893–1895). Studies on hysteria. *Standard Edition* 2.

Caplan, G., and Lebovici, S., eds. (1967). *Adolescence: Psychosocial Perspectivies.* New York: Basic Books.

Deutsch, F. (1957). A footnote to Freud's "Fragment of the analysis of a case of hysteria." *Psychoanalytic Quarterly* 16:159–167.

Deutsch, H. (1944). *The Psychology of Women.* Vol. 1. New York: Grune and Stratton.

———— (1967). *Selected Problems of Adolescence.* New York: International Universities Press.

Erickson, E. H., (1959). Identity and the life cycle. In *Psychological Issues,* vol. 1, no. 1. New York: International Universities Press.

———— (1964). Psychological reality and historical actuality. In *Insight and Responsibility.* New York: W. W. Norton.

Erikson, E. H., ed. (1961). *Youth: Change and Challenge.* New York and London: Basic Books.

Freud, A. (1936). *The Ego and the Mechanisms of Defense.* New York: International Universities Press.

———— (1958). Adolescence. *Psychoanalytic Study of the Child* 13:155–178.

Freud, S. (1905a). Fragment of an analysis of a case of hysteria. *Standard Edition* 7:3–122.

———— (1905b). Three essays on the theory of sexuality. *Standard Edition* 7:133–243.

———— (1920). The psychogenesis of a case of female homosexuality. *Standard Edition* 18:147–172.

———— (1954). *The Origins of Psychoanalysis. Letters to Wilhelm Fliess, Drafts and Notes: 1887–1902,* ed. M. Bonapart, A. Freud, E. Kris. Introduction by E. Kris. New York: Basic Books.

Friend, M. R. (1972). Psychoanalysis of adolescents. In *Handbook of Child Psychoanalysis,* ed. B. B. Wolman. New York: Van Nostrand Reinhold.

———— (1979). Indications and contraindications for the psychoanalysis of adolescents. In *Downstate Twenty-fifth Anniversary Series,* vol. III. New York: Jason Aronson

Furman, E. (1975). Discussion of the present paper at Cleveland Psychoanalytic

Chapter 2

FURTHER REFLECTIONS ON DORA

MELVIN A. SCHARFMAN, M.D.

Probably no case histories in the field of psychiatry have been as widely read as Freud's five major cases. They have been and continue to be read as part of the training of not only psychoanalytic candidates, but also psychiatric residents, psychologists, and social workers. In view of the widespread use of these papers as part of a teaching curriculum, it would seem of considerable importance to view them, both theoretically and clinically, through contemporary eyes. Often the student reads the case histories uncritically, without recognizing that Freud's formulations in these papers differ from our current views. In his consideration of Freud's adolescent patients, Glenn (Part II, Chapter 1 of this volume) attempts to juxtapose the case of Dora described in *Fragment of an Analysis of a Case of Hysteria* (Freud 1905a) and modern perspectives. He points out that at the time he wrote the paper Freud had not adequately conceptualized the adolescent developmental process. Freud's first discussion of adolescence was in the *Three Essays on the Theory of Sexuality* (1905b). Although published the same year as *Three Essays*, the actual writing of *Fragment of an Analysis of a Case of Hysteria* apparently predated that paper: Dora was first mentioned by Freud (1954) in a letter to Fliess written on October 14, 1900: "I have a new patient,

This paper is an expanded version of a discussion of Freud's Adolescent Patients. I: Dora, presented by J. Glenn at the American Psychoanalytic Association Meeting, Dec. 1975.

Society, Feb. 28, 1975.

Grinstein, A. (1968). *On Sigmund Freud's Dreams*. Detroit, W University Press.

Glenn, J., and Urbach, H. (1979). Adaptive and nonadaptive actio cence. In *Downstate Twenty-fifth Anniversary Series*, vol. III Jason Aronson.

Harley, M., ed. (1974). *The Analyst and the Adolescent at Work*. Quadrangle Press.

Jones, E. (1955). *The Life and Work of Sigmund Freud*. Vol. 2. Basic Books.

Lewin, K. K. (1973). Dora revisited. *Psychoanalytic Review* 60:5

Lorand, S., and Schneer, H. (1961). *Adolescents: Psychoanalytic Problems and Therapy*. New York: Hoeber.

Marcus, S. (1976) Freud and Dora: story, history, case history. *tations: Essays on Literature and Society*. New York: Random

Muslin, H. and Gill, M. (1978). Transference in the Dora case. *J American Psychoanalytic Association* 26:311–328.

Pearson, G. H. J., ed. (1968). *A Handbook of Child Psychoanalysi*. Basic Books.

Piaget, J., and Inhelder, B. (1969). *The Psychology of the Child* Basic Books.

Pumpian-Midlin, E. (1965). Omnipotentiality, youth and commit of the American Academy of Child Psychiatry* 4:1–18.

Rogow, A.A. (1978). A further footnote to Freud's "Fragment of a case of hysteria." *Journal of the American Psychoanalyti* 26:330–356.

Schlesinger, H. (1969). Family: a study of family member intera *Psychoanalytic Forum*, vol. 3, ed. J. A. Lindon, pp. 13–6 Science House.

Settlage, C. F., et al. (1974). Position Paper. Commission IX. C American Psychoanalytic Association Conference on Psychoa tion and Research.

Sklansky, M. A. (1972). Indications and contraindications for the of the adolescent. Panel report in *Journal of the American* Association* 20:134–44.

Tanner, J. M. (1962). *Growth at Adolescence*. Oxford: Blackw

a girl of eighteen; the case has opened smoothly to my collection of picklocks''
(p. 325). On January 25, 1901, in another letter to Fliess, he indicated that he
had completed writing a paper which concerned Dora's treatment (p. 325). The
treatment itself had lasted a little over three months, from October 1900 to
January 1901, and the paper was apparently completed in January, 1901. It
seems likely that the writing took place, or at least started, while the analysis
was proceeding.

As Glenn suggests, it is important to keep a historical perspective in mind
in reviewing any of these early writings. It is too easy to be overly critical of
these pioneering, exploratory beginnings of psychoanalysis rather than to engage
in a constructive reevaluation, particularly in areas that will have meaning for
both the current and future generations of psychoanalysts. Freud did not consider
Dora an adolescent. Many people today would also feel that, with an eighteen-
or nineteen-year-old girl, one could essentially proceed as with an adult in
analysis. Glenn points out that it is not the chronological age which determines
whether or not to consider someone an adolescent but rather the other phenomena
he discusses—that the treatment was initiated at the request of a parent, that
Dora was still living at home, that she was very much emotionally tied to her
family, that she was not functioning independently and had not yet made any
commitment to an appropriate love object outside of the family, and that she
had not reached the level of genital primacy. Even if many girls the same age
as Dora at that point in history and in that cultural setting might have been
viewed as adults, Dora clearly was not an adult. Using developmental criteria,
we would consider her a mid-or at best a late adolescent. Probably at that time,
just as now, patients coming from the more educated upper middle class were
more likely to have had a protracted adolescence. I am in agreement with Glenn's
view that Dora was an adolescent and with those aspects of the treatment he
considers from the point of view of her adolescent level of development. I would
like to elaborate a few of those points and add one or two others. In addition,
I will make some points of a more general nature about certain aspects of
feminine development.

Although Freud indicated that he did not wish to discuss the technique of
analysis in this paper, let us first turn to what is a technical aspect. Glenn pointed
to the fact that Freud discussed a great many sexual matters with Dora, including
direct interpretations of some of her behavior as well as of dream content. He
used a good deal of symbolic interpretation without consideration, such as would
be given today or even in his later writings, of the need to deal with defenses.
If one were to use the same style of symbolic interpretation it would be of
interest to note his comments in the above mentioned letter to Fliess that ''the
case has opened smoothly to my collection of picklocks.'' This would suggest

a sexualized view of the treatment, indicating that it was experienced as a penetration. With a virginal adolescent girl, especially a hysterical one, this would create technical problems in the form of increased anxiety and resistance.

In any event, the repetitive sexualized interpretations, occurring so early in the analysis, would have contributed to an erotization of the transference. But it is not this alone that creates the problem for an adolescent patient. Freud confronted the patient with the nature of her attachment to her father as well as to Herr K. At a time when the patient sought to distance herself from certain aspects of her oedipal feelings, such interpretations served the opposite purpose, directing Dora much too quickly back to the precise involvement from which she was struggling to free herself. We know now that one of the developmental needs of adolescents is to defend against revived oedipal attachments. Freud's interventions would have interfered with what was a necessary developmental position at that time. Generally during adolescence too early interpretation of transference reactions or of the displacement of oedipal feelings on to other objects pushes the adolescent into dealing with just those oedipal wishes which they have such great difficulty in handling. Such interventions frequently lead to interruptions of treatment with adolescent patients, particularly because they have difficulty in recognizing the transference as such early in the treatment. Some adolescents, particularly in the course of analysis, develop transient ego regressions and, at such times, experience difficulty in differentiating the transference as such, instead reacting to the analyst as the primary object. They lose the "as if" quality of the transference. Dora's abrupt breaking off of the treatment appears to me in part to be a reflection of this phenomenon. In a way Freud discusses this when he describes the transference aspects of Dora's first dream. He suggests that one stimulus for the dream is Dora's wish for closeness with him—her wish for a kiss from him, which he infers from his addendum to the dream that she smelt smoke when she wakened. The father in the dream thus not only relates to her childhood wishes and serves to protect her from her response to Herr K., but both men express feelings and conflicts she is having with respect to Freud—he is both the source of danger, the seducer, and the rescuer. Freud does not deal with this, which he later acknowledges as an error. Dora herself is unable to distinguish her present feelings from earlier ones—all the men become one, and she has to run away. Transference had indeed developed, an intense, erotized, and ambivalent one. However, the analyst was not discriminated as a transference figure with whom there was also some other relationship, but was rather reacted to as if he were indeed her father or Herr K. Such a reaction is more likely to occur where there have been early repetitive transference interpretations of feelings toward the original parental object. Adolescents attempt to defend against their attachment to the oedipal object by turning toward new objects. In analysis they need to look upon the analyst as a new object, a non-incestuous object, and firmly establish a relationship on that level before they can begin to examine the other distorting aspects of their feelings in the transference (Scharfman 1971). It seems to me that such a development never really occurred in Dora's analysis. We cannot be sure of the reasons for this, since Freud did not indicate if or when he offered specific transference interpretations. From our present knowledge what is applicable to the analysis of an adolescent is that there should not be repetitive attempts early in the analysis to relate reactions to the analyst back to their earlier sources and that one should avoid as much as possible a sexualization of the analysis. With a hysterical girl such as Dora was, this would not be easy even in light of our present knowledge.

Let us turn to another aspect which at least touches upon *countertransference,* although I do not think that term sufficiently describes the phenomena I would like to talk about. Dora was a young woman who, for all of her early attachment to her father, had been severely and intensely disappointed in him. She was disappointed not just in terms of her oedipal wishes, but also, I believe, disappointed as she saw the kind of man her father was. Frau K., about whom Dora certainly knew, was not his first involvement. Freud mentions that the patient's father had signs of neurosyphilis that manifested themselves when the patient was twelve and he had treated her father for this condition. She also knew that it was a venereal infection and at one point connects her mother's leucorrhea with this infection, confusing it with gonorrhea. It is not difficult to imagine that Dora perceived her father as a man who had had many extramarital sexual relationships. Such a father can be perceived by an adolescent girl as a danger, as she becomes aware of her own sexual wishes, especially those still close to oedipal origins. Such feelings are often far more frightening to the adolescent than to the oedipal child because they can be acted upon in reality. In addition to internalized prohibitions, the adolescent looks to the parent for reassurance that this will not happen. Where the parent is involved in their own acting out, the adolescent is threatened that they may do the same.

Dora's father also compromised himself in other ways, as Glenn reminds us. He initiated the treatment at least in part so as to have Dora cease her interference with his relationship with Frau K. He had earlier fostered the relationship with Herr K. as a means of achieving his own aims with Frau K. and had even argued that Dora must have imagined the scene at the lake. Dora's description of her father was that "he was insincere, he had a strain of falseness in his character, he only thought of his own enjoyment, and he had a gift for seeing things in the light which suited him best" (p. 34). Freud writes further:

I could not in general dispute Dora's characterization of her father; and there was one particular respect in which it was easy to see that her reproaches were justified. When she was feeling embittered she used to be overcome by the idea that she had been handed over to Herr K. as the price of his tolerating the relations between her father and his wife; and her rage at her father's making such a use of her was visible behind her affection for him. At other times she was quite well aware that she had been guilty of exaggeration in talking like this. The two men had of course never made a formal agreement in which she was treated as an object for barter; her father in particular would have been horrified at any such suggestion. But he was one of those men who know how to evade a dilemma by falsifying their judgment upon one of the conflicting alternatives. If it had been pointed out to him that there might be danger for a growing girl in the constant and unsupervised companionship of a man who had no satisfaction from his own wife, he would have been certain to answer that he could rely upon his daughter, that a man like K. could never be dangerous to her, and that his friend was himself incapable of such intentions, or that Dora was still a child and was treated as a child by K. [1905a, p. 34]

We can conclude that Dora had experienced a rather severe and painful disappointment in her father along with her intense attachment to him. Yet Freud never indicates that he dealt with this negative aspect of her feelings. He never deals with Dora's adolescent perception of her father, but emphasizes only the positive oedipal attachment that had its origin much earlier in her life, telling her that she knows that her father really loves her. It seems to me that Dora's attachment to Herr K. in fact evolved partially due to her early adolescent disappointment in her father, not only because of her earlier oedipal attachments to him. In the beginning she may have been looking for a version of her father as many early adolescent girls do—someone who would admire her, pay attention to her, buy her presents—all of which, in fact, Herr K. had done. He was the person with whom she was first attempting to distance herself from her involvement with her father. As such, Herr K. seems to be typical of many early adolescent crushes. What then happened was Dora's reaction at age fourteen when Herr K. suddenly kissed her in a directly sexual manner with what Freud assumes to have been her awareness of his erection at that time. When Dora reacted to this with disgust and abruptly left the room, Freud comments that this is a clearly hysterical reaction and that one would expect a young girl of fourteen to experience "a distinct feeling of sexual excitement in a girl who had never before been approached" (p. 28). He writes further:

the behaviour of this child of fourteen was already entirely and completely hysterical. I should without question consider a person hysterical in whom an occasion for sexual excitement elicited feelings that were preponderantly or exclusively unpleasurable; and I should do so whether or not the person were capable of producing somatic symptoms. [p. 28]

It is rather questionable that one would expect such a response in a girl that age when approached by a man who is her father's friend. Freud's expression of that view may be an indication of his own view of women. In any event, it seems to me that at that moment Herr K. became too much like her father, someone interested in women primarily as sexual objects. This happened at a time when she was making some attempt to choose a non-incestuous object with whom she could find some of the satisfactions she had not found in her relationship with her father. Subsequently Dora found out that Herr K. had also had previous extra-marital involvements. This she discovered from the maid who told her just two days before the scene at the lake that Herr K. had propositioned her, seduced her and then lost interest in her. This is part of the background for the scene at the lake. Herr K. used the same words in approaching Dora that he had used in approaching the maid. It is as if she were trying to tell Freud that Herr K. was not the man Freud thought he was. Erikson (1962) discussed this aspect of Dora's treatment from the point of view of the adolescent's need to establish the genetic truth. In this context he discussed Dora's need to return to Freud a year later to let him know she had succeeded in obtaining from Herr K. his acknowledgment that the events had occurred as she described. Erikson feels that this need of the adolescent to establish the actuality of events is related to their developmental concerns with fidelity.

To return to the case, Freud does not consider the possibility that Herr K. wished to use Dora as he wished to use the maid. Instead, in discussing this with Dora, Freud points out that her reaction of anger at the lake occurred because of her jealousy of Herr K.'s attention to the maid. Perhaps so, but one would also think that at another level she felt completely disillusioned in him, another man in whom she could place no trust, just as she was in many ways unable to trust her father. Dora reacted with a conviction that Herr K. was attempting to take advantage of her and use her as he had used the maid. However, Freud goes on to point out that Herr K.'s real intention was marriage, for which there is little evidence. In fact, earlier in the paper Freud notes that Herr K. felt unable to consider divorcing his wife because of his attachment to his child. Freud tells Dora that her motivation was revenge, that she was reacting to being treated like a servant. In that he was probably correct. Dora's feeling may very well have been one of having been insulted and wanting revenge, but she may have been quite justified. Freud later pointed out that Dora's breaking off the treatment was also an act of revenge. Again he may have been correct but perhaps other interpretations are possible.

Even beyond this he at one point suggests that for her father to marry Frau K. and Herr K. to marry Dora might have been a sensible solution. He says, "Indeed, if your temptation at L——— had had a different upshot, this would have been the only possible solution for all the parties concerned." Throughout the paper Freud viewed Dora's attachment to Herr K. as much more than a step in the direction of removing herself from her attachment to her father. He saw her tentativeness and sexual inhibition in the relationship with Herr K. as reflections of neurosis. While we would not be surprised to see a young girl develop a crush on an older man who is a friend of the family, we would also not expect that it would necessarily be a healthy development if such a crush led to a direct sexual involvement. We cannot know anything of Herr K.'s motivation for turning his attentions toward Dora, but one can speculate that they were not entirely motivated out of consideration and feeling for her as a person. He and the other principals are caught up in a complicated melange involving jealousies, competition and revenge. Such situations are not infrequently encountered in our present society. What is more striking and less understandable was Freud's view of this in turn of the century Vienna. Some consideration has been given to this subject by Steven Marcus (1975) who was particularly struck by the fact that such behavior would be unusual in view of the upper middle-class Jewish background of the participants. Freud himself had the same background, one in which such behavior was presumably not acceptable, yet none of this is suggested in his description of the case.

The complications of Dora's treatment involved still other elements. After Dora informed Freud that it was to be her last session she told him about the communication she had had from the maid indicating that Herr K. had had an affair with her.

As Glenn pointed out, Freud made no real attempt to deal with her announcement that this would be her last session. He rather continued with his interpretation, particularly with pointing out that Herr K. really had the intention of possible marriage, going beyond the fact that Dora may have wished for this. Dora then continued her plan to terminate the analysis that day. Was Dora telling Freud something else? Was she telling him that she felt that he, Freud, was not really interested in her, and that she could not trust his intentions? Some of this at least seems to me to be more than just transference, but rather a coincidence with certain elements of reality. In a way Freud was also using Dora and taking advantage of her, however well-motivated his scientific intentions may have been and however much we may have subsequently benefitted. What I have reference to is that he was engaged in using Dora's case as one to confirm the material he had presented earlier in *The Interpretation in Dreams* (1900). He was pursing his interest in dreams and in confirming some of his hypotheses about dreams and about symptom formation using her case. In a letter to Fliess (Freud 1954, Letter 140, p. 326) written just a few days after Dora's treatment ended, he writes "I finished Dreams and Hysteria yesterday, and the consequence is that today I feel short of a drug. It is a fragment of an analysis of a hysteria, in which the interpretations are grouped around two dreams, so it is really a continuation of the dream book. It also contains resolutions of hysterical symptoms and glimpses of the sexual-organic foundation of the whole." In view of Freud's larger aims, Dora's treatment as such may have been of secondary importance. Whatever his intentions for her, he became for her another man whom she could not trust. I hope it will not be misunderstood if I would say that like her father and like Herr K., Freud also had a mistress, even if that mistress was psychoanalysis and science. For Dora it meant something else. Glenn clearly pointed out secondary evidence of this when Dora returned to see Freud a year later. He had no particular interest in resuming the analysis and, in fact, immediately assumed that she was not in earnest in returning to see him. Freud ultimately forgave her for having deprived him of the satisfaction of curing her troubles, rather than suggesting that the treatment be resumed.

To recapitulate, there are several points in the analysis where Freud defended both Herr K. and the patient's father, telling Dora that she really knew how much they loved her. All of this was said to a young woman who had experienced rather intense disappointment in both of these men. Her analysis might have been a chance at having a different kind of relationship with a man. She needed to go through the intermediate phase of development of the younger girl in which she has a relationship with a man that is not immediately sexualized, but rather one in which she feels accepted as a person, while still looking for some derivatives of oedipal wishes in terms of the wish to feel loved, admired, paid attention to. Dora's attempt to find this in the relationship with Herr K. had led to another disappointment and her symptoms had intensified. A requirement to make analysis possible was for her to experience the relationship with the analyst as a new and different level of a relationship with a man, one that she had not experienced before, certainly one that was not so sexualized. Such an experience is necessary in order for such an adolescent girl to develop and be able to analyze the full transference. It is not an end in itself, but a necessary condition to allow specific interpretation of the transference. If her view of the analyst is not differentiated from her view of her father, the analysis is interrupted, sometimes abruptly, when transference affects are too threatening. Because of the shortcomings of analysis and its technical devices at that time and because of some of Freud's own reactions, such was the case with Dora. We cannot then be surprised that when Dora was seen many years later she was a chronically unhappy woman who had never had a satisfying relationship with a man.

It seems to me that there may be some general considerations of the psychology of women involved. Dora became bitter and revengeful after she had been disappointed in her life. A number of similar women whom I have seen have also become bitter and furious with men after their relationship with their fathers fail. Such disappointments, be they from death, divorce, withdrawal or character failing are certainly common enough. They add reality to oedipal disappointment and may foster a regression to an earlier level of difficulty, reviving and intensifying envy and hostility toward men. In many women, such manifestations result from that path rather than from any intense primary penis envy. Freud makes direct reference to this in pointing out that "if a girl is not happy in her love for a man, the current is often set flowing again by the libido in later years and is increased up to a greater or less degree of intensity . . . .When, in a hysterical woman or girl, the sexual libido which is directed towards men has been energetically suppressed, it will regularly be found that the libido which is directed towards women has been vicariously reinforced and even to some extent conscious" (1905a p. 60).

Implicit in this is that where a woman's love for a man results in intense disappointment, regression to earlier positions will occur. Such disappointments may be due primarily to neurotic conflicts and choices, or they may involve reality occurrences, including the nature of the man. This suggests that the analysis of a woman needs to pay particular attention to those aspects of the real nature of her relationship with her father and of other men who have central roles during her years of development that lead to real disappointment. This would seem to be especially important with someone like Dora. Although only a report of a fragment of an analysis, the relationship with her father completely dominates the report. The two other family members, her mother and an older brother, play only minor roles. Freud describes her mother as an uncultured, foolish woman who suffered from "housewife's psychosis." She had no understanding of her children's more active interests. The relations between mother and daughter had been unfriendly for years. Such a woman would have offered little in the way of a positive feminine model for Dora and could have led her toward a more intense involvement with her father. In addition, Freud notes that the brother was closer to the mother. Her brother "had been the model which her ambitions had striven to follow." It seems not unreasonable to assume that there was also early envy and jealousy of him, and that she had some negative feelings about her femininity early in her life would seem a reasonable assumption. Such a girl has a chance to feel more secure in her femininity if her relationship with her father has a positive outcome. When it fails for whatever reason, the girl regresses to her earlier feelings. Dora had an initial positive relationship with her father, but this was not sustained. Instead, he disappointed her rather severely and she became disillusioned in him in her preadolescence and early adolescence. She sought reassurance from another man, Herr K., and was again disillusioned. It is then that resentment of men becomes prominent. Such a viewpoint may offer an addition, or at times an alternative, to Freud's position that penis envy and resentment of the male's role are the bedrock of the analyses of women. Many women may have had real reasons to have been disappointed by their fathers, reasons involving more than penis envy or the inevitable oedipal disappointment. Hopefully, the reconsideration of the psychology of women, which is currently taking place, will include this possibility. Oedipal fantasies are certainly central, but so is the real nature of the father. Both must be clarified to help a patient find her own truth and enjoy her femininity in a relationship with a man.

References

Erikson, Erik H. (1962). Reality and actuality. *Journal of the American Psychoanalytic Association* 10451–473.

Freud, S. (1905a). Fragment of an analysis of a case of hysteria. *Standard Edition* 7:3–122.

———— (1905b). Three essays on the theory of sexuality. *Standard Edition* 7:125–243.

———— (1954). *The Origins of Psychoanalysis*. New York: Basic Books.

Marcus, S. (1975). *Representations*. New York: Random House.

Scharfman, M. A. (1971). Transference phenomena in adolescent analysis. In *The Unconscious Today*, ed. M. Kanzer. New York: International Universities Press.

Chapter 3

THE MISALLIANCE DIMENSION
IN THE CASE OF DORA

ROBERT J. LANGS, M.D.

My focus in this restudy of Freud's case histories will be on the establishment and maintenance of the therapeutic alliance, and the development of a particular type of disturbance in sectors of this alliance that I have termed *therapeutic misalliances** (Langs 1974, 1975a, 1976a, 1976b, 1977). In particular, the contribution of deviations from the basic ground rules and boundaries of the analytic situation to the development of sectors of misalliance will be explored. My main hypothesis is that modifications in the basic framework of the analytic relationship evoke intense responses in the patient and that they characteristically offer him a basis for potential sectors of misalliance with the analyst. It will be my goal to return to Freud's case histories in search of support or refutation of this hypothesis. In order to concentrate on this task, it will be necessary to bypass many other contributing factors to the material that I will study, and I

*This paper is an abbreviated version of Langs (1976b) The term *therapeutic misalliance* is used here because writers have preferred it to the alternative term of *antitherapeutic alliance* offered in earlier writings (Langs 1973a, 1974). The term applies here (1) as part of a ready contrast to "therapeutic alliance," (2) as a means of referring to the therapeutic process in its broadest sense, and (3) as a way of indicating the noninsightful therapeutic efforts inherent in any sector of misalliance.

will be able to counterbalance only briefly my focus on misalliance with references to the indications of positive segments of therapeutic alliance between Freud and his patients (see Kanzer 1952, 1975, and Zetzel 1966).

We may broadly define the therapeutic alliance as the conscious and unconscious agreement, applied in subsequent actual work, on the part of both the patient and analyst, to join forces in effecting symptom alleviation and constructive characterological changes through insight and inner structural change within the patient. In contrast, therapeutic misalliances constitute interactions that undermine such goals or achieve results on some other basis (Langs 1975a). Therapeutic alliances and misalliances constitute a continuum, and at any given moment one or the other may predominate. While often difficult to distinguish, this differentiation is important since sectors of misalliance entail transference gratifications, shared defenses, and mutual acting out, even though they represent mutual and misguided efforts at cure. The determination of the presence of a misalliance is based on a careful and repeated scrutiny of the patient's associations and behavior, and the analyst's subjective awareness. This type of assessment—which I have termed the *validating process* (Langs 1976a, 1976c)—is repeatedly carried out during the course of an analysis and it serves as an indicator of the direction taken by the analytic work at a given moment. The recognition of misalliances is important in that their development undermines sectors of the basic psychoanalytic work and compromises aspects of the outcome of the analysis. It is therefore essential that they be resolved if insight and structural change are to be maximally achieved for the patient. In fact, the development of sectors of misalliance are inevitable in any analytic process and their recognition and analytic resolution are among the most insight-producing and growth-promoting experiences for the patient—and at times for the analyst as well.

Investigations of therapeutic misalliances show that they are often based on deviations in the analyst's usual stance and on errors in technique (Langs 1973a, 1974, 1975a, 1975b, 1976a, 1976c). These findings led to a reconsideration of the framework of the psychoanalytic relationship and of the indications for and complications evoked by deviations and parameters of technique (Langs 1975b). The attempt was made to establish a distinction between valid deviations and others that prove detrimental to the analytic process and are, therefore, best classified as technical errors. Related to this problem is the issue of how to best establish and maintain the therapeutic alliance (Stone 1961, 1967, Greenson 1965, 1967, 1971, 1972, Greenson and Wexler 1969, Arlow and Brenner 1966, Zetzel 1956, 1958, 1966–1969, Heimann 1970, Kanzer 1975, Arlow 1975, Langs 1975a, 1975b, 1976c).

My own clinical observations have indicated that the therapeutic alliance is best maintained and developed through a firm, though not rigid, adherence to the basic ground rules of analysis and through a sensitive maintenance of the psychoanalytic framework. This includes the establishment of a sound therapeutic stance and the use of interpretations; in general, noninterpretive measures of all kinds prove detrimental and the source of misalliances.

In this context, I attempted to define the present, empirically derived optimal ground rules of the psychoanalytic situation. I included the following (Langs 1975b, 1976c): set fees, hours, and length of sessions; the fundamental rule of free association with communication occurring while the patient is on the couch; the absence of physical contact and extra-therapeutic gratifications; the analyst's relative anonymity and the use of neutral interventions geared primarily toward interpretations; and the exclusive one-to-one relationship with total confidentiality. In most clinical situations—including the treatment of adolescents—it is better to adhere to the basic ground rules and to offer interpretations to the patient, rather than to deviate under any circumstances except an emergency. Further, all modifications of the ground rules, even when prompted by necessary human responsiveness or an emergency situation, universally evoked intense responses in the patient. If these went unrecognized and unanalyzed, they tended to have detrimental effects on the analysis and on the patient.

These earlier findings are not a brief for rigidity, but they do indicate the importance of the framework of the analytic relationship and the great influence on the patient of any modification in this basic area. The manner in which the analyst establishes and maintains the boundaries and framework of the analytic relationship reflects important aspects of the management of his own intrapsychic state and fantasies, including countertransference aspects. Further, the proper management of the framework implicitly offers the analyst as a constructive figure for conscious identification by the patient, and creates the conditions for the most viable and uncontaminated unfolding of the patient's transference projections and neurosis—and their interpretation and modification. Impairments in the management of the framework and unneeded deviations in technique tend inappropriately to gratify and offer maladaptive defenses to both patient and analyst, promoting pathogenic interactions and identifications. The present ground rules and boundaries of adult (and adolescent) psychoanalysis contain within them an optimally viable and valid basic hold for the patient (Winnicott 1965) and a corresponding setting for the unfolding of the analytic work.

In taking a backward look and applying current standards to Freud's work, I recognize the extent to which he experimented with the ground rules and was involved in a constant search to establish effective therapeutic principles. These case histories were in no way a detailed account of Freud's analytic technique or of the sessions with his patients. We are therefore faced with a number of limitations to this exploration, and yet it seems possible to benefit from Freud's early ingenious efforts to develop a viable psychoanalytic technique and to learn from the apparent mistakes that he inevitably made. However, despite the inherent difficulties, the attempt to test out current hypotheses based on a retrospective study of Freud's material offers an unusual opportunity to ascertain the extent to which the management of the framework of the psychoanalytic relationship meaningfully contributes to the therapeutic experience of the patient. With these ideas in mind, let us now consider Freud's (1905a) analysis of Dora.

The Clinical Material

In studying the case of Dora for misalliances, I am not embarking upon an entirely original research. Viderman (1974), whose study I discovered after writing this paper, offered a similar but more general approach to some of the issues discussed here. Erikson (1962) utilized aspects of this analysis to develop his conceptualization of reality and actuality both in the analytic situation and for the individual in his life. In attempting to demonstrate that actuality—defined as "the world verified only in the ego's immediate emersion in action"—differed for Dora and Freud, Erikson was studying a dimension of potential misalliance from his own vantage point. Before comparing his findings with my own, however, I will present some pertinent clinical material.

A review of Freud's paper on Dora indicates that there were two main and one related minor "deviations"—by present definition—in analytic technique utilized by Freud and two types of misalliances which developed between himself and Dora, formed partly on the basis of these deviations. Specifically, Freud had treated Dora's father for syphilis and also knew her father's sister and brother; in addition, Freud knew Herr K., the man who had attempted to seduce or marry Dora and who also had referred Dora's father to Freud. Freud's presentation suggests that Dora's father spoke to him directly about Dora prior to the analysis and that he communicated with Freud after the analysis had been completed, and possibly did so during the three months in which the analysis was in progress. In these ways, Freud did not maintain the one-to-one relationship with Dora that many analysts would currently establish (Langs 1973a), and these various third parties to the analysis—directly and indirectly—appear to have been important factors in the outcome of the analytic experience.

A second area of deviation related to Freud's special interest in Dora's sexual material—a modification in neutrality—while a third and more minor "deviation" occurred when Freud experimented with Dora by pointing to a book of matches that he had brought into his consultation room; the role that this maneuver played in the analysis will be discussed below.

In this context, then, the first sector of misalliance between Dora and Freud related to the manner in which Dora entered analysis. Her father brought her to Freud with the evident intention that Freud should actively intervene on his behalf so that Dora would no longer press him to give up his affair with Frau K. As Dora's father gave Freud a history of her problems, he said: "Please try and bring her to reason" (Freud 1905a, p. 26).

Dora, for her part, apparently entered analysis in order to convince Freud that her assessment of the situation with her father was correct and in all likelihood she also hoped to persuade Freud to intervene for her with her father so that he would give up his mistress (Erikson 1962). Dora hoped to establish a misalliance in which Freud would help her to manipulate her father and disrupt his relationship with Frau K. As additional evidence that this was among Dora's motives for seeing Freud, we may note that she had threatened suicide and was first brought to Freud for analysis after a quarrel with her father on this very subject.

Dora was also suffering from a multiplicity of hysterical symptoms and wished to find symptomatic relief from these maladies. This undoubtedly contributed to segments of a viable therapeutic alliance with Freud that fostered the development of the positive aspects of their therapeutic endeavors. However, in addition to possibly being prepared to resolve her inner conflicts and symptoms through the analytic efforts developed by Freud, it appears that Dora also hoped to alleviate these difficulties through the special assistance that she sought from him. It seems likely that Dora's conscious and unconscious motivations for analysis and her conscious and unconscious fantasies related to the means through which she would find symptomatic relief, contributed both to sectors of alliance and misalliance with Freud. This is typical of patients entering analysis, and much depends on the analyst's response.

For his part, Freud was aware of Dora's intended misalliance and while he did not specifically interpret and analyze it, rather early in the analysis Freud pointed out to Dora that her illness was intended to detach her father from Frau K. In so doing, he added that she would recover if this were achieved, but that he—Freud—hoped that her father would not yield to Dora's symptoms, since this would provide her with a most dangerous weapon. This intervention preceded by a short time the appearance of Dora's first dream which conveyed her intentions of terminating her analysis. Freud's comment may have contributed to these intentions since he was, in effect, unconsciously indicating to Dora his unwillingness to participate in her intended misalliance, doing so without providing her insight into the meanings of the misalliance and offering, however indirectly, alternative methods of resolving her difficulties. In a sense, this may be seen as an early effort by Dora to effect a "misalliance cure" (Langs 1975a, 1976a, 1976c)—noninsightful symptom relief effected with the help of Freud. The latter's comment indicates the extent to which he sensed the power of such "cures" and recognized them to be anti-analytic. This interaction and the areas of developing misalliance will, however, become clearer after we outline Freud's apparent contributions to them.

Freud was, of course, interested in helping Dora to alleviate her hysterical symptoms through insight into the unconscious fantasies on which they were based. However, Freud indicated in his presentation that there were other motives which prompted his interest in Dora, and these had the potential for creating sectors of misalliances that could also disturb the analysis. They are evident in Freud's statement: "I was anxious to subject my assumptions [i.e., regarding sexuality] to a rigorous test in this case." As we know, Freud had recently written the *Interpretation of Dreams* (1900) and was looking to apply his new theories about dreams and neurosis clinically. Furthermore, he was working on his *Three Essays on the Theory of Sexuality* (1905b) and was also most eager to test out his hypotheses regarding infantile sexuality in his clinical work with his patients. He was also interested in offering his insight about dreams to the treatment of the neuroses. As Freud himself later stated (1912), therapeutic zeal and vested interests of this kind can prove disruptive to an analysis—in our terms, can create misalliances. Erikson (1962) has written of these concerns of Freud as his quest for genetic truth. He contrasted it with Dora's search for historical truth, as related to her current realities and to the fidelity of those close to her; this served as a means of establishing her identity as a young woman.

Let us now briefly follow some of the highlights of Dora's analysis with a focus on the threads woven out of Freud's "deviations" and the potential efforts toward misalliance of both Freud and Dora. The first communications from Dora, as reported by Freud in his paper, alluded to an attempt at seduction by Herr K. when Dora was fourteen years of age. This had preceded by two years the scene at the lake with Herr K. in which he had proposed to Dora. The latter incident had prompted Dora to rupture her relationship with him and intensified her efforts to separate her father from Frau K. In an earlier experience, Herr K. had arranged to be alone with Dora, and had kissed her, evoking a reaction of disgust. Dora was frightened and Freud considered this to be an abnormal reaction; he very quickly brought out Dora's awareness of erections in men.

From our vantage point, it would appear reasonable to formulate the hypothesis that Freud's personal acquaintance with Dora's father and Herr K. contributed to a very early and intense erotization of her relationship with Freud, as communicated in relatively thinly disguised form in this first communication. If we remember that Dora's father had turned her over to Herr K. as a kind of payment for his relationship with Frau K., we can immediately recognize a very striking parallel between that situation and Dora's initial relationship with Freud. While it is true that Freud failed throughout this analysis, as he readily acknowledged and discussed, to interpret Dora's transference (i.e., primarily genetically or intrapsychically-based) feelings and fantasies toward him, the additional fact that Freud was associated in reality with Dora's father and Herr K. undoubtedly contributed to Dora's and his own conscious and unconscious perception of this relationship (Langs 1973b). His ready acceptance of sexuality and his very early emphasis (intervening and questioning) on this area further heightened Dora's belief that Freud was in some ways not unlike her father and Herr K. Thus, a modification in the analyst's neutrality seems to have contributed to a misalliance with the patient (Langs 1975c).

This delineation of the role of possible unconscious perceptions of Freud and of the interactional dimension of Dora's responses to him help to clarify her ongoing intrapsychic conflicts and unconscious fantasies. The patient's responses to the analyst are always a mixture of reality—as it exists and is perceived—and fantasy, transference and nontransference. Only by delineating the actual nature of the ongoing interaction with the analyst, and especially the implicit and explicit meanings of his interventions and failures to intervene, can one establish the components of reality and fantasy in the patient's reaction to him (Langs 1973b, 1975c, 1976a, 1976c).

The relative neglect of reality factors in the patient-analyst relationship (see also Greenson 1972) and of nontransference elements was not only characteristic of Freud's technique at the time of his analysis of Dora, but persists to the present day. With Dora, he was slow to recognize the transference elements in her communications, and he tended to link them to genetic material without a full appreciation for the implications for his present relationship with his patient (Kanzer 1966). We can still learn a great deal from the consequences of these oversights.

The case history indicates that Dora expressed other concerns that are related to the manner in which she entered analysis and to the fact that Freud knew her father. She spoke of how a governess had pretended affection for her when in reality the governess very much preferred her father and eventually dropped Dora. This may be an indirect representation of her concerns in her relationship with Freud. She may even have fantasied that Freud's primary allegiance was to her father and that there was an alliance between her father and Freud. For her part, Dora continued to attempt to prove that the scene by the lake had been a reality and not her fantasy, and Freud concluded—undoubtedly conveying this to Dora—that she was being completely truthful. As a possible reward for this affirmation, Dora told Freud that she believed that her father was impotent and acknowledged her awareness of fellatio. Freud then quickly interpreted Dora's love for her father and for Herr K., but Dora denied the latter. It was in this context that the first dream was reported.

In it, a house is on fire and Dora's father is standing beside her bed and wakes her. She dresses quickly and her mother wants to stop and save her jewel-case but her father says, "I refuse to let myself and my two children be burnt for the sake of your jewel-case" (p. 64). They hurry downstairs and as soon as Dora was outside, she woke up.

This dream had first been dreamt three times at the lake after Herr K.'s attempt to either seduce or propose to Dora. It is striking that in his analysis of this dream, while Freud is interested in the day residues, he did not fully determine the specific day residues for this dream—the adaptive tasks or stimuli which had prompted it (Langs 1973a). Since they undoubtedly included major precipitates from Dora's ongoing relationship with Freud, this suggests that Freud had a blind spot for Dora's feelings toward him—the so-called transference—since the dream, even to Freud in retrospect, very clearly conveyed Dora's thoughts of fleeing the analysis and her fantasies that she was once more in danger sexually in her analysis with Freud as she had previously been with Herr K. (a repetition of the initial theme of the analysis).

The manifest dream itself and certain of Dora's associations illuminate the theme of potential misalliance—the divergence in therapeutic intentions or means of conflict resolution—in that her mother wants to save her jewel-case, but her father wants to save his children. The associations to jewel-case related to Dora's virginity which she felt had been threatened by Herr K.; she apparently felt similarly threatened by Freud. While the unfolding genetic history provided clues as to the development of the intrapsychic fantasies and needs within Dora that prompted her to sexualize her relationship with Freud and to respond to his technique in an erotic manner, our main efforts here will continue to focus on the generally ignored contributions made by Freud to these sexual anxieties and fantasies, and to the possible misalliance with which Dora was concerned. In this regard, the dream seems to reflect Dora's anxiety regarding Freud's intense interest in her sexual fantasies, his close association with her father and Herr K., and her responsive determination to flee the analytic situation.

The continuum and intermixture of alliance and misalliance is suggested by the apparent dual roles in which Freud is placed in this dream: seducer and protector. This provides evidence that in addition to the sector of misalliance between Freud and Dora, there were important areas of alliance and continued hopes in Dora that Freud would rescue her from her plight—both inner and outer. Further, the manifest dream is concerned with alerting and adaptive responses to danger. On this basis, and in keeping with Dora's subsequent associations, we may also postulate that the dream was prompted by unconscious perceptions of Freud's pressures toward misalliance and Dora's own fears of participating in it and was reported to Freud as part of an effort to call it to his attention and to assist him and herself in resolving it (Langs 1975a, 1976c). It therefore appears that Dora was attempting to save her analysis at the very juncture that she was thinking of abandoning it.

Dora's associations to this dream eventually led to the fact that Herr K. had taken the key to her bedroom and had left Dora unprotected from his intrusions. Freud interpreted her intentions to escape from Herr K.'s persecution, but did not develop a comparable theme for Dora's relationship with himself. Eventually, the anxieties were traced to her feelings toward her father who actually was the middleman in both situations. Freud was also able to point out that Dora was frightened by her readiness to submit sexually to Herr K. and needed to flee him because of this, although he again did not allude to this in the analysis.

It was in this context that Freud attempted his experiment of placing matches where Dora could see them from the couch. When Dora could see nothing, Freud pointed to the matches and discussed how fire was tied to fears of bed-wetting, and they went on to establish that Dora had indeed been a bedwetter in her childhood. Here Freud's interest in genetic truth and in sexuality deflected him from verbalizing Dora's current anxieties and fantasies, although his be-havior did demonstrate an unconscious appreciation for some of the current stimuli for Dora's fantasies and associations. Unconscious perceptiveness of this kind is often evident in otherwise deviant or erroneous interventions of analysts (Langs 1976a). In addition, Freud was unconsciously acting out something akin to Dora's very fear of an uncontrolled analytic situation—fire—thereby sharing this fantasy with her. It is of interest, in view of my finding that deviations in technique almost always evoke attempts by analysands to evoke further devia-tions (Langs 1975b), that Dora later responded with two symptomatic acts of her own—the hiding of a letter from, and thereby playing secrets with, Freud, and playing with a reticule during a session. This latter reflected her masturbatory fantasies and, undoubtedly, her mounting sexual anxieties in the analytic situ-ation and her unconscious perception of Freud's behavior. We may view Freud's use of the matches and Dora's behavior with the letter and reticule as a sector of misalliance in which nonverbal communication and acting out—actually, acting in—was permitted in lieu of verbal communication.

Freud's experiment led to a most revealing addendum to the first dream: Dora had smelt smoke. Freud then connected the dream to himself since he was prone to use the phrase that there could be no smoke without fire, but when Dora directly objected to this intervention, Freud appears to have dropped it. It may well be that here both Freud and Dora shared a defensive misalliance—a dis-placement away from their relationship. Freud did, however, return to this area in a small way when he interpreted Dora's wish to yield to Herr K. and to have a kiss from him, suggesting that she also wished to be kissed by himself. In this context, Freud later made the general comment that transference fantasies cannot be proven, something that seems to reflect his skepticism and difficulties in this area.

Freud then adds that the dream had actually been reported when he and Dora had been working on the topic of masturbation. He then reports that Dora knew of her father's syphilitic diagnosis by virtue of the fact that she had heard her father talking about it after he had seen Freud. She had connected this illness with her father's loose behavior, and we can see again how Freud was, for Dora, undoubtedly identified with her father and with his style of life. Freud did attempt then to tentatively suggest to Dora that he must remind her of Herr K., but he did not consider the possibility that his behavior, in being similar to that of Herr K., was a factor.

The second dream, one that is far more complex than the first, alludes to Dora being in a strange town and then going into a house where she finds a letter from her mother that refers to Dora's having left without her parent's knowledge. She learns that her father is dead and asks about one hundred times: "Where is the station?" receiving the answer, "Five minutes." She sees a woods and then asks a man who replies, "Two and a half hours more." She refuses his company and then sees the station that she is seeking in front of her, but she cannot reach it. She feels anxious and then is at home where a maidservant opens the door and replies that her mother and the others were already at the cemetery.

As indicated by Dora's associations and Freud's analysis, this dream had many allusions to the scene at the lake as well as to Dora's plans to terminate her analysis. Freud delineated three unconscious fantasies in the latent content of this dream: revenge on her father; defloration by force; and waiting until a goal is reached. Associations led to pregnancy fantasies and to sexual curiosity.

In the third session in which this dream was being explored, Dora announced her intention to terminate at the end of the hour. Her associations indicated that in doing so, she was identifying with a governess toward whom Herr K. had made advances and who had succumbed, only to be rejected later by him. Despite her anger, the girl had waited around hoping that Herr K. would pursue her, although he never did. Still ignoring the "transference" implications of this dream and associations, Freud used it to finally convince Dora that she had been deeply hurt by Herr K. who had used similar language in approaching both Dora and the governess. Freud added that it was this hurt that had prompted her to flee from Herr K.—all the while secretly hoping that he would pursue her and convince her that his intentions were sincere. In a sense, by accepting Dora's decision to terminate and by not analyzing the meanings of this decision, Freud enabled Dora to re-enact the incident with Herr K. with one important modification: she was now the aggressor and Freud was the victim. This type of shared acting out of conscious and unconscious fantasies is another common form of misalliance.

In his discussion of the analysis, Freud indicated his awareness that Dora was attempting to have him ask her to continue and thereby to provide her with the substitute gratification that she longed for. In stating this, he was alluding to another kind of misalliance that Dora sought to live out with Freud, one in which she would spurn him and Freud would ask her to remain. This would have entailed the bilateral enactment of another unconscious fantasy related to the experience with Herr K., and while Freud did not gratify this misalliance, he also did not interpret it. In all, Dora had lived out her revenge on both her father and Herr K., as well as undoubtedly some direct hostility toward Freud by terminating in the manner that she did.

Freud emphasized that his failure to master the transference was an important factor in Dora's abrupt termination, although he did not ascribe to it the prime importance that he gave to his failure to explore Dora's homosexual fantasies. He did state, however, that: "Owing to the readiness with which Dora put one part of the pathogenic material at my disposal during the treatment, I neglected the precaution of looking out for the first sign of transference" (p. 118). He then goes on to say that Dora "kept anxiously trying to make sure whether I was being quite straightforward with her, for her father 'always preferred secrecy and roundabout ways' " (p. 118). We see here Freud's own awareness that his special interest in Dora's sexual material had contributed to his neglect of the transference; his comments also seem to reflect his unconscious realization that Dora had strongly identified him with her father, although he does not trace this to the role that her father played in introducing Dora to Freud. We see that, to the very end, this "deviation" in technique contributed to Dora's "transference" fantasies, and to the premature interruption of her analysis. Freud's overriding interest in having Dora confirm his theories of infantile sexuality is also reaffirmed here as a source of misalliance and flight.

In concluding his presentation, Freud describes Dora's return visit some fifteen months after her termination. As Erikson (1962) emphasized, Freud stated that he immediately knew that she was not in earnest, thereby reflecting some difficulty that remained within him regarding his relationship with Dora. In that last interview, Dora described how five months after termination, at the time of the death of one of Herr and Frau K.'s children, she had confronted everyone and was vindicated. The timing of her visit to Freud, however, related to a facial neuralgia that Dora had developed after she had apparently read about Freud's promotion to professor. Without considering deeper reasons as to why Dora returned to see him at the time that she did, Freud "forgave" Dora for not letting him cure her more fully and the interview ended.

Erikson suggested that Dora's vengeance seemed to Freud to be acting out and that this assessment may have been a factor in his feeling that Dora was not interested in pursuing further analysis with him. Further, to extend Erikson's discussion of the importance of establishing a sense of fidelity to assist Dora in affirming her feminine identity, we can see that Freud's associations with Herr K. and her father impaired both his image as a person with whom Dora might identify in a more healthy manner and as the analyst who might help Dora achieve a sense of identity based on a strong sense of fidelity. As Erikson noted, Dora's first dream assigned to her father the role of a hoped-for protector, a role that Dora had no doubt transferred to Freud, but then had difficulty maintaining.

Summary

To summarize, the case of Dora suggests that Freud's "deviations" from present technique through which he accepted a patient under the circumstances of having previously treated her father and having known the man who had attempted to seduce her, along with his continued contact with this patient's father during and after the analysis, violated the one-to-one quality of the analytic relationship. In doing so, it threatened the sense of confidentiality necessary for a proper analytic atmosphere and confounded Dora's image of Freud. This deviation in technique runs like a clear thread throughout the analysis and is directly related to the premature termination enforced by Dora who fled Freud in a manner very similar to her flight from Herr K. The material strongly suggests that Dora was never able to sufficiently differentiate Freud from her father and Herr K., and was never clear as to Freud's motives for seeing her and as to the underlying basis for her interest in her sexual fantasies.

This special interest which modified Freud's neutrality prompted a second sector of misalliance between Freud and Dora, and placed undue emphasis on the patient's sexual associations and on the efforts to search out the genetic dimensions of her infantile sexual life. This was perceived by Dora as strongly seductive and quickly linked to her father and Herr K., and was further reinforced by the fact that Freud had made the diagnosis of her father's syphilitic infection. It appears to have evoked a responsive participation by Dora reflected in her revelation of erotic material which suggests an anxiety-ridden erotization of her relationship with Freud that contributed to her premature termination. Dora was also unable to overcome the suspicion that Freud was directly involved in a misalliance with her father and carrying out the latter's wish to deter her from disrupting his relationship with Frau K. or to have Freud serve as a new potential substitute lover.

References

Arlow, J. (1975). Discussion of Mark Kanzer's "The therapeutic and working alliances," *International Journal of Psychoanaytic Psychotherapy* 4:69–73.

Arlow, J., and Brenner (1966). Discussion of Elizabeth R. Zetzel's "The analytic situation." In *Psychoanalysis In The Americas*, ed. R. Litman, pp. 133–138. New York: International Universities Press.

Erikson, E. (1962). Reality and actuality. *Journal of the American Psychoanalytic Association* 10: 451–474.

Freud, S. (1900). The interpretation of dreams. *Standard Edition* 4/5.

——— (1905a). A fragment of an analysis of a case of hysteria. *Standard Edition* 7: 1–122.

——— (1905b). Three essays on the theory of sexuality. *Standard Edition* 7: 125–243.

Greenson, R. (1965). The working alliance and the transference neurosis. *Psychoanalytic Quarterly* 34: 155–181.

——— (1967). *The Technique and Practice of Psychoanalysis*. Vol. I. New York: International Universities Press.

——— (1971). The 'real' relationship between the patient and the psychoanalyst. In *The Unconscious Today*, ed. M. Kanzer, pp. 213–232. New York: International Universities Press.

——— (1972). Beyond transference and interpretation. *International Journal of Psycho-Analysis* 53: 213–218.

——— and Wexler, M. (1969). The non-transference relationship in the psychoanalytic situation. *International Journal of Psycho-Analysis* 50: 27–40.

Heimann, P. (1970). Discussion of 'The non-transference relationship in the psychoanalytic situation.' *International Journal of Psycho-Analysis* 51: 145–147.

Kanzer, M. (1952). The transference neurosis of the Rat Man. *Psychoanalytic Quarterly* 2: 181–189.

——— (1966). The motor sphere of the transference. *Psychoanalytic Quarterly* 35: 522–539.

——— (1975). The therapeutic and working alliances. *International Journal of Psychoanalytic Psychotherapy* 4: 48–73.

Langs, R. (1973a). *The Technique of Psychoanalytic Psychotherapy*. Vol. I. New York: Jason Aronson.

———— (1973b). The patient's view of the therapist: reality of fantasy? *International Journal of Psychoanalytic Psychotherapy* 2: 411–431.

———— (1974). *The Technique of Psychoanalytic Psychotherapy*. Vol. II. New York: Jason Aronson.

———— (1975a). Therapeutic misalliances. *International Journal of Psychoanalytic Psychotherapy* 4: 77–105.

———— (1975b). The therapeutic relationship and deviations in technique. *International Journal of Psychoanalytic Psychotherapy* 4: 106–141.

———— (1975c). The patient's unconscious perception of the therapist's errors. In *Tactics and Techniques in Psychoanalytic Therapy, Vol. II, Countertransference*, ed. P. Giovacchini. New York: Jason Aronson.

———— (1976a). *The Bipersonal Field*. New York: Jason Aronson.

———— (1976b). The misalliance dimension in Freud's case histories. I. Dora. *International Journal of Psychoanalytic Psychotherapy* 5: 301–318.

———— (1976c). *The Therapeutic Interaction*. New York: Jason Aronson.

Stone, L. (1961). *The Psychoanalytic Situation*. New York: International Universities Press.

———— (1967). The psychoanalytic situation and transference: postscript to an earlier communication. *Journal of the American Psychoanalytic Association* 15: 3–58.

Viderman, S. (1974). Interpretation in the analytic space. *International Review of Psycho-Analysis* 1: 467–480.

Winnicott, D. W. (1965). *The Maturational Processes and the Facilitating Environment*. New York: International Universities Press.

Zetzel, E. (1956). Current concepts of transference. *International Journal of Psycho-Analysis* 37: 369–376.

———— (1958). Therapeutic alliance in the psychoanalysis of hysteria. In *The Capacity for Emotional Growth* pp. 182–196. New York: International Universities Press 1970.

———— (1966). 1965: Additional 'notes upon a case of obsessional neurosis.' *International Journal of Psycho-Analysis* 47: 123–129.

———— (1966–1969). The analytic situation and the analytic process. In E. Zetzel, *The Capacity for Emotional Growth*, pp. 197–215. New York: International Universities Press, 1970.

Chapter 4

DORA'S IMAGERY: THE FLIGHT

FROM A BURNING HOUSE

MARK KANZER, M.D.

Freud's intention in his study of Dora (1905) was only partly therapeutic. His first intention was to apply his discoveries about dreams (largely related to his self-analysis) to clinical problems; beyond that his interest was directed toward what remained most precious to himself, the understanding of normal mental processes. To separate his clinical work from these other motivations is not only impractical but it would deprive it of the spark of creativity and the broad perspectives that always characterized his investigations and has remained a tradition in psychoanalysis.

It was Freud himself who was the first to reassess his treatment of the eighteen-year-old "hysteric." Dora, in the light of what he had learned not only clinically but also self-analytically and in relation to normal mental processes. To the extent that analytic therapy will represent a growth in the experiences and capacities of the analyst as well as the patient, this outcome remains a precedent for analytic treatment since that time. Indeed, we ourselves have not stopped reassessing the Dora case with respect to the patient, the physician and continuing growth of insight into normal mental processes.

All three are brought to bear in this study on the imagery of Dora's first dream, the flight from a burning house with her father, with the emphasis on general characteristics of imagery as emerging from Freud's research as well as the more specific use made of it during the treatment. As such, the present review selects a specific aspect of Freud's own intention, to apply the knowledge of dreams to clinical work, and the reverse, to learn from clinical work matters of significance for the understanding of dreams and imagery.

We shall orient ourselves by setting forth the dream:

A house was on fire. My father was standing beside my bed and woke me up. I dressed quickly. Mother wanted to stop and save her jewel-case; but Father said: "I refuse to let myself and my two children be burnt for the sake of your jewel-case." We hurried downstairs and as soon as I was outside I woke up. [1905, p. 64]

Freud was eliciting universal fantasies as well as Dora's particular ones in this dream. One key to both lies in the ambiguity of symbols, visual as well as verbal. Two readily recognizable universal fantasies in Dora's dream have as subjects the rescue by the father and the fire-water dichotomy. Put together here, rescue by the father from fire is a birth fantasy, alternatively expressed by themes of rescue by mother from the water or oneself rescuing father or mother from fire or water.

The biblical tale of Moses illustrates this universal fantasy. Moses, rescued from the Nile by the Egyptian princess, later rescues his people by leading them through the Red Sea. He rescues them again by bringing forth water in the wilderness when he strikes a rock with a rod, defying God in so doing. Analytic insight into symbols enables us to recognize the phallic exhibitionism and urinary ambition involved in the last action which seems a variant of Prometheus serving his people by bringing fire from heaven. Both are punished by the gods. Fire plays no small part in the Moses chronicle from the time when, as a small child, he was protected from and punished for his ambition (seizing the crown of pharaoh) by being required to put hot embers in his mouth and suffering thereafter impairment of speech (flow of words as urinary equivalent).

Other myths relating to rescue from a burning city include those of Aeneas from Troy and of Lot's wife from Sodom and Gomorrah. The former depicts the hero with his paralyzed father on his back (saving of the father) guided by his mother, the love-goddess Aphrodite, fleeing a city condemned for harboring the adulterous Helen and Paris. Typical primal scene aspects inhere in this and other birth fantasies and the parallels to the story of Oedipus become pronounced as Aeneas encounters Dido, queen of Carthage, who, like the Sphinx, casts herself into the sea on his account, while he continues on to found Rome—to be translated into an incest-free marriage. The new city will ultimately represent a return to the old one. Even closer to Dora's dream however is the story of

Lot's wife who, fleeing the flames that punish the sinful cities of the plains, defies the rescuing father-God by looking backwards and being turned into a pillar of salt. Eurydice must really prefer Hell to the music of Orpheus!

Dora too was ambivalent about leaving Herr K., her would-be seducer, and Freud, who would not seduce her. In her case, as in the other myths we have just cited, the ambivalence is expressed in splittings and reversibility. One is rescued by the good father, one would like to return to the evil father of the primal scene. The manifest content of dream and myth idealizes the former solution, the suppressed content the latter and the conflict and punishment by neurosis—Lot's wife turned to an indecisive pillar of salt (an equivalent to the Medusa reaction and also of her inability to renounce penis envy and obey God's command).

Such universal fantasies may be treated like typical dreams and applied (with reservations) to the particular dream. Indeed, Freud himself might more readily have come to grips with Dora's problems if he had done so. He consistently perceived more readily her desire to flee from him than her desire to remain and be seduced by him, although his own analysis unmistakably demonstrated this. Actually, though he insisted that transferences were taking place between Dora's attitudes to Herr K. and himself, and he tried to win from her acknowledgement of her sexual responsiveness to Herr K., he was singularly unable to press this parallel as far as he himself was concerned. While the world of psychoanalysis has been enriched by his discoveries about transference in the Dora case, less can be said for any discoveries about countertransference he might have made. It was not until a decade later that countertransference-analysis began to occupy his attention. Strachey (1958) has noted the paucity of explicit discussions of the subject of countertransference in Freud's published works (1915, pp. 160–161).

The reader will find Freud's contributions to the subject of imagery most brilliantly worked out in the Dora case, where he employs the material he elicits in order to reconstruct the oedipal period—the foremost task of psychoanalysis, as he saw it. The linking of the fire-water images to universal bodily functions that are prominent during that period and become focused in intimate activities associated with bedwetting, masturbation and primal scene fantasies, was highly original. The application of these insights not only to neurosis and its cure, but also to the hidden significance of objects and actions, opened a new world to the understanding of animism and the normal, if usually undetected, processes of the mind. "Water" linked together the jewel-case of the mother (menaced by fire [sexual passion]), the tear-shaped pearls Dora wished for her ears, the moist female genitals and the punishment for sexual activity through leucorrhea. A grammar of the logic of the unconscious, intuitively grasped by poets and mystics, became available to the scientist, to be used in a variety of disciplines.

Freud was also impressed by the evidence that each thought is accompanied by its contrary (p. 85) and the role of "switch-words" or verbal bridges (to which puns belong as well as parapraxes) in alerting the analyst to hidden currents of thought behind ambiguous words and awkward expressions. Almost every aspect of Dora's dream, as well as her words and actions, obtained new and significant meaning when applied in the opposite sense. Equally significant is the process of selectivity by the analyst in determining the correct sense in the overdetermined material that is placed before him. Freud would ultimately seek to safeguard this by recommendations to adopt a neutral attitude and permit contact on primitive levels of communication through the analyst's evenly suspended attention.

The technique employed with Dora was quite different since she was constantly pressured to confirm the analyst's interpretations and had little opportunity to freely bring forward her own associations, fantasies and ideas. In effect, we learn a great deal about Freud himself through the pressures he uses, partly as the result of views and techniques that have distanced themselves only to a degree from the earlier hypnotic technique and also partly as the result of his own personality organization which was in the midst of an intensive self-analysis at the moment—an aspect to which we shall return.

It would seem useful, in view of the overall purpose of this volume in re-evaluating aspects of Freud's case histories, to take a new look at the emergence of the "flight from the father fantasy" in the context of the particular analytic situation employed at that time. We become more aware of a particular aspect of all symbols: their communicative function and their organizational uses in controlling diverse forces within the individual as well as between the individual and the outside world. The prototype of all imagery in that respect, we suggest, is the total experience in which the cry of the hungry infant elicits the need-satisfying appearance of the mother and the primary unit of language is thus established. Dora, further along in her maturation, was an anxious adolescent, identified with the mother (through the common possession of a jewel case) and calling for rescue by a "good father" who was, in one aspect of the treatment, the analyst himself.

We shall be attentive therefore to the type of communication ensuing from the analysis of this dream image and its inherent language. We are quickly oriented by the first communications. At a moment when the analysis seemed likely to "throw light upon an obscure point in Dora's childhood," the dream, a recurrent one that had begun at L., site of the encounter with Herr K., now claimed attention. The object of meticulously constructing the memory of childhood had to be replaced, with some disappointment one gathers, by a meticulous reconstruction of the attempted seduction.

Little latitude was left to Dora who was expected to proceed as she had been trained to do in the interpretation of dreams. She reported apologetically that an association came to her but unfortunately could not relate it to the dream as it referred to something recent. Freud reassured her by telling her to proceed, since the "recent" material would be found to fit in with the past dream. Thus the present was carefully discounted as an operative factor.

Dora now gave the day residue involving a dispute over keeping her brother locked in at night. (One never learns why the mother was so insistent on this habit.) Father said it would not do: "Something might happen in the night so that it might be necessary to leave the room." (This is presumably a report in Dora's own words rather than the father's.) Freud was "taken aback" inasmuch as this had an ambiguous ring. While the father had an outbreak of fire in mind, Freud suspected "switch-words" which would put the train of thought on another track. (For comments on Freud's train imagery, particularly at this time when his railroad phobia was under self-analysis, see Lewin 1970.) While he does succeed in showing that one track led to bedwetting in childhood (and mastur-bation) both in the brother and in Dora herself, it is possible that still another track—inside the analyst—was entering into the analysis in the form of his intuition and empathy. Elsewhere in this volume, in discussing his response to the Rat Man's screen memory of lying in bed between his parents during the oedipal phase and urinating, we point to the possibility of a similar response.

The brilliant interpretations that follow in the case study bring at one point a footnote: "I added: 'Moreover, the reappearance of the dream in the last few days forces me to the conclusion that the same situation has arisen once again, and that you have decided to give up the treatment—to which, after all, it is only your father who makes you come' " (p. 70n). The footnote, showing awareness of transference aspects of the dream, occurs immediately after Freud has been insisting that she really was tempted by Herr K., an interpretation which she rejected. And at this point Freud is reminded of the ambiguous words about leaving the room and is impelled to an odd experiment in which he exposes a matchbox which Dora failed to notice. This resulted in a pressuring session with Dora acknowledging her bedwetting in childhood after recalling that her brother had been a bedwetter. Freud found himself thinking silently: "How much easier it is to remember things of that kind about one's brother than about oneself" (p. 72)—an idea perhaps not altogether prompted simply by the pa-tient's analysis.

This was followed by Dora offering an addendum to her dream at the next session: that each time she awakened from these dreams, she smelled smoke. Perhaps this subsequent recollection indicated a particularly strong resistance to be overcome; perhaps too it indicated that Dora was responding to Freud's interpretations and, despite her antecedent negations, was interested in getting him to pursue the analysis further. It is also noteworthy that he immediately applied the "smoke" addendum to himself. It showed, he held, that the dream had a special relation to himself: not only was he a "passionate smoker" (like father and Herr K., as it turned out) but he connected it himself to the comment "There can be no smoke without fire," with which he would insist on getting Dora to confirm his interpretations. Then, and with little apparent reason, he not only connected the kiss to one that had passed between Herr K. and herself in the past but to a longing of Dora's to kiss him which had been the exciting cause that "led her to repeat the warning dream and to form her intention of stopping the treatment" (p. 74). Yet at the previous session he had remarked that she came only because her father wished it!

The sudden intrusion of the transference with full force into Freud's mind seems to us remarkable for many reasons. It is apparently a breakthrough of an intuition that responded to Dora's ambiguous words that "something might happen in the night so that it might be necessary to leave the room." From fire he found his way through "switch-words" to water, but was not satisfied. Everything in the dream called for reversal. He applied this rule to Herr K., insisting that Dora wished love-making from him as once from her father. Even as Dora was "naturally" rejecting this idea, Freud—judging by the footnote at this point—found the third current of thought breaking through into his conscious mind. The dream applied to himself. He was putting himself into Herr K.'s place as potential seducer from whom Dora would be resolved to flee. Therefore would he not be applying to himself the message that she really wanted to flee from Herr K. because she wished to return to him (like Lot's wife) to be seduced? Was this why he was not perturbed by the "wish to flee"?

Dora's sudden recollection of the smell of smoke when she awakened from the dream now continued the "fire code" she had been learning from him, to indicate, perhaps that she did accept his interpretation about Herr K. and himself after all. Freud's commentary at this point utilizes a metaphor about the dream based on the body image (see Shengold 1966 on the relationship between the body image and the topographic formulations Freud applied to the structure of dreams): "A regularly formed dream stands, as it were, upon two legs" (p. 71). The dream itself becomes a sexual organ at the top of the legs to be inspected and penetrated (see also Erikson's 1962 interpretation of the significance of the Irma dream for Freud). The second leg, hitherto neglected, rests upon the immediate exciting cause which had attracted relatively little interest up to this point. Now a significant reorientation takes place as though, prompted by a hint from Dora in recalling the smell of smoke, he has been aware all along that his cigar-smoking, his use of the metaphor about searching (in her?) for the fire that produces smoke and (most recently) the strange "playing with fire" experiment, the groundwork has been prepared for permitting both of them to contemplate the thought that the desire for him to kiss her had been the exciting cause of the dream and the warning with it that she was preparing to leave treatment (unless she received it?).

Freud's failure to heed the warning creates the problem that marks the rest of the analysis and its failure. The prospective kiss which excited the dream was not considered "susceptible of definite proof" because of the characteristics of "transference" (?), probably meaning that its true force lay in the earlier episodes that were coming up for analysis (p. 74). Nevertheless, the immediate analysis of the dream closes with conflicts over this matter apparently on his mind. The dream, though old and recurrent, had, he concluded, "gained a new significance connected with the present time . . . .The dream thoughts behind it included a reference to my treatment and it corresponded to a renewal of the old intention of withdrawing from a danger" (p. 93). The recent day residue about locking the brother in a room had served as a mediating link to recall the past. Freud did not suggest that it was mobilizing and representing a significant attitude in the present.

The failure to consider the latter possibility was responsible for the continuance of research into the past and the childhood neurosis as well as the affair with Herr K., which to Dora was apparently frustrating when the "transference" to Freud was making him the most real and important person in her life. Certainly she was in no hurry to leave him. It was only weeks later that the second dream occurred and with it the decision to leave treatment. We are inclined to believe that adequate consideration of the constant indecision during the interlude would have saved the treatment. We shall pass over the second dream (which we see as upholding this hypothesis) and turn to the postscript in which transference is granted a new validity when it has become an insight too late to save the analysis. Freud commented that "the postponement of recovery or improvement is really only caused by the physician's own person. . . . The symptoms disappear a little while later, when the relations between patient and physician have been dissolved" (p. 115). Perhaps one may say that the analyst's insight also occurs later for similar reasons.

The acknowledgment of insight into the transference, withheld previously, caused Freud to reconsider the course of the treatment beginning with the first dream. "When the first dream came, in which she gave herself the warning that she had better leave my treatment just as she had formerly left Herr K.'s house, I ought to have listened to the warning myself" (p. 118). He should have inquired, he decided, as to whether she found anything to suggest that he harbored the same evil designs that Herr K. did. With this in mind, he suggested that perhaps transferences ought to be worked into the analysis at an early stage.

He wondered why he did not in fact intervene in this sense and suggested that "since no further stages of transference developed and the material for the analysis had not yet run dry," he considered that he had ample time before him. Yet he himself had already given us material to suggest another approach—recognition of the stimulation proceeding from his cigar-smoking and his use of the metaphor, "where there's smoke there's fire." These are not merely transferences, as we would see them today; they are part of the working alliance. Glenn and Langs have pointed to his "plain talk" which he regarded as a courageous refusal to be hypocritical where there was in fact a seductive significance for an adolescent girl of that period. The strange matchbox game was probably part of the underlying unconscious dialogue between them in which the theme of playing with fire was implicated. The incessant prodding of the girl for memories and confirmations of interpretations without really permitting her own thoughts to come to the fore was perhaps part of an attitude of parental figures to adolescents at the time and made no allowance for their need to have their own identities recognized.

Was it really an unknown resemblance between Herr K. and himself which made Dora feel rebuffed and take her revenge by leaving him? Could there have been a wish to have her leave him which militated against his recognizing until too late that it would have been possible to do so? Her father called twice to say she really wanted to return, but Freud found no reason to take this seriously. When she returned after fifteen months to say that she wished help, he could see at a glance that she was not serious. He did not know what sort of help she needed. Should he have suggested that he had a warm personal interest in her? Her facial neuralgia at their last interview occasioned only a "brilliant interpretation" that it coincided with her having read in the papers of his promotion to a professorship and a comment that he forgave her for having thwarted his wish to give her a thorough cure. Her own rejection was personally resented and reversed.

In rereading the case histories, it is easy enough to recognize Freud's genius, but a greater tribute will be possible when it is recognized what great personal difficulties he had to overcome and what a rudimentary grasp he had of techniques and psychological principles which would be laboriously acquired. Sometimes a contrast is made between Breuer fleeing from the sexual expectations of Anna O. and Freud courageously facing and accepting the same expectations from his own patients. The courage was all the greater when he had to fight recurrent inclinations to flee and imperceptibly guided patients toward a premature termination—as do so many analysts-in-training today, perhaps all analysts with countertransference problems on occasion.

We are not entirely without other data as to the personal factors that entered into the analysis of this girl. It took place while he was in the midst of that important part of his self-analysis which was recorded in the *The Psychopathology of Every Life* (1901). He had occasion there to make some brief but significant remarks about Dora, whose real name was Rosa, that of his favorite sister and also of the nursemaid she employed for her children. Sister Rosa herself had baby-sat before her marriage when Freud and his wife had gone on vacation. The summer before Dora's analysis began, he had encountered sister Rosa and her husband in Venice. Rosa, after her marriage, occupied an apartment next to his until the growing needs of his family and practice required him to take it over for himself.

The Psychopathology of Everyday Life includes amusing stories of inner determinants that linked the names of Dora and Rosa inescapably—the names being prototypes of switch-words? Glenn has suggested (Part I, Chapter 1) that the dichotomy may lie between mother and nursemaid in Freud's own life. Dora followed the example of Herr K.'s nursemaid in deciding to leave her employ abruptly because he had *not* made love to her. One is inclined to speculate about Dora's brother (a year-and-a-half older than herself) who was so intimately tied up with the dream, and her lack of urinary control. The thought crossed Freud's mind, but was not uttered, that it is easier to remember such matters in connection with a brother than with oneself. Here there is perhaps a link with his own interest in fire-water symbolism. He also evidenced a familiar sign of being personally involved in a work by delaying the publication for four years. Sister Rosa was four years younger than himself. We would be less inclined to juxtapose the two facts if it were not for Freud's own stress, both in the study of Dora and in *Everyday Life*, on the significance of dates.

Conclusions

The imagery of the Dora case is especially singled out for its contributions to the understanding of the formation and functions of images in general, their elucidation through the analytic method and their application in turn to the analytic process. As specific text, Dora's first dream, the flight from a burning house with her father, is chosen for study.

Mythological prototypes abound, especially when the ambiguity of the image, as demonstrated by Freud, is taken into account. Moses rescued from the water by the princess (mother), Aeneas fleeing from burning Troy with his father on his back, Lot's wife fleeing from burning Sodom and Gomorrah with father (God's guidance) but halting her own rescue by looking back—all convey related fantasies amply clarified by analytic research. Birth fantasies, with background preoccupations with sexual contacts between and with the parents, are common to all.

Much of this was demonstrated in relation to Dora's dream, and pioneering work on the primal polarity of fire and water and their relationship to bodily processes and phase-specific problems of maturation was accomplished. The reversibility of images also emerged: fleeing from and running to both images must be explored to fully understand the dream and the myths. Subject and object were split: the good self fled with the good father; the bad self stayed with the bad father. Correspondingly, switch-words assumed great importance in the analytic practice, just as the related parapraxes that were simultaneously absorbing Freud's attention in his investigations on the psychopathology of everyday life.

The present article suggests further that the images have communicative significance from the time of the primal image which arises in the constellation of the cry of the distressed infant and the diatrophic response of the mother. Imagery integrates diverse inner strivings at the same time that it organizes the relation between the inner and outer worlds. Phase-specific continuities evolve. It is noteworthy how the primal language of the image is repeated in Dora's cry of distress and the rescuing action of the father, just as it is to be found in the related myths cited. The manifest contents reveal the acceptable aspects of the situation, the latent contents the unacceptable.

The analytic situation produces the same constellations: orientation toward rescue by the analyst and seeking to convert the relationship into the very danger from which rescue is sought. In the early era of analysis, far from finished with his own self-analysis, Freud was not in a position to distance himself from the interplay of these complexities to solve them all accurately. A particular reaction to the dream is chosen here to demonstrate a block to understanding which arose from the countertransference. The associations to the dream gave Freud a first intuitive glimmer of Dora's sexual transference to himself. Though he followed the associations backward into the past, as was his wont, the forward move into the present continued to impress itself upon his consciousness until he was finally able to recognize that Dora was sexually attracted to him and wished to stay, not merely to flee. Freud's efforts to discount the practical implications of this insight are detailed. Only after the analysis had terminated unsuccessfully was insight permitted to establish itself on a conflict-free basis. Transference is an expectable aspect of the treatment and of the messages conveyed by imagery, not an embarassing complication. Dreams convey valuable pictures of the present two-person relationship.

A splitting device is used to convey part of the problem in the *Everyday Life* volume. Dora—or rather Rosa, her true name as well as that of Freud's favorite sister—comes up for discussion in connection with the "switch-word" relationships between the two women in his mind. The connections of both with nursemaids hints at still earlier connections between his mother and his own nursemaid in early life.

From this standpoint, analysis can be seen as a laboratory for the creation of common images which, applicable in that situation, permit a conflict-free language to be formed between the two participants in the analytic situation. With this recognition, we find that Freud has anticipated us when, in the Dora case, he referred to "the language of hysteria" in which she expressed herself. We find further that her dream images, like her symptoms and thinking, also present her vision of the analyst. His real person, his technique and his countertransferences all find representation there, complementing her own thoughts and behavior. To the extent that this is to be found in the dreams of other persons—and we suggest that it may be quite common—the analyst is presented with a most valuable guide to his own behavior, techniques and countertransferences. He is given material not only for self-analysis but for self-supervision.

That imagery in general reflects the object—the circumstances under which it was created as well as that for which it is at present being used—is a dimension supported by the appearance of universal fantasies as well as the universal appeal of art and literature. Children's fairy tales memorialize forever the cruel aspects of the parent as well as their good and helpful ones in the figures of witches and fairy godmothers. Religion carries this over into demons and protective deities. The task of the analyst is to detect and correct the typical fantasies of the patient and translate them into a more appropriate language for his adjustment to everyday life. He must be able to represent the latter himself.

References

Erikson, E. (1962). Reality and actuality. *Journal of the American Psychoanalytic Association* 10: 451–474.

Freud, S. (1901). Psychopathology of everyday life. *Standard Edition* 6: 241–242.

——— (1905). Fragment of an analysis of a case of hysteria. *Standard Edition* 7: 3–122.

Lewin, B. (1970). The train ride. *Psychoanalytic Quarterly* 39: 71–84.

Shengold, L. (1966). The metaphor of the journey in "The Interpretation of Dreams." *American Imago* 23:316–331. Also in *Freud and His Self-Analysis*. Vol. I of the Downstate Anniversary Series. New York: Jason Aronson.

Strachey, J. (1958) Footnote to Freud's Observations on transference love. *Standard Edition* 12:160–161.

Chapter 5

INTEGRATIVE SUMMARY: ON THE
RE-VIEWINGS OF THE DORA CASE

ISIDOR BERNSTEIN, M.D.

Of all Freud's writings probably the most fascinating, impressive in their clarity and dazzling in the display of his genius are the five case histories. In addition, the sheer beauty of the writing entitles them to be viewed as great literature. They are, of course, more than case histories or reports of analyses: they constitute a stirring account of the discovery of psychoanalysis and many parts read like an autobiographical detective story. The reader cannot help sharing Freud's excitement and delight as facts emerge to confirm and help expand his theories and lend substance to them. The richness of the clinical material is paralleled by the elegance of Freud's dynamic formulations and theoretical constructions. These case histories can be reread with pleasure and provide stimulus for further consideration of the many ideas that Freud advanced. The papers by Drs. Glenn, Langs, Kanzer and Scharfman regarding the Dora case are examples of the productivity they continue to generate.

Freud's case reports can be viewed from three perspectives: historical, clinical and theoretical. Historically, the cases provided the clinical material which Freud needed to develop, demonstrate and validate the scientific basis for psychoanalysis and its therapeutic application. This aspect of the Dora case is briefly considered by the authors of the papers I wish to discuss. However, with the exception of Kanzer, they concern themselves mostly with clinical matters.

Glenn points out (and Scharfman agrees) that Freud's failure to recognize that Dora, Katharina and the unnamed "homosexual woman" were adolescents limited Freud's understanding of them; accordingly, Glenn attempts to remedy this by adding a developmental dimension in his reconsideration of the analytic data concerning these three adolescents. In his attempt to define adolescence in both physiologic and psychologic terms, Glenn defines the *beginning* of adolescence by means of a *physiologic* event, the menarche, and the *end* of adolescence in *psychologic* terms. It would be more consistent with his aim to define beginning and end in *both* physiologic and psychologic terms or to limit himself to psychologic terms. That he does not do so, however, does not prevent Scharfman and Langs and myself from agreeing with him that Dora was psychologically in adolescence at the time Freud saw her. To be more precise, she should probably be placed in mid-adolescence.

In his discussion, Glenn points out that Dora had the typical adolescent dependence on her parents and that this led to a struggle against the analyst who was forced upon her by her parents. Accordingly, she would not only identify Freud with the other adults but would see him as acting in collusion with them. This is quite true, but it ignores the significance of the dramatic appeal for help which a suicidal threat or attempt by an adolescent constitute. We can agree with the authors that the adolescent problems which Dora was attempting to solve were compounded by the behavior of the adults of both families and the prevailing social mores with their ambiguous and hypocritical attitudes about sex and femininity. Dora's efforts to detach herself from her parents led first to Frau K. and then to Herr K. Adolescent crushes are common enough, as Scharfman notes, but when they are used by the important adults for their own instinctual gratifications as was the case with Dora, the results can be disastrous. The outcome can be delinquency, perversion or neurosis; sometimes suicide or psychosis may eventuate. Failure in the struggle against the incestuous urges can result in a shattering of the adolescent's still vulnerable trust in his own controls and precariously balanced self-esteem. The tension created by the threat of regressive or disintegrative pressures and the rage against the adults who have failed as idealized figures to support the adolescent's weakened ego and superego may result in a release of primitive aggression which, if turned against the self, may reach suicidal proportions. Some of this aggression would then be directed by Dora against her own body and contribute to her symptomatology. Aggression would also be directed against the most recent adult figure, the analyst, leading to the wish to destroy the analyst or, at least, the analysis. If one were to criticize Freud's technique here it would be on the basis of his emphasis on the libidinal or sexual conflicts before he analyzed Dora's aggression toward himself. Actually, Freud knew of Dora's hostility and contempt for all doctors before she had even met him. Her ambivalent feelings toward him should therefore have been the first area to be analyzed. It undoubtedly was related to her realistically grounded distrust of all adults and authority figures. Freud intensified the problem by his association with the important adults, especially her father, and by the authoritarian and didactic attitude in his conduct of Dora's analysis. Kanzer comments on this pre-analytic behavior of Freud. Viewed from the historical standpoint, Freud's approach is understandable because these case studies preceded Freud's recognition of aggression as being of equal importance with libido; that step was subsequently embodied in the dual instinct theory with the technical modifications that ensued.

A particularly creative and imaginative response to the material in the Dora case is Kanzer's essay on the imagery of Dora's dream of flight with her father from a burning house. Kanzer uses the dream to illuminate and link symbols, myths, universal fantasies and Dora's analysis. One could hardly ask for a more spectacular illustration of the overdetermination of a mental product. The discussion helps to bring into bold relief some of the very important but less emphasized aspects of analytic insight into normal as well as neurotic mental processes which Freud achieved during his treatment of Dora, for example, the linking of images of fire and water to universal bodily functions during the oedipal period, the use of switch-words or verbal bridges, etc. Kanzer then examines the "flight from the father fantasy" in relation to Dora's analysis. He shows its presence not only in relation to her father but the father surrogates, Herr K. and Freud, and discusses Freud's difficulties in dealing with the transference.

A serious limitation of any discussion of Freud's technique in the Dora case is the fact that Freud did not describe or explain his technical approach. We do not even know whether Dora used the couch. In order to present the material in more coherent and readable fashion, particularly for the exposition of his thesis regarding the psychosomatic basis of hysteria, Freud availed himself of poetic license in describing the manner in which the analytic material was obtained and the order in which he related it to his readers. The present authors and myself are therefore left with the necessity for making inferences about his technique and the status of transference and countertransference situations. However, this is not too different from what sometimes occurs in supervision of analyses. The authors have all had experience with supervision, Glenn and Scharfman particularly with adolescent analyses, and they justifiably draw on that for their criticism and evaluation of Freud as an analyst of adolescent girls. There is no doubt that Freud committed a number of errors in technique. Glenn ably summarizes these and their consequences in his review of the determinants of Dora's leaving the analysis.

Let us imagine Freud, as a beginning and inexperienced analyst of adolescents, to be in supervision. The supervisor would first evaluate the suitability of the patient for analysis by a beginner. Here, the criticism regarding the manner in which she was brought to analysis would be relevant. Another possible source of difficulty could also have been anticipated, i.e., that Freud knew too much about Dora before the analysis started. It led Freud to make a number of formulations and to anticipate matters to an extent where he was relying less on material as it came from Dora than on the information he already had obtained outside the analysis. This is a problem of technique in child and adolescent analysis and there are still differing opinions about the advisability of having extensive historical facts external to the analysis. A too-detailed history of the patient can lead to assumptions or formulations that can interfere with the openness of mind necessary to listen to the patient. In the analysis, it would appear as though Freud were telling Dora that he hardly needed her for the analysis; to her this would be a repetition of previous depreciations of her importance, as though she were a minor character in a play—a crowning insult for a hysteric. I agree with the authors that Freud's eagerness led to premature interpretations which resulted in strengthening of Dora's defenses. It could be that he was carried away by the excitement of discovery that befits an explorer of a new world—the world of dreams and the unconscious.

The supervisor would next ask, "What are you trying to do?" To answer this for Freud, the reply would be, "I am trying to originate and validate the science and theory of psychoanalysis, to demonstrate the correctness of my hypotheses concerning hysteria and to use this patient to do that." To this unconsciously would be added, "and in so doing, I will display all my brilliance to this girl." A supervisor would be compelled to point out the danger of approaching the patient and analytic material in this manner and attempt to moderate the intensity of the analyst's investigative fervor. The supervisor might be tempted to conclude that Freud suffered from fantasies of omnipotence and delusions of grandeur. Hopefully, Freud's genius would have been recognized and he would have been encouraged to proceed with caution. Langs and Scharfman discuss the effect of Freud's motivations on the transference; it provided an element of reality to the transference from the other adults who had used Dora for their own needs.

One helpful suggestion that could have been made, were one able to anticipate later technical knowledge, would be to deal first with resistances. Specifically, analysis of Dora's aggression and the severity of her superego which was based on identification with her compulsive mother would precede the interpretation of her sexual conflicts.

A supervisor would also recognize Freud's approach as too intellectual and didactic and would soon conclude that the major problems had to do with transference and countertransference. It is possible to defend Freud by suggesting that he was appealing to the patient's own intellectual interest as a way of enlisting her active participation in the analysis; this would be in line with establishing a working alliance. Freud criticizes himself for not dealing with the transference problems soon enough. In his postscript he states, "Owing to the readiness with which Dora put one part of the pathogenic material at my disposal during the treatment, I neglected the precaution of looking out for the first signs of transference." Even at that late date, however, he was not aware of his countertransference. I agree with Glenn that the analysis was limited by Freud's lack of the later knowledge of developmental aspects of adolescence. I believe, however, that what was at least equally important for Freud was that his self-analysis was incomplete regarding problems of his own adolescence and that that prevented him from understanding more fully his adolescent patients. This is not an infrequent problem with analysts who have difficulty in dealing with adolescents and the adolescent period of life in their analysands. The lack of knowledge regarding adolescent development did not prevent Aichhorn from being quite effective in his work with adolescents. This could help explain Freud's need to view the adolescent girls as adults, i.e., to skip over their and his own adolescence. A more rationalized explanation would be that Freud was primarily interested in elucidating the structure, dynamics, economics and, to some extent, the genetics of the fully developed (adult) neurosis. Dora was to be the classic example of a hysteric and it was on the assumption that the neurotic structure was fully established in her that Freud proceeded with the analysis. Glenn correctly points out that Dora was not a late adolescent or early adult and therefore her psychic structure was in a state of flux. Freud was seeing her more as what she was developing into and ultimately became as an adult—a hysteric with a masochistic character disorder.

All of the authors deal with the issues of central importance in any analysis: transference and countertransference. Langs, in addition, introduces the term *therapeutic misalliance* to connote the many types of transference and counter-transference reactions and technical errors that may occur in analyses. He does not attempt the difficult job of systematically classifying the errors and their causes. Langs places particular emphasis on the complications caused by Freud's realistic involvements with the families. Reality factors, defenses and resistances, including acting out, may blur the patient's transference reactions so that analysis becomes more difficult. However, I believe that the effort to subsume a variety of extra-analytic or non-analytic behavior under one rubric sometimes oversimplifies the matter rather than truly clarifying it. Consciously applied parameters should be differentiated from inadvertently produced complications. In addition, some of the activities that Langs considers to be errors are not mistakes at all but necessary adaptations to the adolescent condition. Langs does not elucidate the specific adolescent nature of Dora's conflicts and her attempts at solution as clearly as do Glenn and Scharfman. The analyst of adolescents usually must see one or both parents at some point, most commonly at the start of the treatment. Parental support of the analysis, financial as well as emotional, is necessary. Many parents would interfere with their teenage children's treatment if they had not actively participated in the arrangements regarding frequency and cost of treatment. Personal contact by the parents with the analyst can also reassure adolescents, as can providing other sources of information regarding the analyst's reputation and qualifications, his being a reasonable human being of integrity. Indeed, the adolescent who relies on the parents' reality orientation for safety and care may feel unprotected were he to enter treatment without parental confirmation based on their seeing the analyst. This does not mean that complications cannot arise from parental contact. The teenager must be certain that confidentiality is maintained. Langs' discussion of the adverse effects of attempts at manipulation by either the adolescent or the adults is relevant. It is not possible here to more fully discuss the role of parents in the analyses of adolescents. The point is that this very complex matter is not sufficiently dealt with when one states that the parents seeing the analyst creates a "therapeutic misalliance."

It is, of course, of great importance to define the conscious and unconscious motivation of the adolescent and parents when analysis is being considered. As Langs notes, Freud was able to show Dora her wish to disrupt her father's relationship with Frau K. Langs also remarks upon the motivation for insight and relief of suffering that promotes the therapeutic alliance. Dora's unconscious wish to be seduced by Freud as a proxy for Herr K. (and her father) is revealed and defended against in her first dream and prompted her decision to terminate, that is, to flee from the analysis.

So far as the motives of the analyst are concerned, Scharfman suggests that Freud had "another mistress," his interest in science, and this "infidelity" makes him like Dora's father in her eyes. However, it is overstating the case to accept the idea that this would wreck the likelihood of the establishment of a therapeutic alliance. Every analyst has more than a therapeutic motive in analyzing a patient, as Kanzer indicates. Scientific interest with possible contributions to psychoanalytic literature can be present without interfering with the analytic stance of the analyst. In fact, it can help maintain the kind of analytic interest that is helpful. When that interest is too intense or instinctualized or involved with the analyst's fantasies without his awareness, however, it becomes a legitimate reason for concern. In this narrower or more limited sense, we can understand and agree with Langs' reference to Freud's own statement regarding the possible adverse effects of the analyst's ambitious needs on his analytic work. I would also question Langs' equating of Freud's inquiring of Dora about her sexuality as a *real* seduction. This emphasis on the reality aspect is similar to the defensive projection by the patient on to the analyst and the insistence on the reality of the analyst's seductive behavior. It is easier to agree with Langs' later estimate that "The determination of reality and fantasy in Dora's relationship with Freud is a very complex one."

In the first dream, Dora's desires to be seduced or protected are projected on to the father and Freud; however, it is her own indecision as to which she wants and not Freud's behavior, as Langs suggests, that is expressed. As we know, the desire to be saved represents a wish for a child (see Kanzer's remarks about universal fantasies); the unconscious fellatio fantasy and wish for oral impregnation are represented in the latent dream thoughts. This is confirmed in the second dream. Langs' suggestion that the dream was reported to call Freud's attention to the misalliance, I think, states the communicative, rational and adaptive aspect of dreaming more strongly than the material given indicates.

Langs makes a number of cogent observations regarding the complicating effect of Freud's relationship with Dora's parents and their friends, in particular the creation of distrust of him by Dora. It made it difficult for Dora to see Freud as a benevolently neutral figure. What is worse, it blurred for her the distinction between reality and the transference fantasy.

Langs' term encompasses the primary and secondary gain of illness, designated by Freud as paranosic and epinosic gain. The primary gain would be the actual or symbolic gratification of instinctual drives and/or self-punishment. With Dora, the material suggests scopophilic desires with fellatio and incorporative/castrative components; both aggressive and libidinal urges would be gratified. Secondary gain would be manipulative control and revenge against the adults who had subordinated her needs for protection and assistance in dealing with the instinctual upsurge of adolescence to the adults' own needs for gratification.

Glenn describes the dynamics involved clearly. However, I believe that he places undue stress on the aggressive, hostile aspects of the countertransference. He emphasizes the analyst's use of reversal of affect in defending against affectionate feelings toward his patient; aggression appears in place of libido. Glenn also notes that Freud identifies with the aggressor. It is true that Freud was identifying with the aggressor, the rejecting Dora; but he was also involved in both defending against and acting out a phallic exhibitionistic fantasy. Freud, after all, did display his tremendous intellectual and analytic ability with brilliant interpretations and reconstructions; this situation would be conducive to Dora's seductiveness which Glenn refers to and she might stimulate Freud to continue by bringing fresh and provocative material to the analysis. Glenn refers to Freud's narcissistic investment in the analysis and Dora's sharing of the glory in his performance and career. Despite Scharfman's objections to Freud's seeing the conflict in phallic terms as representative of the influence of a Victorian misconception of feminine psychology on Freud, I would agree with Glenn that Dora envied and hated those whom she admired. I further believe that this envy and hatred of the original objects were also directed towards her brother and father. It later found expression towards her husband and son (see F. Deutsch 1957: "contrary to her expectations, he [the son] succeeded in life as a renowned musician"). We could speculate here as to the preoedipal origin of this problem vis-à-vis brother and father. Dora's wishes to incorporate the phallus were recognized early by Freud symptomatically in her nervous cough and aphonia.

I should also like to suggest the possibility of a prepuberty or early puberty trauma—an exhibitionistic display by an important male figure. This could refer to her encounter with Herr K. when she was fourteen years old. Glenn's discussion of psychological and physiological development during the time Dora was growing up reminds us that prepuberty then started about the same age as at present, but that adolescence generally started much later. One might also infer such an incident from her second dream. In it, the thick wood which she entered and there asked questions of a man whom she met could be connected with an early visual sexual experience. There are a couple of references to looking in that dream: she "saw streets and squares" and "she saw a thick wood." The subsequent experience with Herr K. when she was sixteen years old could then serve for Dora as a defensive screen for the earlier event. Her insistence on the truth of the later experience and Herr K.'s part in it could be a way of shifting her guilt about the earlier experience. Also, her wish to repeat the experience with others, including Freud, is typical of a post-traumatic pattern of repeating in an active way what has been previously experienced passively. In her studies of screen memories and of prepuberty trauma in girls Greenacre demonstrated how later traumas can be used defensively to screen earlier ones. Freud refers to Dora's use of a screen memory regarding her brother's part in her having acquired the habit of masturbation. That could relate to a repressed memory of having seen his genitals. These are elements in the history of Dora's illness that bear resemblance to the cases of prepuberty trauma described by Greenacre.

Dora's wish to revenge herself on men would be not only for the disappointment in her relationships with them; it would have earlier origins in her image of herself as lacking the male organ. This attitude would have been culturally represented in her contemporary society's devaluation of women's intellectual abilities and aspirations.

There is general agreement with Freud's own admission that his failure to recognize and interpret the transference early and fully contributed to the interruption of the analysis. His own "acting in" with the matchbox was a provocative bit of behavior. Langs refers to the exhibitionistic and voyeuristic elements in both transference and countertransference, a "misalliance." One could agree with him that this resulted in deviations in technique and that this contributed to the premature termination of the analysis. One would, however, also have to think about Freud's need to state repeatedly his regret at not being able to complete the analysis. Our suspicions would be strengthened by his strenuous denunciation of any scopophilic gratifications by physicians (in his prefatory remarks). Despite his insistence on the need to deal with sexual matters openly, Freud was ignoring the effects on himself of his Victorian upbringing and milieu. Freud underestimated the strength of his own unconscious moralistic attitudes, and this superego conflict could have strongly influenced his decision to discontinue the analysis.

One can see from the preceding papers how many new ideas can be stimulated by a thoughtful rereading of the Dora case. Glenn highlights the advances in technique in the treatment of adolescents as a result of greater knowledge of adolescent development. He discusses the importance of the phase-appropriate struggle for independence from parents, the need of the adolescent to find nonincestuous objects and typical transference and countertransference reactions. Glenn, Langs and Scharfman describe in detail the resulting technical errors. Kanzer uses the material to expand our knowledge of imagery in normal and pathological mental processes and imagery's relation to universal fantasies. Such contributions serve as a testimonial to the enduring vitality of Freud's case history.

References

Deutsch, F. (1957). Footnote to Freud's analysis of hysteria. *Psychoanalytic Quarterly* 26: 159–167.

Freud, A. (1971). Problems of psychoanalytic training, diagnosis, and the technique of therapy. *The Writings of Anna Freud* 7. New York: International Universities Press.

Freud, S. (1905). Fragment of the analysis of a case of hysteria. *Standard Edition* 7:3–122.

———— (1912). Recommendations to physicians practising psycho-analysis. *Standard Edition* 12: 109–121.

Greenacre, P. (1952). Prepuberty trauma. *Trauma, Growth and Personality*. New York: Norton.

PART III

Little Hans

Chapter 1

A FRESH LOOK AT THE CASE OF LITTLE HANS

MARTIN A. SILVERMAN, M.D.

The researches which led Freud to the elaboration of psychoanalysis as a clinical tool for investigating human mental processes were carried out primarily with adult patients. It is curious, therefore, that the first two of the five long case histories which Freud has given us concern not adults but an adolescent and a child respectively. How is it that these two cases were chosen as the first detailed accounts of psychoanalytic treatment to be presented to the public? Approaching the question from an historical point of view might provide partial clarification.

Freud's earliest investigations into the neuroses led to the publication in 1900 of *The Interpretation of Dreams*, the first textbook of psychoanalysis. Freud was well aware of the importance of this work and set out soon thereafter to publish a full-length account of a case study which illustrated the clinical usefulness of the dream in a more detailed fashion than had been possible in the "dream book" itself. A case which aptly suited this purpose involved an eighteen-year-old girl with a variety of hysterical symptoms whom Freud had analyzed during the last three months of 1899. Jones (1955) informs us that although the paper was accepted for publication upon its submission in January, 1901 (the editor of another journal had declined to print it when it was offered to him in 1900), Freud for discretionary reasons held it back for four years before permitting it to be published in 1905 as a *Fragment of An Analysis of a Case of Hysteria* (1905a).

The year 1905 was marked by the publication not only of the case of "Dora" but also of a landmark work, the *Three Essays on The Theory of Sexuality*, a book which, as Strachey (1953, p. 126) has stated, "stands, there can be no doubt, besides his *Interpretation of Dreams* as his most momentous and original contribution to human knowledge" (also quoted by Jones 1955, p. 286). As Freud stated in his preface to the *Three Essays*, he had drawn his conclusions predominantly from psychoanalytic investigations with adult patients and he hoped that knowledge drawn from studies in other fields would eventually be used to test and amplify them.

In accordance with this wish, he requested of the members of the small but growing band of those who were interested in the young science of psychoanalysis that they gather direct observational data concerning the sexual development of children and adolescents. In 1906, he began to receive reports about a three-year-old boy whose father was an adherent of psychoanalysis and whose mother for a brief period had been a patient of Freud's. The reports contained information which Freud shared with the public within the body of two papers, *The Sexual Enlightenment of Children* (1907) and *On the Sexual Theories of Children* (1908).

In January 1908, when "Little Hans," as he came eventually to be called, was four and three-quarters years old, a neurosis broke out which not only provided an opportunity to observe the development of an infantile neurosis in *statu nascendi*, but also responded dramatically to a course of psychoanalytic therapy carried out by the boy's father under Freud's supervision and guidance. An opportunity had presented itself to provide the public with a convincing confirmation of the developmental theory which Freud had promulgated in the *Three Essays* as well as of the efficacy of psychoanalysis as a treatment modality. The *Analysis of a Phobia in a Five-Year-Old Boy* appeared early in 1909 with the express consent of Little Hans's father.

It is evident, therefore, that the cases of Dora and of Little Hans lent themselves to publication because of their eminent suitability as illustrations of central issues contained in two basic communications which Freud had made concerning the theory and practice of psychoanalysis. It is my impression, however, that there is another implication to be found in Freud's decision to use these two cases as the first which he presented in detail in the literature. Psychoanalysis is essentially a developmental theory. Freud found that by tracing adult neuroses back to their genetic roots in the formative years of childhood and adolescence, it was possible not only to unravel the complexities of their makeup and relieve the suffering of those who were afflicted with them, but, even more important, it provided access to understanding the development and functioning of the psychological aspect of man which sets him apart from other animals. Freud was first and foremost a researcher and his decision to turn to an adolescent and a child to help him present the findings of psychoanalysis to the world reflects his abiding interest in exploring and mapping out the details of human psychic development.

Freud probably would have liked to study developmental processes directly in childhood and adolescence, but the opportunity to carry out such an investigation existed only in sporadic instances at the turn of the century. First of all, Freud could not count upon the availability of children with whom he could work psychoanalytically. A society that denied the existence of infantile sexuality also denied the existence in childhood of organized neuroses and psychoses. He certainly could not expect that a world which hurled abuse and calumny upon him for what he told it about the mental life of adults would permit him to work, either analytically or as a direct observer, with little children.

Secondly, it would have been very difficult at that time to study the mental activity of children. In those early days, psychoanalysts depended upon the verbal reports of cooperative, verbal analysands. Not only was the communication of children too little understood at that time, but, as we have come to know only too well, the resistance of children to analysis is far greater than it is in adults, necessitating the use of specialized techniques which had not yet been developed. At that time Freud did not believe that children could participate in an analytic investigation carried out by anyone lacking the degree of respect, trust, and love accorded to anyone other than their parents. It would have been most unlikely to find neurotic children with parents who were both psychoanalytically informed and willing to undertake an analysis of their children's psychological problems under the supervision of a psychoanalyst. Freud, furthermore, seemed to feel that Little Hans's ability to take part in an analytic investigation was itself unusual; he could not have considered it likely that very many other such children could be found. In this regard, Freud seems to have underestimated the capacity of children to recognize the value of exploring that part of their mental activity which is unknown to them (i.e., unconscious) with the help of someone who can help them gain access to it. After all, it was Little Hans himself who told his father that they had only to write down his thoughts and send them to "the Professor" for his nonsense to disappear. Freud was not in a position to know, as we do now, that prelatency children very often are extremely receptive to analytic intervention, rendering psychoanalysis relatively easy.

The successful treatment of Little Hans offered confirmatory evidence of psychoanalytic speculations about the mental and emotional life of children which Freud did not expect to obtain again so easily. It is ironic, therefore, that the publication of the Little Hans case as a presumably *unusual* entry into the psychopathology of childhood paved the way for the eventual development of child analysis and direct observational study of children not only as legitimate activities of psychoanalysts but as invaluable methods of gathering psychoanalytic data to complement that which derives from the investigation of psychopathology in adults.

A Comparison of Child Analytic Approach in 1908–1909 and the Present

When we look back upon the treatment of Little Hans, we can only marvel at the skill with which it was carried out and at the excellent result which was obtained. Any additions or modifications which we might be able to make from the perspective of what we have learned in later years cannot dim the brilliance of that first instance of child analysis. It remains a useful model for the technical management of phobias in the phallic-oedipal period which center about the phase-specific conflicts of that time of life. What we have learned since then, we have gained through techniques and approaches the seeds of which are to be found in the Little Hans paper.

If we were to approach a case like that of Little Hans today, we would do so with the benefit of a greatly expanded body of clinical and theoretical knowledge, much of which has been provided to us by Freud himself. Hans's treatment took place before the development of either the dual instinct theory or the structural theory. With regard to the first of these, the Little Hans case can serve as an apt illustration of Freud's reluctance to accept the presence of a separate aggressive drive in man (Schur 1972). Freud paid considerable attention in the case of Little Hans to the role of aggressive and hostile feelings and even concluded that they played a central role in the boy's neurosis. He stated, for example, that "The fear which sprang from this death-wish against his father, and which may thus be said to have a normal motive, formed the chief obstacle to the analysis until it was removed during the conversation in my consulting room" (1909, p. 112). Later in the paper, he developed a convincing thesis that Hans's anxiety was "to be explained as being due to the repression of Hans's aggressive propensities (the hostile ones against his father and the sadistic ones against his mother)" (p. 140). He even went so far as to raise the idea of an "aggressive instinct" (p. 141) at play, only to reject the idea. At that time, Freud considered aggressive manifestations as fundamentally libidinal. Sadism was not looked upon as a fusion of aggression and sexual drives, but as a sexual expression.

In a similar vein, Freud moved in the direction of a structural point of view with his reflections upon Hans's defensive use of repression and displacement, his punishing himself for wishing to take his mother away from him, and his intense intellectual activity to solve the mysteries of pregnancy and childbirth. He adhered to a prestructual model in his approach to the case, in which he depicted Hans's anxiety as having arisen from a transmutation of libidinal drive tension which was being denied the opportunity to be discharged. In his concluding summary of the origins of Hans's neurosis, for example, he postulated that certain events in Hans's life had provoked genital excitement, hostile and sadistic urges, and jealous yearnings which had led to a "return of the repressed; and it returned in such a manner that the pathogenic material was remodelled and transposed on to the horse-complex, while the accompanying affects were uniformly turned into anxiety" (p. 137). This is very different from the structural (as well as defensive and adaptational) concepts which we would employ today. Freud himself turned back to the case of Little Hans in 1926 in order to revise his formulations to conform with the structural theory which he recently had devised. At that time he largely abandoned the libidinal transformation theory of anxiety, identified anxiety as an attitude arising in the ego consequent to the awareness of danger, and described the ego's institution of defense mechanisms of repression, displacement, regression, and transformation of impulses into their opposite (i.e., fear of retaliation and reversal of aggressive impulses toward the father into tender ones) to ward off the danger. Another important difference between Freud's formulations in 1908 and 1909 and the way we would approach such a case today concerns the importance which we might attribute to oedipal and preoedipal factors. As Anna Freud (1971) has emphasized recently, Freud was preoccupied at the time of the treatment of Little Hans with the psychology of adults rather than of children. His interest in the case centered around the confirmation which it provided of his conclusions about the connection between adult neuroses and antecedent events in early childhood. Since Freud approached the case from the point of view of the adult neurosis, in which unresolved oedipal conflicts had been found to play a pivotal role, it is understandable that he focused his attention upon the phallic-oedipal period which he presumed to be the time when oedipal conflicts materialize (A. Freud 1971). It was not his intention (and certainly not that of Hans's father) to utilize Little Hans's neurosis as an opportunity to explore all of the complexities of child development and child psychopathology.

The analysis of a five-year-old would be carried out today from the point of view of the child rather than that of the adult. It would concern itself more with the overall developmental progression of the child and less with the current symptoms (A. Freud 1965). Attention would be paid not only to the oedipal conflicts themselves but also to the preoedipal factors which have paved the way and themselves contributed to the form and contents of the Oedipus complex as it unfolds in each child. We have learned a great deal since 1909 about the preoedipal period. New information tends to have a seductive effect and, as Arlow (1974) has cautioned, there is a very real danger of our becoming so enamored with the fascinating details of preoedipal development that have been coming to light that we shift our central focus away from the predominantly oedipal conflict situations which are the psychoanalyst's principal concern and attempt to explain neurotic symptomatology in terms of narcissistic transformations and preverbal experiences whose developmental impact remains extremely difficult to assess. The controversial hypotheses contained in Kleinian theory constitute an apt illustration of the problems which are encountered when one attempts to correlate what we think takes place during the earliest months and years with later psychopathological manifestations.

On the other hand, we cannot ignore the data concerning preoedipal development which have been emerging in recent years. The child analyst of today finds himself preoccupied to a great extent with preoedipal issues as he struggles to unravel the problems which his young patient has brought to him. In her introduction to a collection of papers illustrating the work of current child psychoanalysts, Geleerd (1967) expressed surprise at the extent to which preoedipal themes were given consideration in the cases being presented and cautioned the reader to bear in mind that, although these themes occupied the analysts' attention at great length, they did so in a preliminary fashion leading eventually to the analysis of oedipal themes which were seen as occupying a central position in the neuroses under study. Child analysts of today, in other words, continue to recognize the enormous organizing impact *upon the entire personality organization* (Rangell 1972) of the oedipal conflicts which emerge at the height of the phallic phase, but we tend to interest ourselves in the prehistory of those conflicts as well as in their ultimate fate.

Let us turn to the case report of Little Hans's neurosis and take a fresh look at it from the perspective of current understanding of child development and of the evolution of the infantile neurosis. We immediately note that the kind of anamnestic data upon which we have come to depend is very scant in this case report. Freud not only took a very incomplete history; he did not get any historical information at all from the mother, as we would do routinely today. We should like to know more about the early behavioral indications in Hans of the intrinsic drive characteristics (Alpert, Neubauer and Weil 1956) and variations in ego endowment (S. Freud 1937, Hartmann 1939, 1950) which we have come to recognize as important factors in each child's development. We would be interested in the details of Hans's interaction with his primary objects during the crucial early structure-building years (Mahler 1968, Weil 1970) during which central personality characteristics implicating developmental style, core self- and object-representations, the pattern of narcissistic regulation, and the evolution of preferred executive and defensive ego modes crystallize as structural elements which then interact with maturational and experiential factors during the phallic phase to produce oedipal conflicts which vary in each child as to form, content, and available pathways for their eventual resolution (Silverman et al. 1975). Freud's adult-oriented approach to Hans's oedipal struggles, in which he started with the phallic phase, addressed itself to these data only indirectly and very incompletely. In reviewing the Little Hans case at this time, therefore, we will have to make do with a very incomplete body of information in these respects.

When we review the report of the Little Hans case we find, however, that it does contain enough information to permit us to expand Freud's 1909 formulation of the neurosis. Although we do not possess data bearing directly upon Hans's very early life, we do know that at least by his fourth year he was a high-spirited, self-assertive youngster who pursued his aims vigorously and was not easily put off by obstacles in his path. He was an intelligent, verbal, imaginative youngster whose activity expressed itself more in perceptual and intellectual channels than motorically. We might be tempted to trace this back to a congenital activity type characterized by high perceptual activity and relatively low motor activity (Fries and Woolf 1953, Escalona 1963), but without relevant anamnestic data this would be wholly speculative.

What is clear is that by his fourth and fifth years, Hans showed a consistently high level of visual activity in the service both of instinctual drive satisfaction and intellectual mastery. He was a visually alert youngster who took keen notice of things that went on about him, showed sustained interest in observing the eliminative functions of others and in studying the appearance of his own excretory products, attempted repeatedly to solve the mysteries of female genital anatomy by looking as well as by asking questions, kept vigil for hours in the hope of catching a glimpse of the little girl whose charms had smitten him, etc.

Hans's perceptual sensitivity involved the auditory sphere as well. We now know, by his own words, that Little Hans was Herbert Graf, for many years the stage director of the Metropolitan Opera in New York City and the author of three books and numerous articles on operatic production (Rizzo 1972). In choosing his profession, he continued in the musical tradition of his father, Max Graf, a well-known musicologist, critic, and pioneer in the application of psychoanalytic principles to the study of musical creativity. There is a reference in the report of the Little Hans case to the young boy's unusual interest in music even at that time. It might be tempting to relate the selection of a giraffe (spelled the same, but pronounced *zhi-róffa* in German) to the family name of Graf (which means Count, as in Graf Zeppelin or Graf Spey, in German). The young patient upon whom Aarons (1953) reported, however, also used a giraffe to represent his large parents with their supposed, long penises; we do not know his family name.

In addition to whatever intrinsic factors contributed to this particular ego style, there was plentiful enough visual stimulation over the years to explain the development of a hypercathexis of visual activity by the time Hans reached the phallic phase. His mother permitted him to look on when she used the bathroom, at least one aunt fussed grandiloquently over the sight of his genitals, playmates (including two older girls) collaborated with him in mutual scopophilic activity during the summer vacation at Gmunden when he was three and a quarter years old, etc. Hans slept in his parents' bedroom until he was four and a half years old and we certainly have to agree with Freud that he probably witnessed parental intercourse during that time. It is also likely that Hans observed disagreements between his parents (whom we are told eventually dissolved their marriage), which would have contributed to the misinterpretation of the primal scene as a sadistic act, and this probably underlay his horror at seeing horses beaten and his fantasy of beating his mother. His observation (without adequate explanation) of his mother's bodily changes during her pregnancy and of the bloody amniotic fluid following the delivery must also have contributed to his intense, eroticized cathexis of the visual sphere as a major channel for drive expression and ego activity.

Freud has provided enough information for us to attempt an assessment of the status of the drives at the time when Hans entered the phallic phase. We know that he was an affectionate, loving youngster who was capable of intense sensual and sexual excitement and strong libidinal attachment to his objects. We can postulate that a plentiful libidinal endowment (or, viewed in another way, a potential for the emergence of a plentiful libidinal component out of an initially undifferentiated energic reservoir in response to interaction with an average expectable environment) had combined with sufficient favorable experience during the oral phase to lead to a plentiful libidinal cathexis of core self-representations and of core object-representations, from whom he expected to obtain reliable gratification of his libidinal needs.

We know further than Hans's mother infantilized and seduced him into a dependent and increasingly eroticized attachment to her which must have been very powerful. In addition to permitting him to accompany her when she used the bathroom, she still was bathing, drying, and powdering him daily, "taking care not to touch his penis" when he was four and a quarter years of age. His father, too, despite his critique of his wife's "sexual over-excitation" of Hans, was opening Hans's drawers and taking out his penis for him when he had to urinate.

We also know that Hans was given laxatives and enemas "frequently," and there are indications that Hans's father himself struggled with anal-erotic conflicts. He ate foods which were chosen to soften his stools, suggesting a tendency to constipation, and his writings contain plentiful anal imagery (Graf 1942). There are repeated references in the case report to the mother "beating" the baby sister, as well as indications of ambivalence and intermittent sadistic impulses, which suggests that his mother too had significant anal-erotic and anal-sadistic tendencies.

It is remarkable that Freud paid so little apparent heed to the contribution of environmental seduction to the precipitation of Hans's neurosis. He praised Hans's parents for raising him with a minimum of restraint upon the expression of his instinctual drives and came to the mother's defense against the charge of sexual seductiveness levelled against her by the father. According to Rank's summary of Freud's comments during a discussion of the Little Hans case at the Vienna Psychoanalytic Society on May 12, 1909, Freud defended Hans's parents against the charge of having contributed to the development of his neurosis: "not *that* many mistakes were made, and those that did occur did not have *that* much to do with the neurosis. The boy should only have been refused permission to accompany his mother to the toilet. For the rest, neurosis is essentially a matter of constitution" (Nunberg and Federn 1967, p. 235, original italics).

It is unfortunate in that Hans's parents were among the first, though far from the last, to misuse Freud's findings regarding the role of excessive sexual repression in neurosis to rationalize and justify overstimulating their children by acting out voyeuristic-exhibitionistic and oedipal-seductive fantasies with them. Freud's omission probably has contributed to the tendency of some contemporary psychoanalysts to underestimate the neurosogenic impact of parental nudity and related forms of seduction of their children.

Regarding the aggressive drive, we possess an important piece of information. "In very early days," Hans's father said, "when he had to be put on the chamber, and refused to leave off playing, he used to stamp his feet in a rage, and kick about, and sometimes throw himself on the ground" (Freud 1909, p. 54). Whether we postulate an intrinsically high aggressive endowment or speculate that it emerged out of the events of the anal-sadistic phase (Peller 1965), this description of Hans's tantrums illustrates the fact that he entered the phallic phase with strong aggressive as well as libidinal drives.

The details of Hans's passage through the anal-sadistic phase acquire greater significance for us today than they did for Freud in the first decade of this century. We know now that what occurs during the anal-sadistic phase contributes in very important ways to the shape and form of the oedipal conflicts which develop during the oedipal period which follows it (Silverman et al. 1975). The child goes through extremely important subphases of separation-individuation (Mahler 1968), leading to the emergence of critically important self- and object-representations and patterns of narcissistic regulation. The intellectual and motor capacities which blossom during this period provide him with the means with which to carry out an aggressive, self-assertive campaign to acquire autonomous control over his body and its functions. This brings him into conflict with his mother at the same time that he looks to her as his principal love object and relies heavily upon her to provide needed, surrogate ego strength and to be a mirroring, appreciative audience for his narcissistic-exhibitionistic performances (Brunswick 1940, Mahler 1968, Tartakoff 1966). The outcome of these ambivalent internal and external struggles affects his views of himself and of the object world, the degree to which he can rely upon himself to maintain independent control over his libidinal and especially aggressive impulses, and his capacity to weather the inevitable defeats which lie before him in the phallic-oedipal period.

A feature of this which deserves special mention in connection with the Little Hans case is the observation that at the height of the anal-sadistic phase, between fifteen and twenty-four months, children show evidence of a heightened sexual arousal, manifested by masturbatory activity and an interest in the difference between the sexes (Roiphe 1968, Roiphe and Galenson 1972). In a personal communication, Roiphe has stated that parents tend rapidly to repress their observation of this early genital interest. The genital arousal in this early period takes place at a time of intense, narcissistic preoccupation with bodily sensations and functions in a context of incomplete demarcation of self from nonself, a struggle to acquire independent self-control, and an intellectual organization (Silverman 1971) which permits no more than a fuzzy and unstable conceptualization of male and female as finite, independent categories. Roiphe and Galenson (1972) have found that genital arousal in the second year, accompanied by the opportunity to make direct observations of the anatomical differences between the sexes, together with prior or current experiences contributing to either disturbed body image or to faulty object-representation have led to significant castration anxiety without there having been direct threats of castration.

Freud's formulation of Little Hans's neurosis revolved about the impact upon Hans of castration anxiety mobilized by the birth of a baby sister when he was three and a half years old, his mother's threat at about the same time to have his penis cut off if he continued to masturbate, and the impact of his struggle to control powerful masturbatory oedipal yearnings. Freud's impression was that the castration anxiety began with the need to solve the mysteries of pregnancy and childbirth; in later years, prompted by the acquisition of new data, he shifted his emphasis to that of the observation of the difference between the sexes as the most salient factor in mobilizing the beginning of castration anxiety in children (Freud 1925, Peller 1965). In this regard, it is interesting that Aarons (1953) in his account of a case which was otherwise strikingly similar to that of Little Hans, reported that his young phobic patient, who also had experienced the birth of a sister when he was three and a half years old, had begun to express an interest in the difference between the sexes at two years of age (by which time he had had ample opportunity to view his parents' unclad bodies).

The information available to us about Hans's early development, except for the occasional references to his protest against toilet training and the constipation with which it was associated, does not begin until just before the beginning of Hans's fourth year. At that time, Hans was showing an increasing masturbatory interest in his genital sensations and in the difference between the sexes and, either then or soon thereafter, showed signs of an increasing capacity for intense erotic attachment to his love objects, male as well as female, and a spirited determination to obtain possession of them which was to grow and flourish during the next two years. His mother was in the first trimester of a pregnancy which was to culminate both in the loss of his privileged status as her only child and in a vivid demonstration to Hans of his inability to compete either with his active, child-bearing, pre-oedipal mother or with his phallically powerful, child-giving father, a doubly shattering narcissistic blow.

Hans, who was such an observant child, carefully studied the changes in his mother's gravid body and figured out what they meant, as he was to inform his father later on. It is likely that he also was alert to his pregnant mother's narcissistic withdrawal of libidinal cathexis from Hans and her other objects onto herself, a natural reaction to her pregnancy. During the summer in Gmunden, when Hans was between three and a quarter and three and a half years old, he had his mother to himself much of the time, but this ended with the return of the family to the city. Shortly thereafter his sister was born. He reacted with jealousy, anger, an immediate wish for children of his own, and then distress over his sister's lack of a penis. He developed a sore throat and a fever, during which he cried out that he did not want a baby sister. At about the same time, his mother threatened to send him to the doctor to have his penis cut off if he continued to masturbate. We might wonder if the decision to send him to the doctor to have his tonsils cut out, which was performed nine months later, within a month after the outbreak of Hans's phobia, might not have originated during this earlier period. The tonsillectomy might in part have represented a retaliation against Little Hans for expressing anger at the arrival of his baby sister and, presumably, at his mother for having given birth to her after abandoning him for the confinement. I have come across such a sequence in the analysis of a man who learned that at the age of two years he angrily turned away from his mother when she returned from the hospital with a baby. Her response was to notice that he looked pale and to set plans in motion for him to undergo a tonsillectomy.

During the summer following the birth of his sister, the family returned to Gmunden, where again father was absent much of the time for business reasons. This time, however, Hans had to share his mother with his baby sister. He consoled himself by turning to two older girls, with whom he carried out the same kind of pleasurable, mutual observation of bathroom activities which he previously had enjoyed with his mother. He did not give up his interest in his mother, however. He invited her (at four and a half years of age) to touch his penis when she bathed, dried, and powdered him and seduced her periodically into taking him in to her bed by plaintively asking "Suppose I were to have no mummy?"—a comment which also seems to express the angry wish for her to go away, i.e., to die. Later on, just before the outbreak of the phobia and shortly following an anxiety dream in which he once again expressed the fear that his mother would go away, he seductively attempted to interest her in him by quoting an aunt who had praised his genitals. This time, he was unsuccessful. When the family returned from Gmunden, at which time Hans was four and a half (or according to another version given by father, when Hans was four years old and the family moved to a new flat), Hans was evicted from his parents' bedroom. It is likely, in other words, that during his fourth and fifth years, Hans felt seduced by his mother into an intense, sexual longing for her only to have her object to his excitement, threaten to have him castrated for it, and turn away from him to other, seemingly more favored love objects after he had expressed his love for her. How did he deal with the sexual excitement, rage, and narcissistic mortification which he must have felt?

When Hans was four and three-quarters years old, a month before he was to undergo his tonsillectomy (which, therefore, his parents were likely to be discussing at the time and the plans for which may have initiated the outbreak of the phobia), Hans burst into tears while out on a walk with a maid and insisted on going home to caress his mother. The next day, while outside with his mother, he terrified himself with the fear that a horse would bite him and that evening was inseparable from his mother. This marked the beginning of a phobic neurosis characterized by inability to leave the house lest he see a horse and undergo a repetition of this fright.

Freud, operating within the confines of his first anxiety theory and guided by what he had learned from his adult patients about the Oedipus complex, counseled Hans's father, who undertook to analyze the neurosis under Freud's supervision, to tell Hans that his anxiety stemmed from his masturbatory wish to be taken into bed by his mother, whom he loved. Postulating that Hans was driven in part by an attempt to relieve his castration anxiety by seeing a female phallus, he also advised that Hans be informed that his mother did not possess one. Hans's phobic manifestations abated somewhat, but increased again when he developed a prolonged febrile illness and became very much worse after the tonsillectomy.

Slap (1961), in a brief but convincing paper, has called attention to Freud's startling failure to take notice of multiple references to the tonsillectomy in Hans's fantasies. After the tonsillectomy, for instance, Hans shifted to specific fear of a *white* horse; Slap also related the surgical experience to Hans's phobic manifestations, including the fear of lying down in a bathtub, the plumber fantasies and the distress at seeing black leather straps around the mouths and eyes of some horses. Slap speculated that the last anxiety derived from the resemblance between the things Hans saw on the horses' faces and the black surgical masks in vogue at that time in Vienna hospitals.

We also can speculate that Hans's operating upon his rubber doll with a knife might have had the aim of abreacting and mastering the anxiety generated by the tonsillectomy via identification with the aggressor (A. Freud 1936). A child analyst today probably would address himself initially to the reality aspect of the tonsillectomy as a recent trauma which has imposed a demand upon the ego for repair and mastery. After that, he would turn to the unconscious impact of the experience as an apparent carrying out of mother's old threat to have him castrated for masturbating. We know now that tonsillectomy is regularly perceived by a child of Hans's age as a castrative attack (A. Freud 1952, Robertson 1956). It is surprising that Freud, who usually started at the surface in his case histories, discussing external events and the family situation before delving into the unconscious fantasies which they may have stimulated or organized, did not do so with respect to Hans's tonsillectomy.

The German word for tonsils is *Mandeln*, which also means almonds. Testicles are vulgarly referred to in many languages as "nuts." A boy once told me that the doctor had informed him that his enlarged tonsils were "as big as golf balls." When he went to the hospital for his tonsillectomy, he said, he was very worried that "the doctor might reach down too far and take out the wrong balls." Hans may also have noticed or heard that dray horses were generally gelded. His complaint about a girl tearing up his paper ball may also be a reference to testicular injury.

When Hans's father interpreted the fear of being bitten by a white horse as the fear of putting his hand to his penis, Hans readily admitted to masturbating nightly. He reported a dream in which he touched his penis and he and his mother showed their genitals to each other. He expressed the idea of acting this out with the "new" maid (we are not told why the previous maid left). When he followed with a fantasy of taking a crumpled giraffe away from a larger one and with fantasies of smashing through a train window and illegally gaining entry into a forbidden enclosure, Freud concluded that masturbatory, phallic-intrusive, positive oedipal wishes were involved. He told Hans, who was brought to see him, that his ''nonsense'' came from being afraid of his father because he was so fond of his mother. This seemed to relieve the anxiety somewhat, but Hans quarreled with one aspect of the interpretation that had been given him. He stated that he was fond not only of his mommy but of his daddy as well. He said that when his father was away, he feared that he would not come back, and added the information that when he was naughty his mother threatened to leave him and not return. In other words, Hans was ambivalent towards both his parents at that time.

From this point on (the beginning of the month of the anniversary of Hans's own birthday), the analysis took a very different turn. Hans now revealed that it was horses (who pulled heavily loaded carts) who he was afraid would fall down and that he had observed just such an event shortly before his phobia had broken out. He connected the motions the horse had made with his feet with his own habit in prior years of stamping crossly with his feet when his mother interrupted him in his play to have him go to the bathroom and make *lumf*, i.e., to cooperate in her attempts to regulate the evacuation of his bowels. He began to express disgust at anything which reminded him of excretory products. He also described a fantasy in which he climbed onto one of the loaded carts, which he liked to watch as they drove in and out of the yard of the tax office across from his family's apartment house, and was carried off. He recalled seeing a boy strike his foot against a stone and fall down injured while playing at being a horse at Gmunden.

He expressed interest in and fear of the toilet flushing, which reminded him of urination and defecation, and was terrified of sitting or lying down in the bathtub. A fantasy appeared of a plumber removing the bath and sticking a large borer into Hans's abdomen. It soon became clear that Hans was afraid that his mother would drown him in the bath, behind which was the wish that she drown his baby sister. By now it was clear that the preoccupation with *lumf*, which had been so puzzling to his father and to Freud, had been an introductory preamble to the expression of intense, primarily hostile feelings about his mother's pregnancy two years earlier. Freud seems to have missed noticing that the pregnancy theme appeared at the beginning of the month of Hans's own birth, a commonplace observation nowadays. The other factor in the transition to this theme, of course, is the link between rivalry with his father for his mother's attention and similar rivalry with his sister.

Hans expressed disgust with anything that reminded him of feces, i.e., of his sister, fantasized her dropping off the balcony and disappearing, and finally admitted that he wished his mother would drown her in the bath (a contribution to his own fear of being bathed). He became preoccupied with thoughts about life, death, and his sister's birth and expressed fear lest his parents bring more babies "out of the big box" (1909, p. 68). His fear of horses greatly diminished at this point. He told his father that his baby sister had travelled to Gmunden the first time (i.e., before her birth) in a baby box full of babies sitting in a bath. He repaid his father for not telling him the truth about pregnancy and childbirth by telling him tall tales of his own manufacture about these processes.

We can now speculate that Hans's earlier fear of the toilet flushing and his first plumber fantasy in part expressed hostile feelings towards his mother's babies, with wishes to flush them out of her and flush them down the toilet. His fantasy of having his father put him and his sister into the big box, whereupon he would urinate into it suggests the fantasy of urinating into his mother to wash out the babies in her "stork-box," much as she had administered enemas to him in the past to flush out the contents of his bowel. This fantasy probably also formed a transitional link between his anal-sadistic resentment and jealousy of his mother's babies and baby-making capacity and his phallic wish to urinate into his mother to impregnate her. His submission over the years to frequent enemas also contributed to the development of a passive-feminine identification with his mother, and the wish to be impregnated and delivered of babies (see the first plumber fantasy).

At this point, Hans added the last piece to the puzzle of his horse phobia. He complained about his sister's loud screams "when Mummy whacks her on her bottom" and said that "she makes such a row with her screaming" (p. 72). He confessed not only that he had fantasies of beating horses (which, via reaction-formation, had been transformed sometime earlier into distress whenever he saw draymen beating their horses) but also that he wanted to beat his mother with the carpet beater with which she often threatened to punish him. He now revealed that the buses, furniture-vans, and coal-carts whose horses he had feared would fall down and make a row with their feet all were "stork-box carts" (p. 81). This final confession of the wish to beat and destroy the baby sister who had come between him and his mother and to beat his mother to punish her for her perfidy and hurt her as she had hurt him (as well as to take over his father's role as the one who attacked and impregnated her, a role for which his mother had rejected him) seems to have ushered in a phase of integration and working-through, via the elaboration of fantasy, of the pre-genital and genital conflicts contained in Hans's phobia. Hans added that another component of the fear of the horses falling down was the wish for his father to hurt his foot and fall down like his friend Fritzl, presumably so that Hans might take his place in bed with his mother. He described a fantasy of paying the watchman at the tax office to let him ride (naked) on top of a cart, which seemed to express the idea of his possessing the wealth to buy out his father and take his place with his mother. He pushed a pen-knife out between his rubber doll Grete's legs, saying "Look, there's its wiwimaker" (p. 84). This seems to have been an attempt at mastery of his castration anxiety and of his passive submission to the tonsillectomy as well as an attempt to solve the mysteries of impregnation and of childbirth. His father finally gave Hans some information about babies growing in their mothers and being pressed out of them in childbirth like feces (but he did not tell him about the male's part in the process of procreation). Hans proclaimed that ever since the birth of his sister he had wanted to give birth to babies like his mother and that he did not want his mother to have any more children. He expressed the fantasy that his sister belonged to him and to his mother, which can be taken as a reflection both of the pre-genital wish to share control of the baby-making process with his mother and the genital (i.e., oedipal) wish to make babies with his mother in his father's place.

The phobia dissipated and Hans gained the courage to butt his father in the abdomen. This was interpreted to him as a reflection of the wish for his father to die so that he could displace him in bed with his mother. Together, Hans and his father clarified that Hans would like to give his mother a baby. Hans now altered his ongoing fantasy of being a mother with many children to that of becoming their father. In fantasy, he made up to father for taking his mother away from him by marrying him off to his own mother. He expressed the joyous fantasy of taking all his children into the W.C., where he had them watch him urinate and defecate, after which he wiped their behinds and did with them "everything one does with children" (p. 97), a reparative fantasy in which he restored to himself, with reversal of roles, the pleasures he formerly had experienced with his mother. There was even more improvement in his condition after this.

A final fantasy appeared, in which the plumber came and took away his behind and his wiwimaker and gave him new (and presumable bigger and better) ones in their place. With this, the phobia apparently cleared up, except for a residual trace in the form of persistent questions about "what things are made of (trams, machines, etc.), who makes things, etc." (p. 99), an apparent reference to the wish for additional clarification of male and female anatomy and of the role of the male in procreation. As far as we are told Hans's father did not provide this information, nor did he openly analyze Hans's negative oedipal wish to be impregnated by him.

Further Comments About Freud's
Formulation of Little Hans's Neurosis

We have learned a great deal since 1909 about the aggressive drives, pre-oedipal development, and the functioning of the ego. Rangell (1972) is one of many who have written about the role of aggression in the Oedipus complex. Freud himself, in fact, described Hans's aggressive inclinations at length, only to reject the idea that aggressive drives exist separate from libidinal ones.

We have already said a good deal about preoedipal factors, in their own right and as predisposing influences in Hans's Oedipus complex. We can point to oral and anal aspects of his jealousy of his sister and of his envy of his mother's capacity to bear children. Until his sister's arrival, he was a favored, pampered only child who was very much fussed over by his mother (with little opportunity to play with other children to dilute his attachment to her); he shared his parents' bedroom and, not infrequently, their bed. Other adults also found him endearing. Freud was himself very taken with him and trudged up four flights of stairs to present him with a large rocking-horse for his third birthday (Graf 1942). Hans cherished his status as the only child and reacted to his sister's birth with the intense sibling rivalry which is so typical of the only child (see Arlow 1972). His fantastic depiction of his as-yet-unborn sister riding about within the "stork-box" gobbling down meals with great relish and gusto betrays his oral envy of her. His fear that a horse would bite him probably derived in part from the fear of retaliation against him for wanting to orally attack and destroy those who would displace him at the breast (see Arlow 1972, Romm 1955).

Freud was quick to recognize that there were anal-erotic (and anal-sadistic) components within Hans's neurotic organization (e.g., Hans's conflicted preoc-cupation with *lumf* and "wiwi" and his wish to beat his mother), but he did not expressly explore the events within the anal-sadistic period which might have contributed to them. We know, for example, that a struggle took place between Hans and his mother over who was to control the evacuation of his bowels. Hans developed constipation, to which his parents responded by administering lax-atives and enemas. Hans's joking reference to raspberry syrup (used as a laxative) and a gun for shooting people dead (Hans, as his father pointed out in an afterthought, used to confuse the words "shooting" and "shitting" or "*schies-sen*" and "*scheissen*" in the original German) exemplifies his active recollection of those struggles. The battle for control over Hans's excretory functions did not take place *in vacuo*. It occurred at a time when he was going through the practicing and rapprochement subphases of the separation-individuation process and was struggling to achieve independent mastery over his body and its functions (locomotor and intellectual as well as excretory). His neurosis at age four and three-quarters years contains elements which suggest that he was less than optimally successful in achieving a sufficient degree of independent mastery during the anal-sadistic phase. His phobia broke out while he was travelling about the city away from his mother. It interfered from then on with his ability to leave her or even leave the house in which he lived. Hans's restricted freedom of movement and his anxiety about fast-moving horses and the danger of horses falling down suggests the possibility that in addition to fear of loss of sphincter control and anal-sadistic impulses there was specific anxiety about independent locomotion. His recollection of his friend Fritzl falling and hurting himself while playing at prancing about like a horse may have signified more than the oedipal wish to be rid of his father so that he might have his mother to himself. It is possible that Hans also was referring back to his mother's failure to reliably protect, comfort and applaud him as he tried out his newly-discovered locomotor (and intellectual) ability to independently explore his environmental surround during the practicing and rapprochement periods (see Mahler and La Perriere 1965, Mahler 1968). This is consistent with his mother's continuing infantilization of Hans into his fifth and sixth years by performing functions for him which he should have been doing for himself. If we are correct in hypothesizing that Hans's early attempts at achieving individuation, independence, object constancy and internalized self-control were not sufficiently successful, it would help explain the intense separation anxiety and the restricted freedom of activity during the height of his neurosis. We know that Hans's mother assigned him to guard his sister against the danger of falling from the porch, hardly adequate protection for a little girl under two years of age. It is likely that such failure to provide proper protection for the children was expressed in other ways as well and contributed to an inadequate sense of security on Hans's part.

This brings us to a consideration of the ego factors in Hans's phobic disorder. This is a dimension which Freud was unable to explore in depth in 1909. We now know that in a phobia there is failure of the signal function of anxiety with resulting panic, because the ego considers itself unable to effectively control drive tensions which are associated with latent conflicts stirred up by current stimuli (Greenson 1959). The ego does not respond to the demand for work imposed by the drive pressures by mobilizing effective means of discharging them in reality or by successfully suppressing and repressing the urges involved. Instead, it projects and externalizes the inner source of danger, displaces the location of the external stimulus to a symbolic neutral agent, and imposes restrictions upon its own freedom of action in the hope of avoiding impulses which it does not trust itself to be able to control. As Wangh (1959) has pointed out, a phobic defensive system evolves out of a combination of intrinsic and early experiential factors which result in impaired ego control over the drives in the presence of easy object displaceability, a capacity to readily shift cathexis from inside to outside, imaginative creativity in the service of defense, and a predilection for avoidance and regression to dependence upon outside agents to provide external controls.

In Hans's case, the ego's ability to control drive tensions was impaired preoedipally by interference with the development of stable independent mastery over locomotor and excretory functions, instinctualization of sphincter control, and inability to fully resolve the ambivalence conflicts of the anal-sadistic phase. It was impaired further by his parents' seductive hyperstimulation of libidinal and aggressive impulses within him, both pregenitally and genitally. In the phallic phase he was unable to tolerate the narcissistic injury of being displaced by his father as his mother's principal love object or to trust himself to effectively control and regulate the masturbatory sexual excitement and destructive rivalrous impulses mobilized by his oedipal longings. Regression to preoedipal, oral and anal-sadistic longings only reawakened his earlier ambivalence conflicts, the pain of displacement by his younger sister and the incompletely successful struggle to free himself from his dependence upon and identification with his preoedipal, active mother, i.e., to separate and individuate himself from her.

The panic which was generated by his perception of his helplessness led to the imposition of drastic emergency measures. To bolster his attempts at repression of his dangerous longings, he took flight from them by externalizing them, displacing his cathexis from his parents and sister to horses, restricting his freedom of movement so that he could avoid direct contact with them and withdraw to a safe distance from which he could gaze at them from afar, and regressing to dependence upon his parents to watch over and protect him. The shift from motor activity to perceptual and intellectual activity was facilitated both by an already existing inclination in that direction and by a phase-specific intellectual reorganization which led to an increased capacity for abstract fantasy in the place of sensorimotor exploration as a tool of ego mastery (Silverman 1971).

Some Reflections Upon the Treatment of Little Hans

Little Hans was treated by his father, with advice and guidance from Freud. There are inevitable drawbacks to such an arrangement. It is difficult enough to remain neutral and objective when one is not the parent of the child being analyzed. The failure of Hans's father to analyze Hans's negative oedipal, homosexual longings and his failure to provide Hans with information about the male's role in copulation and procreation probably derive in part from the difficulties imposed by Hans's being his son.

There also seems to have been some contribution to these omissions from Freud. Freud did not seem very strongly to urge Hans's father to provide information about the male's procreative role, for example, even though Hans expressly requested it. Freud was in favor of providing Hans with information about "the existence of the vagina and of copulation" (1909, p. 145), but he does not seem to have been inclined to have Hans informed as to the role of his testicles in the baby-making process. While there is no way of knowing all the reasons why he failed to press these points, there is at least one indication that he may have had some inner resistance, which Bell (1961) and Bell, Stroebel and Prior (1971) ascribe to male analysts in general, to exploring the partially passive-feminine feelings and fantasies which are associated with the testicles and their functions. In a much later paper, "The Infantile Genital Organization" (1923), Freud stated the following in a footnote which, according to the editors of the *Standard Edition*, associated his comments directly with the Little Hans case: "It is, incidentally, remarkable what a small degree of attention the other part of the male genital, the little sac with its contents, attracts in children. From all one hears in analyses, one would not guess that the male genitals consisted of anything more than the penis" (p. 142*n*). It is possible that when Hans spoke of his "wiwimaker," his father and Freud understood him to be referring to his penis alone, while Hans actually was referring to penis and testicles, considering them both to be parts of his "wiwimaker." I recall a six-year-old boy who asked during a session for me for me to draw a penis. He was increasingly dissatisfied with my designs and finally burst out "No! No! Draw the *whole* penis! Put on that thing at the bottom with the two balls in it." Another boy, between four and five at the time, showed intense interest in the workings of tools and mechanical devices with moving parts. When I suggested that he was interested in the workings of his penis, he readily assented and launched into a stream of questions about erection, detumescence, etc. Having learned from the other youngster, I asked if he didn't have questions about the rest of his genital apparatus. He was puzzled until I explained that I was referring to the sac at the base of his penis with the "ballies" in it. "Oh," he exclaimed, "you mean that fat thing where the weewee is holded." My experience has indicated to me that young children, after they have figured out that the man introduces something into the woman to impregnate her, egocentrically and as a result of insufficient information at their disposal, often conclude that he urinates into her (see also Freud 1908, pp. 222–224). Since the assumption that the scrotal sac functions as a container for or site of elaboration of urine is a natural one, given its location at the basis of the penis (Glenn 1969), it is not illogical to conclude that it is urine that impregnates the woman. Only education as to the function of the testes can set things straight.

Hans's treatment suffered from lack of analysis of his passive-feminine identification with his child-bearing mother. It would have been very helpful for him to have had an opportunity to learn the details of the male's *active* use of his penis and testicles in the process of procreation.

The feelings and attitudes which Hans's father bore towards Freud must also have influenced him in his handling of Hans's treatment. We know now that his feelings towards Freud varied from worshipful adulation to resentment and skepticism profound enough to prevent him from continuing to associate himself actively with the psychoanalytic movement (Graf 1942), an indication of intensely ambivalent personal feelings which quite probably were partly transferential in nature. At any rate, child psychoanalytic techniques have developed so greatly since 1905 that there no longer exists any justification for analyzing children through their parents, a procedure which is fraught with considerable danger. Glenn and Van Dam, in a panel on the analysis of preoedipal and preschool children (Olch 1971), have listed a number of possible dangers, including interference with the child's efforts to remove himself from dependence upon his primary objects, the risk of sexualizing and aggressivizing the parent-child relationship, and the risk of contributing to the development of a skewed relationship in which the parent offers continual interpretations to the child. The latter, Glenn pointed out, interferes with the child's correction of his view of the parent as omnipotent, hampers defense and encourages the expression of id derivatives. It is both puzzling and unfortunate that the case of Little Hans continues to be used to rationalize such undertakings (see Kessler 1972, Rangell 1950, Furman 1957).

In this connection, I should like to raise a question as to the degree to which Little Hans was treated on the one hand with psychoanalysis and on the other with a kind of family therapy. To what extent can the outcome of the case be attributed to a re-equilibration of the energic, dynamic, topographic and structural organization of the psyche as a result of analysis of internalized conflict and unconscious fantasy and to what extent can it be explained in terms of the effects of Freud's intervention upon the pattern of family interaction? A new relationship was established between Hans and his father as a result of their therapeutic work together. His father became his friend and helper, facilitating ego and superego development, but also entering into a quasi-homosexual relationship which helped to offset and dilute Hans's intensely eroticized, preoedipal and oedipal tie to his mother and which led them into the kind of normal, increasingly sublimated homosexual interaction that we have come to recognize as an essential part of a boy's relationship with his father during the oedipal stage. Looked at from this point of view, it would have been counter-therapeutic for Hans's father to analyze Hans's homosexual longings for him *at that time*, even though his failure to do so was not analytic. Were the analyst someone other than Hans's father, this dilemma would have been circumvented.

I do not wish to imply that Freud made a conscious attempt to induce a reorganization of the family pattern of interaction, as is done in modern family therapy. I also am aware that a certain amount of family reorganization is inevitable in the course of any child analytic treatment. Parents spend time with the child transporting him to his sessions, become more observant of their child and of themselves and try to make salutary changes, etc. Child analysts differ in the extent to which they give advice to parents (or send them elsewhere for guidance), but, as Maenchen has pointed out (Olch 1971), it is difficult and perhaps impossible to avoid advice entirely. What took place in the treatment of Little Hans, however, went far beyond this. Transforming Hans's father into his therapist, under supervision from someone of whom he was in awe (Graf 1942) and who had been Hans's mother's therapist in the past as well, had to affect the family organization to a far greater degree than takes place during the ordinary child analysis of today. When Freud agreed to supervise and oversee Hans's treatment by his father, he provided Hans with a chance to have his father as an ally and an object for masculine identification. Hans was enabled to lean upon his father for auxiliary ego strength, safely work out with him some of the rivalrous tensions that existed between them, and learn from him how to temporarily control his desires and (within the limitations imposed by his father's inability to provide him with all the information which Hans needed) acquire the phallic, masculine secrets which he ultimately would need to win a woman of his own. The talks between them also helped Hans to make use of increasingly abstract intellectual fantasy (from which he had been blocked by the erotization of his visual and imaginative activities), which we know is necessary in the struggle to contain oedipal urges and enter latency (Sarnoff 1971). Freud, as the supervisor and overseer, also served as an auxiliary superego to Hans's parents, helping them to restrain the hyperstimulating, seductive activities which had been fanning the flames of Hans's oedipal strivings. This function is probably present in all child analyses.[1]

1. In a discussion of a somewhat abridged version of this paper presented before the New Jersey Psychoanalytic Society on September 12, 1975, Raymond Gehl correctly called attention to a third source of the rapidly obtained, good result of Little Hans's treatment. Hans possessed impressive ego strengths of the kind that we all hope for in our analytic patients. He was an unusually flexible, adaptable youngster with good frustration tolerance and relation to reality,

The treatment of Little Hans, in short, was not entirely psychoanalytic in nature. The result, nevertheless, was a very good one. There is cause to be concerned about the resolution of Hans's passive-feminine desire to have a baby in identification with his mother but the treatment did succeed in helping Hans accept feminine identifications without panic. Especially if we consider the time at which it was carried out, however, we can only be very impressed with the skill with which the treatment was conducted and the results which were obtained. Hans not only overcame his fear of horses and regained the ability to travel in the street, but he underwent significant ego growth and superego development and moved toward the good relations with both parents and his sister which were so evident when he revisited Freud as a "happy, healthy nineteen-year-old" (Freud 1922, Rizzo 1972).

References

Aarons, A. Z. (1953). Effect of the birth of a sister on a boy in his fourth year. *Psychoanalytic Quarterly* 22: 372–380.

Alpert, A., Neubauer, P., and Weil, A. (1956). Unusual variations in drive endowment. *Psychoanalytic Study of the Child* 11: 125–163.

Arlow, J. (1971). The only child. *Psychoanalytic Quarterly* 41: 507–536.

———— (1974). Panel discussion in "Panel C: The ego and the mechanisms of defense: a review," The Twentieth Annual Freud Memorial Lecture Program, Philadelphia, April 28, 1973. Reported by J. W. Slap. *Journal of the Philadelphia Association for Psychoanalysis* 1: 35–42.

Bell, A. (1961). Some observations on the role of the scrotal sac and testicles. *Journal of the American Psychoanalytic Association* 9: 261–286.

Bell, A., Stroebel, C., and Prior, D. (1971). Interdisciplinary study: scrotal sac and testes: psychophysiological and psychological observations. *Psychoanalytic Quarterly* 40: 415–434.

Brunswick, R. M. (1940). The preoedipal phase of the libido development. In *The Psychoanalytic Reader*, ed. R. Fliess, 231–253. London: Hogarth Press, 1950. Reprinted from *Psychoanalytic Quarterly* 40: 293–317.

Escalona, S. (1963). Patterns of infantile experience and the developmental process. *Psychoanalytic Study of the Child* 18: 197–244.

Freud, A. (1936). *The Ego and the Mechanisms of Defense*. New York: International Universities Press.

---

very fine cognitive and intellectual abilities, an excellent sublimative potential, and a tendency to a very full and stable libidinal cathexis of his object representations. Hans himself contributed greatly to the excellent outcome of the case.

———— (1952). The role of bodily illness in the mental life of children. *Psychoanalytic Study of the Child* 7: 69–81.

———— (1965). *Normality and Pathology in Childhood*. New York: International Universities Press.

———— (1971). The infantile neurosis: genetic and dynamic considerations. *Psychoanalytic Study of the Child* 26: 79–90.

Freud, S. (1900). The interpretation of dreams. *Standard Edition* 4/5.

———— (1905a). A fragment of an analysis of a case of hysteria. *Standard Edition* 7: 1–122.

———— (1905b). Three essays on the theory of sexuality. *Stantard Edition* 7: 125–245.

———— (1907). The sexual enlightenment of children. *Standard Edition* 9: 129–139.

———— (1908). On the sexual theories of children. *Standard Edition* 9: 205–226.

———— (1909). Analysis of a phobia in a five-year old boy. *Standard Edition* 10: 3–147.

———— (1922). Postscript to analysis of a phobia in a five-year-old boy. *Standard Edition* 10: 148*49.

———— (1923). The infantile genital organization: an interpolation into the theory of sexuality. *Standard Edition* 19: 139–145.

———— (1925). Some psychical consequences of the anatomical distinction between the sexes. *Standard Edition* 19: 241–258.

———— (1926). Inhibitions, symptoms and anxiety. *Standard Edition* 20: 75–175.

———— (1937). Analysis terminable and interminable. *Standard Edition* 23: 209–253.

Fries, M., and Woolf, P. (1953). Some hypotheses on the role of the congenital activity type in personality development. *Psychoanalytic Study of the Child* 8: 48–62.

Furman, E. (1957). Treatment of under-fives by way of parents. *Psychoanalytic Study of the Child* 12: 250–262.

Geleerd, E., ed. (1967). *The Child Analyst at Work*. New York: International Universities Press.

Glenn, J. (1969). Testicular and scrotal masturbation. *International Journal of Psycho-analysis* 50: 353–362.

Graf, M. (1942). Reminiscence of Professor Sigmund Freud. *Psychoanalytic Quarterly* 11: 465–476.

Greenson, R. (1959). Phobia, anxiety, and repression. *Journal of the American Psychoanalytic Association* 7: 663–674.

Hartmann, H. (1939). *Ego Psychology and the Problem of Adaptation*. New

York: International Universities Press.

———— (1950). Comments on the psychoanalytic theory of the ego. *Psychoanalytic Study of the Child* 5: 74–96.

Jones, E. (1955). *The Life and Work of Sigmund Freud, Volume 2: The Years of Maturity.* New York: Basic Books.

Kessler, M. (1972). A mother in psychoanalysis treats her son. *Bulletin of the Philadelphia Association for Psychoanalysis* 22: 165–184.

Mahler, M. (1968). *On Human Symbiosis and the Vicissitudes of Individuation, Volume I: Infantile Psychosis.* New York: International Universities Press.

Mahler, M., and La Perriere, K. (1965). Mother-child interaction during separation-individuation. *Psychoanalytic Quarterly* 34: 483–498.

Nunberg, H., and Federn, E. (1967). *Minutes of the Vienna Psychoanalytic Society, Volume II: 1908–1910.* New York: International Universities Press.

Olch, G. (1971). Panel report on "Technical problems in the analysis of the preoedipal and preschool child." *Journal of the American Psychoanalytic Association* 19: 543–551.

Peller, L. (1965). Comments on libidinal organizations and child development. *Journal of the American Psychoanalytic Association* 13: 732–747.

Rangell, L. (1950). A treatment of nightmares in a seven-year-old boy. *Psychoanalytic Study of the Child* 5: 358–390.

———— (1972). Aggression, Oedipus, and historical perspective. *International Journal of Psycho-Analysis* 53: 3–12.

Rizzo, F. (1972). Memoirs of an invisible man—I. *Opera News* 36: 25–28.

Robertson, J. (1956). A mother's observations on the tonsillectomy of her four-year-old daughter (With Comments by Anna Freud). *Psychoanalytic Study of the Child* 11: 410–433.

Roiphe, H. (1968). On an early genital phase: with an addendum on genesis. *Psychoanalytic Study of the Child* 23: 348–365.

Roiphe, H. and Galenson, E. (1972). Early genital activity and the castration complex. *Psychoanalytic Quarterly* 41: 334–347.

Romm, M. (1955). The unconscious need to be an only child. *Psychoanalytic Quarterly* 25: 331–341.

Schur, M. (1972). *Freud: Living and Dying.* New York: International Universities Press.

Sarnoff, C. (1971). Ego structure in latency. *Psychoanalytic Quarterly* 40: 387–414.

Silverman, M. (1971). The growth of logical thinking: Piaget's contribution to ego psychology. *Psychoanalytic Quarterly* 40: 317–341.

Silverman, M., Rees, K., and Neubauer, P. (1975). On a central psychic constellation. *Psychoanalytic Study of the Child* 30: 127–157.

Slap, J. (1961). Little Hans' tonsillectomy. *Psychoanalytic Quarterly* 30: 259–261.

Strachey, J. (1953). Editor's note to "Three essays on sexuality." *Standard Edition* 7: 125.

Tartakoff, H. (1966). The normal personality in our culture and the Nobel Prize Complex. In *Psychoanalysis—A General Psychology. Essays in Honor of Heinz Hartmann*, ed. R. Lowenstein, L. Newman, M. Schur, and A. Solnit, pp. 222–252. New York: International Universities Press.

Wangh, M. (1959). Structural determinants of phobia. *Journal of the American Psychoanalytic Association* 7: 675–695.

Weil, A. (1970). The basic core. *Psychoanalytic Study of the Child* 25: 442–460.

Chapter 2

FREUD'S ADVICE TO HANS'S FATHER:
THE FIRST SUPERVISORY SESSIONS

JULES GLENN, M.D.

Martin A. Silverman's discussion of the *Analysis of a Phobia in a Five-Year-Old Boy* (Freud 1909) is extensive and disciplined. He proceeds from one important point to another, broadening the base that Freud established. I will supplement his paper by concentrating on Hans's diagnosis and Freud's choice of treatment, including his recommendations to the boy's father.

Transient neurotic symptomatology during childhood, which is common, does not always warrant analysis. Analysis is indicated when incapacitating symptoms persist and/or a developmental arrest exists. The analyst must evaluate the environmental situation to determine whether it is likely that the infantile neurosis will clear spontaneously, whether alterations in childrearing practices alone would suffice to stem the disturbance or whether the family pathology would render analysis fruitless. He must also decide whether the child's pathology makes analysis unwise. The innate psychic apparatus must be evaluated; patients with extremely impaired ego functions, childhood schizophrenics for instance,

This paper was prepared for the January, 1977 meeting of the Psychoanalytic Association of New York as a discussion of Martin A. Silverman's "A Fresh Look at the Case of Little Hans" (Part III, Chapter 1 of this volume). I wish to thank Dr. Isidor Bernstein who has provided me with helpful criticism and suggestions for this discussion.

may not benefit from analysis: Indeed the alteration of defenses that occurs in analysis may have a harmful effect. This is not always so, however, since skillful interpretation has strengthened the defensive structure and adaptive mechanisms.

Freud correctly diagnosed Hans as a neurotic child with anxiety hysteria. Except for his circumscribed neurosis, he had a well-functioning adaptive personality structure. There was no question of psychosis or organicity. Although there were areas of developmental arrest—Silverman notes the anal stamp that was retained—these did not appear to be extreme. The treatment was undertaken because of the severity of the phobic symptoms, not their long duration. The decision was, in my opinion, a wise one from the point of view of Hans's development as well as scientific considerations.

Most analytic consultants of the present time would defer deciding the treatment of choice until they had taken a more detailed history of the patient (as Dr. Silverman has indicated) and seen the patient in a diagnostic interview. A consultant would then have several alternative courses: he might decide to wait and see if the infantile neurosis disappeared spontaneously; he might offer the parents advice in regard to childrearing in an attempt to aid the neurosis's resolution and deter future difficulties; or he might suggest psychoanalysis or some other form of therapy.

Freud first offered advice to Hans's father, but limitations of knowledge restricted the extent of his suggestions. He advised Professor Graf to provide Hans with certain information but did not otherwise recommend changes in childrearing. Soon thereafter, when the symptoms persisted, he recommended psychoanalysis of the child. The treatment that Freud supervised was not analysis by today's criteria; it was, rather, a form of psychoanalytic psychotherapy.

Discussion of Freud's advice to Hans's father prior to the institution of analysis is in order. He suggested that Professor Graf tell the child that "all this business about horses was a piece of nonsense and nothing more. The truth was . . . that he was very fond of his mother and wanted to be taken into her bed. The reason he was afraid of horses now was that he had taken so much interest in their widdlers. He himself had noticed that it was not right to be so very much preoccupied with widdlers, even with his own, and he was quite right in thinking this. [Freud] further suggested to his father that he should begin giving Hans some enlightenment in the matter of sex knowledge . . . [He should inform] him that his mother and all other female beings . . . had no widdler at all" (1909, p. 28). In my opinion, these suggestions were inappropriate for the most part.

The first suggestion, that Hans be told of his incestuous wishes, seems unwise to me in that parental interpretations create the difficulties that Dr. Silverman has so ably described. Children often experience interpretations by their parents as license to express their drives openly even when it is maladaptive to do so. Hence reality testing is interfered with and restraint, so necessary to the formation of secondary processes, is impeded. It is difficult for a child to establish an adequate hierarchy of defensive and adaptive mechanisms when he feels urged to discharge drives. Often children read their parents' unconscious intentions correctly when they feel pressed to express themselves, but this may not be the case; the parents may unwittingly carry out detrimental child rearing practices as a result of the misguided belief that interpretation is the best policy.

Some parents frighten their children with remarkably accurate interpretations of id content. A mother, for instance, explained to her son that his fear that his father could die in a plane accident resulted from his desire to destroy his father. This terrified the child. Were such an interpretation suddenly made in the course of an analysis without a great deal of preparatory work, we would judge the technique as faulty. Ego aspects and conflicts were not analyzed. But even if the interpretation were more complete, when a parent acts as analyst trouble may develop.

Accurate interpretations create the impression that the omniscient parents can read the child's mind, thus interfering with his sense of privacy, his sense of reality and, eventually, his sense of autonomy. Difficulty in separating self- and object-representations can occur.

Of course the intellectual atmosphere in analytic circles at the time that Hans was treated required not only private self-analysis, but public statements of one's own dynamics and interpretations of colleague's behavior. The analysts frequently offered each other interpretation of their motives, a disruptive practice which still prevails to a lesser extent. I would suggest that *one* of the reasons for the opposition to Freud was his insistence on interpretation, tactful though it often was. Kanzer (1979) has referred to Freud as the "first psychoanalytic group leader." Of course group and individual therapy breed negative as well as positive transferences which are ill-contained in a scientific organization or among friends.

Interpretations at that time were considered not only enlightening but therapeutic as well. It followed that explanations of one's child's unconscious would be helpful, but how extensively this occurred is uncertain. Even today, however, one hears of parents who consciously or unconsciously include interpretations in their repertory of childrearing practices.

The child subjected to interpretation by his parents may, like patients, become quite resentful. The emergence of patients' hostility often results from a defensive struggle against fantasied sadistic or genital attacks by the analyst; children may react similarly to parents who "analyze" them. Hartmann (1964) has suggested that, in addition, interpretations may lead to a release of aggressive energy for economic reasons; the counter-cathectic energy, which consists of neutralized aggressive energy, will be converted to un-neutralized aggression when a defense is weakened or surrendered.

In any case, interpretations by parents can result in an increase of the child's antagonism which will be difficult to manage outside the analytic situation. Of course, once analysis or supervised treatment through parents is decided upon, interpretations are in order. But Freud's initial suggestion that the interpretation be made was not conceived of as part of a formal therapy. Parenthetically I may add that a possible complication of therapy through parents is that the father or mother will continue to make interpretations to their children after the treatment has terminated.

Freud's second suggestion, that Hans be told that he was right in thinking he should not be so interested in widdlers, including his own, is puzzling in that it is contrary to the liberal attitude that Freud advocated. Far from enabling the unconscious to become conscious, repression was championed. Such a statement would increase the child's guilt and even discourage *interest* in his penis. Hans countered this type of repressive rearing when he later told his father: "But wanting's not doing and doing's not wanting" (1909, p. 31).

Possibly Freud's suggestion that Professor Graf tell Hans that he was too interested in his penis was intended to discourage masturbation. Freud's apparent confusion about prohibiting masturbation stems from uncertainty at that time about the functions and influences of autoerotic activities. The relationship between masturbation and castration anxiety was not fully appreciated at the time. According to Freud, masturbation provided incomplete discharge and therefore led to actual neuroses. But in addition, complete suppression of masturbation led to the transformation of libido into anxiety (Freud 1895). Even in 1912, three years after the publication of Hans's case history, psychoanalysts were still preoccupied with the damage masturbation could cause. Annie Reich (1951) states in her paper on the discussion of masturbation published as *Wiener Psychoanalytischen Vereinigung* (1912): "Most striking is the stress laid by many of the discussants—with Freud as their leader—upon the harmfulness of masturbation" (Reich 1951, p. 81). On the other hand they believed that masturbation was a "satisfactory method in infancy and childhood" (p. 84).

Today we would agree that masturbation in a five-year-old is normal and that its suppression might have ill effects (see A. Freud 1949). Nevertheless it is appropriate for parents to help their children control their autoerotic behavior, to suggest that they not masturbate in public for instance.

Freud, when he supervised Hans's treatment, did not have a clear idea about the difference between parents' educative role and the analytic physician's interpretive function. Even today this confusion persists to a degree. Child analysts debate whether education is appropriate in child analysis. At one time it was generally accepted that education was an essential ingredient of analysis. The preponderance of opinion today is that child analysis optimally should be carried out without educative methods but that this is not always possible. At times a child's serious ego defects make a preparatory educative period necessary before analysis proper can proceed.

As I have indicated, contemporary parents at times do try to "treat" their children by interpreting, usually in an unsystematic way. Sometimes this occurs when the parent is or was an analysand; the parent does to the child what the therapist had done to him. Other motives for parental interpretations include aggression against the child, wishes for an intimate closeness, and an intellectual conviction that this is a sound childrearing procedure. Professionals whose work consists of understanding and interpreting people's behavior and thought may continue their analytic activity at home. Parents who are prone to ignore reality and concentrate on unconscious aspects of their thinking are also prone to interpret deeper aspects of their children's personality.

The final suggestion, that Dr. Graf tell Hans that females lack penises, was bound to frighten the child as it interfered with his use of denial. In fact Hans did become more upset and resorted to defensive reassurances that his mother did have a penis and, further, that penises are "fixed in" (1909, p. 34), a normal development for this age.

It should be noted that even the information that Freud offered to Hans was incomplete and distorted. Hans was to be told that a girl has no penis, thus indicating that she is deficient. The fact is that boys and girls have different organs. A boy has a penis and testicles and a girl has a vulva (including the clitoris), vagina and uterus. A full statement of the differences between the sexes would certainly have been beyond the child's understanding. Nevertheless, an incomplete statement that reinforces a castration fantasy can be confusing. In addition we know that attempts to educate a child about sexual matters frequently fail because the child retains the fantasies appropriate to his developmental stage despite parental enlightenment.

It is also difficult for parents to avoid introducing their own fantasies. Hans's father, when he informed his son about childbirth, told him that it was like having a bowel movement, revealing his own anal conception of the process.

Freud recognized that there were difficulties in parents' providing sex education. At the May 12, 1909, Wednesday evening scientific meeting devoted to sexual enlightenment he warned "that most parents are in general not equipped to be educators" (Nunberg and Federn 1967, p. 230). Then, after referring to the fact that he learned what a child thinks from Little Hans, he recommended that "enlightenment may content itself with contradicting (two) infantile theories'': that conception occurs orally and that sexual activity is sadistic in nature. ''Enlightenment should above all make it clear to them that this is a matter of acts of tenderness, that . . . their parents love each other very much; then the children will not make any demand at all for specific details.'' Small children ''do not ask questions out of a need for causality but for the gratification of certain interests.'' He added that ''as to the process of coitis the older children should find out about it in school, in their science lessons'' (pp. 230–231).

When a child is in analysis, supplying information in conjunction with interpretations may have a palpable therapeutic effect. However, Freud suggested telling Hans about the female's penis-less state prior to the institution of interpretive treatment.

Today the psychoanalytic consultant might well make suggestions about parental practices, specifically about toileting demands and exposure to nudity and parental intercourse. He would suggest that the parents restrain the rigorous toilet training which included the use of enemas. He would recommend that the parents not expose themselves to their child and that he be given a room of his own. Further he would suggest that the parents provide peer companionship for Hans, in nursery school for instance. As Freud recognized, Hans's lack of friends accentuated his longing and stimulated satisfaction through fantasy. Having too few playmates also led the child to seek forbidden satisfaction through incestuous relationships which frightened him. Probably the consultant would have suspected that the impending tonsillectomy was unnecessary. If that were corroborated, he would have recommended that the operation not be performed. This advice might well have prevented the snowballing of Hans's neurosis which grew in intensity following the surgery.

I do not wish to imply that neuroses can be completely explained by parental behavior. Inner conflicts certainly are at the bottom of such disturbances. However, parental practices can accentuate conflicts and encourage maladaptive attempts at resolution. A consultant may be able to recommend means of alleviating conflict and providing adaptive channels of resolution.

References

Freud, A. (1949). Certain types and stages of social maladjustment. In *Searchlights on Delinquency*, ed. K. R. Eissler. New York: International Universities Press.

Freud, S. (1895). On the grounds for detaching a particular syndrome from neuresthenia under the description ''anxiety neurosis.'' *Standard Edition*: 3.

Hartmann, H. (1964). *Essays on Ego Psychology*. New York: International Universities Press.

Kanzer, M. (1979). Freud: the first psychoanalytic group leader. In *Freud's Self-Analysis*, vol. 1 of the Downstate Twenty-fifth Anniversary Series. New York, Jason Aronson. Reprinted from *Comprehensive Group Psychotherapy*, ed. H. Kaplan and B. Sadock. Baltimore: Williams and Wilkens, 1971.

Nunberg, H., and Federn, E., eds. (1967). *Minutes of the Vienna Psychoanalytic Society*. Vol. 2. New York: International Universities Press.

Reich, A. (1951). The discussion of 1912 on masturbation and our present-day views. *Psychoanalytic Study of the Child* 6: 80–94.

Chapter 3

INTEGRATIVE SUMMARY

JULES GLENN, M.D.

Dr. Martin A. Silverman reviews the details of Freud's study of Little Hans from many points of view. He compares Freud's explanations of the boy's pathology in 1909, when he published the case history, with his reevaluation in 1926 when Freud presented the structural theory. He then applies more recent psychoanalytic findings to broaden and enrich our understanding of Hans. In addition, he discusses Freud's technical approach when he supervised the first child analysis.

Regarding theory, Silverman notes that in 1909 Freud believed aggression was an aspect of libido and conceived of anxiety as transformed libido. In 1920, he conceptualized aggression as an independent drive as important as libido and in 1926 he regarded anxiety as the ego's reaction to danger from within or without the organism. Hence, when he reevaluated Hans' pathology in 1926, Freud conceived of his phobia as resulting from the defenses mobilized to guard against forbidden drives and attending anxiety. The conflict centered on the Oedipus complex. Child analysts today would stress preoedipal factors in his neurosis more than Freud did. Silverman warns against the possible abuses of such an emphasis but insists that preoedipal development is important in determining the form of the Oedipus complex. Since Freud's important basic discoveries, child analysts and others have recognized the importance of the child's intrinsic drive characteristics and variations in ego endowment. Conflictual as well as non-conflictual influences on development have been documented. The complicated interweaving of the innate and experiential in determining self- and object-representations, patterns of narcissistic regulation, etc., have been studied.

Freud provided sufficient data to enable us to expand on his formulations. Silverman notes the importance of Hans's visual and auditory perception which may have been determined by hereditary factors, identification with his musicologist father and marked stimulation in his early years (Hans occupied his parents' bedroom until he was four and a half, and his mother exposed herself before him) and which were so well used in the adult Hans's work in the operatic world.

Despite infantilization by his parents, Hans had considerable favorable experience during the oral stage. He entered the phallic stage with an expectation that his objects would be reliable in providing gratification for his ample libidinal urges.

Silverman also discusses Hans's experiences in the anal period—his frequent enemas and his father's expressed interest in defecatory processes. He is surprised at Freud's relative neglect of environmental seduction in the precipitation of the neurosis. Freud apparently carried his disillusionment with the seduction theory too far.

Freud's formulation of Hans's neurosis revolved around the impact on his castration anxiety of his oedipal and masturbatory wishes, the birth of his sister and his mother's actual castration threat. His mother's pregnancy and childbirth stimulated the little boy to try to understand these mysterious events.

Silverman suggests other contributions to Hans's castration complex: the normal development of castration anxiety during the anal phase that Roiphe and Galenson (1972) have brought to our attention; the impact of testicular cathexis and testicular castration anxiety noted by Bell (1961); the perception of the absence of penises when he saw his naked sister and mother. Hans's tonsillectomy must have terrified the boy, but Freud ignored its influence in precipitating Hans's neurosis. Silverman suggests that the operation may have been proposed, unconsciously, as a punishment for the boy's antagonism toward his sibling and that he may have conceived of it as a testicular castration threat. In any case he did react to his hatred for his sister with fear that he might drown or be injured in other ways.

Silverman applies Mahler's (Mahler, Pine and Bergman 1975) recent research to Hans's case. He notes that Frau Graf, who was seductive and intrusive, appeared to interfere with his passage through the stages of separation-individuation. The outbreak of Hans's neurosis was characterized by his wanting to remain with his mother in order to "coax" with her. Perhaps, he suggests, deficiencies in object constancy contributed to the boy's anxiety.

Freud was always cognizant of the interaction between environmental influences and constitutional factors in pathology as well as normality. Although he
recognized the power of physical determinants, he proclaimed that the analyst
must concentrate on the psychogenic aspects in order to cure his patients of their
neuroses. (He also predicted that psychopharmacology would one day afford
effective treatment.)

The environmental determinants that Freud reveals in the case of Little Hans
are imposing: the move from Gmunden (where Hans had many friends who
could help him discharge his libido) to a little apartment (where Hans had few
children his age, and where his attachment to his parents—especially his
mother—grew); his mother's pregnancy and the birth of his sister; his mother's
taking him to the toilet where he could observe her; his mother's castration
threat; primal scene experiences, etc.

In view of the fact that Freud noticed these many environmental stimuli, it
is surprising that he said, during a discussion of sexual enlightenment at the
Wednesday evening meetings, that Frau Graf's sole serious error was to take
Hans to the toilet with her. Apparently, Freud considered the child's upbringing,
including his mother's seductiveness, as essentially normal. Perhaps Freud's
feelings toward Hans's mother, a former patient, prevented him from evaluating
her seductiveness which he observed correctly. Perhaps since Hans's father was
part of the Wednesday evening group, he felt obliged to tactfully underplay Frau
Graf's pathogenic behavior. He probably knew the marriage was unstable; it
later ended in divorce.

Parenthetically we may remark on the early psychoanalytic milieu which
permitted the discussion of the analysis of a colleague's child by a group of
analysts who must have known the identity of patient and parents. These men
possessed the camaraderie of pioneers who were determined to use every available method to further their scientific explorations. They frequently offered each
other interpretations of their motives, an educational but disruptive practice
which still prevails to a lesser extent.

According to the minutes of the Vienna Psychoanalytic Society (Nunberg and
Federn 1962, 1967), Freud did not present Hans's case as an ongoing analysis,
but did discuss aspects of the treatment later (1909) during a meeting devoted
to sexual enlightenment in children. As mentioned, the father-analyst was present. The group seemed conversant with the case.

Despite his awareness of the importance of environmental factors, Freud
missed the significance of Hans's tonsillectomy. This is surprising in view of
Freud's method of analysis. He started at the surface and, after exploring su-
perficial aspects, gradually (more quickly than we do it today, however) helped
expose unconscious determinants of the patient's disturbance. Silverman suggests that when Hans pierced the doll with his knife, he was actively trying to

master a situation in which he would be the victim. Freud was to conceptualize this mechanism in *Beyond the Pleasure Principle* in 1920, and Anna Freud was to show the complex use of defenses (identification and reversal) in identification with the aggressor in 1936. Silverman also notes the mechanism of reversal in Hans's displaced desire to beat his mother and his parodying father's misinformation about sex. Attempts at mastery were also evident when Hans imagined riding a train without father who had missed it. In a later statement Hans reassured himself that father and he did board the train together.

It is interesting that Freud, the consummate observer, described events that could only be explained years later. Even when his theory was inadequate, he provided the raw data on which additions and corrections could be based. Sometimes he even adumbrated future theory as he officially maintained an earlier set of constructs. At the same time that he was asserting that Hans's anxiety was due to damned-up libido, which included aggressive manifestations, he was stating that Hans was afraid of his father who would punish Hans for the evil wishes he harbored against him, thus heralding the structural explanation of anxiety (Freud 1926) and the dual instinct theory (Freud 1920). Freud was describing and naming defense mechanisms even before he fully understood what was being defended. Not until 1926 did he realize that Hans used the displacements which he had described in 1909 to avoid the anxiety resulting from forbidden unconscious wishes. He never differentiated adequately between the projection of Hans's wishes and their externalization.

Silverman assesses Freud's technique—his astonishing application of adult analytic principles to a child's treatment and the limits that his lack of experience imposed. In 1909 Freud believed that only a parent could analyze a child. But by 1920 Hug-Hellmuth was writing about child analytic technique in which play substituted for free association and educational methods were prominent. Freud came to realize that a child would reveal his inner thoughts to an analyst who was not his parent. Melanie Klein (1961) would soon seize on Freud's remarkable capacity to make daring and intuitive insights into the unconscious and design a treatment in which the analyst offered deep interpretations and paid relatively little attention to reality factors and defenses. Anna Freud (1936) would come to emphasize complicated patterns of defense which she insisted must be analyzed in conjunction with drive derivatives and the influence of the environment.

Freud's interest in child observation, which spurred him to watch his own children and then to urge his colleagues to provide him with further data on their families, would develop into the systematic research projects of Anna Freud, Dorothy Burlingham and Margaret Mahler. Freud hardly realized that child analysts as observers and therapists would not merely confirm analytic principles but contribute actively to a growing science.

We need not in this summary review Hans's analysis in the detail that Silverman does so admirably. In essence, the fears of the horse turned out to be displaced expressions of oedipal wishes (the horse represented father whom he wished to hurt and mother whom he wished to beat in a sexual manner as well as injure in anger) and sibling rivalry (the horse symbolized his sister). Many of the details of Hans's fantasies about horses and the trucks they pulled were derived from his thoughts about the birth processes.

Eventually Hans recognized oedipal wishes in which he wanted to give his mother a baby. But, as he was never provided the information about how this was accomplished, he bothered his father with many seemingly unrelated questions.

Silverman observes the inevitable drawbacks when the father acts as analyst. He partially attributes Professor Graf's failure to analyze Hans' negative oedipal homosexual longings and his failure to tell Hans of the male role in copulation to lack of neutrality and objectivity; however, he does not ignore his supervisor's contribution to these lapses.

Silverman finds that Hans's analysis was incomplete, that homosexual attachments and pre-oedipal influences, for instance, were not analyzed. What is remarkable, however, is how complete the analysis was. In just a few months he covered a great deal. Often the patient's rapid improvement limits the scope of analysis. All too often when the therapeutic result is good the patient's parents wish to terminate the treatment before the analyst totally approves. The analyst sees potential troubles that he would like to prevent. He wants to stabilize the changes that have occurred. His scientific curiosity also demands that mysterious and unsolved aspects of the patient's personality be clarified. The parents, satisfied with the result they sought, often do not go along with the analyst's wishes; they solicit the therapist's cooperation in ending therapy. In Hans's case Freud wisely did not press for further therapeutic work. Hans had recovered and further analytic intimacy with his father should have been forestalled. As Silverman and Glenn note, there are serious dangers to a policy of parental interpretation.

A post-analytic peril in this and other cases of treatment through parents, a practice whose impressive results have been reported by Furman (1957), is that the parents may continue their interpretive activity after the therapy has ended and without the restraining influence of the advising therapist. Such a practice was quite likely in the atmosphere that I have described in which a colleague's mutual interpretation was deemed wise.

After suggesting that the parent as therapist may produce a skewed relationship with his child, Silverman considers that perhaps the treatment's effectiveness can be attributed not only to interpretative processes but also to alterations in the family configuration. Father became a friend and helper, facilitating ego and superego development and diluting the child's tie to his mother.

Glenn, in his discussion of Silverman's paper, affirms Freud's diagnosis: Hans suffered from a childhood neurosis, anxiety hysteria in particular. He expresses doubt as to the propriety of analysis when the neurosis is of short duration and when no serious developmental arrest has been observed. Rather, he suggests, attempts at environmental alteration might be considered. If this approach failed to deter the symptoms or a serious disturbance were uncovered, analysis could be initiated. Indeed Freud did not carry out an analysis as we understand it today. The treatment consisted of a judicious combination of child psychotherapy and parental advice. The subtlety and sophistication of this first "analysis" of a child invokes our admiration and envy.

Glenn is critical of Freud's advice to Professor Graf prior to the start of the analysis. That advice confused the parental educative role and the analyst's interpretative function. Freud's suggestion that Hans be told of his incestuous wishes appears to be consistent with the intellectual milieu of the day. Mutual interpretation amongst colleagues was considered helpful scientifically and personally. Today we know of the disruptions that interpretation to colleagues, friends and family can cause. Freud's second suggestion, that Hans be told he was too interested in his widdler, appears to arise out of confusion about the possible ill effects of masturbation. His third suggestion, that Dr. Graf tell him that females have no penises, frightened Hans in that this incomplete information accentuated his castration fantasies.

A present-day analytic consultant, if he elected to offer parents advice, would probably suggest that toilet training practices be altered and that the parents not expose themselves to the child. Inquiry about Hans's forthcoming tonsillectomy might have revealed that it was unnecessary. Hence a traumatic operation might have been prevented.

The modern consultant can thank Freud's patient, Little Hans, as well as Freud himself, for teaching us how the child thinks. From these promising beginnings, child analysis has emerged as a potent therapeutic procedure. The application of analytic knowledge has helped alleviate and prevent emotional disturbances in present-day Hanses.

References

Bell, A. (1961). Some observations on the role of the scrotal sac and testicles. *Journal of the American Psychoanalytic Association* 9: 261–286.

Freud, A. (1936). *The Ego and the Mechanisms of Defense*. New York: International Universities Press.

Freud, A., and Burlingham, D. (1939–1945). *Infants Without Families*. New York: International Universities Press.

Freud, S. (1920). Beyond the pleasure principle. *Standard Edition* 18: 7–64.

———— (1923). The ego and the id. *Standard Edition* 19: 12–66.

———— (1926). Inhibitions, symptoms and anxiety. *Standard Edition* 20: 87–175.

Furman, E. (1957). The treatment of under-fives by way of parents. *Psychoanalytic Study of the Child* 12: 250–262.

Hug-Hellmuth, H. (1921). On the technique of child analysis. *International Journal of Psycho-Analysis* 2: 287–305.

Klein, M. (1961). *Narrative of a Child Analysis*. New York: Basic Books.

Mahler, M. S., Pine, F. and Bergman, A. (1975). *The Psychological Birth of the Human Infant*. New York: Basic Books.

Nunberg, H., and Federn, E., eds. (1962). *Minutes of the Vienna Psychoanalytic Society. Volume I: 1906–1908*. New York: International Universities Press.

———— (1967). *Minutes of the Vienna Psychoanalytic Society. Volume II: 1908–1910*. New York: International Universities Press.

Roiphe, H., and Galenson, E. (1972). Early genital anxiety and the castration complex. *Psychoanalytic Quarterly* 41: 334–347.

PART IV

The Rat Man

Chapter 1

THE TRANSFERENCE NEUROSIS OF THE RAT MAN

MARK KANZER, M.D.

What has become familiarly known as the "Rat Man" is the classical "Notes Upon a Case of Obsessional Neurosis" (1909) described by Freud, which represents an early phase of psychoanalytic theory and technique. As Kris (1951) points out, it reflects the "conspicuous intellectual indoctrination" of patients which prevailed at the time, and the little emphasis on reliving in the transference which analysis was later to acquire. Nevertheless, Freud stressed even in this paper that transference is the effective therapeutic agent; it it interesting, however, from the standpoint of the evolution of analytic thinking that he did not then clearly apprehend the transference significance of many of the exchanges between the Rat Man and himself. In reconstructing this stage of analytic technique, it appears that much of the intellectual indoctrination then considered necessary and compatible with the "mirror role" of the analyst was actually, on an unconscious level at least, a recognition of the resistances and a more or less active intervention which modified the patient's attitude toward the physician. The Rat Man contains remarkable material for a study of the intuitive processes by which Freud explored the minds of his patients, as well as of the clinical experiences that determined the direction analytic formulations were to take.

In introducing us to his methodology, Freud cited Alfred Adler, "formerly an analyst," as having drawn attention to the peculiar importance of the very first communications made by patients. He then confirms this observation by giving the evidence of homosexual object choice in the Rat Man's initial remarks. Freud did not, however, draw from this the apparent inferences with respect to the developing transference; moreover, at that time homosexuality was not connected with ego and superego functioning. Thus, for example, the introductory words of the Rat Man referred to a friend to whom he always used to go when tormented by some criminal impulse, to see whether this man would regard him as a culprit. The friend, however, would give him moral support by assuring him that he was certainly of excellent character and merely in the habit of taking a dark view of himself. That this introductory communication embodied the motivation for seeking treatment, and made clear the need to appease and yet deceive the superego—thereby offering an unmistakable focal point for detecting and dealing with resistance—is substantiated by the subsequent course of the analysis.

The remainder of the first analytic session seems also, in retrospect, to raise some doubts as to the strictness with which the patient conformed to his "pledge" to follow the rule of free association. He is reported to have given a detailed history of his early childhood sexual experiences, a circumstance surely not unrelated to the fact that he had read *The Psychopathology of Everyday Life* and had selected Freud as his therapist for this very reason. These memories were likewise not devoid of interest from the standpoint of formulating the initial dynamics of the transference and the resistances. They abounded in voyeuristic fantasies which were coupled with fears of being observed. There were recollections from childhood of misgivings that the patient's parents could read his thoughts, an idea that must have had immediate pertinence to the analysis, and which reached a climax in his confession of the obsessive thought that his father, upon understanding his son's secret fantasies, would die. Presumably, the battle lines with the analyst were thus drawn.

The next interview, with the famous narrative of the encounter between the patient and the sadistic army officer who precipitated the patient's neurosis, was no mere anamnestic account, as it was considered, but was already a flowering of the transference. The story of the Rat Man, it will be recalled, concerned a neurotic military man who became violently agitated when a mess hall conversation turned to a sadistic punishment practiced in the East, wherein a pot containing rats was turned upside down over the buttocks of criminals. Shortly thereafter, the patient had developed obsessional doubts over the details of payment on a package that was brought to him by the same officer who had described this exotic torture with apparent relish.

During the recital of these events the patient became so perturbed that he frequently had to break off and rise from the couch. The analyst sought to come to his assistance by supplying details that the analysand could not verbalize: "I went on to say," Freud records, "that I would do all I could . . . to guess the full meaning of any hints he gave me." This guessing game apparently opened the way to an amusing and evidently unsuspected bit of acting out. When the young man approached the crucial details of the rat punishment, he was able to draw Freud into a dialogue that was actually a reproduction of the proceedings described. As he falteringly told how the rodents were applied to the buttocks, he rose again from the couch, exclaiming with signs of horror and resistance, "They bored their way in. . . ," but could proceed no further. At this point Freud intervened and completed the unspoken thought by suggesting, correctly, that the rats had found their way into the anus.

Actually, the analyst was being seduced into the role not only of the cruel officer, who told the story, but also of the rats which invaded the victim's body. The rules of the analysis clearly lent themselves to interpretation of the unconscious as a forcible violation of the patient's mind—a point already foreshadowed in the preceding session by recollections of the Rat Man's concern as to whether his parents had once been able to read his thoughts: "I made him pledge himself to submit to the one and only condition of the treatment," Freud noted, "—namely, to say everything that came into his head, even if it was unpleasant. . . ." The analysand, even as he described the rat punishment, pleaded to be released from this vow: "I assured him that I myself had no taste whatever for cruelty and certainly had no desire to torment him" Freud added with apparent feeling for the subtle accusation thus brought against him, "but that naturally I could not grant him something which was beyond my power. . . . The overcoming of resistances was a law of treatment and on no consideration could it be dispensed with."

The patient, with cunning typical of the obsessive neurotic, managed to twist the analytic rule into an instrument suited to his own purposes; moreover, the analyst was persuaded to condone a violation of the pledge by permitting the patient to arise from the couch and actively join in the violation by revealing the contents of his own mind rather than discovering those of the patient—namely, by himself speaking the magic words which were the equivalent of the action: "into the anus."

Freud observed: "At all the more important moments while he was telling his story his face took on a very strange, composite expression. I could only interpret it as one of *horror at pleasure of his own of which he himself was unaware.*" The full significance of this pleasure might have been gleaned from the fact that ". . . the patient behaved as though he were dazed and bewildered. . . . He repeatedly addressed me as 'Captain'. . . ." This Freud explained (completely overlooking the alternative) as ". . . probably because at the beginning of the hour I had told him that I myself was not fond of cruelty like Captain M. . . .''

At the next session, the patient was still in conflict over a vow—this time, with regard to an obsessive ritual he had concocted for payment on a package delivered to him by the captain. This had precipitated his flight from the army encampment and refuge in Vienna, where he had sought relief from his guilt, first from a friend and then from Freud. His account of this affair during the session arouses the suspicion that again this was no mere anamnesis but had definite transference implications. Now that the analyst had taken the place of the cruel captain, was the patient planning anew to break a pledge (to undergo treatment), flee from Vienna and return to camp? He did, at any rate, tell Freud during this hour that he had originally sought a physician only to receive from him a certificate which would have enabled him to return to the Army and carry out the terms of his obsession. Such shuttling back and forth between persons and places is characteristic of this type of neurosis. Freud comments: ''Many months later, when his resistance was at its height, he once more felt a temptation to travel to P——— after all, to look up Lieutenant A. and to go through the farce of returning him the money.''

The succeeding interview presumably saw the continuance of the inner debate as to the patient's ability to rely upon and confide in his physician. Fears of his own aggression and of retaliatory hostility preoccupied him. He reminisced about the sudden death of his father and his own ensuing guilt: his parent had passed away as the young man lay resting for an hour (death wishes toward Freud?); nevertheless, he had never quite accepted the reality of his father's death, and on hearing some witticism, would find himself thinking, ''I must tell father that'' (the analytic rule?). When he walked into a room, he would expect to find his father in it (analyst's office?); at other times, however, he became so depressed by self-reproaches about his father's death that only the reassurances of a friend that he was not guilty were helpful—a circumstance which leads back to the patient's very first communications and his need to seek out persons (including Freud) who would attest to their confidence in him. The friend or analyst, as unconscious surrogate father, could reassure him of his innocence in no more convincing way than to demonstrate, by their existence, that he had not killed them.

Freud responded to this with a lengthy theoretical discourse on the relationship between idea and affect in the neuroses, in order to persuade the patient that his sense of guilt must indeed have had some valid unconscious justification, and to induce him to search within himself for the explanation of his self-reproaches. Thus, analysis was sharply differentiated from the reassuring techniques which the young man had evolved for himself and which would have been gratified by most other forms of therapy. Nevertheless, reassurance was given indirectly by Freud, for when the patient inquired as to the value of discovering his hidden motives, he was told that his troublesome feelings would probably be dissipated in this way.

This implied absolution was followed by the confession, vague and tentative, of misdemeanors in childhood. Freud at once seized upon this and assured him at great length that precisely the incidents which occurred in early life were of the greatest importance and that the patient would discover for himself the laws of the unconscious. (In what sense this was meant is not quite clear, since the Rat Man was already acquainted with Freud's writings.) This intellectual explanation seems to have been accompanied by some signs of approval and satisfaction on the part of the analyst; moreover, the patient was again invited, in a friendly way, to prove his capacity for self-analysis. Actually, the analysand next reacted with suspicion; he wished to know whether the procedure thus advocated could really undo such long-standing ideas. Thereupon he was assured that Freud had formed a good opinion of him—a statement to which he reacted with "visible pleasure." In short, far more than theoretical expositions were employed by the therapist during this interview.

In any case, the resistance seems to have been lessened by these exchanges. At the beginning of the next session the patient renewed his earlier statements that he believed his parents could read his thoughts (a tribute to the deftness of the analyst?), and bolstered his courage at last to confess a childhood fantasy concerning his father's death. This recollection could now be conceded, since Freud had already guessed and shown tolerance of this idea. The latter was not yet satisfied, however, and after some further prodding and reassurance by means of "theoretical explanations," further confessions were forthcoming.

Freud comments in a note that "It is never the aim of discussions like this to create conviction. They are only intended to bring the repressed complexes into consciousness, to set the conflicts going in the field of conscious mental activity, and to facilitate the emergence of fresh material from the unconscious." The Rat Man reacted to Freud's expositions with the now well-known tendency of the obsessive to draw the therapist into further intellectual explanations in the course of which the fundamental rule is increasingly reversed. In this instance, however, Freud neatly avoided the trap set for him by the patient's questions and remarked that surely the latter must have some answers prepared and need but follow the trend of his own thoughts to discover them.

There followed a chain of associations from, first, matters that might not be communicated to the father, to, second, envy of a younger brother, and, third, to recollections of an incident in which he had enticed this brother to look into the barrel of a gun, whereupon he had pulled the trigger. The interpretation of the transference here may be made both actively and passively: in the tacit struggle over penetration of each other's minds, the patient both intended and feared aggression in his relation with the physician; the "rat punishment" had thoroughly infiltrated the unconscious significance of the fundamental rule and the analytic task was to expose and dislodge it.

Freud pursued his course in this situation by insisting that the recollection of the incident with the brother was merely a cover for hostile intentions towward the father; in this way, the problem of concealed aggression was kept in the foreground. The analyst's theoretical comments constituted a sharp probing instrument; the patient himself was, in the imagery of his own unconscious, pressed increasingly into the plight of a cornered rat. At this juncture, he lamented his own "cowardliness," but Freud mitigated his plight by telling him that he ought not consider himself responsible for the residue of infantile dispositions within himself. In this way, the patient managed to convert into analytic terms his habitual disposition to persuade a respected friend to assure him that he was not really a criminal despite his reprehensible impulses.

Unfortunately, Freud concluded his formal presentation of the case at this point in order himself to discuss the theoretical aspects of obsessional neuroses, into which the Rat Man gave him such unprecedented insight. Some further references, however, enable us to glean a few details of the subsequent analysis. The memory of injuring the brother after persuading him to look into the gun barrel has unmistakable sexual implications which are probably illuminated by a strange ritual which the patient had at one time practiced. During his student days, and after the death of his father, he had developed the habit of interrupting his studies between twelve and one at night, and opening the door as though someone were standing outside. Then he would take out his penis and contemplate it in the looking glass.

Freud supposed, in explanation, that the patient was expressing ambivalence toward his father, seeking to please him by his diligence in studying late at night, but at the same time affronting him by his sex play. Certainly this incident suggests some transposition of the earlier one with the brother, who was lured under false pretenses into looking at the gun (penis). Transference implications also may be discerned in the one-hour interval during which the patient alternated between conforming to and defying his father's wishes (the fundamental rule): opening the door to confront the father's ghost which, as we have previously seen, had settled itself on the figure of the analyst; struggling to control his exhibitionism (the urge to confess to the therapist, with ultimate sexual aims); and even in the role of the mirror (mirror = analyst?).

Evidence accumulated to justify Freud in declaring that "it was only over the painful road of transference that [the patient] was able to reach conviction" of the truth of the theoretical postulates. He dreamed that he saw his analyst's daughter standing before him with two patches of dung instead of eyes, which Freud interpreted as meaning that he would marry the girl not for her beautiful eyes but for her money. (Various other possibilities arise if we consider the dream figure as the Rat Man himself.) Supplementary fantasies came in the form of visions of Freud as a wealthy and powerful man whose interest in the young man arose out of his desire to have him as a son-in-law. A testing of this hypothesis took place in the form of acting out: "How could a gentleman like you, sir," he asked, "let yourself be abused by a low good-for-nothing wretch like me? You ought to turn me out." The occasion was then seized for violating and reversing the analytic rule by rising from the couch and striding up and down, watching the analyst and averring that he feared attack for his impudence—a situation that presented an advanced counterpart of the first session in which Freud was tacitly lured into enacting the part of the cruel captain and of the rat penetrating the anus. The transference elements were now more clearly to be discerned.

In retrospect, we may say that at this stage in the development of psychoanalysis, there was not yet a full appreciation of the extent to which memories of the past were represented by or constituted actual reflections of attitudes in the present. Reconstructions of former events were entered into in preference to a dynamic analysis of the immediate transference, a danger which Freud had recently come to see in the case of Dora, but whose application he had not yet entirely grasped. The footnotes on the Rat Man do indeed discuss the fact that "childhood memories" are distorted and consolidated with the events of later years; much remained, however, to be worked out with respect to the resulting implications.

The predilection for reconstructing the past also played a large part, as may be noted in the Rat Man's case, in the disposition to theoretically indoctrinate the patient and to the subsequent need to find supplementary means of providing him with emotional conviction. Transference interpretations, focused on the immediate affect (aggression toward and distrust of the analyst), are more apt to touch the affective core of the resistance, and fit more frequently with the rule that resistance shall be interpreted before content. Nevertheless, in retrospect, it may be seen with what skill and intuition Freud's theoretical explanations took cognizance of and dealt with the transference.

References

Freud, S. (1909). Notes upon a case of obsessional neurosis. *Standard Edition* 10: 155–318.
Kris, E. (1951) Ego psychology and interpretation in psychoanalytic therapy. *Psychoanalytic Quarterly* 20: 15–30.

Chapter 2

EGO ORGANIZATION IN OBSESSIVE-COMPULSIVE
DEVELOPMENT. A STUDY OF THE RAT MAN, BASED
ON INTERPRETATION OF MOVEMENT PATTERNS

JUDITH S. KESTENBERG, M.D.

This paper is a sequel to a previous publication which attempted to demonstrate "how the observation of patterns of motility and thought can contribute to the understanding of the sequence of developmental phases in general and to the genesis of obsessive organization in particular" (1966, p. 151). At that time I described movement patterns from which one could interpret the Rat Man's drive organization. In the present paper I will draw from Freud's descriptions of his patient's movements and action-thoughts (Laban 1960) to attempt a re-construction of his ego organization. Following this, I shall construct an account of his development in clinical terms.

In the 1966 paper I suggested that Freud stressed the central role of the phallus and thus gave direction to the patient's thoughts away from pregenital interests towards a genital organization. In the present paper, I shall show that Freud traced the central role of the baby in the image of the rat, but did not connect it to the patient's wish to deliver his undescended testicle. Using Laban's (1947, 1960) concepts of motion factors related to space, gravity, and time and Lamb's (1961) interpretations of their use and structure (Ramsden 1973), I shall show in each subsection how Freud's technique was (and still is) based on the analyst's own adaptation to reality and adjustment to objects.

Introduction

The essential unity of movement and thought is especially transparent in obsessives (Freud 1909). Without claiming a one-to-one correlation between movement, feeling, action, thought, and language, one can derive information about the regulation of one of the systems through the study of the other. Moreover, there is genetic unity between them. For instance, the maturation of movement patterns, serving adaptation and adjustment to objects, keeps pace with the maturation of related cognitive structures (A. Freud 1965, Piaget and Inhelder 1969, Kestenberg 1965, 1967, Kestenberg et al. 1971). They evolve from one another and reinforce each other to support specific developmental tasks (Kestenberg 1975).

In the second year of life, at the height of the anal-sadistic phase, the increased aggression promotes differentiation between feeling, thought, and action (Hartmann 1939). At first, the child's thoughts are "action-thoughts" and only gradually does he transform them into "word-thoughts" (Laban 1960). Defenses which hitherto have been primarily motor, transfer their sphere of operation into the area of ideation and verbalization. To the degree that obsessives think in action-thoughts and use motor defenses, their symptomatology evidences not only id- but also ego-regression. They tend, as the Rat Man did, to transpose sequences of actions from their childhood into their adulthood.

All mental processes are accompanied to some degree by a reinforcement from the motor apparatus (Birdwhistell 1970). Even repression is accompanied by minute pressing actions that represent on the outside what the patient is trying to do on the inside. Kanzer (1966) described the way in which acting out betrays its derivation from phase-specific forms of motility. Anna Freud (1966) warned us not to confuse obsessive repetition with pre-ego mechanisms which arise from repetition compulsion. In the latter, we encounter high-frequency oscillating rhythms, such as sucking and mouthing. The former is modeled after the anal-sadistic rhythm of holding, straining, and expelling. Derived from this rhythm is the obsessive's attempt to learn, like a child, by repetition of holding and throwing; leaving his mother and returning to her, as if still engaged in the "rapprochement" subphase of separation-individuation (Mahler 1968, Mahler et al. 1975).

The motor development of children destined to become obsessive is frequently ahead of other ego functions. Impelled to move and learn through movement, they oppose their mothers early and may be weaned prematurely. The interaction with the mother reduces itself to a struggle for dominance. Thoughts which would ordinarily be used to devise means for overcoming obstacles, may become sidetracked into finding ways of ridding oneself of confining adults. Words are used as weapons and learning becomes arrested in defensive actions, isolated from identification with the loved adult. Parents who abstain from battling and encourage verbalization in lieu of impulsive actions (not only in the child but also in themselves) promote harmonious advances in development and conflict-free learning. This educational stance is the prototype of the analyst's position which avoids disapproval of acting out and, instead, helps to transform acting into remembering. Freud's minute descriptions of the Rat Man's behavioral sequences, his affects, his facial expressions and movements show in some detail that the Rat Man resorted to early modes of learning and was not, at first, accessible to explanations. The detailed descriptions of Freud's interventions give us a glimpse of the methods by which he opened the way for his patient's resumption of adult learning and adaptation.

Before attempting to draw on data from movement analysis to reconstruct the Rat Man's ego organization, I shall briefly summarize my previous attempt to assess his drive organization.

Brief Summary of the Reconstruction of Obsessive Drive Organization (1966) and Its Application to the Analysis of the Rat Man.

Rhythms of tension changes can be seen throughout life. In successive stages of growth, differentiation, and integration, we note the predominance of certain rhythms over others, as, for instance, an oscillating (sinus rhythm) in the oral, a holding-straining-expelling in the anal-sadistic, and a running-type rhythm in the urethral phase that follows. In transitions from one phase to the next, there are growth-crises in which divergent trends overlap and vie with one another. "The resulting increase in aggression enhances differentiation. A steady influx of genital impulses promotes integration. The role of the mother during these developmental changes is to anticipate and support more advanced patterns and organizations" (Kestenberg 1966, p. 158).

After the passing of pregenital phases, in a preoedipal phase—called "inner-genital"—a disequilibrium, similar to that Freud had termed delirium in the Rat Man, is resolved, with internal sensations acting as inner organizer and the mother as outer organizer of development. Integration of pregenital and early genital drive-components must be accomplished and the preoedipal baby-wish must be traded for an "ideal" penis-wish before phallic dominance can take over.

Implicit in my 1966 account of the Rat Man's neurosis were the following assumptions: (1) he was overstimulated in the transition from the oral-sadistic to the anal-erotic subphase; (2) his aggression was increased by too intense struggles with his caretakers; (3) in transition from the anal-sadistic to the urethral-erotic subphase, his aggression was not mitigated; (4) during the inner-genital phase, he suffered from a severe disequilibrium which could not be resolved by a harmonius integration of conflicting trends; and (5) he entered the phallic phase with an ambivalent anal-sadistic organization.

In the following, more extensive reconstruction, I shall draw on the preceding findings and, in order to focus on the Rat Man's ego organization, I shall introduce ego-controlled movement patterns (expressive of affects, used for defenses and learning, for adaptation to external reality, and for reaching objects and building relationships). Tables (1, 2, 3) explaining the classification, relation, and interpretation of movement patterns will be provided in an appendix.

Because each subsection will deal with movement patterns serving separate areas of ego functioning, and because their developmental lines will have to be traced to early latency, a certain amount of repetition and overlapping cannot be avoided. The same is true of the last section of this paper which, based on the previous movement analysis, collates clinical data to reconstruct the Rat Man's early development.

The Contribution of Movement Patterns to the Rat Man's Ego Organization. A Developmental Approach

Affect Control

In the neonatal phase, the infant's caretaker provides the primary objects (Balint 1960) which the child needs for comfort (air, light, warmth). By attunement with the rhythms of his needs (expressed in tension changes), the mother helps the child to feel safe and to respond to her in kind. By adjusting to his breathing and to the shape of his body and by helping him to adjust to hers, she makes herself available as a model for identification. As they breathe, they grow towards one another and shrink away. Through this interaction and the coordination between tension- and shape-changes, needs become coordinated with environmental conditions and with the first kinesthetic feelings of togetherness. An integration between bodily functions and maternal care brings on the first manifestations of psychic content. In the *neonatal* phase, the principal physical apparatus for affect expression—tension- and shape-flow—give rise to ego feelings (Freud 1923, Kestenberg 1971, Mahler 1971). Bound flow of tension is felt as inhibition and shrinking of shape as restriction of contact; together they indicate displeasure. Free flow is felt as freedom to move and growing of shape (e.g., in inhalation) as transcending one's own boundaries; together they indicate pleasure (Glaser 1970, Kestenberg 1976). These movement factors are based on elasticity and plasticity of tissues. They are reduced in various states of dimmed consciousness. The older the infant, the less he is subject to states of reduced vitality in which tension feels neutral and the body feels shapeless—Table 1:9 and 9.9—the principal motor ingredients of deanimation (Schossberger 1963).

Through interaction between the learning infant and the teaching mother, the child's feeling tones become more pronounced and neutral states decrease in quantity. Freud's repeated allusions to his patient's vagueness, the indistinctness of his speech or his dazed appearance, suggests that the Rat Man used neutral flow to numb his feelings. Freud's persistent interest in the patient's state of mind helped to decrease his use of deanimation and flattening of affect as defenses.

In the *oral* phase, the baby learns to steady himself by keeping his tension on an even level and to readjust his position by small changes in tension (Table 1:2 and 3). Coordinated with these self-soothing techniques is the transformation of frowning in discomfort into smiling with comfort and pleasurable stimuli. By the end of the first year, the infant can calm himself by lowering his tension while he lengthens, craning his neck and extending his arms (Table 1:6 and 6.6). By gaining control over small intensities of tension and over small changes in shape, he becomes capable of mirroring his mother's expressions and gestures. However, if too many people interact with him, he becomes overstimulated, dazed, and loses control over his expressiveness. Still worse is lack of a model for imitation, which produces a masklike facial configuration (Spitz and Wolff 1946). A certain amount of deanimation occurs in everyone—child and adult—making it possible to deal with inanimate matter without fear. When the child gains control over neutral flow, and can evoke and relinquish it at will, he also becomes capable of animating the inanimate and treating it as if it were a person or an animal. When, at the end of the first year, the baby becomes overstimulated by a plethora of inner and outer stimuli, he can protect himself by temporary alterations of consciousness and by a deanimation which reestablishes his partially lost protective barrier against stimuli. Animating and deanimating the world is an important pastime of the oral-sadistic child who studies the consistency of things and turns back to his mother to bite, touch, and explore her.

Shengold (1967, 1971) postulated that "rat people" are overstimulated. The Rat Man felt flooded by associations while his affective range was constricted. He sometimes acted like a bewildered one-year-old who views the world with a remote expression on his face.

In transition from the oral to the *anal* phase, the baby twists and squirms and exhibits through changes in facial expression fine readjustments of tension. Readjusting and controlling small intensities of tension, he may widen into a smile or lengthen and broaden his chest like a clown (Table 1:4, 6 and 4.4, 6.6). During the anal-sadistic phase he develops control over high intensities (Table 1:5.5). He stoops as he strains, and cowers on the floor when angry (Table 1:5.5). Turning from passive to active he can now induce temper tantrums which used to overwhelm him. He revolts against his mother, increasing his resistance in proportion to the mother's countertention and counter-opposition. When, with his mother's support, he can end the anal-sadistic phase without too great ambivalence, he becomes capable of regulating tension intensity in the medium range rather than in its extremes. At the same time he reduces the contrasting feelings of grandiosity and self-denigration and begins to have a balanced self-representation. Instead of feeling ''so big'' and soon after ''so small,'' he gets to know his right size. The Rat Man behaved as if he had never successfully completed the anal-sadistic phase. He did not have good control over middle ranges of affectivity. He veered from agitation to indifference or daze, and from fantasies of achieving a high position to feeling disgraced or abandoned.

At the end of the second and the beginning of the third year, when the child accomplishes transition from the anal to the *urethral* phase, he experiments a great deal with gradations of tension changes. In the beginning of this phase, he prefers gradual changes of tension which are coupled with bulging into things. He may be best characterized as a ''lordotic straggler.'' In the next, urethral-sadistic, subphase, he tends to shoot out abruptly and to hollow, as if he had become empty inside (Table 1:7 and 7.7). In transition from one subphase to the next, these tendencies overlap and vie with one another. Lack of coordination between self-expression through tension changes and shape changes can become trying to the toddler but more so to his mother. He may start an activity abruptly and bump into things, then he may pull his belly in and gradually bend down, inspecting the floor. In the midst of poking things and examining them in a leisurely fashion, he may abruptly drop what he held and fall into a musing state as if depleted of energy. He may step backwards and forwards, not being able to make up his mind where to go and what to do. His mother becomes confused by his unpredictable actions and moods.

If one looks at the Rat Man's train ride back to Vienna from this point of view, one finds a decided similarity between his indecisive movements and the unpredictable affects and haphazard roaming of the ''dawdling and dashing'' two-year-old who has not been able to resolve the problems of the urethral phase. The Rat Man would abruptly veer from one idea to another and make up for his inability to settle down in a gradual manner by endless repetitions or reversals. He would repeatedly "drop" the project of marrying and unaccountably and abruptly return to it. His conflicts were expressed in the simultaneous use of clashing patterns, for example, when he offended people by abruptly and impatiently butting into them, without preparation (Table 1:7 and 8.8).

Through successive pregenital phases, the child masters the rudiments of control over tension- and shape-flow changes. Although he has begun to co-ordinate them after a fashion, a correspondence between feelings of tension and self-feelings is yet to come. Entering the *inner-genital phase,* he temporarily loses control over the apparatus of affectivity. He is emerging from his baby cocoon and the newness of being brave and big, as opposed to being a scared baby, makes it difficult for him to progress without regression (A. Freud 1965, Kestenberg 1975). His rhythms of tension-flow are varied and the qualities of tension and body-shape veer from harmonious to clashing and from combination to diffusion. He seems to revive and mix up all of his previously organized feelings. He stares, wiggles, jumps, stoops, dashes away, and dawdles. He is poised, agile, delightful to be with, angry; he talks nonstop and becomes monosyllabic in turn. His regressive bouts are especially disquietening because he can be "clearheaded and shrewd" like the Rat Man, accessible to reasoning, and proud of his adultlike control. On the other hand, he may feel very small or very big, henpecked and deprived, or expansive, with everything in the world belonging to him and him alone. He may get into everything, disturbing order, while insistent that none of his belongings be touched or disturbed. He may talk loudly and whisper, mixing up feelings so that one can hardly know whether he is happy or sad. His expressions are like "hybrids between two species" of feeling. The affective confusion that invades his thinking resembles the Rat Man's delirium.

The recovery from the disequilibrium of the two-and-a-half-year-old is accomplished through a reintegration of clashing and inappropriate affects (Kestenberg 1967b). Gradually or in spurts his "delirium" gives way to reasonableness. The influx of inner-genital rhythms tends to have an integrative effect. Their characteristic graduality is combined with low intensity of tension, giving the impression of patience and calm (Table 1:6 and 8). In coordination with these tension qualities, the child tends to bulge out and lengthen his torso as if he were imitating the bearing of a pregnant woman (Table 1:8.8 and 6.6). He organizes his affectivity by becoming tender like his mother and by developing a sense of inner shape, feeling the way he imagines her to be: filled with a growing and moving baby. Through identification with his mother he resorts more and more to verbalization rather than to screaming or impulsive grabbing. However, the calming effect of impulses, emanating from the inner-genital organs can be disturbed: (1) by too many aggressive, pregenital urges; (2) when the mother herself is high strung and impatient or worried; or (3) when there is an impairment or illness in an inner-genital organ.

In such cases, the disequilibrium is prolonged and can lead either to progressive disorganization or to a tendency to become disorganized under stress. The Rat Man was subject to all three adverse conditions; as a result he tended to become confused to the point of a "delirium."

In normal development, an influx of very intense waves of tension, which radiate from inner-genital organs into the outer, frustrates the child and gives rise to aggression. Aggressive impulses to expel the imaginary baby and mutilate it put an end to the friendly preoedipal relation to the mother. A denial of inner-genital organs ushers in a preoccupation with the phallus. Unable to achieve an equilibrium, the Rat Man very likely entered the phallic phase with a regressive revival of an anal-sadistic organization. Intense affects became imbued with a desire to dominate and the wish for a baby was distorted by his disgust with feces. A denial of the inner-genital organs could not be accomplished because of a continuing preoccupation with an undescended testicle. As a result, the Rat Man must have entered the phallic phase with a predisposition for feminine-anal identification.

In normal development, the *phallic-oedipal* child gives up the dyadic preoedipal relation with his mother and turns to his father instead. The onrush of phallic rhythms brings to affects an exuberating quality that acts as an antidote against the bad feelings of disappointment, related to the mother. Intrinsic in the now predominant phallic rhythm is intensity of tension in free flow, which develops abruptly and drops just as abruptly (Table 1:2, 5 and 7). What was felt as an inner shape in the preceding phase, is experienced now as a solid anchor point. Shortening and hollowing (thinning) (Table 1:5.5 and 7.7) at the waist counteracts and supersedes the feeling of length and fullness (Table 1:6.6 and 8.8) which corresponded to the idea of pregnancy in the preceding phase. The phallic child's torso and pelvis become one solid structure, with head and limbs acting as its extensions. This underlies the image of the body as a phallus (Lewin 1933); it constitutes an impregnable, closed system. Negative oedipal fantasies distort this representation only to a limited degree. When a boy wants to be filled by his father's penis, he anticipates that he will exhibit to the naked (penisless) mother a great phallic body, stiff and solid and subject to her admiration. However, when penetration is wished for in identification with a degraded, filthy, anal mother, there results a permanent danger to the phallic closed system and a corresponding lowering of self-confidence and self-esteem. The ensuing impairment of affect control that persists into latency may be the first manifestation of obsessive-compulsive symptomatology.

No doubt, the Rat Man's phallic phase, built as it was on an anal rather than a genital integration, was permeated by intense clashes between phallic-sadistic and feminine-anal impulses. A periodic regression to a delirium, which seemed to repeat the disequilibrium of the two-and-a-half-year-old, brought forth mixtures and alternations between oral, anal, urethral, inner-genital and phallic impulses. The plethora of impulses interfered with the formation of a stable superego. In *latency*, when an appropriate, harmonious affect regulation usually comes under the control of the ego and superego, the Rat Man's unstable superego and ego overladen with defense mechanisms combined to solidify an obsessional dissociation of affects.

Freud's detailed description of his patient's facial expressions and movement as well as the analysis of his feelings suggests that, in every stage of development, the Rat Man's affect-regulation was disturbed. He suffered from flattening of affect and feelings of constriction, poor modulation of self-expression which made seeking contact ineffective, and diminished ability to soothe and console himself by lowering tension. He veered from agitation to feelings of deanimation accompanied by omnipotent self-aggrandizement alternating with self-denigration. He exhibited insufficient impulse control which made him feel open to attack from within and without, and basic impatience coupled with intrusiveness made him impetuous and obnoxious. Failure in maternality transformed tender approach into attack; failure to feel exuberant and proud of his phallic masculinity prompted him to act like a little boy in relation to women and like a woman in relation to his father. Finally, he was unable to stabilize the feelings which are normally governed by a stable superego.

By explaining to the patient the "one and only condition of the treatment," namely, the fundamental rule (saying everything, be it unpleasant, unimportant, irrelevant, or senseless), Freud helped the patient to become cognizant of his feelings. The patient's first communication was indeed full of precise descriptions of his feelings in relation to an older friend, the prototype of his analyst. Freud paid attention not only to his patient's affects, but was keenly aware of his own. He was astonished by the discovery that the Rat Man's father had died several years previously; he was taken aback by the patient's confession that his compulsive thought applied not only to his female friend but also to his father. At times he attempted to reassure and guide the patient by telling him about his own feelings.

The less the Rat Man used his affects for undistorted self-expression, the more he exploited them for defensive purposes. Out of the early form of affect manipulation there arose more complex defensive structures which, through incessant repetition, prevented the unfolding of mature adaptive patterns and learning.

Learning, Defenses, and Adaptation to External Forces

The newborn is incapable of actions. He responds to inner and outer stimuli by changes in tension and shape. Gradually the child learns to adapt to space, gravity, and time; in this process he adjusts his tension in such a way that his reality oriented goals can gain freedom from drive pressure. When interest in space, gravity (experienced as weight), and time is added to the regulation of tension (expressive of needs, drives and affects), the child becomes simultaneously oriented to the outside and the inside. He controls his tension in order to accomplish new tasks without fear. When actions are no longer defensive and learned skills have become automatized, movement patterns, called *efforts* (Laban 1947, 1960, Kestenberg 1975), are used in the service of adaptation without concern for bodily functions. Freud's patient referred to his explanations as similar to his own "efforts of thought." Freud's interpretations were indeed comparable to these modes of adaptation through movement. In contrast, the Rat Man's thoughts were comparable to *precursors of effort* which are used in defensive actions and in learning (Kestenberg 1967, 1975). According to Freud (1923) and Hartmann (1939), defenses operate with drive energy while adaptive ego functions avail themselves of neutral or neutralized energy. Since learning makes use of the same motor patterns as do early defenses, it is likely that learning through movement also operates with instinctual characteristics. While all efforts and their precursors are available in the first year of life, those that pertain to the *control of space*, are practiced more than others in the oral phase. To pay *attention* to the space around us, we can focus sharply, cutting directly through space or we pay heed to whatever passes by, approaching space through indirect routes (Table 3:1 and 2). Before we can pay attention in this manner, we use precursors of efforts to deal with space. Making sure that we do not steer off course, we keep our tension on an even keel to channel pathways in space or we make adjustments in the flow of tension to become flexible and pursue circuitous pathways (Table 2:1 and 2).

The Rat Man found it very difficult to pay attention to his studies and to his own thoughts. A glimpse at the map depicting the roads and locations pertaining to the patient's journey from the scene of military maneuvers to Vienna, reveals that his ideation and his actions followed the same pattern. He withdrew attention from the fact that he owed money to the post office clerk. Instead, he channeled his thoughts towards the fulfillment of his oath to pay Lieutenant A., and to this end he tried to learn his whereabouts. Freud suggested that he was attracted to the landlord's daughter as well as to the post office clerk at the location where he sought to find the lieutenant. Instead of acting in a forthright, direct manner, the Rat Man used channeling as a mode of isolation and for the purpose of learning the location of his creditor. Had he taken into consideration all the information given to him, he could have used an indirect route to make an appropriate selection for his travels. Instead, he squirmed, manipulated facts, and followed random associations, using a defensive flexibility which allowed him to avoid the truth rather than learn the facts.

It was impressive to perceive to what degree the Rat Man's isolation and avoidance mechanisms resembled the young infant's manner of learning orientation in space. At first, the infant hits and misses, then he watches his hand, then keeps it in even flow in preparation for channeling a pathway to the object (Piaget and Inhelder 1948, Kestenberg 1975). When he no longer needs to isolate one section of space from another in order not to miss, he ceases to pay attention to his hand and his arm automatically choses a direct route. The infant first readjusts his tension levels and avoids extraneous stimuli to make possible a flexible pursuit of a moving object before it vanishes from sight. When he no longer needs to avoid certain sections of space by adjusting his tension accordingly, he automatically moves in an indirect manner and his gaze shifts easily in circuitous pathways. The Rat Man seemed arrested in the process of learning orientation in space, using irrational isolation and avoidance to accomplish his goals without fear. Freud not only analyzed the patient's "protective measures" but he also fostered adaptive, secondary process thinking by giving him a model for attentive investigation and by encouraging him to heed memories of external events. So great was the Rat Man's need to revert to experimentation with space that he could not confine it to thought alone but had to roam about Freud's room as if he were still a toddler. Freud's interventions organized this endeavor into focusing on a clearly defined account of a childhood event. Kanzer (Part IV, Chapter 1) feels that the current interaction with the analyst should have received more direct focus before the patient's attention was directed to the infantile sources of transference. I am concerned with the fact that Freud consistently directed his investigation to the sources of irrational behavior. He helped convert infantile, repetitive defensive actions into current true efforts of thought (secondary process thinking).

Control of space, which underlies logical thinking (Piaget 1930), must develop at least to a rudimentary degree before the infant can appraise the impact of action upon external events. By incessant practicing designed to combat *gravity*, the toddler in the anal-sadistic phase becomes capable of *intentional* acts. As he learns to appraise his own weight and the weight of objects, he strains to pull himself up, becomes vehement, throws things down and uses his fingers gently to pick up small objects (Table 2:3 and 4). Eventually he becomes capable of using strength and lightness in a rudimentary way (Table 3:3 and 4). He becomes determined to do things his own way and he plays with commands and prohibitions, before he can internalize them.

The Rat Man seemed incapable of a strong conviction or action. He made up commands and prohibitions and acted out obedience and disobedience in a playful way, reminiscent of the toddler when he imitates his mother's disciplinary actions. His potential for a light approach to serious matters was revealed in his weaving jokes and word distortions into symptoms, but only towards the end of his treatment could he laugh when Freud interpreted this technique. Identifying with the aggressor (his father or mother), he became very intense and his movement and facial expression revealed vehemence rather than strength. He managed to become gentle in a reaction-formation against violence, but was not, at first, lighthearted like his father. He did not stabilize the ego functions which are derived from adaptation to gravity, such as evaluating the effect of force upon the environment, weighing the relative importance of issues, taking a stand or taking responsibility for one's convictions. Instead he retained the power struggle of the omnipotent toddler who has not yet learned to appraise himself realistically.

Freud not only analyzed the patient's identification with the aggressor and his reaction formations, he also described the "peculiar indeterminateness of all his remarks" (p. 167) and presented himself as model for developing strength. He actively sought to bring about a sense of conviction in the patient, which would be based on the patient's own working over the material he reclaimed from repression (p. 181). By using metaphors and telling stories, he also showed the patient how to attack problems lightly without forcing issues and winning of arguments. Sometimes Freud fell short of his own ideals, when he fed the patient intellectual information about psychoanalytic theory and even became argumentative himself (p. 179). What I am concerned with here is Freud's own sense of conviction which he conveyed to the patient and his consistent endeavor to help the patient develop an independent judgment.

Efforts dealing with space and weight establish a stability and dependability on the basis of which the child can begin to make changes in time. In the urethral phase, he is concerned with *decision-making* and in this process he learns to deal with *time*. One of the outstanding characteristics of the Rat Man was his indecision. Unable to time his actions by accelerating or decelerating (Table 3:5 and 6), he allowed thoughts to attack him when ideas "flashed through his mind" (Table 2:5). To avert their threat, he had to institute counterphobic measures which were equally sudden, or to undo dangerous decisions by hesitating (Table 2:5 and 6). Rushing around and dawdling, he acted like a two-year-old who runs away suddenly or hesitates to enter a room because he is shy of strangers. These defenses are created when the meaning of time is still rudimentary. The Rat Man seemed arrested in this type of learning and, within the context of his neurosis, was not able to cope on this level with time in a realistic fashion. Freud not only analyzed his counterphobic and delaying defenses, but through his own decisiveness, steered him towards the completion of learning so that he could deal with time realistically. Timely in his interpretations, Freud was able to postpone them when uncertain. When he did speak, his assurance contrasted with the Rat Man's excessive doubt. A notable exception was Freud's uncertainty and forgetfulness, "owing to complexes of my own."

In the inner-genital phase, the child frequently combines gentleness with hesitation, which gives a subtle quality to his reaction formations (Table 2:4 and 6). After an initial period of disequilibrium, he learns to accept explanations, assimilating and making deductions step-by-step. The outcome of this type of learning is the integration of relaxation and patience with reaction formations and delaying tactics on one hand and with lightness of spirit and ability to take time on the other. These principal ingredients of *maternality* were lacking in the Rat Man. Although he was capable of acting in a concerned, protective way, he could neither sustain these traits nor integrate them. His reaction formations suffered from an instability, characteristic of the early anal phase, and his aggressive type of defenses far outweighed his consideration for others. Freud gave free vent to his own maternality when he fed the hungry patient or praised him. By today's standards, these actions are not considered therapeutic, but a kindly, permissive, quasi-maternal attitude, as displayed by Freud, has remained the basic psychoanalytic stance.

In the phallic phase, the child learns in flashes and attacks problems with sudden fervor (Table 2:5). His sudden, gentle motions (Table 2:5 and 4) reinforce his denial, and his repression is modeled after sudden and vehement actions (Table 2:5 and 3). A preferred combination of acceleration and strength (Table 3:5 and 3), used for such tasks as hammering and punching, evolves from outbursts of intense feelings (Table 1:7 and 5). Trying to emulate the phallic characteristics of his father, the Rat Man responded to the ensuing castration fears by regressing to a cowardly, anal-sadistic feminine position. As a result, he would argue and submit, stand up and literally fall down in a delirious manner. Freud's *fatherly* attitude, which often backed his demands for performance without delay, may have accelerated and strengthened the patient's father-transference. However, it also laid the foundation for the analysis of excessive counterphobic and counteraggressive defenses, which had interfered with the internalization of reasonable commands and prohibitions. Their attenuation paved the way towards a mitigation of the patient's severe superego.

The latency child synthesizes precursors of effort into complex structures, which form the basis for his defense clusters and learning skills (Table 2). Differentiating sharply between clashing patterns, he can separate affective, defensive and adaptive functioning to conform to exigencies of reality (Kestenberg 1975). Upon entering latency, the Rat Man synthesized conflicts into symptoms and he was forever trying to differentiate between internal and external reality. Freud was able to analyze his conflicts by helping him to sever faulty connections and synthesize data according to their meaning. He accomplished this by giving direction to the therapeutic alliance that enabled him to lead the patient out of his intense transference-neurosis into remembering, working through and learning to adapt to reality.

Defenses, Object-Related Learning and the Building of Object Relationships

Making use of the intrinsic affinity of tension- and shape-flow patterns, body needs and drives are structured by corresponding modes of object seeking (A. Freud 1965). Defenses, which make learning possible, are given direction by centripetal and centrifugal motion-vectors that create two-way traffic between the self and the object. Adaptation to the forces of external reality is structured by more complex, multidimensional relationships. For instance, indirect attention is given scope for action when it can spread through a wide area of space in search of the moving and vanishing object (Table 3:2 and 2.2).

In the oral phase when the child practices the *channeling* of pathways in space, his task is accomplished in a conflict-free manner when he learns to reach horizontally *across the body*, past the midline (Table 2:1 and 1.1). His reaching arm becomes a bulwark for *isolation* from outside interference. When the Rat Man, in the transference, acted out the memory of being beaten by his father, "he behaved like someone in desperate terror trying to save himself from castigations of terrific violence; he would bury his face in his hands, cover his face with his arm . . .." His impulse to cut his throat was an idea modeled after "channeling and cutting across the body" (Table 2:1 and 1.1). Among its many determinants, it probably contained a defense against the impulse to attack the interfering old woman.

Flexible turns and twists of the body, often used in *avoidance* and escape combine with shifting *sideways* to become a model for distortions and displacements. An example for such a complex mechanism, derived from movement, is the Rat Man's distorted representation of the baby-penis as a rat, which he displaced from his own body to that of his lady or that of his father.

Channeling by barring access to the throat or chest are used in all direct methods of self-defense; flexible avoidance combines with displacement away from the body to learn how to bypass the opponent and thus have him suffer harm indirectly.

Many of the Rat Man's repetitious protective devices resembled the young child's first attempts to learn to communicate with his mother. This transaction is habitually performed in the horizontal plane, the table or feeding plane (Kestenberg et al. 1971). The baby's gaze shifts across the room and sideways as he channels pathways and flexibly avoids obstacles that hide his mother from view. Eventually, he learns not only to spot her in space, but also get hold of her *directly*, extending his arms and *enclosing* the space around her (Table 3:1 and 1.1). Holding her in space in that manner is a model for framing her image to keep it in his mind. Getting to her *indirectly* through *spreading* in space allows the baby to find his mother even though she is not in his direct line of vision (Table 3:2 and 2.2). Finding her becomes the model for remembering her image even though she is absent. After a while these patterns "enclosing directly" and "spreading indirectly" become means of *communication* in reality and in fantasy. The Rat Man seemed incapable of successful communication with his lady, Gisela, or with Freud. He was forever preoccupied with finding ways to reach Gisela, and he suffered in her absence like a small child, separated from his mother. His verbalizations were vague, sometimes unintelligible. Freud not only led him to the source of the imaginary obstacles he had put in his own way, he also taught him to speak directly to the point and to cover small areas of thought rather than pursue a "train of thought" which tormented him endlessly and clarified nothing. He not only traced his devious, repetitious displacements, but he also drew his *attention* to methods of *exploration,* which covered wide areas and came upon facts via indirect routes.

In the anal phase, children learn to use gentle motions with *upward* swings, such as are used for picking up lint or crumbs (Table 2:4 and 4.4). They combine *straining* or vehemence with *downward* motions to let themselves down from a standing position (Table 2:3 and 3.3). At the same time, upward movements give structure to the gentleness, used in *reaction formations* against impulsive or defensive vehemence, employed in actions, such as pushing or throwing down. Soon, looking up to find the mother's face and looking down to find the lower parts of her body become supplemented by *ascending* and *descending* in the vertical plane. When climbing up on one's mother and getting down from her lap give shape to light and strong efforts to possess and relinquish her, the vertical plane establishes itself as a vehicle for *confronting* the adult with the child's intent (Table 3:4 and 4.4; 3 and 3.3). Presenting what he thinks, making himself understood and understanding mother, enables him to erect permanent, stable self- and object-representations.

The stability of the Rat Man's relationships was undermined by oscillations. He developed an obsession for understanding, while at the same time no one could understand him. He picked up a stone on the road to protect his lady, but soon replaced one absurd action by another and returned the stone to its original site. Acting like a toddler who stoops to pick up, then throws the object aside and returns to play with it again, he used directions in a random fashion as he struggled to retain an intact image of his lady. His learning was severely disturbed since he had difficulties in coding and decoding structured messages. This pertained to his own and to Freud's explanations. Freud's stability and his capacity to structure his convictions and to discriminate between the relative importance of issues—in addition to his continuous efforts to shape clear images of the patient and his family—facilitated the Rat Man's transition from a playful use of defenses from the second year of life to the employment of harmonious sets of adaptive interpersonal methods of *explaining* and *understanding*.

During the urethral phase, children begin to draw appropriate conclusions from their understanding of relationships. Their many *sudden* moves *backwards* and their frequent *hesitations* to come *forward* (Table 2:5 and 5.5; 6 and 6.6) come at the peak of their rapprochement crisis (Mahler 1968, 1975), when they renew their efforts to separate from the mother. Backtracking to avert stumbling over obstacles and being uncertain about proceeding are used both for defenses and for learning. By the end of this phase, toddlers have learned to make decisions, on the basis of which they will *accelerate* when they *retreat* from an adversary and *decelerate* when they *advance* to meet a friend (Table 3:5 and 5.5; 6 and 6.6). They have grasped the rudiments of *operational* thinking and they realize or intuit that a slow escape is useless and that rushing a friend may alienate him. They have learned to coordinate their decisions and anticipations with patience versus impatience and with intrusiveness versus shyness (Table 2; Table 1). This enables them to retreat gracefully when mother leaves and to anticipate her return in relation to fixed events (after lunch or before breakfast).

During his obsessive acting out, the Rat Man was incapable of functioning operationally. Like a two-year-old he rushed ahead impatiently and backtracked, hesitating and relying on an ''adult'' to guide him. He seemed unable to anticipate other people's reactions, did not trust his own memory and did not draw conclusions from data available to him. Rejected by his cousin, Gisela, he would retreat and return to her in an oscillating fashion. Not until the end of his treatment did he decisively give up his plan to marry her. Freud's sense of time, coupled with his extraordinary capacity to *remember* and *anticipate*, helped his patient to assemble the events of his life in an orderly, meaningful sequence. Guided by Freud, the Rat Man began to perceive how the members of his family changed in time. He reinstated the severed connections between the past and the present and was eventually able to give up infantile wishes and make decisions from the vantage point of an adult self-representation.

During the inner-genital phase (Kestenberg 1975), the child deals with his internal genital impulses by externalizing them onto objects in the world. Reaching for them with upward and forward motions, he frequently manipulates them in a gentle and hesitating manner (Table 2: 4.4 and 6.6; 4 and 6). This helps him to build models, on the outside, of organs that he can neither see nor touch.

In this process he develops a double image of himself—as a baby and as a mother. His relationship to her is reflected in his frequent advancing and ascending to her (Table 3:6.6, and 4.4). Identifying with her goals and aspirations, he begins to incorporate the qualities of deceleration and light touch into his rudimentary ego-ideal of a benign mother (Table 3:6 and 4). Freud was able to integrate a light and leisurely approach with confronting the patient regarding his thoughts and actions. Looking up to and identifying with Freud, the patient developed a tolerance for infantile wishes and became a willing partner in the analytic process. Within this setting, Freud could analyze the meaning of the rat as a child, conceived and delivered by the Rat Man. Eventually, the patient was able to talk about his mother, as she was now and had been in the past.

In the phallic phase, denial and repression become coordinated with the negation of false, acceptance of new, and elimination of extraneous information, which are all necessary for systematic learning (Freud 1925). These are, at first, modeled after experiences of quick backtracking, looking upwards with glee or pushing down vehemently (Table 2:5 and 5.5; 4.4 and 4; 3:3 and 3). Under the guidance of his father, the phallic child mends his ways, asks many "whys," accepts or rejects explanations and confronts people with his flashing ideas (Table 3:6.6 or 5.5 and 3.3 with 5). Identifying with his father, he becomes convincing and makes decisions on the basis of past experiences. These qualities in the Rat Man were overshadowed by defensive doubts, rationalizations, and compulsions to understand. At the time, Freud felt an urgency to convince the patient of the validity of his new ideas. When he argued in this way, the Rat Man responded by explaining and arguing in a similar fashion. Excepting these occurrences, Freud could combine his ability to impart information in a decisive manner with his talent to connect the present with the past. Identifying with him, the patient became a more reliable and self-assured informant.

During latency, the child is engaged in practicing old ways to resolve conflicts; at the same time he learns many new ways to adapt. The shaping of his relationships is founded on his ability to move simultaneously in all directions and planes. A multidimensional, solid body image underlies the multifaceted network of affective, defensive and adaptive ego functions, which constitutes the core of the child's self-representation (Jacobson 1964). The Rat Man's self-appraisal and self-esteem were conflict-ridden and unrealistic. Freud's encouragement of self-analysis, combined with a reappraisal of family members, gave the patient a chance to revise his old and consolidate his new self- and object-representations.

Freud's capacity to adapt and relate was the mainstay of the therapeutic alliance with the patient. The change in the Rat Man's ego organization during treatment can be seen with greater clarity when it is viewed against the background of Freud's stable ego traits. This, in turn, permits us to scrutinize Freud's analytic work and select clues for the reconstruction of the Rat Man's neurosis as it evolved in successive developmental phases until it culminated in obsessive symptoms in latency.

Reconstruction of the Rat Man's Early Development

There are phases in development in which the child and his parents have a second chance to make up for previous failures and complete unfinished developmental tasks (Erikson 1959, Kestenberg et al. 1971, Kestenberg 1974). One of these is the inner-genital phase which starts with a disequilibrium and proceeds to a reintegration of conflicting and outmoded solutions of old and new conflicts. By creating a new baby—in fantasy—the child corrects all the errors of pregenital phases. It appears that the Rat Man did not have the opportunity to recuperate from pregenital traumatizations. He did attempt a phase-specific unification of pregenital and early genital trends by creating an imaginary baby. However, he was not able to rid this image of disturbing, sadistic features. Neither was he able to give up the baby and establish a transfer from the overvaluation of baby to a pride in the phallus. Freud did remark that the patient's rat complex disappeared after he understood the meaning of the rat as a baby. However, he did not connect the rat-baby to the patient's undescended testicle.

In the following reconstruction of the Rat Man's development, I shall link up clinical data with insights gained from looking at his ego organization through the eyes of a movement observer. I shall try to show that the Rat Man's inability to cope with his inner-genital defect prevented him from restructuring his pregenitally tinged ego organization and did not allow him to overcome the trauma of his sister's death.

In nineteenth century Vienna it was customary to employ a wet nurse, who was entirely devoted to the infant. Such a caretaker might have given the Rat Man the opportunity to form a good need-satisfying, symbiotic relationship and could have given him a good start for the subsequent phases of separation-individuation (Mahler 1968, Mahler et al. 1975). One gets the impression that, at the end of his first year, things changed. Perhaps it was difficult for him to merge the images of his nurse, sisters, grandmother, and the many nurses in the family with the image of his mother. No doubt, he was subjected to conflicting commands, prohibitions and sanctions since the time he embarked on practicing independent locomotion. Predisposed to a precocious motor agility and stimulated by his sisters, he must have become a continuous object of criticism.

Early creepers become disoriented in space and may not be able to find their way back to their mothers on whose laps they need to rest and refuel (Mahler and Furer 1963). With many people in the way, the spatial confusion is compounded and the child becomes especially vulnerable to object loss. Losing sight of a familiar person frequently leads from initial agitation to feeling dazed and unable to enjoy play.

One gains the impression that things were quite hectic in the Lorenz household, with sisters, nurses, maids, relatives, and parents picking the child up and shoving him out of the way, overstimulating him and abandoning him. When his mother became pregnant again and his father annoyed at the prospect of a new expenditure, they may have withdrawn their attention from the hitherto overvalued only son. Did he begin to feel then that "it was always the same with him; his fine and happy moments were always spoiled by something nasty"? Did he already feel flat and constricted and lose interest in paying attention and exploring without worry? Isolating and shielding himself, using avoidance and displacement as strategic defenses, and surreptitious learning methods were probably reinforced by early training, customary at the time. One can conjecture that, in trying to free himself from the confinement of the potty, he would fall down with the receptacle still attached, its contents dropping on his rear end. Were such mishaps the sources of later fantasies that fecal objects were moving and reentering the body?

At the end of the oral phase, self-expression becomes enriched by mimicking the facial mobility and intonations of caretaking adults. Attentive exploration becomes the basis of rudimentary communication by gestures and sounds. I imagine that, at that time, the little boy was forced to oscillate between mimicking one person after another. This could have overwhelmed and confused him, making it difficult for him to modulate his feelings. It is likely that his attention was frequently disrupted and his explorations put to an end by forceful removal.

Despite this gloomy picture of the end of his first and the beginning of his second year, there are indications that the little boy found means of ingratiating himself and avoiding punishment by making abundant use of derivatives of anal-erotic drives. Borrowing from observations of babies in that phase, one can picture him twisting, turning, and teasing, making his mother angry by biting her or wiggling out of her arms to reach something forbidden, dropping things and whining to get them back. He may have hit mother's face, poked her eyes, pinched her cheek, and pulled her hair. A teaser and a show-off, through his antics he could have made the adult's angry face change into a smiling or laughing one. Freud's vivid description of the Rat Man suggests that underneath his somber, tortured facade was an impish word-twister and subtle sleight-of-hand magician, who could make small things appear serious and big things funny. Thus, he could transform transgressions, usually frowned upon, into amusements for the adult. The adult who fell for it would support a rhythmic game of doing and undoing which prepared the ground for a rhythmic superego, easily bribed by silly behavior and word-twisters.

In the anal-sadistic phase, the unruly baby becomes transformed into a "horrible" toddler. Defending his right to self-determination, he commands obedience from his own body, from inanimate objects, and from people. He fights tiredness and tries to subdue the limpness or inertia that befalls him from sheer exhaustion. He gets up and falls, picks up things and throws them away violently. Some get lost or broken, some are removed by his mother. Infuriated by her "insubordination" and faithlessness when she pays attention to other people or leaves him, he screams or attacks her. When she admires him, he becomes gentle and looks up to her in counteradmiration. He brings her gifts and takes them away. Innumerable times he climbs up on her, demanding to be held or carried. Being down feels like being thrown down and a request to descend from a high place (like a window sill) gives rise to feelings and ideas such as the Rat Man's who "as he was standing on the edge of a steep precipice . . . suddenly received the command to jump over, which would have been a certain death." In his intensely revengeful fantasies the child makes his mother small and helpless and throws her down. He may want to soil or break her like one of the inanimate objects she had been trying to protect from his careless or reckless maneuvers. By the time he can express himself in words rather than actions, he may—like the Rat Man—furiously call his persecutor: "You lamp! You towel! You plate!" He may associate these germinal ideas with feces falling down the toilet and he may veer between identifying them with his mother and with himself.

Ordinarily, during the anal-sadistic phase, high tension states alternate with relief, and feeling small or put upon gives way to optimistic elation (Table 1:5 and 6; 5.5 and 6.6). Identification with the aggressor is mitigated by reaction formations, and violent struggles transform into a determination to convince—by showing and explaining—to understand and be understood. However, these ego gains undergo regression or distortion when the toddler's inner conflicts are intensified and made real by external struggles with his caretakers. Contending with a domineering mother who demands cleanliness, commands good behavior, prohibits bad actions and imposes severe sanctions, the child learns to project his forbidden wishes onto her.

At the height of his anal-sadistic phase, the Rat Man's mother delivered a baby boy, very likely with the assistance of Dr. P. It is not too far-fetched to assume that, in the little boy's mind, mother and doctor produced a dirty, mouselike (ratlike) fecal baby, and his father had to pay for it. At that time, the older child's reaction formations must have centered on remaining clean, on allowing the baby to survive instead of sending it back into the rectum, and thus transforming his retaliatory angry wishes into protective ones. At the same time, his curiosity must have been considerably aroused by the home delivery of the baby, from which he felt excluded. The exposure to his mother's smells and disgusting secretions must have increased his scopophilic anal impulses. As a result, his reaction formations were weakened and his adaptive functions invaded by an array of defenses which interfered with his efforts to understand and be understood.

Almost all the defenses of this period are played out in actions or action-words. A toddler will prepare himself to do something forbidden by shaking his head and saying "no-no," echoing his mother's intonation. He may repeat such actions over and over in an effort to convert a prohibition into a command. Play with sounds, derived from spitting, bubbling, eructation, flatus, etc., leads to alliteration. These word-defenses begin as jokes and become progressively more complicated as the child achieves greater efficiency with language. They become particularly pronounced during the inner-genital phase when play on words becomes the child's own creation. They come to a peak in early latency at the time when learning to read and write is drawn into the child's defense structure.

The Rat Man not only used word distortions like a toddler, but some of his compulsive acts seemed literally lifted from events that must have occurred in the second year of life. When he knocked his foot against a stone, lying on the road, he was obliged to put it out of the way to protect his cousin from harm. It soon occurred to him that the idea was absurd and he returned to put the stone back where he found it. This seems to be a replica of a daily nursery experience when the mother puts away a toy for fear that the child will trip over it. It is not uncommon for the child to retrieve the toy and put it right back where he can easily knock his foot against it and stumble. This is not only an act of defiance, but also part of an ongoing experimentation with losing, picking up, dropping, knocking, and throwing objects, falling over them and making them fall. Many provocative actions are used as means to find out or confirm what is forbidden. In his many symptomatic actions, the Rat Man was trying unsuccessfully to differentiate between good and evil, important and unimportant, his own wishes and commands from others, aggressive actions and loving concerns. He behaved as if he had never completed the goals of the anal-sadistic phase. It seems likely that he moved into subsequent developmental phases without a stabilization of affects that counteracts ambivalence, and without enough of a rudimentary differentiation between action and thought that makes a two-year-old capable of intentional role-playing without fear.

In transition from the anal-sadistic to the urethral phase, the toddler begins to mobilize himself so that he can start to operate on his own for much longer periods of time than he could before. He still needs a trusted adult to contain him at the end of his uncertain journey into the unknown. However, to learn the rudiments of timing and sequencing of actions (Table 3: 5 and 6; 5.5 and 6.6), he has to experiment without too much interference. Becoming a ''do it myself'' specialist, he runs off when he pleases and in the wrong direction, dawdles when called, becomes impatient and runs off again, overshooting his destination, or falling and wetting himself. While in the previous phase his experimentation could be distorted into a struggle for domination, at this time it can be hindered by a struggle for initiative. There is less opposition to ''what'' to do and much more to ''when'' to do it, in what sequence and direction. When an adult becomes his partner in the struggle for initiative, he unduly prolongs the period of learning to make simple rational decisions and to anticipate consequences of actions. Instead of learning to take turns and giving way to others, the child may want to be first in everything and do it faster than others without applying himself to the task or giving it sufficient time. Instead of learning to wait for his mother's return, he may not be able to separate from her without anger, sorrow, and regressive clinging, or by counterphobic rushing away from her before she leaves.

It seems that the Rat Man's urethral phase was, from the start, overladen with conflicts. Still envious of his baby brother and competitive with his sister Kathryn, he regressively intermingled oral and urethral as well as anal wishes and defenses against them. His dream about a herring stretching out from Freud's mother (his grandmother?) to Freud's wife's (his mother?) anus, was constructed in a manner familiar in the life of a two-year-old. Building bridges to people, he treats them like pull-toys which he can manipulate via visible connections. Herring as food, a smelly fecal object, and as a fish, living in water, holds a special fascination for him because of its amazing mobility. In his fantasy, the fish is a bridge between himself and his mother, his grandmother and his mother, leading back to himself. By pulling on grandmother, he can bring mother back (Kestenberg 1971). This idea presages the fantasy of the umbilical cord as a penis, belonging to mother and child. Through a confluence of urethral and inner-genital ideation, there emerges the little fish (sperm-Samen) swimming in the testicle which contains urine (Kestenberg 1968). In the Rat Man's dream-tooth, which dripped and looked like a bulb (orchid-testicle)—we find condensed the infant's feeling the tooth inside his gum and salivating, a two-year-old's hope that the absent testicle will descend like his molars did, and his fear that he will lose teeth (= testicles) like his sisters did in their latency.

In the third year of life, the Rat Man must have been preoccupied with the role of his absent testicle. Seeing and perhaps playing with Kathryn's genitals, comparing them with his own, looking at his mother's protruding abdomen and his father's big (and his brother's little) penis and scrotum must have aroused his curiosity and prompted him to link his observations to dribs and drabs of conversations. Very likely, the doctor and his parents talked about his undescended testicle and became concerned when no change was noted at the age of two. He must have understood that he had a defect, comparable to that of his sisters, but not the same. That he was different and no one could help him must have been a severe blow to his narcissism at a time when ambition and initiative to achieve are at their height.

By the time the Rat Man entered the inner-genital phase, his feeling of integrity, his capacity to work unassisted and to trust rather than doubt his love objects must have been already impaired.

Ordinarily a maternal ego is born in this phase, out of the matrix of memories of babyhood and consistent identification with the caretaker. The child searches in his own body for something he could make a child from, a child who would become a bridge to the beloved mother of his babyhood (Kestenberg 1971). The little boy associates babies with his testicles which, by virtue of their mobility, attain a quality of independent beings. He feels the mother's baby is really his. Earlier ideas of making a baby out of feces and urine were linked with things that were thrown out of the abdomen and disappeared. The idea of the inner-genital-baby grows out of sensations inside the pelvis and emerges in the form of a shaped object one can play with. A testicle that can be up by the groin and down at the bottom of the scrotum is shaped and tender, like a miniature baby. The child's pride in his generativity is one of the principal factors that gives its special features to new drive—and ego—integration. What began as exploration and curiosity about babies is transformed into a thirst for knowledge and a capacity for verbalization of new discoveries; determination leads to internalization, from which questions arise, reverberating into new thoughts, and initiative comes into the service of creativity, through which early fantasies of childbearing and later oedipal epics will be woven.

Unfortunately for the Rat Man, he had little chance to come under the spell of the inner-genital phase which would have helped him to become creative rather than obsessed with creation. His self-esteem shattered because of his testicular defect and his older sisters denying him the wish to be a mommy, he did not have a chance to become maternal without conflict. He turned his attention away from the front of his body and, regressively, hoped to create a dental-fecal-testicular baby. The gnawing, dirty rat-baby was in his own likeness, the image of a baby that would not come out of hiding.

The Rat Man's choice of an infertile woman as a love object resulted from the externalization of his feeling empty and defective (Bell 1964, Blos 1960).

This is a method of defense, used profusely by the three or four-year-old to combat the pregenital-early-genital disequilibrium. For the Rat Man, externalization did not suffice as an aid towards a new integration. He had to resort to pregenital, primarily anal-sadistic, forms of organization as he tried to form an intact body-image. The theme of the restoration of the missing testicle, to have two instead of one, reverberated through many of his compulsive constructions. He equated his testicles with fecal babies and with women. He was preoccupied with two women, one who prepared his food and one whom he wished to marry. He could not settle on one. The dream-herring connected two women: the mother = good egg h healthy testicle and the grandmother = dead egg = lost testicle. Freud's daughter cut the connection, aiding in the delivery of a healthy child = Freud's science, which cured the patient's infertility. The daughter, as evidence of Freud's fertility = healing powers, had two dung eyes = fecal testicles (Bell 1964). The Rat Man tried to integrate various body parts and functions to create an image of the inside of his body. Of the two rats (teeth, feces, urine), one (the inner testicle, equated with the unseen ovary) bored itself into a person's rectum. Once introduced into the body, the animals became the victim's own possessions which could be delivered at term. In all such constructions there was an attempt to create a unisex, with men able to bear and deliver babies like mother. One can imagine the little Rat Man standing up against his older sisters and trying to prove that he too "can be a mother."

The disequilibrium that ushers in the inner-genital phase reveals itself also through the invasion of pregenital components into language and thought. To the oro-anal play with sounds, is added the fluidity of urethral modes of expression, with words running together, making speech unintelligible or dysfluent. When the developmental tasks of achieving rudimentary forms of communicating, understanding, and operating have been completed in pregenital phases, the inner-genital child, guided by his mother, desexualizes and reintegrates the drive derivative components of speech and thought. The Rat Man behaved as if he were still in the midst of a disequilibrium from which he was trying to liberate himself. His obsessive play with words was an aborted communication which changed normal decoding into guesswork instead of an operational procedure. His reproaches and doubts about his recovery seem to have been based on a transference from his "syphilitic" father, who created his defect, and from the doctor, who promised a cure and did not keep his word. Oaths are derived from testimony, based on the idea that those who lie or do not keep their promises will have the testicle upon which they swore withered (Silving 1964). The Rat Man's oath that he must pay the wrong man—on the strength of the cruel captain's misinformation (lie?)—may well have been derived from thoughts about his own lies about masturbation. Perhaps he also anthropomorphized his healthy testicle as a "head-man" (literal translation of "Hauptmann," the German word for "captain") and blamed it for not instructing the other to take the "right" route into the scrotum. The chances are that he first masturbated in response to his sister's seductions, watching (in the mirror?) whether his one testicle will go up and then come down bringing the other with it (see the compulsion to leave the door open for his dead father [= procreator] to come back while he masturbated in front of a mirror. It is not uncommon for a three-year-old girl to look in the mirror, trying to see what she has below—an open door. Boys of this age become aware of the unseen "doors" they have in their groins and imagine that babies are delivered by this route. The Rat Man's doubt about the death of his father had, as one of its components, the eternal question of the cryptorchic child: "Is the hidden testicle dead?" It is noteworthy that his anagram "GLEJSAMEN" developed as a reaction to masturbation. In analyzing it he "deceived" Freud by not accounting for the letter "E" and the faintly present letter "I" (after the "J"). Together they spell "EI", the German word for "EGG" = testicle. Similarly, there was an error in the translation of "VIELKA" as "OLD," when in reality it means "BIG," referring to a female. The condensation "WLK" may have been derived from the Polish word *Wilk*, meaning *wolf*. Wolves were believed to steal human babies and care for them in the forest (Gesell 1940–1941). It brings to mind the possibility that the Rat Man, in competition with his mother and his big sister, had entertained the thought of stealing a child (Julie?) and bringing it up as his own baby-testicle. Loving children as he did and choosing an infertile girl as his prospective wife betrayed his persistent failure in identification with the preoedipal mother and his inability to resolve the problems of the inner-genital phase. Not until Freud accepted his "defect" without alarm and helped him understand the many "misalliances" he had constructed, was he able to get rid of his delirious disequilibrium and of his need to construct obsessive solutions to an insoluble problem.

Normally, the child ends this phase by denying his inner-genitalia and by denigrating his mother and babies. As a final act, he may "deliver" his imaginary baby with violence, thus expelling and "killing" what was inside of him. He transfers his interest from the inside to the outside and begins to overvalue his phallus, his own and his father's. The Rat Man's entry into the phallic phase was disturbed not only by his failure to achieve a normal integration between pregenital and early genital functions, but also by the circumstances of his older sister's illness and death. No doubt, he had not only had sexual encounters with Kathryn, but also had many times resented her superiority and wished her dead. As many children of his age are prone to do, he must have turned his sorrow at her death into its opposite. Thus, it struck him "as very comic" that he associated the letter "W" in "WLK" with a song sung by his sister: "In my heart there sits a big sorrow" (*Weh* in German). His guilt gave rise to ideas of dying instead of her. He must have entertained the thought that she was "pregnant" with the cancer that killed her. He toyed with the idea of introducing an orally-aggressive animal like a crab (the German word for "crab" is *Krebs* = cancer) into his own body. He veered between his murderous impulses against his father (= doctor) and his sister (= his cousin, Gisela). These were followed by thoughts of self-torture and suicide. As a result, his masturbation was fraught with fears of castration or death, enhancing negative-oedipal feelings and reviving his previous wish for a child. Diffuse pregenital regressions distorted his phallic conflict between masculinity and femininity into ambivalence towards father and mother and into doubt about his sexual identity. Masculine traits of determination and decisiveness, usually coupled with the ability to confront and anticipate (Table 3), were wanting. The synthetic function, usually operative in the early phallic phase, failed him. Instead, a repetitious questioning, reevaluating and wavering, characteristic of the anal-sadistic and urethral-sadistic phases, respectively, took over.

Normally, the later phallic phase brings on projection of repudiated wishes and incorporation of commands and prohibitions into the newly differentiated superego. From the identification with the aggressive father through sudden spurts of vehemence (Table 2), the child progresses to mastery over time and strength (Table 3). He becomes motivated to perform stunts, to do well in sports and at school, often under the tutelage of his father. From backstepping and cowering in fear, there develops a facility to escape danger or use these patterns as preparations for attack (Tables 2 and 3). The strength of impulses leads to strength of conviction and to high principles; the suddenness of their onset becomes a model for automatic decision-making (see epigenetic sequence in Table 3). The orderly progression of these ego functions is accomplished via the differentiation between right and wrong, with the superego taking over the punitive functions. The Rat Man never did complete the learning process that leads to the automatic evaluation and choice in everyday life. Consequently, his superego was distorted into a rhythmic structure which alternated permission with threat. Instead of identifying with his father and internalizing his commands, he primarily identified with his preoedipal, ambivalent mother and his sister Kathryn, whom he tried to revive.

In normal development, the regression in early latency (Bornstein 1951) provides a basis for the softening of superego demands and building new sublimations. Out of orality there develops the wish to incorporate wisdom, out of anality a good capacity to work, and out of urethrality the ambition to achieve. From inner-genitality there emerges the creative urge, and the intrusiveness of the phallic child is transformed into the capacity to penetrate deeply into the unknown. The latency child's good balance between synthesis and differentation (Kestenberg 1975) allows him to use complex clusters of ego functions all at once and break them down into discrete components when necessary.

The Rat Man's regression in early latency ushered in compulsive symptoms. His learning was impaired; he could not draw on earlier achievements to consolidate them on a higher level. His ability to communicate, to present his thoughts and to conclude operations in a logical way was severely disturbed. With his superego easily externalized and in need of reinternalization, he became overdependent on his mother. He went to her to complain about his erections, sensing the connection with his wish to see girls naked.

The Rat Man's curiosity did not sublimate into a wish to learn, and his quest for knowledge expressed itself in compulsive questioning, typical for the toddler who asks repetitiously: "What's this?" His lack of understanding was supported by weak repression which reinforced rather than diminished the compulsion to understand. This symptom constituted a variation of the morbid latency idea that his parents knew his thoughts because he had spoken them aloud without hearing them himself. Thus, what was hidden in him was revealed. The parents knew the whereabouts of his testicle despite his wish to conceal it. One can recognize here the derivation from overhearing parents speak about forbidden matters which—they assume—a child would not understand. Taunting parents for such an assumption by compulsive questioning or by feigning lack of knowledge is not uncommon for precocious toddlers. This is a typical example of regressive, retaliatory defensive behavior, which interferes with learning and counteracts internalization in latency.

The Rat Man's father scorned and ridiculed him because of his learning disturbance. The Rat Man thought his laziness would kill his father (p. 300). On the other hand, he equated learning with sexual transgression. He justified his wish to kill his father by blaming him for his sister's death. At the same time he connected his sexual exploration with her subsequent death. His guilt was perpetuated when he did with governesses and little girls what he had learned from Kathryn during his good moments with her. When, at the beginning of his adolescence his precarious defenses broke down, a new disequilibrium could not be met by a reintegration. In love with a little girl, he became obsessed with his father's death. Later his tutor disappointed him because he was interested in one of his sisters and had deceived him when he praised his talents. At the end of his adolescence, he consolidated his compulsive organization by falling in love with Gisela, a substitute for Kathryn, and by becoming again obsessed with his father's death. The disorganizing delirium came to a peak when, long after his father's death, he was returning from military service, free to resume his relation with his mother and his sister-substitute. More than ever did he revert to actions which helped him revive the time before Kathryn became ill and died. He looked to Freud as he had looked to his tutor, his older friends, and the father of his early childhood to help him restore to life his dead testicle and his dead sister.

Conclusions

In a previous paper (1966) I tried to show that obsessive thoughts betray their derivation from actions in the rhythm with which they operate. I postulated that the disintegration of personality, described by Freud as "delirium," seems to be the result of the breakdown of the fragile anal-genital integration, which the Rat Man instituted during his inner-genital phase.

In this paper, I presented the maturational sequence of ego-controlled movement-patterns serving affect regulation, learning and defenses, adaptation to reality and the building of relationships. I used them as aids in assessing the Rat Man's ego-organization, as it might have unfolded in successive developmental phases. I concluded that the Rat Man's affect control was alternately excessive and insufficient and that the exuberance and high spirits of the phallic phase must have bypassed him. His selective ego-regression prompted him to perpetuate early modes of learning. Endless attempts to restructure the ego and the superego through symptomatic acting out led him to literally lift childhood actions from the past into the present.

Freud's superb organization of thought and action provided a model for the reorganization of the Rat Man's ego. The analyst's adherence to the rules of space and time and his emphasis on acceptance of all matters as subject to analytic scrutiny, provide the analytic setting with a balance of stability and mobility. This balance is one of the ingredients that makes psychoanalysis different from other forms of therapy.

It is remarkable how one can trace tenets of psychoanalytic technique, now taken for granted, from the manner Freud addressed his patient, modeling for him the principal adaptive functions of the ego: attention, investigation and exploration; intentionality, determination, and confrontation; and decision-making, timing and anticipating (Lamb 1961, Ramsden 1973).

It is equally remarkable to see in Freud's analysis of the Rat Man how many mistakes can be made without endangering the analysis of a patient (Kanzer 1952, Langs 1976, Zetzel 1966). This is contingent on the analyst's capacity to observe the fundamental tenet that analysis be conducted within the framework of current reality, in which constancy of space, weight, and time is preserved and upheld by the analyst and the patient.

Trying to reconstruct the main trends in the Rat Man's life on the basis of developmental data—derived from movement studies—I got the impression that he might have had a chance to recover from pregenital traumata during the inner-genital phase that follows the pregenital phase and precedes the phallic (Kestenberg 1975). However, the new pregnancy of his mother and his inability to cope with his testicular defect did not allow for a successful reintegration of conflicting trends that usually ushers in the phallic phase. The illness and death of his older sister, Kathryn, reinforced his regressive ruminations about life and death, connected to his desire to revive the dead and give birth to a live baby-testicle. An anal-sadistic-genital organization led to an overemphasis of the negative aspects of the Oedipus complex and to the perpetuation of learning disturbances which became manifest in latency. The creation of the rat as a symbol for food = herring, feces = money, testicle = baby = woman and penis brought about a symptomatic reconciliation of various conflicting trends. The repetitive theme was the wish to recover his lost testicle = baby. The obsessive attempts to dedifferentiate its meaning reevoked old defenses and acting out, in which the most common denominator was the Rat Man's intense preoedipal identification with his pregnant mother and his deceased sister.

Addendum

Holland's (1975) paper about the Rat Man has come to my attention after the completion of mine. His findings prompt me to add this short note.

Trying to define the identity theme for the Rat Man, he characterized it as a "*need to control benevolent goings out and catastrophic comings in*" (italics mine), worked out in "myriads of details of behaviour." Without referring to it (or knowing it?) he postulated an all-encompassing struggle to undo the "catastrophic coming in" of the testicle and to bring about a "benevolent going out" (coming down) of the lost body part.

Using a developmental approach, which correlates nonverbal with verbal behavior, one can detect the contributions of each developmental phase in the evolution of a central theme. From the predominant organizers of a theme one can reconstruct the core problem of a neurosis without losing sight of its many determinants.

More than six decades ego, Freud outlined the core of the Rat Man's delirium as emerging from his wish for a child. A few days after the patient told him that all bad in his nature came from his mother's side, Freud introduced the theme of mother-transference by stating: "He has been able to identify himself with his mother in his behavior and treatment transference." The patient brought back an old dream: "His father had come back. He was not surprised at this [strength of wish]. He was immensely pleased. . . ." His mother reproached him for being away so long. The theme of the missing progenitor (father-testicle) emerged here in context with the patient's identification with his mother, who bore many babies despite the father's objections. Just two days later the patient wished death upon the ill Dr. P., the same physician who might have delivered all babies, but could not cure Kathryn and, no doubt, could not bring back the dead father and the missing testicle. All ideas converged upon the theme of illness, death, healing, and reviving, with the motor components of going and coming back giving structure to thoughts-efforts.

Table 1

Tension-Flow reflecting needs, drives and affects	*Shape-Flow* expressive of self-feelings, such as comfort-discomfort or attraction-repulsion to stimuli
Tension Qualities Intensity Factors	affine - related to	*Shape Qualities* Dimensional Factors

1) *Bound Flow* (Inhibition)	1.1) *Shrinking* (Discomfort, withdrawal)
2) *Free Flow* (Lack of restraint)	2.2) *Growing* (Comfort, approach)
3) *Even Level of Tension* (Indifference, sameness, poise, a.o.)	3.3) *Narrowing* (constriction, shying away)
4) *Adjustment of Tension Level* (Affect modulation)	4.4) *Widening* (Expansion, seeking)
5) *High Intensity of Tension* (Intensity of feeling)	5.5) *Shortening* (Becoming smaller, downcast)
6) *Low Intensity of Tension* (Low intensity of feeling)	6.6) *Lengthening* (Becoming bigger, elated)
7) *Abrupt Change of Tension* (Impulsivity)	7.7) *Hollowing* (Emptying, feeling rejected)
8) *Gradual Change of Tension* (Patience)	8.8) *Bulging* (Feeling full, satiated, gratified)
9) *Neutral Flow of Tension* (Loss of elasticity, deanimation, loss of distinctness of feeling)	9.9) *Neutral Shape* (Loss of plasticity, feeling and looking shapeless, losing structure)

Table 1. Tension and Affine Shape Qualities combine to give content and structure to *affects*. Lack of affinity between them connotes an intrasystemic conflict between feeling safe or afraid and feeling at ease or feeling malaise.

Table 2

Precursors of Effort Reflect modes of (a) defenses against drives and (b) learning modes	Affine Sets of Learning Patterns	*Directions in Space* Express modes of (a) defenses against objects and (b) object-related learning
1) *Channeling* = Keeping tension levels even to follow precise pathways in space Precursor of directness, used in isolating, disconnecting and learning to define	Learning to define issues and preventing distractions	1.1) *Moving Across the Body* in one direction of the *Horizontal Plane* Barring access to the body, preventing distractions
2) *Flexible* = Changing tension levels to move around in space Precursor of indirectness, used in twisting, avoiding and in learning by association	Learning by association and by generalization	2.2) *Moving Sideways* in one direction of the *Horizontal Plane* Displacing, eluding, generalizing
3) *Vehement or Straining* = Increasing tension to overcome difficulties in dealing with weight Precursor of strength, used in defensive attacks and in learning to conquer problems	Learning to attack problems through explanations	3.3) *Moving Downward* in one direction of the *Vertical Plane* Provoking, putting down learning to explain
4) *Gentle or Delicate* = Decreasing tension to feel confident in dealing with weight Precursor of lightness, used in reaction formation, appeasement and in learning without resistance	Learning with ease, seeking out explanations	4.4) *Moving Upward* in one direction of the *Vertical Plane* Looking up, trying to please, seeking guidance.
5) *Sudden* = Increasing or decreasing tension abruptly to beat time Precursor of acceleration, used for defensive rushing, for counterphobic defenses and in learning by sudden insight	Learning by illumination, derived from past events	5.5) *Moving Backward* in one direction of the *Sagittal Plane* Preparing to protect oneself, backtracking and remembering

6) *Hesitating* = Increasing or decreasing tension gradually to prolong time

Precursor of deceleration, used for defensive postponing, dawdling and in learning in a deliberate manner

Learning to make step by step deductions with proper sequencing and by anticipating consequences

6.6) *Moving Forward* in one direction of the *Sagittal Plane* Testing, initiating,

Table 2. Precursors of Effort and Shaping of Space in Directions combine to give structure to *defenses and to learning modes* with special reference to establishing and maintaining motor *contact with people and objects.* Lack of affinity between these patterns connotes intrasystemic conflicts between certain defenses, associated with learning and modes of attaining or relinquishing contact.

Table 3

Effort Reflects coping with the forces of external reality: space, weight and time	Affine Sets of Patterns	*Shaping* Expressive of multifaceted relationships of objects, which structure adaptation to reality
Space Effort:	Used in *communication and investigation*	*Shaping in the Horizontal Plane* (Aid to balance)
1) *Directness* (focused attention; to the point; discrimination; visual fixation)		1.1) *Enclosing* (exploration of small areas of space, especially in dyadic relationships and with stationary objects)
2) *Indirectness* (General attentiveness; alertness to changes; listening)		2.2) *Spreading* (exploration of large areas of space, especially in multiple relationships and with moving objects)
Weight Effort:	Used in *presentation, understanding and explanation*	*Shaping in the Vertical Plane* (Aid to stability)
3) *Strength* (intentionality; determination)		3.3) *Descending* (confronting people; demanding cooperation)

4) *Lightness* (intentionality; light touch; tact)

4.4) *Ascending* (confronting them with one's aspiration and looking up to theirs)

Shaping in the Sagittal Plane (Aid to mobility)

Time Effort: Used in *operations and procedures*

5) *Acceleration* (decision, unambiguous, without alternative)

5.5) *Retreating* (anticipating consequences on the basis of past experiences, also terminating)

6) *Deceleration* (decision with deliberation)

6.6) *Advancing* (anticipating consequences of actions, initiating)

Table 3. Efforts and Shaping Space in Planes combine to give the motor basis for *communication, presentation and operation* (Ramsden 1973). They mature at the same time as the cognitive structure which supports secondary process thinking, symbolization and deductive reasoning. Observers of young children often infer the existence of such precepts from motor behavior, conveyed through efforts and shaping. Lack of affinity between effort and shape connotes an intrasystemic conflict between coping with internal and external reality and relations to self and objects. There is an *epigenetic* sequence in the maturation of:

1) Tension-Flow   Rhythms (Table 1)
2) Precursors of Effort (Table 2)
3) Effort (this table) and

1.1) Shape-Flow Regulation (Table 1)
2.2) Directions in Space (Table 2)
3.3) Shaping in Planes (this table)

Clashes between 1, 2 and 3 reflect intersystemic conflicts between drives, defenses and reality testing.
Clashes between 1.1, 2.2 and 3.3 reflect intersystemic conflicts between self-feelings, object-directedness and multifaceted relationships.

REFERENCES

Balint, M. (1960). Primary narcissism and primary love. *Psychoanalytic Quarterly* 24: 6–43.

Bell, A. (1964). Bowel training difficulties in boys. *Journal of the American Psychoanalytic Association* 3:577–590.

Birdwhistell, J. (1970). *Kinesics and Context*. Philadelphia: University of Pennsylvania Press.

Blos, P. (1960). Comments on the psychological consequences of cryptorchism. *Psychoanalytic Study of the Child* 15:395–429.

Bornstein, B. (1951). On latency. *Psychoanalytic Study of the Child* 6:279–285.

Erikson, E. (1959). *Identity and the Life Cycle*. New York: International Universities Press.

Freud, A. (1965). *Normality and Pathology in Childhood: Assessment of Development*. New York: International Universities Press.

———— (1966). Obsessional neurosis: a summary of psychoanalytic views. Presented at Congress. *International Journal of Psycho-Analysis* 47:116–123.

Freud, S. (1909). Notes upon a case of obsessional neurosis. *Standard Edition* 10: 153–257.

———— (1923). The ego and the id. *Standard Edition* 19: 3–66.

———— (1925). Negation. *Standard Edition* 19: 235–239.

Gesell, A. (1940–1941). *Wolf Child and Human Child*. New York: Harper.

Glaser, V. (1970). Das Gamma-Nervenfaser System (GNS) als Psycho-Somatisches Bindeglied. *Atemschulung als Element der Psychotherapie*. Darmstadt: Wissenschaftliche Buchgesellschaft.

Hartmann, H. (1939). *Ego-Psychology and the Problem of Adaptation*. New York: International Universities Press, 1958.

Holland, N. N. (1975). An identity for the Rat Man. *International Review of Psycho-Analysis* 2: 157–169.

Jacobson, E. (1964). *The Self and the Object World*. New York: International Universities Press.

Kanzer, M. (1952). The transference neurosis of the Rat Man. *Psychoanalytic Quarterly* 21: 181–189.

———— (1966). The motor sphere of transference. *Psychoanalytic Quarterly* 35: 522–540.

———— (1976). Freud's "human influence" on the Rat Man. This volume, Part IV, Chapter 6.

Kestenberg, J. S. (1965, 1967a). *The Role of Movement Patterns in Development*. Reprinted from the *Psychoanalytic Quarterly* by the Dance Notation Bureau, N.Y., 1970.

———— (1966). Rhythm and organization in obsessive-compulsive development. *International Journal of Psycho-Analysis* 47: 151–159.

———— (1967b). Phases of adolescence. I. *Journal of the American Academy of Child Psychiatry* 6: 426–463.

———— (1968). Outside and inside, male and female. *Journal of the American Psychoanalytic Association* 16: 457–520.

———— (1971). From organ-object imagery to self and object representations. In *Separation-Individuation: Papers in Honor of Margaret S. Mahler.*, eds.

pp. 75–99. New York: International Universities Press. McDevitt and Settlage.
———— (1974). Child therapy, child analysis and prevention. Tape produced by
Psychotherapy Tape Library, N.Y.
———— (1975). *Children and Parents. Psychoanalytic Studies in Development.*
New York: Jason Aronson.
———— (1976). The role of the transitional object in the development of the
body image. In *Between Reality and Fantasy: Transitional Objects and Phe-
nomena,* eds. S. Grolnik and L. Barkin with W. Muensterberger. New York:
Jason Aronson.
Kestenberg, J. S., Marcus, H., Robbins, E., Berlow, J., and Buelte, A. (1971).
Development of the young child as expressed through bodily movement. I.
Journal of the American Psychoanalytic Association 19: 746–764.
Laban, R., and Lawrence, F. C. (1947). *Effort.* London: MacDonald and Evans.
Laban, R. (1960). *The Mastery of Movement.* 2nd ed., revised and enlarged by
L. Ulman. London: MacDonald and Evans.
Lamb, W. (1961). Correspondence course in movement assessment. *Unpub-
lished.*
Lamb, W. and Turner, D. (1969). *Management Behavior.* London: Duckworth.
Lewin, B. (1933). The body as a phallus. *Psychoanalytic Quarterly* 2: 24–27.
Mahler, M. (1968). *On Human Symbiosis and the Vicissitudes of Individuation.*
New York: International Universities Press.
———— (1971). A study of the separation-individuation process and its possible
application to borderline phenomena in the psychoanalytic situation. *Psy-
choanalytic Study of the Child* 26: 403–424. New York: Quadrangle.
Mahler, M., and Furer, M. (1963). Certain aspects of the individuation-sepa-
ration phase. *Psychoanalytic Quarterly* 24: 483–498.
Mahler, M., Pine, F. and Bergman, A. (1975). *The Psychological Birth of the
Human Infant.* New York: Basic Books.
Piaget, J. (1930). *The Child's Conception of Physical Causality.* New York:
Harcourt.
Piaget, J., and Inhelder, B. (1969). *The Psychology of the Child.* New York:
Basic Books.
Ramsden, P. (1973). *Top Team Planning.* New York: Wiley.
Schossberger, J. (1963). Deanimation, a study of the communication of the
meaning by transient expressive configuration. *Psychoanalytic Quarterly* 32:
479–532.
Silving, H. (1964). *The Oath. Essays on Criminal Procedure.* Buffalo: Dennis.
Shengold, L. (1967), The effect of overstimulation: rat-people. *International
Journal of Psycho-Analysis* 48: 403–415.

———— (1971). More about rats and rat people. *International Journal of Psycho-Analysis* 52: 277–289. This volume, Part IV, Chapter 3.

Spitz, R., and Wolff, K. M. (1946). Anaclitic depression: an inquiry into the genesis of psychiatric conditions in early childhood. *Psychoanalytic Study of the Child* 2: 313–342.

Zetzel, E. (1966). Additional notes upon a case of obsessional neurosis: Freud 1909. *International Journal of Psycho-Analysis* 47: 123–129.

Chapter 3

MORE ON RATS AND RAT PEOPLE

LEONARD SHENGOLD, M.D.

In a previous paper (Shengold 1967) I dealt with cannibalistic manifestations in adults who had undergone traumatic experiences as children—experiences that had resulted in ego regression and distortion, and in fixation on and regression to oral sadism and masochism. These manifestations include fears and wishes of being devoured associated with a particular vulnerability of the anal area; a characteristic "cannibalistic" rage associated with the overstimulated state; the tendency to seek repetition of overstimulating experiences—and the massive defensive efforts needed to deal with all these: pervasive and intense isolation (isolation that is associated with vertical ego splits); autohypnotic states; denial and lying; and the turning of impulses alternately upon others and upon the self. These people have a split superego serving the opposing needs to repeat and to be punished for the cannibalistic experiences. I call these patients "rat people" because, like Freud's Rat Man patient, they use the imago of rodents to carry connotations of overstimulation and cannibalism. I intend in this paper to explore rat symbolism, and to say something more about ego distortions in the "rat people."

Rats, Cannibalism and Overstimulation

I begin with a literary quotation which connects rats, oral sadism and overstimulation. It comes from *Torture Garden* by Octave Mirbeau, which I believe to be the source of the story that obsessed Freud's famous patient, the Rat Man (Freud 1909). This story was told the Rat Man by a sadistic army captain, who

> "had *read* [my italics] of a specially horrible punishment used in the East . . . the criminal was tied up . . . a pot was turned upside down on his buttocks . . . some *rats* were put into it . . . (the Rat Man is speaking and these hesitations are his) . . . and they . . ."—he got up again and was showing every sign of horror and resistance—"*bored their way in* . . ."—Into his anus, I [Freud] helped him out.

This remark of Freud's is cited by Kanzer (1952) as evidence of Freud's countertransference. The difficulty of saying "into his anus" is demonstrated by its not being specifically stated in the Mirbeau story either. I think this evasion marks the special resistance evoked by the cannibalistic "vulnerability" of the anal zone; it appears to be the principal site for the overwhelming stimulation (experienced as a being eaten into and a being eaten up) that can go on to ego dissolution.

Torture Garden was published in Paris in 1899, seven years before the Rat Man's encounter with the captain. During those years the book was widely read in Europe, having acquired a pornographic notoriety; it is, however, the work of a serious artist (Wilson 1950). The book has a climactic episode about a rat torture; the garden is in China, the torturer Chinese; and the heroine, Clara, obsessed by torture, asks him: "What is this torture of the rat? . . . Can you describe it to us?" (Note the hesitations that are so similar to the Rat Man's: these interstices are simultaneously attempts at isolation and a supplying of holes to be penetrated, i.e., "peristaltic language.")

> The Torturer answers, "You take a condemned man, charming lady . . . or anybody else . . . you take a man, as young and strong as possible, whose muscles are quite resistant; in virtue of this principle: the more strength, the more struggle—and the more struggle, the more pain! Good! I don't know if I'm making myself understood? Then in a big pot, whose bottom is pierced with a little hole . . . a flowerpot, milady . . . you place a very fat rat,*

---

*In the Rat Man's version (see below and Freud, 1909), the one rat becomes "some rats." We do not know if this is his distortion or the sadistic captain's. What does this multiplication mean? There are many possibilities: defensive (e.g., obfuscation) and revelatory (e.g., two as a female symbol), etc. One defensive meaning involves the keeping away from the *one* rat as the biting phallus. The Rat Man talks of both "the rat punishment" and the "punishment of the rats" but when the rat becomes singular it is clearly phallic: "when he was wishing Constanze the rats he felt *a rat* gnawing at his own anus and had a visual image of it" (Freud 1909).

whom it's wise to have deprived of nourishment for a couple of days, to
excite its ferocity. And this pot, inhabited by this rat, you apply hermetically,
like an enormous cupping-glass, to the back of the condemned by means of
stout thongs attached to a leather girdle about the loins. Ah ha! Now the plot
thickens!'' He looked maliciously at [her] out of corners of his lowered lids,
to judge the effect his words were producing. ''And then?'' said Clara simply.
''Then milady, you introduce into the little hole in the pot . . . guess what?''
The good fellow rubbed his hands, smiled horribly, and then continued: ''You
introduce an iron rod, heated red hot at the fire of a forge . . . and when the
iron rod is introduced, what happens? Ha Ha! Imagine what must happen,
milady.'' ''Oh, come on, you old gossip!'' . . . ''A little patience,
milady . . . Well, you introduce into the pot's hole, an iron rod, heated red
hot . . . the rat tries to escape the burning of the rod and its dazzling light.
It goes mad, cuts capers, leaps and bounds, crawls and gallops over the man's
flesh, which it first tickles and then tears with its nails, and bites with its
sharp teeth, seeking an exit through the torn and bleeding skin. But there is
no exit. During the first frenzied moments, the rat can find none. And the
iron rod, handled cleverly and slowly, still draws near the rat, threatens it,
scorches its fur. Its great merit lies in the fact that you must know how to
prolong this initial operation as much as possible, for the laws of physiology
teach us that there is nothing more horrible to the human flesh than the
combination of tickling and biting. It may even happen that the victim goes
mad from it. He howls and struggles; his body . . . heaves and contorts,
shaken by agonizing shudders. But his limbs are firmly held by the chains,
and the pot, by the thongs. And the movements of the condemned man only
augment the rat's fury, to which the intoxication of blood is often added. It's
sublime, milady. Finally, for I see you're anxious to know the climax of this
wonderful and jolly story; finally—threatened by the glowing rod and thanks
to the excitation of a few well chosen burns, the rat ends by finding an exit,
milady. Ah ha ha! . . . you see, I'm proud of the interest you take in my
torture. But wait! The rat penetrates the man's body, widening with claws
and teeth the opening he madly digs, as in the earth. And he croaks, stifled,
at the same time as the victim, who, after a half-hour of ineffable, incom-
parable torture, ends succumbing to a haemorrhage—when it isn't from too
much suffering or even the congestion caused by a frightful insanity. In all
cases, milady, and whatever the final cause of this death—you can be sure
it's extremely beautiful!''

The anal erotism and the oral sadistic libido that are associated with the
obsessions of the Rat Man are set forth here (The Rat Man told Freud of a dream

of his involving oriental torture which he had dreamt in 1906—before the meeting with Captain N.): also the connotations of overstimulation and cannibalism. First, the rat is overstimulated with the red-hot iron rod (the danger throughout is that of a penetrative invasion by a phallus equipped with flesh-eating power); the rat "goes mad" and tears and *bites* at the man's flesh, finally making a cannibalistic anal penetration after unbearably overstimulating the victim with the "prolonged" and "horrible . . . combination of tickling and biting." Both rat and victim are overstimulated and die. Both are helpless in the face of increasing torment. The basic story of the victim's being eaten and anally penetrated by the rat is also present in displacement in relation to the glowing rod and the rat (here as victim); symbolically, it is presented through the heated iron rod and the flowerpot with the hole in its bottom; in attenuation the theme is repeated by way of the Torturer's teasing method of telling his story to the enthralled, overexcited Clara.

The Rat as Carrier of the Tooth

The words *rat* and *rodent* originate in tooth-connoting concepts. They are derived from the Latin *rodere*: to gnaw, consume. Related roots are *radere* (Latin): to scratch, and *radona* (Sanskrit): tooth (*Webster's Unabridged*, 1960).

The rat imago appears as a leading motif in the study of oral sadistic and masochistic phenomena (*tooth* phenomena). Lewin (1950), referring to the regression seen in pharmacothymic stupors, writes: "The wish to be eaten sometimes makes its appearance starkly in the delirious hallucination of menacing animals, large and small." Rats are especially common in the hallucinations of DTs. The rat is a "tooth-carrier" endowed with the power to creep back and forth from level to level of libidinal development, from one erogenous zone to another, biting and being bitten. The rat is one of the most common of many imagos that are first of all cannibalistic: carriers of the destructive tooth. These include the natural wolf, snake, spider; and the monstrous sphinx, vampire, werewolf. These are biting, sucking, crunching, devouring creatures. "We get to look upon the child's fear of being devoured, or cut up, or torn to pieces . . . as a regular component of its mental life. And we know that the man-eating wolf . . . and all the evil monsters out of myths and fairy stories flourish and exert their unconscious influence in the phantasy of each individual child" (Klein 1933).

The rat is a very ancient animal. Remains of rats and men have been found together in fossils of the glacial period (Zinnser 1935). There are no references to rats as such in classical or biblical literature; the term for *mouse* was used to indicate both kinds of animal. Some patients make no differentiation between

mice and rats; more frequently, the mouse has more benevolent (or less destructive) connotations, e.g., its uses as a symbol of pubic hair and as a term of
affection in some languages. Most often, however, the mouse is rat-as-victim
(e.g. the Witch's song in Act III of Humperdinck's *Hänsel und Gretel*: "Kommt,
kleine Mäuslein, kommt in mein Häuslein." Also see clinical example (Patient
1 given later in this paper). The special designation for the rat was adopted in
European languages only after the great invasions from Asia by the black rat
in the twelfth and thirteenth centuries. The black rat probably exterminated the
prevailing indigenous rats and brought with it the devastating medieval plagues.
(*Encyclopaedia Britannica*, 1961, vol. 18). The brown rat, *Mus norvegicus*,
swept over Europe in the early eighteenth century and has in its turn killed off
the black rat in most parts of the world.

The resemblance between men and rats has often been pointed out, usually
in relation to a tribute to their similar intraspecific destructive competitiveness.
Lorenz (1966) indicates in rats "the collective aggression of one community
against another" as a model of what now threatens mankind. Both species
demonstrate intraspecific *murderous* aggression: "the gradual, relentless progressive extermination of the black rat by the brown has no parallel in nature
so close as that of the similar extermination of one race of man to another"
(Zinnser 1935). There are other similarities:

> The difficulties of combating the most successful biological opponent to man,
> the brown rat, lies chiefly in the fact that the rat operates basically with the
> same methods as those of man, by transmission of experience and its dissem-
> ination within the close community. [Lorenz 1966]

The rat is usually described in literature as evil, and is detested. It persecutes
and is persecuted, and evokes intense destructiveness. "Rats are, indeed," wrote
Charles Lamb, "the most despised and contemptible parts of God's earth. I
killed a rat the other day by punching him to pieces and I feel a weight of blood
on me to this hour." With a number of quotations, I want to illustrate how the
rat is connected with overstimulation and cannibalism.

The rat is destructive and voracious: "Ratborne diseases have resulted in the
deaths of more people during the last 5000 years than the combined casualties
of the wars taking place over those years" (Barker 1951). "Most rats kill birds
or animals for their flesh and blood; others simply have a lust for killing" (Mills
1959). "Their diet is omnivorous; they eat anything, including human
flesh . . . when driven by hunger they are so ravenous that neglected babies
have been killed and eaten by them . . . [There are] a few cases of able-bodied
men who have suffered a like fate when attacked by hordes of rats" (*Encyclopedia Americana*, 1957, vol. 23).

The rat is fecund so that if left unchecked it can overwhelm other species: "They bear, four or five times in the year, four to ten young, which can in turn breed in six months" (*Encyclopaedia Britannica*, 1961, vol. 18). "The terrible rate at which the rat increases explains the slow process of extermination, despite the vast sums expended. It has been calculated that two rats, if left unchecked, would in the course of three to four years multiply into 20 millions" (Protheroe 1940).

The rat is especially ferocious towards its own kind:

They change into horrible brutes as soon as they encounter members of any other society of their own species . . . What rats do when a member of a strange rat-clan enters their territory . . . is one of the most horrible and repulsive things which can be observed in animals . . . with their eyes bulging from their sockets, their hair standing on end, the rats set out on the rat hunt. They are so angry that if two of them meet they bite each other . . . (The strange rat) is slowly torn to pieces by its fellows. Only rarely does one see an animal in such desperation and panic, so conscious of the inevitability of a terrible death, as a rat which is about to be slain by rats. It ceases to defend itself. [Lorenz 1966]

(In this description of the "rat hunt" are found both the sadistic fury and the terrified masochistic submission that can be evoked by the rat.)

The rat, like all rodents, has amazing teeth: "[They] have a set of fierce looking gnawing teeth . . . [these] incisors sharpen themselves to chisel-like points as they are used. The owner rapidly grinds down these teeth with incessant gnawing, but they never wear out. A rodent's incisors continue to grow as the fingernails of people do" (Hegner 1942). "The rat's incisors grow at the rate of five inches a year" (Mills 1959).

The rat must use his teeth or they can cause his death:

Should a member of this group have the misfortune to break a chisel tooth, he is often doomed to death. The broken tooth fails to meet the tooth opposite; both teeth grow unhindered. Since they are no longer ground off against each other, they grow wildly, sometimes circling the victim's face, locking his jaws, and causing starvation. [Hegner 1942]

The rat is continuously teething: "The incisors grow, calcify and erupt continuously throughout the life of the animal" (Schour and Masser 1949).

The rat is a fit object on which to project cannibalism. It is particularly linked with anal erogeneity because of its association with dirt and disease. Man has had continually to deal with the rat because of its omnipresence, its destruc-

tiveness and its great fecundity that makes extermination necessary but ineffec-
tual. So the rat is both persecuting and persecuted. The problem of the continual
increase in the number of rats, emphasized by the historical invasions of rats
on a grand scale with accompanying cataclysmic deadly plagues, makes the rat
particularly suited to represent, by allusion, overstimulation (too-muchness).
And cannibalism is invoked. The linkage of rats, teeth and biting is evidenced
by folklore from all parts of the world. And in relation to the rat's remarkable
teeth, it may be said, paraphrasing Freud's dictum, that they must bite others
or they will literally bite themselves.

Meanings of The Rat to the Rat Man

The Rat Man came to Freud complaining about an obsession and compulsive
actions that had begun when he was on military maneuvers, after the sadistic
army Captain N. (who, in my opinion, had read Mirbeau's *Torture Garden*)
told him about the rat punishment and had also said something about paying
back money that was owed to a third person. The violent symptomatic reaction
that followed was analyzed by Freud:

> in the short interval between the captain's story and his request . . . to pay
> back the money, rats had acquired a series of symbolic meanings, to which,
> during the period that followed, fresh ones were continually being added

Rats, Freud says, are associated with anal eroticism. They are connected with
dirt (feces, money), infection (venereal disease), and with cruelty and sadism.
Rats mean teeth and biting (the Rat Man felt that a rat was feeding off his
father's corpse) and cannibalism. There is a condensation of meanings from the
oral-sadistic and anal-sadistic libidinal stages. Most "rat phenomena" of the
Rat Man (and of "rat people," for that matter) can be stratified in terms used
by Fliess (1956): the erogeneity involved is anal, but the libido is oral-sadistic.
This instinctual aim is destructive and ultimately cannibalistic; if turned against
the self, the aim is to be destroyed and eaten.

The rat was equated with the penis by the Rat Man, especially in relation to
anal intercourse (and sadistic intercourse). Here phallic power is equated with
cannibalistic penetration—the penis has teeth and can bite (e.g., rat = syphilis
that eats into the body). The rat as a phallic symbol is not only destructive (as
are such symbols as knife, spear, club, gun) in contrast to more benign phallic
symbols (stick, necktie, umbrella, balloon), but is specifically cannibalistic.

Rats can (like the penis: the "little one") represent children, but these are
dirty, biting, raging children. As vermin, rats can symbolize unwanted siblings

or unwanted children who evoke rage. As in *The Pied Piper of Hamelin*, or like Ibsen's poor unwanted *Little Eyolf* (1894)—crippled, like Oedipus, by his parents' selfishness. He is regarded by both parents as an unwelcome sibling rather than as their child. He bites at his parents' consciences and is finally lured to his death like a rat by the Rat wife, who had introduced herself prophetically by saying, "I humbly beg pardon—but are your worships troubled with any gnawing things in your house . . . for it would be such a pleasure to me to rid your worships' house of them." Many of the ambiguous meanings of the rat for the Rat Man can also be found in Ibsen's play.

The law of talion applies to rats—if they bite, they can be bitten: "But rats cannot be sharp-toothed, greedy, and dirty with impunity; they are cruelly persecuted and mercilessly put to death by men" (Freud 1909). If rat = penis, destructivity towards the rat involves castration. If rat = child, destructivity towards the rat involves murder.

I would like to stress the ubiquitous oral sadism and masochism in all these meanings that Freud and his patient found for rats: rats bite into the anus; the rat-penis has teeth; rat-children bite and are bitten. The basic fantasy of castration here is that involving the *biting off* of the penis; intercourse is a *biting into* the cloaca.

The rat can stand for subject or object, part-subject or part-object. The Rat Man, "a nasty little wretch who was apt to bite people when he was in a rage," was also subject to the rat: "He remembered being castigated by his father at age three to four because he has bitten someone" and this had been taken as a castration threat. The father, here the rat-persecutor, is—in the fantasies of the adult Rat Man—himself eaten by a rat. Father, mother, analyst could all be rats who could bite and be bitten. (Melanie Klein [1932] on children's terrors: "the real objects behind those imaginary terrifying figures (evoking cannibalism) are the child's own parents, and those dreadful shapes . . . reflect the features of its father and mother.")

Implicit in the clinical material and explicit in the rat torture is the association of overstimulation and rage with rats.

Ego Regressions in the Rat Man and in "Rat People"

Some of the regressive ego manifestations I have described in "rat people" (Shengold 1967; see also Shuren 1967) are demonstrated in Freud's Rat Man. Freud (1909) outlines the symptoms and defenses of obsessive-compulsive neurosis and their dynamic antecedents. I have written of the *intensity* and *massiveness* of the isolation needed by people who were seduced and beaten as children to split off and contain the impulses involved in, and the memories of,

their traumatic overstimulating experiences. In the Rat Man paper, Freud describes two kinds of isolation. There is disconnection between thought and
affect, which is one of the mechanisms involved in disconnection between idea
and idea. Freud says:

> Repression is effected not by means of amnesia but by a severance of causal
> connections brought about by a withdrawal of affect. These repressed con-
> nexions appear to persist *in some kind of shadowy form* . . . and they are thus
> transferred, in a process of projection, into the external world, where they
> bear witness to what has been effaced from consciousness [my italics].

The disconnection between thoughts can also be accomplished by "inserting a
time interval" between them (Freud 1909). Where such isolation is massive and
intense, as with "rat people," vertical splits occur in the mental apparatus,
making possible such phenomena as the Orwellian "double-think" that is con-
ditioned—again by rat torture—on to the victim-hero of *Nineteen Eighty-Four.*
Freud tells of the Rat Man:

> He then went on to say that he would like to speak of a criminal act, whose
> author he did not recognize as himself, though he quite clearly recollected
> committing it. He quoted a saying of Nietzsche's: " 'I did this,' says my
> Memory. 'I cannot have done this,' says my Pride and remains inexorable.
> In the end—Memory yields." [Freud 1909.] Orwell's description, in his novel
> *Nineteen Eighty-Four,* even includes the use of autohypnosis: "double-think:
> to know and not to know, to be conscious of complete truthfulness while
> telling carefully constructed lies, to hold simultaneously two opinions which
> cancelled out, knowing them to be contradictory and believing both . . . to
> forget whatever it is necessary to forget, then to draw it back into the memory
> again at the moment when it was needed, and then promptly to forget it again,
> and above all to apply the same process to the process itself . . . consciously
> to induce unconsciousness, and then once again to become unconscious of
> the act of hypnosis you had just performed."

However, the "yielding" for the Rat Man still leaves the memory in the "shadowy" form described by Freud above and he goes on to tell it to Freud. These
"shadowy" memories make for two kinds of knowing: "for he knows (things)
in that he has not forgotten them, but he does not know them in that he is
unaware of their significance." Economic considerations in relation to these
splits are conveyed by:

He could not help believing in the premonitory power of dreams, for he [the Rat Man] had several remarkable experiences to prove it. Consciously he does not really believe in it. (The two views exist side by side, *but the critical one is sterile.*) [My italics.]

Freud gives another example in his early work *Studies on Hysteria* (1893–1895), quoting the following dialogue between himself and his patient, Miss Lucy R. Freud had asked about her relationship with her employer (he knew, though she did not, that an incestuous attachment was involved):

> Freud: "But if you knew you loved your employer, why didn't you tell me?"
> Lucy R.: "I didn't know—or rather I didn't want to know. I wanted to drive it out of my mind and not think of it again, and latterly I believed I had succeeded."

In a footnote written apparently somewhat later, Freud adds,

> I have never managed to give a better description than this of the strange state of mind in which one knows and does not know of a thing at the same time. It is clearly impossible to understand it unless one has been in such a state oneself. [Freud 1894]

Freud goes on to tell about the "very remarkable experience of this sort" he once had, and ends with a memorable turn of phrase appropriate to Oedipus, the discoverer of the Oedipus complex, and to everyone:

> I was afflicted by that *blindness of the seeing eye* which is so astonishing in the attitude of mothers to their daughters, husbands to their wives and rulers to their favourites [my italics].

For Freud this was an occasional, an exceptional, experience, but for *rat people* it represents a kind of thinking that (as in Orwell's *Nineteen Eighty-Four*) can dominate their mind and their world. Orwell shows how "double-think" is aimed at the abolition of memories of the past.

By means of isolation and with the use of autohypnotic states involving alterations of consciousness (Breuer's "hypnoid states": see Fliess 1953, Dickes 1965, Shengold 1967), vertical splits in the ego take place—one major one is the split between the cognitive and the experiencing ego (see Shuren 1967, whose formulations are based on clinical material similar to mine). A functioning of the ego necessary for the subjective feeling of identity—the ability to feel what is there to be felt—is disrupted by this split; the personality is compartmentalized, not completely but in the "shadowy" fashion Freud mentions so that there are provisional and alternating personae that can take over with slight alterations of consciousness.* Freud describes the compartmentalization in the Rat Man twice. In the published case history he states his

> impression that he [the Rat Man] had, as it were, disintegrated into three personalities: into one unconscious personality, that is to say, and into two preconscious ones between which his consciousness could oscillate. His unconscious comprised those of his impulses which had been suppressed at an early age and which might be described as passionate and evil impulses. In his normal state he was kind, cheerful, and sensible—an enlightened and superior kind of person—while in his third psychological organization he paid homage to superstition and asceticism. Thus he was able to have two different creeds and two different outlooks upon life.

This is more succinctly put, without the topographical (here really descriptively used) explanation, in the case record not meant for publication: "He is made up of three personalities—one humorous and normal, another ascetic and religious and a third immoral and perverse." In my patients these "psychological organizations" (between which the patient can shift, thereby disrupting the ordinarily taken for granted consummation of feeling what is there—preconsciously—to be felt) are kept separated by "hypnoid states"—alterations of consciousness. For example, a patient says: "I know that I hate you and I want to bite off your penis but that part of me is wrapped in cellophane." When fully "awake" (the hypnotic wrapping dissolved), these feelings can be acknowledged—the patient can "know" she hates in the experiential sense of the word. When analysis works for these people, the autohypnotic (largely defensively used) symptomatology is given up and the synthetic function of a "knowing" ego is free to blend the disparate "personalities" and the contradictory trends.

---

*The complete absence of the split is seen, taking his statements in a reverse order, in Walt Whitman's affirmation of identity: "I am the Man; I suffered; I was there."

A Shakespearean Revenge Fantasy
of Cannibalistic Castration

A passage from *Macbeth* illustrates the universality of the rat meanings found in the Rat Man case.

The witches in *Macbeth* represent the bad primal parent (see Shengold 1963): mendacious, destructive and terrifying—a phylogenetic figure whose counterpart in present-day reality can be a psychotic or psychopathic parent who attacks his children. The witches are ambiguously sexed, though primarily feminine (like the Sphinx; see Shengold 1963). Banquo says to them, "You should be women, and yet your beards forbid me to interpret that you are so." These "weird sisters" are to lead Macbeth to his destruction as well as to his murderous career. Like the bad primal parent they are liars, luring Macbeth on with seemingly sure guarantees of his invincibility. Just before they meet Macbeth and Banquo at the beginning of the play, the first witch and her sisters come on stage. The first witch is in a rage of oral frustration:

> A sailor's wife had chestnuts in her lap
> And mounched and mounched and mounched.
> "Give me," quoth I.
> "Aroint thee witch!" the rump-fed ronyon cries.

"Rump-fed" shows that the witch's hunger is for flesh, not just for chestnuts, and that anal erogeneity is involved. The witch wants to use her teeth and "mounch" on the chestnuts in the lap (genital area) of the orally satisfied object. The witch goes on to her plan of revenge which involves a transformation into a cannibalistic castrating rat:

> Her husband's to Aleppo gone, master o' the *Tiger*
> But in a sieve I'll thither sail,
> And like a rat without a tail
> I'll do, and I'll do, and I'll do.

The thrice iterated "do" echoes the thrice iterated "mounched." The witch-as-rat will now castrate (the rat is castrated) with her teeth—first her vampire intent:

> I'll drain him dry as hay . . .
> Weary sev' night, nine times nine,
> Shall he dwindle, peak, and pine . . .

Finally the castration:

> Look what I have.
> 2nd Witch: Show me!
> 1st Witch: Here I have a pilot's thumb,
> Wracked as homeward he did come.

(I:iii:3–29)

Teeth and Teething

To investigate further the rat as tooth-carrier, I want to deal with some of the phenomena connected with teeth and teething. There is much folklore linking rats, mice and teeth—especially in relation to the losing of teeth. This will be presented below. I mention it here to underline the impact of the amazing teeth of the rodent on human psychology where these teeth figure as an element in the external world that is used to express what is going on in the body.

Abraham (1924), in describing the second oral stage of libido development, pointed out that the development of the teeth coincides with the influx of sadism that occurs during that stage.

Undoubtedly the teeth are the first instruments with which the child can do damage to the outer world. For they are already effective at a time when the hands can at most only assist their activity by seizing and keeping hold of the object . . . the teeth are the only organs (small children) possess that are sufficiently hard to be able to injure objects around them. One has only to look at children to see how intense the impulse to bite is. This is the stage in which the cannibalistic impulses predominate.

Abraham quotes a comment of van Ophuijsen's who believes "that certain neurotic phenomena are due to a regression to the age when teeth were being formed."

Subsequently, despite much that has been written on biting and oral sadism, the phenomenon of teething has been strangely neglected in psychoanalytic literature. Kucera's article (1959) is an exception. He points out that pleasure sucking is interfered with by teething, and that this intensifies the sadistic effect of the coming in of the teeth on the infant. He goes on to say that the "experience which is regularly provoked during teeth eruption can be looked upon as the key situation for the origin of primary masochism, as its physiological organic foundation." Without going into the moot questions of the existence and the origin of primary masochism, I want to deal with the *experience* of teething.

With the teeth painfully forcing their way through the mucosa of the gum, the infant can be said to bite himself (and experience being bitten) before he can bite anything else. Both during, and of course after, the eruption of the tooth, the infant bites himself. Tooth eruption produces the experience of being simultaneously the subject and the object of the biting for the owner of both the tooth and the surrounding mucosa. Of course, one cannot empathize with the child here since the ego at the time of teething is in a rudimentary state with incomplete differentiation of subject and object, of inside and outside. This differentiation is taking place during the oral sadistic phase of libido development. (Painful teething usually takes place between six months and a year and a half; however, teething accompanies all the stages of libido development: the last baby teeth to come in, the second molars, usually erupt in the first half of the third year. The permanent teeth begin to come in when the child is about six [Spock 1957].) During this phase the infant has to deal with an instinctual access of aggression which must be fused with libido. To deal with the frustration of need satisfaction and with overstimulation, a loving mother is needed to counteract the danger of a breakthrough of the stimulus barrier at the time of access of the aggressive instinct (see Hoffer 1950, Mahler 1952). Active discharge of the aggressive drive takes place by way of the teeth and the body musculature. Passive oral masochism is also experienced in the body (registering therefore in the forming body ego fundamental to the ego) in part by way of the teeth and their adjacent mucosa. It is probable that the phylogenetic significance of the tooth and of the teething experience is much greater than the ontogenetic. A look at animal life with evolution in mind, or at what Tennyson calls "Nature red in tooth and claw," tends to suggest this. The continuously teething rat also epitomizes a primal common ancestor for man. I do not know that child observers have sufficiently "looked at" teething. The change to tension and unpleasure of a hitherto predominantly pleasure-giving erogenous zone at a time when the ego is beginning to coalesce may be more significant than has been thought.

Cannibalistic Wishes, Infantile Experiences, and Teething

Teething might furnish an "ontogenetic root for the subjective reality of the cannibalistic act," the existence of which is questioned by Fliess (1956) who states that the second oral phase is the only phase of libido development where direct instinctual gratification is denied. Although the child does not discharge his oral impulses by eating the flesh from the breast, he does bite himself when he is teething, and the breast when he has teeth, at a time when "I am the breast—the breast is part of me" (Freud 1941). Lewin (1950) points out that the infant's wish to be devoured is not based on direct infant observation, but is "a heuristic fiction . . . a construction based on inference." Klein (1933) asserts that the fear of being eaten is *experienced* during the first year of life and that it is due to the projection of active oral-sadistic wishes on to the parent. Simmel (1944) speaks of cannibalistic fears and wishes as associated with the infant's identification with food. The food that is incorporated becomes a part of the baby's ego, becomes a part of the baby, and the baby "might be considered as eating himself." Autocannibalism, then, stems from the time that the mother's breast is still regarded as part of the body ego of the child. About the baby at the breast during this period, alternately chewing at his fingers and toes, Lewin (1950) states: "one may say, with license, that it indulges thereby in an act of autocannibalism." I would ask the same license for my formulation of teething as involving autocannibalism which supplements rather than supplants the other constructions.

Teething as a Physiological Prototype of Projection

Teething also provides an experience of *discharge* of painful tension in the infant's first year (with an experiencing ego present):

> Fell sorrow's tooth doth never rankle more
> Than when it bites but lanceth not the sore
>
> *(Richard II*, I, iii, 301–2)

says Shakespeare. But when the tooth actually breaks through the mucosa of the gum, tension is discharged and the "sore" is "lanced."* Perhaps this conditions some of the fantasies of explosive cannibalistic penetration, passive and active, that one gets from patients who have undergone experiences of overstimulation and, compulsively and repetitively, crave for a discharge of tension as if they were addicts—any kind of destructive penetration is sought out as a means of getting rid of the overstimulation.

At any rate, the infant can—*after* tooth eruption—bite others as well as bite himself. Aggression can be turned outwards, and also projected on to the en-

---

*There is at least one instance in literature in which rats deliver the victim from a traumatic and unendurable situation (= discharge of tension): rats bite through the ropes to release the prisoner in Poe's story, "The Pit and the Pendulum." I am grateful to Dr. Mark Kanzer for pointing this out to me. For clinical material illustrating the craving of penetration to discharge the overstimulated state ("Fuck me to death!" one patient cried), see Shengold (1967).

vironment so that a tension felt "within" becomes "without"; the eruption of the tooth acts like a material projection onto the environment. The tooth cannot only be used against others, but others can be endowed with it. Freud (1920) says about internal stimuli (like the drive representatives of oral masochism),

> there is a tendency to treat them as though they were acting, not from the inside, but from the outside, so that it may be possible to bring the shield against stimuli into operation as a means of defense against them. This is the origin of projection . . .

The eruption of teeth can be seen as an experience that helps bring this about.

Teeth and Castration Anxiety

There is much in the psychoanalytic literature about teeth and the phallic phase of libido development (e.g., tooth dreams referring to masturbation). These "teeth phenomena" usually involve the falling out of the teeth rather than their eruption, and they invoke castration anxiety. I believe that it is because teeth can also connote the terror of passive masochistic annihilation that they can evoke the "surprising, strong resistance" pointed out by Freud (1900). The resistance is in part ascribable to castration anxiety, but in addition the resistance relates to the intrapsychic phenomena connected with the "tooth experience" earlier than the falling out of teeth: the biting and being bitten associated with the eruption of teeth. The two can coalesce; e.g., Fliess (1956) wonders "whether castration is not in the last analysis conceived of as effected through biting?"

The phenomena related to teething have also been surrounded by a "surprising, strong resistance," and not only by psychoanalysts whose very few contributions I have already mentioned. The fact of physiologically painful teething, familiar to any parent, has been minimized and even denied by generations of dentists and pediatricians (cf. Kucera 1959).

The Object Endowed with a Tooth

Fliess (1956) has pointed out how oral sadistic libido is regularly discharged in subsequent stages of libido development in situations both normal and pathological, so that any erogenic zone can be infused with cannibalistic libido. Any combination of sudden access of defused aggression and an ego regression, involving an impending loss of control of the instinctual access, means, if it goes far enough, a return to traumatic passive cannibalistic terror. In relation to the anal stage, for example, the Rat Man's terror concerns the rat *biting* its way into his body through his anus. The rat's many meanings for the Rat Man have been reviewed; it is above all the carrier of the tooth and thereby gains its full terrifying power. In dealing with another symbol that can be endowed with a tooth, the spider, Abraham (1922) (without stating that he does so) stratifies the meanings of a spider—with each added statement bringing in more terrifying connotations. The spider symbolizes the destructive phallic mother. It also symbolizes her destructive phallus, which can castrate. Abraham then quotes Nunberg, who states that the spider sucks blood, and finally quotes Freud, who adds that the female spider devours her mate—eats cannibalistically and thereby castrates by biting. The symbol for the phallic mother becomes terrifying when the phallus is endowed with teeth that can castrate and devour.

The tooth equips, accompanies, and is the prototype for penetrative, devouring objects at any stage of libidinal development, involving any erogeneity that discharges oral sadistic libido. Differentiated objects that can be tooth-carriers are: the penetrative, castrating phallus of the parent (father or phallic mother); the fecal mass of the second anal stage that is clearly "not-me." The fecal stick that is "me: not-me"; and the breast-mouth are the earlier subject and/or object that can be charged with cannibalistic libido. So both subject and object are equippable with teeth. This involves erogenous zones, partial object and subject: fantasies of the breast with teeth, vagina dentata, rectum dentata, urethra dentata (Keiser 1954), phallus equipped with a mouth (Fliess 1956). Fliess states: "the mouth of this stage (second oral stage) is transferable on to all subsequent dominant erogenic zones." Subject, object and erogenous zone can all be represented by cannibalistic creatures like the rat which will appear, in analysis, in the associations of patients who have had traumatic overstimulating experiences.

Material from Myths and Folklore Illustrating
the Endowment of Objects with a Tooth

The following myths about mice and rats demonstrate the connection between the projection of cannibalistic aggression and the teeth. I quote from Frazer (1890) on "contagious magic":

Thus in many parts of the world it is customary to put extracted teeth in some place where they will be found by *a mouse or a rat*, in the hope that through the sympathy which continues to exist between them and their former owner, his other teeth may acquire the same firmness and excellence as the teeth of these rodents. In Germany it is said to be almost a universal maxim that when

you have a tooth taken out, you should insert it in a *mouse's hole*. To do so
with a child's milk tooth . . . will prevent the child from having toothache
[my italics].

Lewis (1958) quotes folklore about the loss of teeth and mice and rats from
Russia, Germany, Costa Rica, Oceania and from Polish Jews. Frazer has examples from Jews, Germans, Singhalese and Americans.

In this folklore the tooth is projected upon the rodent (literally), as in earlier
development aggression is projected upon the mother to form the bad mother
and the bad "not-me." To put it genetically, the breast is endowed with teeth:
this is the basic meaning of the rat (into whose hole the lost tooth is to be put).
The bad toothed breast is a projected part of the self at first, invested with
narcissistic libido—part-self, part-object. After the establishment of object relations and a sense of self, the fear of being eaten and the sources of overstimulation are felt clearly as coming from the outside. This is eventually evidenced
by the castration fear of the oedipal period which is, in regressive terms, so
involved in these myths about losing teeth. The parent will not castrate the child
if he loses, or has knocked out (as in puberty initiation rites), the penetrative
tooth that symbolizes the penis. At a more regressive level, these myths are
about not biting so as not to be bitten: The rat, not me, has the tooth.

Clinical Illustrations

The rat imago is used by patients who have been and continue to be overstimulated: beside themselves with rage; longing for a discharge to escape the
traumatic state of too-muchness. I have described the concomitant ego and
superego regressions. I want to add to previously published descriptions (Shengold 1967) one literary and two short clinical examples.

A reading of Dostoyevski's *Notes from Underground* is to the point. The
Underground Man characterizes himself repeatedly as a "mouse" (he is predominantly masochistic), who lives in a rat hole-cloaca "underground." He
gnashes his teeth, longs to bite; he suffers from toothache and finally enjoys it.
He vents and courts spite: "There in its nasty, stinking underground home our
insulted, crushed and ridiculed mouse promptly becomes absorbed in cold,
malignant and, above all, everlasting spite." We see the vertical ego splits at
work and at war in the Underground Man:

When petitioners would come to me . . . I used to grind my teeth at them,
and felt intense enjoyment when I succeeded in making anybody unhappy.

[He then says that he is conscious of not really being a spiteful man and that he wants to be loved.] I was lying when I said just now that I was a spiteful official. I was lying from spite. I was simply amusing myself with the petitioners . . . and in reality I never would become spiteful. I was conscious every moment in myself of many, very many elements absolutely opposite to that. I felt them positively swarming in myself, these opposite elements. . . .

The concomitant lack of identity and inability to love (like all "rat people") are set forth:

Even in my underground dreams I did not imagine love except as a struggle. I began it always with hatred and ended it with moral subjugation, and afterwards I never knew what to do with the subjugated object.

The poor Underground Man is himself predominantly the Mouse, "the subjugated object," although he confesses how he tormented and rejected the mousy young girl Liza after getting her to love him.

Patient 1

A young woman came to analysis complaining of pervasive feelings of worthlessness based on her reaction to what she called her "bad" sexual impulses which were sadomasochistic and accompanied by great anger. These sexual impulses were ruthlessly suppressed in action, but at times the excitement was overwhelming and she felt compelled to masturbate. Her rage was rarely experienced although she was almost always aware it was there (the knowing and not knowing of the Rat Man). The rage would usually get discharged (and could be felt) against herself; she could act the role of a martyr and provoked people to treat her as one. Although her cruel impulses were conscious and were manifestly sexual in her masturbatory fantasies, they had no real significance for her. They were divided off from her "official" personality; she was generally regarded, and with good reason, as a gentle and kind person (cf. the Rat Man). But when subject to rage and sexual excitement, she would go into an autohypnotic state and often would provoke something to happen. Sometimes she took a masochistic role, as when she "found herself" inviting a strange and suspicious looking man into her apartment simply because he had rung the bell. Sometimes she would do something sadistic, but it was almost always disguised. In the analysis she was continually inviting and expecting rage and sexual attack but this was blocked off from her responsible awareness by her hypnoid states; what happened when she was "wrapped in cotton wool," as she put it, did not count. It became clear that she wanted to be raped in her altered state of consciousness. This meant wishing a repetition of experiences from childhood with her sadistic and seductive father. The alterations of consciousness effectively deprived her of identity when she was the subject of her repeated overstimulated states. As the analysis proceeded and began to clarify this, she talked of herself as two personalities (as with the Rat Man these were in addition to her usual personality), which she called The Rat and The Mouse. To be The Mouse meant to be the little girl victim of her cruel father. As the Mouse she craved to have something violent and sexual done to her to end the traumatic overexcitement and provide a discharge. Her Rat personality was especially disowned; as the Rat she was aware of the wish to bite and to revenge herself—specifically she wanted to castrate by biting: to bite off the penis of the person who was over-stimulating her. One day she talked of her excitement on reading Marlowe's *Edward II*, a play about a homosexual king who is killed by having a red-hot poker shoved up his anus. She wanted this done to herself, she wanted to do it to the analyst. In the Edward II story are some of the elements of the rat torture of *Torture Garden*: the red-hot poker, the anal penetration that kills. The rat was present in the patient's identification of herself as The Rat—the possessor of the cannibalistic penetrative "toothed" penis that is seen as having the power to discharge the overstimulated condition. As a child she had many times sat on her father's lap and felt his erection. She was compelled to repeat this—to crave both to be the victim (the Mouse) and also to reverse roles—to become "The Rat" and do it to "the king."

In subsequent analytic work the patient was able to feel fully, to remember fully and then to integrate the Mouse and Rat personae and thus undo their power.

Patient 2

A young Jewish man tells his analyst that when he was in the waiting room, he had walked to the window. Another patient, a woman, was then behind him; he had wanted to stare at her but had refrained. (It had been established many times that women in the waiting room were incestuous objects, belonging to the analyst.) As he looked out of the window far down at the street below, the patient had had the fantasy that the woman behind him would say, "Don't jump—fall!" As he reported this, he felt that it was a kind of joke, but not a funny joke. Actually he had had a momentary impulse to jump. He then went into a resistant autohypnotic state, almost falling asleep. He "woke up" with the following: "I suddenly think of a story I read. It was about one of Freud's patients he called the Rat Man. Hungarians or Ukrainians put some rats upside down on his buttocks . . . God . . . how cruel. But . . . but the story . . . excited me (he reproduces the pauses of the Rat Man). I felt that maybe if I could get away with it, I would do it." At this point in the analysis the patient had not acknowledged his own predominantly passive anal cravings. Although the ambiguity of "I would do it" allows for an expression of his being the rat-victim, he consciously meant that he would like to give the rat-treatment to someone else. But it had been the woman *behind* him in the waiting room that he had fantasied wanting him to fall (= to become a woman), and it was the arousal of anal excitement with the fantasy of a destructive penetration that had brought on his hypnosis.

The patient had distorted the "Oriental torture" mentioned in the Rat Man case and connected it to Eastern Europe—to the Hungarians and Ukrainians that were his own ancestors. He associated to Hungarians and Ukrainians as being anti-Semitic; they would do things to Jews like him. But he himself had a Hungarian name, and was a Jewish anti-Semite. The hated analyst (who is "behind him") is also Jewish. The anal erogeneity is associated with active and passive sadistic wishes. The patient went on to talk of his childhood traumatic experiences as the recipient of his mother's enemas.

His being at once a Jew and an anti-Semite was typical of the splits in this man's personality. He, like Patient 1, was generally regarded (and thought of himself) as a kind and good-natured fellow. He too was subject to altered states of consciousness which defended him against the acknowledgement of his wishes and body feelings, while allowing for the repetitions of the past experiences on which these were based. He too performed and suffered cruelties that he refused to recognize.

One day, a high point in the analysis, he had felt great anger towards me and this was accompanied by fully acknowledged anal excitement. The next day he came in disturbed and hypnotic; with no mention of the previous session he went on to talk of his anger towards the whole world. His hypnoid state deepened and he actually went to sleep and had a dream on the couch: he dreamt that his mother-in-law was standing beside him. He woke, told me the dream and became very upset at the continuing hypnosis and "sleepiness." Then he said: "Now I remember yesterday's session, but it's so vague. The man who had those feelings in his anus is someone else." Later in the session, following long silences, I asked him about his dream: "What comes to mind in relation to your mother-in-law?" "What dream? What mother-in-law?" he asked in consternation. He had completely suppressed the dream of ten minutes before. As he remembered it he said poignantly, "My God! how bizarre! I'm not a person. I live in pieces."

Summary

I have reviewed some of the meanings of the rat imago for patients who have been seduced and traumatized as children. The rat is used as a hallmark for active and passive cannibalistic impulses, chiefly associated with anal erogeneity. I have stressed the importance of the tooth as the primal aggressive tool and speculated about the significance of teething. Some of the ego pathology of "rat people" was described and exemplified, especially their extensive use of alterations of consciousness that makes possible vertical ego splits consisting of unacknowledged but powerful "personalities" that appear and disappear. These people operate under the sway of the compulsion to repeat past traumata whose central content appears to be overstimulation.

References

Abraham, K. (1922. The spider as a dream symbol. In *Selected Papers*. London: Hogarth Press, 1949.
———— (1924). The development of the libido. In *Selected Papers*. London: Hogarth Press, 1949.
Barker, W. (1951). *Familiar Animals of America*. New York: Harper.
Dickes, R. (1965). The defensive function of an altered state of consciousness: a hypnoid state. *Journal of the American Psychoanalytic Association* 13: 365–403.
Fliess, R. (1953). The hypnotic evasion. *Psychoanalytic Quarterly* 22: 497–511.
———— (1956). *Erogeneity and Libido*. New York: International Universities Press.
Frazer, J. G. (1890). *The New Golden Bough*, ed. Gaster. New York: Criterion, 1959.
Freud, S. (1893–1895). Studies on hysteria. *Standard Edition* 2.
———— (1900). The interpretation of dreams. *Standard Edition* 4/5.
———— (1909). Notes upon a case of obsessional neurosis. *Standard Edition* 10: 55–318.
———— (1920). Beyond the pleasure principle. *Standard Edition* 18: 7–64.
———— (1941). Schriften aus dem Nachlass. *G.W.* 17.
Hegner, R. (1942). *A Parade of Familiar Animals*. New York: Macmillan.
Hoffer, W. (1950). Oral aggressiveness and ego development. *International Journal of Psycho-Analysis* 31: 156–160.

Kanzer, M. (1952). The transference neurosis of the Rat Man. *Psychoanalytic Quarterly* 21: 181–189.

Keiser, S. (1954). Orality displaced to the urethra. *Journal of the American Psychoanalytic Association* 2: 263–279.

Klein, M. (1932). *The Psychoanalysis of Children*. London: Hogarth Press, 1949.

——— (1933). Early development of conscience in the child. *Contributions to Psycho-Analysis*. London: Hogarth Press, 1948.

Kucera, O. (1959). On teething. *Journal of the American Psychoanalytic Association* 7:284–291.

Lamb, C. (1799). *Selected Letters*, ed. Matthews. New York: Farrar, Straus, 1956.

Lewin, B. D. (1950). *The Psychoanalysis of Elation*. New York: Norton.

Lewis, H. A. (1958). The effect of shedding the first deciduous tooth upon the passing of the oedipus complex of the male. *Journal of the American Psychoanalytic Association* 6: 5–37.

Lorenz, K. (1966). *On Aggression*. New York: Harcourt, Brace.

Mahler, M. S. (1952). On child psychosis and schizophrenia. *Psychoanalytic Study of the Child* 7: 286–305.

Mills, E. (1959). Rats, let's get rid of them. (U.S. Dept. of Interior circular, no. 22.)

Mirbeau, O. (1899). *Torture Garden*. New York: Citadel Press, 1948.

Protheroe, E. (1940). *New Illustrated Natural History of the World*. New York: Garden City Press.

Schour, I. and Masser, M. (1949). The teeth. In *The Rat in Laboratory Investigation*, ed. E. J. Farris and J. Q. Griffith. Philadelphia: Lippincott.

Shengold, L. (1963). The parent as sphinx. *Journal of the American Psychoanalytic Association* 11: 725–751.

——— (1967). The effects of overstimulation: rat people. *International Journal of Psycho-Analysis* 48: 403–415.

Shuren, I. (1967). A contribution to the metapsychology of the preanalytic patient. *Psychoanalytic Study of the Child* 22: 103–126.

Simmel, E. (1944). Self-preservation and the death instinct. *Psychoanalytic Quarterly* 13: 160–185.

Spock, B. (1957). *Baby and Child Care*. New York: Duell, Sloan.

Wilson, E. (1950). In memory of Octave Mirbeau. *Classics and Commercials*. New York: Farrar, Straus.

Zinnser, H. (1935). *Rats, Lice and History*. New York: Little, Brown.

Chapter 4

REFLECTIONS AND SPECULATIONS ON THE

PSYCHOANALYSIS OF THE RAT MAN

STANLEY S. WEISS, M.D.

Freud's *Notes Upon a Case of Obsessional Neurosis* (1909), commonly known as the case history of the "Rat Man," is a classic of psychoanalysis. Jones (1959, p. 166) reported that he was "spellbound" as he listened to Freud's presentation in April 1908 at the Salzburg Conference. Freud spoke for four hours and Jones described it as "an intellectual and artistic feat." To this day, the Rat Man continues to hold the interest of all students of psychoanalysis.

The "Rat Man Case History" is also unique since we possess an "Addendum: The Original Record of the Case" (Freud 1909, pp. 253–318, *passim*), almost four months of Freud's daily notes from which he extracted the analytic data for his paper and from which he drew his theoretical conclusions. We are very fortunate to have this document, incomplete as it is, since it was Freud's practice throughout his life to destroy all material on which publication was based.

In this brief communication, I wish to (1) focus on the transference of the Rat Man; (2) examine Freud's technique at the time; (3) indulge in a few speculations about the role of the Rat Man's "Jewishness" in his neurosis, taken primarily from material in the daily notes which did not find its way into Freud's publication. In regard to the transference, I will suggest that Freud conceptualized transference at the time as a series of isolated phenomena that replayed significant memories, fantasies, and events of childhood. Further, I plan to demonstrate that Freud overlooked during this early analysis preoedipal and oedipal mother transferences and certain of the patient's antagonistic feelings toward Freud himself which were manifested in anti-Semitic references and the defensive use of identification with the aggressor. However, the successful analysis of the Rat Man was a major scientific step forward in Freud's evolving technique and theories of psychoanalysis.

At the time of the Rat Man's psychoanalysis, which commenced October 1, 1907, Freud was enlarging and deepening his important discovery of transference and experimenting with technical maneuvers as he continued his basic research into the science of psychoanalysis.

Obsessional neurosis was the main topic of the 1965 International Psychoanalytic Conference in Amsterdam, at which many important contributions were presented (1966). However, what I wish to report in this brief paper has not been emphasized in the literature and, hopefully, can deepen our appreciation and understanding of this famous patient.

The Rat Man, as is well-known, visited Freud to get relief from a painful and tormenting obsession that his father (who, Freud was surprised to learn, had died nine years earlier) and his lady friend, Gisela, were being eaten by rats that gnawed into the body through the anus. The obsessional fear broke out during Army maneuvers at which the Rat Man had especially wanted to prove his manliness; instead, he became terrified upon hearing about a rat torture from a sadistic captain. Most likely as a symbolic castration, he lost his glasses at this time, even before hearing the captain's account of the torture. He became flooded with anxiety concerning the payment for a new pair of glasses that was sent to him. He had to keep the rats away from his father and lady friend by carrying out an absurd, difficult ritual that he set up to pay for the new glasses. The rat fear became the core of the analysis and Freud tells us that in slightly less than a year the Rat Man's condition was restored to normal.

The Rat Man knew something about Freud's family and scientific work at the outset and came to him with certain attitudes and a preformed transference that would very quickly crystallize into a transference neurosis. The Rat Man had heard of Freud's sexual theories and had leafed through *The Psychopathology of Everyday Life* (Freud 1901). He was obviously impressed with Freud's work. His sister had once stated that Freud's brother, Alexander, would be a good catch for the Rat Man's lady friend, which had made him quite angry. The Rat Man also possessed important misinformation about Freud. He supposed, as he told Freud later, that a great misfortune had once befallen the family in Budapest. Allegedly, a brother, who was a waiter, had committed a murder and had been executed for it. The Rat Man thought, prior to starting his analysis, that Freud whose family had murderous impulses, would fall on him like a beast of prey to search out what was evil in him. Since the surname Freud was relatively rare in Central Europe, it is understandable why the Rat Man associated the story with Sigmund Freud. The latter knew that the patient was referring to a Leopold Freud, whose crime dated back to his own third or fourth year. During the analysis, he humorously remarked, to the Rat Man's relief and pleasure, that he had never had any relatives in Budapest. An interesting coincidence may have reinforced the patient's associating Freud and rats. Although the Rat Man was analyzed at 19 Berggasse, he might have known that Freud's first office for a few years was at 7 *Rat*hausstrasse.

Presenting himself to Freud after his failure to prove during Army maneuvers that he was a competent soldier like his father, his attitude was that of an angry, castrated, and defeated son. Thus, when Freud told him the fee, the Rat Man muttered to himself, "So many florins, so many rats." This angry thought, implying that Freud should be given the rat treatment—not only one rat or even two rats as mentioned by the cruel captain, but a rat for each florin—was not verbalized at the time. Therefore, we could say that the first interview started with certain negative as well as positive transference reactions.

We are told that the Rat Man had the idea that persisted throughout his life that his parents could read his thoughts; consequently, he must have felt that Freud also had this power. During the Rat Man's youth, it was not uncommon for parents in Vienna to encourage this idea. This was a well-accepted child-rearing practice at the time (Spitz 1974). It is also not an uncommon fantasy of many of our patients today, even though, of course, our child-rearing practices in this regard have changed.

During the session, the Rat Man spoke (after Freud's later discovery of the superego, analysts would say "confessed") of sexual activities with governesses, Fräulein Peter and Fräulein Lina, and with his mother in the past, but did not verbalize his thoughts and feelings about Freud and the fee in the present. He therefore felt he had to be punished and it is not surprising that at the end of the second session, the patient behaved as though he were dazed and bewildered and repeatedly addressed Freud as "Captain." The transference neurosis was now in full bloom but in this session the Rat Man, not Freud, was the victim being invaded anally by Freud who was seen by the patient as rat, cruel captain, and sadistic father (Kanzer 1952, Part IV, chapter 1).

Most likely the Rat Man as a child viewed in reality, or surely in pictures, his officer-father in full uniform with the long sword carried by every noncommissioned officer in the Austrian Army. The idea of his penis being cut off had tormented the Rat Man for years and his castration anxiety appears to have revolved around swords. The Rat Man, we know, possessed two Japanese swords made of a large number of Japanese coins that hung at the head of his bed. Such swords were very popular as decorative wall hangings with young men at the time (Spitz 1974). During the Rat Man's lifetime, dueling which led to inca-pacitation or even death was a normal part of life in Austria and it was shameful to refuse a duel. The Rat Man, we know, had a number of fantasies of challenging to a duel a Lieutenant who was a bully and who struck recruits with the flat of his sword if they failed to execute certain maneuvers. He had also challenged a fellow student in his first year at the university but this was never carried through. The Rat Man, Freud tells us, had the idea of making a funnel-shaped hole in his head to let what was diseased in his brain come out. His father, who was full of stories of his soldiering days, used to talk of the "Nuremberg Funnel," an instrument of torture kept in the Nuremberg Museum in which water is poured down the victim's throat. It is evident that the Rat Man came to Freud with an unconscious fear that Freud would forcefully penetrate his body.

Freud's genius and intuition gave him the ability to observe transference phenomena in a scientific and empathic manner, without reacting personally, before he understood all the aspects, richness, complexity, and cohesiveness of the transference. However, Kanzer (1952; Part IV, chapter 1 of this volume), in an important paper on the transference neurosis of the Rat Man, written before Freud's original record of the case had been published, noted that Freud did not know during the second session that he was being seduced into playing the part of the cruel captain by helping the Rat Man reveal significant parts of the story of the torture. During this emotionally charged session, Freud verbalized for his patient the idea "into the anus," words that were highly instinctualized for the Rat Man.

Shengold (1967) further pointed out that "rat people," a name attached to patients with dynamics similar to Freud's Rat Man, frequently start analysis with a "galloping" transference (see Shengold Part IV, chapter 3). They are immediately and intensely set up to relive the traumata of the overstimulation of childhood. His father spoke of the Nuremberg Funnel torture during the Rat Man's childhood and a transference was readily established when the captain spoke of the rat torture during Army maneuvers. We also know that during childhood the Rat Man usually slept with his parents. Possibly in the context of overstimulation and marked castration anxiety, it is significant that his sister Katheryn (four or five years older than the patient) died when he was four, an early object loss for the patient. We also learn from the original record that he had an undescended testicle which may well have enhanced the castration image.

I believe the Rat Man's transference was partly mobilized by the activity of Freud himself as part of his evolving technique at the time. The classic procedure of today was far from fully developed. We know that the treatment lasted only eleven months and could not be considered a full-length psychoanalysis by today's standards.

Resistance was pointed out or connected to its genetic roots. At this time, Freud also believed that sound and correct intellectual explanations could overcome resistance. For instance, Freud mused, "Strangely enough, his belief that he really nourished feelings of rage against his father has made no progress in spite of his seeing that there was every logical reason for supposing that he had those feelings." At times, resistance if not felt to be too strong would not be given any analytic scrutiny. Freud reported in one session that "he apparently had only trivialities to report and I was able to say a great deal to him to-day." Freud had not yet clearly conceptualized the force and strength of an unconscious and persistent internal resistance.

During the Rat Man's psychoanalysis, interpretations were limited to the unconscious. Transference interpretations were tentatively made and limited primarily to the positive transference. Current transferences, especially negative transferences, were frequently dismissed or displaced into the past and not permitted to win attention in the present. For example, Freud reported "A fresh transference: My mother was dead. He was anxious to offer his condolences, but was afraid that in doing so an impertinent laugh might break out as had repeatedly happened before in the case of a death. He preferred, therefore, to leave a card or me with 'p.c.' (pour condoler) written on it; and this turned into a 'p.f.' (pour féliciter)." Freud interpreted this bit of negative transference towards him and about his beloved mother by immediately displacing it to the patient's mother. "Hasn't it ever occurred to you that if your mother died you would be freed from all conflicts, since you would be able to marry?" The patient retorted in an angry and frightened way, "You are taking a revenge on me. You are forcing me into this, because you want to revenge yourself on me." Could we speculate that the Rat Man at this point suddenly became aware of his attack on Freud and Freud's attack in return which was contained in a correct but ill-timed interpretation? Is it fair to surmise that the Rat Man by verbalizing a death wish against Freud's beloved mother inflicted pain on Freud and that unconscious anger and hurt were warded off by an interpretation which contained a death wish against the patient's mother? Can we consider this an early example of countertransference which Freud conceptualized a few years later (Freud 1910)? Though Freud did not fully, consciously grasp the full significance of many of his immediate responses, they often rested on a keen intuitive basis and were carefully evaluated by noting the patient's responses. Freud's process of treatment, as with all analysts since, was a scientific and therapeutic exploration of patient and self.

Freud, in the original record of the case, spoke always of *a* transference or transferenc*es*. For example, "He interrupted the analysis of the dream to tell me some transferences." The "next session was filled with the most frightful transferences. . . ." The concept of a transference neurosis representing a new illness with a cohesive structure which is at every point accessible to intervention and can be cured by the therapeutic work was only conceptualized at a later period (Freud 1914). At the time of the Rat Man's psychoanalysis, Freud was looking for past memories and not concentrating primarily either on the real or transferred attitudes of the patient to himself. Thus, the technique was largely determined by the concept of the therapeutic process at the time; that is, to seek the past memory directly or to study the forces from past experiences entering into object attitudes at the moment. For instance, Freud notes that, "I had told him earlier, by way of clearing up a transference, that he was playing the part of a bad man in relation to me—that is to say, the part of his brother-in-law." Many of our beginning candidates who fail to place Freud's concepts of technique with the Rat Man in historical context have difficulty in allowing the negative and positive transference to blossom fully and attempt to "clear it up" by interpreting the transference prematurely, which corresponds to this early period of analytic discovery.

As further evidence of the activity of the analyst at the time, Freud requested during the eighth session that the Rat Man bring a photograph of his lady with him to the next analytic hour. During the following hour, Freud observed that the patient was in a violent state of conflict—should he abandon the treatment or surrender his secrets? The Rat Man's strong defenses against exhibitionistic impulses, which were evident in the first session when he associated to his sexual activities, were, once again, mobilized by Freud's request. He apparently took the request to bring in the picture as a command that he would have to relinquish his woman as well as his sexual activity, which he would not do without a struggle. The Rat Man related that after having intercourse on two occasions he had thought, "This is a glorious feeling! One might do anything for this—murder one's father, for instance!"

Freud did not understand at the time how activity, as compared to the later analytic technique of a more passive stance, might mobilize transference, and he apparently did not understand the negative transference significance of the story the Rat Man told him during the ninth session. The Rat Man had recalled that when he was in a Munich sanitarium, he had a room next to a girl with whom he had sexual relations. The second time he was there he hesitated to take the same room because it was large and expensive. When he eventually made up his mind to take it, he was then told that a professor had already done so. "May he be struck dead for it! he thought." The analyst apparently had difficulty at this time in seeing that the death wish was aimed at "Professor" Freud himself.

The Rat Man also imagined a deputy judge (himself) naked and a woman (Freud's daughter) practicing "minette" (fellatio) upon him. Freud did not interpret the negative transference but "repeated my lecture of last Saturday on the perversions." The negative transference which, of course, involves an aggressive attack upon the analyst, is not easily seen by many of our analytic candidates and psychiatric residents, even though they have the benefit of Freud's discovery. It is not surprising that it took Freud a longer time to come to grips with the negative than with the positive aspects of the transference. Schur (1972) also has noted that Freud could understand positive transference much more readily than he could negative transference. Freud (1937) mentions the limited horizon of analysis in those early days and that he might have missed some very faint signs of a negative transference of a patient successfully analyzed who later became antagonistic and reproached him for having failed to give him a complete analysis.

At another time during the analysis, Freud reported that the Rat Man was hungry and was fed. Four sessions later he felt, as he handed Freud his fee, that he ought to pay for the meal as well and suggested 70 kronen. This sum was derived, Freud noted, from the farce at the Budapest Music Hall in which a weak bridegroom offered a waiter 70 kronen if the waiter would undertake the first copulation with the bride. The Rat Man also thought that Freud had made a profit out of the meal since the patient had lost analytic time because of it and the analysis would last longer. In essence, he felt that he had been short-changed. We might note that Freud's brother who, the Rat Man believed at the beginning, was a waiter and murderer, was now directly associated with Freud himself as one who fed the hungry patient. Another instance of preclassical technique appeared when Freud gave him Zola's *Joie de Vivre* to read, apparently because the hero's problems resembled the patient's. It was most likely only a sympathetic gesture, but Freud might have thought the novel would also stimulate new associations and memories.

We know that money was important to the Rat Man, as it was to his mother, to whom he turned over his inheritance. She, in turn, gave him an allowance. He had to ask her permission before starting analysis because of the need to discuss the fee with her. He would also be irritated with friends over money matters and would dislike it very much if the conversation turned in the direction of money. In the preliminary neurosis prior to the analysis, the payment of money to a young lady at the post office for the forbidden glasses played a most important role. The Rat Man's difficulties with money passed readily over into the transference neurosis.

A significant association to rats (*Ratten*) was installments (*Raten*). To understand the importance of the association *Raten*, it is helpful to know that in South Germany and, most likely, in neighboring Austria, it was primarily the

Jewish businessman who was beginning to develop installment buying as a legitimate business practice for the working middle class (Niederland 1973). This was not the installment buying which developed rapidly following World War I and involved an interest charge but was a part payment agreement between the businessman and his customer. The Rat Man showed Freud his uneasiness and fear about installment buying by reporting that, before the analysis, he had offered security for a friend who had to pay a sum of money in twenty installments, and had got the creditor to promise that he would let him know when each installment fell due so that he should not become liable under the terms of the agreement to pay the whole amount in one sum (p. 288). Therefore installments (*Raten*) might have linked Freud, the Jewish analyst who at regular intervals expected payment, to the rats (*Ratten*) and to the father who had been a gambler (*Spielratte*) and the mother with a rattail hairdo and, of course, to marriage (*Hieraten*). Freud noted that the Rat Man ''is beginning to behave like a miser, though he has no such inclination. He found difficulty, too, in making his friend an allowance.'' Could we speculate that the Rat Man, like many obsessive patients in analysis, had difficulty in paying his analytic fee? However, Freud makes no mention of any overt problem that his patient had with the fee. Nevertheless, the stinginess and retentiveness of anally fixated people was well-known to Freud (1908).

Thanks to Freud's daily notes, we can see that the Rat Man used several Jewish terms during the analysis, upon the meaning of which I would like to now briefly focus. These intimately involve the transference and the Rat Man's ambivalent feelings and struggle about his Jewish identity.

At one time he thought, ''20 *kronen* are enough for the *Parch*.'' *Parch* is translated in a footnote to the text as a Jewish term meaning futile person. However, the translation is somewhat inaccurate and what should be emphasized is a ''dirty, sly, low-grade person who should be avoided'' (Rosten 1970, p. 284). Here, the Rat Man was clearly attacking Freud for taking his money. Freud could very clearly see the patient's identification with his mother but not at this time the aggressive attack that was being directed towards himself both as ''mother'' and ''Jewish analyst.'' After the father's death, the mother had told her son that she would be economizing to replace the capital which had been spent during the father's illness. Despite a foul smell from her genitals, she stated that she could not afford frequent baths, thus making him very angry. He himself carried cleanliness to excess.

The Rat Man used the Jewish term *Miessnick*, meaning ugly creature, to describe Freud's daughter and he told Freud a joke involving the word *Schügsenen* (the Viennese Yiddish term for the more commonly used *Schiksa*) which is correctly translated as gentile girls.

Where did the Rat Man's use of Jewish terms come from and what were their meaning? Freud clarifies this by telling us that the Rat Man's mother was an adopted daughter of a well-to-do Jewish family named Rubensky. The Rat Man's father was a first cousin of his mother prior to her adoption. Both parents were obviously Jewish and Yiddish was most likely spoken at home. The father used to give in a joking way an exaggerated picture of the conditions in which they lived when they were young. The Rat Man's mother would occasionally chaff the father by telling him how he had been the suitor of a butcher's daughter before he married the daughter of a wealthy Rubensky. Any sign of his father's lack of education greatly embarrassed the Rat Man. The social stratification within minority groups is dynamically very important. Harsh feelings and prejudice are often expressed toward the self and towards members of the various cultural levels within the group. The aggression mobilized within the levels of the majority group is more easily directed outward.

In the transference, the Rat Man felt that Freud, like his mother wanted him to follow in his father's footsteps and marry one of the wealthy Rubenskys. (In the original record, it is clearly mother's wish. However, in the case history [pp. 198–199] Freud presents it as the wish of both parents.) He dreamt that Freud's daughter had dung in place of her eyes. Of course, Freud interpreted this dream correctly as the Rat Man's wanting to marry Freud's daughter, not for her beautiful eyes (the young Emma Rubensky supposedly had beautiful eyes), but for her money. What Freud did not fully appreciate at the time was the hostility the Rat Man felt and expressed as he viewed the analyst as his Jewish mother who was pushing for this union between her son and a wealthy and respectable Jewish family. In the fantasy that Freud wanted him to become his son-in-law is the wish to get close to Freud, bow to his mother's wish, and follow in his father's footsteps by marrying into an influential Jewish family. However, he is ambivalent about the marriage because of his ambivalence about his Jewishness. The Rat Man struggled with the wish to give up completely his Jewish identity. Several years before his analysis, he felt violent self-reproaches, suddenly fell on his knees (a praying position never used by Jews), conjured up pious feelings and determined to believe in the next world and immortality. His father, we are told, had never consented to be baptized but much regretted that his forefathers had not relieved him of the problem of being Jewish. He had often told the patient that he would make no objections if he wanted to become a Christian (p. 302). Vienna was a city with a strong Jewish influence as well as strong anti-Semitic feelings.

It appears that the Rat Man was in conflict not only over whether to marry into a respected Jewish family like Rubensky or Freud, but he also wanted to do what his father couldn't—and give up his Jewishness and the problems that it caused. Possibly his compulsive prayers might have been a mockery of the Jewish prayers from his strong religious period during adolescence, and the ambivalence and shame the adult Rat Man felt about being Jewish might have passed over into the daily analytic ritual of the new science of psychoanalysis. Freud, therefore, became the omnipotent, powerful, Jewish father-God who could read the Rat Man's thoughts and mete out love or destruction—a return from the dead of the loved and hated father of the Rat Man's early childhood.

As a three- or four-year-old and at the time of his sister's fatal illness, the Rat Man had done something naughty for which his father had given him a beating. The little boy flew into a terrible rage and hurled abuse at his father even while he suffered his blows. He screamed, "You lamp! You towel! You plate! and so on" (p. 205). During the transference neurosis, the Rat Man began heaping the grossest and filthiest abuse upon Freud and his family (p. 209). His vocabulary had obviously grown as his hatred of Freud was replayed in the safety of the analytic office. Thus, during the Rat Man's psychoanalysis, Freud, the ideal of the Jewish physician, writer, and creative scientist, became demoted from the omniscient Almighty to the oedipal father who deserved the rat torture, castration, and even death.

The Rat Man's father had recognized one of the officers under whom the patient was serving as son of an officer under whom he himself had served. He told a story which the Rat Man repeated to Freud. Once, at Pressburg, the train could not enter the town owing to a heavy snowfall. The patient's father armed the Jews with spades so that they could clear the snow. This was permitted although they were as a rule forbidden access to that part of town. The officer was pleased, but the Rat Man's father replied angrily, "You rotter! You call me 'old comrade' now because I have helped you, but you treated me very differently in the past" (p. 305). Presumably the father also had difficulties in the Army because he was Jewish. In this meaningful and rich association, the Rat Man also tells Freud, who does the very important and necessary analytic spadework by digging into the patient's mind, that Freud himself, like the Rat Man, has to overcome many difficulties because of being Jewish. Could we speculate at this point that the cruel captain might have sadistically teased the young officer because he was Jewish?

Certain patients whose analysts possess specific identifying characteristics, such as an accent, name, or physical attributes that reveal something obvious of the identity of the analyst, often use phrases, words, anecdotes, etc., that attempt to link themselves to the analyst as well as to mock and attack him. The negative transference can be revealed if the analyst will pursue the associations. Apparently, at this time in the development of psychoanalysis, Freud did not pay much attention to the Jewish words and phrases used by the Rat Man.

Conclusion

Freud, the discoverer of analytic technique, was still struggling and experimenting methodologically with the Rat Man. Today we might say that the treatment was a combination of psychoanalysis and psychotherapy. However, that observation would not do justice to the magnificence of this historically important early analysis. Freud, the discoverer of transference, was making further progress in understanding the complexity and subtlety of this phenomenon.

Today it is apparent that Freud did not yet fully understand or clearly conceptualize various aspects of the transference, superego, and ego defense at the time of the Rat Man's treatment:

1. The cohesive structure of the transference neurosis is a new edition of the infantile neurosis formed in and by the analytic situation. Freud conceptualized transference as a series of isolated phenomena that replayed significant memories, fantasies, and events of childhood.

2. The negative transference manifested itself by derogating Freud in the role of a waiter and by attacking in subtle fashion Freud's Jewishness.

3. The preoedipal and oedipal mother transference directly related to the analyst. It is apparent in the original record that Freud could clearly see himself as a replacement for the Rat Man's father but had difficulty seeing himself as representing the patient's mother.

4. Analytic activity may mobilize transference reactions, especially in patients with a background which predisposes to intense transference manifestations.

5. Important superego aspects of his patient's pathology, for example, the idea of a patient confessing "sinful" behavior during the first session under the guise of free association and feeling as if analytic suggestions were analytic commands, were not yet fully understood.

6. The important defense of identification with the aggressor was not perceived. The Rat Man changed from fear of the cruel captain to violent, biting attacks upon Freud. Later, in *Beyond the Pleasure Principle* (1920), Freud spoke of children passing from a frightening or traumatic event passively experienced to the activity of play during which revenge is taken by unleashing aggression on a new object.

Such shortcomings, which would soon be overcome, do not detract from the genius, intuition, and creative ability that Freud showed in mastering practical as well as theoretical problems presented by this case of obsessional neurosis.

Unfortunately, the Rat Man lost his life in World War I and could not contribute personally to follow-up studies. However, through the original record of the case, Freud and his immortal patient have given us added analytic data

214   STANLEY S. WEISS, M.D.

for study, reflection, and speculation.

References

Freud, S. (1901). The psychopathology of everyday life. *Standard Edition* 6.
——— (1908). Character and anal erotism. *Standard Edition* 9: 169–175.
——— (1909). Notes upon a case of obsessional neurosis. *Standard Edition* 10: 153–318.
——— (1910). The future prospects of psycho-analytic therapy. *Standard Edition* 11: 139–151.
——— (1914). Remembering, repeating and working through. *Standard Edition* 12: 147–156.
——— (1920). Beyond the pleasure principle. *Standard Edition* 18: 7–64.
——— (1937). Analysis terminable and interminable. *Standard Edition* 23: 216–253.
Jones, E. (1959). *Free Association—Memories of a Psycho-Analyst*. New York: Basic Books.
Kanzer, M. (1952). The transference neurosis of the Rat Man. *Psychoanalytic Quarterly* 21: 181–189. This volume, Part IV, Chapter 1.
Niederland, W. (1973). Personal communication.
Plenary Papers, Discussion and other papers on obsessional neurosis (1966). *International Journal of Psycho-Analysis* 47: 116–212.
Rosten, L. (1970). *The Joys of Yiddish*. New York: Simon and Schuster.
Schur, M. (1972). *Freud: Living and Dying*. New York: International Universities Press.
Shengold, L. (1967). The effect of overstimulation: rat people. *International Journal of Psycho-Analysis* 48: 403–415.
——— (1971). More on rats and rat people. *International Journal of Psycho-Analysis* 52: 277–288. This volume, Part IV, Chapter 3.
Spitz, R. (1974). Personal communication.

Chapter 5

THE MISALLIANCE DIMENSION
IN THE CASE OF THE RAT MAN

ROBERT J. LANGS, M.D.

The present paper is an effort to continue the investigation of sectors of misalliance between Freud and his patients, and their relationship to deviations in technique as measured by the template of current psychoanalytic standards. The Rat Man case (Freud 1909) is unique among Freud's writings in two respects that are pertinent to this study: a summary of each of the first seven sessions of the analysis is available in the published presentation of the case, and further, through some unusual circumstance, Freud preserved the notes for the first three months of the analysis; these were subsequently published in Volume 10 (pp. 253–318) of the Standard Edition. This material therefore presents us with a rare opportunity to view aspects of Freud's technique as he practiced it in 1907. In fact, this material is so rich that it will be necessary to be highly selective and focus almost exclusively on what is relevant to the main theses of this paper. The present study can be supplemented by the papers of Zetzel (1966), Kestenberg (1966), Grunberger (1966), and especially the careful investigation of the relationship between the Rat Man and Freud presented by Kanzer (1952), a study which foreshadowed many of the findings and formulations to be presented here.

In Freud's interaction with the Rat Man there are two types of deviations from current classical technique. The first concerns the nature of the interventions that Freud made and, in general, reflects deviations in Freud's neutrality, level of activity, and degree of anonymity. The second includes specific deviations in technique such as feeding the Rat Man and lending him a book. Here, I will more briefly review the first group of "deviations" or variations in technique since they have been rather thoroughly considered by Kanzer (1952), and will focus more extensively on the relatively unexplored second group.

Sectors of misalliance may be initiated by the patient or analyst; most often they derive from a circular interaction between the two. If we first examine the Rat Man's initial communications to Freud, we can identify their potential for misalliance; we will then be able to investigate Freud's responses to these efforts and to follow the subsequent interaction.

The Published Paper

While the Rat Man's conscious wish was to be relieved of his obsessional symptoms through treatment by Freud, he very quickly revealed in his initial communications an unconscious wish for misalliance which had several meanings. His first words upon beginning his analysis alluded to a friend who gave him consistent moral support by reassurances that he was not a criminal and that his conduct was irreproachable. In the Rat Man's earlier years, a student had reassured him but had subsequently betrayed him, using his relationship with the Rat Man to get close to the latter's sister.

In this way, the Rat Man revealed an unconscious motive for treatment related to his wish to obtain direct reassurance from Freud in a manner that would bypass the analysis of the unconscious fantasies on which his obsessional—and other—symptoms were based. In addition to this aim, the material reflects the potential for a homosexual transference with active and passive, and as later borne out, masculine and feminine, sadistic and masochistic features. Any effort by the Rat Man to gratify these transference fantasies and wishes in his relationship with Freud could form the basis for a sector of misalliance—unconscious shared efforts to achieve symptom relief through means other than insight. In addition, in the third session of the analysis, when Freud was attempting to directly reassure the Rat Man, the latter revealed a conscious wish to obtain a certificate from Freud to the effect that he should be permitted to live out the requirements of his obsessions in order to maintain his state of health. Further, by anticipating Freud's betrayal, the Rat Man showed not only his mistrust of his analyst, but also his intense masochistic wishes to be harmed or wronged.

In all, then, these various deviant motives for treatment, and the search for transference gratifications that they entailed, created strong potentials for sectors of misalliance with Freud. Transference expressions are both maladaptive efforts at self-cure (Freud, as quoted by Ferenczi 1909), and the communications that make insight through the interpretations of the analyst. Much will therefore depend on the analyst's responses to the patient's attempts to directly gratify his transference wishes; any conscious or unconscious compliance by the analyst will establish a sector of misalliance. In this context, we may now examine the manner in which Freud responded to his patient and trace subsequent interaction for data related to modifications in the frame of the analysis (as measured by present standards), sectors of misalliance, and the patient's unconscious perceptions of, and primarily nontransference reactions to, Freud.

At first, Freud listened. The Rat Man's associations went to his early sexual history, manifestly because he had read some of Freud's writings. The first image was one of the Rat Man as a child creeping under his governess's skirt, a memory that may reflect his unconscious view of the analysis. Similarly, his reference to telling his mother of his erections and his feeling in childhood that his parents knew his thoughts presumably contain fantasies about his analytic relationship. The hour culminates in a thought that through his voyeurism something might happen—for example, that the Rat Man's father might die.

In the second session, the Rat Man began to tell the well-known story of the rat punishment and the cruel captain. He became agitated and asked Freud to spare him, walking around the office. Freud stated that he could not grant such a wish and as the Rat Man had difficulty in describing the punishment, Freud joined in with guesses such as impalement and a reference to the rat's boring into the anus of its victim. As Kanzer (1952) noted, Freud had very quickly joined the Rat Man in acting out on some level the very torture and interaction that was so disturbing to the patient. In our terms, Freud had joined in a sadomasochistic, homosexual misalliance with the Rat Man, one that would afford the latter gratification on many levels and evoke further reality-based—primarily nontransference—responses to Freud based on these actualities. This was most striking when the Rat Man called Freud "Captain," which Freud did not analyze but rather responded to with reassurance. Other versions of this sadomasochistic and mutually defensive sector of misalliance appeared in later sessions, especially in Freud's intellectual explanations and the Rat Man's challenging and questioning responses (Kanzer 1952).

The fifth session contained a great deal of this intellectual interplay and ended with Freud's expression of a good opinion of the Rat Man. The consequences of this seductive "deviation" in technique (as defined by present standards) are striking: in the next hour, the Rat Man spoke again of his fear that his parents could guess his thoughts and alluded to his love of women—undoubtedly as a defense against the homosexual anxieties and fantasies stirred up by Freud's remarks. An allusion to his father's death followed, with the comment that the sister of a friend whom he knew as a child would then be kind to him. This association, which seems to express defensive hostility toward Freud, may also reflect the Rat Man's unconscious perception of Freud's focus on his death wishes against his father (Langs 1975c), an aspect of the material that may well have received undue attention in Freud's interventions.

Freud responded by suggesting a suicidal fantasy to the Rat Man who was not convinced by it, and who insisted upon his love for his current lady friend. When Freud became theoretical, the Rat Man became agitated and defended his love for his father. After considerable arguing, Freud escaped the current situation by a reconstruction related to the Rat Man's childhood hostilities toward his father. This was characteristic of Freud's technique at the time, in that Freud consistently avoided the day residues and current precipitants of his patient's transference reactions, nor did he take cognizance of any realistic perceptions and reality-based reactions to himself (Kris 1951, Kanzer 1952). It was in this setting that, in the following session, Freud made the comment to the Rat Man that since his disturbing impulses were from his childhood, the Rat Man was not responsible for them. The Rat Man was extremely dubious of this unconsciously sought reassurance—and sector of misalliance—and Freud attempted to prove it to him.

It is here, however, that the initial report of the analysis ends, although there are isolated allusions to the analytic work in the subsequent discussions presented by Freud. In particular, the Rat Man is described at one point as walking around the room after Freud had pressured him about his hostility toward his father. At this time, the Rat Man said that he should be turned out and expressed a fear of being beaten by Freud. In addition to the transference elements, these communications reflect accurate conscious and unconscious perceptions of the aggressive elements in Freud's technique. It was this material that led directly to the rat ideas and to the overdetermined series of derivatives related to the unconscious meanings that rats had for the Rat Man. While his associations clearly reflect both transference meanings and unconscious perceptions of Freud (the nontransference element) that contributed to the revelations and underlying implications of the rat fantasies, their analysis was made almost entirely in symbolic and genetic terms. Thus, it appears likely that these constellations of distorted and perceptive responses to Freud, including their contribution to sectors of misalliance, contributed to the expression of the Rat Man's nuclear pathogenic unconscious fantasies.

Thus, the reported case material indicates that Freud participated with the Rat Man in several sectors of misalliance that bypassed the quest for insight and inner change. These centered around a homosexual misalliance in which sa-

domasochistic fantasies were acted out on some level, and also included unconscious attempts by the Rat Man to obtain sanctions and reassurances regarding
his disturbed ideas and behavior, and Freud's offering of such.

The case report raises an important additional issue. The data suggests that
at the junctures of "technical deviations" by Freud, such as the moment when
he expressed a positive opinion of his patient, there was a striking outpouring
of material rich in unconscious fantasy content. However, a proper understanding
of this content could be made only if the adaptive context—Freud's remark—was
thoroughly appreciated (Langs 1973b). Both Kanzer (1952) and Zetzel (1966)
have made particular note of the productivity of the Rat Man in regard to
derivatives of unconscious fantasies, emphasizing that this indicated a viable
therapeutic alliance and a strong therapeutic atmosphere. While this may be the
case, as I have shown elsewhere (Langs 1974, 1975b, 1976), deviations in
technique and the development of misalliances are among the most certain
sources of productive material from patients. Stimulated by the extensive unconscious meanings of such alterations in the otherwise secure and safe boundaries of the patient-analyst relationship, unconscious fantasy activity and
communication are utilized as a prime means of adapting to such traumas. Thus,
in assessing such material, the precipitant and context must be recognized in
order to properly evaluate its sources and meanings. In this way, deviations and
momentary sectors of misalliance can lead to productive analytic work—though
only if they are identified and the analyst's actual contributions to them are
rectified as they are being worked through with the patient (for a different, but
related viewpoint, see Viderman 1974).

In tracing the effects of Freud's "deviations" and his possible
countertransference-based interventions, and the sectors of misalliance to which
they contributed, it has been necessary to bypass the indications of significant
sectors of a viable therapeutic alliance between Freud and the Rat Man. In
addition to the signs of sincere, mutual respect, there is a quality to the meaningful and analyzable unfolding of the Rat Man's associations that indicate its
secure presence. In addition, the frequency with which the Rat Man appears to
have genuinely confirmed many of Freud's interventions point in this direction.
Admixtures of sectors of alliance and misalliance in varying proportions are
characteristic of all analytic work. As a result, insightful cures will intermix
with misalliance cures (Langs 1975a), so that the basis for symptom modification
must be investigated in terms of its antecedents and its underlying basis. As we
would expect, the former type of symptom alleviation, insight cure, generally
proves far more stable and adaptively useful for the patient than the misalliance
cure. The data offered by Freud does not, however, offer a sufficient basis to
specify the contributions from each of these spheres to the Rat Man's improve-

ment. There is evidence in both directions; however, Freud's more constructive work with this patient should not be overlooked in the course of our study of his "deviations" and the sectors of misalliance that they helped to create. Freud's original case records will afford us an opportunity to obtain some specific additional data pertinent to these issues, so let us turn to it directly.

The Original Case Record

This record starts with the eighth session since the previous hours had been presented in the published report. The notes begin with a reference to a bad day (apparently, a bad session) in which resistances predominated after Freud asked to see a photograph of the Rat Man's lady. The patient thought of leaving analysis as an alternative to the surrender of his secrets. His next communication refers to a prayer by which he protected himself and others from harm, and he then recalled an experience in a mental hospital where he wanted a room next to a young lady with whom he was having an affair. He had wished that the professor who held this room would be gone; subsequently, the professor had a stroke and died. The request for the photograph would be a deviation in current standard analytic technique—our template—and the consequences are clear: resistance, thoughts of leaving analysis, fear of surrender, magical protection against the seducer, and death wishes.

As the notes proceed, there are frequent descriptions of struggles between the Rat Man and Freud. The patient would not reveal his lady's name and Freud actively persuaded him to do so. A little later on, Freud made some apparently gratuitous comments including a speculation that the Rat Man's lady had been seduced by her step-father. This led to a period of intensified masturbation by the Rat Man and to requests by him to be dismissed from the analysis. When Freud responded by attempting to explain transference, a forty-minute struggle ensued during which the patient was angered by Freud's forcefulness. There followed a series of blatant sexual fantasies which involved Freud and his family—undoubtedly in part as a response to Freud's aggressiveness and se-ductiveness. Some analytic work then proved feasible with this material, mo-mentarily turning the sector of misalliance based on modifications in Freud's neutrality into positive therapeutic endeavors, but when Freud eventually re-assured the Rat Man regarding his frightful fantasies, the patient specifically described his mistrust of Freud. The material during this period also indicates that the Rat Man and some of his family knew members of Freud's family.

The Postcard

It was in December of the analysis that Freud described several specific "deviations" in technique. The session of December 8, for example, began with an allusion to a *rendezvous* between the Rat Man and a dressmaker which ended in premature ejaculation. The Rat Man became depressed and this was reflected in "transferences in the treatment." There were references to each of the Rat Man's parents as related to their son's coarseness, and a pursuit of the "transference" led to material about a relative who would set the Rat Man up in business if he would marry one of his daughters. Freud apparently interpreted these associations in terms of the genetics of the Rat Man's illness, missing the likely tie to a later-reported "deviation" that had already occurred: a postcard that Freud had recently sent to the Rat Man. The latter responded with great irritation with Freud, expressed by direct insults. He accused Freud of picking his nose, refused to shake hands with him, thought that a filthy swine like Freud needed to be taught manners, and added that the postcard that Freud had sent to him, which had been signed "cordially," was too intimate.

Ignoring the implications of this "deviation" in technique, Freud continued to relate this material to the genetics of the Rat Man's choice of a love object. The Rat Man responded with a fantasy that Frau Professor F. should lick his "arse" and by seeing Freud's daughter with two patches of dung in place of eyes. Freud's symbolic translation of the Rat Man's love of his daughter for her money was a continuation of his disregard for the current precipitants in his relationship with the Rat Man for the latter's dreams and fantasies. It was in this context that the Rat Man referred to standing up against his mother's complaints about the money that he had spent.

From there, the material goes to the theme of the rats, and Freud noted that the Rat Man avoided relating this theme to his mother. One meaning evoked at this time had to do with laughing at his father, whose lack of education greatly embarrassed the Rat Man. His father was uneconomical while his mother was able to economize. The Rat Man referred to the way in which he secretly supported a friend and Freud saw this as an identification with his father who had behaved in the same way with their first lodger. While his father seemed to be a kindly man, the Rat Man was ashamed of his father's simple and soldierlike nature.

We may pause here and offer an alternate formulation of this material (see also Zetzel 1966). The entire sequence seems to have been evoked by Freud's cordial postcard which apparently had a strong homosexual meaning for the Rat Man and evoked considerable anxiety, erotic fantasies, and anger. The postcard fostered fantasies that Freud wished to be more personally involved with the Rat Man and to have him as a member of his family. As an apparent defense against this seductiveness, the Rat Man became quite enraged with Freud and attacked him for his attempts to become too intimate with him. The mixture of defensive fury and wishes for gratification are reflected in the fantasy that the professor—obviously a representation of Freud—should lick his "arse." The dream or fantasy of Freud's daughter with the patches of dung in place of eyes is to be viewed here as—among its many meanings—a reflection of the Rat Man's unconscious perception of Freud's blindness to the interaction between the two of them. As I have shown elsewhere (Langs 1974, 1975b, 1975c), it is particularly in situations where the analyst has made a technical error or has deviated from the usual and appropriate boundaries of the therapeutic relationship, and has in addition failed to recognize and acknowledge his deviation, that the patient unconsciously perceives the error as well as the analyst's failure to recognize it. In this context, allusions to blindness and failures to perceive are extremely common—a finding that is remarkably borne out in this material. These communications may also be viewed as efforts by the Rat Man to alert Freud to his blind spot and to "cure" Freud of the difficulties that he was having in understanding his patient. Characteristically, attempts to maintain misalliances are accompanied by efforts to modify them; this is generally true of both patient and analyst (see Langs 1975a, 1976).

It may be noted once again that I am putting aside other contributions to the sequence that I have just analyzed. For example, the Rat Man's anger at Freud also probably related to the hours that he had missed because of Freud's vacation and to the envy of the women whom he seems to have fantasied to have been with Freud. This may well have been another determinant of the material related to the Rat Man's mother, and other contributions to this sequence could also be developed. Central to the ideas that I am attempting to develop from this clinical material, however, is the striking similarity between the sequence of the Rat Man's associations and behaviors following the receipt of the postcard and reactions of patients currently in psychoanalysis to comparable alterations in the framework of the analytic relationship (Langs 1975b, 1976). It is also rather typical that a patient responding to such behavior on the part of his analyst avoids direct references to the deviation, embeds it indirectly in his associations, and accepts the inappropriate gratifications and misalliance generated by it. Only later will he unconsciously attempt to modify the misalliance through further tangential references to the deviation and its consequences, with communications designed to indicate the disruptive effects of the misalliance. Finally, it should be remembered that the Rat Man's specific intrapsychic responses to this deviation were clearly determined by his own inner conflicts and unconscious fantasies; each patient responds to his analyst's efforts to create sectors of misalliance in keeping with his own needs and character structure.

The next communications touch upon the Rat Man's mother's inappropriate attitude toward money and the patient's ability to stand up against her. References to poor mothering are also extremely common when the analyst has deviated, and we must therefore suspect that the Rat Man's ability to stand up to his mother evolved in part as a reaction to Freud's unconscious and inadvertent seductiveness, and the Rat Man's defenses against it. The references to the Rat Man's father's lack of education and lack of understanding may be viewed as another indication of the patient's unconscious perception of Freud's failure to understand the current interaction, and his efforts to help Freud to modify this problem.

In all, then, it is remarkable to find that the notes written by Freud permit an understanding of the Rat Man's response to an extension of today's usual boundaries between the patient and analyst in terms entirely in keeping with formulations derived from more current studies of such modifications in the framework of the analysis (Langs 1973b, 1974, 1975b, 1976). Once again we see that such occurrences are extremely productive of associations replete with derivatives of unconscious fantasies and perceptions, but they can only be properly understood and analyzed based on a clear appreciation for the correct adaptive context and precipitants for the material (Langs 1973b). It also seems clear that there are inherently sound safeguards in the specific tenets which constitute today's ground rules and boundaries—the frame—of the psychoanalytic relationship and situation. The sensitivity of the Rat Man to alterations in this frame, which to some extent was not that of Freud at the time, appears to support such a thesis.

The Feeding

It was at the end of this month that Freud began a session with the note that "He (the Rat Man) was hungry and was fed." Let us first detail the sequence that proceded this experience and the reactions that followed, after which we will be able to formulate the repercussions of this particular "deviation" in technique which took the form of a direct, noninterpretive gratification of the patient.

In general, in the preceding sessions the Rat Man was concerned with his anger at his father in a way that suggested "transference" reactions. It is notable that the Rat Man had been upset by the illness of Dr. Pr., the physician who had taken care of both his father and himself (in the session following the hour of December 28, Freud alluded to an interruption in the analysis because of the death of Dr. Pr.; there is some confusion regarding the date of this session). In this earlier hour, there were fantasies of Pr.'s death and of both killing him and keeping him alive—an allusion to the Rat Man's fantasies of omnipotence. Dr. Pr. was then connected to the death of the Rat Man's sister, Katheryn, since he was the physician in attendance at the time; this brought the Rat Man to what undoubtedly was one of the major traumas in his early childhood and a focal point of his neurotic illness—a factor that Freud had some difficulty in exploring and crystalizing (Zetzel 1966). The Rat Man's guilt over his sister's death was linked to the death of a dressmaker who had committed suicide when the Rat Man had spurned her. This then led to an account of the beginning of the Rat Man's obsessional thinking in which his father's death and his relationship with the lady played a prominent role. There were allusions to suicidal fantasies and intense self-reproaches, particularly because of thoughts that his lady was a whore. The theme of religion emerged (while unclear, it appears that the Rat Man's parents were Jewish, and that his mother had been adopted by a Jewish family) and the struggle with the temptation to marry a Jewish woman was mentioned. His oath to not masturbate in his teens and the incidents in which he would open the door for his dead father while exposing himself in a mirror were reported at this time. This latter material was disconnected and unintelligible to Freud who attempted to explain it in terms of the Rat Man's defiance of his father by masturbating. This was only partially confirmed and the associations in this sequence ended with a reference to an earlier incident in which the Rat Man had spied upon a naked girl and felt guilty.

It was thus that the hour of December 28 began with the feeding. The Rat Man then continued his story of his stay at Unterach where the voyeurism had occurred and where he had, he now added, suddenly decided to make himself slimmer through long bouts of running which included stepping to the edge of a steep precipice and having the fantasy of jumping over. Next came mention of his service in the Army and a fantasy of how he could measure his love by examining his response to the question: if his father collapsed, would he fall out of ranks to help him? His father's death was mentioned, as was a lieutenant who was a bully and who struck his men with the flat of his sword. The issue of standing up to such a man and the fear of being horsewhipped came next, and the patient described fantasies of challenging him to a duel. Then came a reference to a superior officer of his father's who had been extremely nasty until a time when the patient's father armed the Jews of a particular town with spades to clear the snow for the army train, and this officer had praised him. The father was critical of such praise.

The next associations alluded to the Rat Man's compulsion to talk at Unterach and to his obsessions of counting and protecting, including magical efforts to protect his lady from illness and to understand every syllable that was spoken to him. The counting-anxiety in thunderstorms pointed to a fear of death and the running in the sun had a suicidal quality to it—factors which Freud pointed out and were confirmed by the Rat Man. There followed further memories of suicides in his family, including one that occurred over an unhappy love affair.

The Rat Man himself had sworn that because of his mother he would never kill himself, even if disappointed in love. At this point, Freud noted that the suicidal fantasies must have been self-punishment for his having wished his lady friend—his cousin—dead during his rage. Freud then gave him Zola's *Joie de Vivre* to read, apparently because the hero of this novel was perpetually occupied with thoughts of his own and other peoples' deaths. It was in this context that the Rat Man described his obsessional experience with the stone that might have overturned his lady's carriage—an incident in which he had moved the stone and then returned it to the position where it might do damage.

It was, as I noted, in the following hour that the reference to the interruption owing to the illness and death of Dr. Pr. occurred. This led to rat wishes and hostile thoughts, and to the fantasy of Dr. Pr. sexually assaulting his sister Julie. Freud considered this to represent the Rat Man's envy over medical examinations and did not relate it to either the feeding or the loan of the book. The Rat Man's father had hit Julie when she was ten and said that she had an arse like a rock. Freud apparently interpreted the Rat Man's rage against his father, but noted that there was no confirmation of this intervention. Instead, a "transference" fantasy was reported: "Between two women—my wife and my mother—a herring was stretched, extending from the anus of one to that of the other. A girl cut it in two, upon which the two pieces fell away (as though peeled off)." The only associations to this fantasy were that the Rat Man disliked herring intensely and that when he had been fed by Freud recently, he had left the herring untouched. The girl was one whom the Rat Man had seen on the stairs and had taken (apparently correctly) to be Freud's twelve-year-old daughter.

The following hour began with a reference to an invitation from his sister to go to a play with her. This invitation angered him and he wished upon her the rat torture. In the face of the Rat Man's rumination, Freud was very active and attempted to link the rat fantasy to the patient's earlier episode with anal worms. In doing so, Freud attempted to connect the story of the herring to enemas given at that time, once again devoting himself to genesis at the expense of the current interaction. Much of this went unconfirmed and the reader could profitably turn directly to this material to see the many new associations that reflect the Rat Man's unconscious fantasies and perceptions in interaction with Freud. I will confine myself to some very striking allusions. There was a reference to a cousin who had shown the Rat Man a large worm in his stool, to which he reacted with disgust. While Freud was attempting to interpret fantasies of the Rat Man to the effect that his masturbation had caused his sister's death, the patient continued to allude to exhibitionistic material such as actually showing his mother an erection and voyeuristic recollections of nude girls.

At this point, homosexual memories of mutual exhibitionism and voyeurism were reported. Reference to a recent episode of diarrhea was connected with the herring episode (the material in the remainder of the sessions recorded by Freud repeatedly returns to the incident of being fed and its repercussions). This theme was further developed through an image of the Rat Man being caught with his pants down and a reference to the girl, viewed indirectly as a prostitute, who had cut the herring in half. This led to allusions to pubic hair and Freud offered some apparently extraneous comments about the way in which women at that time gave no care to their genital hair—a possible countertransference reaction. Freud's house was seen as one that was run by two women, and the Rat Man reported a fantasy that two women had prepared the meal that Freud had fed him.

In the next hour, there were allusions to prostitutes and Jewishness; homosexual play with a brother was reported, as was a series of sexual fantasies which Freud linked to the Rat Man's mother. In the experiences with his brother, the latter's penis had come into contact with the Rat Man's anus. Then, in the following hour, the Rat Man reported a fantasy of kicking Freud's child, which was again related by him to the herring. Next came the fantasy of impregnating his own sister and the thought that Freud had made a profit from the meal he had served the Rat Man, since the latter had lost time and the therapy would last longer. The Rat Man also felt that he should pay an additional fee for the meal. Embedded in this material was a fantasy that linked the fee for the meal to a bridegroom's offer to a waiter that the latter have the first copulation with his wife and he paid for it. Here, the Rat Man said that whenever Freud praised any of his ideas he was very pleased, but that a second voice went on to say "I shit on it."

In the next hour, the Rat Man reported a dream that he went to the dentist to have a bad tooth pulled. One was extracted but it was not the right one. Further, in a subsequent session, there were references to a young girl cousin who had been inappropriately touched under her bedclothes by a doctor.

The Rat Man's responses demonstrate and confirm a wide range of previously reported observations and formulations based on contemporary clinical material (Langs 1973a, 1973b, 1974, 1975a, 1975b, 1975c, 1976). Once again, I will stress the consequences of the deviations and their contributions to the unfolding of this material, and I will not attempt to establish the manner in which this source of the patient's conscious and unconscious fantasies and perceptions of Freud interdigitated with other stimuli for this sequence. I would stress at the outset, however, that it is characteristic for patients to be directly and, more frequently, indirectly preoccupied with the impact of a major deviation in the framework for long periods of time, especially when it has gone unnoticed and unanalyzed.

To select the main points relevant to the hypotheses under exploration in this paper, the material suggests that the Rat Man's moment of hunger occurred at a time when he was dealing with some very traumatic memories and some very disturbing feelings toward Freud. Some of this may have been evoked by the apparently seductive postcard sent by Freud to the Rat Man, the effects of which had remained unanalyzed. Since Freud's focus at this point in his technique was on the genetic roots of symptoms and so-called transference fantasies, he almost entirely overlooked the current precipitants of the Rat Man's reactions toward him and had no extensive clinical experience in distinguishing his patients' primarily intrapsychically determined fantasies about him (transferences) from their conscious and unconscious realistic, veridical perceptions (nontransferences) (Langs 1973a, 1976).

The feeding provided obvious transference gratification and was the basis for a sector of misalliance which disturbed the Rat Man to some extent, although he participated in and accepted gratification from it. This generous and seemingly supportive measure, which transgressed the usual current boundaries of the patient-analyst relationship, was responded to in a wide variety of ways; there are a number of indications that it evoked intense anxiety in the Rat Man and considerable concern regarding what might further happen between himself and Freud. Thus, he had quickly responded to the feeding by alluding to suicidal fantasies developed in the context of the need to slim himself. The anxiously accepted incorporative gratification had to be rejected on some level, even at the cost of his life.

Among the many other frightening fantasies that this feeding had evoked in the Rat Man—all with clear meanings relevant to the analytic relationship—were death wishes toward his father, the mention of the lieutenant who was a bully and the fantasies of challenging him to a duel, the use of the Jews as menial help, the rejection of the favorable comments made by his father's superior officer to him, and the ultimate linking of the suicidal fantasies to an unhappy love affair and to the need for punishment. The feeding, as this material indicates, was seen in part as a dangerous homosexual seduction and attack, to which the Rat Man reacted with great mistrust and rage.

Rather than interpreting this material, Freud responded by giving the Rat Man a second gift—that of the book. Now the Rat Man's unconscious perception of Freud's behavior became clearer and was more vividly expressed in the derivatives in the sessions. A relatively undisguised fantasy, in which the doctor who had recently died was assaulting the Rat Man's sister sexually, shows the mixture of unconscious perception with genetic (transference and fantasied) contributions that deviations of this kind usually evoke in patients (Langs 1975b, 1975c, 1976). The rich imagery involved in the herring fantasy and in the Rat Man's dislike for herring reflects, among other things, the patient's dreaded wish to be seduced.

There is also considerable additional material related to the rejection of seductive invitations and continued efforts by the Rat Man to communicate his fantasies and anxieties regarding Freud's feeding of him. There is a reference to the greatest fright in his life, when he thought his mother's stuffed bird was alive. In his fantasies, the Rat Man felt that Freud was behaving like a prostitute—or using his patient as one—and was attempting to seduce him. This prompted him to defend himself against his own passive feminine wishes which had evoked, and were being further stirred up by, Freud's behavior. A good deal of this material culminates in the conscious fantasy that Freud had profited inappropriately from the feeding which was equated by the Rat Man with an offer from a bridegroom to have another person copulate with his wife. These are by no means entirely transference-based fantasies, but are clearly related to the realistic seductive overtones of the situation; they are a mixture of reality and fantasy. It is of interest that the Rat Man alluded at this time to another "deviation" from neutrality in Freud's technique, namely, Freud's praise of him. Again, he indicated his need to reject this praise.

As is so typical of patients involved in an unanalyzed interaction of this type, the material culminates in a dream in which a dentist pulls a wrong tooth. This dream expresses very succinctly the Rat Man's unconscious perception of Freud's technical errors (Langs 1975c, 1976), and his continued efforts to aid Freud in resolving them.

Discussion

To offer a general conclusion, this material supports the thesis that deviations in technique and extensions of the patient-analyst relationship beyond the usual boundaries—alterations in the frame—evoke extremely significant and intense responses on a fantasied and behavioral level in all patients. The analysis of the patient's responses generally takes precedence over all other analytic work except for emergencies (Langs 1975b). In a viable analytic atmosphere with a generally good therapeutic alliance such as that created by Freud with the Rat Man, these analytic experiences can be extremely moving and meaningful. Failure to deal with this area when it is pertinent will generally leave the analytic situation in apparent chaos, and promote regressive and acting out responses in the patient. It is striking to see the number of times that the Rat Man failed to confirm Freud's interventions since they did not deal with the deviations in technique.

While the Rat Man's associations were extremely productive and there are many recognizable derivatives of unconscious fantasies once the main context for this material is understood, there is little indication in these pages of a general confirmatory responsiveness on the patient's part.

Because of Freud's failure to analyze the Rat Man's reponses to his extensions of the boundaries of their relationship, the Rat Man continued to express derivatives of unconscious fantasies related to these "deviations" in the month of subsequent sessions detailed by Freud. There remained within him the overriding need to adapt to these experiences and to resolve the intrapsychic anxieties and conflicts that they were evoking in him.

In all, there were several sectors of misalliance created by Freud's extra-analytic behavior. Both Freud and the Rat Man shared major defenses against an awareness of the conscious and unconscious meanings of what had transpired between them, and there were some shared efforts to accomplish symptom alleviation through sanction and the gratification of the Rat Man's neurotic behavior and needs. The notes also portray the homosexual and sadomasochistic qualities in the misalliance sector which directly gratified many of the Rat Man's pathogenic unconscious fantasies, and also evoked considerable anxiety. The many allusions to exhibitionistic and voyeuristic fantasies also characterized an element of the misalliance in which Freud and the Rat Man alternately played the role of voyeur and exhibitor, as well as seducer and seduced. It was largely Freud, however, who played the active, penetrating, seductive, overgratifying role that the Rat Man invited, accepted, and then defended himself against.

Freud's "deviations" in technique and the sectors of misalliance that they generate—and the Rat Man's and Freud's efforts to perpetuate as well as modify these misalliances—contributed to the ongoing flow of the patient's associations. The presentation by Freud provides evidence that, in addition to these determinants, his valid interventions and a variety of life experiences of the Rat Man also contributed significantly to this material. All of the adaptive stimuli were processed by the Rat Man in keeping with his own intrapsychic needs, conflicts, and fantasies. A full comprehension of this material and its transference and nontransference components is feasible, however, only if the precipitants and actualities that have been identified here are recognized and understood. In this way, the derivatives of the Rat Man's unconscious fantasies find meaning both in terms of his current adaptive reactions and their genetic basis. Further, on this basis reality and fantasy, perception and misperception, can be sorted out in a way that fosters the patient's grasp of inner and outer realities and generates insight into his own intrapsychic disturbances.*

---

*Beigler's (1975) thinking is in keeping with my observations and conclusions regarding the Rat Man. His article was published after this paper was written.

Summary

The consequences of an extensive variety of modifications in present standard psychoanalytic technique in Freud's work with the Rat Man have been explored, especially in regard to contributions to sectors of misalliance between the patient and analyst. Most of these modifications in the basic framework evoked intense adaptive responses in the Rat Man, with both transference and nontransference, fantasied and perceptive, components. The findings support the thesis that patients are extremely sensitive to modifications in the framework, and that the analysis of these reactions, and the rectification of unneeded deviations, where feasible, are prime analytic tasks.

References

Beigler, J. (1975). A commentary on Freud's treatment of the Rat Man. *The Annual of Psychoanalysis* 3: 271–285.

Ferenczi, Sandor (1909). Introjection and transference. In *Further Contributions to Psychoanalysis*. New York: Bruner, 1950.

Freud, S. (1909). Notes upon a case of obsessional neurosis. *Standard Edition* 10: 153–320.

Grunberger, B. (1966). Some reflections on the Rat Man. *International Journal of Psycho-Analysis* 47: 160–168.

Kanzer, M. (1952). The transference neurosis of the Rat Man. *Psychoanalytic Quarterly* 21: 181–189.

Kestenberg, J. (1966). Rhythm and organization in obsessive–compulsive development. *International Journal of Psycho-Analysis* 47: 151–159.

Kris, E. (1951). Ego psychology and interpretation in psychoanalytic therapy. *Psychoanalytic Quarterly* 20:15–30.

Langs, R. (1973a). The patient's view of the therapist: reality or fantasy? *International Journal of Psychoanalytic Psychotherapy* 2: 411–431.

———— (1973b). *The Technique of Psychoanalytic Psychotherapy*. Vol. 1. New York: Jason Aronson.

———— (1974). *The Technique of Psychoanalytic Psychotherapy*. Vol. 2. New York: Jason Aronson.

———— (1975a). Therapeutic misalliances. *International Journal of Psychoanalytic Psychotherapy* 4: 77–105.

———— (1975b) The therapeutic relationship and deviations in technique. *International Journal of Psychoanalytic Psychotherapy* 4: 106–141.

———— (1975c). The patient's unconscious perception of the therapist's errors.

In *Tactics and Techniques in Psychoanalytic Therapy*, Vol. II, Counter transference, ed. P. Giovacchini. New York: Jason Aronson.

———— (1976). *The Bipersonal Field*. New York: Jason Aronson.

Viderman, S. (1974). Interpretation in the analytic space. *International Review of Psycho-Analysis* 1: 467–480.

Zetzel, E. (1966). Additional 'notes upon a case of obsessional neurosis.' *International Journal of Psycho-Analysis* 47: 123–129.

Chapter 6

FREUD'S "HUMAN INFLUENCE"
ON THE RAT MAN

MARK KANZER, M.D.

It is a noteworthy fact that Freud's three lengthy case reports which teach us most about the details of his technique—Dora (1905), The Rat Man (1909), and the Wolf Man (1918)—were all antecedent to the delineation of the transference neurosis (1914). (The Wolf Man case was actually jotted down in 1914 with observations on the transference neurosis as a retrospective lesson, just as the analysis of Dora had given new recognition to the significance of transference.)

Only the Rat Man comes close to fulfilling criteria for a full-fledged analysis even by earlier standards. If, after eleven months, Freud reported that "therapeutic success" was achieved, he meant really that the pragmatic outcome had weakened the patient's disposition to trace the causes of his illness "thread by thread" as Freud would have preferred. Nevertheless the fascination and instructiveness of the treatment has retained it as a prime teaching instrument in analytic curricula. There would be even more to impart, however, if the material could be placed in accurate historical perspective.

Such a review of the case has been made all the more desirable through the supplementary notes which were found among Freud's papers after his death (1909, pp. 259–318). The discovery of the material is itself testimony to its particular significance, since usually "it was his practice, after one of his works had appeared in print, to destroy the records of the case" (Strachey 1955, p.

253). Previously, there had been available only detailed reports of the first seven sessions, while material from the others had been scattered throughout the work. The extended chronicle adds some three months of consecutive observations, and offers an unparalleled opportunity to follow the unfolding of the analytic process in terms of Freud's techniques and theoretical orientation. Moreover, and of special interest for this study, it permits a remarkable closeup of his personal interactions with the patient.

To be sure, we must recall that even authentic records may prove uncertain guides. Thus Freud (Nunberg-Federn 1962) himself, introducing the Rat Man to his own followers as early as October 30 and November 7, 1907 (treatment had begun on October 1), and on subsequent occasions (making it the first continuous case study in analytic history), referred to the treatment as an example of a "changed technique" in which "the psychoanalyst no longer seeks to elicit material in which he is interested, but permits the patient to follow his natural and spontaneous trains of thought" (p. 227).

This statement is puzzling for two reasons: (1) Exactly the same point had been made with respect to Dora several years earlier (1905, p. 12), and (2) Freud scarcely permitted much spontaneity, as we would understand it today. Perhaps the first point is to be explained by the consideration that new followers may have still been oriented to his older work, while with respect to the second, progress in the understanding and application of free association was still taking place. This latter aspect is clarified by Freud himself in a review (1920) in which he divided the past history of psychoanalytic therapy into three phases:

"At first the analyzing physician could do no more than discover the unconscious material that was concealed from the patient, put it together, and, at the right moment, communicate it to him. Psychoanalysis was then first and foremost an *art* of interpreting" (italics mine). (See, for example, the Dora case and the masterly but quite directive reconstruction of the significance of the jewel case in her dreams.) An inquisitorial note enters into remarks that the patient was "obliged to admit" the force of the analyst's comments, and a new fact was uncovered "which I did not fail to use against her."

"Since this [approach] did not solve the therapeutic problem, a further aim quickly came into view: to oblige the patient to confirm the analyst's construction from his own memory. . . inducing him by *human influence*—this was where suggestion operating as 'transference' played its part—to abandon his resistances" (italics mine). (The Rat Man and the Wolf Man serve as the prime examples here.) A third phase, embodied in the paper "Remembering, Repeating and Working Through" (1914) would rely essentially on neutrality and interpretation of the transference neurosis to achieve its results.

Our own focus will be directed to the human influence which Freud exerted upon the Rat Man as part of the "art" of interpretation which avowedly made use of suggestion and still displayed not a little of the argumentativeness of the encounters with Dora. Nevertheless, we are in a position to place this phase in a historical context through Freud's own restrospective evaluation: "But it became ever clearer that the aim which had been set up—the aim that what was unconscious should become conscious—is not completely attainable by that method." The patient must pass through a stage of repetition of the repressed until a transference neurosis is formed which makes it possible to recall the past with a sense of conviction. Only then can therapeutic success be achieved.

Commentators do not often underline sufficiently the important differences in the use of transference for suggestive purposes in the second phase and the new use to which it was put when directed, not to the immediate recall of memories, but to the understanding of behavior in the analytic situation (i.e., the transference neurosis). Thus, when the Rat Man dreamed, after a real encounter with Freud's daughter, that he saw her before him with two patches of dung instead of eyes, Freud translated this to mean thoughts of a marriage for money rather than beauty. Now, he insisted, the Rat Man must accept an earlier interpretation to which he had been resistant—namely, that at one time he reacted neurotically to his father's demand that he wed for money (as father had done with mother) rather than love. In the official text, Freud leaves the matter with the rather unrevealing comment that the patient "could no longer remain blind to the overwhelming effect of the perfect analogy between the transference phantasy and the actual state of affairs in the past." In the supplementary notes, however, we find no evidence that the patient was really overwhelmed or even influenced by the interpretation, but rather that the dream was part of a series of attacks on Freud and his family, which showed a shifting emphasis from the past memories to current feelings that had to be dealt with before convincing interpretations could be made.

The need to invoke a special element of "human influence" to make an interpretation acceptable might have been reduced had the truly vital sphere of interaction between patient and analyst received more direct focus, as in the third phase. Thus, when the Rat Man brought forward a fantasy that Freud's mother was dead and that his wish to offer condolences was inhibited by the fear of breaking into "an impertinent laugh," Freud suggested that the material really related to the patient's desire for the death of his own mother. "You are taking revenge on me," the Rat Man cried out. Whether or not he correctly sensed a retaliatory motive, the hostility to Freud was sidestepped by the one-sided emphasis on the past, which could only have stirred up further exasperation and desire to involve the analyst personally that the Rat Man clearly was evincing.

There was evidence that Freud, as might have been expected, was indeed more involved than he knew, and the present-day reviewer may see signs of this in the data dealing with the course of the analysis. Actually, such a reconstruction was undertaken in 1952 when material relating to early phases of the treatment was reexamined in terms of more current concepts of transference neurosis (Kanzer 1952). Evidence of early transference neurosis formation was adduced when the patient cast the analyst in the role of the rat torturer. Freud's intuitive attempts to cope with the resistances were also subjected to scrutiny. In 1966, after the hidden chronicle was brought to light, Elizabeth Zetzel reassessed the progress of the case from the standpoint of the therapeutic alliance. We believe it would be useful at this time to extend our own previous studies to include the later stages of the treatment, drawing on the new material and considering the therapeutic alliance (which we construe rather differently than did Zetzel) within the total picture.

Where previously we have seen in Freud's helpfully "guessing" the thoughts of the patient about the "rat torture" (during the second session) a transference gratification achieved through mutual acting out, it should also be acknowledged that it was a contemporary form of promoting the formation of a therapeutic alliance. Freud himself would have considered it a means for inducing an "effective transference" which would come about if "one exhibits a serious interest in (the patient), carefully clears away the resistances that crop up in the beginning and avoids making certain mistakes" (Freud 1913, p. 139). We have maintained elsewhere that precisely such activities permanently implant seeds of the therapeutic and working alliances (Kanzer 1975).

Both transference neurosis and therapeutic alliance have antecedents in the past history and cultural settings of both partners—ultimately in their infantile neuroses and constructive parent-child relationships. Elsewhere in this volume, Stanley S. Weiss delineates common bonds between Freud and Lorenz (the Rat Man) which lent nuances to their speech not explored in the analysis—oriented as it was to the uncovering of unconscious oedipal memories. Pre-therapeutic determinants of the nascent transferences and countertransferences included certain relationships between the two families, common outlooks of the time in the Viennese community, and a degree of acquaintance on the part of the patient with Freud's teachings on sex.

Along such lines, we shall attempt to assess the fuller range of interactions during the analytic process and especially the nature and manifestations of the "human influence" which Freud exerted. Thus, in the fourth session, the patient told of "nonsensical" feelings of guilt toward his dead father which an earlier confidant (object of a form of transference) had regularly dismissed as transparently absurd, but without achieving lasting relief. Freud now jolted him by refusing exoneration and maintaining instead—with the conspicuous "intellectual indoctrination" of which Kris (1951) spoke—that there was indeed justification for his self-reproaches, but it existed only in the unconscious and had to be brought to the surface. In addition to this accusation and assumption of the role of omniscience, Freud's response involved the use of imagery and metaphors that could not have but shaken the patient deeply.

When the Rat Man inquired as to the therapeutic advantages to be gained by bringing into consciousness his elusive self-reproaches (a preliminary stage of negotiation?), Freud pointed to the now famous archeological trophies that filled his office and explained that, whereas their burial in a tomb had been the cause of their preservation, a disintegration had begun after they had been dug up. This "illustration" is rendered all the more significant by the fact that it was applied not only to a sense of guilt over the father's death but to recent fantasies about his returning to life. We have previously suggested, in line with our delineation of the transference neurosis in this case, that this fantasy was related to transferences now being made from the father to the analyst (1952). One may also wonder about Freud's countertransferences and the admiration often accorded this particular metaphor: are objects in tombs pathogenic and their disinterment therapeutic? Freud had his own apprehensions about father's return to life (Kanzer 1969).

Surrounded by objects from the tomb, he must have seemed the very model of the resurrected father demanding confession and holding out combined possibilities of punishment and forgiveness. This conception is reinforced by a recent article by Major (1974) who declares that Freud's term, in offering to "guess" the Rat Man's thought was "erraten", (to "divine"). With the "rat" syllable, and "divining" to confirm the patient's idea of his omniscience, the session must indeed have been converted for the moment into a confrontation with the father's ghost, whose return he would invite by masturbating before a mirror.

At the end of the fourth session, the patient still expressed doubt that it would be possible to bring to the surface such remote events in his own life, but Freud responded that despite the difficulties "his youth was very much in his favor, as well as the intactness of his personality. In this connection, I said a word or two upon the good opinion I had formed of him, and this gave him visible pleasure" (p. 178). Zetzel (1966) and others have cited this incident as a notable means of directly encouraging a patient in the interests of furthering a therapeutic alliance, but perhaps it could also be looked upon as a reparative maneuver after the traumatizations consequent upon the archeological admonitions. A more neutral approach, devoid of both the injurious as well as supportive aspects of "human influence," could surely have brought out and ultimately interpreted the current aspects of death wishes to the father as applicable to the analyst.

It is to be acknowledged, however, and studied with interest, that Freud's tacitly threatening and cajoling admonitions did indeed begin to loosen the defenses. The Rat Man now recalled an occasion when the thought of advantages to be gained by his father's death had occurred to him: the inheritance of wealth and the opportunity to marry the girl of his choice. Other memories of a similar nature came to the fore, but the patient held up as an argument contrary feelings of love for his father. Thereupon, Freud offered an "intellectual" explanation of ambivalence, but accompanied it with another telling metaphor. He chose to cite the well-known lines of Shakespeare's *Julius Caesar*: "As Caesar loved me, I weep for him; as he was fortunate, I rejoice at it; as he was valiant, I honor him; but, as he was ambitious, I slew him."

The same lines had played a part in Freud's own dreams and analysis of an ambivalent relationship to a nephew, a year older than himself. More deeply still, a sense of guilt over the death of a younger brother, Julius, was apparently involved. The question may be raised as to whether some similar ambivalence was now becoming apparent in relation to the patient who responded, rather intriguingly, to Freud's illustration by bringing into the next session (the seventh) the memory of a situation in his childhood quite similar to the interplay between Freud and his young uncle during boyhood days. "My (one year younger) brother and I used to fight a lot when we were children. We were very fond of each other at the same time, and were inseparable" (Freud 1900, p. 184). May not such episodes have contributed to leanings of Freud toward a belief in telepathy?

When Freud thereupon told the Rat Man that such reminiscences about hostility between brothers may be screens for deeper memories of hostile feelings between father and son (see also Shengold 1971), was he not drawing on self-analysis to educate his patient? A little later, Freud's involvement at a point where the patient's life showed resemblance to his own found him forgetful of the patient's communication and wondering if the communications had come from him or "another patient." (It is our experience that the "other" in such circumstances is often the analyst himself.)

Freud's self-analytic acumen did not fail him as he recognized that he had been troubled by the account of the death of Katheryn, the patient's sister, in childhood. This had stirred up "complexes of my own" (almost certainly with respect to the death of his own little brother Julius). Another intersection with the patient's past occurred at the point where he recalled lying in bed between his parents and losing control of his bladder. This had provoked a memorable beating from his father. (There are variants of this story as is typical with screen memories.) The boy responded with such fury that his father desisted from beating and remarked in wonder, "The child will be either a great man or a great criminal."

Or, Freud adds, a neurotic. His own father, faced with a similar situation when little Sigmund at seven or eight, "before going to sleep, disregarded the rules which modesty lays down and obliged the calls of nature in my parents' bedroom while they were present." The father passed judgment: "This boy will come to nothing." This had been "a frightful blow to my ambition, for references to this scene are still constantly recurring in my dreams" (1900, p. 216). In both instances, urinary self-assertion as a challenge to the father in the primal scene at the height of the oedipal period seems to have been the occasion for a substitutive castration and change in personality. In the case of the Rat Man, it was definitely to be numbered among the events determining the rat phobia.

Freud does not oblige us by directly confirming the self-analytic supplement. However, he does insert a lengthy footnote raising a more general question as to the relationship between historical truth and psychological truth which was of recurrent interest to him and important for psychoanalysis, relating to the need to search for facts or fantasies. "We *frequently* come across instances of this kind' , he averred in [italics mine], which crucial early experiences emerge from the shadows of memory. Referring apparently to the different versions of the Rat Man's trauma (did his own seem like one more?), he stressed their common origin in the fantasies consequent upon the "nuclear complex" of the neuroses. This was the first reference to the "nuclear complex" in the sense of the Oedipus complex. It is apparently an example of the sublimation into scientific insight of combined insights into the processes within the patient and himself.

Commentary

Older frames of reference by which Freud judged his use of "human influence" to achieve results during the "second stage" of psychoanalytic treatment (1910–1914) show the dependency upon intuition and the biases resulting from lingering conceptions of the need to uncover specific unconscious memories of sexual traumata as the goal of treatment. The current interplay of feelings with the patient was imperfectly comprehended under the concept of "transference" and resistance. The patient's disinclination to yield up a picture of his lady upon demand was regarded as a "resistance"; in the later phase it would have been regarded as an intrusion on the part of the therapist.

Some, like Zetzel, now stress the "kindly" aspects of the therapeutic alliance as against the coldness and rigidity of his neutrality. The fact is, however, that the analyst, forced to rely upon "human influence" rather than more firmly established criteria for interventions, could be stern or out of contact with the patient. Thus, human influence in turn could be erratic and disruptive to treatment. This is examined in greater detail in other contributions to this volume. It is our impression that the breaking off of the records on the Rat Man some three weeks after the eventful "herring dinner" showed that a serious disruption of the therapeutic alliance had resulted from this "warm" and "one-to-one" impulse that was injected at a critical turn in the proceedings (see, for example, Langs' paper, Part IV, chapter 5 of this volume).

Freud's "intellectual indoctrination" of the patient often arises at points in which it actually injects images and metaphors that influence the patient—sometimes helpfully, sometimes adversely—during the proceedings. Conversely, the patient often used language and images (see, for example, Weiss's analysis of his Jewish terms) that were of considerable import but not regarded as of interest in relation to the goals of the analytic process at the time. It seems to us very possible that so-called "negative therapeutic reactions" may result from failure to be aware of the influence of these factors.

Summary

Parallels between incidents in the patient's life and Freud's have been discussed, toward a clearer understanding of the history of psychoanalysis. Sometimes Freud detected and was able to analyze countertransferences that resulted. On one occasion, at least, he was able apparently to empathize on the basis of a similar experience and to recognize, as a result, the existence of universal fantasies that guided him away from the too direct pursuit of specific memories of traumata.

References

Freud, S. (1900).The Interpretation of Dreams. *Standard Edition* 4–5.

Freud, S. (1905). Fragment of an analysis of a case of hysteria. *Standard Edition* 7: 7–122.

———— (1909). Notes upon a case of obsessional neurosis. *Standard Edition* 10: 155–327. (1913) On beginning the treatment. *Standard Edition* 12: 123–144.

———— (1914) Remembering, repeating and working-through *Standard Edition* 12: 147–156.

———— (1918). From the history of an infantile neurosis. *Standard Edition* 17: 7–122.

Kanzer, M. (1952). The transference neurosis of the Rat Man. *Psychoanalytic Quarterly* 21: 181–189. Part IV Chapter 1 of this volume.

Kanzer, M. (1969). Sigmund and Alexander Freud on the Acropolis. *American Imago* 26: 324–354.

———— (1975) The Therapeutic and the working alliances *International Journal of Psychoanalytic Psychotherapy* 4: 48–73.Kris, E. (1951). Ego psychology and interpretation in psychoanalytic theory. *Psychoanalytic Quarterly* 20: 15–30.

Major, R. (1974) The language of interpretation, *International Review of Psycho-Analysis* 1: 425–436.

Nunberg, H., and Federn, E. (1962). *Minutes of the Vienna Psychoanalytic Society.* Vol. 1, Chapter 16, Freud and His Self-analysis. Volume 1 of the Downstate Twenty-fifth Anniversary Series, New York: Jason Aronson 1906–1908.

Shakespeare, W. (1901). The Tragedy of Julius Caesar. In *The Complete Works of William Shakespeare* XI: 24–158.

Shengold, L. (1971) More on rats and rat people. *International Journal of Psycho-Analysis* 52: 277–288. Part IV, Chapter 3 of this volume.

Strachey, J. (1955) *Standard Edition of Freud* 10: 253–257.

Zetzel, E. (1966). The analytic situation. In *Psychoanalysis in the Americas*, ed. R. E. Litman, pp. 86–106. New York: *International Universities Press.*

Chapter 7

INTEGRATIVE SUMMARY

MARK KANZER, M.D.

An early attempt to update the Rat Man case was made when Kanzer (1952) sought to apply to the first sessions the concept of the transference neurosis which Freud did not actually introduce until his paper on "Remembering, Repeating and Working-Through" in 1914. Where Freud's interventions had been traditionally regarded as merely stimulating the patient to recall thhhe forgotten past, the use of the transference neurosis model revealed a hitherto unemphasized relationship to the analyst as transference object and real person from the very beginning of treatment. Later, with the advent of the concept of neutrality and the infiltration of the analytic situation with emergent regressive behavior from the past, such findings became more generally recognized.

With the publication in the *Standard Edition* of the original record of the treatment in 1955, momentous new opportunities became available for bringing Freud's pioneering and brilliant but aging classic into alignment with modern views, thus enhancing its contemporary value as a teaching instrument. Whereas he had usually destroyed his notes after the publication of a case, these had been preserved and were discovered only after his death. They now provide us with an unrivalled opportunity to learn of the actual interchanges between a patient and Freud during a session, as well as some of his reflections during and between sessions. As such they offer biographical and self-analytic as well as case material.

In a commentary on these notes a decade later, Elizabeth R. Zetzel (1966) stressed new opportunities to evaluate the role of the mother and preoedipal stages of development which had not been afforded by the official presentation of the case. The impact of relationships to siblings also lent detail to the formative years which could be depicted now more accurately with respect to their normal as well as pathogenic aspects. Freud himself could be seen to a greater extent as a real person, warmly interested in the patient, aware at times of counter-transference difficulties, and utilizing encouragement and educational measures. Interested in promoting the concept of the therapeutic alliance, Zetzel (1966) maintained that his interventions, while sometimes justifying the later more neutral technique, may also have been helpful.

Judith S. Kestenberg in the same year (1966) used the ''Rat Man'' to illustrate her views on ''Rhythm and Organization in Obsessive-Compulsive Development.'' She wrote: ''Freud's vivid description of the Rat Man's verbal and motor behavior highlighted the changing quality of thought and movement during the course of treatment,'' and she pointed out and proceeded to correlate his adult behavior with typical patterns of early development. The phobic fear of the rat gnawing in his anus organized a confluence of such early motor rhythms. His running aimlessly about Freud's office when frightened reproduced similar behavior on other occasions and was suggestive of a toddler's agitation (or, I would add, the scurrying of a rat). Kestenberg traced, in turn, from the Rat Man and other cases, more general determinants of adult pathology.

In the present volume, she enlarges on her earlier study in a new article, ''Ego-Organization in Obsessive-Compulsive Development,'' which draws on many years of observations on infants and young children. Freud's own descriptions of his patient, as she points out, do not confine themselves to verbal reports but show keen interest in his facial expressions, bodily movements, and displays of affect. ''The Rat Man behaved as if he had never completed the oral-sadistic phase successfully,'' she declares. ''He did not have a good control over middle ranges of affectivity. He veers from agitation to indifference or daze, and from fantasies of achieving a high position to feeling disgraced or abandoned.'' Kestenberg is calling attention here, as did Freud and others, to the fragmentation of the Rat Man's personality, which attests to processes of isolation and ego-splitting in his development.

She approaches both the pathology and the progress in therapy from a phase-specific standpoint. Particularly original is her appraisal of the patient's problems over his undescended testicle, which receives only passing mention in Freud's supplementary journal and none in the original case history. She points out, for example, that the magic word coined by the Rat Man to keep apart the name of his girl friend and the idea of semen (Glejisamen) contains two letters to which he offered no associations—the "e" and the "i" in the first portion. Put together, they constitute "ei" or egg, which can allude either to the testicle or the feminine reproductive cell. The girl friend had been deprived by operation of her ovaries. From this data Kestenberg suggests a need to control goings in and comings out of the body—the rat gnawing its way in as the testicle and the fulfillment of the wish to bear a baby. (It is of interest that Norman H. Holland (1975) postulates an identity problem for the Rat Man based on a need to control catastrophic goings-in to the body and benign goings-out. He does not invoke the role of the testicles.) Kestenberg also applies her concept of the testicles to the consequences of the none-too-benign taking-in of a supper fed to the Rat Man by Freud. Later the patient dreamed that a girl cut in half a herring which he had refused to eat (i.e. created two testicles).

Kestenberg, with modern teachings on the child-mother unity in mind, postulates that, like a good parent fortified with patience, understanding, and compassion, Freud furthered the more normal rematuration of the patient after fixation points had been loosened. He countered his fuzzy thinking with precise formulations, taught him to form new object- and self-images and served as a dependable model in place of the confused and disturbed parents. Analyzing himself as he went along (his own laughter, incredulity, and conflicts), he was able to transmit such self-scrutiny to the Rat Man as well.

Leonard Shengold in two papers (1967, 1971) has found in the Rat Man case the illustration of a seduced and traumatized child who develops cannibalistic fantasies as an adult and tends to find in the rat, the bearer of the tooth *par excellence*, a symbol of his own ferocious orality. He belongs to a group Shengold calls "rat people." His wide-ranging commentaries further bring under consideration the experience of teething, which bears most interestingly on the fantasies of devouring and being devoured described by Bertram D. Lewin (1950) in his concept of the "oral triad" folklore, and tales about rats, and as well, a remarkable exposition about the "hero" of this cult, the Rat itself, together with facts about its history and behavior which bring truth and fiction remarkably close together.

Several of the commentators stress the splitting of the ego as a structural aspect of the Rat Man's neurosis. (It is also apparent that there was a splitting of the superego.) Shengold delineates a "vertical" splitting of the ego linked to the use of isolation as a defense against the memories of severe trauma which the individual is prone to repeat. Alterations of consciousness are associated with these vertical splits and become the occasion for powerful components of the personality to emerge and disappear again (like their rodent counterparts) without the ego having to take responsibility for them (in contrast, but not necessarily in contradiction to other portrayals of the ego as seeking to control comings-in and goings-out). The ego fragments that recur represent tenuous remnants of the past associated with the breast and with feces and other objects (urine, testicles) that come and go.

The splitting and alteration of consciousness themes are also to be found in the paper on "Reflections and Speculations on the Psychoanalysis of the Rat Man" by Stanley S. Weiss. He notes that the symptoms of confusion of thought (allied to alterations in consciousness) actually began with the loss of his eyeglasses and the dilemmas involved in recovering and paying for new vision. That brought Lorenz to Freud at the beginning of treatment. Splitting of the ego was further indicated early in the analysis with the recollection that in childhood Lorenz believed that his parents understood his thoughts. (A self-observing portion, I should add, derived during superego formation from the parents, was reexternalized.) These self-observing powers were next split off and delegated to the analyst. In the course of treatment this function, hitherto pervaded with guilt, would be appropriated by the ego again with the permission of the tolerant analyst (taming the severe superego).

The mechanism of ego-splitting may also be detected behind the denial of his Jewish identity which was a feature of Lorenz's thinking and entered covertly and undetected into the transference. Weiss places at our disposal important aspects of Viennese thinking of the era which, in fact, formed a common frame of reference for both analysand and analyst. The belief that parents could read thoughts was consciously instilled in children by Viennese parents of the time. (René Spitz was an informant on this and other material.)

Jewish identity entered into the outbreak of the patient's neurosis when he was engaged in military maneuvers in the Austrian army and seeking (as his father had done successfully) to demonstrate that people with his own background could hold their own under such conditions. Weiss points to a special vehicle of Lorenz's ambivalence in this matter—the word *Rat* within the term *Raten* (rates or installments). Jews were especially connected with the introduction of installment purchase into the Viennese business world. Analytic payments were linked with installment buying when, even in making financial arrangements with Freud at the beginning of treatment, the thought flashed through Lorenz's mind, "So many florins, so many rats." Each florin was to turn into a rat and penetrate Freud's anus—thus linking both rats and money to anal fantasies. He also sneered at Freud as a *Parch* who was worthy only of a 20 crown tip. While the *Standard Edition* translates this as a "futile person" (1955, p. 298), Weiss cites a Jewish definition which conveys a Jewish slur apparently more in consonance with the patient's feelings.

In general, Weiss points out, Freud was not at home with manifestations of negative transference at the time and allowed the split-off aggression of the patient to be hidden behind these Jewish terms and allusions. He might otherwise have recognized the link that was forming between the patient's ambivalent religiosity of adolescence and the analytic "rituals" which he both mocked and revered as he put Freud in place of father returned from the dead and, even, of the omnipotent Father-God of the Jewish religion.

The more detailed frame of reference into which analytic data may now be filled increasingly widens the significance of "first communications" from the patient, extending back beyond the first session on the couch to the preliminary interview and beyond that to the personal history of the individual. Where Freud stresses (correctly) the implications of a bisexual orientation, Kanzer calls attention to Lorenz's initial mistrust and deceptiveness. Zetzel remarks upon his need to get his mother's permission before undertaking the treatment. Weiss points out the early information he had acquired even before consulting Freud and the influence of the Jewishness of both men.

Robert J. Langs discusses the concept of *misalliance* relating to a patient's expectations that contrast with therapeutic aims and press for a different type of relationship with the analyst—whether as sex partner, inflicter of the rat torture or gullible object of deception. The relationship of a resistance to a misalliance seems comparable to that of an interpretation to a construction—a wider and more integrated view of psychic processes results. In a kindred way Langs speaks of the analyst's "deviations" from standard technique, as in the "guessing game," the demand for the lady's picture and name, Freud's sending the patient a postcard or lending him a book, and the particularly intriguing "herring meal" which he was impelled to feed him. Zetzel (1966) saw in the latter an expression of the analyst's warmth in a one-to-one relationship. None of the authors in this chapter (each, needless to say, choosing his own subject matter without prior discussion and usually from different viewpoints) found the matter so innocuous; doubt must be cast both on the analyst's undiluted warmth and the patient's benefit therefrom. Jerome S. Beigler (1975) finds that the feeding produced "an emotional storm," an impression with which the present commentator (Kanzer) fully agrees.

Langs makes the significant point that the patient is often aware of the analyst's deviations, perhaps through a disturbance that results in the state of empathy between them. His dreams may offer a clue that the analyst should heed. Thus, the dream of Freud's daughter appearing before the Rat Man with dung in place of eyes is related, Langs believes, to the frequent symbolism of a blind person in a dream as a reproach to the analyst. Similarly, a dream in which a dentist extracted the wrong tooth is seen as conveying this same message on another occasion. On the other hand, Merton M. Gill (personal communication) feels that Freud may well have had a keener awareness of events than he indicated in his writings and suggests that his reminding the Rat Man at the time of the "guessing game" that he was *not* the cruel captain was in part at least an indirect interpretation of a transference resistance. He is in favor of interpretations where indicated even quite early in the analysis as a means of limiting the intensification of disturbing emotions. Our fuller understanding of initial communications supports this view.

Kanzer, in a study of "Freud's 'Human Influence' on the Rat Man," undertakes to examine his views and techniques from the contemporary (1909) standpoint of psychoanalysis and in relation to problems that shaped its subsequent lines of advance. He points to several similar experiences of the patient and of Freud himself as given us in self-analyses—reactions to the loss of a dead sibling, for example, and voiding in front of the father as the critical expression of oedipal defiance. At some points, obvious countertransference results, at others empathy, and at least once (with respect to reflections on the relationship between historical and psychic reality) a conflict-free insight that redounded to the advantage of psychoanalysis. The "human influence," however, tended to be irregular and arbitrary and permeated even "intellectual indoctrinations" with suggestive metaphors and images. The advance to neutrality is seen as a means of controlling personal irrelevancies, increasing genuine empathy with the patient and promoting the course of the analytic process.

References

Biegler, J.S. (1975). Treatment of the Rat Man. *Annual of Psychoanalysis* 3: 271–283.

———— (1914). Remembering, repeating and working through. *Standard Edition* 12: 147–156.

Freud, S. (1909). Notes upon a case of obsessional neurosis. Original Record of the Case. *Standard Edition* 10: 251–318.

Holland, N. (1975). An identity for the Rat Man. *International Review of Psycho-Analysis* 2: 157–169.

Kanzer, M. (1952). The transference neurosis of the Rat Man. *Psychoanalytic Quarterly* 21: 181–189. Part IV, Chapter 1 of this volume.

Kestenberg, J. (1966). Rhythm and organization in obsessive-compulsive development. *International Journal of Psycho-Analysis* 47: 151–159.

Lewin, B.D. (1950). *The Psychoanalysis of Elation.* New York: Norton.

Shengold, L. (1967). The effects of overstimulation: rat people. *International Journal of Psycho-Analysis* 48: 403–415.

————— More about rats and rat people. *International Journal of Psycho-Analysis* 52: 277–288. Part IV, Chapter 3 of this volume.

Zetzel, E. (1965). Additional notes upon a case of obsessional neurosis: Freud 1909. *International Journal of Psycho-Analysis* 47: 123–129.

PART V

The Schreber Case

Chapter 1

SCHREBER: FATHER AND SON

WILLIAM G. NIEDERLAND, M.D.

Previous studies of the Schreber case, begun several years ago, led me to postulate two crucial events in Schreber's adult life as the factors precipitating both his illnesses (Niederland 1951). His candidature for the *Reichstag* in 1884 was in my view the precipitating cause of his first psychosis, and his promotion, almost a decade later, to the position of *Senatspräsident*, of the second. I also called attention—among the various as yet obscure aspects of the case history—to the markedly different course and outcome of the two illnesses: the one relatively mild and transient in character, ending in recovery after less than a year; the other rapidly developing into a severe, lifelong psychosis. Freud (Freud 1911) was uncertain about this difference but was inclined to attribute the course and outcome of the second psychosis to the male climacterium because Schreber was in his early fifties at the onset. I laid stress on the events mentioned above and suggested that in both illnesses, "under the impact of a threatening reality which imperiously demanded of Schreber an active masculine role in life, his latent passive-feminine tendencies broke into consciousness, and he fell ill'' (Niederland 1951).

In studying the case I limited myself previously to the *Denkwürdigkeiten*, to Freud's famous analysis (Freud 1911) of it, and to the subsequent contributions of other authors, among the most notable those by M. Klein (1946), Katan (1950,1952,1954), Nunberg (1952), Baumeyer (1955–1956), Macalpine and

Hunter (1955). I then began to extend my investigations and to include certain findings pertaining to the life and work of Schreber's father (Niederland 1960). Unfortunately chapter III of the *Denkwürdigkeiten*, dealing with Schreber's early family relationships, was deleted as "unfit for publication," and very little else is said in the book about its author's childhood or adolescence. Therefore I pursued another route of investigation to acquaint myself, if possible, with some circumstances of Schreber's upbringing.

Having learned that Schreber's father had been a prolific writer, I reviewed as many of his printed works as I could find in the libraries and collections accessible to me, altogether nine out of almost twenty written by Schreber senior. I also read several editions of the *Ärztliche Zimmergymnastik* (Schreber 1865), mentioned in the son's memoirs as well as in the analysis of the latter by Freud. I extracted further supplementary data from a published biography of the father (Ritter 1936), from unprinted biographical material which I received from Germany (some from Dr. F. Baumeyer and Mr. F. von Lepel of West Berlin), and from a rather detailed obituary written by L.M. Politzer (1862) a few months after the elder Schreber's death in 1861.

Though the material reviewed by me is by no means insignificant in volume or content, I wish to make it clear from the outset that data are still scarce and so far add up to little objective information about the son's early life. As fragmentary as these newly gained data are, they nevertheless appear to be not entirely devoid of meaning or interest for the psychoanalyst and the psychiatrist familiar with Freud's analysis of the *Denkwürdigkeiten*. Some of these data may enable us—as Freud had suggested—to trace certain details of Schreber's delusions to their sources and to correlate a number of hitherto obscure passages in the description of his delusional system with certain ideas, principles, and the lifework cherished by his father.

Daniel Paul Schreber was the second son of a social, medical, and educational reformer. The father, Dr. Daniel Gottlieb Moritz Schreber (in some of Dr. Schreber's books the middle name is spelled Gottlob instead of Gottlieb) (1808–1861), was a physician, lecturer, writer, educator, and clinical instructor in the medical school of the University of Leipzig. He specialized in orthopedics and later became the medical director of the orthopedic institute in that Saxon city. He was particularly interested in problems about the upbringing of children, physical culture, methodical body building through gymnastics, preventive medicine, school hygiene, and public health. Politzer (1862) called him "a physician, teacher, nutritionist, anthropologist, therapeutic gymnast and athlete, and above all, a man of action, of tremendous enthusiasm and endurance. . . .." Freud, in speaking of Schreber senior, stated that his memory is kept green to this day by the numerous Schreber Associations which flourish especially in Saxony. . . . His activities in favor of promoting the harmonious upbringing of the young, of securing coordination between education in the home and in the school, of introducing physical culture and manual work with the aim of raising the standards of hygiene—all of these activities exerted a lasting influence upon his contemporaries. His great reputation as the founder of therapeutic gymnastics in Germany is still shown by the wide circulation of his *Ärztliche Zimmergymnastik* [Medical Indoor Gymnastics] in medical circles and the numerous editions through which it has passed.

It is evident that in describing the father's fame and work, Freud refrained from saying more about the man's personality; nor did he mention any of the other books published by Dr. Schreber. This was in conformity with Freud's "policy of restraint" explicitly stated in his monograph, a policy to which Freud both wisely and deliberately adhered while writing about the memoirs of the younger Schreber. It is most likely due to this rule of restraint that Freud spoke of Schreber senior in the general terms that he did. Several of Dr. Schreber's children and members of his family, Professor Paul Flechsig, and others were still alive at the time of Freud's publication. It could hardly have escaped Freud's attention that there was more to this remarkable man, his character, influence, and work.

As almost fifty years have passed since the appearance of Freud's paper and nearly a century since the elder Schreber's death, we are today in a position to deal more fully with the raw material provided by the father and the son. Unhampered by Freud's need for restraint, we can endeavor to amplify, with the help of the additional information now available, certain analytic observations pertaining to the famous case. More specifically, I propose to focus attention on those correlations between paternal and filial mental productions which have not hitherto appeared in the psychoanalytic literature.

One of the popular books written by Dr. Schreber was published in Leipzig a hundred years ago. It is a guidebook for parents and educators. Its long-winded title reads: *Kallip'die oder Erziehung zur Schönheit durch naturgetreue und gleichmässige Förderung normaler Körperbildung* (Schreber 1865). Several equally verbose subtitles are added to the main title. After the author's death the book was reprinted and renamed *The Book of Education of Body and Mind;* it was also called Dr. Schreber's *Erziehungslehre.* I have chosen this volume for particular consideration because it is almost exclusively about the upbringing of children from infancy to adolescence. It also contains passages which indicate that the methods and rules laid down by Dr. Schreber were not merely theoretical principles offered in book form for the public, but that they were also regularly, actively, and personally applied by him in rearing his own children—with telling effect, as he reports with paternal pride. Indeed, he ascribes to his use of these methods a lifesaving influence on one of his children. The main body of Dr. Schreber's educational system is condensed in his often repeated advice to parents and educators that they should use the maximum of pressure and coercion during the earliest years of the child's life. He emphasizes that this will prevent lots of trouble later on. Subjecting the child at the same time to a rigid system of vigorous physical training and combining methodical muscular exercises with measures aimed at physical and emotional restraint, will promote both bodily and mental health.

A more detailed scrutiny of the book permits us to form some tentative ideas about the early upbringing of young Daniel Paul and the general setting, emotional and otherwise, in which he grew up. The reproduction of a few illustrations from Dr. Schreber's *Erziehungslehre* will serve better than words to indicate the nature of his educational methods and their forceful application by him.

Dr. Schreber seems to have been obsessively preoccupied with the posture of young children. Dr. Schreber was particularly concerned with active measures aimed at developing and maintaining the straightest possible posture at all times—whether standing, sitting, walking, or lying; he constructed certain orthopedic apparatus to achieve these ends. (It is possible that this preoccupation stems from the frail state of health which seems to have afflicted Dr. Schreber in his own youth. The biographical material contains a few oblique references to this as well as to his small stature. These circumstances may have contributed, I believe, to his great devotion to physical culture, calisthenics, fresh air, etc.) In his instructions concerning the posture of children between two and eight years of age, he is very strict and demands that children of this age group acquire and maintain a tensely erect posture *(eine straffe Haltung)*. In another passage, referring to the same age group as well as to older children, the great importance of an absolutely straight and supine posture during sleep is stressed.

Figure I shows Dr. Schreber's apparatus for the enforcement of this posture during sleep and its application *in situ*. Figures II and III illustrate the enforcement of a straight posture in the sitting position by means of Dr. Schreber's *Geradehalter*. About the latter we are told by its inventor that "it is made of iron throughout. . . preventing any attempt at improper sitting. . . . It comes in two forms, one recommended for private use [in the home] and one, in a more simplified form, for use in schools, particularly for the first two grades in elementary school." Later the *Schrebersche Geradehalter* was further modified by his friend and co-worker, Dr. Hennig, as shown in Figure IV. Another of Dr. Schreber's body building and muscle strengthening inventions is the

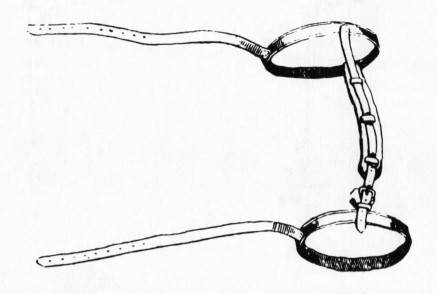

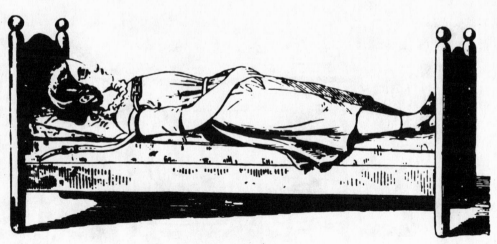

FIGURE I

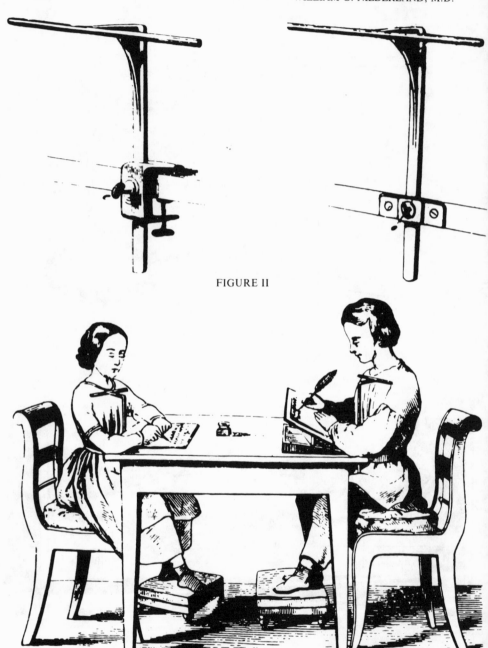

FIGURE II

FIGURE III

FIGURE IV

FIGURE V

*Pangymnastikon.*The construction and application of this apparatus are described in a special volume entitled "The Pangymnastikon, or the whole gymnastic system condensed into one apparatus, or all gymnastic exercises brought within the compass of a single piece of apparatus as the simplest means for the complete development of muscular strength and endurance" (Schreber 1862). These books, like several others by Dr. Schreber, are filled with anatomical illustrations and numerous figure drawings showing the human body in a variety of positions, gymnastic exercises, etc. It is noteworthy in these drawings that when the body is horizontal the figure is usually also drawn rigid (Figure V), and the text emphasizes both posture and endurance.

Besides elaborate prescriptions for daily gymnastics and methodical calisthenics, in word and picture, we find in the *Erziehungslehre* detailed rules for every action during almost every hour in the regular routine of the child's life. There are minute and inflexible instructions for the child's behavior, for its orderliness and cleanliness which "must be made the supreme law," for specific walking exercises through which the child is ritualistically put before breakfast or lunch, with "no deviation allowed from the once established procedure," and with immediate punishment threatened if the child does not strictly follow the rules. In that case "breakfast or lunch is to be withheld from it."

In a lengthy paragraph, "systematic and constant admonishments as well as exercises" are recommended for the proper pronunciation of words and syllables. Great care has to be taken that bad speaking habits, such as "smacking of tongue and lips, inhaling noisily through the nostrils, sniffling through the nose during the act of breathing are energetically put down." Equally to be combated are "the beginnings of passion" which from the very start require *direktes Niederkämpfen*. Disciplinary measures including corporal punishment are indicated at the slightest infringement and "at the earliest age. . . because the ignoble parts of the child's crude nature must be weakened through great strictness."

Dr. Schreber then reminds his readers that they should never forget to compel the child, when it has been punished, "to stretch out its hand to the executor of the punishment"; this ensures the child "against the possibility of spite and bitterness." He recommends that a blackboard be hung in the children's room on which should be recorded each child's act of disobedience, forgetfulness, etc., throughout the month. "At the end of the month, in the presence of all, a family session should be held" before the blackboard, and punishment or praise, as the case may be, should be given to each child on the basis of the marks and notes recorded. Finally, he assures parents and educators that the docility and submissiveness of children brought up in this fashion will be such that there will no need for a continuation of this treatment after the fifth or sixth year of life; nor will parents have to worry, he adds in another chapter, about *gefährliche stille Verirrungen,* that is, that the child will masturbate later on.

To estimate the influence of such paternal precepts and disciplines on the son, it is well to bear in mind that a century or so ago similar notions were widely held in medical and nonmedical circles. We owe to Spitz's historical survey of masturbation a graphic description of such ideas. Spitz points to the sadism "characteristic of the campaign against masturbation" during the second half of the nineteenth century and to the practices of mechanical restraint and corporal punishment which were given strong support by many authoritative physicians at that time. The very popularity of Dr. Schreber's books proves the point. With due allowance to the *Zeitgeist,* it is nevertheless obvious that the father's psychopathology, as evidenced in his writings, must have had a direct and presumably massive impact not only on the public who held his writings in high esteem for several decades, but especially on his own family.

At least three biographical facts can be adduced to demonstrate the accuracy of this assumption. First, Dr. Schreber was a reformer who by his own admission drove some of his children, presumably his sons more than his daughters, into a state of complete submission and passive surrender, making them the earliest targets and examples of his aggressive efforts aimed toward the development of a better and healthier race of men. While the authoritarian regimentation of children, with its emphasis on coercing disciplinary measures, was probably typical of the country and the era in which Dr. Schreber lived, it is a matter of record that the straps, belts, and other forms of mechanical restraint were his personal inventions. They obviously sprang from his own pathology, were recommended and applied by him, rationalized as educational reform, and at least some of his children were subjected to this "holy" purpose. In fact, the frequent exhortations in Dr. Schreber's books against the "softness" of life, the "decadence" of the world, and the threatening degeneracy of youth—his often repeated warnings and appeals to parents, educators, school and government authorities—themselves indicate that such regimentation of children was even then becoming outmoded. The fact that, analytically speaking, Dr. Schreber was crusading against masturbation and other *gefährliche Verirrungen* leading to physical and mental "softness" in children, does not require further elaboration. The violent, sadistically tinged methods used by him in this fight prevented at least one of his children from establishing an identity for himself, particularly a sexual identity, and is recorded throughout the *Denkwürdigkeiten.*

The second assumption that there were strong sadistic components in Dr. Schreber's personality and behavior does not rest on the material extracted from his books alone. It receives direct support from an independent contemporary source. One of the medical reports on Daniel Paul Schreber which Baumeyer (1955–1956) recovered in Saxony some years ago has an annotation which reads:

"Der Vater (Schöpfer der Schrebergärten zu Leipzig) litt an Zwangsvorstellungen mit Mordtrieb." ("The father [founder of the Schreber Gardens in Leipzig] suffered from compulsive manifestations with murderous impulses.") In a personal communication, Dr. Baumeyer has expressed his agreement with my opinion that this illuminating statement (contained in the medical report of the Sonnenstein Asylum, where the son was confined after his second breakdown) must have been based on information given to an attending psychiatrist in the Asylum by some close member of the Schreber family, because the father had died more than thirty years before the entry was made.

My third biographical point refers precisely to Dr. Schreber's death and to what seems to have preceded it. In the late 1850s, probably in 1858 or 1859, according to his biographer, Ritter (1936), Dr. Schreber suffered a serious accident when a heavy iron ladder fell on his head in the gymnasium where he did his customary calisthenics. He seems never to have fully recovered from the sequel of this injury which are described by Ritter as "a protracted, chronic head condition, the exact medical diagnosis of which is not known." The biographer then raised the pertinent question as to "whether actually this ladder accident or possibly a severe nervous breakdown" unconnected with the head injury may have been the basis of his illness. A letter written by one of Dr. Schreber's daughters (Baumeyer 1955–1956) to the Sonnenstein Asylum in 1900 also mentions "the fall of an iron ladder in the gymnasium on the head [of the father] some months before the onset of a strange disease of the head," and she hints that there were some marked changes in her father's character. At any rate, the cautious wording "strange disease of the head" and Ritter's outspoken allusion to a breakdown seem to indicate a mental illness, or at least an undiagnosed illness accompanied by prevalently mental symptoms, which began when the father was fifty or fifty-one years of age. He died—and here we have the clinical diagnosis and the date—of intestinal ileus on November 10, 1861. A later autopsy revealed a perforation of the intestines in the area of the appendix.

Comparing the data about the illnesses which afflicted both the father and the son as each of them entered the sixth decade of life, and reviewing further the characteristics of certain mental productions of both men, it becomes difficult to avoid the recognition of some noteworthy similarities in the two. The father, following an injury to his head, falls ill in his fiftieth or fifty-first year with what his daughter and his biographer alike call a strange disease of the head *(Kopfleidens)*. He dies at the age of fifty-three. The son, Daniel Paul, also becomes sick at the age of fifty-one and his chief symptoms initially are complaints about his head, softening of the brain, that he would die soon, etc. In November, 1893, he is admitted, with his second and chronic disease, to the Leipzig University Psychiatric Clinic where he makes a suicidal attempt that same month. Two years later, when he has reached the age of fifty-three, he records in his memoirs a marked deterioration of his condition in these words, "The month of November, 1895, marks an important time in the history of my life. . . . During that time the signs of transformation into a woman became so marked on my body that I could no longer ignore the imminent goal at which the whole development was aiming. . . ."

Though the sick son does not explicitly say so in this passage, we know that the development of which he speaks was aiming at the union of himself, as a woman, with the deified father. At the age of fifty-three, he connects this delusional goal chronologically with the month of November, the month his father died at the age of fifty-three. Scrutinizing the medical reports found by Baumeyer (1955–1956) further, one notes, perhaps with some initial surprise, that the three important hospitalizations in the younger Schreber's life occurred in or about the month of November. In different years of course, but all because of rather acutely developing mental symptoms necessitating his hospitalization just then. To be sure, coincidental factors cannot be ruled out; nor can it be ignored that the onset of the first two illnesses leading to hospitalization followed, on each occasion, external life events which were discussed in some detail in my previous paper (Niederland 1951). But had not the father's mental difficulties and overt nervous symptoms also followed an external event in *his* life, namely, the sudden head injury in the gymnasium? Could not those external events in the son's life, especially his rather sudden and highly emotionally charged promotion at the age of fifty-one, have been unconsciously equated by the patient to the very "blow on the head" which struck the father with such deleterious consequences at approximately the same age? In his memoirs the son time and again speaks of all sorts of blows directed at his head, often in connection with noise and spoken words.

Be that as it may, there are other factors to consider with respect to the introjected paternal image which remained "enshrined" in the son's ego and whose "release" can be traced in part through the chapters of his memoirs. (I am borrowing these graphic terms from Bychowski's formulations of the mechanisms here involved [Bychowski 1956]. In one of the very few passages in the *Denkwürdigkeiten* in which the son refers to his father's work directly and in an undistorted fashion, he mentions the *twenty-third* edition of the paternal *Ärztliche Zimmergymnastik*. It is therefore worth noting that the memoirs consist of *twenty-three* chapters, including the introduction, and not counting the various postscripts and addenda. The finished manuscript of the memoirs was handed to the Saxonian Court of Appeals (which had to decide on rescinding the tutelage) in precisely *twenty-three* copybooks written by the younger Schreber. In court the latter countered one of the main objections against publication of his memoirs with the following pointed argument recorded in the legal proceedings: "The publication of the Memoirs is planned, according to preliminary agreement with the publisher Nauhardt in Leipzig, in the form of a contract on the basis of a commission, *the same form of publication in which his father's Medical Indoor Gymnastics appeared. . .*" (italics added).

As the father's writings were prompted by his missionary zeal to spread information on physical health and body building everywhere so that a stronger race of men would result (the father's *Erziehungslehre* was expressly dedicated to the welfare of future generations), so the son, during his illness, appears to have been driven by the introjected paternal image in the direction of the same aspirations. In the introductory remarks to and in various chapters of the memoirs the younger Schreber expresses his certainty that the publication of his experiences of miracles, God, rays, etc. will be a blessing to humanity. His sole aim, he declares, is to spread truth and further knowledge for the good of mankind. The father, with no little apostolic grandeur, strives for the development of better health and hygiene in an earthbound way, as it were; the son in his delusional elaboration of these precepts does so *in an archaic, magical way.* The father's books are replete with anatomical illustrations and figure drawings. The sick son, during the years of hospitalization, often draws human figures on paper and fills pages of his own book with ruminations on drawing and sketching.

Throughout the *Denkwürdigkeiten* there are numerous references to God's "writing-down-stystem" which the patient himself finds "extraordinarily difficult to explain to other people. . . as it belongs even for me to the realm of the unfathomable." I am inclined to trace the origin of this divine "system" to the father's handwritten notes, manuscripts, books, lectures, and to see in it also the psychotic, regressively deified elaboration of the paternal blackboard which, with its ominous marks and notes, probably played such a menacing role in the patient's childhood. We owe in some measure the appearance of the memoirs to this "writing-down" method originally used by the father and later taken over by the son.' Long before the younger Schreber began writing the full text, he kept notes in shorthand, jotted down his thoughts and experiences on scraps of paper, later making annotations in copybooks. If he had not made ample use of "God's writing-down-system," the *Denkwürdigkeiten* would possibly never have been published, at least not in their present form.

It seems therefore permissible to think of the memoirs as representing, in a sense, the younger Schreber's complex struggle for identification with his father as well as his battle against it, a struggle which accompanies and intensifies his homosexual conflict, so clearly elucidated by Freud. With this premise we can attempt to arrive at a fuller understanding of those bizarre ideas in the son's delusional system which, directly or indirectly, appear to be derived from the introjected paternal image. These ideas constitute archaic elaborations of certain paternal characteristics and procedures, as experiences introjected early in life and later "released" in the memoirs by the son. The introjection of his autocratic father's methods re-emerge as delusional or hallucinatory entities in the son's archaic regression and are recorded by him in a number of autobiographical, relevant, but usually quite obscure passages through the *Denkwürdigkeiten*. Many of the divine miracles of God affecting the patient's body become recognizable, shorn of their delusional distortions, as what they must originally have been modeled on: the infantile, regressively distorted image of the father's massive, coercive as well as seductive manipulations performed on the child's body, as represented in Figures I through V.

The father's apparatus of belts and body straps give new sense and meaning to such divine miracles as "being tied-to-earth," "being tied-to-celestial-bodies," or "fastened-to-rays." The "chest-compressing-miracle," described in the memoirs as one of the most horrifying assaults against his body, also becomes clearer if viewed in its relation to the paternal apparatus shown in Figures II and III. The "coccyx miracle" repeatedly mentioned in the son's book refers, I believe, to the strict rules governing sitting down enforced by the father. The seductive character of these paternal manipulations is clearly shown by the expression *"Menschenspielerei"* (play-with-human-beings) which Schreber connects, even in his preface, with the miracles and the stimulation caused by them. Other miracles which during the early years of hospitalization affected the son's "whole abdomen, the so-called *putrifaction of the abdomen,"* caused the *"obstruction of my gut,"* and apparently gave him the feeling of "being dead and rotten" (italics in the original). These seem to refer to the shocking impact of the terminal ileus to which the father quite suddenly succumbed. The very night of his death the father had been scheduled to lecture before the Leipzig Pedagogical Society. The son was then nineteen years of age.

As is well known from psychotic patients, and as I have shown elsewhere with regard to Schreber (Niederland 1951), the son was by no means without insight into some of these connections. About his identification with the father he states for example: "God is inseparably tied to my person through the power of attraction of my nerves. . . . There is no possibility of God freeing Himself from my nerves for the rest of my life." In another passage he writes: "I had the 'God' or 'Apostle'. . . in my body, more specifically in my belly." Note that the word "apostle" is used directly here by the son. In German idiom, the father was a *"Gesundheitsapostel"*.

Of particular interest in the father's *Erziehungslehre* is the emphasis on early and massive bodily stimulation (through manipulations, exercises, appliances, etc.) which, at a somewhat later age, is combined with religious observations and practices. The child should be taught, Dr. Schreber explains, to turn "at the end of every day its mind to God, to review the feelings and actions of the day. . . in order to mirror its inner self in the pure rays of God, the loving and universal father. . .." Dr. Schreber also recommends the mandatory teaching of human anatomy in direct conjunction with religious education in public schools. Several italicized pages in the concluding chapters of the *Erziehungslehre* deal in a rather obscure and mystical way with *dem rein Göttlichen* (the purely divine) and with the merging, in truly religious feeling, of two types of *Strahlen* (rays) to a point of complete union. Whether these notable passages in the father's work formed a sort of starting point for their later elaboration by the son into the equation *rays = father = God*, and also into the Schreberian divine hierarchy with its florid anatomical-religious peculiarities is difficult to decide, though I am inclined to see also here important interrelationships which invite further investigation.

After having clarified the meaning of some of these obscurities in Schreber's memoirs, we may also understand more fully a few of his frequent complaints. When he protests, for instance, against "the enormous infringement of man's most primitive rights," or when he accuses Professor Flechsig that "you, like so many doctors [father], could not completely resist the temptation of using a patient as an object for experimentation," we may legitimately connect the feelings expressed here with the massive coercive aspects of his early upbringing. By way of pointing more sharply to the patient's own wording, I am also inclined to see in these statements a confirmation of my earlier stated view that Dr. Schreber, the father, physician, educator, and reformer, quite likely chose his male children as objects for his reformatory "experimentation," as the son so aptly puts it. In fact, the first son, Gustav, committed suicide; the second son, Daniel Paul, became psychotic and later "the most quoted patient in psychiatry" (Macalpine and Hunter 1955). The three daughters apparently remained well. This outcome, completely unknown to Freud, essentially corroborates Freud's main thesis about the case.

Freud, who presumably had no information about the patient's childhood, nevertheless discovered from the memoirs that their author must have found "his way back into the feminine attitude which he had exhibited toward his father in the earliest years" of his life. Freud also postulated on purely theoretical grounds that the brother might have been older than the patient. We now know that Freud was correct on both counts.

As incomplete as these more recently accumulated data still are, they enable us to clarify a number of obscurities in the *Denkwürdigkeiten* and to throw new light on certain peculiarities in Schreber's delusional system. In reconstructing and retracing the early elements of this case history, our next task will be to focus further attention on the early traumatic relationship with the father, on the nature and genesis of the divine miracles, and on the meaning of the cosmic myths common to both father and son.

Summary

A preliminary study derived from a biography, nine of seventeen or eighteen published works, and other material related to the lifework and character of the father of Daniel Paul Schreber is presented. It yields a number of facts that permit partial reconstruction of certain childhood influences and later events in the life of the author of the *Denkwürdigkeiten* which became part of his delusional system. It also makes clear the source of some of the hitherto obscure passages in the son's record of his psychotic delusions.

References

Baumeyer, F. (1955–1956). Der Fall Schreber. *Psyche* 9:513–536.

Bychowski, G. (1956). The ego and the introjects. *Psychoanalytic Quarterly* 25:11–36.

Freud S. (1911). Psychoanalytic notes upon an autobiographical account of a case of paranoia *Collected Papers*, vol. 3:387–466.

Katan, M. (1950). Schreber's hallucinations about the "little men." *International Journal of Psycho-Analysis* 31:32–35.

———— (1952). Further remarks about Schreber's hallucinations. *International Journal of Psycho-Analysis* 33:429–433.

———— (1954) The importance of the nonpsychotic part of the personality in schizophrenia. *International Journal of Psycho-Analysis* 35:119–128.

Klein, M. (1946). Notes on some schizoid mechanisms. *International Journal of Psycho-Analysis* 27:99–110.

Macalpine, I. and Hunter, R. A. (1955). *Daniel Paul Schreber—Memoirs of My Nervous Illness*. Cambridge, Mass.: Robert Bentley.

Niederland, W. G. (1951). Three notes on the Schreber case. *Psychoanalytic Quarterly* 20:579–591.

———— (1960). Schreber's father. *Journal of the American Psychoanalytic Association* 8:492–499.

Nunberg, H. (1952). Discussion of M. Katan's paper on Schreber's hallucination. *International Journal of Psycho-Analysis* 33.

Politzer, L. M. (1862). *Daniel Gottlieb Moritz Schreber*. Jahr. f. Kinderheilkunde V.

Ritter, A. (1936). *Schreber—Das Bildungssystem eines Arztes.* Erlangen: Inaugural Dissertation.

Schreber, D.G.M. (1858). *Kallip·die oder Erziehung zur Schönheit durch naturgetreue und gleichmässige Förderung normaler Körperbildung.* Leipzig: F. Fleischer.

——— (1862). *Das Pangymnastikon.* Leipzig: F. Fleischer.

——— (1865). *Ärztliche Zimmergymnastik.* Leipzig: F. Fliescher.

Spitz, R.A. (1952). Authority and masturbation: some remarks on a bibliographical investigation. *Psychoanalytic Quarterly* 21:490–527.

Chapter 2

THE "MIRACLED-UP" WORLD

OF SCHREBER'S CHILDHOOD

WILLIAM G. NIEDERLAND, M.D.

Among Freud's famous case histories, his study of the Schreber case (1911) holds a special position for various reasons:

It is a clinical textbook of analytic discoveries and psychodynamic formulations in the field of psychotic illness. As Strachey has recently stated (1958), Freud's monograph on Schreber is "in many ways the forerunner of the metapsychological papers on which Freud embarked three or four years later."

Though it is in its entirety a clinical study, the Schreber analysis deals with the productions of a patient who as a person was as unknown to Freud as Freud to him, and about whose childhood, early experiences, family relationships, etc., Freud knew next to nothing. Indeed, Freud tells us that his analysis of Schreber's *Memoirs* (1903, 1955) made use of only one fact not given in the book, i.e., the patient's age at the time he fell ill.

Moreover, it is the analysis of a printed report, and represents—along with Freud's other literary-historical writings during that epoch—one of the first examples of a growing number of analytic studies in the fields of literature, history, biography, i.e., of what today is called pathography.

With reference to Schreber's childhood, Freud spoke tersely of "the shadowy sketch of the infantile material" that he had found in the *Memoirs*. In the introductory paragraphs as well as in other parts of his paper, Freud also encouraged analytically trained observers to familiarize themselves more thoroughly with the circumstances of Schreber's life because such greater familiarization would enable them "to trace back innumerable details [of the patient's autobiography] to their sources and so to discover their meaning."

Prompted by these remarks and availing myself of a certain amount of newly accumulated information about Schreber's life and antecedents (collected partly by Baumeyer [1956], partly by myself [1959], I have recently undertaken a study of such potential sources and of the material derived from them. Furthermore, focusing attention on those obscure aspects of the *Memoirs* which have hitherto remained unexplored, I have tried to correlate these passages with certain newly established childhood data which promise to be of value in our efforts to arrive at a better understanding of some peculiarites in Schreber's delusional system. As all attempts to discover the famous chapter III originally deleted from Schreber's printed text have proved futile, my work along these lines has been limited to an inquiry into the early traumatic relationship between Schreber *poere* and Schreber *fils*. Though this type of reconstructive approach is necessarily handicapped by significant shortcomings—nothing relevant, for instance, is known about Schreber's mother—it nevertheless seems a legitimate approach, since it is based on the only childhood material at present available to us as well as on Freud's main thesis in this case: "Here we find ourselves. . . on the familiar ground of the father-complex."

Indeed, as it is the father who, transformed into the superior figure of God, stands in the center of the son's delusional system, and as it is also the father whose character and influence can now be more fully appraised on the basis of our additional background material, it may be expected that some heretofore inaccessible formations in Schreber's delusional system, especially those directly derived from the father-son situation, will now become analytically and genetically comprehensible. This approach, with all its unfortunate lack of maternal data, appears even more promising in the light of Schreber's own statements that he is primarily concerned with "the relationship between God and myself" and with ideas formed by him as a result of his "impressions and experiences about. . . the essence and attributes of God. . .." In the following pages, these paternal "essence and attributes" as well as "the *lasting* conditions" (italics in the original) caused by them in the son will be further investigated.

A Reconstructive Survey of
Schreber's Early Experiences

If there existed a biographical outline of Schreber's life before he fell ill at the height of an impressive professional career, it would be relatively easy to

give an anamnestic account of the events which ultimately led to his hospitalization (and eventual death) in an insane asylum. So far, no such account is
possible. What is known adds up to very few reliable, albeit relevant data on
his childhood. From Baumeyer's report (1956) we learn that Schreber had been
a brilliant student at school and that his memory always was and remained
"excellent" through all the years of his illness. To the same source we owe
these pertinent facts about Schreber's early family constellation:

Father: Daniel Gottlieb Moritz Schreber, physician and educator, 1808–1861
Mother: Name and origin unknown, 1815–1907 [After the completion of this
    paper I learned the name of Schreber's mother: Pauline, n9ee Haase. Thus,
    Schreber's confused sexual identity appears concretized, as it were, in his
    two given names, Daniel Paul(ine)—*nomen est omen*.]
Brother: Gustav, 1839–1877, apparently unmarried, committed suicide
Sister: Anna, 1840–1914, married
*Patient: Daniel Paul, 1842–1911, married 1878 (one year after the brother's
    suicide)*
Sister: Sidonie, 1846–1924, unmarried
Sister: Klara, 1848–1917, married

From Baumeyer's communication we know further that the patient had shown
"a hasty, restless, nervous nature. . . from childhood on," as reported in a
letter by Schreber's youngest sister in 1900. This letter also stresses her brother's
rich intellectual gifts and his goodhearted, friendly personality. No further objective data about the patient's early life are available except the fact that the
Schreber family were Protestants and lived in comfortable economic circumstances.

In one of the few passages of the *Memoirs* in which the patient himself refers
to his childhood directly, we are told:

Miracles of heat and cold were and still are directed against me. . . always
with the purpose of preventing the natural feeling of bodily well-
being. . . . During the *cold-miracle* the blood is forced out of the extremities,
so causing a subjective feeling of cold. . . during the *heat-miracle* the blood
is forced towards my face and head. . . . *From youth accustomed to enduring
both heat and cold, these miracles troubled me little. . . ."* [italics added]

These and other remarks induced me to inquire more closely into the nature
and genesis of the "divine miracles" performed upon Schreber's body. Since
one set of miracles is recorded here by Schreber in connection with a childhood
reminiscence, I shall return to this point later. The quoted passage also provided

me with specific evidence concerning the reality of certain childhood events or experiences which may have played a role in the production of such fantasies. Upon realizing the importance of the "historical truth" (Freud 1938) for the origin of at least some of these phenomena, I determined to submit the life and character of Schreber's father to further scrutiny in an effort to trace, if possible, the early history of the paternal contributions to the son's psychopathology. My investigations along these lines were facilitated when I found relevant, if scattered bits of childhood material in the father's printed works. Several of his books (1839, 1852, 1858) offer lengthy descriptions of the particular methods and educational procedures used by him in the upbringing of his children. A summary report on this part of my study is published elsewhere (1959).

Apart from a regimented, rigidly disciplined type of education which seems to have been Schreber's lot from early infancy, he appears to have been forced into complete submission and passive surrender by a father whose sadism may have been but thinly disguised under a veneer of medical, reformatory, religious, and philanthropic ideas. The presence of overt murderous impulses in the father is documented in one of the case histories published by Baumeyer (1956). Schreber *p9ere* did more than invent unusual mechanical devices for coercing his children into submission, presumably his sons more than his daughters. On the basis of ample evidence found by me in Dr. Schreber's own writings, it is clear that he also used a "scientifically" elaborated system of relentless mental and corporeal pressure alternating with occasional indulgence. This methodical sequence of studiously applied terror interrupted by compensatory periods of seductive benevolence was combined with ritual observances which as a reformer he incorporated into his over-all missionary scheme of physical education.

From the multitude of examples enumerated in the father's various books, I mention here only a few previously unreported by me, since they concern events in Schreber *fils'* early life. To start with the son's above-quoted statement about his being accustomed "from youth to enduring both heat and cold," we learn from the father's textbook on child care (1852) that ". . . beginning about three months after birth the infant's skin should be cleaned by the use of cold ablutions *only,* for the purpose of physically toughening up the child from its earliest days." While it is advisable to administer warm baths to infants up to the age of six months, "one may then pass to cool and cold *general* ablutions which should be performed at least once daily and for which the body should be purposefully prepared by prior local applications of cold water" (italics in the original). From the fourth or fifth year of life cold baths are the accepted rule.

In an earlier volume entitled *Das Buch der Gesundheit (The Book of Health)* (1839), Schreber senior recommends that children's "eyelids, eyebrows, and temporal areas be treated daily with cold water," which in his view will make for sharper vision. In a later text (1858) he instructs parents to wash the eyes of their babies thoroughly a number of times a day with a little sponge through the first several months of life. This book also offers detailed advice on how to combat crying in young children:

> . . . crying and whimpering without reason express nothing but a whim, a mood, and the first emergence of stubbornness; they must be dealt with positively, through quick distraction of attention, serious words, knocking on the bed (actions which usually startle the child and make him stop crying), or if all this be to no avail, through the administration of comparatively mild, intermittently repeated, corporeal admonishments. It is essential that this treatment be continued until its purpose is attained. . . . Such a procedure is necessary only once or, at most, twice—and then one is master of the child forever. From then on one glance, one word, one single menacing gesture are sufficient to rule the child. . . .

The whole problem of the "cry baby," of later moodiness and stubbornness in children can thus be settled, according to Schreber senior, during their first year of life. This is also the best time to train the young child "in the art of renouncing." The mode of training here recommended is simple and effective: While the child sits in the lap of its nurse or nanny, the latter eats and drinks whatever she desires; however intense the child's oral needs may become under such circumstances, they must never be gratified. Not a morsel of food must be given the child besides its regular three meals a day. The father is particularly strict in this situation. He relates an episode "in my own family" when a nurse, with one of the Schreber children sitting in her lap, was eating pears and could not resist the impulse to give a small piece of the pear to the begging child, though this had been strictly *verboten*. The nurse was immediately fired, and since news about this drastic action spread quickly among the children's nurses then available in Leipzig, the father writes, from then on he had "no further trouble with any other such erring maids or nurses."

In a different connection Dr. Schreber (1858) states: "Physical diseases in children . . . are decisive tests of the inner sense, true character tests." He then reports another incident from his family life. Because of its revealing character I wish to quote the account of this occurrence in the original:

> Eines meiner Kinder war in dem Alter von 1½ Jahr in einer Weise erkrankt, dass das einzige auf Lebensrettung hoffen lassende, noch dazu gefahrvolle Heilverfahren nur bei vollständig ruhiger Fügsamkeit des kleinen Patienten möglich war. Es gelang, da das Kind an den unbedingtesten Gehorsam gegen

mich von Anfang an gewöhnt war, während ausserdem das Leben kes Kindes nach menschlicher Berechnung höchstwahrscheinlich unrettbar gewesen wäre. [One of my children had fallen ill at the age of one and a half and the only treatment, though a dangerous one, giving any hope for saving his life was possible only through the completely quiet submissiveness of the young patient. It succeeded, because the child had been accustomed from the beginning to the most absolute obedience toward me, whereas otherwise the child's life would in all probability have been beyond any chance of rescue.]

The two episodes, the pear incident and the child's illness, seem to me particularly illuminating. They indicate that the strict rules set down in Dr. Schreber's writings, far from being theoretical educational concepts, were literally, meticulously, and often personally enforced in the upbringing of his own children. In other words, here we have samples of those actual and concrete experiences for which we have been searching in our effort to learn more about the childhood of the young Daniel Paul. It is quite possible, indeed, that the child in question who showed "the most absolute obedience" toward the father already at the age of one and a half was our patient himself. The gender used in the Germany text *("des* kleinen Patien*ten")* makes it clear that it was a male child. It may also have been the elder brother, of course. If so, the experiences of the younger brother cannot have been much different; for the father who so proudly announces to the world the lifesaving success of his educational system can hardly be expected to have refrained, in the case of the second son, from using measures closely resembling those which had served him so well for the first.

It is beyond the scope of this paper to examine in detail the relative merits or demerits of such practices, the question of their application in infancy, their impact on the development of the body ego, and a host of other problems they pose. Suffice it to say that we will presently encounter certain psychic derivatives of these experiences as components of some of the "miracled-up" delusional formations which fill the pages of the *Memoirs*.

It is obvious, then, that the child who was later to become "the most-quoted patient in psychiatry" (Macalpine and Hunter 1955) had already undergone a notable degree of traumatization when he entered his third or fourth year of life. About that time the father, bent as he was on his stated goal "to eradicate the child's crude nature. . . and to put down its ignoble parts," embarked on a more complex and more ambitious program of regimented upbringing. He brought to bear on the child the whole system of medical gymnastics, calisthenic exercises, orthopedic appliances, and other regulatory practices which he had invented himself and which I described in some detail elsewhere (1959). During those years the young boy seems to have been subjected to what Sylvester (1959) has named "gadget experience," that is, a combination of ego-disruptive experiences which comes from the usage of mechanical contraptions on the child's body, for orthopedic or other purposes, and which can result in serious distortions of the child's body image, ego structure, reality testing, and object relations. That the sometimes crippling effects of such early "gadget experience" did not fully materialize during Schreber's childhood—the sister's testimony, if correct, suggests a comparatively mild form of childhood neurosis—and were only later "miracled up" during his psychotic illness, may be due to several circumstances. One of these may have been the fact that the father, with all his compulsive rigidity and authoritarian strictness, applied his mechanical contraptions and his other methods of physical and mental restraint as a rule intermittently, i.e., limited to a number of hours during the day or night. Also the effects of the father's alternating practices—periods of enforced passivity followed by intense physical activity—have to be considered. An illustration of this procedure will be presented below in connection with my discussion of Dr. Schreber's rules for the sitting or resting child.

Another relevant factor appears to be connected with the father's psychopathology in a more direct way. The latter's defensive struggle against his own sadism frequently transpires in his texts on child care. For instance, he insists that all manipulatory practices and coercive actions on the child's body be performed *iucunde*, as he puts it, that is, in a manner pleasurable and enjoyable to the child. The impact of this procedure on the child's psychosexual development, the intense overstimulation thus produced, the premature interference with libidinal needs in general, and the emphasis on the homosexual libido in particular, the peculiar mixture of once brutally enforced, then again pleasurably induced passivity—all these do not require further analytic elaboration. Nor is it surprising to find among the elder Schreber's prescriptions further suggestions along these lines, for instance, his recommendation of enemas as "the most subtle form of laxative." He is tireless in his campaign against masturbation, which necessitates "incessant vigilance" on the part of parents and educators, because it is "this insidious plague of youth. . . which makes the unfortunate [youngsters] stupid and dumb, fed up with life [*lebensmüde*], overly disposed to sickness, vulnerable to countless diseases of the lower abdomen and to diseases of the nervous system [*Nervenkrankheiten*], and very soon makes them impotent as well as sterile." The son's version of these paternal threats and dire pronouncements forms an essential part of the *Memoirs*, even as their original title indicates: *Denkwürdigkeiten eines* NERVENKRANKEN. We may well be justified in recognizing in this title the reminiscences (or may we say, confessions?) of one who saw himself, long before his delusions took on a religious-mythical character, sick and impotent as a result of masturbation. This is indicated in the language of the medical report accompanying the *Memoirs:* "He thought he was dead and rotten, suffering from the plague, [with] all sorts of horrible manipulations being performed on his body. . .." That Schreber felt that masturbation had something to do with his illness is also shown by the label *Pestkranker* he applied to himself, thus employing the very term *Pest* (plague) which the father uses to characterize the plague of masturbation. The patient further reports: "At various times I had on my body fairly definite signs of the manifestations of plague."

Another factor of considerable import in Schreber's early life must have been the voice of the father, not merely in the usual sense as the guiding and directing voice of his childhood, but more specifically as the chief instrument of the father's multifold activities as a fiery preacher and orator, as an indefatigable teacher and emitter of verbal exhortations, injunctions, and blandishments. Politzer (1862), in his obituary, emphasizes the father's restless energy and missionary zeal. From all we know, the elder Schreber, rather than being an ordinary physician and orthopedist, was really a reformer with a mission, an educator with a single goal, or, in the son's terminology, an "Apostle" and "God"—a verbose and talkative sort of "God," we may perhaps be allowed to add. In this respect, too, the father's writings are the best testimony. Through most of his books runs a note of relentless sermonizing, and one can almost hear his voice in his long-winded sentences, admonishing, lecturing, scolding, and exhorting. An interesting question arises here: Was Schreber's choice of profession, law, influenced by these experiences or rather by the fact that the paternal grandfather had been a lawyer, or by both?

On the basis of our knowledge to date, it is not possible to answer this question. Reviewing this sketchy outline of the nature and extent of the paternal influences to which the young Schreber was exposed, it also must be noted that the data presented are open to various inferences. With regard to the authoritarian way of upbringing, the antimasturbation campaign, the paternal harangues, the spirit of the times—*der Zeitgeist*—has to be considered. One might reason that the elder Schreber was the type of "symbiotic father" whose all-pervasive presence, usurpation of the maternal role, and other domineering features (overtly sadistic as well as paternalistically benevolent, punitive as well as seductive) lent themselves to their fusion into the bizarre God hierarchy characteristic of the son's delusional system. As to the significance of the collected data, it seems to me that the sources of information from which they are derived are pertinent and reliable. Our reconstructive approach based on these sources provides us with enough material to be included in an evaluation of Schreber's childhood experiences, and our exploration of these experiences is apt to throw new light on the early traumatic relationship between father and son.

In the next section of this paper I propose to examine one aspect of this relationship, the origin of the "divine miracles," from a psychoanalytic angle. I will attempt to demonstrate how some of Schreber's childhood experiences mentioned above emerge in the form of "miracled-up" delusions during the psychotic process and are projected in various chapters of the *Memoirs* . It is as if the pages of the manuscript Schreber filled with his delusional descriptions had served him as a welcome screen for the externalization and concretization of his fantasies. (The word *miracled up—angewundert* in the original—constantly used by Schreber in this connection, is in a sense indicative of this mechanism; in part a neologism, the term not only suggests the startling appearance of something unexpected, but also the subject's act of externalizing this inner percept and then staring wonderingly at it as a miraculous, incomprehensible, and at the same time concrete phenomenon of the outer world.)

The Genesis of the "Divine Miracles"

In one of his last papers Freud (1938) writes about the genetic approach in psychoanalysis: "What we are in search of is a picture of the patient's forgotten years that shall be alike trustworthy and in all essential respects complete." He then advances the proposition that there is a kernel of historical truth in psychotic delusions, that "in them something that has been experienced in infancy and then forgotten re-emerges—something that the child has seen or heard at a time. . . and that now forces its way into consciousness." According to Freud, part of the analytic process "consists in liberating the fragment of historic truth from its distortions and its attachments to the actual present day and in leading it back to the point in the past to which it belongs." Waelder (1951), later applying this concept to the clinical study of paranoia, sees the paranoid symptoms as a "return of the denied," and I have recently (1958) expanded these views with respect to certain auditory-tactile sensations experienced by the child during the first years of life.

This approach, then, first made by Freud, to the historical truth (albeit distorted) in the mental productions of psychotic patients, would appear to contribute much to a fuller understanding of such productions. The "divine miracles" which abound in Schreber's *Memoirs* are a case in point. There are literally hundreds of these miracles scattered throughout its text, and chapter XI entitled "Bodily Integrity Damaged by Miracles" offers a detailed description of many of them. The opening paragraph of this chapter reads:

From the first beginnings of my contact with God up to the present day my body has continuously been the object of divine miracles. If I wanted to describe all these miracles in detail I could fill a whole book with them alone.

I may say that *hardly a single limb or organ in my body escaped being temporarily damaged by miracles, nor a single muscle being pulled by miracles,* either moving or paralyzing it according to the respective purpose. Even now the miracles which I experience hourly are still of a nature as to frighten every other human being to death. . . . In the first year of my stay at Sonnenstein sanatorium the miracles were of such a threatening nature that I thought I had to fear almost incessantly for my life, my health or my reason. . . . [In a footnote Schreber adds:] This, as indeed the whole report about the miracles enacted on my body, will naturally sound extremely strange to all other human beings, and one may be inclined to see in it only the product of a pathologically vivid imagination. In reply I can only give the assurance that *hardly any memory from my life is more certain than* the miracles recounted in this Chapter. *What can be more definite for a human being than what he has lived through and felt on his own body?* Small mistakes may have occurred as my anatomical knowledge is *naturally only that of a layman.* . . . [italics added]

The patient's mode of experiencing his inner stimuli as being of outside origin and the hypercathected quality of these experiences are here stated with extraordinary sharpness.

A word is needed on Schreber's reference to himself as a layman. He does so throughout his book. I have found that, whenever he mentions his status as a layman, he directly or indirectly alludes to his relation with his father, the physician and orthopedist, whose domain is human anatomy. The first sentence of the first chapter (entitled "God and Immortality") of the *Memoirs* contains the same apologetic statement about "I as a layman" in matters of anatomy and health, as if the son dared but hesitatingly and fearfully to enter the discussion of this subject, that is, the father's medical and personal domain.

In fact, the whole chapter XI deals with the changes in Schreber's own anatomy which were brought about by God's miracles constantly performed on his body. The son enumerates a long list of such miracles beginning with the threatened emasculation of his genitals, proceeding to the removal of various inner organs, to the damages inflicted on his head, chest, abdomen, and nerves, and ending with the enactment of miracles on his muscles and skeleton, including his coccyx bone. In examining the nature of these miracles, the analyst cannot fail to note marked similarities between the miracles listed in the *Memoirs* and the physical manipulations which Schreber had experienced during childhood at the hands of his father. Here are two examples:

One of the most horrifying miracles was the so-called *compression-of-the-*

chest-miracle [the son reports] which I endured. . . . It consisted in the whole chest wall being compressed, so that the state of oppression caused by the lack of breath was transmitted to my whole body. . . . Next to the *compression-of-the-chest-miracle*, the most abominable of all miracles was. . . "the head-compressing-machine". . . which compressed my head as though in a vise by turning a kind of screw, causing my head temporarily to assume an elongated almost pear-shaped form. It had an extremely threatening effect, particularly as it was accompanied by severe pain. The screws were loosened temporarily but only very gradually, so that the compressed state usually continued for some time. [The German names of these two miracles—*das sogenannte Engbrüstigkeitswunder* and *Kopfzusammenschnürungswunder*—point almost directly to the "historical truth," i.e., to the paternal manipulations. Especially the second term, *Kopfzusammenschnürungswunder*, graphically portrays the act of tying the head with a rope or belt].

Superficially viewed, all this might appear to be a typical manifestation of the "influencing machine" which occurs in the persecutory delusions of many schizophrenics. However, closer examination of the available sources has convinced me that there is a realistic core in this delusional material. The historical truth about these two miracles can be found in the following paternal practices described in Dr. Schreber's books.

The father, obsessively preoccupied with the children's postural system, invented a series of orthopedic apparatus, the so-called *Schrebersche Geradehalter*, to secure a straight and upright body posture day or night. One of these contraptions consisted of a system of iron bars fastened to the chest of the child as well as to the table near which the child was sitting; the horizontal iron bar pressed against the chest and prevented any movement forward or sideward, giving only some freedom to move backward to an even more rigidly upright position. I believe that this device, apparently applied for several hours every day, constitutes the fragment of historic truth recognizable in the "compression-of-the-chest" delusion. In order to ensure a proper growth of the skull, especially of the jaw, chin and teeth, the father also constructed a helmetlike *Kopfhalter* which by his own admission was apt to produce "a certain stiffening effect on the head," and should therefore be worn only one or two hours per day. I am inclined to regard this contraption as the historical forerunner of the son's delusional "head-compressing-machine," which obviously caused him to complain that "the compressed state usually continued for some time" after its enforced use. To enhance the effect of the helmetlike *Kopfhalter* or to prevent any tilting of the head forward or sideward when the helmet contraption was not applied, the child had to wear leather belts tied by buckles around the head and shoulders for the entire day. It seems to me that this device in the son's delusional (and perhaps not so delusional) elaboration was felt as compressing the "head as though in a vise by turning a kind of screw" and finally as producing "in the skull a deep cleft or rent roughly along the middle. . .." Another heavy belt was used at bedtime to make sure that the child remained in a supine position all night long. This belt was fastened to the bed and ran tightly across the child's chest, thus keeping his body posture straight as well as supine through the night. Also this gadget may well have contributed to make the "compression-of-the-chest-miracle" one of the most horrifying ones recorded by Schreber. It may also have been the nucleus of truth around which further delusional ideas developed, namely, the "tying-to-earth" or "tying-to-celestial-bodies" miracles occurring in the *Memoirs*. The tying of the patient's body to such "celestial bodies" expresses here in the concretized language of the schizophrenic the thinglike quality as well as the projection of the unresolved libidinal ties with the deified father.

The heat- and cold-miracles discussed earlier were connected by Schreber himself with concrete events he had experienced in his childhood, i.e., with the spartan type of his upbringing. The genesis of other miracles is not always so clear and has to be reconstructed from the available material. In chapter XI, for instance, we read that "my eyes and the muscles of the lids which serve to open and close them were an almost uninterrupted target for miracles." The prescriptions of Schreber's father included a whole system of eye-washing, eye-sponging, lid-cleansing procedures. This system, which was put into action several times a day beginning in the postnatal period, has already been mentioned. Katan (1950) interprets Schreber's description of the "miracled-up, cursorily made little men" dripping down on his head and eyes as symbolic of a nocturnal emission. This may well be so, if the phenomenon of the mysterious "little men" is viewed mainly from the standpoint of the genital libidinal organization. By displacement the eye readily becomes a symbol of the genitals, male as well as female. Evidently Schreber's delusions are the end products of complex mental processes into which instinctual drives, introjective-projective mechanisms, libidinal conflicts, regressive contributions from multiphasic sources, and restitution processes are fused to become a single entity, possibly in the manner of the Galtonian photographs, of which Lewin (1953) speaks in a different context. In my present approach, I chose to omit the investigation of those areas, as significant as they are, and to follow instead Freud's suggestion, that is, to focus attention on the demonstrable fragments of "historical truth" as one element in Schreber's delusional formations.

While the instinctual drives, therefore, are unquestionably basic for the formation of the phenomena which Schreber reports, these phenomena cannot be fully understood ontogenetically without taking into account the memory traces laid down by the paternal manipulations during infancy. Both Schreber *poere* and *fils* seem to be particularly interested in treatments administered to the eyes, the former *prescribing* more and more procedures to ensure their proper functioning, the latter *describing* more and more miracles performed on them. A comparison of the paternal and filial texts makes it difficult, at times, to know exactly where the father's medical mythology ends and the son's delusional mythology begins.

The father, for instance, aside from the ophthalmological prescriptions in his regular textbooks (1839, 1858), devotes a supplementary booklet to *The Systematically Planned Sharpening of the Sense Organs* (1859b), in which he insists on all sorts of ocular exercises during childhood, such as quick distraction of visual attention, forcing "the child to focus on sharp objects, on detailed observation of little objects, on [visual] comparisons of these among themselves, on estimating distances, etc." In the son's "miracled-up" world, such early experiences seem to emerge in th following context (chapter XI): "Whenever I showed signs of being unwilling to allow my eyelids to be pulled up and down and actually opposed it, the 'little men' became annoyed and expressed this by calling me 'wretch'; if I wiped them off my eyes with a sponge, it was considered by the rays as a sort of crime against God's gift of miracles. By the way, wiping them away had only a very temporary effect, because the 'little men' were each time set down afresh [on the eyes]."

Given the archaic language of the primary process, a clearer description of the later vicissitudes of those early eye manipulations can hardly be expected: the conflict-producing situation, the intense stimulation, the guilt, the masturbatory and homosexual libidinization of what must have been felt originally as attacks on the body integrity. Even the paternal sponge used in the daily eyewash appears here. Nor are there omitted the father's statements that his manipulations are really of the greatest benefit for and a genuine blessing to the child, a "gift of miracles," any rebellion against which is considered by the rays (father) as a serious crime.

In a later passage (chapter XVIII), Schreber complains about his father's practices of forcefully distracting his visual attention and directing him to observe little objects: "As often as an insect. . . appears, a miracle *directs the movements of my eyes*. I have not mentioned this miracle before, but it has been regularly enacted for years. Rays [father], after all, want constantly to see what pleases them. . . . My eye muscles are therefore influenced to move in that direction toward which my glance *must* fall on things just created or else on a female being. . ." (italics in the original). In a footnote, Schreber adds that "miracles direct my gaze (turn my eyes) to the desired object."

Waelder's (1951) formulations of "noisy counterclaims" and of the "return of the denied" are applicable to much of this delusional material. The conflict-producing, scopophilic impulse aimed at instinctual gratification—Schreber discusses his looking at insects, things just "created" or to be created, etc., in the context of copulation, the sight of females, and voluptuousness—is warded off through denial and expressed through the counterclaim: "Rays want constantly to see what pleases them. . .," that is, foremost a female being. In the "return of the denied" the instinctual impulse reappears in connection with "the desired object," while utilizing the "historical truth," namely, that originally the father had instructed the son to look, to observe, to follow the movements of objects with his eyes, and the like.

To turn to other aspects of the "divine miracles," it is worth noting that the father's more voluminous writings, especially those which had an enormous popular appeal at the time of their publication and passed through numerous new editions subsequently, are replete with anatomical material. Almost one third of the *Buch der Gesundheit* is devoted to human anatomy. It contains thirty-four anatomical pictures, several of them full-page and in color. These pictures show the human figure *in toto* or in segments, now portions of the viscera and abdomen, now dissected parts of the skull, brain, skeleton, or the like. The books *Kallipäedie* (1858), *Medical Indoor Gymnastics (1865)*, *Pangymnastikon* (1862), and *Anthropos—The Miraculous Structure of the Human Organism* (1859a), contain hundreds of anatomical illustrations showing the human figure in an endless variety of positions and physical exercises. It is further noteworthy that most of this anatomical material is composed of male figures without a trace of genitals; a few isolated illustrations in those short book sections which deal with the secretory and urinary functions of the organism show the genitals—viewed not *in toto*, but rather as dissected, separate parts of the human anatomy. I learned only recently that the father himself served as the model for the illustrations in the *Pangymnastikon* (Ritter 1936).

The disruptive impact of all this on the young Schreber's body image is "miracled up" in chapter XI. It reads like a highly condensed, symbolized, archaically distorted, yet essentially correct version of many of the paternal physical maneuvers to which the young Schreber was subjected, a sort of "primary-process" catalogue of those remote infantile experiences, shaped, altered, and strongly cathected ("deified") by the father-son conflict. In this sense, chapter XI can be understood as an archaic textbook of the father's as well as Schreber's own anatomy: gullet and lungs, pharynx and stomach, abdomen and intestines, muscles and bones are "pictured" just as methodically, if delusionally, as they are in the father's anatomical texts and illustrations. The "picturing of human beings" is mentioned in the chapter itself (as well as in other parts of the *Memoirs)*, though in contrast to the father's works there are no anatomical illustrations in them. (We know, however, from the case histories discovered by Baumeyer, that Schreber used to draw human figures during the years of his confinement in the insane asylum.) These findings lend strong support to Katan's (1950, 1954) views that the father not only represents the boy's ideal of masculinity, but also that the God who persecuted Schreber represented part of Schreber himself and that God's genitals represented Schreber's genitals.

The impairment of the body image is further "miracled up" in the delusional reduction of Schreber's height. One of the miracles caused "a change in my whole stature (diminution of body size)," he writes. Mittelmann (1958) has pointed to the serious impairment of the body image as a result of motor restriction in childhood. Greenacre (1955) finds that such subjective sensations of changed total body size or of the size of certain body parts occur in individuals who at critical periods in early life have been "subject to external stresses of a nature which upset the integrity of the self-perception." The presence of such external stresses in Schreber's childhood has been amply documented. It is likely that the reduction of the son's body size also is another expression of identification with the father's body who was a man of small stature. I am inclined to view, partly in accordance with Katan, the "little men" as representing Schreber's homosexual objects, modeled on the father's body which appears "miracled up" in the hundreds of anatomical "little-men" illustrations mentioned above.

The connections between the father's actual handling or observing the child and the "miracles" later enacted on the adult patient are lucidly stated in Schreber's description of the "miracles" performed on his muscles and skeleton. Here, again, the original text is required to understand its full meaning: "An allen meinen Muskeln wurde (und wird noch jetzt) herumgewundert, um mich an allen Bewegungen oder jeweilig der Beschäftigung, die ich gerade vornehmen will, zu verhindern." The German *herumgewundert* carries the connotation of *herummachen* or *hantieren*, i.e., manipulating. The text says, "All my muscles were (and are still today) miracled around in order to prevent all my movements or any activity which I am about to perform." Here the effects of the father's interference with the child's motor activities are indicated. In "miracling up" these events, Schreber notes that attempts are made at "paralyzing my fingers when I play the piano or write, and at damaging my kneecap to the point of destroying my capacity to march, when I walk around in the garden or in the corridor." As to the attack on Schreber's capacity to march—in the original *Marschfähigkeit*—I found evidence in the father's writings that cufflike iron braces may have been applied to the child's legs to prevent the development of bowed legs.

Among the various miracles directed against his bones, Schreber lists those which resulted in his "skull repeatedly sawn asunder. . . and partly pulverized" (through the action of the "head-compressing machine"?) and in damage to his ribs (caused by the "compression-of-the-chest-miracle"?). Ultimately, these are variations of the castration theme which he mentions first. This part of his story culminates in the description of the *coccyx-miracle:*

> Its purpose was to make sitting or even lying down impossible. I was not allowed to remain for long in one and the same position or at the same occupation; when I was walking, they attempted to make me lie down, only to chase me promptly from my reclining position when I was lying down. The rays seemed to lack any understanding of the fact that a human being, since he really exists, *must be somewhere.* . . . I had become an unwelcome person for the rays (for God), in whatever position or posture I would find myself or whatever activity I would engage in [italics in the original.]

Without any further comment I now wish to compare this account of the coccyx-miracle with certain rules laid down by the father for the child's postural system. After explaining the proper mode of sitting during childhood, that is, straight and upright at all times, Dr. Schreber insists that the act of sitting down be carried out *gleichseitig*, that is, on both buttocks simultaneously. He warns parents and educators alike that the child's tendency to sit down *ungleich* (unevenly) has to be fought against because of its harmful effects on the spinal column. Then he continues:

> . . . one must see to it that children always sit straight and on both buttocks simultaneously, . . . neither first on the right nor on the left side. . . As soon as they begin to lean back, it is time to change their sitting position to an absolutely still, supine one. . . . It is important to train children of this age [from two to seven] to acquire absolutely straight posture and movements, because it is more difficult to achieve this at a later age. When children are tired, they should be made to lie down. But if they are up and around, they should be forced to hold themselves erect in walking, standing, playing, and in all their activities. This can best be done by insisting that as soon as a child behaves in a relaxed or lazy way, he is made to lie down, if only for a few moments. [as a punishment.]

Of interest in this reconstructive approach to Schreber's early history are the vicissitudes of the castration threat which he experienced as a young boy. To paraphrase Hartmann and Kris (1945), one may say with regard to the Schreber home: *There always was castration in the air.* The father's aggressive and coercive actions; the orthopedic contraptions; the disrupted, dismembered, and dissected aspects of the human body; the violence and authoritarian impetus of the injunctions; the sequence masturbation-pest-sterility-insanity (castration)—all belong in this setting. As to the castrative aspects prevailing in Schreber's early life situation, I came upon evidence that such threats were not limited merely to their appearance in word and picture. They were part, so to speak, of the boy's actual environment from the age of two. In 1844, the father became the owner and director of the orthopedic institute in Leipzig. Under Dr. Schreber's management the institute soon grew into a well-known *Heilanstalt,* which was repeatedly enlarged and to which orthopedic patients from many countries flocked. Ritter (1936) reports that these crippled and mutilated people mingled freely with the Schreber children, joined them in the garden of the institute, took part in their games, etc. These early experiences in the orthopedic *Heilanstalt,* together with their castration aspects, must have been connected with and then blended into the patient's later experiences in the *Nervenheilanstalt* where he expected "unmanning," was in fear of being put to death, saw himself "dead and rotten," and felt that he was suffering from general paralysis. The last-mentioned condition is said to have played a role in the brother's death in 1877. Be that as it may, it is likely that among the inmates of Dr. Schreber's *Heilanstalt* during those early years of our patient's life there were at least some who, superficially viewed, resembled certain paretics, paraplegics, catatonics, etc., in Dr. Weber's *Heilanstalt* half a century later. Schreber's confusion with respect to this situation is recorded in his case history. Also his expectation, immediately on entering the asylum, of being tortured, manhandled, and mutilated is probably overdetermined as well as "concretized" through his childhood contacts with amputees and otherwise physically damaged people in the father's orthopedic institute. A similar "concretizing" element may have played a part with regard to the paternal predictions of impotence and sterility resulting from masturbation. The lack of offspring in Schreber's marriage may well have been experienced as the verification, inexorable and ominous, of the father's dire predictions and may thus have become an important factor in precipitating the illness.

A miracle not mentioned in chapter XI, but frequently occurring in the case history, is the "bellowing miracle." Whether its kernel of truth is based on the father's activities as a lecturer and orator, on his sermonizing, haranguing, and other vocal pursuits (the father even prescribes "systematic, constantly repeated [verbal] admonishments" to combat poor pronunciation of words or syllables by children), I am not prepared to say. That there exists a direct connection between the father and the "bellowing miracle" is shown by the occurrence of the latter in relation to the sun: Schreber bellowed and shouted at the sun. At one time two suns appeared in the sky—a possible allusion to both father and elder brother. My assumption that the latter played a role in the delusion of the two suns is supported by Schreber's statement that the other sun was derived from the Cassiopeia group of stars (chapter VI). In the preceding chapter he speaks of the "Brothers of Cassiopeia."

I wish to conclude this part of my paper by briefly discussing two enigmatic miracles which, I suggest, can be made intelligible through an inquiry into their "historical truth." At one point during his illness Schreber not only thought of himself as being dead and decomposing; he also fantasied that a newspaper had been put into his hands in which he could read his own obituary notice. Since undoubtedly no such report existed, we must ask ourselves—in order to arrive at the truth (albeit distorted)—whose obituary actually *was* published and *was* read by the Schreber family at the time of *whose* death? Needless to say, this delusion must refer to the father's, and probably also the brother's death notices in the papers. Those who will object to my assumption of such a far-reaching identification may be interested in learning more about the father's death. He died of acute ileus *(Darmverschlingung)* on November 10, 1861, after a brief hospitalization of a day or two. More than three decades later, the son tells us that precisely "on November 8 or 9th, my illness began to assume a menacing character. . . the following day we travelled [from Dresden] to Leipzig, direct to Professor Flechsig at the University Clinic. . .." That same night of November 10 or 11 (1893), the sick son made the first suicide attempt, had himself hospitalized in Leipzig, and felt that he was dead (the father had died in a Leipzig hospital). I found that at that time some Leipzig newspapers had erroneously reported November 11, 1861, as the day of the father's death. Even this uncertainty seems to be reflected in the son's description of his own hospitalization, thirty-two years later. His otherwise very detailed report in the *Memoirs* (chapter IV) does not make it clear whether he was hospitalized on November 10 or 11, 1893. There he made another suicide attempt, a few days later, and soon began to believe that he was suffering, among other symptoms, from *Darmverschlingung*, i.e., ileus, the very disease to which the father had succumbed. The details of these events can be found in chapter IV of the *Memoirs*. It is perhaps not surprising to note that all three of Schreber's hospitalizations, though widely separated in years, took place during the month of November. He also gives this month of a later year, 1895, as the date on which the connection between his emasculation and redeemer ideas was established, and he began to reconcile himself to the former.

A striking fragment of truth is concealed, I believe, in Schreber's delusion of the end of the world. In his lengthy discussion of this catastrophe the figure 212 appears, the lifespan allotted to the earth in his delusional system being 212 years. This cryptic number becomes comprehensible when viewed against the background of Schreber's early family constellation. A glance at my outline of Schreber's chronological (numerical) position in his relation to the siblings (see above) will show that two siblings preceded Schreber and two siblings followed him, with himself as the middle child, to wit: 2-1-2. We have here in all likelihood the emergence of his "historical" sibling situation condensed in and attached to a numerical element, which in turn is attached to the delusional idea of the end of the world, which itself contains another nucleus of truth in its complex structure. As I have discussed elsewhere (1956), in Schreber's fantasy of the *Weltuntergang* the fantasy or experience of birth ranks as a considerable item, probably modeled on the birth of his younger siblings.

"Margraves of Tuscany and Tasmania"

In this section I shall attempt to demonstrate that one of Schreber's delusions, besides dealing with the infantile father-son conflict, reflects elements of his unresolved relationship with his mother whose personality and/or influence have otherwise remained conspicuously absent from the *Memoirs*.

The known facts about Schreber's adulthood—that he became the presiding judge of the Saxonian Superior Court, was married for a number of years, and ran for an important political office—make it appear likely that prior to his breakdown he must have attained a measure of adequate ego functioning and may also have reached or at least approximated the state of genital organization. Freud has brilliantly elucidated the dynamics and vicissitudes of Schreber's inverted oedipal relation to his father. Thus we may legitimately ask: Where is Schreber's positive Oedipus complex? Where in the autobiographical *Memoirs* are its precipitates or vestiges? Though it is hazardous to try to reconstruct this phase of Schreber's life on the basis of a single delusional utterance, I am inclined to assume that his oedipal problem finds expression in the fantasy that the Schrebers, who belonged to "the highest aristocracy of Heaven," bore the title of "Margraves of Tuscany and Tasmania."

Freud connects this fantasy with the frustration Schreber suffered in his marriage. "It brought him no children," Freud writes, "his family line threatened to die out, and it seems that he felt no little pride in his birth and lineage." Here, incidentally, lies another kernel of historical turth; one of Schreber's ancestors, the physician and botanist Johann Christian Daniel von Schreber (1739–1810), was knighted in 1791. Baumeyer mentions that his co-worker, Ayem, believes that this fantasy may be connected with the events of Canossa. Nonetheless, this still leaves unanswered the question of the origin of the delusional title "Margraves of Tuscany and Tasmania." Of course, one may be tempted to dismiss the fantasy with a reference to its obvious clang association. Apart from the fact that Schreber's recorded clang associations are of a more direct nature and appear in a very different setting (usually as isolated, bisectional formations, that is, "Santiago-Carthago"), his choice of such specific geographic-historical areas as Tuscany and Tasmania, presided over and owned by the Schreber nobility, invites investigation. Moreover, the circumstance that this delusion concerns not Schreber's body (like many of his other fantasies) but his family arouses our interest. In expanding Freud's and Baumeyer's notions and inquiring more closely into the content of the delusion, I have come to understand it as a delusionally distorted derivative of the "miracled-up" vestiges of Schreber's lost Oedipus complex. Since such vestiges must be derived from the original oedipal constellation, their analysis may provide us with information on Schreber's Oedipus complex. (Katan [1954], exploring the patient's prepsychotic phase, focuses attention on the loss of the positive Oedipus complex in schizophrenic illness, a loss which results in a marked reinforcement of the pregenital fixations, weakens contact with reality, and increases the state of narcissism. These findings throw further light on Schreber's choice of the megalomanic title.)

At this point, a somewhat lengthy historical detour becomes necessary. It is important for the English-speaking reader to realize that the episode of Canossa, though belonging to medieval history, stood at the center of a furious political battle called *Kulturkampf* which dominated the domestic scene in Germany during the 1870s and 1880s. Not only does Schreber's candidature for the *Reichstag* fall into that period, but also part of his cosmology with its multiple references to Catholicism and Protestantism, to the Jesuits and the Pope, with his fear that Protestant Saxony would be taken over by the Catholics and the subsequent spread of this fear to the planets, the solar system, and the universe—all this is linked up in Schreber's mind with the *Kulturkampf*. The political personalities which Schreber mentions by name in the early chapters of the *Memoirs*, such as Bismarck and the Pope, the Cardinals Rampolla and Galimberti, were protagonists in that heated controversy. Chapters V through VII are incomprehensible unless these facts are taken into account. According to Schreber, the "Catholicizing of Saxony and Leipzig" was imminent. The intensity of his conflict is revealed in the asylum material which tells of Schreber's own plans to convert to Catholicism. Thus, since he took an active part in politics and was a candidate for election to Parliament in 1884, the year he fell ill for the first time, he found himself in the midst of a major emotional and political crisis. An essential aspect of his conflict was, as I have shown in a previous paper (1951), that *running for the Reichstag meant running against Bismarck,* the most powerful father figure then in Germany who all his life was sternly opposed to parliamentary (that is, filial) intrusion. Another factor aggravating Schreber's difficulties must be related to the circumstance that at the very time he saw himself, his family, and his country endangered by the spread of Catholicism, the reigning king of Saxony actually was a Catholic.

As one studies the early chapters of the *Memoirs*, one finds them filled with archaic descriptions of the *Kulturkampf* situation. This is hardly surprising, because Schreber had just lived through the controversy before falling ill. The turbulent events had obviously reactivated his own unconscious conflicts, as evidenced by his personal participation in the struggle, the extreme delusional elaboration of the events, the naming of some of the chief protagonists in the *Kulturkampf*, etc. Let us return now to the delusional title of "Margraves of Tuscany and Tasmania" and ask once more: why this particular combination?

The second part of the fantasy, Tasmania, does not present too much difficulty. As every student of colonial history knows, the island of Tasmania was originally a British penal colony. Schreber, a prominent jurist versed in law as well as history, must almost certainly have been aware of this fact. The question of sending convicts to remote areas overseas was widely discussed in Europe, and Tasmania was known as the "jail of the Empire" during the mid-nineteenth century. To the public mind such penal colonies with their population of criminals were places of horror, of which an old chronicler said: *"Hic homines patricidae habitant"* ("here live men, murderers of their fathers"). Schreber's choice of Tasmania, then, signifies in all likelihood prison and punishment.

This asumption receives support from the analysis of a parapraxis appearing in another of Schreber's delusions. In enumerating the various *Kulturkampf* figures Schreber lists the above-mentioned Catholic dignitaries as "Cardinals Rampolla, Galimberti, and Casati. . .." So far as I could ascertain, there was no Cardinal Casati. The only person of that name, a contemporary of the two prelates and also of Schreber, was the explorer and geographer Gaetano Casati (1838–1902) who for a time joined the African expeditions of Emin Pasha and later of Stanley. While serving under Emin Pasha, he was taken prisoner by the natives, tied naked to a tree and tortured. Left to his fate, he managed to escape, and later published an account of his and Emin Pasha's adventures, *Dieci Anni in Equatoria*, which was translated into German in 1891. Schreber knew Italian quite well and wrote letters in Italian at Sonnenstein asylum (Baumeyer). Some of Schreber's descriptions about strange travels ("I traversed the earth from Lake Ladoga to Brazil"), about the outbreak of devastating epidemics, etc., resemble—shorn of their massive delusional distortions—the accounts of Casati's and Emin's African exploits. (Emin Pasha's first expedition started from Lado, a region west of the upper Nile adjoining Lake Albert. In 1878, he became governor of the Equatorial Province and made his headquarters at Lado where he was joined by Casati. In 1885, Emin Pasha and Casati were driven out of Lado by the Mahdist revolution and encountered serious difficulties with the authorities, hostile natives, dangers from epidemics, etc. Lake Ladoga is, of course, situated between Finland and Russia which Dr. Schreber "traversed" in his young years as the personal physician of a Russian aristocrat; Dr. Schnitzer also began his medical career as the personal physician of a nobleman, the Turkish governor of Dalmatia, with whom he traveled through parts of the Ottoman empire.)

These reports, one may speculate, became fused with Schreber's reminiscences of stories related by his father concerning the latter's early travels in Russia and other countries. Though I cannot prove that Schreber read Casati's book, perhaps during his stay at the asylum, it is practically certain that he knew about the harrowing experiences of Emin Pasha and Casati, since the former—originally a physician of German-Jewish extraction by the name of Eduard Schnitzer—became a sensation in the Germany of those days due to his colorful career, fame, travels, and tireless efforts aimed at reform. In this respect Dr. Schnitzer-Emin Pasha was not unlike Dr. Schreber, our patient's father, and Casati, Emin's assistant, not unlike the patient himself. Both Casati and Schreber *fils* were the sons of physicians. Both were imprisoned and tortured, the one in the African jungle, the other—according to his own thinking—in the Sonnenstein asylum. There exist, however, more parallels between the two older men, Emin Pasha and Schreber's father. They both came from the eastern parts of Germany, both were graduated in medicine at approximately the same age, both went abroad shortly after their graduation, the former to Turkey and the latter to Russia. In 1858 or 1859, about three years before his death, Dr. Schreber suffered a serious head injury, possibily a skull fracture, from an iron ladder which fell on his head. In 1889, three years before his death, Emin Pasha met with an almost fatal accident which caused the fracture of his skull. He was murdered in Africa in 1892, a fact widely discussed in Germany.

All these facts were undoubtedly known to Schreber. The delusional fusion of Dr. Schnitzer (Emin Pasha)—Dr. Schreber (father, God), as hypothesized here, would explain to an extent Schreber's allusions to his persecution by Jews, baptized Jews, and Slavophiles. Emin Pasha was a baptized German Jew from Silesia, originally a Slavic province. Admittedly somewhat stretching a point, it is not unthinkable that Emin Pasha's sudden and violent death in 1892 had its repercussions on Schreber's precarious condition at that time. Emin Pasha's murder, occurring during Schreber' s prepsychotic phase, could have reactivated Schreber's unconcious conflicts regarding his own oedipal crime. Instead of being exiled as a *convict* to Tasmania for having killed the father, he was made *presiding judge* in October 1893. (Other factors operative at that time in Schre-

ber's life were discussed by me in some detail elsewhere [1951, 1959].) A
month later he landed in his own "Tasmania," i.e., in the mental hospital.

Be that as it may, if Tasmania means punishment, it seems permissible to
regard Tuscany as signifying crime. Historical Tuscany with its capital Florence
has frequently had the same reputation which in Biblical times was attributed
to Sodom and Gomorrha, Nineveh, etc., places of sin, strife, incest, and homosexuality. Schreber's single statement about the "Margraves of Tuscany and
Tasmania" characteristically occurs in the midst of a lengthy discourse on "soul-
murder" and on "a battle arising out of jealousy between souls already departed
from life." The connection between "soul-murder" and homosexuality has been
demonstrated by Freud. With respect to the "battle arising out of jealousy,"
we have to return to Schreber's emotional state during the *Kulturkampf*. The
violent crisis in Germany had revived strong feelings about that earlier episode
in which a similar struggle between the secular powers, represented by the
Emperor, and the religious forces, represented by the Pope, had culminated in
the Emperor's utter humiliation and defeat at Canossa in Tuscany in 1077. There
are few moments in German history that have impressed later generations as
intensely as the spectacle of Henry IV, the Emperor, standing in the courtyard
of Canossa as a suppliant before Pope Gregory VII and Mathilde, Marchioness
of Tuscany, Mistress of the castle of Canossa and then the most powerful lady
in Europe. In fact, the defeat of the Emperor had been brought about by the
alliance between the Pope and Mathilde of Tuscany. The Pope was accused of
having intimate relations with Mathilde. Bismarck, in a famous speech before
the Reichstag in 1872, revived the episode of Canossa when he exclaimed,
"Nach Canossa gehen wir nicht" ("To Canossa we shall not go"), thus giving
rise to what some historians have called the *furor protestanticus* in the Protestant
German circles to which the Schreber family belonged.

The evidence that certain aspects of the Canossa story became part of
Schreber's delusional system is based on various remarks contained in the *Memoirs*. I shall analyze here only the statement, which appears in chapter VII, that
"after the death of the present Pope and of an interim-Pope Honorius, a further
conclave could not be held. . .." (Schreber uses here the expression *Zwischen-
papst* which in the translation by Macalpine and Hunter is erroneously rendered
"intervening Pope," whereas the German word clearly denotes the interim
quality or *interregnum* character of this reign—an unmistakable allusion to the
brother's *"interregnum"* after the father's death. By using the term *Zwischen-
papst*, Schreber places a stamp of dubious, transient quality on the brother's
"reign.") Since there is but one interim- or anti-Pope Honorius in the history
of the papacy, this can refer only to the anti-Pope Honorius II (1061–1071)
whose successor, Gregory VII, was the victor of Canossa. Thus "after the death

of the present Pope" must refer to Honorius's predecessor, Pope Nicholas, who died in 1061 (Schreber's father died in 1861), and the naming of the interim-Pope Honorius must mean the *"interregnum"* of Schreber's brother Gustav, which came into being "after the death of the present Pope," that is, after the death of Schreber's father in 1861. The event of Canossa took place in 1077 (Schreber's brother died in 1877). The year 1877, then, marks the end of the brother's *"interregnum,"* and Schreber was now in line to become the male head of the family. If my previous interpretation of the sequence "Cardinals Rampolla, Galimberti, Casati" is valid, the same chronology holds true in this statement. Rampolla and Galimberti, then Papal Secretary of State and Apostolic Legate respectively, represent Schreber's father and brother, while Casati who was tied to the tree is the patient himself. His precarious state is indicated by his remark: "A further conclave could not be held because Catholics had lost their faith." The intensity of Schreber's conflict is revealed by this projection of his uncertainty and perplexity onto the Catholics, possibly also by his marriage in 1878, which followed his brother's suicide with conspicuous speed. Schreber could not accept the active masculine role, 1877, because such a role would have made him not merely the brother's successor, but also the usurper of the father's position; or, in terms of Canossa, 1077, he would have become Honorius's successor Gregory, the *triumphator* over the Emperor (father) and supposed lover of Mathilde (mother).

The sequence of events proves the point. When Schreber is called upon to assume the "presidency" in his family setting, he is unable to do so. Standing as a candidate for election to parliament, he cannot go through with it and falls ill for the first time. Promoted to the presidency of a high court almost a decade later, he again feels threatened and breaks down the second time. The threat of becoming a father himself, and in his own right, drives him back into the libidinized subjugation to the deified father of his early childhood (Niederland 1951) and the disrupted development of his ego in those years.

Nor does the Canossa story end here. Two dramatic episodes soon followed. First the Emperor's eldest son, Konrad, rebelled against his father, waged war against him, and had himself crowned king. Several years after Konrad's death the Emperor's second son, Henry (like our patient, his father's namesake and second son!), revolted against the father who was taken prisoner by the son and forced to abdicate. Both sons' rebellions were actively supported by Marchioness Mathilde of Tuscany. Also involved was the Emperor's wife Praxedis whom the Emperor suspected of having engaged in an illicit love affair with his son Konrad. The Empress openly admitted that she had committed adultery, but only at the behest of her husband, the Emperor. Historians disagree on the veracity of the accusations, but hold that all these machinations, then publicly discussed and repeatedly negotiated before the *Reichstag,* contributed to the downfall of the Emperor. Whether Schreber was familiar with all the details of the Canossa story is hard to say. As a jurist and student of history he probably was. There is little doubt that he was an avid and thorough reader, accustomed in his studies to going back to prime sources. Later, during "sleepless nights in the cell [of the asylum]," he tells us, "I produced my historical and geographical knowledge. . .." It can be said with certainty, however, that Schreber knew about Canossa at least as much as the average German highschool student in that generation knew—and that included most of the essential events, their protagonists, dates, and the unrestrained passions connected with them. To the analytic observer the emotional impact of the Canossa affair is clear. Its implications and aftermath contain the dynamic aspects of a highly involved oedipal constellation.

In view of Schreber's excellent memory enhanced by the schizophrenic's hypermnesia for names and dates, in view also of the availability of withdrawn object cathexes for reinvestment in his restitution attempts aimed at regaining the lost objects via word representations, a full inquiry into such verbal formations as the "Margraves of Tuscany and Tasmania" appeared to me of some importance. Since in schizophrenia words and verbal ideas assume the role of objects, the analytic evaluation of these formations can supply us with information concerning the wishes, strivings, and conflicts attached to them. In the case under consideration, Schreber's choice of the delusional title with its particular names and historical-personal connotations seems to contain those vestigial elements of the "battle arising out of jealousy" in which past and present, history and individual fate, oedipal and preoedipal components coalesce. If my decoding of these elements is correct, the vestiges of Schreber's Oedipus complex which are concretized, as it were, in the enigmatic title, can be understood in this way:

Margraves—the rebellious sons who in alliance with the powerful Marchio-
         ness (mother) humiliate and overthrow the father
Tuscany—the scene of the father's utter humiliation and defeat
Tasmania—the place of punishment for the oedipal crime.

Summary

Until recently very little was known about Schreber's childhood. Nor do the limitations of our knowledge permit us now to reconstruct Schreber's childhood along longitudinal lines. Nevertheless, investigations based on the *Memoirs* and their analysis by Freud, on the recent contribution by Baumeyer, and on new authentic material accumulated by the present author have enabled us to review the patient's relationship with his father in the light of childhood events. More specifically, in correlating certain formations of Schreber's delusional system with experiences in his early life, it has been possible to arrive at the kernel of "historical truth" in the genesis of such formations, thus illuminating hitherto unintelligible aspects of the *Memoirs.*

Schreber's childhood appears to have been characterized by passive submission to the father's forceful, overpowering, often sadistic (though not entirely unaffectionate) behavior; by early traumatization through exposure to bizarre "gadget experiences," to bodily overstimulation alternating with mechanical restraint, heightened kinesthetic and contact perceptions, impairment of the body image, etc.; by direct and indirect castration threats resulting from the paternal antimasturbation campaign and Schreber's childhood years in the father's orthopedic institution. Through the investigation of these experiences various heretofore obscure features of Schreber's pathology, particularly the so-called "divine miracles" enacted on the patient's body throughout his illness, can be traced ontogenetically to their traumatic origin in the early father-son relation. An attempt is also made to connect one of Schreber's megalomanic fantasies about his family ("Margraves of Tuscany and Tasmania") with vestiges of his lost positive Oedipus complex.

In conclusion, I suggest that another dimension may now be added to the analysis of the *Denkwürdigkeiten:* the understanding that at least a number of Schreber's delusions represented fantasies about or distorted memories of the real experiences to which he was subjected by his father during childhood and which Schreber treated as present reality during his illnesses.

References

Baumeyer, F. (1956). The Schreber case. *International Journal of Psycho-Analysis* 37:61–74.

Casati, G. (1891). *Zehn Jahre in Equatoria und die Rückkehr mit Emin Pasha* [*Dieci Anni in Equatoria e il Ritorno con Emin Pasha, Milan*]. Bamberg: Reinhardt-Stöttner.

Freud, S. (1911). Psychoanalytic notes upon an autobiograhical account of a case of paranoia (dementia paranoids). *Standard Edition* 12:9–82.

———(1938). Constructions in analysis. *Collected Papers*, 5:358–371. London: Hogarth Press, 1950.

Greenacre, P. (1955). *Swift and Carroll.* New York: International Universities Press.

Hartmann, H. and Kris, E. (1945). The genetic approach in psychoanalysis. *Psychoanalysis Study of the Child 1:11–30.*

Katan, M. (1950). Schreber's hallucinations about the "little men." *International Journal of Psycho-Analysis* 31:32–35.

———(1954). The importance of the non-psychotic part of the personality in schizophrenia. *International Journal of Psycho-Analysis* 35:119–128.

Lewin, B. D. (1953). Reconsiderations of the dream screen. *Psychoanalytic Quarterly* 22.

Macalpine, I. and Hunter, R. A. (1955). *Daniel Paul Schreber—Memoirs of My Nervous Illness.* Cambridge: Robert Bentley.

Mittelmann, B. (1958). Psychodynamics of motility. *International Journal of Psycho-Analysis* 39:191–199.

Niederland, W. G. (1951). Three notes on the Schreber case. *Psychoanalytic Quarterly* 22.

———(1956). River symbolism, Part I. *Psychoanalytic Quarterly* 25.

———(1958). Early auditory experiences, beating fantasies, and primal scene. *Psychoanalytic Study of the Child* 13:471–504.

———(1959). Schreber: father and son. *Psychoanalytic Quarterly* 28:151–169. Part V, Chapter 1 of this volume.

Politzer, L. M. (1862). D. G. M. Schreber. *Jahrb. Kinderheilk.*, V.

Ritter, A. (1936). *Schreber—Das Bildungssystem eines Arztes.* Inaugural Dissertation, Universität Erlangen, Germany.

Schreber, D. G. M. (1839). *Das Buch der Gesundheit [The Book of Health].* Leipzig: H. Fries.

———(1852). *Die Eigentümlichkeiten des kindlichen Organismus [The Characteristics of the Child's Organism].* Leipzig: Fleischer.

———(1858). *Kallipädie oder Erziehung zur Schönheit [Callipedics or Education for Beauty].* Leipzig: Fleischer.

———(1859a). *Anthropos—Der Wunderbau des menschlichen Organismus [Anthropos—The Miraculous Structure of the Human Organism].* Leipzig: Fleischer.

———(1859b). *Die planmässige Schärfung der Sinnesorgane [The Systematically Planned Sharpening of the Sense Organs].* Leipzig: Fleischer.

———(1862). *Das Pangymnastikon [The Pangymnasticon].* Leipzig: Fleischer.

———(1865). *Ärztliche Zimmergymnastik [Medical Indoor Gymnastics].* Leipzig: Fleischer.

———(1883). *Das Buch der Erziehung an Leib und Seele [The Book of Training Body and Soul].* 3. Aufl. Leipzig: Fleischer.

Schreber, D. P. (1903). *Denkwürdigkeiten eines Nervenkranken.* Leipzig: Oswald Mutze.

Schreber, J. C. D. (1818). *Memoriae Perillustris Academiae Naturalis Curiae Praesidis.* Universität Erlangen, Germany.

Strachey, J. (1958). Preface. *Standard Edition* 12.

Sylvester, E. (1959). In panel: Psychological consequences of physical illness in childhood, reported by V. Calef. *Journal of the American Psychoanalytic Association* 7:155–162.

Waelder, R. (1951). The structure of paranoid ideas. *International Journal of Psycho-Analysis* 32:167–177.

Chapter 3

FURTHER DATA AND MEMORABILIA
PERTAINING TO THE SCHREBER CASE

WILLIAM G. NIEDERLAND, M.D.

This paper is a continuation and extension of previous studies on various aspects of Schreber's delusional system and its intricate relations to his father's life and work (Niederland 1951, 1959a, b,1960). In it I wish to offer further material and documentary evidence pertaining to the famous case. In doing so I am aware that the method of presenting and using findings collected from outside sources, and not from the patient himself, differs from the accepted analytic method of gaining access to such data which in analysis, of course, originate from one source alone, i.e. the adult patient. In applied analysis, in child analysis, and also during psychotic episodes in the treatment of adult patients, the method of gaining access to important material may legitimately change. I therefore hold that the procedure I employed in my search for source material on Schreber—the systematic collection and analytic evaluation of authentic data derived from *all* available sources—is both permissible and useful. It corresponds to the approach chosen by more illustrious predecessors (Freud, Jones, Greenacre, Eissler, etc.) in their respective fields of applied psychoanalytic investigation, and also enables us to correlate in the present case certain

Read at the 33rd Annual Meeting of the Eastern Psychological Association, Atlantic City, N.J., April 1962.

pathogenic events in Schreber's early life with some of his bizarre delusional formations in adulthood and thus to demonstrate what Freud (1911, 1938) has called the "historical truth" in a number of these heretofore unintelligible phenomena.

If, for instance, the analytic study of some of the patient's more conspicuous delusions reveals such an unmistakable relation to his father's child-rearing practices as is exemplified in my findings on the otherwise incomprehensible *Kopfzusammenschnürungswunder* and *Steisswunder* (the "head-being-tied-together-miracle" and "coccyx miracle"), I think that we are justifed in assuming that the origin of these Schreberian productions is to be found in the early traumatic father-son relationship. It is difficult to avoid the conclusion that these "divine miracles" described in the *Denkwürdigkeiten* in considerable detail and without too much psychotic distortion are derived from, or at least modelled on, the father's medical-orthopedic procedures as the precursors of the later delusions. One has, in fact, only to drop the word *wunder* in the first neologism, i.e., *Kopfzusammenschnürungs*(wunder), in order to arrive at the realistic core of its meaning in the patient's actual childhood experience, when the father as a physician and constructor of a formidable array of orthopedic apparatus contrived and applied a helmet-like tying device called a *Kopfhalter* to the child's head. (Schreber also speaks of *Kopfzusammenschnürungsmaschine*, thus directly pointing to a mechanical head-tying apparatus which, according to him, was applied to his skull.) Or, to understand the origin and meaning of the "coccyx miracle" one has but to compare the respective passages in the writings of Schreber *p9ere* and *fils*. Here is the father's forceful description of how children have to sit (Niederland 1960):

> . . . one must see to it that children always sit straight and on both buttocks simultaneously. . . neither first on the right nor on the left side. . . . As soon as they begin to lean back [on the chair], it is time to have them change their sitting position to an absolutely still, supine one. . . . It is important to train children of this age [from two to seven] to acquire absolutely straight posture. . . they should be forced to hold themselves upright and erect. . . . This can be achieved by insisting that as soon as a child behaves [sits] in a relaxed or lazy way, he is made to lie down, if only for a few moments. . . .

The delusional elaboration of this paternal coercion with respect to sitting and lying down can be found in chapter XI of the *Denkwürdigkeiten* where the "coccyx miracle" is explained in the following way:

> Its purpose was to make sitting or even lying down impossible. I was not

allowed to remain for long in one and the same position or at the same occupation; when I was walking, they attempted to make me lie down, only to chase me promptly from my reclining position when I was lying down. The rays [God, father] seemed to lack any understanding of the fact that a human being, since he really exists, *must be somewhere*. . . . [italics in the original]

As I have noted elsewhere, such comparative observations can be helpful in clarifying various other obscure phenomena emerging during Schreber's illness. A case in point is his frequent reference to those mysterious "little men" that have been the subject of much discussion in the literature (Freud 1911, Katan 1950, Macalpine and Hunter 1955). I am greatly indebted to Dr. Robert C. Bak who was the first to draw my attention to their connection with the numerous drawings in the father's *Ärztliche Zimmergymnastik* and other books which, indeed, are filled with drawings and sketches of little human figures in a great variety of physical poses, gymnastic exercises, calisthenics, etc. That these figures represent in all likelihood the realistic precursors of the delusional "little men" later on can also be seen from the specific wording which the patient uses whenever he refers to them and their puzzling appearance. He calls them *hingemachte kleine Männer*, that is, men made or drawn (in the sense of produced), thus employing terms which point to their anal-sadistic derivation in his own thinking as well as to their relation to the bewildering little men-figures in the father's literary productions.

Other delusional formations which Schreber reports, such as being at times without a stomach ("I existed frequently without a stomach," he writes in the *Memoirs*, chap. XI), that his "gullet and the intestines were torn and vanished," that his skull was sawn asunder and perforated, and the like, appear to be connected with certain anatomical illustrations in the father's medical books. During the years following the patient's birth these books were published or reprinted. In early childhood the patient must have seen them in manuscript or galley proof form and must have been overawed by the sight of vivid illustrations of dissected bodies and body parts (see D. G. M. Schreber 1859). Since the father's anatomical volumes and medical writings were abundantly and colorfully illustrated, they must have acquired for Schreber the meaning which picture books and illustrated fairy tales generally have in childhood. The one difference perhaps is that the very copiousness of the dissected body material (over which the father as physician and orthopedist presided) lent itself to become fused with the body-building and body-coercing paternal practices *in concretu*, as it were, and added to the ever present castration threat in the early Schreber home. This was located in a wing of an orthopedic-surgical *Heilanstalt* for deformed patients

(Niederland 1959a, b), and this lent itself to the elaboration of florid castration and sado-masochistic fantasies in a setting of surgical orthopedic gymnastic practice.

The illustration (Fig. I) from Dr. Schreber's *Pangymnastikon* suggests the probable derivation of another "miracle" in the *Memoirs*, Schreber's puzzling *Mehrköpfigkeit*. In chapter VI the patient reports:

> . . . there was a time when souls in nerve-contact with me talked of a *plurality of heads*. . . which they encountered in me and from which they shrank in alarm, crying "For heaven's sake—that is *a human being with several heads.*" I am fully aware how fantastic all this must sound to other people; and I therefore do not go so far as to assert that all I have recounted was objective reality; *I only relate the impressions retained as recollections in my memory.* [Italics added]

This picture shows heads coming out of one body in the fashion indicated by the patient. His statement about "impressions retained as recollections" also suggest a measure of subjective awareness as to the possible origin of his delusional fantasies. Be that as it may, the findings seem to demonstrate Schreber's early childhood experiences not only as the "kernel of truth" of some of his later delusions, but also as the core of the psychotic material "miracled up" by the patient during his illness. In his restitution efforts, with the help of such experiences, he attempted to regain the lost objects and to re-establish his unresolved infantile ties with them. One of the main features of this attempt at restitution consists, as Freud has shown, in an effort to recapture the lost objects by reinforcing the cathexis of verbal and non-verbal representations standing for them. Hence the plethora of names and dates in Schreber's productions, especially the multitude and deification of the names representing the father; hence also the great number of "divine miracle" formations, their frequent repetition, neologistic naming, and detailed description in a steady flow of verbal material and delusional imagery in Schreber's book.

It is well to remember that until a few years ago Schreber had been like a man without a childhood, a patient without a past. It is one of the ironies of analytic research that "the most frequently quoted patient in psychiatry" (Macalpine and Hunter 1955) has left virtually no data about his early life and that our inferences regarding his childhood and adolescence must be based on reconstructions. In this respect, of course, our patient is not unlike other psychotics who rarely, if ever, furnish sufficient evidence about their developmental years and early family relations. Freud, to be sure, in analyzing the *Denkwürdigkeiten*, soon discovered "the shadowy sketch of infantile material"

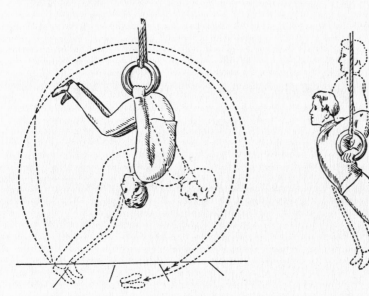

FIGURE I

in them, as he put it, and left in his own words to us latter-day analysts the task of filling in the gaps and supplying additional data for a fuller understanding of the case history.

In pursuance of this task I wish to record some new, as yet fragmentary, but otherwise well-substantiated information which has come to light with respect to Schreber's mother, about whom nothing was known until very recently and who only now has become the subject of a valuable analytic study by White (1961). In the course of my search for authentic background material on the Schreber family I was fortunate enough to obtain a letter written by the patient's eldest sister, Anna, which dates back to 1909—two years before the death of the author of the *Denkwürdigkeiten*. This letter contains the following remarks about her parents and their close relationship during her childhood: "Father discussed with our mother everything and anything; she took part in all his ideas, plans, and projects, she read the galley proofs of his writings with him, and was his faithful, close companion in everything." Granted a loyal daughter would tend to depict the parental relationship in such a harmonious fashion after the lapse of so many years (the father died in 1861, the mother in 1907). However, the apparently casual remark on her mother's working on the paternal manuscripts in personal collarboration with their author—that is, the very writings which are replete with the minute prescriptions, orthopedic procedures and

anatomical drawings later transmuted by the patient into the raw material for
the "divine miracles"—led me to reflect on the likelihood that the mother must
have thus become, from the patient's point of view, the willing and active
participant in the paternal practices, manipulations, and coercive procedures
performed on the patient. It thus becomes likely, as has already been postulated
by other authors, that the peculiar complexities of Schreber's God, the central
figure of the *Denkwürdigkeiten,* with its division into anterior and posterior
"forecourts", upper and lower deities, and various other attributes, represent
the condensed, archaically distorted fusion of both parental images in the son's
delusional system. God, in this system, would then be the delusional composite
of both father and mother, both projected and later regained as objects through
the restitution attempts via the delusional fantasies about miracles and other
"divine" maneuvers enacted on the patient's body. The fact that, according to
the sister's testimony, the mother helped and actively participated in those partly
coercive, partly seductive procedures whose nature and significance I have
discussed in my earlier papers, seems to lend support to this conclusion.

Further support along these lines comes from the discovery of new material
regarding the patient's mother as well as from the *Denkwürdigkeiten* themselves.
In the latter, in his angry outbursts, Schreber calls the sun and God a whore.
With regard to the mother, whose name was *Pauline (née Haase)* I found that
she was herself the third child of a prominent physician and professor of medicine
in Leipzig, precisely as was her son *Paul,* our patient. During his illness Paul
delusionally changed his sex to that of the mother and hallucinated about being
"Miss Schreber." Other striking examples of Schreber's confusion regarding
both his own sexual identity and the identity of paternal and maternal figures
are contained in the following data obtained by me from the municipal archives
in Leipzig: the maternal grandmother of the patient was *Juliana Emilia Haase,*
wife of the physician and professor just mentioned. In the *Denkwürdigkeiten*
the patient transforms his grandmother into a practicing male physician named
Julius Emil Haase. It may be said with certainty that, at least on the basis of
my documentary material extending over more than a century of the Schreber
genealogy, no male person of this name exists in his lineage, and that we are
confronted here with a retroactive delusional change of sex by the patient, similar
though in reverse to his own change of sex during the psychosis. He employs
the same reversal, narcissistically elaborated, in the case of his paternal grandmother whose name was *Friederike née Grosse;* in a delusional footnote she
becomes *Friedrich der Grosse.* The footnote can be found in chapter II of the
Memoirs, which deals with the delusionally exalted lineage of the Flechsig and
Schreber families (the Schrebers had once had the title "Margraves of Tuscany
and Tasmania") and with an occurrence "between perhaps earlier generations
of the Schreber and Flechsig families which amounted to soul murder". Ac-

cording to information I have recently received from the Stadtarchiv Leipzig the grandmother *Friederike geborene Grosse* died on December 30, 1846. It is likely that this was for our patient, then four-and-one-half years of age, his first experience of the death of a close family member. The patient was born in 1842.

To return to the division of God into an upper and lower one or into a superior and inferior deity, named by the patient Ormuzd and Ahriman respectively and spoken of by him as the "hierarchy of God's realms," the role of the patient's elder (and only) brother in the structure of this delusional aggregate should be recalled. Freud already mentioned the probability that Schreber's peculiarly composed God in a sense had derived from paternal and fraternal roots contained in the delusional material. The new data confirm Freud's assumption. The brother, Daniel Gustav became the head of the Schreber family after the father's sudden death in 1861. He committed suicide in 1877 a few weeks after his promotion to become *Gerichtsrat* (judge) at a provincial Saxon Court in Bautzen. Since the otherwise reliable Baumeyer (1956) suggests that the brother was a chemist and says nothing about the mode of suicide, I may be permitted to quote verbatim from the *Stadtarchiv*-Bautzen in Saxony which in its collection of municipal documents pertaining to the year 1877 has the following entry:

Schreber, Daniel Gustav, Dr. Jur., Kgl. Gerichtsrat in Bautzen, laut Kirchenbuch St. Petri, Bautzen, gestorben 8. Mai früh, 38 Jahre, ledig. Selbstmord durch Erschiessen. [Schreber, Daniel Gustav, Doctor of Law, Royal Judge in Bautzen, according to church register St Peter, Bautzen, died on 8 May, in the morning, 38 years old, unmarried. Suicide by gunshot.]

Several newspapers in Saxony under the date of May 10, 1877 carried similar notices; some also mentioning that melancholia or depression must be regarded 'als die Ursache des traurigen Ereignisses' *(Chemnitzer Tageblatt,* 10 May, 1877, No. 111, p. 4). The newspaper further emphasizes that the suicide occurred only a short time after the brother's nomination. I consider this last point as well as the obituaries in the newspapers important, since Schreber delusionally indicates in his memoirs not only that he read his own *death notice* in the newspaper, but also that his 1893 breakdown occurred a short time after his promotion to become Senatspräsident. The identification aspects and their far-reaching effects in the Schreber case, with which I dealt previously, are particularly impressive here; various multiple cross-identifications are readily discernible in Schreber's pathology. In the *Memoirs* they are often expressed by the occurrence of certain names, dates, and more specifically by anniversary reactions. All this can only be alluded to here, since their detailed consideration would require a separate study.

The sister's letter is of interest also with respect to some other aspects of

Schreber's symptomatology. She describes in it in some detail how everything in the Schreber home was *gottwärts gerichtet* (oriented towards God), how God was present in their childhood world at all times, not merely in their daily prayers, but in all their feeling, thinking, and doings. She concludes the letter with the words: "All this was finished with the sudden death of our beloved father. . . *unser Kinderparadies war zerstört.*" Here we may perhaps be permitted to view this statement as a non-delusional version of her brother's archaic "end-of-the world" fantasy and to contrast it with his delusional restitution attempt at recapturing the lost childhood paradise through the reunion with God-father-mother-brother, i.e., through the formation of his particular God-aggregate of upper and lower parts, anterior and posterior courts, as the composite deified representation of the early objects.

In this respect certain features of Schreber's pathology, in particular the great number of the "divine miracles" derived from or modelled on the early paternal-maternal manipulations, can also be understood as complex manifestations of a compelling, regressively reinstinctualized need to recover or recreate at all costs the lost objects, something we are used to encounter in certain transference reactions of a stormy nature. These transference reactions, in relation to Schreber's physician, Dr. Flechsig, his assistants and orderlies, are graphically described in the *Denkwürdigkeiten* and served Freud as valuable landmarks in his analysis of the case. The father of the patient was indeed an extraordinary man. Some of the passages about religion in the elder Schreber's books read as though written by one who, while not an ordained priest and not fond of dogma, had seen in a mystical way the true light of God. In studying his writings, I found that he was fond of lecturing and sermonizing to his children on the human body, the wonders of nature, and the relations of God to the universe, elaborating especially on the phenomena of magnetic attraction and repulsion in which he saw the expression of basic cosmic forces governing the universe. He built on these phenomena of attraction and repulsion a sort of popularized pseudophilosophical system of his own, his *Weltanschauung*, writing and lecturing about it extensively. It is noteworthy that in the son's delusional cosmology the paternal *Weltanschauung* reappears. Though distorted, condensed, and concretized, it emerges throughout the text of the *Memoirs* in a readily recognizable fashion as a conglomeration of philosophical, theological, and cosmological speculations in which divine rays, attraction to and repulsion by God, magic attributes of the deity, personal "nerve contact" with the latter, and similar ideas predominate. The non-delusional raw material of most of this can be found in the father's medical and philosophical writings. To give only two examples here:

The father, in discussing the span of human life on earth, indicates two hundred years as the maximum age which human beings may attain in time to come. The son's delusional description of the end of the world contains this figure, two hundred years, as the approximate time limit set by him for the occurrence of the anticipated event. Again, one of the father's books has the sub-title *Der Wunderbau des menschlichen Organismus* (the miraculous structure of the human organism). The term *Wunder* appears in the *Denkwürdigkeiten* not only in constant connection with God's miracles, that is, the father's "miraculous medical" actions; it also is quoted directly by the son as *wundervoller Aufbau* and then explained by him in an almost insight revealing footnote: "Again an expression which I did not invent. . . . The term *wundervoller Aufbau* was suggested to me from outside." From the sister's letter and other sources the origin of these notions becomes clear. The father, a passionate educator and eloquent talker, took his children on frequent strolls, citing to them with paternal pride and sermonizing insistence the wonders of God, of the world, and of the body. During and after such lectures the children were questioned in minute detail as to their understanding of the cited wonders and the one who, like our ever-obedient patient, knew the correct answers, received paternal praise.

Of interest is the onset of Schreber's first illness, about which little has been known until now. Freud, letting the patient speak for himself and strictly adhering to his self-imposed "policy of restraint," only pointed to Schreber's passing remark about his candidature for the Reichstag in 1884. With respect to this candidature for election as a member of parliament, I wish to supply some of the following data. Schreber was then running for the Reichstag as the avowed candidate of the *Nationalliberale Partei* (National Liberal party) which was in opposition to Bismarck's autocratic and reactionary r9egime in Germany. After a political campaign in which Schreber actively participated, the election took place on October 28, 1884. Schreber was defeated, with an overwhelming majority voting against him (14,512 against 5,762), and a local newspaper in his election district—Chemnitz in Saxony—carried the somewhat scornful headline about his candidature: *Wer kennt schon den Dr. Schreber*—who after all knows Dr. Schreber? A few weeks later, in November 1884, he fell ill with his first sickness, which has been described as a hypochondriasis or a condition characterized chiefly by hypochondriacal complaints. The recently accumulated material indicates that Schreber, following his defeat, suffered from a severe depression, considered himself incurable, had difficulties in talking and walking and made two suicidal attempts. He was hospitalized for approximately six months (Baumeyer 1956). He undoubtedly also had various hypochondriacal symptoms and, for instance, thought that he was going to die "any moment." On the basis of the old medical records communicated by Baumeyer (1956) it is clear that depressive and hypochondriacal manifestations were present during this first illness and that the depression was connected at least chronologically with Schreber's election defeat. Shortly after his unsuccessful campaign he developed a serious disorder which, among other symptoms, included speech disturbances and difficulties in walking, i.e., manifestations in all probability related to his active yet unsuccessful participation in the election campaign.

My data further suggest at least *one* reason for Schreber's disastrous political-personal situation (and his subsequent hospitalizaton) which resulted from his participation in the unsuccessful campaign. There is evidence that the Schreber family was in political difficulties with the governmental authorities in Saxony during the 1840s, especially during the revolutionary years 1847 and 1848, when the patient was five years of age or so. As I have explained elsewhere (Niederland 1959b), the turbulent political events in Germany during the 1880s seem to have revived in him memories and anxieties connected with his childhood experiences during the 1840s. In connection with his political campaign of 1884 these memories seem to have contributed to a regressively intensified reliving of the castration fears of his oedipal years. These years, as mentioned above, had also been marked by political events and considerable uncertainties connected with fears of personal and political persecution.

Turning to the outbreak of Schreber's second and lasting illness in 1893, its chronological connection with his promotion to Senatspräsident has been duly noted and has often been commented on in the literature. But here also a second, perhaps equally important, factor must now be added. Schreber's brother, *Daniel* Gustav, as we have seen, committed suicide a short time after his nomination as *Gerichsrat*. The patient, *Daniel* Paul, tried to do the same a few weeks after his nomination to an even higher juridical position and, prevented from physical suicide, succumbed to lifelong mental illness. The father died in his early fifties in a Leipzig hospital on November 10 or 11, 1861. Thirty-two years later the patient, likewise in his early fifties, had himself hospitalized in a Leipzig hospital on November 9 or 10, thinking himself dead and making several suicide attempts. The presence of strong intrafamily identifications is evident here (Niederland 1959a) and is linked with typical anniversary reactions.

In closing this brief presentation of supplementary material I wish to reiterate that I do not claim that the data so far accumulated throw light on the nature of Schreber's psychosis. Suffice it to say that some of them appear to be useful in our effort to unravel a few of the many obscure features in the clinical picture and to make hitherto incomprehensible aspects of Schreber's delusional system accessible to further investigation. It is well to bear in mind that *Denkwürdigkeiten*, in Freud's view an "invaluable book," is no casual text of reminiscences. It contains not only the patient's mental productions, but also reveals on closer scrutiny the matrix from which they are formed.

References

Baumeyer, F. (1956). The Schreber case. *International Journal of Psycho-Analysis* 37:61–74.

Freud, S. (1911). Psycho-analytic notes on an autobiographical account of a case of paranoia. *Standard Edition* 12:9–82.

———(1938). Construction in analysis. *Collected Papers* 5:358–371.

Katan, M. (1950). Schreber's hallucinations about the "little men." *International Journal of Psycho-Analysis* 31:32–35.

Macalpine, I., and Hunter, R., trans. and eds. (1955). *Daniel Paul Schreber. Memoirs of My Nervous Illness*. London: Dawson.

Niederland, W. G. (1951). Three notes on the Schreber case. *Psychoanalytic Quarterly* 20:579–591.

———(1959a). The "miracled-up" world of Schreber's childhood. *Psychoanalytic Study of the Child* 14:383–413. This volume, Part V, chapter 2.

———(1959b). Schreber: father and son. *Psychoanalytic Quarterly* 28:151–169. This volume, Part V, chapter 1.

———(1960). Schreber's father. *Journal of the American Psychoanalytic Association* 8:492–499.

Schreber, D.G.M. (1839). *Das Buch der Gesundheit*. Leipzig: H. Fries.

———(1859). *Anthropos—Der Wunderbau des Menschlichen Organismus*. Leipzig: H. Fleischer.

———(1862). *Das Pangymnasticon*. Leipzig: H. Fleischer.

White, R. B. (1961). The mother-conflict in Schreber's psychosis. *International Journal of Psycho-Analysis* 42:55–73.

Chapter 4

TEACHING FREUD'S CASE HISTORIES:

THE SCHREBER CASE

JULES GLENN, M.D. and IRVING RUBINS, M.D.

Introduction

Freud's case histories have been integrated into the psychoanalytic curriculum in many ways. At one end of the spectrum classes examine these papers as autonomous articles with little reference to later developments in analysis. At the other extreme, a course in theory or psychopathology will include the histories among the many sources of information, but will omit detailed study of them. Institutes differ regarding the optimum place of these articles in the curriculum.

Disagreements exist as to whether the case histories should be taught in a single course in the first year of classes, as they frequently are. Arlow (1973) has been an ardent proponent of the early teaching of analytic theory and technique as understood and practiced today. He has suggested that courses like Freud Case Histories, taught at the beginning of training, lead students to accept Freud's early conceptualizations which, although historically important, include many outmoded constructs and methods. The candidates then start their supervised analyses armed mainly with knowledge of theory and procedures that are dated.

However it is possible to create a balanced curriculum in which the students learn valid up-to-date concepts along with the historical development of psychoanalysis. Freud's Case Histories can be a key course in which early concepts are juxtaposed against and integrated with modern views. Five of Freud's cases (Dora, Little Hans, the Rat Man, the Wolf Man and the "homosexual woman") provide exquisite analytic material (Freud 1905, 1909a, 1909b, 1911, 1914, 1920). A sixth paper, on Schreber (Freud 1911), includes Freud's clear summaries of parts of the long and often confusing autobiography of a paranoid man. Freud and other analysts have used Schreber's work as clinical data from which important analytic conclusions can be drawn. Indeed, first year students, having no clinical analytic experience themselves, appreciate reading Freud's masterful descriptions, especially when they can utilize his cases as a basis for learning theoretical and technical concepts in a clinical context. Through his vivid reports theory can come alive.

A reciprocal enrichment can emerge. Freud's cases can be used to understand established theory, and information recently obtained can clarify certain of Freud's clinical findings. The increased knowledge of child development that psychoanalytic observers of children (for example, Hoffer 1949, A. Freud and Burlingham 1944, Spitz 1965, Benjamin 1961, Escalona 1968, Mahler 1968, Brody and Axelrod 1970, Galenson and Roiphe 1971) have uncovered can cast light on observations previously made by Freud.

In this paper we will describe how we taught one segment of a Freud case history in a course at Downstate. In this segment the class discussed the Schreber case from a variety of perspectives. We will show how Freud's explanations of pathology can be elaborated and supplemented with the help of recent knowledge of schizophrenia, information about Schreber's rearing collected by Niederland (1974) and present concepts of child development. During the course different metapsychological points of view were presented and integrated. However, since this is an elementary course, a full explanation of these aspects could not be achieved.

First we must provide some background so that the reader will see how the Freud Case History course fits into the first year curriculum at Downstate. Then we will delve into the details of the classes in which the Schreber case was discussed. An element of particular interest is our contrasting Freud's simple developmental scheme of 1911 with modern views.

Downstate's First Year

At present Downstate's curriculum consists of four years of courses, each year being divided into three ten-week trimesters. The Freud Case Histories course, which lasts twenty weeks, is taught in the second and third trimesters of the first year.

A diagram of the first year courses in 1975–76 will demonstrate their temporal relation.

1st Semester	2nd Semester	3rd Semester
Psychoanalytic Theory I	Selection of Cases for Analysis	Psychoanalytic Theory II
The Interpretation of Dreams	Chapter VII of *The Interpretation of Dreams*	Child Development
Psychoanalytic Methodology	Freud's Case Histories	Freud's Case Histories
Psychoanalytic Technique		Continuous Case Seminar

The reader will observe that when the Freud Case Histories course starts, the students have already been exposed to two pedagogical approaches. Some courses emphasize contemporary integrations of the past and present theory while others follow the historical approach. The courses in Psychoanalytic Theory present Freud's concepts in historical sequence but do not ignore the relation between early and later theory. In Theory I, given prior to the Freud Case Histories, students study early analytic constructs, particularly libido theory. In Theory II, concomitant with the latter part of the Freud Case Histories course, they examine concepts developed from 1910 to 1920, that is, prior to the systematization of ego psychology. (Theory courses continue the historical study in the second year.) The first semester course on *The Interpretation of Dreams* stresses seeing Freud's original insights in present day terms. Present concepts are emphasized in the Methodology course, in which the instructor's analytic case material is studied from a contemporary vantage point, and in the technique course. Some students start doing supervised analyses in the second half of the first year, thus providing a source for the continuous case seminar presentation.

The Freud Case Histories Course

As we have indicated, the Freud Case Histories is a twenty-week course taught in the second and third trimesters of the first year. Each class is one hour and twenty minutes long. The students spend the final three weeks on the Schreber case after having considered Dora, Little Hans, the Rat Man and the Wolf Man in that order. When this segment of the course is reached, the candidates are accustomed to skipping from one metapsychological viewpoint to another, from Freud's early conceptualizations to his later views and to present theory and knowledge. Theories of normal and pathological personality organization have been discussed and technical issues in regard to the previous cases have been considered as well. The classes are seminars rather than lectures and hence contain the dangers of confused and desultory discussions as well as opportunities to integrate the many areas that comprise psychoanalysis.

The Segment of the Course on Schreber

Before going into the details of the three classes on Schreber, we will provide an overview of the material covered.

During the three classes on Schreber, Freud's observations and theories were examined in some detail. The class studied the homosexual wishes behind Schreber's delusions, the defenses (disavowal, reversal and projection) that determined the symptomatology, and the significance of decathexis and restitution in paranoid schizophrenia. Freud's suggestion that masochism played a role in paranoid ideation (elaborated by Bak 1946) led to a discussion of the continuity between non-psychotic masochism, borderline states and frank psychotic delusions.

Although the importance of homosexuality, of Schreber's intensive libidinal attachment to his father, was clear recent knowledge of the development of schizophrenia requires one to take more notice of preoedipal determinants. Freud's schemata of early development at the time he wrote the Schreber case and in *On Narcissism: An Introduction* (Freud 1914) were seen to be inadequate and incomplete. To provide a broader picture of development, the instructors introduced current concepts of development based to a great extent on direct observations of children. Although time limited the depth in which the class could study the works of Arlow and Brenner (1964), Mahler (1968), Mahler and La Perriere (1965), Spitz (1965), Jacobson (1964), Kohut (1971), Kernberg (1975) and others who have expanded Freud's observations and enriched theory, sufficient data could be presented to help understand some of the problems that psychoses pose.

The developmental point of view supplemented the economic as students examined cathexis and decathexis at different stages. It also supplemented the structural and dynamic viewpoints as the class studied alterations in the psychic structure of the growing child.

In particular, differing concepts of primary and secondary narcissism and object relations cast light on normal and pathological development. Questions about cathexis—when it was of the self, the self-representation, the representations of self-objects or more maturely conceived object-representations—helped clarify the various configurations.

Paranoid schizophrenics regress to the symbiotic stage, i.e., to an early state of narcissism in which self-representation and object-representation are indistinct from one another. The child feels at one with the mother and hence omnipotent. Despite the feeling of power that may result from such a regression, the psychotic is in danger of losing his identity as he feels fused with his early object or pre-object or its symbolic representation (for example, the sun or the ocean).

The earliest object that the child perceives, the mother, must play a greater role in the genesis of schizophrenia than Freud suggests in the Schreber paper.

With these facts in mind, the class reevaluated the significant roles of Schreber's mother and father in the patient's development. Schreber Senior appears to have been a more significant presence than most fathers and may have intruded himself into the child's early object-representations as a *symbiotic father*, to use Niederland's (1974) apt term. This is in addition to the inevitable representation of the mother as an early object or pre-object. Further, sadistic child rearing practices carried out by the father and his agents, mother and maids, must have stimulated young Schreber's masochism. Certainly as Niederland (1974) had discovered and documented, these practices appeared in disguised forms in the patient's symptomatology.

The failure of the patient's mother to protect him from excessive external and internal stimulation when he was an infant is another factor which may have led to the precocious but brittle defense formation that Bergman and Escalona (1949) contend occurs in many childhood schizophrenics. Misunderstanding of or faulty reaction to many of the child's cues must have resulted from the father's interference with the mother's natural responses to her son.

As the reader can see, during the segment of the Freud Case Histories Course in which Schreber was studied, the class shuttled between earlier and later ideas of Freud and present concepts regarding normal and pathological development. Attempts were also made to integrate the various metapsychological points of view and to provide clinical data to make the theory come alive.

In studying the other case histories, technical issues, as formulated when at the time that Freud treated his patients and at the present, were clarified as well.

I. The First Class

The students were assigned the first two sections of Freud's paper on the Schreber case for the first class. Despite their reluctance to reproduce the contents of their reading as a basis for discussion they did so. The following recapitulation will serve to orient the reader and help him recall Schreber's illness.

Schreber suffered from three episodes of emotional illness. His first, at forty-two years of age, occurred after he lost in an election for the Reichstag. Dr. Flechsig, whom Schreber and his wife came to admire tremendously, successfully treated the patient for the condition which was diagnosed as hypochondriasis.

His second illness, at fifty-one, occurred between his appointment in June to the position of Senatspräsident (judge presiding over a division of a Court of Appeals) and October, when he was to take office. Premonitions of the serious illness heralded the actual psychosis. He dreamed that his old illness was returning. On another occasion, while half asleep, he felt it would be nice to be a woman submitting to copulation.

The illness per se started in October of that year. Schreber returned to Flechsig's clinic in November after a period of sleeplessness. He suffered from hypochondriasis, delusions and hallucinations. He believed his brain was becoming soft, that he had the plague, was decomposing and, indeed, was dead. He felt he was being tortured by Dr. Flechsig whom he called a soul murderer. Religious delusions, which we will discuss further, appeared.

At fifty-eight, after he had been transferred to other institutions, he instituted legal action to obtain a discharge from the hospital. When he was sixty the court determined that he was sufficiently recovered socially and could be released. His memoirs, which he had written while hospitalized, were published when he was sixty-one.

A third illness occurred when Schreber was sixty-five. In May of that year his mother died and in November his wife had a stroke. The patient himself died at sixty-nine.

After outlining Schreber's history, the class discussed his delusions as they appeared in the memoirs, following Freud's concepts.

Schreber's delusions included belief that he must redeem the world. This could occur after he was transformed into a woman through divine miracles which produced specific damage to his body. He believed he had lived for a long time without a stomach or intestines, but that rays had replaced the destroyed organs. Female nerves passed into his body.

At first Schreber believed that Flechsig persecuted him and that God was his ally. Later God became the persecutor. The patient emerged as a victor over God because the "order of things" was on his side.

Many indications of a female identity appeared. Voices insulted Schreber as he became a woman, calling him "Miss Schreber." Previous ideas that he had to be emasculated fused with the idea that he had to redeem the world; now the "order of things" demanded his emasculation. He would then be impregnated by the divine rays so that he would create a new race of men. At times Schreber dressed as a woman and looked at himself in the mirror. He believed he had developed breasts and female genitals, indeed, that he had become the wife of God.

According to Schreber, men have bodies but the human soul is composed of nerves which are threads. God himself is nothing but an infinite number of nerves, which are very intense rays, related to the sun and the starry heaven. Ordinarily God draws *dead* souls to him and these unite with God in the "Forecourts of Heaven". On rare occasions, however, God enters into a relationship with a gifted *living* person. A bond of this type occurred between God and Schreber. The nerves of the live man, Schreber, developed a state of intense excitement and attracted God's nerves. This threatened God, who could not free himself, and He, now imperfect, retaliated, causing Schreber great suffering. God demanded a constant state of excitement and it was the patient's duty to provide this. Schreber said that if he incidentally attained some pleasure, this was slight compensation for the suffering and deprivation he experienced.

After summarizing Schreber's delusions, the class made preliminary attempts at interpreting them, based mainly on Freud's explanations.

Schreber's homosexuality was apparent to all and was documented from facts presented in his memoirs. After Flechsig cured Schreber of his first illness, the patient experienced affectionate feelings for him. The premonitory dreams early in his second illness were signs of Schreber's love for Flechsig, of his desire to become a woman and return to Flechsig. The cause of the second illness would therefore appear to involve an accentuation of homosexual desire, an outburst of "homosexual libido" as Freud says.

Defenses against homosexuality appeared: (a) Schreber displayed an increased interest in his wife; and (b) God became the displaced object to whom he was attached.

Later in his paper Freud demonstrated how the delusion of persecution involves defenses against homosexuality. One of the series of mechanisms that Freud discussed involves the use of negation, reversal and projection.

I love the man.
I do not love the man (negation).
I hate the man (reversal).
The man hates me (projection).
And therefore persecutes me.

Reversal, it was noted, involves the mobilization of opposite instinct fusions as a defense.

But why the outburst of "homosexual libido"? Freud suggested three possible causes:

(1) The male climacteric. (The class rejected this possibility.)

(2) Transference from Schreber's dead brother and father to two aspects of Flechsig (the lower and upper Flechsig in Schreber's delusional system).

(3) Later in the paper Freud suggests that Schreber's frustration about having no children resulted in a wishful fantasy of becoming a woman and producing children.

The class suggested several additional possible precipitating events:

(1) The threat of success. Schreber had been appointed to a high and prestigious office just prior to the onset of his second illness.

(2) Failure. Schreber had lost his election to the Reichstag prior to his first illness.

(3) Object loss. The patient's mother died and his wife suffered a stroke prior to the onset of his third illness. Further, his illnesses developed on or near anniversaries of his father's death, which occurred in November, 1861. It was suggested that possibly the threat of success or the blow of failure was unconsciously equated with object loss. Could it be that when Schreber unconsciously felt he had lost an important person in his life he reacted with an intense need for union with someone, with his mother or his father? This would account for his identification with women, his desire for union with a father surrogate, his homosexuality.

II. The Second Class

In preparation for this class the students finished reading Freud's paper on Schreber.

The second class started with an instructor outlining the issues that had been raised in the first session and with the expectation that the class would seek further insight into unresolved problems.

The instructor then asked the class to present Freud's formulae for Schreber's various delusions. As we had already stated the formula for the development of paranoia in men in our first class discussion on Schreber. (It does not appear necessary for the purposes of this paper to present the formulae for the production of erotomania, alcoholic delusions of jealousy, delusions of jealousy in women, and megalomania. The reader is referred to p. 63ff. of Freud [1911].) this was easily done and the importance of negation, reversal and projection became obvious. It was observed that Freud used the term *repression* to cover many defenses. One student asked why projection was such a prominent feature in paranoid schizophrenia. Another student supplied the correct answer: that the marked confusion between self-representation and object-representation in schizophrenia made projection and identification prominent defenses.

The teacher then turned to Freud's discovery that in paranoid schizophrenia there is initially restitution. (Although paranoid schizophrenia was not discussed systematically and in detail in the year described, it had been considered more fully the previous year. It was generally agreed that today Schreber would be diagnosed as a paranoid schizophrenic.) The instructor asked whether anyone could suggest another determinant of world destruction fantasies. One student said that the aggressive drive (a later conceptualization of Freud's) could account for it, that the patient's hatred could result in fantasies that all would die. The class then engaged in a discussion of cathexis and decathexis. It was pointed out that the economic point of view was under consideration here. Other metapsychological points of view were listed, including the genetic and the developmental.

The students asked whether the sun was a male symbol as Freud contended, or whether it could also be a female symbol. This introduced the possibility that Freud had overlooked the importance of the mother in the development of Schreber's pathology. Clinical and mythological examples of the bisexual meaning of the sun emerged. The important issue of the role of the mother in schizophrenia was put aside for future consideration.

Cathexis was defined as the attachment of psychic energy to the self, the self- or object-representation. It was decided that tone could cathect the object-representation but not the object itself, though it is possible to cathect parts of the self or of the self-representation. Early in the history of analysis, local cathexis of parts of the body, e.g., the arm of an hysteric, was taken for granted. Today we consider the cathexis to be of the *representation* of a part of the body. There was some question in the class, however, about whether there could be local cathexis, for example, of the genitals. At this point the issue of local physiological changes being equated with cathexis, which is a psychic concept, arose. Some students thought it in accordance with a recognition of the body-mind unity to consider physical energy charges as equivalent to psychic cathexis. However the controversial nature of such a hypothesis was emphasized. Someone said that in psychosomatic disorders the body itself was cathected.

Other forms of cathexis were also mentioned: attention cathexis, cathexis of wishes, cathexis of the ego as a structure within the personality.

Decathexis was then discussed by the class. Schreber's decathexis of the world (strictly speaking, his decathexis of the *representation* of the world) eventually led him to imagine that the world had disappeared, had been destroyed. One student became dissatisfied with the explanation of decathexis of the outer world in economic terms, and suggested that viewing decathexis as a regression to an early stage of development would be more useful. The instructor agreed that this was a useful approach, and that the developmental point of view supplemented the economic. We must ask: What is the state of cathexis in the earliest periods of an infant's life? Before this topic was discussed by the class, one student warned that a schizophrenic might regress not to a state of normal infancy, but to a stage distorted by a schizophrenic disorder that had already started in infancy.

We turned to the developmental scheme outlined by Freud in his paper on Schreber. According to Freud, the earliest stage, the auto-erotic, was followed by the narcissistic stage and then by object choice. The narcissistic stage gave rise to homosexuality, to a choice of object who was like the subject, especially insofar as they had similar genitals. In the stage of object choice, a heterosexual object was selected.

It was generally agreed by the class that this simple scheme was not realistic and it was pointed out that Freud changed his concept of development when he wrote his paper on narcissism (Freud 1914). According to this conceptualization the child progresses from Primary Narcissism to Secondary Narcissism to Object Cathexis; hence Primary Narcissism seems to be the equivalent of Auto-eroticism. According to this formulation, during Primary Narcissism the cathexis is entirely of the self. Later, the outside world becomes cathected. Cathexis is then withdrawn from the outside world and directed again toward the self, creating a Secondary Narcissism. This scheme did not appear to the class to be well conceived because subtleties regarding cathexis were not taken into account. Freud did not semantically differentiate between cathexis of the self and cathexis of the self-representation.

A chart outlining early development as described by different analytic authors had been distributed to the class and was at this point subject to scrutiny. While this complex chart could not be studied in detail in the three sessions at our disposal, it served to alert the students to the complexities of development. Libidinal stages were omitted on the assumption that the students understood these well and could integrate them into the total chart. It is reproduced below.

It appears that the terms *autistic phase* (Mahler), *undifferentiated stage* (Hartman, Lowenstein and Kris, Freud), *nondifferentiated stage* (Spitz), *auto-eroticism* (Freud, Kohut), and *primary narcissism* (Freud, Jacobson) delineated the same early stage lasting about the first two months of life. During this stage the ego and id are not differentiated, nor is the external world differentiated from the self. Inner and outer worlds are a blurred continuity. Cathexis of self-respresentation as differentiated from object-representation does not occur. According to Jacobson (1964), cathexis is of the self, that is, of the body; this constitutes *primary narcissism* in her terms. After this early stage there is a gradual development and separation of self-and object-representations, as described by Spitz and Mahler (the latter in her observations on the symbiotic and separation individuation stages).

The schizophrenic regresses to stages in which self-and object-representation are poorly differentiated. At that stage the main object in the environment and hence the object-representation is that of the mother rather than the father. Freud's analysis of Schreber emphasizes the patient's relation to his father and

Mos.	Mahler	Benjamin	Spitz, etc.	Piaget	Kohut
0	0–1 Autistic stage	0–4 wks. High stimulus barrier	0–3 Undiff. phase (HLK) (F*) = Ego and id not separated	0–1 Reflex period Conditioning begins	Autoerotic (F) Stage of Fragmented Self*
1	Start Symbiotic Stage (to 1–½ years)	4 wks.- Low Stimulus barrier	Nondiff. phase (Sp) = I and Non-I not separated as well		Ego Nuclei (G)
2		2–½ mos. Stimulus barrier rises (psychological)			
3	1–		Primary narc. (J) (F2) Smile; start of non-I (pre-object)	1–4 Combination of reflexes Hand-mouth-eye coord. Start of intentional thumb sucking: of ego and id (Hoffer)	
4		2–½ mos.			
5		Start Separ. individuation	Indiscriminate smile stops. Only to parent		
6	5–10	Differentiation subphase		4–8 Circular reactions (kick or push object to make it move) start of obj. Permanence	
7	Stranger reaction	Stranger anxiety peaks			
8	Stranger reaction	Stranger anxiety peaks	Stranger anxiety: separation of self from non-self; separation of self-rep. from object rep. (J)		Start of stage of cohesive self: idealized parental imagos and grandiose self*
9				8–12 Means and ends: Obj. permanence look behind screen	
10	Start of practicing sub-phase (10–15)	Separation anxiety peaks			

Key:F-reud (1938). F§ -Freud (1911). F3- Freud (1914). HLK-Hartman, Loewenstein, & Kris. Sp-Spitz (1965). J1-Jacobson (1965). G2-Glover (1956).

Other references: Benjamin (1965); Piaget and Inhelder (1969); Kohut (1971); Mahler and La Perriere (1965); Mahler (1968).

*Dates are not provided by Kohut (1974).

does not take the patient's relationship to his mother into account. As there is little information about Schreber's mother in his autobiography, Freud, and Niederland after him, apparently felt constrained to concentrate on the patient's father.

III. The Third Class

The reading assignments for this class were several articles by Niederland (1974) Bergman and Escalona (1949), Bak (1946) and Freud (1922).

Using the previously distributed chart outlining early development as conceptualized by different authors, students were encouraged to attempt to integrate or reconcile the views of Kohut and of Mahler (they were more familiar with the latter tham the former). Difficulty arose with what was felt to be Kohut's loose usage of Mahler's terms and a confusion due to the uncertainty of the timing of his stages. Kohut (1971) states that the stage of the cohesive self occurs between the late symbiotic and early separation-individuation stages. As the former occurs later than the latter, the class was confused. The teacher stressed the concept of the overlapping of phases in any developmental schema—for example, while the symbiotic phase, during which mother and child are perceived as one, runs from about four weeks to five months. Significant remnants of symbloses persist to eighteen months did beyond. Symbolic tendencis thus overlap with the separation-individuation phase which begins at about five months and proceeds to the object constancy phase at three and a half years. He further underlined the previously expressed idea that it was unlikely that the feelings of the adult schizophrenic are the same as the feelings of the normal developmental fragmented self phase described by Kohut. Nevertheless, it was pointed out that the concepts of *regression* and *developmental arrest* are of great value in one's understanding of schizophrenia. Certainly Schreber, seeing himself as united with God, the father, did not feel like a complete and independent person.

The group was asked which signs and symptoms in Schreber could be explained by regression to earlier stages. Grandiosity, it was argued, parallels the symbiotic stage of Mahler and Kohut's stage of the appearance of the cohesive self, stages in which the grandiose self and the idealized parental image prevail.

A student suggested that the appearance of world destruction fantasies indicated regression to the autistic state for two reasons. First, he thought the appearance of enormous aggression implied an early state. Second, when all libido is withdrawn from objects, an autistic state exists. The teacher objected, doubting that a delusion of world destruction, which contains within it the knowledge of the world's existence, could be a regression to an autistic stage. He suggested the regression would be to a later period, the symbiotic stage, in which the representations of the world were cathected.

A student presented the view that symptoms can never literally fit within a specific stage of development because they include the self-perception of regression—for instance, the feeling of loss of the world necessarily includes the memory of its presence before the regression. Another student suggested that the world destruction fantasy was itself evidence of an adaptive recathexis because the world's absence was noted, but this did not seem to meet with general acceptance.

The teacher now summarized, stressing that Freud's emphasis on cathexis and decathexis employs the economic point of view, one of the many metapsychological approaches. Ideally one should examine a psychic phenomenon in all its metapsychological aspects. Today metapsychology includes structural theory which had not been developed when Freud wrote about the Schreber case. The instructor compared the integration of early Freudian ideas into modern theory with an analogous view of physical science, where Newtonian physics is subsumed in modern physics.

He also made several other points. (1) He did not believe that primary narcissism is a useful concept, because there is no self-representation to cathect in earliest infancy. However one may define primary narcissism as a stage of cathexis of the *self* rather than the self-representation, as Jacobson does. (2) He reminded the group that poor reality testing and primary process thinking, characterized by illogicality, extreme mobility of cathexis, symbolism and condensation, were the most important signs of regression to earlier stages of ego development. (3) In general, when a child feels threatened with separation, even in the course of normal separation-individuation, he feels furious. This is part of the normal developmental process. In the schizophrenic child the intensity of rage is greater, probably due to inborn factors.

A student asked whether qualitative or quantitative differences determine the child's response. In the instructor's view probably both were present. Schizophrenia is a physical or physiological disorder, in which the drives are increased and the ability to handle these drives is diminished. Environmental factors reinforce or deter the basic biological disturbances.

A student agreed that most likely constitutional factors play an important role in the etiology of schizophrenia. He asserted that, despite lack of proof in the case material at hand, a careful observer would have detected evidence of pathology in the patient's childhood. He felt that Schreber regressed to a point in which he was fixated in part as a result of constitutional factors, and that the regression was not total.

This comment led to a discussion of the concepts of developmental arrest and fixation. It was pointed out that the term *fixation* has two meanings: remaining at a certain point in a line of development; or being prone to go back to that point. Currently we often call the first type of fixation "developmental arrest." Such arrests are generally partial.

The students were asked to reexamine the dynamics of the precipitating events in Schreber's ilness. They proposed the hypothesis that the patient perceived his appointment to a prestigious judicial post as a challenge to the oedipal father, mobilizing castration anxiety and causing consequent regression. Some students doubted that Schreber had progressed to the oedipal stage and suggested a preoedipal view of the situation in which the appointment created an imagined threat of separation from mother. In either case, unconscious psychic conflict and anxiety led to the institution of defenses, including regression.

It was agreed that the prospect of increased responsibility, as in the judicial appointment, implied increased separation, leading to rage, terror, and a defensive need to fuse with mother, i.e., to regression. Fury with the object may cause regression to a state of fantasized fusion in order to preserve the object, be it an oedipal or preoedipal object. As the discussion enlarged the child's pre-oedipal relationship with his mother was emphasized. (See White 1961 for an examination of the "mother conflict in Schreber's psychosis.") A student thought that Schreber's mother must have been adequate, as Schreber functioned well, as far as we know, for many years.

The instructor urged the group to evaluate Freud's emphasis on the father. He specifically asked about William G. Niederland's discovery regarding Schreber's childhood experiences with his father, mother and nurse. How did these experiences affect his illness?

The group was fascinated by Niederland's revelations. They readily related the disciplines and apparatuses used by the father to the symptoms the son complained of in his illness. The patient's feelings of compression of the chest and head were seen to be derivatives of the braces and bars that his father had advocated children wear and which the patient himself must have worn. The hallucinatory sensations of hot and cold were connected with the cold baths at an early age, the coccyx miracle to sitting posture exercises, and the eye miracles to the eye ablutions and exercises. The class reacted to the sadistic attitude of the "educational" process with feeling.

The teacher asked whether these extraordinary experiences alone could cause schizophrenia. Certainly such experiences could influence development, much more so if they occurred in the preoedipal period. In Schreber's case they obviously influenced the form the disease took. The teacher stressed the sadistic nature of the situation, since, as Niederland observed, the father had prescribed applying painful measures with friendliness. (Dr. William G. Niederland, in a personal communication, corrects the use of the term *friendliness* here. He states that Schreber's father used the Latin word *iucunde,* which means "pleasurably," but which "in the German context the prescription *iucunde* has the definite meaning of stimulating the young child manually, making it feel very good, stimulated, loved, bodily excited, sensitized physically, etc. . . . *Iucunde* has a libidinal connotation.")

The class was asked whether sadism in the father encouraged masochism in the child and whether this could lead to paranoia. (Bak's [1946] article on this subject had been assigned reading.) The response indicated that most of the class had not read the article and that those who had were not gripped by it. Because the students complained of difficulty in following Bak's formulations and remained unconvinced, it was felt that clinical illustrations might clarify the points Bak made. A clinical vignette was introduced in which a patient at first appeared to be severely masochistic and then, despite therapeutic efforts, became overtly paranoid. In paranoid states unconscious masochistic wishes may appear in delusional form. The patient, whose reality testing is deficient, becomes convinced that he is being mistreated by others; his fantasies are projected and treated as reality. It was noted that most masochists do not become paranoid, but that the analyst may have difficulty determining whether a patient is simply masochistic or paranoid as well.

The group contributed experiences of their own along these lines and added that Freud observes in his paper, "Some Neurotic Mechanisms in Jealousy, Paranoia, and Homosexuality," that paranoid patients read the unconscious of others. This phenomena had been seen clinically by them. A student suggested that paranoid people are extremely sensitive to their environment.

The teacher drew attention to the work of Bergman and Escalona who observed that the stimulus barrier of a group of schizophrenic children was very low, thus making them extremely sensitive to external stimuli. In contrast to normal children, they develop defenses precociously and these defenses are "brittle." Schizophrenia emerges when, under traumatic circumstances, these defenses "crack." In other cases the mother fails to protect the child against excessive stimulation with a similar result—the premature development of very vulnerable defenses. Could this be true of Schreber? Excessive stimulation began relatively early in his life.

This discussion turned the group's attention back to Schreber's elusive mother. A student asked whether her compliance with her husband's sadistic educational methods indicated that she, too, was sadistic. He added that in view of the mother's obvious failure to protect her child, there was no need to postulate a defective stimulus barrier.

The teacher repeated that there *was* early overstimulation—for instance, the cold ablutions in infancy. (According to Benjamin [1965] there is a period which starts at one month and lasts until two and a half months during which the stimulus barrier is particularly low and the child is especially vulnerable to overstimulation.) In addition, the teasing frustration of the child's drives produced internal overstimulation. The class recalled that Schreber's father insisted that the child's nurse eat while next to the baby and not feed him. The fact that Schreber's father fired a nurse for feeding the child on one such occasion affirmed the father's omnipresent intrusiveness. The father interfered with the mother carrying out her natural jobs.

Students, now heatedly involved in the discussion, suggested that the mother received little support, little narcissistic supplies from her husband, and this interfered with her ability to give to the baby. Schreber senior probably provided a rigid schedule for his wife as well as his children. Students suggested that the father burdened her with non-maternal duties and that there was insufficient room for her in the rearing of the children. The teacher agreed that following her husband's rules compromised her ability to make use of normal maternal empathy. Misinterpretation of the child's needs—miscuing—frequently occurs in schizophrenic development.

Students stressed further that the children were only professional items to the father. (Commenting on this, Dr. William G. Niederland states that Schreber's father regarded the children as extensions of his body rather than as "professional items." The father had usurped the mother's role in many ways; he loved the children in both a paternal and maternal way, frequently taking them on walks, playing with them, holding them like a mother, etc. Indeed, Schreber's father actually believed that his gadgets, which compressed parts of the body, were health-protective and preventative methods against kyphosis, prognathia, scoliosis and other orthopedic deformities which he, as an orthopedist, had to treat so often. There was no orthopedic surgery at that time, only apparatuses. At the same time that he was a libidinal object, this same father was the dreaded castrator of his male children. The resultant confusion must have been enormous, Dr. Niederland concludes. [See Part V, chapters 1, 2 and 3; Niederland 1959a, 1959b, and 1963].) They felt that the elder Schreber did not see his children as people with individual needs. The teacher supported this idea. Schreber's statement that God did not understand living people was probably derived from a childhood impression that father did not understand his son.

The mother, generally, is the most important person in the infant's life, but in Schreber's case there was early confusion. The father so intruded himself into the child-rearing process that he became an extraordinarily important object. When Schreber was a very small infant he undoubtedly was not aware of his father's tremendous influence on his mother and nurse and hence the father was not incorporated into the representation of the very early pre-object or object. Later the father imago probably fused with the mother imago. In contrast,

Niederland states that the child viewed his father as a kind of mother, a "symbiotic father," from the beginning.

Discussion

We have proposed that the Freud Case Histories course can integrate knowledge obtained early in the curriculum in other courses. It can also add to such knowledge. Freud's excellent case histories can be a boon to the student with little or no analytic experience. His clinical observations can make theoretical concepts come alive. They can be the basis for teaching the historical background of modern concepts and satisfy the student's need for knowledge of the present status of analytic thinking. The case histories course can integrate the clinical observations and the many metapsychological points of view. The theory of normal and abnormal development can be presented in conjunction with technical precepts.

To accomplish these aims the instructor must be aware of the state of analysis at the time Freud published his cases and be able to reinterpret Freud's clinical material in the light of present knowledge. He must be willing to observe Freud's shortcomings at the time he wrote the cases and later. The instructor must teach psychoanalysis in the same spirit that Freud did, acknowledging difficulties, seeking additional observations and more satisfactory constructs. In doing so he will enable students to view Freud's theoretical concepts and practical suggestions in ways that are helpful to them in their clinical work. The danger of accepting Freud's early, incomplete and sometimes incorrect concepts and methods will be diminished. The possibility that the students will be able to think for themselves, unhampered by a dogmatic adherence to Freud's views, while appreciating his brilliant accomplishments, will be enhanced.

References

Arlow, J.A. (1973). The influence of the psychoanalytic curriculum on supervision. In *Training Analysis. Report of the Second Conference of the Chicago, Pittsburgh and Topeka Institutes*, ed. I. Ramzy. Topeka, Kansas: Topeka Institute for Psychoanalysis.

Arlow, J.A., and Brenner, C. (1964). *Psychoanalytic Concepts and the Structural Theory*. New York: International Universities Press.

Bak, R. (1946). Masochism and paranoia. *Psychoanalytic Quarterly* 15:285–301.

Benjamin, J. (1965). Developmental biology and psychoanalysis. In *Psychoanalysis and Current Biological Thought*, eds. N. C. Greenfield and W. C. Lewis p. 57–80. Madison and Milwaukee: University of Wisconsin Press.

Bergman, P., and Escalona, S. K. (1949). Unusual sensitivities in very young children. *Psychoanalytic Study of the Child* 3/4:333–352.

Brody, S., and Axelrad, S. (1970). *Anxiety and Ego Formation in Infancy*. New York: International Universities Press.

Escalona, S. K. (1968). *The Roots of Individuality*. Chicago:Aldine.

Freud, A. (1966). *Normality and Pathology in Childhood. Writings of Anna Freud.* 6. New York: International Universities Press.

Freud, A., and Burlingham, D. (1944). *Infants without Families*. New York: International Universities Press.

Freud, S. (1905). Fragment of an analysis of a case of hysteria. *Standard Edition* 7:3–122.

———(1909a). Analysis of a phobia in a five-year-old boy. *Standard Edition* 10:3–149.

———(1909b) Notes upon a case of obsessional neurosis. *Standard Edition* 10:153–318.

———(1911). Psychoanalytic notes on the autobiographical account of a case of paranoia (dementia paranoides). *Standard Edition* 12:8–82.

———(1914a). From the history of an infantile neurosis. *Standard Edition* 17:3–122.

———(1914b). On narcissism. An introduction. *Standard Edition* 14:69–102.

———(1920). The psychogenesis of a case of female homosexuality. *Standard Edition* 18:147–172.

———(1922). Some neurotic mechanisms in jealousy, paranoia and homosexuality. *Standard Edition* 18:223–232.

———(1938). An outline of psychoanalysis. *Standard Edition* 23:141–207.

Galenson, E. and Roiphe, H. (1971). The impact of early sexual discovery of mood, defensive organization and symbolization. *Psychoanalytic Study of the Child* 26:195–216.

Glover, E. (1956). *On the Early Development of Mind*. New York: International Universities Press.

Hartmann, H., Loewenstein, R., and Kris, G. (1964). *Papers on Psychoanalytic Psychology.* Psychological Issues Monograph 14, Vol. IV., No. 2, ed. H. J. Schlesinger. New York: International Universities Press.

Hoffer, W. (1949). Mouth, hand and ego-integration. *Psychoanalytic Study of the Child* 3/4:49–56.

Jacobson, E. (1964). *The Self and the Object World*. New York: International Universities Press.

Kernberg, O. (1975). *Borderline Conditions and Pathological Narcissism*. New York: Jason Aronson.

Kohut, H. (1971). *The Analysis of the Self*. New York: International Universities Press.

Mahler, M.S. (1968). *On Human Symbiosis and the Vicissitudes of Individuation*. New York; International Universities Press.

Mahler, M. S. and La Perriere, K. (1965). Mother child interaction during separation-individuation *Psychoanalytic Quarterly* 34:483–498.

Niederland, W. G. (1974). *The Schreber Case. Psychoanalytic Profile of a Paranoid Personality*. New York: Quadrangle

Piaget, J. and Inhelder, B. (1969). *The Psychology of the Child*. New York: Basic Books.

Spitz, R. A. (1965). *The First Year of Life*. New York: International Universities Press.

White, R. B. (1961) The mother conflict in Schreber's psychosis. *International Journal of Psycho-Analysis* 42:55–73.

Chapter 5

A STRUCTURAL APPROACH TO PARANOIA
(JACOB A. ARLOW AND CHARLES BRENNER)
AN ABSTRACT

ABSTRACTED BY JULES GLENN, M.D.

In 1964 Jacob A. Arlow, long admired for his remarkably lucid instruction at the Downstate Psychoanalytic Institute, and Charles Brenner published *Psychoanalytic Concepts and the Structural Theory*. In that monograph they demonstrated that the rigorous application of insights derived from structural theory clarifies otherwise baffling clinical observations and contradictory theoretical constructs.

Because *Psychoanalytic Notes on an Autobiographical Account of a Case of Paranoia* contains Freud's (1911) major contributions to the understanding of psychoses, Arlow and Brenner review it extensively and critically in their final chapter, "The Psychopathology of the Psychosis." They also discuss Freud's later writings on the subject (1924a, 1924b, 1924c).

Applying the structural theory (Freud 1923, 1926), they confirm Freud's basic assumption that the psychic processes in neuroses and psychoses display a fundamental unity.

Arlow, J. A., and Brenner, C. (1964). *Psychoanalytic Concepts and the Structural Theory*. New York: International Universities Press. Chapter 10 (pp. 144-178) is entitled The Psychopathology of the Psychosis.

Freud emphasized the economic factor in explaining the withdrawal from the environment, which he considered an essential characteristic of psychosis. The patient withdraws libidinal cathexes from the mental representations of the objects in the world about him, and hence experiences them as unreal or destroyed. As the libido is withdrawn from object-representation, the ego, self or body organs are hypercathected, producing megalomania or hypochondriasis.

Freud stated that the shift of cathexis from object-representations to the self involved a regression to an early narcissistic stage through which infants normally pass. After an initial period of withdrawal, psychotics attempt to reestablish contact with the outer world by pathological means; their efforts at restitution produce delusions and halucinations as they recathect object-representations.

An important difference between neurotics and psychotics then is that whereas repression in the former bars wishes and fantasies from consciousness, in psychosis repression also deprives the object-representations of their cathexis.

Having outlined Freud's theory of psychosis, Arlow and Brenner challenge its assumptions and proceed to apply Freud's later concepts, particularly the structural theory, to create a basic reformulation.

Maintaining that there is a basic unity between the psychopathology of neuroses and psychoses, they nevertheless find certain distinguishing qualities. (1) Psychotic patients show greater evidence of regression to prephallic pregenital aims and are "more likely to show evidence of the persistence to an unusual degree of prephallic wishes and gratification throughout childhood and into adult life" (p. 155). Nevertheless they warn against underestimating the significance of phallic derivatives in psychosis. (2) Aggression and conflicts over aggression are more prominent in psychoses. (3) Ego and superego disturbances are more severe and more widespread in psychoses, as a result of regression or maldevelopment. In defending against anxiety psychotics rely on regressively altered ego and superego functions.

Arlow and Brenner state that a psychotic break with reality (which they maintain is not universal among these patients) results from severe disturbances of ego functions. This explanation, which is quite different from Freud's theory of decathexis, is based on Freud's later conceptualizations regarding psychic structure, the importance of aggression, the role of anxiety in psychic conflict and the defensive functions.

The authors present a clinical illustration of their thesis. A psychotic woman responded to conflict over angry sadistic impulses toward her husband by entering a stuporous state in which she remained immobile and silent and did not even think. This defensively motivated disruption of ego functions was much greater than would occur in a neurotic patient. Disruption of voluntary motility, external sensory perception and conscious thought resulted in severe withdrawal from external reality.

It should be noted that the extremely disruptive defensive maneuvers that psychotics mobilize can guard against conflicts over libidinal as well as aggressive drives.

The authors describe mildly psychotic patients, seen in office practice, in whom failure of integrative capacity causes disruption of relationship with the environment. Mental representation of external objects remain strongly cathected; fixations on original objects of childhood, on parents and siblings, remain quite intense during their entire lives. The disturbed ego functions serve defensive purposes. Disruption of continuity of mental life is intended to avoid severe anxiety or guilt.

Other patients defend themselves against dangerous wishes by becoming confused and disorganized in their ability to think and understand; disturbed object relations inevitably results.

The authors note that regressive ego disturbances serve instinctual and superego aims as well as defensive ones. They facilitate expression of rage, for instance, and provoke punishment at the hands of those they irritate.

Turning again to world destruction fantasies, which Freud explained as due to decathexis of object-representations, Arlow and Brenner propose that they are products of defense against intense aggression. Rather than acknowledge his own desire to destroy, which would arouse guilt and anxiety, the psychotic mobilizes defenses, as projection, and believes that God or natural forces, etc., have wrought havoc. The wish is perceived as real. When the defenses fail to achieve their purpose the delusional patient's anxiety appears, a fact that Freud's theory of decathexis does not explain.

In evaluating Freud's explanation of megalomania as a result of hypercathexis, the authors note that, contrary to what one would expect, many psychotic patients suffer from abnormally *low* self-esteem. It would appear that narcissistic libido has been depleted rather than increased.

Once again Arlow and Brenner find the defensive value of the delusion. The patient rejects the possibility that he is a helpless person who would perish without his parents. Instead he declares himself omnipotent. He combats anxiety about being weak, helpless or castrated by a wish-fulfilling fantasy of omnipotence and a regressive alteration of the ego function of reality testing.

Hypochondriacal symptoms in psychotic patients have a structure similar to neurotic hysterical conversion symptoms. They are "the expression in body language of a fantasy which is itself a compromise between an instinctual wish which has given rise to anxiety and conflict, and the defense against the wish" (p. 173). In both conditions reality testing may be seriously impaired. In the psychotic condition the degree of ego disturbance is considerably greater than in neurosis.

Similarly the delusions and hallucinations which Freud attributed to restitutive mechanisms are better explained as results of defenses against conflict over instinctual wishes and/or self-punitive needs. The failure of reality testing typical of these psychotic manifestations serves to avoid or minimize anixety. The patient regards the hallucinatory sensory experience and the delusions as actual events which justify instinctual expression.

In chapter 6 of their *Concept of Regression and the Structural Theory* Arlow and Brenner lay the groundwork for the discussion of regressive phenomena in psychosis. They define regression as "the re-emergence of modes of mental functioning which were characteristic of the psychic activity of the individual during earlier periods of life" (p. 71). They emphasize that the process, which is universal and generally temporary, is not a global one. Even in psychotic patients regressions are generally specific and discrete rather than total. This holds true for drive, ego and superego aspects, any one of which may be affected. All ego functions are not involved at once. Nor does the regressed schizophrenic *become* a small infant. As Arlow has stated (personal communication), one should not speak of regression to an earlier time, but of the reactivation of primitive mechanisms.

In summary then Arlow and Brenner confirm Freud's statement that neurotic and psychotic disturbances display a fundamental unity, but they reject his theory that decathexis of object-representations is the essential feature of psychosis. They apply knowledge of the structural theory and modern concepts of conflict, anxiety and defenses, which were developed after Freud's economic theory of psychosis, and derive a comprehensive understanding of these serious disturbances.

References

Freud, S. (1911). Psycho-analytic notes on an autobiographical account of a case of paranoia (dementia paranoides). *Standard Edition* 12:9–82.

———— (1923). The ego and the id. *Standard Edition* 19:12–66.

———— (1924a). Neurosis and psychosis. *Standard Edition* 19:149–153.

———— (1924b). The loss of reality in neurosis and psychosis. *Standard Edition* 19:183–187.

———— (1924c). A short account of psychoanalysis. *Standard Edition* 19:191–209.

———— (1926). Inhibitions, symptoms and anxiety. *Standard Edition* 20:87–172.

Chapter 6

INTEGRATIVE SUMMARY

JULES GLENN, M.D. and MARK KANZER, M.D.

The Schreber case provides rich but limited material not ordinarily available to the analytic institute classroom. As Freud noted, flagrantly psychotic persons like Schreber are ill suited for the rigors of psychoanalytic treatment. Freud had tried to treat a number of schizophrenics (or paraphrenics, as he called them) at the insistence of hopeful parents, but he remained pessimistic about the therapeutic possibilities. At the time that Freud was writing about Schreber, Jung was bemoaning the suicide of one of his schizophrenic analytic patients, but hoped that he would be able to analyze the fantasies of future psychotic analysands with more precision and thus cure them (see McGuire 1974). Today we recognize that successful therapy requires modifications so great the the treatment, although based on psychoanalytic knowledge, is not psychoanalysis per se.

Schreber's memoirs provided Freud with extraordinarily clear descriptions of the patient's thinking processes and fantasies such as few students or analysts have available. Unfortunately censors deleted the sections about his family and childhood. However, William G. Niederland's research has been invaluable in providing material that enabled him to elaborate on and correct aspects of Freud's theory.

Niederland (personal communication) has said that, examining the Schreber case, "the students gradually see and learn not only more and more about young Schreber's life and early upbringing; they also note how analytic research and acquisition of knowledge proceed, step by step, piece by piece—as it is indeed the fact with every clinical analysis, i.e., with the patient on the couch.''

We have selected three of the many excellent articles which comprise Niederland's careful research into the childhood determinants of Schreber's illness (see also Niederland 1974). Freud relied on Schreber's written Memoirs (see Macalpine and Hunter 1955) for his data, whereas Niederland studied Schreber's father's numerous writings and other biographical material as well, thus uncovering many kernels of truth around which specific symptoms were organized.

Glenn and Rubins (chapter 4) outline Freud's summary of Schreber's disturbance and the dynamics he discovered. Freud demonstrated the special processes of thought related to Schreber's homosexuality that permeated his psychosis. Schreber imagined that his body was deteriorating and that he was turning into a woman as part of God's scheme to create a new race of men. His intense libidinal attachment to God manifested itself through the action of mysterious rays and eventually in ecstatic feelings. To defend himself against the intensified homosexuality he developed delusions of persecution, delusions of grandiosity and delusions of world destruction. Freud brilliantly showed the role of reversal and projection in the appearance of persecutory ideas. He also revealed the importance of defensive withdrawal of cathexis from the representations of the external world in the production of world destruction fantasies.

Niederland's research uncovered the general milieu and the specific events in Schreber's childhood that led to his symptomatology. If Freud had these data available he choose a ''policy of restraint'' and deliberately excluded these facts from his study, thus protecting members of Schreber's family from embarrassment and pain.

Niederland reports in ''Schreber; Father and Son'' (chapter 1) that Schreber senior was a physician, lecturer, writer and educator, a proseletizer who advocated childrearing procedures that became highly regarded. He applied these strict and inflexible methods to his children including the author of the *Memoirs*. Niederland noted that the elder Schreber's sadistically tinged attempts to subjugate his children led to the patient's feminine attitude toward his father which Freud had reconstructed. In his psychotic state Schreber imagined being transformed into a woman as means of uniting with a deified father. Niederland reports many similarities between father and son, results of the patient's introjection of and identification with his ambivalently loved father. For instance, both became ill in their early fifties of sickness involving real or imagined pathology of the head. Schreber's relapses occurred in November, the month of his father's death. Father's writings were prompted by a missionary zeal to develop a stronger race of men through the child rearing procedures and exercises he advocated; the son stated that his own book would spread truth and further knowledge for the good of mankind. Indeed according to his beliefs, his psychosis served to produce an improved race.

The bizarre ideas of the son's delusional system appear to be derived from the introjected paternal image. Many of the father's characteristics and procedures appeared as archaic, elaborate, psychotic derivatives. The father's apparatuses for maintaining perfect posture appeared in delusional form as divine miracles of "being tied to earth," "being tied to celestial bodies" or "fastened to rays." The "chest compressing miracle" derives from an apparatus which actually pressed on the child's chest.

Further, Schreber's father suggested that the child be taught to turn at "the end of every day its mind to God. . . in order to mirror its inner self in the pure rays of God, the loving and universal father." Here we find not only the rays which were included in the son's delusional system, but the suggested identification of rays, God and father.

In "Further Data and Memorabilia" (chapter 3) Niederland provides additional evidence that in Schreber's attempts at restitution of his destroyed world he called on memories from childhood "to regain the lost objects and to reestablish his unresolved infantile ties with them." This sound concept of restitution differs from Freud's at the time he wrote about Schreber. Freud wrote: "It was incorrect to say that the perception which was suppressed internally is projected outwards; the truth is rather. . . that what was abolished internally returns from without" (1911, p. 71). Later however Freud stated that there is a kernel of truth in delusions, that something the child saw or heard reappears. Indeed, as Niederland demonstrates, images from his father's books appear in the son's adult delusions.

Niederland introduces another very important contribution when he contends that not only was Schreber attempting union with his father and brother; he also attempted to unite with his lost mother. The peculiarly constituted God of Schreber contained derivatives of father, brother and mother. There is evidence that father and mother worked closely together.

Returning to questions about the events that precipitated Schreber's illnesses, Niederland suggests that when he ran against Bismark's party for a seat in the Reichstag and lost, he regressed to the oedipal period with its intensified castration fears. The fact that when Schreber was five his family had had difficulties with government officials facilitated that regression. In additon, Niederland adds, Schreber identified with his brother, who, commited suicide after being nominated for office.

We may note that Niederland demonstrates the prominent use of primitive mechanisms like introjection, adds proof of Schreber's attempts at union with his mother, notes the depression that characterized his early symptomatology and documents the effects of early overstimulation. Niederland emphasizes the oedipal and implies that the Oedipus complex was distorted by preoedipal influences.

In "The 'Miracled Up' World of Schreber's Childhood" (chapter 2) Niederland reconstructs many of the patient's very early experiences and offers us many illustrations of the influence Schreber's father's behavior had on his son's delusions. Schreber senior had advocated cold ablutions from the age of three months in order to toughen the child. This led to Schreber junior's delusion that heat and cold were being directed against him, but, because he was used to these stimuli, he could tolerate their noxious influence. Schreber's father also recommended training the child in the art of "renouncing" during the first year of life. This was to be accomplished by such acts as refusing the child food while his nurse ate with the child on her lap. The elder Schreber was proud of his children's complete submission by one and a half years of age! As Niederland emphasizes, by the time the boy entered his third or fourth year he had undergone a notable degree of traumatization which must have impaired his ego development. Indeed, Niederland states that Schreber's father dominated the family and usurped his wife's role to the extent that he could be called a "symbiotic father" whose sadistic and seductive qualities appeared in the bizarre God of Schreber's delusions. In addition Schreber's father sought to suppress masturbation and advocated the use of enemas. The family mixed with deformed patients of the orthopedist father. Castration was in the air in many forms.

As there is little information about Schreber's mother, it was difficult for Niederland, who adhered to known facts in his theory building, to demonstrate her role in the psychosis. Nevertheless he attempted to ferret out of Schreber's delusion that his family belonged to the highest aristocracy of Heaven and bore the title of "Margraves of Tuscany and Tasmania," elements of Schreber's unresolved relationship with his mother. He concludes that the Margraves represented rebellious sons who, in alliance with a mother surrogate, overthrew the father; that Tuscany was the scene of the father's defeat; and that Tasmania was the place of punishment for the oedipal crime.

Thus, although Niederland recognizes Schreber's regression from the positive to the negative Oedipus complex, he emphasizes oedipal rather than pre-oedipal conflicts.

Glenn and Rubins describe how they taught the Schreber case to first year analytic students. The concepts that emerge are relatively simple, suited to an elementary course. Nevertheless, in addition to revealing pedagogical methods, their article fills in some of the conceptual gaps in the studies of Freud and Niederland. They present speculations regarding Schreber's preoedipal relationships with his mother as well as his father. They point to Freud's incorrect conceptualization of early narcissism. Freud felt that paranoid patients regress to a state of narcissism in which they love persons similar to themselves, i.e., to a homosexual period. Today we know that in the earliest stages of life, the mother is the infant's pre-object and then his object. It is to an autistic and or symbiotic stage that the schizophrenic regresses. In Glenn and Rubins' teachings certain facts that Niederland has presented acquire somewhat different significance. The repeated early overstimulation emerges as preoedipal traumata which burst through the stimulus barrier to produce a fragile ego, this in accordance with the studies of Bergman and Escalona (1949). Glenn and Rubins also suggest that Schreber senior's interference with the mother's empathic care for her children resulted in miscuing as well as deficient satisfaction. The Schreber family can be classified as a "skewed family" (Lidz 1973). (Kohut [1971] makes a similar point about the Schrebers.) In this configuration one parent is extremely egocentric and fosters a strange and unreal family atmosphere, "forcing the children to fit into it and even accept distorted perceptions of events" (p.33), while the other parent tolerates the bizarre child rearing practices of the first. (Usually, according to Lidz, the mother is the strange parent, but in the Schreber family the father acquired that role.) The class's assumption that Schreber's illness had a biological base contradicts neither Freud's nor Niederland's developmental approach.

Although it is beyond the scope of this book to fully explore the complexities of psychotic disturbances, we can elaborate on some salient psychoanalytic concepts which Glenn and Rubins consider in their chapter.

Arlow and Brenner (1964) reevaluate the Schreber case in *Psychoanalytic Concepts and the Structural Theory*. They point out that Freud, studying Schreber when the libido theory dominated psychoanalytic thinking, emphasized economic aspects. The decathexis of objects and increased libidinal cathexis of the self accounted for delusions of world destruction, megalomania, hypochondriasis and other psychotic symtpoms. They also note Freud's statements (1) that the shift of cathexis from objects to self involved a regression from a normal libidinal postion to the stage of narcissism and (2) that restitutive mechanisms, i.e., recathexis of object-representations, play an important role in the formation of delusions and hallucinations. Throughout their discussion they correct Freud's terminology and differentiate object from object-representation and self from self-representation.

Arlow and Brenner emphasize the deficiencies of Freud's early theory and, applying the structural point of view, demonstrate that many of the manifestations of psychosis result from defenses against libidinal and aggressive drives and the anxiety engendered by them. (In 1911 Freud had not yet postulated an aggressive drive that was not merely a manifestation of libido.) Hence they interpret a particular patient's stupor as a defense against fear of rage toward her husband, not as a simple consequence of object decathexis. The revelation in analysis of the frightening wishes can, they assert, afford therapeutic relief.

Their thesis is compelling and need not exclude the economic aspects of regression. Certainly defensive regression can result in the reorganization of the psychic economy as primitive pre-object representations grow in importance. As a patient regresses to early narcissistic states, self-and object-representations may become confused; symbiotic and even autistic phenomena (Mahler 1968, 1975) may prevail. Aspects of the early stages have been described by different analysts, creating a more or less coherent picture of infancy.

Spitz (1965) for instance drew attention to the child's beginning differentiation of the I from the non-I as the baby's first social smile appears. He and Benjamin (1965) discovered an initial high threshold to external stimuli followed by a period of greater sensitivity to stimuli. Although in general Freud's concept of *narcissism* has been confirmed, some corrections are needed. Even the small infant pays attention to (cathects) the outer world to a degree. With time external cathexis increases as pre-objects and then objects are more clearly perceived. An analyst may surmise what an infant's feeling of fusion is like when he hears an adult patient describe the Isakower phenomenon (Isakower 1938), a regression to such an early state. We regret that we can but hint at the rich observations and constructions of infant development described by A. Freud (1965), Mahler (1968, 1975), Spitz (1965), Benjamin (1965), Piaget and Inhelder (1969), Hartmann (1964) and of course Freud.

Although Arlow and Brenner observe that psychotic people undergo ego regressions and assert that their libidinal impulses may be primitive, they do not emphasize developmental arrest or fixation sufficiently. They are correct in their insistence that defenses play a central role in pathogenesis, but, while emphasizing defenses and the "reactivation of primitive mechanisms," they pay insufficient attention to certain *experiences* of the regressed patient. They discount the importance of temporal regression. They correctly state that in megalomania denial can ward off fears of weakness and helplessness, but this does not preclude concomitant regression to an early narcissistic state. The drives defended against and expressed in psychosis, the defenses resorted to and the adaptive mechanisms that emerge are primitive indeed. Oedipal configurations are distorted by powerful preoedipal influences. Defusion and deneutralization release aggressive forces more potent and less controllable than in neuroses. Longstanding ego distortions due to biological disturbances, family influences or both make it difficult for these patients to prevent intense conflict. When such conflict appears primitive defenses attempt to contain it with pathological consequences. (It should be noted that the ego distortions per se give the patient's personality a pathological ring.)

The superego too can be primitive and severe, like some superego precursors. Delusions of persecution appear to be based in part on regression to a time when prohibitions and punishments were external. Superego factors also contribute to the masochistic basis for persecutory delusions which Bak (1946), elaborating on a suggestion of Freud's (1917), has so clearly described.

Glenn and Rubins follow Arlow and Brenner's emphasis on the importance of defenses and the significance of aggression in Schreber's pathology. They too suggest the delusions of world destruction reveal intense hostility. They note that Freud, even before the emergence of the structural theory, described such defenses as repression, projection, displacement, regression and reversal to explain Schreber's delusions.

Discussing the precipitating events that led to Schreber's illnesses, they point to his fear of success which, implicitly, has a superego component. But guilt over surpassing the oedipal father, documented by Niederland, is but one factor, according to them. Psychotics' fear of loss of the preoedipal mother further intensifies anxiety and produces hatred and regression to stages of fantasied union with mother.

There is a wide range of pathology which encompasses the most seriously ill primitive schizophrenics, ambulatory psychotics who suffer from disabling delusions but remain out of hospitals, borderline states and neurotic disturbances. Analysts rarely see patients whose developmental arrest is so all pervasive that they have never achieved a degree of oedipal involvement. Schreber regressed from an oedipal level (undoubtedly quite distorted and strewn with primitive wishes and fantasies) to a preoedipal libidinal organization with the further appearance of primitive ego and superego manifestations. Analysts often see borderline patients in whom regression and developmental arrest, although marked, are less severe, and more mature aspects of the personality are retained.

The question arises as to whether the psychopathology of schizophrenia involves a "psychological deficiency state" or whether the types of conflicts and defenses we see in neuroses account for psychotic disorders (London 1973a, 1973b, Arlow and Brenner 1964). We contend that the existence of deficiency in the schizophrenic does not preclude the presence of inner conflict. A biological deficiency can make the schizophrenic patient especially vulnerable to psychic conflict and can facilitate the use to a pernicious extent of primitive defenses—regression, projection, and denial. Biological disturbance in conjunction with environmental stress (or extreme external stress alone) can lead to developmental arrests or fixations, can interfere with the stability of secondary process thinking, self- and object-representations, and neutralization of drive energies (Hartmann 1964). We can direct therapeutic efforts to amelioration of physiological pathology as well as to building psychic structure (through fostering identifications for instance), resolving psychic conflict and supporting adaptive defenses.

We cannot possibly review the many recent contributions to the borderline condition (Blum 1972, Dickes 1974, Frosch 1964, 1970, Kernberg 1975, Kohut 1971, for instance). The many stimulating theoretical and clinical concepts that appeared in the Schreber case study and in later papers by Freud produced a profusion of research that has furthered our knowledge. The concept of narcissism, originally described in *Leonardo Da Vinci and a Memory from his Childhood* (1910) and extended in the Schreber work in "On Narcissism" (1914), and in other papers, has been continuously refined and fruitfully applied.

Let us return to the question of the suitability of "Psycho-analytic Notes on an Autobiographical Account of a Case of Paranoia" as a vehicle for teaching analytic students.

On the one hand, Freud's analysis contains brilliant observations on Schreber's memoirs. It provides students with data not ordinarily available in the institute classroom. The painstaking research of Niederland supplies supplementary information that enables one to confirm and correct Freud's commentary. The student can appreciate scientific theory building in operation: with added data, explanations often have to be altered. The healthy critical attitude that emerges may strengthen the student's desire for research and for improved formulations while retaining that which is sound. He will incorporate Freud's scientific open-mindedness and his desire for repeated reevaluations, thus promoting creative thinking. And reading and discussing Freud's brilliant insights which bring order to Schreber's confused ideation is an enriching experience.

On the other hand the degree to which Freud's observations and concepts have to be supplemented may be excessive. Today we know that preoepidal ego, aggressive and libidinal factors play a major role in schizophrenia, paranoid ideation and homosexuality. The significance of the early mother-child relationship may be paramount. Because Freud failed to emphasize these sufficiently the instructor and students must provide clinical and research data to demonstrate present knowledge. Would it not be wiser for a teacher of a course in psychoses to present clinical descriptions on which up to date formulation can be made from the start? Having material from patients whom the doctor had actually seen (in contrast to Schreber whom Freud never interviewed) will, in addition, diminish the need to speculate and discourage conjecture that, without great caution, a class may actually stimulate. *Non liquet.*

References

Arlow, J.A., and Brenner, C. (1964). *Psychoanalytic Concepts and the Structural Theory.* New York: International Universities Press.

Bak, R. (1946). Masochism and paranoia. *Psychoanalytic Quarterly* 15:285–301.

Benjamin, J. (1965). Developmental biology and psychoanalysis. In *Psychoanalysis and Current Biological Thought,* eds. N.C. Greenfield and W.C. Lewis. Madison and Milwaukee: University of Wisconsin Press.

Bergman, P. and Escalona, S.K. (1949). Unusual sensitivities in very young children. *Psychoanalytic Study of the Child* 3/4: 333–352.

Blum, H.P. (1972). Psychoanalytic understanding and psychotherapy of borderline regression. *International Journal of Psychoanalytic Psychotherapy.* 1:46–59.

Dickes, R. (1974). The concepts of borderline states: an alternative proposal. *International Journal of Psychoanalytic Psychotherapy* 3:1–27.

Freud, A. (1965). *Normality and Pathology in Childhood.* New York: International Universities Press.

Freud, S. (1910). Leonardo da Vinci and a memory of his childhod. *Standard Edition* 11:63–137.

———(1911). Psycho-analytic notes on an autobiographical account of a case of paranoia (dementia paranoides). *Standard Edition* 12:9–82.

———(1914). On narcissism: an introduction. *Standard Edtion* 14:73–102.

———(1917). "A child is being beaten." *Standard Edition* 17:179–204.

Frosch, J. (1964). The psychotic character: clinical psychiatric considerations. *Psychiatric Quarterly* 38:91–96.

———(1970). Psychoanalytic considerations of the psychotic character. *Journal of the American Psychoanalytic Association* 18:24–50.

Hartmann, H. (1964). *Essays on Ego Psychology.* New York: International Universities Press.

Isakower, O. (1938). A contribution to the psychopathology of phenomena associated with falling asleep. *International Journal of Psycho-Analysis.* 19:331–345.

Kernberg, O. (1975). *Borderline Conditions and Pathological Narcissism.* New York: Jason Aronson.

Kohut, H. (1971). *The Analysis of the Self.* New York: International Universities Press.

Lidz, T. (1973). *The Origin and Treatment of Schizophrenic Disorders.* New York: Basic Books.

London, N.J. (1973a). An essay on psychoanalytic theory: two theories of schizophrenia, part I: review and critical assessment of the development of the two theories. *International Journal of Psycho-Analysis* 54:169–178.

————(1973b). An essay on psychoanalytic theory: two theories of schizo-phrenia, part II: discussion and restatement of the specific theory of schizo-phrenia. *International Journal of Psycho-Analysis* 54:179–193.

Macalpine, I., and Hunter, R.A., trans. and eds. (1955). *Memoirs of My Nervous Illness* by D.P. Schreber. London: Dawson.

Mahler, M.S. and Furer, M. (1968). *On Human Symbiosis and the Vicissitudes of Individuation: Infantile Psychosis*. New York: International Universities Press.

Mahler, M.S., Pine, F., and Bergman, A. (1975). *The Psychological Birth of the Human Infant*. New York: Basic Books.

McGuier, W., ed. (1974). *The Freud/Jung Letters*. Princeton: Princeton University Press.

Niederland, W. G. (1974). *The Schreber Case*. New York: Quadrangle.

Piaget, J., and Inhelder, B. (1969). *The Psychology of the Child*. New York: Basic Books.

Spitz, R.A. (1965). *The First Year of Life*. New York: International Universities Press.

PART VI

THE WOLF MAN

1. THE BORDERLINE CHILDHOOD

OF THE WOLF MAN

HAROLD P. BLUM, M.D.

Freud's Wolf Man remains a favorite teaching case, and it is certainly the most detailed, documented, and exciting of his case histories. The analysis, lasting more than four years—1910 to 1914—was a long, detailed, in-depth study for that early period, when very short analyses were customary. The case history is an extraordinary clinical document, recording original discoveries and the solution of complicated enigmas of symptom and character, personality developement, and regression. The many layers of meaning are presented vividly and with great clarity and cohesion. The rich data and pioneering formulations have fostered new insights and the appreciation of new problems.

Never again was Freud to provide clinical material of such sweep and depth. He referred to the case in numerous other publications—in one of his last papers, "Analysis Terminable and Interminable" (1937), he critically commented on the Wolf Man's therapeutic result and the need for further periods of treatment. The case touches on a host of questions regarding psychoanalytic theory and technique (the termination of treatment, the limits of analyzability, the importance of the primal scene, the fundamental significance of the infantile neurosis for later adult disturbance, etc.). It is also a fascinating study of Freud at work with a most challenging patient, a patient from a different social, cultural, and language milieu. It was a transcultural analysis with universal relevance.

One has the impression in reading the Wolf Man that the analysis was more enriching for Freud than it was for his famous patient, a reflection of Freud's scientific and literary genius, and possibly also an indication that the analysis was primarily elucidated and organized in the mind of the analyst.

The voluminous data relevant to the Wolf Man span a period of more than sixty years, providing the lengthiest longitudinal case study opportunity in psychoanalysis. The case history is complemented and extended by the subsequent analytic report of Ruth Mack Brunswick (1928), the observations of the patient by other analysts, Muriel Gardiner's (1971) long-term follow-ups, and the patient's own comments and recollections.

The case of the Wolf Man has always been approached with diffidence, perhaps because of our reverence for Freud, and certainly because the patient was alive and bore a special status—a ward of psychoanalysis with a unique analytic identity.

When I was a candidate, the case was taught with almost unquestioned acceptance of Freud's formulations and adherence to his established early views (1914) and those of Brunswick (1928). Neither Freud's nor Brunswick's study has ever been up-dated in terms of structural theory and ego psychology, despite the vast growth in psychoanalytic knowledge since this case history was published.

The Wolf Man was not analytically observed or treated during his childhood. Freud derived knowledge of his infantile neurosis from the patient's analysis as an adult. Indeed, he did not, unfortunately, present his patient's adult neurosis, so that we are missing this important set of primary data. The analytic method, of course, was different in those days and this influenced the data obtained. Freud noted that the patient was far from an ideal case and was cautious ''. . . of the distortion and refurbishing to which a person's own past is subjected when it is looked back upon from a later period'' (1918, p. 9). The Wolf Man, at the age of eighty-three, wrote the recollections of his childhood at the urging of Dr. Gardiner. He had previously avoided writing about his adolescence and childhood, despite having written other autobiographical commentary.

With the advantages of hindsight, follow-up, and the perspective of more than half a century of analytic development, the Wold Man's personality disorder merits further inquiry. Re-examination of the data suggests new connections and hypotheses. There is, of course, also a danger in overexploiting a classic case history. Referring to the classic cases of Freud, Anna Freud reminds us that ''. . . the very familiarity which analysts began to feel with these patients allows the temptation to deal with them in their imagination as if they were their own patients, to wish to know everything about them, to test the interpretations given, to probe beyond the conclusions drawn, or wherever possible to reconstitute

once more the original data from which the author's abstractions had been made"
(Gardiner 1971). Even though the Wolf Man has been able to cooperate and to
provide additional reminiscences and commentary, there are still dangers of
speculation about him that must be acknowledged. Freud called his paper "From
the History of an Infantile Neurosis," and the infantile disturbance is of special
significance. The concepts of infantile neurosis and developmental disturbance
were to undergo further differentiation, and exert a compelling influence on later
analytic theory.

In this presentation I shall review the Wolf Man's infantile illness and some
of its determinants and consequences and will assume the reader's familiarity
with the Freud and Brunswick clinical reports. I shall attempt to demonstrate
that the Wolf Man's childhood disturbance was a severe borderline disturbance
which provided the foundation for a borderline adolescence and for what I regard
as his adult borderline personality. "From the History of an Infantile Neurosis"
may be viewed as the history of a borderline childhood with episodes of infantile
psychosis. Indeed, the case might be described as, "From the History of an
Infantile Psychosis." The psychotic states of adult life were regressive revivals
of the infantile psychosis (Frosch 1967). The paranoia was not recapitulated in
the original analytic transference to Freud, but was a post-termination regressive
decompensation primarily triggered by Freud's illness (and perhaps the illness
and infertility of the Wolf Man's wife). The "transference psychosis" did not
appear in the regressive analytic situation, but after termination. The borderline
case is often unable to terminate and may require continuing periods of therapeutic support to maintain ego integration.

I am using the word borderline to describe a condition close to psychosis,
with severe ego impairments but without the irreversible disorganization and
structural fragmentation of psychosis (Kernberg, 1967). The borderline case,
such as the Wolf Man, may have a tendency to severe regression with psychotic
episodes. The borderline case cannot easily be distinguished from mild psychosis
with functional recovery and reintegration. Frosch (1967) considered the Wolf
Man a probably psychotic character, a designation very close to borderline
psychosis.

In 1937, Freud expressed reservations about the outcome of his analysis and
noted further illness of a paranoid character. In his initial interview with Freud,
the Wolf Man had offered to defecate on his head and participate in rectal
intercourse (Jones 1955). Freud mentioned his previous diagnosis (by Kraeplin
and others) as "manic-depressive insantiy." In the analytic situation, Freud
(1918) describes him as, ". . . for a long time unassailably entrenched behind
an attitude of obliging apathy" (p. 11). Freud observed the patient's inveterate
narcissism and his intense and constant ambivalence. "The contrast between the

patient's agreeable and affable personality, his acute intelligence and his nice-mindedness on the one hand, and his completely unbridled instinctual life on the other, necessitated an excessively long process of preparatory education, and this made a general perspective more difficult" (p. 104). Severe characterological disturbance was observed: "no position of the libido which had once been established was ever completely replaced by a later one. It was rather left in existence side by side with all the others, and this allowed him to maintain an incessant vacillation which proved to be incompatible with the acquisition of a stable character" (p. 27). Serious sado-masochistic trends were observed in his identification with the suffering Christ, in his torture and beating fantasies, and his depressive and masochistic self-reproach. Freud (1919) referred to the Wolf Man in his classic paper "A Child Is Being Beaten." With prophetic insight he observed: "People who harbour phantasies of this kind develop a special sensitiveness and irritability towards anyone whom they can include in the class of fathers. They are easily offended by a person of this kind, and in that way (to their own sorrow and cost) bring about the realization of the imagined situation of being beaten by their father. I should not be surprised if it were one day possible to prove that the same phantasy is the basis of the delusional litigiousness of paranoia" (p. 195). The paranoid states that subsequently erupted occasionally, the hypochondriasis and life-long depressions, the tendency to act out his fantasies, the lack of ego synthesis and cohesive personality organization, recurrent crises requiring supportive intervention—all point toward a borderline personality. This would be consistent with the preanalytic picture of the totally crippled adult patient, unable even to dress himself, with his later dependence upon continued therapeutic contact and upon the psychoanalytic movement. (There was a possible transformation of his identity into the Wolf Man of psychoanalysis.) On the other hand, he has had sufficient personality resources to benefit from the psychoanalytic and psychotherapeutic help and to demonstrate a functional adaptation far beyond the invalidism that might have left him confined to a mental hospital.

The borderline syndrome or personality had not been conceptualized at the time of the Wolf Man's analysis, nor was there child analysis or detailed observational studies of borderline and psychotic children. The study of the infantile neurosis and childhood disturbance in the Wolf Man case, in fact, did much to stimulate the development of systematic child analytic investigation. Freud elucidated the Wolf Man's childhood problems as the background of the subsequent adult disturbance, and reconstructed the primal scene as an underlying traumatic experience with important developmental consequences.

The Wold Man presented a broad spectrum of disturbances throughout his childhood and adolescence. The many symptoms and dysfunction in early childhood would be analogous to a later pan-neurosis. There was an infantile anorexia of unknown dimensions and duration. After age three-and-a-half, his personality underwent a transformation, and he became irritable and violent. This sharp transformation occurred after his nurse's castrating reproach for masturbating and his attempt to suppress masturbation. But it is significant that it developed during separation from his parents (Gardiner 1971, pp. 5, 170). Freud noted the anal-sadistic regression and cruelty that followed the suppression of masturbation, but had not then formulated his theory of ego regression or alteration. The child took offense on every possible occasion, raging and screaming like a savage or lunatic (p. 15). He could not be consoled, was suspicious and distrustful. At his fourth birthday on Christmas, he had his famous anxiety dream of white wolves sitting quite still in a tree outside his window. He awoke in terror lest they eat him. Freud connected this nightmare at age four and the subsequent wolf phobia with his witnessing the primal scene two and a half years earlier and with his repudiated feminine wishes. Prior to the dream, his sister had teased and frightened him by showing him pictures of an upright wolf with claw extended.

He tormented insects and people, had fantasies of being beaten on the penis, and enjoyed beating horses. Yet, if a horse was beaten, he began to scream. At four and a half his wolf phobia was replaced by obsessional symptoms involving intractable praying and ritualistic signs of the cross, kissing of holy pictures, and preoccupation with anal blasphemies. He developed respiratory rituals of inhalation and exhalation, associated with making the sign of the cross. Torturing others and self-tormented, he was fearful of injury and death.

He was both aggressor and victim and constantly feared attack, as he had in his nightmare. He was terrified of the primal scene as an exciting beating and castration and, I believe, as a mutually destructive devouring. He defended against his cruelty and sadism with obsessive piety and masochism. The obsessional symptomatology continued until about age ten, waning during the period of his German tutor. Under the tutor's influence, he gave up his obsessional piety and the last obsession with heaps of dung. The tutor also discouraged him from his cruelties to animals and his continued practice of cutting up caterpillars. The panic, torture, temper, and screaming reactions with uncontrolled, protracted rages are suggestive of a borderline child with the *anlage* of ego deviation (A. Weil 1953). He resembled the atypical child, described by Geleerd (1958), who easily withdraws into fantasy, is prone to severe tantrums and expectations of attack, and who needs the presence of the love object to hold on to reality.

The Wolf Man's later nightmarish anxiety may be related to the earlier tantrums. Geleerd (1958) described the panic underlying the flooding rages in borderline children. This is traumatic anxiety with ego helplessness. Omnipotent control is sought as salvation from the utter defenselessness of the ego. The screaming is a cry for help and an expression of helplessness.

The borderline or psychotic child may manifest disturbance and dysfunction in a number of areas, rather than the typical symptoms of adult psychosis. The hyperirritability and excitation is a consequence of not only masturbatory excitement, but a general lack of ego modulation of impulses and affects. The borderline has been overstimulated and traumatized, or has a constitutional defect in binding or synthesis which invites traumatization (Weil 1953, Bender 1968).

Freud related the Wolf Man's fear of being eaten to his fear of and unconscious wish for homosexual gratification from his father. I believe his phobia and overwhelming anxiety can now be related to his conflicts over symbiotic fusion and his regressive tendency to global identifications, which involve merger with the object. This is evident in his nightmare state's extending into everyday life, his attacks of visual hallucinosis, and his withdrawal into a veiled state of narcissistic retreat. The impairment of the separation-individuation process is related to the fear of being devoured and overwhelmed by the object. There appears to have been a persistent fixation to the oral triad of devouring, being eaten, and fused sleep (Mahler 1971, Lewin 1950).

Freud (1918) regarded the aftermath of the patient's condition as a defect following on an obsessional neurosis. It is now known that childhood obsessional neurosis often represents severe personality disorder and that many obsessive children become psychotic as adults (A. Freud 1965, p. 152).

Because the Wolf Man's childhood was characterized by a persistent, constricting, and very severe obsessional neurosis, one wonders if the popular pseudonym for the case in terms of the transient wolf-phobia is at all appropriate. The title "Wolf Man" is overdramatic and misleading in its clinical implications.

I would suggest that in addition to the symptoms and inhibitions, the defect Freud mentioned may be regarded as an ego defect. This patient displayed narcissistic vulnerability and detachment, disturbed object relations and impulse control, apathy and affective impoverishment, and a tendency to severe regressive response. The neurotic and obsessive overlay to the severe personality disturbance did not prevent a rapid recrudescence of symptoms by the time of puberty at age thirteen. It is questionable whether there was ever a period when he was totally asymptomatic. After the obsessions subsided, at about age ten there were depressions, with peaks at five o'clock in the afternoon. At thirteen he developed a nasal catarrh and acne. Pubertal acne and blushing were exceedingly painful to this hypersensitive patient. He was also very concerned with his nasal discharge—a forerunner of the later concerns with gonorrheal discharge, and then again with his nose, during the paranoid episode and treatment by Ruth Mack Brunswick. Wealthy, privileged, and sensitive, he had always been teased at school. Troubled by acne and blushing, and obsessed with his nose and skin, he stayed away from school. He became more and more seclusive in adolescence and preoccupied with the care of his body and clothes (Brunswick 1928, p. 287).

There is no question that his pubertal crisis and the childhood period before his nightmare both involved a struggle against masturbation and the dread of castration. However, the severe phallic conflicts both defended against his preoedipal problems and contributed to the failure of more adequate oedipal and adolescent solutions. In turn, the presumed underlying disturbance of separation-individuation interfered with healthy adolescent development—he was a solitary, depressed, and distrustful adolescent. His panic about his nose at thirteen reappeared with delusional intensity at age thirty-seven. He then looked slovenly and harassed, according to Brunswick, "as if the devil were at his heels as he rushed from one shop window to another to inspect his nose" (1926, p. 290), constantly studying his face and nose in mirrors (p. 302). The gonorrhea revived his fear of phallic damage, earlier displaced upward to fears concerning nasal damage and abnormal nasal discharge. His genital infection and discharge reinforced his hypochondriasis and fantasies of castration. Freud's case begins with a breakdown of the patient following the attack of gonorrhea at age eighteen.

A psychoanalytic developmental framework was only in its early stages of evolution during Freud's lifetime. An overview of the Wolf Man's earlier childhood and adolescence demonstrates developmental disruption. Between three and four, following what normally should have been the consolidation of object constancy, he was agitated, beset by beating fantasies, was cruel, distrustful, screaming, and raging. His nightmare and phobic anxiety of wolves at age four became a generalized apprehension, extending from wolf pictures to people, with fears of being stared at and teased. This resulted in screaming when feeling stared at, as he had awakened screaming from his nightmare—an *anlage* of later ideas of reference and derivative, also, of the primal scene. The succeeding obsessional neurosis, at approximately ages five to ten, was associated with continued overt sado-masochism and depressions. Depression and hypochondriasis continued into adolescence, with distrust and seclusion. The (preadult) narcissistic disorder and impairment of object and reality relationships are consistent with the borderline syndrome.

Preoedipal influences have molded the oedipal conflicts of the borderline personality. The picture is often confused because of the coexistence of various developmental phases and the fluctuation between symbiotic strivings and more advanced ego interests and achievements. The borderline syndrome may include deviant, regressive, and mature personality traits (Ekstein and Wallerstein 1954).

Separation-individuation has progressed, but is incomplete or deviant (Frijling-Schreuder 1969). Regressive defense carries the danger of personality disruption, and the untamed omnipotence and aggression threaten the survival of object relationships (Blum 1972).

The Wolf Man's borderline childhood was the foundation for his vulnerability to uncontrolled regression. His disturbance underwent various changes, but essentially it persisted, with periods of remission and exacerbation, into the patient's adult life. Not every childhood ego disturbance eventuates in a borderline adult personality; the outcome depends on further developmental vicissitudes. A borderline adult personality such as the Wolf Man, however, emerges from a borderline childhood and adolescence. His adolescence did not consolidate a more cohesive personality organization with ego growth, but culminated in severe regression and withdrawal.

The primal scene and castration anxiety are major threads running throughout the patient's disturbance, his symptoms, and his character disorder. Freud, in addition, presented numerous contributing factors (A. Freud 1971). These included anorexia and fears of being devoured, anal-urethral fixations, experiences of seduction and early castration threats, fears giving way to guilt—which transforms sadism into masochism—and passive homosexuality (with feminine identification in the primal scene).

Brunswick re-emphasized the importance of the primal scene experience for the Wolf Man's subsequent disturbance. His voyeurism-exhibitionism, his fears of looking and being looked at, and his sexual preferences were all related to the primal scene. Brunswick maintained the basic formulation that he had not resolved his hostile fear of his father and his longing for homosexual gratification in identification with his mother in the primal scene. Being stared at as the wolves had stared at him in his nightmare was a projection of his own staring at the primal scene.

Freud recognized the prevasive importance of the primal scene for his patient and even reconstructed its exact setting: the Wolf Man's age, the hour it occurred, as well as the Wolf Man's awakening response of having a bowel movement. The Wolf-Man was eighteen months of age, suffering from malaria, and witnessed coitus *a tergo* at five in the afternoon (when fever recurred), the hour at which his subsequent depressions reached their peak. There were five wolves in the Wolf Man's drawing of his dream, although he reported six or seven of them.

In his later years he complained that the world was hidden from him by a veil which was torn only after defecation following an enema. The Wolf Man, born on Christmas in 1886, relived the primal scene with impregnation and his own rebirth when the veil was torn. The veil, as Greenacre (1973) observed, was also a wall of denial. The window in the dream and the veil represented his wish to see and his blinding denial. His envelopment in the veil was also a withdrawal into sleep and symbiosis. Here was a dramatic depiction of the Wolf Man's narcissistic detachment, intolerance of narcissistic frustration, and fantasy of an intrauterine escape to the safety of fusion with his mother. His sense of reality and the structure and organization of his life were threatened from early childhood.

Brunswick denied that any new memories had occurred in her treatment and emphasized remnants of the homosexual father transference to Freud. Harnik (1930), however, pointed out that there were new findings which had not been previously reported. This led to an interesting exchange between Harnik (1930, 1931) and Brunswick (1930, 1931),* following the first publication (1928) of her five months of analysis with the Wolf Man in 1926.

The Wolf Man told Brunswick that after his nightmare at age four he couldn't bear to be looked at and would scream if he felt a fixed stare. "He would fly into a temper and cry, 'Why do you stare at me like that?' An observant glance would recall the dream to him with all its nightmare qualities" (Brunswick 1928, p. 289). Harnik suggested it was the recovery of this new memory that was the favorable turning point in his treatment with Brunswick. The diagnostic and prognostic significance of a "childhood paranoia" was not then appreciated by either Harnik or Brunswick. Harnik criticized Brunswick's singular reliance on the primal scene as an explanation of the Wolf Man's symptoms and character, regarding the newly recovered memory as a screen for infantile masturbation. He disputed her insistence that only unresolved transference to Freud was uncovered during her treatment of the Wolf Man's paranoia. Harnik almost recognized the severe childhood regression after the nightmare and, citing the anorexia and insistent wishes to be fed via gifts, postulated on oral fixation.

Although their dialogue seems naïve and incomplete today, Harnik was groping toward preoedipal problems and the Wolf Man's regressively disturbed sense of reality in childhood. The Wolf Man reported to Freud that, following his nightmare, it took quite a long while before he was convinced it had only been a dream. Freud commented on the particular significance of the sense of reality, stating that the dream related to an occurrence that really took place and was not merely imagined (1918, p. 33). The reality of the occurrence (the primal scene) was strongly emphasized, in Freud's view, in marked contrast to the unreality of the fairy tales of the wolves. There was no comment in that period about when, in terms of his development, the child was able to differentiate

The author expresses his appreciation and gratitude to Dr. Helen C. Meyers for her translation of the Harnik-Brunswick dialogue.

dream from reality. But the Wolf Man's pavor nocturnus continued on into his waking, daily activities. He tended to sleep and dream, so to speak, while awake: the nightmare experienced had invaded reality. (The Wolf Man's famous dream may not have been an anxiety dream [of REM sleep], but a symptomatic nightmare.) Nightmares, with their pervasive terror of attack and helplessness, are reminiscent of paranoia, especially when the boundaries between sleeping and waking, fantasy and reality, have been blurred. The regression of the sleeping nightmare could not be reversed and regulated in the child's waking life.

This childhood syndrome is a template and model of the Wolf Man's adult paranoia. The case may depict a paradigmatic infantile prototype of paranoia, at three and a half to four years of age: "taking offense on every occasion, raging like a lunatic," beating fantasies and sado-masochistic behavior, distrust and ideas of reference, fears of attack with merger of nightmare and reality, fears of helplessness with passive omnipotence and projection of aggression.

The analysis of the nightmare led to the reconstruction of the primal scene. Was this single early primal scene such a traumatic developmental influence for this patient? The patient grew up on a vast estate on which animals copulated and were castrated; impregnation, birth, and death must have been commonplace. The child undoubtedly knew of the gelding of horses and the castration of rams. The deadly danger of infection was known from his own illness, his mother's pelvic complaints, and the lethal inoculations of the vast sheep herds during an epidemic. He observed sheep breeding, and we can assume he was repeatedly exposed to instinctual activity.

There are further problems. Can we at present accept the formulation that an infant of eighteen months, suffering from malaria, undoubtedly with fever and severe stress reactions, could record the primal scene? Infants with malaria may be subject to delirium, febrile convulsions, coma, or exhaustion. Just what was the trauma—the malaria, or the primal scene, or an obscure combination of both, along with unknown vectors concerning parental care and complications? The primal scene was a major determinant of the Wolf Man's disorder, but there are issues of vulnerability, phase specificity, and overdetermination, with interrelated causes and effects.

The complications included the lack of parental empathy and appropriate responses, ego immaturity, general overstimulation, malarial fever, and possible swaddling. The Wolf Man assumes he was swaddled,* which, if true, could have been an important developmental influence and have contributed to the motionless figures in his dream. The physical illness and incapacity could have

The author expresses his appreciation and gratitude to Dr. Muriel Gardiner for transmitting his questions to the Wolf Man.

severe traumatic and sado-masochistic implications, which would also influence any concurrent primal scene experience. A serious and extended malaria at eighteen months, as opposed to a single primal scene experience, could lead to ego disturbance and the developmental disruption of separation-individuation. The nearly lethal pneumonia at age three months may also have had unknown psychobiological side effects. Certainly the role of malaria and the earlier pneumonia as possible traumatic experiences in their own right was not appreciated. We do not know the severity, duration, or sequelae of the malaria, or the number of attacks or recurrences.

The reconstruction of the primal scene under these complicated circumstances strained Freud's credulity as it does ours today. This early model of reconstruction remains highly controversial.

Perhaps the most famous and detailed reconstruction, it was a major stimulus to later research on analytic reconstruction. Freud himself continued to struggle with the question of reality versus fantasy and retrospective falsification versus retrospective reactivation of the primal scene. He suggested that the remembered primal scene at eighteen months became a fresh traumatic experience at the time of the nightmare preceding his patient's fourth birthday on Christmas eve (1918, p. 109). In his final recapitulation (p. 121), Freud left open the possibility that the Wolf Man had retrospectively introduced a fantasy of his parents copulating into his observation of them together at eighteen months of age. Certainly the Wolf Man's statement about having witnessed, at eighteen months of age, upon awakening, the primal scene repeated three times, must be viewed with serious reservations. The child's concept of the number three and of a sequence of three distinct experiences develops considerably later than the age of eighteen months. Judging from the early scenes of sexual seduction with Grusha (his nursemaid) and his sister and the many servants on the vast Russian estate, as well as opportunities presented by the animals, it would seem that there was early, repetitive exposure to instinctual overstimulation and early castration threats.

The primal scene, sexual seduction, masturbation, and related danger cannot be viewed in isolation from his parents. There is insufficient attention in the case reports to the Wolf Man's sharing a bedroom, first with his old nurse (Nanya) and sister, and then with his Nanya (Gardiner 1971). The developmental implications of the intimacy and voyeurism-exhibitionism of this sleeping arrangement are not explored. Nor should the child's interpretation of the primal scene be dissociated from other facets of the parent-child relationships and the parent's relation to each other. The reaction to the primal scene would depend upon the child's developmental phase, his psychic structure, and his own ego-edited reaction to the total experience.

Was Freud's reconstruction of this single primal scene a return to a theory of traumatic parental seduction in neurosogenesis? If trauma, with malaria, rather than primal scene in isolation, is emphasized at eighteen months, then this is trauma at the time the basic mood develops, substantially deriving from trust or distrust. It is the rapprochement subphase of separation-individuation, when language, secondary process, and other ego functions are rapidly differentiating and vulnerable to injury (Mahler 1971).

Freud was always aware of the limitations of his theory and technique. With the growth of psychoanalytic knowledge, many early explanations are obsolete and incomplete. The case of the Wolf Man was originally presented in terms of the castration complex and particularly the negative Oedipus complex. The preoedipal factors influence and contribute to the core oedipal problems. The relationship with the father and the fear of his homosexual love for the father are seen as paramount in the patient's conflicts (Freud 1918, p. 32). The mother-child relation and maternal influence (as in the other Freud case histories) is in the background and is hardly considered. Problems of the two mothers, his peasant Nanya and his hypochondriacal mother, who was only close to him when he was ill, are not developed. His Nanya may even have spoken a different dialect. There were a series of governesses whose impact and consequence were relatively unknown. We know that the patient identified with his hypochondriacal mother who was preoccupied with her pelvic and bodily complaints. She was self-absorbed, not involved in the day-to-day childrearing, and unable to exert a healthy, maternal direction of the household. She apparently knew little of, or did not control, the patient's sister's teasing and attempts to seduce him.

His father was also unable to provide healthy, paternal direction and stimulation, for he suffered from a manic-depressive psychosis. The father was frequently physically away in sanitoria and in all probability committed suicide, as did the patient's sister, before the Wolf Man underwent analysis with Freud. The father was the model of a castrated cripple, represented by the deaf and dumb servant who was unable to communicate because his tongue had been cut out. The patient identified with his psychotic, immobilized father. Was the father mute during periods of depressive psychomotor retardation? Was the father's "affectionate abuse" of the child as innocent as it seemed, along with his oral threats to gobble him up? Did the father's psychosis contribute to the atmosphere of unbridled instinctual life and possible exposure to the primal scene? How sensitive and understanding were these parents, especially when one recalls not only the mother's narcissistic hypochondriasis, but her comments to her son when she took him to the sanitorium to see his psychotic father? "He had not seen his father for many months, when one day his mother said she was going to take the children with her to the town and show them something that would very much please them" (Freud 1918, p. 67). His father was gravely depressed and the boy found him pathetic. What was the child previously told about his father's absence, illness, and character change?

One of the Wolf Man's earliest memories was of being alone with his nurse at two and a half and witnessing the departure of his parents and sister. There were not only repeated separations from his parents, but a lack of warm parental involvement and participation in his life. These early relationships are of crucial importance for understanding the Wolf Man's later object relations and ego development. The paranoid psychosis of Schreber and the paranoid episodes of the Wolf Man are all too often discussed in their original formulations without reference to infantile ego development and the early mother-child relation. What is stressed is the feminine attitude toward the father, regression from negative oedipal fantasies, and primitive defenses against homosexual wishes. Preoedipal conflicts, ego development, and early self- and object-relations had not yet received systematic study.

A great deal more would have to be understood about the Wolf Man's narcissistic detachment and feelings of entitlement and insatiable demanding. His being born in a caul, the favorite and only son; his rebirth as a replacement for his Nanya's dead baby, born at Christmas; his identification with the Christ child, and his being considered Freud's favorite case were narcissistic gratifications, no doubt reinforced by his fame and position in psychoanalytic history and the special interest and support of psychoanalysts. Had the early distrust and detachment, the veiled wall which separated him from the world, been overcome in his years of treatment and support (psychological and economic) by various psychoanalysts?

Nor can the inherited and constitutional predisposition to severe emotional disturbance in his family be overlooked. There is an extraordinary passivity and rigidity that not only appeared in the analysis of the Wolf Man and his later life history, but was already present in what we know of his earlier childhood—that is, the stillness in his wolf dream and drawing. He clung with tenacity to any position, giving it up only under great duress and when offered a substitute, on which he then became very dependent. This was apparent in his giving up the phobia for the obsessions and later giving up his religious interests for his German tutor. The analysis with Freud did not move until the imposition of a termination date. Freud tells us, "he immediately gave up working in order to avoid any further changes, and in order to remain comfortably in the situation which had been thus established" (1918, p. 11).

At that time Freud thought the patient's resistance and fixation had given way under the inexorable pressure of the termination limit. "All the information, too, which enabled me to understand his infantile neurosis is derived from this last period of work, during which resistance temporarily disappeared and the patient gave an impression of lucidity which is usually attainable only in hypnosis'' (p. 18). The hypnotic compliance and apparent lucidity did not alter the deeper personality deformations and what Freud called the patient's ''psychic inertia.'' Freud also referred to the concept of *entropy* (p. 116), which, in thermodynamics, tends to make certain physical changes irreversible and which psychologically opposes the undoing of what has already occurred.

If the Wolf Man was swaddled for nine months according to the cultural custom (Erikson 1963), this may have further contributed to his passivity and masochism, and even his later identification with Christ on the cross. The possible influence (negative and positive) of swaddling on his personality is unknown. His pervasive passivity, however, would appear to be related to constitutional factors and to developmental failures rooted in his early object relations and identifications. His passive beating wishes and masochistic fantasies were considered derivatives of unconscious female identification in the primal scene. These beating fantasies, however, are also indicative of an early sado-masochistic relationship to the mother and a severe disturbance in ego and drive development (Novick and Novick 1972). The Wolf Man's analysis preceded but also stimulated the formulation and elaboration of the psychoanalytic theory of aggression.

The Wolf Man's fear of helplessness and passivity, his fear of being devoured, were also related to his wish to be devoured into sleep, into a veil of narcissistic withdrawal and symbiotic reunion. His preoedipal conflicts are now apparent in his clinging, ambivalent, masochistic tie to the preoedipal mother. He demonstrates the vulnerability of some borderline patients to severe regression and their rather typical conflict between the wish to fuse and fear of fusion with loss of the object and identity. Freud may very well have been an idealized self-object (Kohut 1971) as well as an auxiliary ego. This patient became paranoid when Freud developed cancer. His own devouring aggression and destructive wishes might now destroy the formerly omnipotent object—and himself. Did Freud refer him to a female colleague to reduce the unconscious threat of castration by the therapist or, perhaps, also to encourage the development of supportive, maternal transference?

The nature of the actual object relation and transference relation with Brunswick are not clarified in her terse treatment (five months) and reported ''supplement'' to the case. The maternal, narcissistic, and symbiotic transferences were neither understood nor identified. Explanations depended upon the homosexual father transference described by Freud. Even though Brunswick was also Freud's patient, the probable sister transference is not elaborated. She mentions his attachment to his preschizophrenic sister in her later analytic treatment of the Wolf Man. Brunswick's insistence to the Wolf Man that he was not

Freud's favorite case must have had special significance for these two patients of Freud. She largely ignored his status as Freud's famous case and Freud's financial support of this special patient as well as his presentation to the Wolf Man of a volume containing the patient's immortal case history with a personally inscribed dedication in 1919, and additional analysis without fee in 1920.

Whom did Freud unconsciously represent for this narcissistic, omnipotent patient identified with Christ? Was it true that Brunswick was only an extension of and proxy for Freud, God the Father? His referral to Brunswick was doubtless felt as both a rejection and the presentation of a free but poor substitute for Freud, his lost idealized object. The Wolf Man was unable to express his rage at the "rejection" or his gratitude for the bestowal of free further treatment. To him, Brunswick probably represented Freud and the psychoanalytic movement. Her explanations and formulations adhered to Freud's early published views, not an extension of them. She did not reconsider the transference implications of the patient's personality transformation, transfer, and new female therapist. In addition to mother or sister, was Brunswick his Nanya into whose care he was entrusted by his sickly mother; his English governess who supports and controls him with his nurse-wife; or a composite of these infantile objects?

The Wolf Man was fixedly studying his face in the mirror and may well have developed a narcissistic (mirror?) transference (Kohut 1971) to Brunswick. The threatened loss of Freud had fractured his ego stability with regression to magical mirror self-object ties (Shengold 1974). His recovery could be related to the formation of a narcissistic object relationship with her, with fantasies of protective omnipotence and an archaic narcissistic transference "cure." A replacement and transfer of the narcissistic transference to Freud and to psychoanalysis can also be inferred.

His withdrawal disguised his insatiable demands for oral-dependent gifts and narcissistic supplies. Brunswick may have intuitively provided empathic mirroring responses, reliability, reality, and a vital auxiliary ego during his psychotic regression. In the psychosis there was probably a fusion of the grandiose self and ideal object and, with narcissistic rage, the persecutory transformation, splitting, and projection of the unintegrated, aggressively devalued self-object. The regressive retreat moved from narcissistic but differentiated object-representations to fusion of self- and object-representation. The Wolf Man's narcissistic transference to Brunswick was determined by his desperate need to re-establish narcissistic equilibrium and symbiotic relationships when faced with Freud's loss. The Wolf Man's relationships to his analyst were determined primarily by his personality disorder rather than the special nature and research goals of his treatment (see Offenkrantz and Tobin 1973). Freud's fascinating technical variations in the treatment of the Wolf Man are beyond the scope of this paper, as are the countertransference issues (Kanzer 1972). There would, of course, be particular countertransference problems for anyone undertaking the treatment of one of Freud's patients, now "Freud's famous case." The technical problems are also corollary to questions about this patient's ego resources and analyzability.

His rapid improvement with Brunswick's help is reminiscent of the hypnotic lucidity of the terminal phase of treatment with Freud and the brief additional analysis (four months) with Freud, in 1920. Freud, recapitulating the problems of the case with characteristic foresight, did not focus on the Wolf Man's homosexuality, but drew attention to the patient's pathological narcissism:

> He broke down after an organic infection of the genitals had revived his fear of castration, shattered his narcissism, and compelled him to abandon his hope of being personally favoured by destiny. He fell ill, therefore, as the result of a *narcissistic* "frustration." This excessive strength of his narcissism was in complete harmony with the other indications of an inhibited sexual development: with the fact that so few of his psychical trends were concentrated in his heterosexual object-choice, in spite of all its energy, and that his homosexual attitude, standing so much nearer to narcissism, persisted in him as an unconscious force with such very great tenacity. Naturally, where disturbances like these are present, psychoanalytic treatment cannot bring about any instantaneous revolution or put matters upon a level with a normal development. . . .[1918, p. 118]

The Wolf Man's narcissistic disorder has been elaborated by Gedo and Goldberg (1973).

Mack Brunswick (1928) corroborated the veiled state of the patient as a womb fantasy and noted, ". . . throughout the psychosis, the veil of the earlier illness enveloped the patient, nothing penetrated it" (Gardiner 1971, p. 300).

During the paranoid regression, the primary nature of his feminine identification (in a symbolic primal scene) became apparent. Brunswick reported (p. 301): "Dr. Wulff, who knew and attended the patient and both his parents. . . said, 'He no longer plays the mother, he is the mother down to the last detail.'"

This was a global identification based upon and only a step from merging with his maternal object. His use of the mirror represented his merging femininity and protected his identity against re-engulfment. Here, castration anxiety both screened and evoked the anxiety of disintegration. His facial concerns represented the danger of castration and femininity, but also the deeper danger of loss of differentiation of self and object.

In the window of his nightmare, in looking and being looked at in the mirror, he attempted to face his conflicts, to find his narcissistic object, and confirm his identity. The persecutory nightmare was repeated in the adult paranoia and followed by reparative efforts at ego mastery of the dread of borderline regression into narcissistic fusion.

Summary

The case of the Wolf Man has been surveyed in terms of psychoanalytical theoretical developments subsequent to 1918 and 1928. The Wolf Man affords an extraordinary opportunity for longitudinal developmental study. It is suggested that the patient suffered, not from an infantile neurosis, but from a borderline condition with episodes of infantile psychosis. The infantile psychotic episodes recurred in the paranoid states of adult life. The Wolf Man's famous dream is re-examined as a nightmare in terms of ego response and later revival of analogous ego states. Freud's reconstruction of the primal scene at eighteen months is reviewed with particular attention to the possible traumatic role of malaria and the effect of trauma during the rapprochement phase of separation-individuation. Problems of separation-individuation, and narcissistic disorder and regression are emphasized.

References

Bender, L. (1968). Childhood schizophrenia: a review. *International Journal of Psychiatry*. 5:211–219.

Blum, H. (1972). Psychoanalytic understanding and psychotherapy of borderline regression. *International Journal of Psychoanalytic Psychotherapy* 1:46–59.

Brunswick, R. (1928). A supplement to Freud's "History of an infantile neurosis," in *The Wolf-Man by the Wolf Man*, ed. M. Gardiner. New York: Basic Books.

Ekstein, R. and Wallerstein, J. (1954). Observations on the psychology of borderline and psychotic children. *Psychoanalytic Study of the Child*, 9:344–369.

Erikson, E. (1963). *Childhood and Society*. New York: W. W. Norton.

Freud, A. (1965). *Normality and Pathology in Childhood. The Writings of Anna Freud*, Vol. 6. New York: International Universities Press.

———(1971). The infantile neurosis: genetic and dynamic considerations. *Psychoanalytic Study of the Child*, 26:79–90.

Freud, S. (1918). From the history of an infantile neurosis. *Standard Edition* 17:3–122.

———(1919). A child is being beaten. *Standard Edition* 17:175–204.

———(1937). Analysis terminable and interminable. *Standard Edition* 23:209–253.

Frijling-Schreuder, E. (1969). Borderline states in children. *Psychoanalytic Study of the Child* 24:307–327.

Frosch, J. (1967). Severe regressive states during analysis. *Journal of the American Psychoanalytic Association* 15:491–507.

Gardiner, M, ed. (1971). *The Wolf-Man by The Wolf-Man*. New York: Basic Books.

Gedo, J. and Goldberg, A. (1973). *Models of the Mind,* Chicago: University of Chicago Press.

Geleerd, E. (1958). Borderline states in childhood and adolescence. *The Psychoanalytic Study of the Child* 13:279–295.

Greenacre, P. (1973). The primal scene and the sense of reality. *Psychoanalytic Quarterly* 42:10–41.

Harnik, J. (1930). Kritisches über Mack Brunswick's "Nachtrag zu Freud's 'Gesichte einer infantilen neurose." *Internat. Zeitschrift für Psychoanalyse* 16:123–127.

————(1931). Erwiderung auf Mack Brunswick's Entgegnung. *Internat. Zeitschrift für Psychoanalyse* 17:400–402.

Jones, E. (1955). *The Life and Work of Sigmund Freud,* Vol 2. New York: Basic Books.

Kanzer, M. (1972). Review of *The Wolf-Man by the Wolf-Man*. *International Journal of Psycho-Analysis* 53:419–421.

Kernberg, O. (1967). Borderline personality organization. *Journal of the American Psychoanalytic Association* 15:641–685.

Kohut, H. (1971). *The Analysis of The Self*. New York: International Universities Press.

Lewin, B. D. (1950). *The Psychoanalysis of Elation*. New York: W. W. Norton.

————(1930). Entgegnung auf Harniks kritische Bemerkungen. *Internat. Zeitschrift für Psychoanalyse* 16:128–129.

————(1931), Schlusswort. *Internat. Zeitschrift für Psychoanalyse* 17:402.

Mahler, M. S. (1971). A study of the separation-individuation process and its possible application to borderline phenomena in the psychoanalytic situation. *The Psychoanalytic Study of the Child,* 26:403–424.

Novick, J. and Novick, K. (1972). Beating fantasies in children. *International Journal Psycho-Analysis* 53:237–242.

Offenkrantz, W. and Tobin, A. (1973). Problems of the therapeutic alliance: Freud and the Wolf-Man. *International Journal of Psycho-Analysis* 54:75–78.

Shengold, L. (1974), The mirror as metaphor. *Journal of the American Psychoanalytic Association* 22:97–115.

Weil, A. (1953). Certain severe disturbances of ego development in childhood. *The Psychoanalytic Study of the Child* 8:271–287.

Chapter 2

FURTHER COMMENTS ON THE WOLF MAN:

THE SEARCH FOR A PRIMAL SCENE

MARK KANZER M.D.

As Harold Blum has stated, the Wolf Man case offers us a transcultural analysis with universal significance (1974; Part VI, chapter 1 of the present volume). A work of art as well as a scientific treatise, it is like a Shakespearean play that is seen with increased perception by each successive generation. Admonitions against its continued use as a teaching instrument are bound to have little effect in relation to its lasting fascination and instruction as an entrance to the world of psychoanalysis itself. Perhaps it can be compared to a path through the wilderness in comparison with a modern highway. The spirit of discovery ranges itself against advanced theory and technique.

Nevertheless modern views on the oral triad, the "veil" of the Wolf Man as a "waking dream screen," separation-individuation, narcissism and the borderline case, may profit and find validation in this study which will not permit itself to become old. As an alternative, we may look at it with fresh eyes and re-frame the picture. We believe that much has been done along these lines in the present chapter. There is no illusion that it contains the last word on the subject.

How far we have come since 1930, when the issue was raised by Harnik as to whether the subsequent analysis of the Wolf Man by Brunswick had uncovered "new memories" or done anything but resolve some remnants of transference to Freud! The potentials of structural psychology or child analysis or even Freud's second instinct theory seem scarcely to have been developed when the debate was couched in such terms, we may take for example, the dream during the Brunswick analysis in which the wolves were ranging fiercely up and down behind a wall, and a woman (a partial representation of Dr. Brunswick) was apparently planning to open the door to let them in. This was a reproduction of the original wolf dream and the door, as she recognized, corresponded to the window in that famous dream. Brunswick leads the associations back to the age of four and still tries to reconstruct the primal scene, refute critics who question the validity of the dream, and elicits the fear (which Harnik regarded as *the* "new contribution" of the analysis) that if he spies upon the parents in coitus, father (the wolves) will devour him—a regressive representation of his desire to take mother's place in the sex act.

How easily one might have taken anothe view of the same dream! Brunswick had been more successful than she knew: she had mobilized the wolves, so stationary in the original dream, and brought them into the present. She had thus complied with the conditions Freud postulated after contemplating the unsatisfying results of the patient's analysis—to bring the past back not directly through memory but through acting out, preferably in the analytic situation itself (1914). The analyst is opening the door lifting the defenses that have long kept the wolves in check. She will be destroyed, the dream warns; both of them will be destroyed if this occurs. One analytic approach seeks literal genetic reconstruction of a past trauma; the other functionally appraises the current transference neurosis which includes but is not merely a literal reproduction of an infantile sexual trauma.

But is it only the father's rage that is to be warded off? Is it not that of the child himself? The patient was now visibly raging like a wolf and threatening to shoot Freud and Brunswick. Strangely, neither she nor Freud (who supervised her) considered that the past was returning through acting out in this fashion. Neither was his theory of aggression being used. The primal scene rage reaction of the little Wolf Man was finding an outlet at last, the rage that came to be represented in passive staring instead of devouring them, and then in projection of the dangerous oral aggression into the passive staring wolves.

Brunswick's treatment of the Wolf Man is indeed curious to modern eyes. Is it merely analysis of the unresolved transference to Freud, as she thought, to insist that he was not the favorite patient and to invoke Freud himself as authority? Even if correct, this goes outside the analytic situation to interpret the resistance and is a psychotherapeutic confrontation with reality. But what criteria could be invoked to deny that he was *a* or *the* favorite patient of the master, who so distinctly had favorites among his followers and who was treating the Wolf Man with a particular eye to refuting his own critics? Blum has recounted evidence of his favoritism (as we have also done in our review of the Gardiner book) and now we will merely add that Helene Deutsch describes how she was discharged with little notice by Freud to make way for the return of the Wolf Man in 1919 (Deutsch 1973, p. 133).

As we would now recognize, Brunswick's insistence that the Wolf Man was not Freud's favorite patient was not only an assault on his imperiled reality testing but also on the working alliance with both Freud and herself. (She too was under treatment by Freud at the time!) As a result she neither understood his disturbed behavior nor could control it, as she acknowledged, and had to ascribe it to psychosis. A functional approach would have clarified the reactions he was undergoing to this intervention and at least restored understanding between them. Fortunately the patient was able to work this through on his own, as indicated by a dream which she recognized as portending improvement. In this, she took the place of the mother but took icons from the wall and smashed them. Originally the mother had quieted his oedipal stage unruliness and promoted superego formation by reading the New Testament to him and initiating the ritual of kissing the icons before retiring.

Brunswick seems correct in seeing an important reversal of the past: the patient is no longer required to adopt a masochistic identification with Christ; (is not this something new in the analysis—even if not a memory?). True to the consecration of the past, however, she does not connect the dream with her destruction of his idolization of Freud. For one thing, this relieved his need to identify with the truly suffering Freud whose illness was a prime determinant of the present phase of the neurosis. Another factor, however, could be evidence in the dream that mother preferred him to father: only the two of them were left; just as the two of them had participated in the Bible-reading for moments of gratifying bestowal of her attention on him alone. Was not the icon-kissing an enforced reconciliation to ward off the wolf dream? The guilt of destroying father was mother's alone. He could feel safe from oedipal reprisal, as do so many "heroes" of family romances who are abetted by heroines in achieving their goals.

Nevertheless, for Brunswick, the Wolf Man was never permitted to form an image of himself as other than identifying with, rather than possessing the mother. Later, when he had a dream that he was lying in bed with her while Freud was seated behind them, she recognized the primal scene and a wish to be identified with her while the father performed intercourse from behind. She did not consider the possibility that he might be taking father's place in the primal scene and—in a complete reversal—compelling father to witness them from the rear! This too would have added something to the criteria of analytic progress had these included the desire to master the past instead of merely reliving it. It would have strengthened the emergent positive Oedipus complex instead of submerging it in renewed insistence that the patient wished only to identify with her in the primal scene. Little Hans was to be the paradigm of phobias resulting from the positive Oedipus complex, the Wolf Man the paradigm of phobias resulting from the negative Oedipus complex, despite evidence and admissions that the "oedipuses" of both children were mixed.

The publication of the Wolf Man's own account of the analytic experience and his impressions of Freud is a unique but desirable precedent. The analytic process is a two person relationship and the view of only one of the participants, while for practical reasons the only one usually made available, will achieve fuller dimensions when complemented by the other. This is all the more important in this instance where Freud deliberately restricted himself to delineating the infantile neurosis and bypassed the adult neurosis and contemporary aspects of the analysis, as though the infantile neurosis were an independent entity which was merely reflected in the events of the present! Conversely, what actually happened in the present between patient and analyst, insofar as it was not a transference replica, was of little significance. Apparently Freud could speak to the Wolf Man of his own family, his difficulties with his followers, his favorite books and his views on many subjects without considering that this interfered with the task of recalling infantile memories. Such isolated treatment of past and present could only lend to the dilemmas Freud faced at the end of the treatment.

He could speak of the patient as wrapped in "obliging apathy" (as far as reconstruction of the past was concerned) when he was in fact clamoring to be permitted to interrupt treatment to go in search of Therese at last. The crisis probably was due in good part to another factor that Freud did not consider of significance for the therapeutic work. The patient had come from Russia in the company of a psychiatrist, Dr. D., who had recommended him to Freud. One gets the impression from the case history that Dr. D. drops out at this point, but that was not at all the case. He remained with his wealthy client, spending most of the day and night with him where Freud had access only for an hour. He taught him to gamble and find diversion in Vienna; when the analyst went on vacation, Dr. D. did not desert him but took him to gambling resorts in Germany and also to Spain. In the fall of 1910, after some nine months of a companionship which may well have served as a protection against agoraphobia (and the appearance of the wolf, i.e., Freud), he returned to Russia. Left alone to face the brunt of the analysis, the patient's panicky insistence on being permitted to make his way to Therese in Munich (which could also have been looked upon as a return to the infantile neurosis and situations in which his parents had deserted him) left Freud no choice but to comply. Further visits took place periodically and in time he brought her back to Vienna but did not marry her for that would have countermanded analytic tenets against making decisions during treatment!

The "termination"—first of so many that lay ahead—was noteworthy. He brought Therese to visit Freud for the first time. He also gave Freud a "farewell gift" (not mentioned in the text) which Freud for theoretical reasons felt would underline the separation; male patients supposedly find it difficult to accept otherwise the gift of health from a male analyst. The gift was interesting—an Egyptian figurine with a mitered hat which thereafter took its place in Freud's collection. She would permanently hold a place for the donor in the office, one might assume, and also represented a trade for the new wife. The miter may well be of special significance in this connection.

It is of interest here to review the article of Eva Rosenfeld (1956) in which she directly links the wolf dream with the erarly dream of Freud in which he saw his mother, sleeping or dead, carried by two figures with bird beaks, in the style of Egyptian deities (1900, pp. 583–584). She surmises, from the associations to the former dream, that the wolves had already eaten the tailor of the fairy tale who had escaped by climbing a tree. It was this fairy tale that had instigated the dream, but now we find evidence of a wish that had been overlooked, i.e., that the wolves (in whom we have remarked the little boy's aggression) would climb up and devour the tailor (in German, *Schneider* or circumciser, castrator). To the extent that the tree is a phallus, it has now become the property of the child instead of the father. Rosenfeld's inference about the wish to devour the father (in conjunction with our own about the desire to castrate him and take mother away) receives further support from her comparison of the wolves to totem animals and the sons of the primal horde who devour the father.

For Freud, the thrust of his effort to reconstruct the Wolf Man's primal scene, which he would have regarded as decisive in his disputes with Jung and Adler, encountered obstruction not only in the elusiveness of the scene but through questions in his own mind as to whether he was dealing with real experiences, fantasies or products of his own constructions (which included his own possible fantasies). In addition, as Rosenfeld indicates by linking his Egyptian bird-god dream with the Wolf Man's, he may have been troubled by counter-identifications, fusing reactions to his own primal scene with that of the patient and seeking to recover his own primal scene indirectly in that way. The circumstance in Freud's home as a child when he shared a room with his parents and younger siblings until the age of three would have been conducive to concern with dating the Wolf Man's primal scene at about the same age (see Schur 1972, p. 21).

Rosenfeld indicates the all-pervasiveness of the bird-god dream for Freud. She finds it the point of departure for his abiding interest in Egypt and his argument that Moses was an Egyptian. His interest in antiquity and archeology would be related sublimations. Lewin (1970) was of the opinion that during his self-analysis, Freud literally supposed that the lost memory would be recovered visually, with dreams as the intermediary link. Thus the past would be "brought to life," as Freud so frequently phrased it.

The failure to establish with certainty the age at which the Wolf Man witnessed the primal scene (a term introduced for the first time in this study) and the question as to whether the experience was real or not—a doubt which Freud's critics have never ceased to exploit—became inordinately important for him. All theory and technique are in fact influenced by this dilemma and in fact the theory of therapy was changed when he terminated the treatment of the Wolf Man with acknowledged feelings of dissatisfaction (1914). "I admit that this question [about the reality of the primal scene] is the most delicate question in the whole domain of psychoanalysis," he averred. "No doubt has troubled me more; no other uncertainty has been more decisive in holding me back from publishing my case" (1918, p. 103). The usual telltale delay of four years between writing his findings and publishing them took place.

An apparent allusion to his critics, Jung and Adler, whom he had not quite vanquished, as well as to his personal disappointment in the self-analytic quest to recover the primal scene—the earliest memories to be dredged up, he thought—are reflected in his statement that "the description of such early phases and of such deep strata of mental life has been a task which has never before been attempted; and *it is better to perform the task badly than to take flight before it*" (1918, p. 104; my italics).

Yet another telltale characteristic of Freud's personal involvement in his work was to be found in the feeling that he could not present it in his usual lucid and persuasive style; perhaps he could not persuade himself. During the interval between finishing his writing of the case and his publishing it, he elaborated still another possibility for explaining the primal scene—the influence of in-herited memories: "It seems to me quite possible that all the things that are told to us today in analysis as fantasy—the seduction of children, the influencing of sexual excitement by observing parental intercourse, the threat of castration (or rather castration itself)—were once real occurrences in the primaeval time of the human family, and that children in their fantasies are simply filling in gaps in individual truth with historical truth" (1916–17, p. 371). By shifting the primal scene to the sphere of psychogenetic memories, it was placed beyond the recovery of the analyst.

Freud's references to the Wolf Man recur in no less than six articles between 1913 and 1937 (Strachey 1918, p. 5) and indirectly in other articles as well; we may well say that he was indeed the case likely to come to mind as Freud sought illustrative material. Analysts, continuing their preoccupation with him, are perhaps fulfilling in this respect their own archaic heritage, namely a disposition to empathize and identify with Freud's own thinking. Perhaps he fills in gaps in individual truth at the moment with historical truth.

Summary

Brunswick's analysis of the Wolf Man is reviewed and reveals far-reaching progress which was unrecognized inasmuch as the goals were too limited (resolving residua of transferences to Freud by recalling the primal scene in greater detail) and the interpretations a deterrent. The emergence of the positive Oedipus complex was consistently regarded as a wish to identify with, not possess mother.

There is also evidence that through the Wolf Man, Freud was in quest of his own primal scene. His disappointment led to basic changes in theory and technique (1914) and to the consignment of the primal scene to the sphere of inherited memories.

References

Blum, H.P. (1974). The borderline childhood of the Wolf Man. *Journal of the American Psychoanalytic Association* 22: 721–742. Part VI. Chapter 1, this volume.

Brunswick, R.M. (1928). A supplement to Freud's "History of an infantile neurosis." *International Journal of Psycho-Analysis*. 9: 439–476.

Deutsch, H. (1973). *Confrontations with myself*. New York: Norton.

Freud, S. (1900). The interpretation of dreams. Standard Edition 415.

————— (1914). Remembering, repetition and working through. Standard Edition 12: 145–156.

————— (1916–1917). Introductory lectures on psychoanalysis. Part 3. Standard Edition 16.

————— (1918). From the history of an infantile neurosis. Standard Edition 17:3–122.

————— (1937). Analysis terminable and interminable. Standard Edition 23: 209–253.

Gardiner, N., ed. (1971). *The Wolf Man by the Wolf Man*. New York: Basic Books

Harnik, J. (1930). Kritisches ueber Mack Brunswick. *Intern. Ztschr. PsA*. 16: 123–127.

Kanzer, M. (1972). *The Wolf Man by the Wolf Man* (Gardiner). Book review. *International Journal of Psycho-Analysis*. 53: 419–421.

Lewin, B.D. (1970). The train ride. *Psychoanalytic Quarterly* 39: 71–89.

Rosenfeld, E. (1956). Dream and vision. *International Journal of Psycho-Analysis*. 37: 97–105.

Schur, M. (1972). *Freud: Living and Dying.* New York: International Universities Press.

Strachey, J. (1955). Introduction to Freud's "From the history of an infantile neurosis." Standard Edition 17: 3–6.

Chapter 3

THE PATHOGENIC INFLUENCE OF THE
PRIMAL SCENE: A REEVALUATION

HAROLD P. BLUM, M.D.

The primal scene has been so important and intrinsic to clinical psychoanalysis that it has become a basic concept whose definition, developmental role, and clinical significance has usually been taken for granted. Our literature is replete with reports of primal scene disturbance, and the pathogenic influence of the primal scene has been invoked and derived as a major determinant in virtually all forms of psychopathology. This applies, for example, to neurosis with learning inhibition, sexual dysfunction, and sleep disturbance. As a ubiquitous factor in the explanation of all forms of psychological disorders, Esman (1973) wondered if the primal scene explained everything—and, therefore, nothing. He doubted the pathogenic effect of witnessing the primal scene that Freud had repeatedly asserted.

The concept of the primal scene has been extended to the most varied derivatives and transformations. The configuration of the primal scene has represented not only the parents in the act of copulation, but also regressive and associated infantile meanings (Edelheit 1971). The primal scene schema traces secondary

This article is a modification of the author's introduction to the panel on the Pathogeneity of the Primal Scene which Dr. Blum chaired at the May 1977 meeting of the American Psychoanalytic Association. [See also Blum 1979.]

transformation in myth, crucifixion, fantasies, etc. To refer to the primal scene on all developmental levels, whether fantasied or real, or single or patterned exposure, or to remotely related derivatives may result in a conceptual confusion in which the primal scene may represent all things at any time. This diffuse definition may also partially account for differences in the frequency and significance of the primal scene reported in the clinical material of different analysts. The expanded meaning and application of the concept have raised new questions concerning its definition, its relation to developmental phase and role, as well as its relation to trauma, personality disorder, sadomasochism, and sublimation.

I believe the primal scene should be differentiated from its precursors and derivatives. Historically and conceptually, the primal scene fantasy was related to the infantile neurosis and oedipal conflict. The primal scene fantasy of parental intercourse is a phallic-oedipal phenomenon. It may have the most varied and disguised regressive or sublimated transformations. The phallic phase primal scene fantasy is not the oral triad or fused dyad of symbiosis or conjoint anal act of defilement or excretion. The primal scene should also not be confused with the negative Oedipus complex of the male and its regressive masochistic manifestations, although primal scene fantasy may have any or all of these regressive infantile interpretations. Ego immaturity, congnitive confusion and persisting libidinal fixations can still be discerned in the oedipal child's distorted theories of sexual relations and reproduction.

Just as the primal scene inevitably elicits reactions of rejection and exclusion, or of intrusion and inclusion, there are serious problems on a theoretical level as to what to include in the basic concept of the primal scene and its scope and boundaries. The primal scene is a crystallization of the oedipal drama, a condensed representation of passionate attachment and conflict in the oedipal triangle between parents and child. In the literal drama, the fantasy of the primal scene figures prominently in the classic novels and plays. The drama and dance, in form and content, may be traced to the primal scene with actors, audience, acts, action, and performance, as well as physical and psychological barriers between the actors and the audience. These barriers represent not only the doors and walls of the bedroom but the prohibitions against participation in parental sexual activity, the taboo against incest.

Condensing the passions of the Oedipus complex, the primal scene represents active and passive, male and female, phallic and castrated, the bisexual combination of masculinity and femininity, and the child's double identification with the parental partners in incestuous intercourse.

Primal scene curiosity leads to questions concerning pregnancy and birth, and the origins of babies and parents. The confused child (as depicted in a popular limerick) wonders "who does what, how, why, and to whom?" Some primal scene fantasies refer to being present at the moment of creation of self and sibling. The primal scene is not synonymous with the Oedipus complex; but it represents the dramatic tension, conflicts, disappointments and questions of the oedipal child, and via displacement and condensation may represent any oedipal derivative. Many derivatives of the primal scene occur right in the parental bed where children are allowed to rest or sleep, where games, study and group reading occur, and where the family watches TV and practices playful togetherness. ("Incest is the game the whole family can play.") Other oedipal derivatives, such as the fantasy of castration or punishment in the act of intercourse, may be represented in primal scene imagery.

Freud's discussions of the primal scene are indicative of his continuing preoccupation with issues of early seduction and trauma, and searching efforts to find the difference between fantasy and actual traumatic experience. Two important questions related to the traumatic effect of the primal scene concern its proposed universal interpretation in sado-masochistic terms, and the difference between the primal scene as a universal fantasy and the primal scene as an actual experience and observation.

When had the fantasies developed and what are the effects of actual overstimulation, genital exposure, and parental seduction? Freud overlooked neither the difference nor the interplay between reality and fantasy. He wrote (1908) of the reality influences and the shaping of the children's theories concerning sexuality and in particular the primal scene. Referring to fragments of truth in the children's sex theories Freud noted "the sex battle" that may actually precede the sexual act, and stated, "In many marriages the wife does in fact recoil from her husband's embraces, which bring her no pleasure, but the risk of a fresh pregnancy. And so the child who is believed to be asleep (or who is pretending to be asleep) may receive an impression from his mother which he can only interpret as meaning that she is defending herself against an act of violence. At other times, the whole marriage offers an observant child the spectacle of an unceasing quarrel, expressed in loud words and unfriendly gestures; so that he need not be surprised if the quarrel is carried on at night as well, and finally settled by the same method which he himself is accustomed to use in his relations with his brothers and sisters or playmates. Moreover, if the child discovers spots of blood in his mother's bed or on her underclothes, he regards it as a confirmation of his view. . ." (pp. 221–222). Freud's remarks are crucial to contemporary psychoanalytic reconstruction.

As Anna Freud noted (1967), trauma itself had lost its original and very specific meaning and had come to refer to almost any pathogenic event rather than to those instances in which the ego was overwhelmed. We may be in the same situation with respect to the primal scene and our evaluation of its pathogenic influence. We have to consider whether the primal scene is universally traumatic. As in the case of trauma, it is necessary to apportion pathogenic responsibility correctly to outside and inside forces (A. Freud 1967), and to determine the circumstances under which the primal scene may be pathogenic.

Freud was concerned with what would now be called the phase-specific effects of trauma and problems concerned with trauma at different levels of development. The Wolf Man's terrifying identification with the castrated mother in the primal scene at eighteen months was reconstructed upwards to the oedipal phase. In this explanatory postulate, which was not the only one used by Freud, the activation of the primal scene experience at age four in the Wolf Man's nightmare had the same effect as a phase-specific recent experience (Freud 1918). Freud also raised questions of inherited dispositions in the form of phylogenetic memories and primal fantasies, as well as the opposite question of retrospective falsification of later impressions into early childhood and their sexualization after the event. Freud was nevertheless inconclusive about the role of primal scene fantasy versus reality, i.e., the reality of primal scene exposure. These are still somewhat controversial issues, though we have a much different view of the role of trauma in the complex overdetermination of symptoms and character disorder in contemporary psychoanalysis. Primal scene trauma is usually only one of many traumatic elements in pathogenesis. We must take into account multiple factors and functions, and patterns of strain as well as experiences of shock (and the later change of meaning and function).

Anna Freud's (1951) observations of the telescoping effect of memory and of the preformed coital play of children reared in war nurseries (perhaps akin to Freud's "phylogenetic memories") cast doubt about the reconstruction of a single infantile primal scene shock such as described in the case of the Wolf Man. Trauma may be elaborated in fantasy, and the fantasies themselves may be disguised and acquire new interpretations during the course of development. The primal scene itself may be incorporated into a later screen memory, or may be a screen memory for other traumata, serving a screening or defensive function.

Issues surrounding the primal scene concept at different developmental levels are as controversial as questions concerning the effects of the frequency and intensity of primal scene stimulation. Primal scene fantasy is associated with the oedipal phase, but primal scene exposure may occur in any phase. The effects of the primal scene must be quite different at different levels of development, and quite different when the primal scene is an oedipal fantasy or a phase-specific oedipal trauma. The meaning and effects of the primal scene as a phase specific trauma, or the primal scene experience as an out-of-phase form of overstimulation are still matters of debate.

Besides the pathological consequences of the primal scene, Freud (1925) also commented upon the arousing, stimulating influence of the primal scene on the child's entire sexual development. The developmental role of primal scene fantasy, so often discerned in childhood and adolescent masturbation fantasies, must also be considered in terms of age appropriate influences and the consolidation of sexual identity and object choice. Moreover, could the repeated experience of the primal scene sometimes spur developmental mastery and sublimation in the resourceful child who does not remain overwhelmed?

What is the effect of primal scene exposure under cultural conditions which sanction the child's passive participation as spectator and in which the parental reaction is seemingly without anxiety or guilt? Is it true that primal scene exposure need not be interpreted as sado-masochistic and need not be traumatic as has sometimes been proposed (Esman 1973)? How can such questions be reconciled with the universality of the incest taboo and with the fact that unconscious guilt is unavoidable and is intensified with the active or passive incestuous involvement in primal scene experience?

Would not such guilt and the need for punishment, the violent passions that are inflamed in the child exposed to the primal scene, and the likelihood of preoedipal regression support the child's sado-masochistic interpretation of the primal scene experience? The child's experience of overstimulation and frustration, narcissistic injury and rage would also contribute to and blend with sado-masochistic fantasy, as would his belief that his parents have deceived and betrayed him. If there has been genital exposure, there may be perceptual shock and heightened castration anxiety—reinforcing the fantasy or reality of sexual assault. If primal scene exposure is not regarded as pathogenic, how do we account for the primitive defenses, perceptual and reality disturbances, perverse fixations and repeated acting out associated with primal scene experience in clinical and applied psychoanalysis?

Psychoanalysts will continue to wrestle with these issues and questions.

References

Blum, Ho Po (1979). On the concept did consequences of the primal scene. *Psychoanalytic Quarterly* 48: 27–47.

Edelheit, H. (1971). Mythopoiesis and the primal scene. *Psychoanalytic Study of Society* 5:212–233.

Esman, A. (1973). The primal scene: a review and a reconsideration. *Psychoanalytic Study of the Child* 28:49–81.

Freud, A. (1951). Observations on child development. *Psychoanalytic Study of the Child* 6:18–30.

———— (1967). Comments on psychic trauma. In *Psychic Trauma*, ed. S. S. Furst. New York: Basic Books.

Freud, S. (1908). On the sexual theories of children. *Standard Edition* 9:209–226.

———— (1918). From the history of an infantile neurosis. *Standard Edition* 17:3–122

———— (1925). Some psychical consequences of the anatomical distinction between the sexes. *Standard Edition* 19:248–258.

Chapter 4

THE MISALLIANCE DIMENSION ON
THE CASE OF THE WOLF MAN

ROBERT J. LANGS, M.D.

Freud's Case Report

In writing of the Wolf Man, Freud's primary purpose was to demonstrate the importance of the infantile neurotic factors in subsequent emotional illnesses—the Wolf Man had reported a dream from the age of four which proved to be the key to his symptoms as child and adult. This was an important matter for Freud since his theory of infantile sexuality was being challenged by Adler and Jung. However, in addition to this primary purpose, Freud utilized the material to develop a series of brilliant observations of great diversity, including the first references to the concept of the primal scene, discussions of the important issue as to whether traumatic memories were essentially realities or fantasies, remarks on the development of the ego, a clarification of the libidinal developmental phases, and further observations on obsessional neurotic formations.

For our purposes, the reported case is of interest because of Freud's use of several deviations in technique, one of which would probably be defined today as a parameter—though it could not be analyzed after its actualization—evoked in response to ego pathology in the Wolf Man (Eissler 1953, Freud 1937). Two deviations arose when the Wolf Man had persisted over most of the initial three years of his analysis in remaining deeply entrenched in resistances. At a point where Freud felt that the Wolf Man's attachment to him was quite strong, he set a fixed termination date—the parameter—and also promised to relieve the Wolf Man of his constipation of many years. As Freud describes it, the Wolf Man responded with a plethora of material which permitted the analysis of his infantile neurosis as well as his adult difficulties, and this enabled him to terminate the analysis on a successful note.

While Freud had virtually nothing to say about the Wolf Man's relationship with him, we may extract some pertinent data from his case report. In doing so, the reader finds himself in the midst of a great wealth of material that seems pertinent to the Wolf Man's relationship to Freud, material that has an immediate "feel" for transference and nontransference implications. This impression was also developed by Offenkrantz and Tobin (1973), who suggested that there were problems in Freud's therapeutic alliance with the Wolf Man because Freud had a dual interest in his patient, that of research as well as that of helping him to alleviate his symptoms. They felt the Wolf Man's likely knowledge of Freud's research interest in him had created a narcissistic transference which enabled the patient to continue to function, and that this *narcissistic misalliance*—as I would term it—was later replaced by a similar alliance with Brunswick. These authors also noted the lack of "transference" discussions in Freud's case report and suggested that the wolf dream had as one of its current day residues, the Wolf Man's awareness that Freud was presenting aspects of his case to the small group of followers with whom he met in Vienna.

Freud's discussion of the Wolf Man centers around his childhood dream and its relationship to primal scene experiences and fantasies. Central here was the Wolf Man's feminine identification and wish to copulate with his father, and the castration anxiety that this entailed. Freud noted that the Wolf Man drew a scene from this dream and that he kept this drawing—the first allusion to a "deviation" in technique. In this context, the Wolf Man's first recorded association to the dream related to a follower of Pasteur who had inadvertently killed many sheep on the Wolf Man's grazing lands when he was a child, doing so through innoculations which, instead of being preventative, proved fatal. The Wolf Man's dread and mistrust of Freud are strongly hinted at in this association, and Freud described his awareness that a father transference predominated throughout this analysis, though the suspicious and hostile elements were not developed (Kanzer 1972).

However, in light of what was to follow, one can wonder about the reality precipitants for the Wolf Man's mistrust. Related to this aspect of the "transference"—more correctly, the patient's total relationship with Freud—are the Wolf Man's openly expressed fears that Freud would eat him up, and the patient's need to look at Freud during the first weeks of the analysis, during which he was in a sanatorium. References to coitus *a tergo*—the means of intercourse in the reconstructed primal scene—also lent itself strongly as a representation of the relationship with Freud, who noted that the wolf dream which contained this element was reported in many variations throughout the analysis. This suggests that many current day residues in the relationship between Freud and the Wolf Man prompted the repetitive communication of this particular dream (Langs 1971). In addition to the unconsciously perceptive aspects of these dreams, there were undoubtedly transference elements, including contributions from the Wolf Man's feminine identification and his identification with Christ—he was born on Christmas—particularly in the sense that Christ was permitted by his father to die. Further, in his identification with his mother, the Wolf Man imagined himself with bowel problems and bleeding and had many blatant castration anxieties.

At termination, the Wolf Man recalled that he had been born with a caul, a fact which allowed him the illusion of being a special child of fortune. The associations reported by Freud indicated that the primal scene material now expressed the Wolf Man's fantasied conditions for recovery, namely, that if he submitted as a woman to his father and gave him a child, he would be cured.

From this material, it is possible to suggest that Freud's modified parameter of setting an irrevocable termination date prompted, in part, a sector of misalliance with the Wolf Man in which Freud became the God (father), who promised cure and who brought matters to an end (death), and in which the Wolf Man became the victim, Christ. In addition, as had occurred with the Rat Man (Kanzer 1952), it would appear that the promise of cure and the insistence of a forced termination did, in reality, gratify a whole range of passive feminine fantasies related to the primal scene dream and experience, and its intrapsychic consequences. Thus, we may speculate that the Wolf Man obtained in part a countertransference or misalliance cure (Barchilon 1958, Langs 1975a), or that he responded with alleviation of his symptoms because of a narcissistically gratifying or defiant misalliance with Freud (Offenkrantz and Tobin 1973). In addition, insight and inner change may well have played a role; here, I am attempting to delineate additional facets of the Wolf Man's initial apparent recovery. In this context, the Wolf Man may be seen as having submitted in a feminine manner to Freud and as having produced a child for him—the wolf dream and its analysis—and thereby a cure in part through a misalliance and mutual inappropriate gratification (Kanzer 1972).

The case as reported by Freud does not seem to permit speculation beyond this point. If we now turn to the Wolf Man's memoirs and recollections of Freud, we may offer some additional formulations. In doing so, however, we must proceed with caution; Brunswick (1938) felt that the Wolf Man had distorted

Freud's stance on several important matters—a problem to which I will return later.

The Wolf Man's Memoirs and Recollections

In his memoirs, the Wolf Man described his first experience in Russia with a therapist who was a hypnotist. This physician saw him and treated him in a very special manner, but proved uninterested in him personally and more concerned about having the Wolf Man, who was a teenager at the time, influence his family to give this psychiatrist-neurologist a large contribution of money. As Brunswick (1928) has pointed out, the Wolf Man attempted to provoke poor care from many of the physicians who treated him, but at the same time he was, in reality, often treated badly. These experiences served to generate and to reinforce his intrapsychic mistrust and the unconscious fantasies on which it was based. In the context of this statement, I want to emphasize again that in attempting here to trace out some of the reality factors in the Wolf Man's psychopathology I will of necessity not attempt to counterbalance my discussion with the complementary understanding of the Wolf Man's intrapsychic pathology which was independent of, and which then interacted with, these reality stimuli. As we now know, both the reality stimuli and the intrapsychic set and response must be known in order to fully account for any particular symptom or fantasy; historically, it is the former dimension of the Wolf Man's problems that have been relatively neglected and because of this, it will be my main focus.

It was a Dr. D. from Russia who brought the Wolf Man to Freud; the Wolf Man was so impressed with Freud that he immediately decided that he wanted to be analyzed by him. According to the Wolf Man, he remained in analysis only because Freud agreed to permit him to marry Therese, the woman he loved, although Freud said that this decision had to be analyzed before it could be consummated. The Wolf Man stated further that the analysis was at a standstill until Freud agreed to this marriage, and that he had to delay the marriage because he wanted to finish his analysis with Freud and felt that the latter would not agree to this if he acted prematurely; for him, the actual end of his analysis was tied to Freud's agreeing to the marriage. The Wolf Man indicates that Freud saw Theresa with him before the analysis ended and that he had a positive picture of her. These "deviations" which, as Kanzer (1972) described it, the Wolf Man "forced upon" Freud (it is not uncommon for patients to attempt to evoke deviations from their analysts), added to the dominant-submissive, mutual gift-giving sector of misalliance that I have already formulated as obtaining between Freud and this patient.

In addition, the Wolf Man returned to Freud some five years after he had completed his analysis. At that time, he claimed he felt fine, but Freud told him that more analysis was needed. We learn from Brunswick (1928) and Jones (1955) that the Wolf Man's constipation, which Freud, true to his promise, had cured, had returned; Freud apparently felt that this was due to some unresolved transference fantasies. The additional period of analysis lasted several months and because the Wolf Man was now relatively destitute, Freud agreed (offered?) to treat him without a fee.

In the Wolf Man's recollections of Freud, there are some relevant comments. His apparently valid (Kanzer 1972) image of Freud is that the latter did a considerable amount of educating and explaining. In addition, the Wolf Man was privy to a number of personal comments from Freud, such as a remark related to Freud's son's fracturing a leg and allusions to other patients by name. The Wolf Man pointed out that Freud had commented that friendliness between the patient and analyst may overstep certain boundaries and thereby interfere with analysis, but this patient's description of their relationship suggests that Freud permitted himself a great latitude in extra-analytic contacts and comments with his patients. The Wolf Man felt much like a co-worker with Freud, and based this feeling on Freud's discussions with him of politics, art, and the opponents of analysis; on Freud's direct advice against his becoming a painter; and as we learn later from Brunswick's report (1928), especially on his advice that the Wolf Man not return to Russia in 1919. Because he felt that there was a danger of the patient being stuck in the "transference" with too close a tie to his analyst, Freud requested that each of his patients upon termination give him a gift in order to decrease his feelings of gratitude. Interestingly, the Wolf Man gave Freud a female Egyptian figure which he reports having seen in pictures of Freud's office taken many years later.

The multitude of deviations and extensions of the boundaries of the patient-analyst relationship described by the Wolf Man undoubtedly promoted a seductive atmosphere, a submissive and passive-feminine stance in the Wolf Man, and an unconscious image of Freud as seductive, masculine, and powerful—with reactive instinctual stirrings. With these kernels of reality (Niederland 1959), the Wolf Man's related unconscious responses cannot be considered entirely in terms of transference—i.e., displaced fantasies and projections from the Wolf Man's past; they contained important valid unconscious perceptions and were also in part meaningful adaptive responses to the actual situation with Freud. This myriad of misalliances and transference gratifications went unrecognized, uncorrected, and unanalyzed by Freud; their repercussions and their influence on the Wolf Man's psychopathology and fantasy life went unmodified. The consequences of this became clearer in the analysis with Brunswick (1928) to which I will now turn.

Ruth Mack Brunswick's Report

The Wolf Man was sent by Freud to Brunswick because of the patient's delusion that he was the victim of a nasal injury caused by electrolysis therapy performed by a Professor X. It was apparent to Brunswick (1928) from the outset that the source of the problem was an "unresolved transference" to Freud, and it is this that we will study.

As background, Brunswick (1928) reported that after his brief period of analysis in 1919, which was undertaken without a fee as was her own analytic work with the Wolf Man, Freud collected money from the Wolf Man each spring for six years. The Wolf Man had accepted this in a dishonest manner by concealing the possession of jewels he thought of considerable worth, although they later turned out to be less valuable than expected.

In 1923, after Freud's first minor mouth surgery, the Wolf Man saw Freud and was shocked by his appearance, responding with a period of increased masturbation. A later operation was more serious, which the Wolf Man knew and was disturbed by.

In writing his own case history for Brunswick after her analytic work with him had been completed for the moment (he returned to her sporadically afterwards), the Wolf Man described a series of visits to dentists who differed in their opinions regarding his oral problems and the treatment required; one had pulled the wrong tooth. During his analysis, Freud had referred the Wolf Man to Professor X. for obstructed sebaceous glands, and in the period before his analysis with Brunswick, the Wolf Man went to several dermatologists who offered him divergent opinions as to the nature of his problem and suggested different forms of treatment. It was a diathermy treatment by Professor X., however, that left the Wolf Man scarred and delusionally preoccupied with his nose. Another treatment by Professor X. had led to the flow of blood and the feeling of ecstasy. Brunswick described the connections between the Wolf Man's concern with his nose and identifications with both his mother, who had a wart on her nose, and his dead sister, who was concerned with her pimples. There were other genetic connections which I will not trace out. Of interest to us is a dermatologist the Wolf Man consulted whose office was near Freud's. Thinking the Wolf Man to be a man of means, he charged him his usual fee, and the Wolf Man was elated that he was able to pay him like a gentleman rather than being treated gratis.

During the three years that these delusional symptoms were alternately exacerbating and remitting, one remission occurred after Freud had written to the Wolf Man asking him some additional questions regarding the wolf dream. In addition, this request prompted the Wolf Man to recall several new childhood memories, including an operation performed on stallions and the manner in which a sixth toe was removed from a child after birth. Soon after receiving this letter, the Wolf Man went to a dermatologist who criticized the work of Professor X. and who told him the damage would be permanent. This led to an intense depression; the obsessional-delusional thought that now preoccupied the Wolf Man was a question as to how Professor X., who was one of the most well-known dermatologists in Vienna, could be guilty of such irreparable injury to him. He wondered if this were an accident, negligence, or unconscious intension, and he hated X. as his mortal enemy. From the first, both Brunswick and the Wolf Man knew that this question and the fantasies—and I would add, unconscious perceptions—embedded in it referred indirectly to Freud.

In describing the course of this five-month analysis, Brunswick initially reported that the Wolf Man's deception of Freud, and his refusal to discuss with her either his nose, the dermatologist, or Freud, proved to be early "impregnable" resistances. His first dream, which was not described in detail although many others were, was a version of the wolf dream in which there were grey wolves; they were associated with the grey police dog owned by Freud. That the Wolf Man's delusions related to Freud was unmistakable. The second dream is described more specifically. In it, the Wolf Man is at the prow of a ship carrying a bag containing his wife's jewelry and a mirror. He leans against the rail and breaks the mirror, and realizes that he will have seven years of bad luck. It had been seven years since he had been analyzed by Freud and it was suggested that the broken mirror related to his feelings that his face was damaged. The possible allusions to the Wolf Man's objections to the narcissistic misalliance between himself and Freud, and to the analyst as a mirror, were not considered.

The heart of the analysis centered around Brunswick's exploration of what she considered to be the Wolf Man's grandiosity regarding his personal intimacy with Freud and his deep suspiciousness of Freud's advice that he not return to Russia, which the Wolf Man felt had led to the loss of his fortune. When Brunswick told the Wolf Man that it was impossible for Freud to have made such explicit statements, there was little response. It appears likely, however, that Freud had indeed made comments along these lines, though how explicit they were is an open question. Gardiner (1971), Kanzer (1972), and Offenkrantz and Tobin (1973) have all suggested that there were realistic aspects to the Wolf Man's perceptions of his relationship with Freud; one cannot validly discuss his feelings entirely as transference distortions or delusions.

Getting nowhere in her attempts to devalue the Wolf Man's belief in his special relationship with Freud, Brunswick boldly informed the Wolf Man of the death of Professor X., and this led to the revelation of blatant fantasies of revenge on him with denial regarding their connection to Freud. Brunswick then proceeded to systematically destroy the Wolf Man's belief in his favored position with Freud, using information obtained from Freud and from her own direct observations of Freud and the Wolf Man. Ignoring the many grains of truth on which the Wolf Man founded his impressions, including his idea that Freud and Brunswick had discussed him (this was true, although apparently not to the extent that he believed), Brunswick repeatedly denied his contentions. She soon provoked dreams in which she appeared indirectly in a masculine and powerful role, and in a devalued manner. The Wolf Man made threats to kill both Brunswick and Freud. Then, for reasons that were unclear to Brunswick, except for the fact that she felt that she had destroyed his Christ fantasy, positive dreams began to appear and the Wolf Man's delusion was eventually resolved. In this context, a dream of a doctor forcing things onto the Wolf Man appeared, and eventually he felt that he could forgo the gifts from Freud because they were not worth the passivity involved. In his final dream of the analysis, the patient is walking with the second dermatologist who treated him; the physician is speaking of venereal disease. The Wolf Man mentions the doctor who had overtreated his gonorrhea and the dermatologist says it was not he but another. To the very end, despite his symptomatic resolution, the Wolf Man was mistrustful and critical of physicians. While Brunswick notes that Professor X. played right into the Wolf Man's fantasies—reinforced them in reality—and that the gifts from Freud represented sexual satisfaction from the Wolf Man's father, the influence of these realities on the Wolf Man were not traced out.

In considering the sectors of misalliance that developed between Freud and the Wolf Man, the cumulative material from many sources suggests that each of the "deviations" in technique, however benignly motivated, fostered and enhanced a series of pathogenic unconscious fantasies and identifications that interfered with a lasting inner resolution of the Wolf Man's psychopathology. These noninterpretive measures may well be the unconscious but realistic basis for the Wolf Man's belief that Freud had treated him wrongly and had left him crippled—castrated—for life. These kernels of reality were undoubtedly subsequently distorted and elaborated by the Wolf Man on the basis of his inner pathology and fantasies, but their full analytic resolution would have required a recognition of their veridical aspects. By pressuring the Wolf Man into a passive feminine position which intensified his castration anxieties and undoubtedly his fears of annihilation (note the dream of the broken mirror), Freud aggravated the Wolf Man's anxieties and conflicts in this area and thereby inadvertently contributed to the delusional symptomatology.

While that symptomatology has been previously clearly related to Freud, heretofore it has not been especially noted that there were valid elements to these beliefs, that they were the basis for a pathogenic sector of misalliance between Freud and the Wolf Man and that they were fostered by the former's extraneous interventions. The clearest prior statement along these lines was made by Flarsheim (1972) who briefly suggested that the Wolf Man's paranoid residual transference reactions to Freud stemmed in part from the latter's forced termination of the analysis. Flarsheim relates this consequence to the generally adverse reactions in patients to any forcible technical device used to control them. More generally, Greenacre (1959) has noted that deviations in technique tend to undermine the patient's autonomies and thereby foster narcissistic and other pathological misalliances. The material from the Wolf Man clearly supports her thesis. In addition, this material supports the observations that I have made elsewhere regarding the relationship between deviations in technique, sectors of misalliance, and difficult to analyze regressive episodes in patients (Langs 1973a, 1975, 1976).

While fraught with problems, it seems of value to make a tentative effort to formulate the basis for the development and resolution of the Wolf Man's delusional symptoms. To do this, it will prove helpful to recall that in order to fully comprehend the intensification of a patient's pathological unconscious fantasies, anxieties, and disturbances in ego functioning, we must have an in-depth appreciation for the nature of the stimuli and trauma with which he is dealing (the adaptive context; Langs 1972, 1973a). In addition, we must have a full picture of the intrapsychic conflicts that these precipitants have stirred up within the patient and his available adaptive resources and shortcomings—in brief, his intrapsychic responses and their contribution to his behavioral and fantasied reactions. However, the intrapsychic components are not fully intelligible without a full recognition of the interactional aspects (Langs 1973b, 1976). A similar model of the importance of the adaptive aspects of unconscious fantasies (and transference) was implicit in Freud's comprehension of the relationship between day residues and dreams (Freud 1900, Langs 1971).

Certain stimuli are inherently traumatic, and among these, deviations and errors in technique are especially important for patients in analysis (Langs 1973a, 1975a, 1975b, 1976). Such deviations generally entail pathological gratifications, the sharing of defenses, overstimulation, and inappropriate sanctions—in addition to any positive features they may have. They evoke, as we have seen in each of these case studies, a mixture of gratification and fear, and lead to acting out and other regressive responses. The deviant behavior fosters an image of—and an unconscious identification with—the analyst as a seductive, aggressive, and otherwise poor therapist, all elaborated intrapsychically within the patient according to his own personality, pathology, conflicts, and conscious and unconscious fantasies and memories. In all, in order to identify the transference and primarily intrapsychic elements in these reactions, we must first be able to delineate precisely the nontransference or reality aspects.

This situation is further aggravated by the analyst's unawareness of the countertransference aspects of his deviation when this is present, and his failure to recognize the relationship between the patient's pathological reactions and fantasies and his noninterpretive interventions. As a result, he is unable to correctly interpret the patient's unconscious fantasies and perceptions; he has missed his role in evoking them. Thus, he also cannot provide the patient the cognitive mastery verbalized insight might afford him. In all, both his basic "hold" (Winnicott 1958)—as expressed in effecting a secure frame and implicitly offering himself as a model of someone ("an object") who can properly manage the analytic situation and therefore his own inner state—and his ability to offer correct interpretations are impaired. Many regressive episodes and stalemates in analysis stem from such unrecognized sources.

We can speculate that a stalemate created in part by factors such as these may have existed between Freud and the Wolf Man. This was based initially on a variety of "deviations" and variations in technique—including direct advice, seeing the Wolf Man's fiancée, and discussing personal matters in Freud's life. The later forced termination, gifts, and the free analytic sessions may then have contributed to the fixity of the sectors of misalliance, and to the intensely negative perceptions of Freud as a malicious and destructive physician who had wronged him. They also fostered unresolved ambivalent fantasies and attitudes toward Freud that reflected the patient's own inner pathology as well. With the occurrence of Freud's illness and the threat of his loss, the Wolf Man's unmastered conflicts, anxieties, perceptions, and guilt seem to have intensified, as did his longings for fusion and his murderous hatred. The delusional symptom that developed at this time expressed many dimensions of the unresolved transference and in addition, of the sectors of misalliance—the mutually fostered sense of merger and identification, the belief and extension into fantasies that he (the Wolf Man) had been damaged, the revenge on Freud turned against himself, the Wolf Man's actual need for further treatment, and the exhibitionistic-voyeuristic, sado-masochistic dimensions of the misalliance. Through the symptom, the actual contributions of Freud—nontransference and reality—are represented in disguised form, as well as their intrapsychic elaborations and other fantasied contributions from within the Wolf Man. Because of the Wolf Man's own propensities and due to the nature of the "deviations," this patient's symptom highlights the actual damage done to patients by unneeded modifications in the frame—an aspect evident also in my studies of Dora and the Rat Man. Elsewhere, I first termed such symptoms in patients *iatrogenic syndromes* (Langs 1974)—here, iatrogenic paranoia—and more recently (Langs 1976), *interactional neuroses or psychoses*. These designations are meant to stress the contributions from the analyst to the patient's symptoms, and, from the technical viewpoint, the need for rectification of such contributions in addition to the analysis of their repercussions for the patient.

Brunswick was an extension of Freud for the Wolf Man and undoubtedly represented another of his gifts—Freud had sent him to her and he was again seen without a fee. The transference and nontransference responses evoked by these realities were not analyzed in her work with the Wolf Man, but instead her efforts were designed to destroy the Wolf Man's pathological misalliance with Freud (represented as his Christ fantasy), and in all likelihood, this was replaced with a more benign, less anxiety-provoking misalliance with herself (Offenkrantz and Tobin 1973). Freud may have intuitively aided in this resolution by not continuing to work with the Wolf Man and by sending him to a woman analyst. The final dream of his analysis with Brunswick seems to express this more benign but continued misalliance: the Wolf Man is walking with the second, less damaging doctor, and another is blamed for his poor work, while there is a mysterious allusion to a third doctor. In a sense, the Wolf Man perpetuated this misalliance and the impaired autonomy that it entailed in the many years that followed.

Concluding Comments

Freud's parameters with the Wolf Man have previously been alluded to many times as a model deviation in technique (Eissler 1953), although as Stone (1961) noted, the forced termination did not meet all of the essential criteria defined by Eissler because there was no opportunity to resolve its effects through subsequent analytic work. Both Gardiner (1971) and Brunswick (1928) noted that this termination left the Wolf Man with unanalyzed and pathogenic feelings and fantasies toward Freud. The recognition of such adverse sequellae to parameters and deviations suggests the need to reconsider their indications and clinical applications (Langs 1974b, 1976).

Our observations lend support to the formulation that the manner in which the analyst creates and maintains the analytic setting and relationship is continuously and unconsciously monitored by the patient. These ground rules and boundaries reflect crucial aspects of the analyst's identity and functioning, and deeply influence the patient's sense of security and trust, the important ongoing identificatory aspects of his relationship with the analyst, and the nature of the patient's intrapsychic fantasies, unconscious perceptions and projections. We may tentatively suggest again that the present basic ground rules of analysis as defined earlier (see Langs 1973a, 1975b) offer an optimal therapeutic hold, a maximal chance for an interaction designed for the inner benefit of the analysand, and the ideal setting within which his intrapsychic fantasies, pathology and transference expressions may be safely expressed, analytically resolved and worked through.

I will conclude with a quote from Freud which describes the spirit in which this series of papers have been written and alludes to the hopes for future studies that it may stimulate:

> As a rule, however, theoretical controversy is unfruitful. No sooner has one begun to depart from the material on which one ought to be relying, then one runs the risk of becoming intoxicated with one's own assertions and, in the end, of supporting opinions which any observation would have contradicted. For that reason it seems to me to be incomparably more useful to come back to dissentient interpretations by testing them upon particular cases and problems. [Freud 1918, p. 48]

References

Barchilon, José (1959). On countertransference "cures." *Journal of the American Psychoanalytic Association* 6:222–236.

Brunswick, Ruth Mack (1928). A supplement to Freud's "History of an infantile neurosis." In *The Wolf-Man by the Wolf-Man*, ed. M. Gardiner. New York: Basic Books.

Eissler, K. R. (1953). The effect of the structure of the ego on psychoanalytic technique. *Journal of the American Psychoanalytic Association* 1:104–143.

Flarsheim, A. (1972). Treatability. In *Tactics and Techniques in Psychoanalytic Therapy*, ed. P. Giovacchini, New York: Jason Aronson.

Freud, S. (1900). The interpretation of dreams. *Standard Edition* 4/5.

——— (1918). From the history of an infantile neurosis. *Standard Edition* 17:3–122.

——— (1937). Analysis terminable and interminable. *Standard Edition* 23:211–253.

Gardiner, M. (1971). The Wolf-Man in later life. In *The Wolf-Man by the Wolf-Man*, ed. M. Gardiner. New York: Basic Books.

Greenacre, P. (1959). Certain technical problems in transference relations. *Journal of the American Psychoanalytic Association* 7:484–502.

Jones, E. (1955). *The Life and Work of Sigmound Freud*. Vol. 2. New York: Basic Books.

Kanzer, M. (1952). The transference neurosis of the Rat Man. *Psychoanalytic Quarterly* 2:181–189.

——— (1972). Book Review of *The Wolf-Man by the Wolf-Man*. *International Journal of Psycho-Analysis* 53:419–421.

Langs, R. (1971). Day residues, recall residues, and dreams: reality and the psyche. *Journal of the American Psychoanalytic Association* 19:499–523.

——— (1972). A psychoanalytic study of material from patients in psychotherapy. *International Journal of Psychoanalytic Psychotherapy* 1:4-45.

—————— (1973a). *The Technique of Psychoanalytic Psychotherapy*. Vol. I. New York: Jason Aronson.

—————— (1973b). The patient's view of the therapist: reality or fantasy. *International Journal of Psychoanalytic Psychotherapy* 2:411–431.

—————— (1974). *The Technique of Psychoanalytic Psychotherapy*. Vol. II. New York: Jason Aronson.

—————— (1975a). Therapeutic misalliances. *International Journal of Psychoanalytic Psychotherapy* 4:77–105.

—————— (1975b). The therapeutic relationship and deviations in technique. *International Journal of Psychoanalytic Psychotherapy* 4:106–141.

—————— (1976). *The Bipersonal Field*. New York: Jason Aronson.

OOffenkrantz, W., and Tobin, A. (1973). Problems of the therapeutic alliance: Freud and the Wolf-Man. *International Journal of Psycho-Analysis* 54:75–78.

Stone, L. (1961). *The Psychoanalytic Situation*. New York: International Universities Press

Winnicott, D. W. (1958). *Collected Papers*. London: Tavistock Publications.

The Wolf-Man (1971). My recollections of Sigmund Freud. In *The Wolf-Man by the Wolf-Man*, ed. M. Gardiner, pp. 135–152. New York: Basic Books.

Chapter 5

LERMONTOV AND THE WOLF MAN

EUGENE HALPERT, M.D.

It is the purpose of this paper to examine the Wolf Man's identification with the poet and writer Mikhail Yurievich Lermontov. This examination offers evidence of a specific global identification of the Wolf Man's and hopefully sheds further light on the workings of the Wolf Man's mind while at the same time permitting some comments on Lermontov.

Any attempt at further exploration of the Wolf Man's case has certain inherent difficulties. Anna Freud (1971) warned about the temptation bred by familiarity with the case "to test the interpretations given, to probe beyond the conclusions drawn" (Gardiner 1971, p.x). Blum (1974) also comments on these difficulties and speaks of each analyst's feelings for Freud and his case histories which plays some role in any analyst's writing about them. Despite these difficulties it is possible, particularly with the new fund of information made available with the publication of *The Wolf-Man by the Wolf-Man* (1971) to validly explore and enrich our understanding of this most important case. Indeed, as implied by Blum (1974), all the advances made since the publication of the case in 1918—the advent of structural theory, the advent of child analysis and child observation and the various advances in ego psychology—demand such reevaluations.

In this vein Blum reexamined Freud's difficult and complex case in order "to demonstrate the Wolf Man's childhood disturbance as a severe borderline disturbance which was the foundation for a borderline adolescence" (p. 723) and adulthood. In attempting to demonstrate the severity of the Wolf Man's ego

defects, Blum speaks of the Wolf Man's "regressive tendency to global identifications, which may involve merger with the object" (p. 727).

Before proceeding, it behooves us to remember that Freud wrote this case
history with a specific purpose in mind and in adhering to his purpose stated
that he would restrict himself to the presentation of the infantile neurosis. His
primary purpose in publishing the case when he did was to answer the criticisms
of both Jung and Adler who, each in his own way, denied the existence of
infantile sexuality. Freud stated:

> What is in dispute, therefore, is the significance of the infantile factor. The
> problem is to find a case which can establish that significance beyond any
> doubt. Such, however, is the case which is being dealt with so exhaustively
> in these pages, and which is distinguished by the characteristic that the neurosis
> in later life was preceded by a neurosis in early childhood. It is for that very
> reason indeed that I have chosen to report on it. [1918, p. 54]

And in this task Freud succeeded. The material of the case, the wolf dream, the
associations, fantasies, and transferences presented all contributed to the chain
of analytic evidence that illustrated the existence of infantile sexuality in this
patient, and the form and content of it's successive phases. The evidence also
illustrated the role played by these sexual factors in the development of neurotic
structures such as phobias and obsessions in this patient's childhood and adulthood.

That the Wolf Man suffered from something more severe than a neurosis, that
he had certain ego defects more indicative of what today we would call a
borderline or psychotic illness, is a thought that seriously troubled Freud. Though
he didn't use the term in his case history, Freud obviously wondered whether
the Wolf Man might have been suffering from what Freud would have called
a *narcissistic neurosis* (psychosis). He wrote:

> When the news of his sister's death arrived, so the patient told me, he felt
> hardly a trace of grief. He had to force himself to show signs of sorrow and
> was able quite cooly to rejoice at having now become the sole heir to the
> property. He had already been suffering from his recent illness for several
> years when this occurred. But I must confess that this one piece of information
> made me *for a long time* uncertain in my diagnostic judgment of this case.
> It was to be assumed, no doubt, that his grief over the loss of the most loved
> member of his family would meet with an inhibition in its expression, as a
> result the continued operation of his jealousy of her and of the added presence
> of his incestuous love for her which had now become unconscious. But I

could not do without some substitute for the missing outbursts of grief. [1918, p. 23]

Freud was alarmed about the Wolf Man's diagnosis and therefore about his analyzability because of the apparent defect in the Wolf Man's ability to cathect an object. This apparent defect weighed more heavily on Freud than all the other pathology which was obvious from the time of the first consultation. To appreciate the significance of this we must remember that at the time of the first consultation Freud was confronted with a twenty-three-year-old man from another country and culture who had never worked and had no profession, who had nothing to hold him in Vienna, who was immensely wealthy, whose father had been repeatedly hospitalized and diagnosed as a manic depressive by none other than Kraepelin, whose family was riddled with mental illness and who himself had been mentally incapacitated for several years to the degree that he had to be dressed and was given enemas regularly by an attendant, and who (in Jones's words) "initiated the first hour of treatment with the offer to have rectal intercourse with Freud and then to defecate on his head" (p. 274). I wonder who reading this would recommend analysis as the treatment of choice to such a patient. And yet both the patient and psychoanalysis profited from Freud's recommendation.

Returning to the question of the diagnosis and Freud's misgivings about it, they were resolved in the following manner:

A few months after his sister's death he made a journey in the neighborhood in which she had died. There he sought out the burial-place of a great poet, who was at that time his ideal and shed bitter tears upon his grave. This reaction seemed strange to him himself, for he knew that more than two generations had passed since the death of the poet he admired. He only understood it when he remembered that his father had been in the habit of comparing his dead sister's works with the great poet's. He gave me another indication of the correct way of interpreting the homage which he ostensibly paid to the poet by a mistake in his story which I was able to detect at this point. He had repeatedly specified before that his sister had shot herself; but he now was obliged to make a correction and say that she had taken poison. The poet, however, had been shot in a duel. [1918, p. 23]

I have quoted Freud at such length on this matter not only to illustrate Freud's own diagnostic doubts about the Wolf Man and how these doubts were resolved, but also because what Freud reported presents the opportunity to study the Wolf Man's relationship to the poet whose grave he visited. Not only was his sister identified with this poet, but the poet was also the Wolf Man's ideal, an ideal with whom he was intensely identified. The study of this identification will reveal the Wolf Man's tendency to fuse with an object, confirming much of what Blum (1974) has written as well as confirming some of Freud's dynamic formulations. It also will offer some insight into what some of the Wolf Man's ego strengths may have been, ego strengths that may have contributed to Freud's initial positive appraisal of his analyzability.

Until the publication of the Wolf Man's memoirs (1971) the identity of the poet at whose grave he wept, an event so crucial to Freud in reassuring him that his patient was not psychotic, was unknown. As we now know the poet referred to is Lermontov. In the section of his memoirs entitled "Recollections from My Childhood," the Wolf Man wrote, "Professor Freud, in my case history, has dealt with Herr Riedel's influence on my attitude to religion, and also with my identification with Lermontov" (p. 21). In a lengthy footnote to this sentence Muriel Gardiner wrote:

On May 5, 1970 after the Wolf Man had completed this chapter of his Memoirs, he wrote me that he had something else that he wanted to tell me, ". . . . In 1906 when I was studying at the St. Petersburg U., I went to a student party . . . . I have never thought that I had any physical resemblance to Lermontov—perhaps a little about the eyes. Now a student I didn't know at all looked at me attentively and said to another student: Look at our colleague. What an extraordinary unbelievable resemblance he has to Lermontov! Astonishing that there can be such a similarity, the same face, these eyes . . . . As there really was no such resemblance, it seems that this student had somehow, in some mysterious way, divined my identification with Lermontov. [1971, p. 21]

How much of this incident is memory and how much is distorted by wishful thinking is of course impossible to say. The important thing, I think, is that after sixty-four years the identification with Lermontov was still so important to him that he remembers proudly at the age of eighty-three how once when he was nineteen someone mistook him for Lermontov. The intensity and totality of this identification is indicated not only by the cherishing of the memory, but by the belief that he was so infused by Lermontov that someone could *see* it by looking at his eyes. There are other indications of this identification scattered through the writings about and by the Wolf Man. We have direct evidence from Freud's case history that the Wolf Man was well acquainted with Lermontov's writings in childhood. In writing about another dream of the Wolf Man's Freud said:

In this earlier dream he saw the Devil dressed in black and in the upright posture with which the wolf and the lion had terrified him so in their day . . . . The patient had soon guessed that this Devil was the Demon out of a well known poem, and that the dream itself was a version of a very popular picture representing the Demon in a love scene with a girl. [1918, p. 69]

The poem referred to must have been Lermontov's "The Demon." Not only do the titles match but according to critics such as Mirsky (1966), "In the second half of the nineteenth century it was probably the most universally popular poem in Russia" (p. 135). The chances for the Wolf Man's thorough familiarity with "The Demon" are enhanced even further by the fact that it became the libretto for a Russian opera by Anton Rubinstein. This opera was first performed in Petersburg in 1875 so that the cultured and widely read Wolf Man certainly had the opportunity to know the poem not only by reading but by seeing it performed in operatic form. Indeed the Wolf Man's uncle Basil was at one time married to a woman who was a prominent Russian opera singer. In addition the content of the poem resonates with the inner struggles of the explosive, passionate young Wolf Man. It tells of the devil falling in love with a beautiful, virginal girl and then destroying her by seducing her because of his jealous rage over her relationship with her guardian angel. Lermontov struggled over this poem indicating both the importance and the conflictual nature of the content for him; rewriting it eight times over a period of eleven years. Even after his last version of "The Demon" was written, he continued the theme, writing a satire on the poem called "A Fairy Tale for Children" (1839). In it a devil stands looking at the sleeping form of a girl. Of the devil Lermontov wrote:

I haven't always seen in just this form
The Enemy of pure and holy feelings.
My youthful mind was often preyed upon
By a mighty image. . . . [Lermontov 1839, p. 72]

Here indeed was plenty with which the wild passionate child, given to tantrums, could identify. The Wolf Man, too, as a youngster, tried to combat and exorcise the enemy of his pure and holy feelings; the sexual demons which beset him, via his numerous religious obsessions.

But the reasons for the identification with Lermontov are many, and here a brief resume of the artist and his work is necessary. Though most Western readers are relatively unfamiliar with him, he was and evidently remains, one of the most popular poets and authors within Russia. Though primarily a poet, he also wrote plays and is perhaps best known for his novel *A Hero of Our*

Times which is considered a masterpiece by many and is also considered by many as the beginning of the Russian tradition of the psychological realism in the novel. Mersereau (1962) quotes Tolstoy as saying that "Taman," one of the stories forming *A Hero . . .* was "artistically the most perfect work in Russian literature" (p. x). The hero of the title, Captain Pechorin, is an officer in the Caucasus who uses people, particularly women, to suit his narcissistic needs. But the hero is also curious about himself, introspective, verbal and capable of making valid self-observations as in a passage in which he wonders why he is trying to make a woman fall in love with him. At one point he says:

> I look upon the sufferings and joys of others only in relation to myself as on the food sustaining the strength of my soul. I am no longer capable myself of frenzy under the influence of passion, ambition with me has been suppressed by circumstances, but it has manifested itself in another form, since ambition is nothing else than the thirst for power, and my main pleasure—which is to subjugate to my will all that surrounds me, and to excite the emotions of love, devotion, and fear in relation to me—is it not the main sign and greatest triumph of power? [1958, p. 123]

It is not the narcissism that I wish to call attention to here but the verbal ability, the introspectiveness and insight—qualities that the Wolf Man must have sought and which he may well have manifested to some degree even in the midst of his illness, when Freud first saw him. If so, this would then help explain Freud's recommendation for analysis.

To move from Lermontov's work to his life is practically not to move at all, for not only is his writing clearly autobiographical but his life sounds so like a wildly improbable romantic piece of fiction as to have been dreamed up by a Hollywood press agent or a romantic Russian poet. Born in October of 1814, the only child of an extremely wealthy heiress and a not so wealthy retired army officer, he was killed, or more correctly, arranged for himself to be killed in a duel, twenty-six years and ten months later in July, 1841. His mother died before he was three, and his wealthy and socially superior maternal grandmother won a protracted battle with his father for his custody. A somewhat sickly childhood included trips to the Caucasus. At the age of eleven he began writing poetry. Eventually, at age twenty, through his grandmother's influence he entered the Czar's Hussars where he got into difficulties with all kinds of pranks including writing pornographic poetry. In the rigid autocratic atmosphere of the times, this was not only immature but dangerous. Then in 1837, when he was twenty-three, Pushkin, one of his literary idols, was shot in a duel. Lermontov felt Pushkin had been provoked into this duel by those around the Czar, and he wrote an elegy to Pushkin which made that accusation. This poem earned him not only his first great literary recogntion, but the emnity of the Czar. Then, as now, writers and intellectuals in Russia who dissented were not treated too kindly. Then, as now, the writings were circulated in handwritten copies around the capital. Lermontov was arrested and held incommunicado. Finally he was sent to the front in the Caucasus. At that time the Caucasus were roughtly the equivalent of our Wild West at the time of the Indian wars. There he distinguished himself with brilliantly brave suicidal abandon in hand-to-hand front line combat. Returning to Petersburg after a few months he again got into difficulty by provoking a pistol duel with the son of the French ambassador. When his opponent missed, Lermontov fired into the air. This duel caused the Czar to send him back to the front. It was while on his way to the front, at Piatygorsk, that he provoked the duel that ended his life. That he wished and foresaw this is evidenced by these lines from a poem entitled "A Dream" (1841) written a few months before his death:

> The heat of noon, a gorge in Daghestan—
> I lay there with a bullet in my chest.
> My deep wound was still streaming, and my blood
> Oozed, drop by drop by drop, over my chest. [Deutsch 1966, p. 69]

The points upon which the Wolf Man's identification with Lermontov are based are numerous. Both came from extremely wealthy, landed Russian families, were raised in privilege, surrounded by servants, private tutors and vast estates. Both were only sons, Lermontov had no siblings and the Wolf Man of course had his own older sister. Both had numerous sexual encounters with prostitutes and servant girls. Lermontov became a soldier and an officer who fought heroically in combat and the Wolf Man's latency and prepubertal daydreams were full of martial themes. Freud (1918) wrote that in sublimating his sadism, the Wolf Man at age ten "developed an enthusiasm for military affairs, for uniforms, weapons and horses, and used them as food for continual daydreams" (p. 69). Lermontov's poems and stories are often laid in a military setting with an officer as the main character. Thus Lermontov's works and his life provided just the right diet to fuel the military daydreams of the prepubertal Wolf Man.

To continue with the bases for the Wolf Man's identification with Lermontov, the latter was a creative artist and the former aspired to be one. Lermontov observed himself and others and brooded introspectively in his works on his narcissism and sexual difficulties. Certain other specific unconscious fantasies which appear in derivative form in the life and work of Lermontov were shared by the Wolf Man. For example, the poet's provocation of the Czar and of his opponents into duels, the image of being shot in a duel which recurs in Lermontov's works served to vicariously satisfy the Wolf Man's unconscious fantasies described by Freud (1918) of being penetrated anally by his father.

It is the massive global nature of the identification to which all of the above factors contributed, that supports Blum's (1974) contention of the severity of the Wolf Man's ego defects and his "regressive tendency to global identifications with the object" (p. 727). I believe that this fusion is illustrated not only in the Wolf Man's belief that someone could divine his identification with Lermontov by looking in his eyes but also in the way he chose his wife.

In a chapter entitled "Castles In Spain," the Wolf Man (1971) recounts his meeting and falling in love with his wife Therese. The year was 1908 and he had gone to a sanatorium recommended by Kraepelin:

> It was carnival time, and on the evening of the day I moved into the sanatorium a fancy dress ball for the staff and nurses was to take place. Dr. H and I were also invited to this ball. Watching the dancers I was immediately struck by an extraordinary beautiful woman. She was perhaps in her middle or late twenties and thus a little older than myself . . . . Her blue black hair was parted in the middle, and her features were of such regularity and delicacy that they might have been chiseled by a sculptor. She was dressed as a Turkish woman, and as she was a definitely southern type, with somewhat oriental characteristics, this costume suited her very well and could hardly have been better chosen . . . . I was so fascinated by this woman that I kept wondering how this apparition from the Arabian Nights could ever have become one of the people employed in a Bavarian sanatorium. During the next days I could not help thinking again and again of the exotic appearance of this enigmatic woman. [1971, p. 49]

He goes on to relate how he learns that this woman, who would become his wife, had a mother of Spanish birth. "The information that Therese's mother was Spanish interested me particularly since it gave me the clue to her noticeably Mediterranean features" (p. 50). Later on the Wolf Man writes:

> Therese told me now about her Spanish origin. It was a romantic story. Her father was German. Her maternal grandmother, a Spanish woman, was married the first time to a Spanish officer who was said to have been killed in a duel. [1971, p. 54]

And a page later he wrote, "The knowledge of Therese's Spanish background caused me to transpose her in my mind not only to that faraway country but also into a long bygone era, in which she seemed to fit better than in the present'' (p. 55).

The Wolf Man explains his fascination with the fact that Therese was of supposedly Spanish origin in several ways. First he recalls that in his analysis with Freud the Spanish theme was traced to his opera singer aunt, who though she was Polish, had toured and sung in Spain and who, when he was seven, told him tales of Spain during a visit. Also at the same age he saw this aunt sing the part of Rosina in the "Barber of Seville." Freud, he tells us, interpreted the aunt as a displaced mother figure and the Spanish interest as an oedipal one.

The Wolf Man himself adds that he felt that he identified Therese with someone in an artistic production; with the woman in Leonardo da Vinci's painting "La Belle Ferronnierre" who also parted her hair in the middle. He says:

> I saw a great resemblance between this portrait and Therese and it was this resemblance which permitted me to associate my love for Therese with my tendency toward artistic sublimation. [1971, p. 56]

I am suggesting that there was another association to an artistic work, this time a literary work, *A Hero of Our Time*, that contributed to and helped to determine the Wolf Man's immediate attraction to Therese. I would call attention to the facts that he first sees her at a gala occasion, that she is dressed in a Turkish costume, he is intrigued by her oriental looks and feels she is an apparition from the Arabian Nights. His excitement is heightened by stories of a Spanish background, including a Spanish officer who is killed in a duel. He feels she belongs to a faraway country and a bygone era.

Compare the above to the first story in Lermontov's *A Hero of Our Time,* "Bela," in which the hero, Captain Pechorin, falls in love with the young Circassian princess, Bela. This comes about when Pechorin is invited to a gala event, a Circassian wedding, where there is a good deal of dancing, singing and drinking. There he sees Bela, the younger sister of the bride, for the first time. Lermontov describes her and her tribe as an oriental people, Tartars. "With these Asiatics, you know, it is the custom to invite one and all to their weddings'' (p. 12). The *World Book Encyclopedia* notes that the:

> Circassians are the tallest, and the darkest of the peoples of Caucasia. . . . The Circassians have always been noted for the fierceness of their warriors and the beauty of their women. . . . Circassian women were once sold into Turkish and Persian harems by their fathers. Upper class Circassians are Moslems. [p. 433]

Lermontov wrote further:

And indeed, she was beautiful: tall, slender, with black eyes which resembled those of a mountain gazelle and practically peered into your soul. Lost in thought, Pechorin did not take his eyes off her, and quite often she would steal a glance at him from under her brows. [1958, p. 13]

Given the fact that he met Therese at the hospital a scant two years after he describes feeling so infused with Lermontov that the identification could be seen in his eyes, it is not difficult to picture the Wolf Man identifying with Pechorin and through him with Lermontov as he stood gazing at the beautiful dark haired woman in the Turkish (Circassian) costume and felt that she had stepped out of some oriental tale. This attraction to oriental maidens recurs in *A Hero of Our Time*.

The Wolf Man cherished the belief in his wife's Spanish background and the romantic stories surrounding it and was stunned to learn some years after her death, when he visited her brother in 1939, that this was his wife's fantasy. He was so troubled by this bit of news, which had so meshed with his own fantasies, that it seems likely that when he wrote to Wurzburg in 1947 for records of her birth, ostensibly because he needed them to obtain his Austrian citizenship, he was still unconsciously trying to determine her origins. As he himself notes this was nine years after her suicide. This underlines for us the importance of her fantasy for his own, in—I suggest—maintaining his identification with Lermontov.

One reason behind the maintenance of the Wolf Man's extensive identification with Lermontov was the necessity of warding off the more regressive identification and fusion with the primary object, his hypochondrical mother. We know from Brunswick (1928) that during his paranoid psychotic break, the Wolf Man established a regressive fusion with his mother. Various authors, including Greenson (1954), Jacobson (1954), and Slap (1959), have written about the struggle of certain patients, usually though not invariably borderline or psychotic, against fusion with the threatening, hated primary object. One mechanism available to the ego in such a defensive struggle is identification with another more suitable object. For the Wolf Man Lermontov was such a figure. Lermontov was an active man; a poet, a novelist, a soldier, a hero, but above all he was a man and thus provided an identificatory shield against the regressive fusion with his hypochondrical mother.

Perhaps one last observation may be made in regard to the meaning of the Wolf Man's crying at Lermontov's grave. Freud felt that this confirmed the Wolf Man's capacity to experience and feel for an object (his sister) other than himself. But is this all there was to those tears? Was it his sister he was crying for, or himself as his sister as Lermontov (one reason for his identification with Lermontov not mentioned thusfar was his wish to be his sister so as to find favor with his father), or himself as Lermontov. Here his reaction to his wife's suicide is pertinent and revealing. Gardiner writes:

> Now, this bright April day in 1938, as I sat down in my living-room and he, unable to restrain himself, moved restlessly about, I tried to make out the words coming through his sobs and tears. At last I understood them: "My wife has killed herself. I've just come from the cemetery. Why did she do it? Why did this have to happen to me? I always have bad luck, I'm always subject to the greatest misfortunes. [1971, p. 312]

This is not a man weeping for the loss of a loved object, but a man weeping for himself. He is the injured party. He bemoans *his* bad luck, *his* misfortune. His concern is: Why did this have to happen to *me*? The concern is narcissistic. Could it have been otherwise at Lermontov's grave?

Summary

The Wolf Man's identification with the poet Mikhail Lermontov is traced in some detail and used to illustrate the regressive, all encompassing nature of the Wolf Man's identifications and the severity and nature of his pathology as well as the restitutive stabilizing function this particular identification served. Some comments on the life and works of Lermontov are also made.

References

Blum, H.P. (1974). The borderline childhood of the Wolf Man. *Journal of the American Psychoanalytic Association,* 22:721–742.

Freud, A. (1971). Foreward. In *The Wolf Man by the Wolf Man,* ed. M. Gardiner. New York: Basic Books.

Freud, S. (1918) From the history of an infantile neurosis. *Standard Edition* 17:1–122.

Gardiner, M. (1971). *The Wolf-Man by the Wolf-Man.* New York: Basic Books, Inc.

Greenson, R.R. (1954). The struggle against identification. *Journal of the American Psychoanalytic Association* 2:200–217

Jacobson, E. (1954). Contribution to the metapsychology of projective identification. *Journal of the American Psychoanalytic Association* 5:61–92.

Jones, E. (1955). *The Life and Work of Sigmund Freud.* Vol. II. New York: Basic Books.

Lermontov, M. (1839). A fairy-tale for children. Trans. by G. Daniels, *A Lermontov Reader*. New York: Macmillan

———— (1840): *A Hero of Our Time*. Trans. by V. Nobokov, and D. Nobokov, New York: Doubleday

———— (1841): A dream. Trans. by B. Deutsch. *Two Centuries of Russian Verse*, ed. A. Yarmolinsky. New York: Random House, 1966.

Brunswick, R. M. (1928). A supplement to Freud's "History of an infantile neurosis." In *The Wolf Man by the Wolf Man*, ed. M. Gardiner, New York: Basic Books

Merereau, J. (1962): *Mikhail Lermontov*. Carbondale: Southern Illinois University Press.

Mirsky, D. (1966). *A History of Russian Literature*, New York: Alfred A. Knopf.

Slap, W.S. (1959): Identification in the service of denial. *Journal of Hillside Hospital* 8:284–289

Chapter 6

INTEGRATIVE SUMMARY

JULES GLENN, M.D. and MARK KANZER, M.D.

In "The Borderline Childhood of the Wolf Man," Harold P. Blum revaluates the voluminous data we possess on the Wolf Man, who has been studied for more than sixty years. Blum applies modern knowledge derived from child analysis, child observation, studies of ego psychology, preoedipal influences, narcissism and borderline conditions to elucidate this famous patient's pathology. In addition to Freud's (1918) original paper, he draws on Ruth Mack Brunswick's reanalysis, the Wolf Man's own account of his life and analysis, and the observations of psychoanalysts who have examined him (Gardner 1971).

Blum demonstrates that "the Wolf Man's childhood disturbance was a severe borderline disturbance which provided the foundation for a borderline adolescence and . . . adult borderline personality." He notes that the Wolf Man developed a "transference psychosis" fourteen years after he ended treatment, a reflection of the borderline patient's inability to form a true ego integration and his consequent vulnerability to regression under disturbing conditions. It is significant of his continued dependence on Freud that the latter's cancer stimulated paranoid ideation and reactivated hypochondriacal identifications and trends.

Blum uses the word *borderline* to describe a condition close to psychosis, with severe ego impairments but without the irreversible disorganization and structural fragmentation of psychosis.

The Wolf Man manifested the characteristics of a borderline case as an adult.

Among the evidence of this, according to Blum, are his utter helplessness when he started analysis; his "obliging apathy" during much of his analysis; his inability to develop a stable character because he could never completely replace a libidinal position with a later one; sado-masochistic fixations; prolonged hypochondriacal episodes, longstanding depression and tendencies to act out; failures in ego synthesis, etc. There is also some evidence (Jones 1955, pp. 274, 447) that the Wolf Man made a bizarre offer during their initial meeting to defecate on Freud's head and to participate in anal intercourse.

The patient's infantile disturbances also bear the stigma of severe pathology which can be labelled borderline or even psychotic. Childhood schizophrenics usually do not suffer from the secondary symptomatology (delusions, hallucinations, etc.) that adult schizophrenics do. They manifest pathology in numerous areas, as the Wolf Man did as a child. At three and a half years of age, after a separation from his parents and a seduction, he underwent a personality transformation and became irritable and violent. Sadistic, suspicious and distrustful, he screamed and raged. At four he developed a wolf phobia following the famous wolf dream. Then at four and a half severe obsessive-compulsive symptoms replaced the phobia. All these symptoms of a pan-neurosis remind one of children diagnosed variously as borderline, atypical or schizophrenic. Many severely obsessive children, for instance, later develop clear-cut adult schizophrenia. The borderline child, like the Wolf Man, has been overstimulated and traumatized by his environment or by constitutional defects. We may add that the Wolf Man's childhood pneumonia and malaria possibly produced minimal brain damage.

As an adolescent the Wolf Man was seclusive, depressed and disturbed. When he first saw Freud he was extremely ill; he became openly paranoid when Brunswick started to treat him.

In assessing borderline states Blum suggests that pre-oedipal influences mold the oedipal conflicts and that several ego and libidinal developmental phases coexist. Deviant, regressive and mature traits are present at once. So it was, he asserts, with the Wolf Man.

Having established the Wolf Man's borderline condition, Blum evaluates the significance of the primal scene at one and a half and the wolf dream at four, central issues for Freud. The fears that followed the dream, according to later evidence, had a paranoid quality. The child was terrified of being stared at, possibly, as Harnik suggested, a reaction to forbidden masturbatory wishes.

Blum casts doubt on the accuracy of the construction of the primal scene, but acknowledges its heuristic scientific value. (Freud was also skeptical, a fact that Kanzer discusses further.) A child of one and a half, Blum asserts, could not perceive the details of the primal scene that Freud and his patient reconstructed;

for one thing, the concept of "three," the number of times he supposedly saw his parents have intercourse, would not be available to an infant. The confusion of a febrile child suffering from malaria also would interfere with the perception of details. Blum suggests that the many observations of animals copulating or being castrated or dying and not the few observations of parental intercourse had the traumatic effect. Quite possibly the many traumatic events were telescoped into a few. He adds that the malaria itself must have been a trauma, as were many other events the patient experienced. There were seductions, illnesses, castration threats and a possible constitutional vulnerability to overstimulation.

The primal scene, seduction, masturbation and related dangers cannot be viewed in isolation from the child's relationship with his parents and his developmental level. The primal scene-malaria experience took place at one and a half during the rapprochement subphase of separation-individuation when basic moods, trust and distrust develop. Many ego functions are vulnerable at that time as well.

Other important preoedipal pathogenic factors include the patient's having had two "mothers"—his Nanya and the hypochondrical biological mother who was unable to exert a healthy influence or to protect him. His emotionally ill father and his separations from his parents must have played a role as well.

At the time that Freud wrote about the Wolf Man, preoedipal conflicts, ego development and early self- and object-relations had scarcely been studied in the sense we understand them today. Freud emphasized the negative oedipal fantasies and defenses against homosexual wishes, and related the patient's identification with the mother of the primal scene. Blum calls attention to preoedipal determinants of his passivity, masochism and compliance. The Wolf Man's fear of helplessness and passivity are also indications of a wish to be devoured in sleep, to enter a state of symbiotic union.

Narcissistic as he was, could not the Wolf Man have become paranoid when threatened with the loss of Freud as an idealized self-object (see Kohut 1971)? He must have feared his destructive wishes toward Freud and himself when his analyst developed cancer. Analysis with a woman may have reduced an unconscious fear of castration. It may also, Blum continues, have allowed for a supportive maternal transference. At that time, of course, symbiotic maternal narcissistic "transferences" were not appreciated.

It is curious, as both Blum and Kanzer emphasize, that Brunswick denied that the Wolf Man was a favorite of Freud despite palpable evidence that he was: Freud had given him a personally inscribed copy of his case history and had helped support him financially.

Blum suggests that the Wolf Man, whose own ego stability was threatened by Freud's illness, turned to Brunswick to reestablish narcissistic equilibrium and needed symbiotic relationships. Indeed Freud, as Blum notes, anticipated the future insights into the complexities of narcissism when he wrote: "He fell ill . . . as a result of a *narcissistic* 'frustration.' This excessive strength of his narcissism was in complete harmony with the other indications of an inhibited sexual development" (Freud 1918, p. 118).

Mark Kanzer, examining the wealth of data in the Wolf Man's several analyses, first turns his attention to Ruth Mack Brunswick's treatment of the then-paranoid patient. He observes that she thought that she had uncovered nothing essentially new. Indeed her tendency was to cover old ground in more than one sense. Interpreting a new version of the wolf dream mainly in terms of the past, she neglected the reality behind the Wolf Man's belief that he was a favorite patient of Freud and failed to interpret his present lupine rage at her. Nor did she explore the possibility that another dream in which the patient's mother removes holy icons from the wall could also be understood in relation to the present. Kanzer suggests that her interpretations were insufficient in that she did not explore the possibility that her destroying his idealization of Freud eliminated him from the oedipal triangle and allowed the patient to feel affectionate toward his woman analyst. The Wolf Man's passive homosexual wishes, emphasized by Freud, are examined at the expense of his aggressive masculine desires. The emergence of the positive Oedipus complex was consistently regarded as a wish to identify with, not possess the mother.

The analysand's own report of his analysis casts light on his adult neurosis which Freud intentionally kept in the background. We learn of Freud's telling the patient a great deal about his own personal life and interests, apparently without believing this would interfere with the recollection of infantile memories, a prime aim of analysis. We also learn that the Wolf Man spent much time, vacations included, with the psychiatrist who had accompanied him from Russia and recommended Freud. This must have diluted and split the transference and prevented intense pain on separation. The Wolf Man's panicky insistence that he reach Therese, his wife-to-be, when this physician returned to Russia and left him in Freud's care must have reflected a fear of the transference and aimed at avoiding separation anxiety.

Kanzer points out that in his eagerness to reconstruct the past, Freud gave insufficient weight to the present which, as he himself later emphasized (1914), should be analyzed as a vivid re-experiencing of the infantile.

The analyst's activity influences the patient's dreams and fantasies when the analyst errs, as Robert J. Langs points out in his discussions of "misalliances" that follow Freud's "deviations" from what later became standard technique. The patient shows awareness in his dreams and associations of the analyst's mistakes and tries to warn him through certain symbols—blindness, pulling the wrong tooth and the like. The pulling of the wrong tooth as a criticism of the analyst figures in the Brunswick supplement. In responding to Freud's interpretations of the primal scene, the patient tells of a Pasteur follower who innoculated sheep on his father's estate and killed off the herds. The warning of Brunswick not to open the door to the wolves might be cited as another instance. Of course the analyst's helpful presence may also appear in dreams, fantasies and other derivatives. The Wolf Man's apparent approval of Brunswick's smashing icons could be cited as a "corroborative dream."

As we know Freud learned technique from his patients who also helped him conceptualize the procedure. Frau Emmy von N. supplemented Freud's hypnotic method by spontaneously unburdening herself without being hypnotized. She then reproduced memories and new impressions which led "in a quite unexpected way to pathological reminiscences" (Breuer and Freud 1893–1895, p. 56). Strachey states in a footnote: "This is perhaps the earliest appearance of what later became the method of free association" (1893–95, p. 56). And Anna O. coined the terms *talking cure* and *chimney sweeping* (p. 30) which Freud in turn used.

Nevertheless we must be cautious in attributing an omniscience to Freud's patients that they did not possess. The patient may fear the analyst's noninterpretative intrusion when he feeds him, suggests that the analysand offer a gift or makes a decision as to whether the patient should marry. The patient may then timidly or boldly use a dream to communicate his reservations and anxiety, a procedure that must be differentiated from the patient's knowingly and accurately espousing correct technique. The analyst may then realize that he is frightening the patient unnecessarily or obfuscating the transference. He may then interpret the patient's reactions to his interventions as well as alter his own behavior in the future.

The analyst must recognize when present reality contributes to the patient's imagery, but should not overlook the influence of the past in the creation of transferences. A proper and accurate balance between the recognition of reality and fantasy in the patient's analytic productions is essential to optimum analytic techniques.

Turning to another area crucial to analytic understanding, the evaluation of *past* reality, Kanzer examines Freud's uncertainty as to whether the primal scene actually occurred. To Freud the thrust of the reconstruction of the Wolf Man's infantile neurosis and the primal scene seems to have become not so much his theoretical controversy with Adler and Jung but the indecision in his own mind as to whether the scene was literally "real" or a fantasy. He continues for years to waver between the one and the other and we get the impression that this problem has become highly personal, that through the Wolf Man he is working out this area in his own self-analysis. It spreads to questions of theory and technique. "I admit that this is the most delicate question in the whole domain of psychoanalysis" (1918, p. 103), he averred. "No doubt has troubled me more; no other uncertainty has been more decisive in holding me back from publishing my conclusions." (Four years intervened between writing and publishing the case—one of the characteristic signs of Freud's feeling of personal involvement in his work.)

Another characteristic of Freud's personal involvement in his work is the feeling that he cannot get it to yield to his otherwise lucid and persuasive expositions—he cannot be persuaded himself. He was dissatisfied with his presentation of the Wolf Man and he makes the significant statement that "the description of such early phases and of such deep strata of mental life has been a task which has never before been attacked; and *it is better to perform the task badly than to take flight before it*—a proceeding which moreover (or so we are told) *involves the coward* in risks of a certain kind. I prefer, therefore, to put a bold face on it and show that I have not allowed myself to be held back by a sense of my own inferiority" (1918, p. 104; italics ours).

The feeling of uncertainty spreads beyond the question of the reality of the primal scene to questions of theory, technique, literary style, and now finally—though cryptically mentioned—the "holy war" with his own "wolves," Jung and Adler, at whom he jousts with the case which, in his own mind, is as unconvincing as his childhood endeavors to comprehend the primal scene. The reference to "cowardice" probably relates to Jung's recommended solution: to win converts to analysis by doing away with sexual explanations and finding more glib and readily accepted explanations of the neuroses. The reference to the sense of inferiority obviously involves Adler. Freud's own final solution was a third one: the primal scene was neither quite real nor quite a fantasy but had phylogenetic components. "It seems to me quite possible that all the things that are told to us today in analysis as fantasy—the seduction of children, the inflaming of sexual excitement by observing parental intercourse, the threat of castration (or rather castration itself)—were once real occurrences in the primaeval times of the human family, and that children in their fantasies are simply filling in gaps in individual truth with historical truth" (1918, p. 371).

Safely ensconced in "archaic heritage," despite all the teachings of contemporary biologists, the reconstruction of the past found its ultimate barrier beyond accessibility (or responsibility) by the analyst. In *Analysis Terminable and Interminable* (1937), which still brooded over the Wolf Man, the ego—and not merely the id—was given roots in hereditary endowment. The problem of historical truth and its relation to psychic truth would remain without ultimate solution but would continue to be a driving force for Freudian problem-solving to the end of his days.

Kanzer, then, suggests that Freud found it "safer" to turn to the inherited archaic heritage as a basis for primal scene fantasies. We may ask whether Freud could have been defending against the return of repressed childhood memories of the actual primal scene. We know that Freud's family occupied a single room when he was an infant (Schur 1972); he must have actually and repeatedly witnessed intercourse at a very early age. Of course, in the specific instance of the Wolf Man, there was, as Blum documents, reason to doubt that the one and a half year old child could perceive the details of his parents' sexual activity when he had malaria. In any case, Kanzer emphasizes, Freud appeared to be in quest of his own primal scene.

Analysts continue to assess the influence of primal scene observations and fantasies in a panel on the Pathogeneity of Primal Scene at an American Psychoanalytic Association meeting in May, 1977. We have included in this volume the introductory remarks of the panel chairman, Harold P. Blum, which place the Wolf Man's analysis in perspective. He lists among the issues that require study: the question as to whether observations of the primal scene need be pathogenic; the effects of such experiences in other cultures; the role of primal scene experiences during the preoedipal and oedipal periods; the influence of primal scene exposure on mastery and sublimation; and the differentiation of traumatic and other disturbing influences of the primal scene.

Eugene Halpert adds a historical note in Lermontov and the Wolf Man. He provides a good deal of information pointing to the patient's intense interest in the poet Lermontov at whose grave he wept a few months after his sister's death. Lermontov, a well-known Russian romantic poet and adventurer, was the idol of the Wolf Man throughout much of his life. Quoting from both the works of Lermontov and the Wolf Man's own reminiscences, Halpert demonstrates a striking massive global identification and, in so doing, reveals the primitiveness of the Wolf Man's personality and neurosis.

References

Breuer, J., and Freud, S. (1893–1895). Studies on hysteria. *Standard Edition* 2.

Freud, S. (1916–1917). Introductory lectures on psycho-analysis. *Standard Edition* 16.

———— (1918). From the history of an infantile neurosis. *Standard Edition* 17:7–122.

———— (1937). Analysis terminable and interminable. *Standard Edition* 23:216–253.

Gardiner, M., ed. (1971). *The Wolf-Man by The Wolf-Man*. New York: Basic Books.

Jones, E. (1955). *The Life and Work of Sigmund Freud*. Volume 2. New York: Basic Books.

Kohut, H. (1971). *The Analysis of the Self*. New York: International Universities Press.

Schur, M. (1972). *Freud: Living and Dying*. New York: International Universities Press.

Part VII

Summary: and Conclusion

Chapter 1

NEW DIMENSIONS IN HUMAN RELATIONSHIPS

MARK KANZER, M.D.

In Freud's first psychotherapy cases, largely pursued with a cathartic technique (Breuer and Freud 1893–1895), empathic observations began to shape self-analysis and patient-analysis interrelatedly. With Frau Emmy von N., his first case, the drama of intercommunication is established in his initial interview with the forty-year-old widow suffering from tics and "hysterical deliria" since the death of her husband fourteen years earlier. "Every two or three minutes (during an otherwise intelligible description of her problems) she suddenly broke off, contorted her face into an expression of horror and disgust, stretched out her hand towards me, spreading and crooking her fingers, and exclaimed, in a changed voice, charged with anxiety: 'Keep still!—Don't say anything!—Don't touch me!' " (p. 49). The drama is inherent in the tersely phrased and unadorned description of these events and it must have been difficult for the inexperienced and young practitioner (in his early thirties) to feel "uninvolved."

Freud arranged to see Emmy daily—later a routine procedure in psychoanalysis—drawing upon the earlier experience of his senior colleague, Joseph Breuer, with the famous Anna O. His first efforts to explain to the patient (and himself) the cause of her symptons were empirical and naive, but capable of evolving rapidly. The evolution was mediated in no small part by his flexibility, his empathy and his desire to aid the patient. This prelude to an "analytic atmosphere" was rewarded with the patient's confidences and even her attempt to dominate him. We see free association and benevolent listening as keystones to a more permanent technique being launched as Emmy refused to brook untimely and irrelevant interruptions of her communications. Even under hypnosis, she "said in a definitely grumbling tone that I was not to keep on asking her where this and that came from, but to let her tell me what she had to say. I fell in with this and she went on without preface (to tell of her reactions to her husband's death and the irrational blame she placed on her child as a result)" (p. 63). Within two weeks, free association of this sort was leading the way to an understanding of the traumatic origin of symptoms, the role of sexual frustration, the deep-seated and concealed hatred within a family, all of which commonsense questioning would never have revealed.

Freud was accumulating a background for the more purposeful interviewing of future patients, but also for a key to his own relationship to the patient that would provide inexhaustible insights into the workings of the mind and into the subtle communications between the two partners in the analytic situation. For when, in response to his attempts to relieve her unconscious guilt by moralizing reflections, she proved quite impervious, he compared her sadly to "an ascetic medieval monk, who sees the finger of God or a temptation of the Devil in every trivial event of his life and who is incapable of picturing the world even for a brief moment or its smallest corner as being without reference to himself" (pp. 65–66). A metaphor about the Devil was not only enhancing his style and contributing to a picture of the patient but, as has been shown elsewhere (Kanzer 1961), was attesting to an unmentioned inner crisis, part of the beginnings of self-analysis, in which Freud himself, like an ascetic medieval monk, reacted to the dawning awareness of patients' sexual preoccupations with himself which shaped all their thoughts while in his company and forced reciprocal preoccupations upon himself. It is most instructive, from the standpoint of the history of ideas, to see how he was able to desexualize his insight into terse scientific conclusions more than a decade later when he stated that "when I instruct a patient to abandon reflection of any kind and tell me whatever comes into his head, I am relying firmly on the presumption that [there is a purposive, directive] idea of which the patient has no suspicion—one relating to myself" (1900 pp. 531–532). Every thought, during free association, unbeknownst to the patient, is directed toward the analyst.

By 1895, Freud was ready to leave the cathartic form of treatment behind him and embark on his own methodology—psychoanalysis—though this would not really take definite form for years to come. For some time he had been in a unique and unrecognized form of self-analysis with Wilhelm Fliess (1954). This self-analysis crystallized in connection with his analysis of "Irma" (Emma) which marked an event of major importance—the discovery of the "secret of dreams" through the analysis of one of his own dreams that took up in semi-recognizable form the problem of whether he had treated this patient correctly through his new-found method. In the "dream of Irma's injection" which he resolved on the morning of July 25, 1895, he takes a position intermediate between a patient (Irma) with whom he identifies and physicians who treat her with an admixture of physical and psychological therapies. The results of his own analysis of the dream were crucial for the future of his science: he corrected an injustice to the young woman whom, for personal reasons that he had not faced up to, he had discharged incorrectly from treatment; he found an approach to reconciliation with his own "analyst," Dr. Wilhelm Fliess, after a crisis of confidence; and he applied his newfound understanding of dreams to perfect his techniques of self-analysis as well as patient analysis (Freud 1900, pp. 106–120; Erikson 1962; Schur 1966, 1972). In his self-analysis of the Irma dream (also called the "specimen" dream of psychoanalysis), Freud not only became the first self-analyst but also the first self-supervisor in analytic history.

The pursuit of the meaning of dreams and its application to the treatment of patients was still in the foreground of his interests at the end of 1900 when he undertook the treatment of "Dora," an eighteen-year-old girl with hysterical symptoms. She was the be the first of the "classical cases" which he was to bequeath to posterity, though her treatment was to last only three months and was to be remembered as much for what he failed to understand until the treatment was over as for the understanding he showed during the treatment. The post-therapeutic insight came in the form of a new recognition of the role of transference during the analysis.

In our volume, the review of the "Dora" case (1905) begins with a survey by Jules Glenn of Freud's adolescent (female) patients: Katharina, Dora and the "homosexual woman." The post-Freudian developments that he stresses are: the recognition of the special psychology of adolescents since 1905; the need to acknowledge their strivings for independence which conflict with their alternating manifestations of dependency on the parents at that stage; and the special problems of relating to females which, especially in recent times, many have criticized in Freud.

Already in relation to "Irma" and the specimen dream, Freud himself pointed out that behind the figure of this patient lay concealed representations of his mother, his wife and his oldest daughter, a formidable combination to be overcome in achieving a conflict-free attitude to a patient who, as a young widow, was making formidable demands on him in her own right. These complex problems were scarcely diminished in the case of Dora, who, as Glenn demonstrates in "Notes on Psychoanalytic Concepts and Style in Freud's Case Histories," awakened within him countertransferences relating to his favorite sister Rosa as well as to a nursemaid who had played a very important role in his childhood.

At that time, Freud was in the throes of a crusade against the hypocrisy of society which instigated sexual guilt in young people, not least of all by depriving them in childhood of the facts about conception and childbirth. This too may be regarded as an outcome of self-analysis. He undertook single-handedly to confront hypocrisy with "truth." He dubbed the parts of the body by their recognizable names and was able to demonstrate that in discussing sexual behavior plainly with Dora, he was teaching her nothing new even when the topic of perverse practices came up. It was the beginning of the sexual revolution of the twentieth century, so much of which has been linked with Freud's name. Yet it was already apparent with Dora, as Glenn points out (as do other contributors to this section), that the freedom which he proudly heralded had its darker side. The girl, sufficiently mistrustful of the sexual licentiousness of her own father and of a would-be seducer, Herr K., was understandably impressed by other possible motives Freud might harbor besides that of being a crusader against social hypocrisy.

Glenn, as well as Robert J. Langs and myself, who also contribute to the Dora section, reviews the flight of the girl from treatment and is persuaded that Freud did far less than he might have to deter her from this course. In the case of the eighteen-year-old "homosexual woman" some two decades later, Freud showed, according to Glenn, many of the same shortcomings that characterized his lacunae in empathy with Dora, indicating an area in which failures of self-analysis and patient-analysis complemented each other. Robert J. Langs, using concepts of misalliance and deviation to describe Freud's deflections from the later classical techniques, examines the famous dream in which Dora escapes in the company of her father from a burning house—recognized only later by Freud as heralding her departure from treatment—and demonstrates the fears and wishes she nourished with respect to Freud as potential seducer. Where Freud ostensibly sought to link the origin of anxieties about fire to early childhood bedwetting problems, a game of "playing with fire" which he felt impelled to introduce (at a time when analytic rules were less fixed) indicated a shared fantasy that was part of an ongoing and unconscious sex game between them. (In my paper in this section, I point out a correlated early recognition by Freud that Dora was considering a flight from treatment—an insight that was not permitted to receive proper attention until this event had actually come to pass.) Such mutual teasing and alienation is not uncommon in the relationship of adolescents and their parents, mutually surveying each other with greater awareness of sexual attractions and barriers.

In my paper I also take up Dora's dream of fleeing from Freud's office especially in the light of the symbolism and universal fantasies involved. There are two universal fantasies here, rescue by the father (childbirth) and the fire-water dichotomy that intrigued Freud so much over the years and was certainly associated with a significant event of his own childhood when he displeased his father by urinating before his parents in their bedroom. Almost as a by-product of his clinical work which still remained a continuation of his dream studies, Freud traced the origin of the fire-water dichotomy and their sexual symbolism to common bodily experiences—an unprecedented and eventful approach. The flight from the burning house has mythological prototypes—Lot's wife, Aeneas and his father Anchises (where the son rescues the father), Brunhilde and Siegfried, and many similar themes that carry us into the present day. Dora's dream may be viewed, I suggest, as a continuation of the frightened child's effort to conjure up the image of the mother as a basic pattern for the dream work itself. There is a primal ambiguity of visual images here, analogous to that for primal words, which Freud saw elsewhere in his discussion of this dream. What he did not see, however, was the ambiguity of the flight *from* and flight *to* himself conveyed by this very dream. Had he considered and interpreted this message, it might have led him to rescue the analysis itself. The fire imagery in the dream, on the basis of Freud's own associations, indicates countertransference problems; it also allows us to see in dreams a portrayal of the analyst as well as of the patient. Such implications should be of the greatest significance for revealing the on-going transference and countertransference attitudes and keeping in close touch with the patient's mental processes.

Melvin A. Scharfman, in a discussion of Jules Glenn's chapter, adds to the revealing metaphors that transmit images from Freud's mind to the patient's, and now to us, when he quotes him as writing to Wilhelm Fliess (Freud 1954) at the beginning of her treatment that "I have a new patient, a girl of eighteen; the case has opened smoothly to my collection of picklocks." Both sexuality and illegal entries, conveyed by this image, indicate that this outlook was at work during the treatment—a common enough circumstance for which the analyst is better prepared than Freud by the collection of picklocks his self-analysis (and training analysis) has provided. Another metaphor may be added. At the end of the treatment, Freud again reported to his "analyst": "I finished 'Dreams and Hysteria' [a title for the case history that he contemplated] yesterday, and the consequence is that today I feel short of a drug" (1954, p. 326). He knew well enough from his own experiences with cocaine the dangers of a daily addiction to which one succumbs and against which one struggles. It was his own version of the mutual experience that Dora recorded so ambivalently in the "flight from the burning house" dream.

Scharfman points to elements other than the transference in the analysis that may have transmitted Freud's feelings and strengthened Dora's distrust. Was it really true, as Freud thought, that a normal girl of fourteen will feel only sexual excitement and not disgust when a married man, an ostensible friend of the family, pressed himself against her body? The question also arises among the contributors, with different viewpoints expressed, as to whether the interest of Freud in using Dora as an instrument for his theoretical investigations was helpful or in conflict with his therapeutic intentions. In a summary of Part II Isidor Bernstein argues that the case histories must be seen in a total context where they rate highly as gems of literature, education and theory that are integrally related to Freud's therapeutic viewpoint and the historical progression in which "Dora" is embedded. To the personal interplay between Freud and this patient, he adds the former's apparent desire to dazzle and overwhelm the young girl with his brilliance.

In a telling and illuminating comparison, Bernstein compares Freud to an analyst in training today who reports his experiences with this case to a supervisor. Freud's contact with the father before the analysis, his reliance on information that came from sources other than the patient and a propensity for premature interpretations would have drawn admonitions. Freud's "interpretations" were often, in fact, intellectual expositions on which he insisted with the authority of a parent or teacher (a phase of his behavior that still carried over the hypnotic tradition which, with growing reliance on free association, would be self-corrected). Bernstein also cites the subsequent history of Dora after the analysis as an example of the permanent embitterment that may characterize patients in later life when analysis has left them with their sense of self damaged by feelings of disappointment and rejection. Freud did not sufficiently appreciate the benefits of his treatment in her confrontations with her elders after the termination or he might not have let her go with the hurt remark that her triumph had been to deprive him of the satisfactions of carrying the cure to completion.

With Dora, Freud was opening up the field of adolescent analysis, if only in an incidental way. With "Little Hans" (Herbert Graf) he made the daring leap into child analysis with fuller knowledge of the implications. Motivated as always by the desire to explore new territory, he was aware of the opportunity, through direct analysis of a child, to confirm or disprove the assumptions that he had drawn from the memories and symptoms of adults. In connection with this enterprise he called upon his followers to report their own observations, thus promoting a group project in place of his usual lonely research.

Little Hans was the five-year-old son of a mother who had been Freud's patient and a father, Max Graf, a noted Viennese music critic who had become his disciple and took part regularly in the Wednesday night meetings that became the Vienna Psychoanalytic Society. Once again, as in several other cases, we find Freud taking patients from his own circle for treatment—a practice subsequently frowned upon but inevitable at a time when Freud was known only among his intimates.

With this five-year-old boy, Freud's capacities for inventiveness in the face of established standards were much in evidence as he converted the father into the therapist who would place himself under his own supervision. Martin Silverman, in "A Fresh Look at the Case of Little Hans," reviews the results from the standpoint of today's more rigorous procedures. He notes that Freud paid little attention to a recent tonsillectomy undergone by the child, though there is ample material to suggest its influence. He also takes the opportunity, through the equation of the tonsils with the testicles (the German word for tonsils is *Mandeln*—almonds, nuts) to indicate that the castration anxieties of the little boy included the testicles as well as the penis.

Little Hans, as Silverman points out, was treated before Freud came to regard aggression as a separate instinct; and his recognition of the negative Oedipus complex and of negative transference was correspondingly limited. Nevertheless, he was able to place the death wishes against the father in the context of the libido theory and give them fundamental clinical importance during the analysis. Similarly the developmental viewpoint (which would include attention to the preoedipal period and superego formation in addition to the oedipal phase) was not yet delineated. Nevertheless, Silverman feels that the case material permits us to reconstruct these major facets to a considerable extent. There had been considerable development of scoptophilic elements from the preoedipal period which carried over into the oedipal. Perhaps the efforts of his parents, under the influence of Freud's liberal teachings, was a factor here. Silverman suggests (and we have encountered a similar problem with Dora) that the seductiveness involved in the new freedom was overlooked. Information about the oral and anal phases is sufficiently provided to bring the child's personality formation into a modern line-of-development approach. The impact of the birth of a sister can now be more readily assessed in relation to the fuller longitudinal and cross-section views that Silverman offers.

Silverman concludes that the outcome of the treatment was remarkably good, even if it involved a considerable amount of family therapy rather than psychoanalysis as we would understand it today. No small part of the benefits was to be found in bringing father and son together in lasting mutual understanding and affection. Toward the end of the treatment, the boy himself was able to take the lead in promoting the development of the analysis. In the future, though the parents were divorced, the son followed the father into the field of music, where he enjoyed an outstanding career.

We get many glimpses of Freud as a human being both in the course of the treatment of Little Hans and in material that sheds light on his relationship with the Graf family. The father describes how Freud trudged up four flights of steps on the occasion of the third birthday of his little son and Freud's future patient to carry him a large rocking horse—an omen of things to come. There is obvious strong personal feeling when he remarks that people will assume that Hans, since he is neurotic, is a "degenerate" with hereditary taints (1905, p. 141). While admittedly partisan with respect to the child, he takes occasion to deny that he is unique so as to protect other little neurotics from similar prejudices should their conditions become known. Today, in fact, as Glenn points out, we might regard his problems as a transient manifestation of the maturing process and feel that advice to his parents about his upbringing is all that is needed.

The ultimate lesson that Freud wishes to convey from the publication of the cases is neither theoretical nor clinical; it is cultural. He expresses the hope that educators, learning from such instances the inner problems of children, will deal with them sympathetically and with understanding rather than repressive measures. The social aim must be considered a major motive of Freud in dealing with all his cases, along with his tireless research aims, empathy and inventive approach. Yet self-analysis had its limitations, just as did person analysis—perhaps these even acted as a spur to new efforts and discoveries, as happened with Dora. It is sad to record that Max Graf, still venerating Freud, had to report forty years later that the day had come when their friendship ended. "I was unable and unwilling to submit to Freud's 'do' or 'don't'—with which he once confronted me—and nothing was left for me to do but to withdraw from his circle" (1942, p. 475). Perhaps his own counteridentifications with Little Hans were worked through at that moment.

The "Rat Man," so-called because of an obsession that rats would bore their way into his anus and that of his father (already dead) and his "lady," was the first adult male to be enlisted in Freud's classical case histories. He was also the first to become the subject of analytic clinical conferences (without his knowledge) when Freud presented him on several occasions to the members of his Wednesday night group (Nunberg and Federn 1962). Some of the ideas of the latter found their way into Freud's subsequent publication, testifying to the fact that psychoanalysis was ceasing to be a one-man science.

Treatment was begun in October 1907, some seven years after Dora had begun hers. The technique of free association had advanced and the libido theory was more clearly formulated. Despite Freud's greater appreciation of transference, however, he did not see it as an indicator of this relationship to the patient except as a mere unrealistic reflection of an earlier oedipal relationship. Consequently, he was not apt to stress the patient's feelings about himself or keep attuned to their contemporary problems in adjustment. Nor did he consider the possibilities of *countertransference*—the term itself was not coined until October, 1910. Fundamental theoretical and clinical concepts remained to be elucidated in the future, yet the Rat Man is the most fully reported of all Freud's cases, the analysis lasting eleven months.

An exciting supplement was added as late as 1955 when the *Standard Edition* published a journal, long hidden in Freud's files, which recorded actual details of the treatment over a three-month period. It is by far the most direct and authentic transcript of daily analytic sessions, verbal interchanges with patients and glimpses of Freud's own personality in an analytic setting that we possess. The differences between the official and the unofficial case histories are often striking—for example, the mother scarcely emerges from the shadows in the official portion but her role is quite prominent in the unofficial portion. The intense transference (and real) hostility of the patient becomes evident only in the latter, while Freud's tactics and actual choice of words, which are of fundamental significance, are best sought there.

The task of updating the case and suggesting areas of empathic and counter-transference responses by Freud begins in our volume with my 1952 paper, "The Transference Neurosis of the Rat Man." The "transference neurosis," as distinguished from the transference, was a product of Freud's later experience and taught him to look more carefully into the patient's current behavior, especially in relation to himself. In that paper I point out different sequences in which the transference neurosis was operating during the Rat Man analysis and the intuitive way in which its manifestations were handled in contrast to the more purposeful measures and interpretations that would be undertaken at a later time.

The article was written before the 1955 disclosure of the hidden journals and the promulgation of concepts of the therapeutic alliance by Zetzel (1956) and Greenson (1965). In this volume, I add a follow-up commentary which takes the journal into account and gives consideration to certain aspects of the alliances. The title of the paper, "Freud's 'Human Influence' on the Rat Man," derives from Freud's own review of the evolution of his technique (1920). In a first phase, to which Dora belonged, the analyst interprets the hidden memory, which the patient is expected to confirm. In the second phase, he notes the appearance of transference but uses it almost exclusively to confirm the existence of earlier memories and to persuade the patient by means of the suggestive force granted him by the transference ("human influence") to accept the interpretation.

In this paper, I also suggest that a sign of "human influence" is the extensive theoretical explanations with which Freud would enlighten his patients. Ernst Kris (1951) described this as "intellectual indoctrinations." A scrutiny of these explanations, however, finds them rich in metaphors and often illustrating backgrounds in Freud's own life which make their significance for himself quite striking. For example, he illustrates the meaning of ambivalence by a quotation from *Julius Caesar* which he had used elsewhere to demonstrate his own ambivalence, or creates a tomblike atmosphere by pointing out objects in the office that had been excavated from tombs while admonishing the patient to acknowledge the death wishes he had once nourished toward his father. The patient responds with thoughts of the father coming to life.

Robert J. Langs designates as a "misalliance" the expectation—carried over from previous relationships—that the analyst would dismiss as absurd the notion that he had committed acts for which he harbored apparently excessive guilt. Such a "sector of misalliance" had to be corrected by a true alliance dedicated to promoting insight rather than covering it up. Langs also explores as "deviations" from the correct course of an analysis such interventions as requiring of the patient that he give Freud a picture of his lady and reveal her name, or feeding him supper on a particularly inappropriate occasion. This latter cannot really be called a mere manifestation of the analyst's kindliness which did no harm when we examine all the consequences (Zetzel 1966). Langs' alternative constructions are supported by detailed studies of the contexts in which such interventions took place.

Stanley S. Weiss, in "Reflections and Speculations on the Psychoanalysis of the Rat Man," is one of several contributors who extends the patient-analyst relationship backwards into its prehistory shortly before their actual encounter comes about. As with other Freud patients, there had been direct or indirect personal contacts: the Rat Man had some acquaintance with Freud's writings, he had been told incorrectly that his brother, a waiter, had been hanged for murder, and there had once been some talk of a marriage between his own sister and Freud's brother. Weiss goes beyond this however to sketch certain tacit links between them on the basis of Viennese, and particularly Viennese Jewish, customs at the time. René Spitz and William G. Niederland were among Weiss's informants.

Proceeding toward the actual precipitation of the condition that brought the patient for treatment, Weiss presents the evidence of the ordeal it had meant to him to be in military training and to follow in his father's footsteps by showing that a Jew could stand up to such stresses in an anti-Semitic environment. The story of the rat torture would have fallen on especially receptive ears, especially as his own father had once described the Nuremburg funnel torture in which the body is forcibly penetrated. The loss of his glasses, which precipitated the neurosis, was symbolic of castration as well as a loosening of contacts with reality, and the problem of paying for them touched off deep-seated conflicts about money, especially those relating to his Jewish identity. Many remarks that he made to Freud achieve new sharpness when their original Jewish meanings are given (which Weiss does), and a sneering anti-Semitism of his own (identification with the rat-aggressor) becomes an important element in the developments between them.

The approach of Weiss (supplemented by analogous contributions by myself and Langs) shows how inadequately informed Freud had been on the basis of the libido theory when, in outlining the importance of the first communications, he had chosen to fix upon the conflicts over heterosexual and homosexual inclinations that these revealed. Appropriate to the wider understanding that we now possess is the contention by Merton M. Gill, long a member of the Downstate faculty, and Hyman L. Muslim (1976) that early interpretations may not only be justified but necessary to deal adequately with resistances. They suggest moreover that an intervention by Freud early in treatment, when he told the Rat Man that he himself was not disposed to cruelty, may have been not an intuitive reassurance, as my 1952 paper assumed, but rather a conscious and indirect interpretation. Certainly there is no reason to object to the notion that both conscious and unconscious considerations may have prompted a remark that seems more a reassurance than an interpretation. Gill and Muslim also hold that when Freud, on the same occasion, told the patient that he could no more give him the right to withhold his thoughts any more than he could give him the right to have the moon, since both depended on laws of nature and were beyond his power to influence, he was not avoiding personal responsibility for the fundamental rule (as I suggested) but justifiably underlining the impersonal aspect.

This could indeed be a valid consideration, but the particular wording on this occasion does not seem to me strictly impersonal—analysis raises the question as to why the moon was involved!—and was promptly followed by evidence that Freud could indeed modify the fundamental rule by agreeing that the Rat Man need not divulge everything. He need only offer hints and Freud would "guess" the rest of the sentence. To term this "acting out with the patient" has also drawn criticism from Zetzel (1966) and Major (1974) which seems obscure and derived from the notion that Freud could not have been inconsistent. Major's exposition does seem to have real merit in that it adds still greater force to my view by translating the word *guess* into the original German, *erraten* which, Major tells us, means "to divine" and further invokes the rat as an instrument of divination by boring his way into the patient's mind. We should note that Freud had already placed the fundamental rule in the same category of natural (or supernatural) forces as the orbiting moon, and that strongly suggestive forces of "human influence" were indeed being brought to bear on a patient whose neurosis made him disposed to superstition and belief in the magical properties of thought. Had he not said earlier in that same session that as a child, he believed his parents knew his thoughts because he spoke them out loud without his hearing himself do it? Almost immediately this seems to have been tested out in his claim that he could not tell Freud what was on his mind and the demonstration by the latter that he could indeed "divine" the contents by the merest hints and even without the use of the fundamental rule as ally. Such interplays of suggestions and countersuggestion are a common part of the analytic process, requiring to be raised in time from empathy to full consciousness and logical exposition. The capacity to modify the fundamental rule is indeed sometimes not only a possibility but a necessity.

The borders of the analytic situation widen as Leonard Shengold and Judith Kestenberg introduce the genetic viewpoint into the proceedings. Shengold (1967, 1971) has found in the Rat Man an illustration of a seduced and traumatized child who develops cannibalistic fantasies as an adult. In the rat, a gnawing voracious animal, he discovers a symbol of his own ferocious orality. Shengold designates as "rat people" an entire category of persons who might be said to share the rat as "totem animal." In surveying the "rat people," he discusses the infantile experience of teething as a painful penetration "into" the self by the tooth and its relation to the sense of devouring and being devoured, so well known to analysts through the "oral triad" of Lewin (1950). He likewise amasses a notable collection of folklore and tales about rats which build up a consistent image of the "bearer of the tooth," the rat, whose real character and habits are remarkably like the symbolic form he has come to represent to humans.

In a metapsychological exposition, Shengold stresses a splitting of the ego in the "Rat Man," which he finds linked to the original use of isolation as an intense and massive defense against memories of severe trauma. Alterations of consciousness become occasions for a reopening of patched-over splits through which warded off portions of the ego appear and disappear like their autosymbolic counterparts, the rats. With them come remnants of the past (breast images, excrement, etc.) that emerge and vanish without the ego having a sense of control of responsibility over parts of itself. (See also in this connection Kestenberg's discussion of the influence of undescended testicles on the Rat Man's fantasies and symptoms.) The couch situation may produce an alteration of consciousness that can bring on the "galloping transference" we find in the Rat Man.

Judith S. Kestenberg contributed to our understanding of the Rat Man through a unique approach as early as 1966. She found in his behavior and symptoms typical patterns of early motor development in the child. The phobic fear of the rat gnawing into his anus drew upon early efforts to establish control over sphincter movements and sensations that seemed outside the self. His running about Freud's office when frightened reproduced, she suggested, the agitated flight of a frightened child. Now, with another decade of observation and experiment behond her, Kestenberg contributes to this volume an article on "Ego-Organization in Obsessive-Compulsive Development." Freud, she notes, did not confine himself to verbal interchanges with this patient but carefully observed his facial expressions and bodily movements. He doubtless influenced the Rat Man through his own facial expression, his laughter, the feelings of surprise that he describes, and spontaneous behavior that revealed him as an interested, compassionate and intelligent new object who, like a parent, could influence him to form new self- and object-images through which he could complete the process of maturation interrupted by his neurosis.

Kestenberg, like some of the other contributors to this volume, is impressed by the recent recognition, promoted largely by Anita Bell (1961), of the role of the testicles in male development. The undescended testicles of the Rat Man, which Freud mentions only in passing in the unofficial records of the treatment, seem to her a key to the puzzling incantation of the patient, *Glejisamen*, which he knew to be associated with semen. There were two letters to which he could offer no associations—the "e" and the "i." She puts them together to form the German *Ei* or "egg" (testicle) from which the semen derives and which must be kept apart from his lady for fear of fertilizing her. The rat, in one of its many aspects, is seen as a testicle that has intruded into his body. Kestenberg also finds in the testicles a key to a puzzling dream in which a girl cuts a herring into two portions (the testicles).

The Schreber case is actually based on the autobiography of a paranoid judge whom Freud never treated or even met, but his elucidation of the man's story and the conclusions he draws about the processes involved in paranoia rank among his greatest intellectual achievements. The uncovering of data with respect to the judge's eccentric father and the realistic nucleus in childhood experiences of many of Schreber's strangest delusions presented by William G. Niederland must count among the most valuable researches ever made into Freud's case histories and the propositions he put forward to explain them. The best known and most controversial of Freud's teachings on paranoia have related to his tenet that unconscious homosexuality was at the innermost core of paranoia and that the symptoms represented attempts to ward off insight into the homosexual desires. The psychosis (during one breakdown) occurred with the return of the repressed in the form of a conscious fantasy that it must be an enjoyable experience to be a woman submitting to the act of intercourse.

While there certainly could have been no "countertransferences" in Freud's involvement with the Schreber case, it would appear to have taken up the thread of unanalyzed transferences left over from his own analysis with Fliess, which had ended with a negative and not entirely paranoid charge by the latter that Freud had appropriated for himself Fliess's own teachings on bisexuality—certainly a "loaded" topic. Part of Freud's sense of loss was mitigated by a new attachment which soon formed to Carl Jung and was destined to end on as unpleasant a note, with charges and countercharges, as the relationship to Fliess. Freud acknowledged a repetitive drive to pursue such cycles in his intimate relationships with men. Oddly enough, it was precisely Freud's interpretation of the Schreber case, and particularly its sexual aspects, that Jung found unacceptable (see Leonard Shengold's review of the Freud-Jung correspondence, and my comments on the correspondence between Freud and Emma Jung, in our earlier volume, *Freud and His Self-Analysis*).

In the interval between the break-up with Fliess (1901–1902) and the break-up with Jung following the latter's rejection of the Schreber case (1912), Freud undertook two or three semi-autobiographical studies in the field of literature and the arts—notably on Wilhelm Jensen's *Gradiva*, which drew him closer to Jung in the halcyon days of their early attachment. *Gradiva* deals with an archeologist (a study that was one of Freud's own great passions) who, to encounter a girl from his own home town whose existence he resolutely bans from consciousness, travels to the ruins of Pompeii and develops the delusion that she is now a revenant from the days when the eruption of the volcano extinguished all life in the Roman city. Freud takes delight in interpreting the dreams of the young man as though he were a real person and in demonstrating the unconscious skill of the girl in helping the sick youth to regain his mental health—naturally, with the traditional happy ending. Freud himself often had been attracted to Pompeii in his travels and, as James Strachey comments, he was fascinated by the analogy between the historical fate of Pompeii (its burial and subsequent excavation) and the mental events with which he was so familiar—burial by repression and excavation by analysis. The analysis of *Gradiva* would have permitted Freud, long a victim of travel phobias, to relax his more scientific controls and engage safely in counteridentifications with a patient.

The analysis of Leonardo briefly anteceded the Schreber study and postulates a sublimated form of homosexuality for the Renaissance genius with whom identifications may be surmised (see Jones 1955, p. 78). The work was completed in the spring of 1910 and was notable, among other things, for its introduction into scientific literature of the concept of *narcissism* which the Schreber study extended. During the summer Freud undertook his annual travels to the south, this time in the company of Sandor Ferenczi, a favored disciple whom he analyzed intermittently. Their companionship was not always pleasant, especially as Ferenczi now took the opportunity to press Freud to confide in him about personal matters, thereby fulfilling every analysand's fantasy of reversing the relationship. Freud was not to be drawn into this dangerous game; Ernest Jones published a pertinent letter that Freud wrote Ferenczi on October 6, 1910, stating that he had not overcome his *countertransference* to his former patient (Jones 1955, p. 83)—the first use of the term. He further added that since his traumatic experience with Fliess, he was reluctant to "uncover my personality completely" and that "a part of homosexual cathexis has been withdrawn and made use of to enlarge my own ego. I have succeeded where the paranoiac fails." (He could internalize the analytic function instead of relying on the "fiction" that Fliess was his analyst.)

The understanding that went into the Schreber analysis later undoubtedly drew on just this ability to sublimate as Schreber had been unable to do. Self-analysis is evident at two points in Freud's writings on Schreber. Near the end of the study, he coolly makes a comparison between the delusions of the latter and certain of his own concepts whose similarity he notes—namely, Schreber's postulates about the rays of God and his own about the vicissitudes of the libido. There is no reason to doubt, as he suggests, that the paranoiac can have as the basis of his delusions an endopsychic perception of his true inner processes that the scientist must more impersonally formulate.

Typically, Freud is not content with a clinical study even of such vast import as the understanding he was able to bring to paranoia. The symbols of the sun and animistic forces that preoccupy the paranoiac are in fact the favorite subjects of myths and spread to the religious beliefs and power structures of empires. This provides Freud with an opportunity for a little joke about the myth that the eagle subjects his young to an ordeal through which he must prove his heritage—to look boldly into the sun. The jest involves the dissident Adler (eagle) and Jung (young) who were not proving their lineage at the moment. Freud would soon be working out his feelings to the dissidents in such semi-autobiographical works as *Totem and Taboo* and *Moses and Monotheism* in which ,as in the sun and moon (see Rat Man interchange) identifications (also to be found in his explicitly recognized identification with the Biblical Joseph, son of Jacob) a certain cosmic grandiosity inheres. The conversely meek and reasonable side of the founder of psychoanalysis is shown when he ends this period of stress in 1914 with a work *On the History of the Psychoanalytic Movement* in which he disclaims personal glory with the concluding statement that "Men are strong so long as they represent a strong idea; they become powerless when they oppose it" (p. 66). Yet is he quite rejecting cosmic magic when he takes leave of the dissidents with the words: "I can only express a wish that fortune may grant an agreeable upward journey to all those who have found their stay in the underworld of psychoanalysis too uncomfortable for their taste" (p. 66)? The dispatch of the dissidents to heaven does not sound like an entirely benevolent wish!

In the decades following the publication of the Schreber case, Freud continued to criticize and revise his own theories. The introduction of the structural point of view in the 1920s forms the basis for reevaluation of Freud's concept of psychosis by Arlow and Brenner (1964) whose findings are abstrated in this volume by Jules Glenn. They contend that Freud overemphasized the economic metapsychological approach and underemphasized the importance of conflict and defense. They assert that the role of decathexis is disproved by clinical observation and that application of Freud's findings regarding neuroses to more malignant disorders can explain the psychopathology. Glenn and Rubins, in teaching the Schreber case to analytic students, attempt to integrate Freud's economic view and the later structural theory. They also emphasize that advances in knowledge of child development have corrected the theory of development that Freud espoused when he wrote the Schreber paper. The significance of interactions with and representations of the preoedipal mother in schizophrenia has been elucidated since Freud's writings on Schreber.

The "Wolf Man," whose analysis covered the period from 1910 to 1914 when Freud's authority was being challenged by the dissidents among his followers, provided a "test case," in his controversies with Jung and Adler, to prove that the neurosis had its origins in infantile sexuality. The "dream of the wolves" which his wealthy young Russian neurotic reported provided evidence that an infantile neurosis was at the core of his present symptoms. It was the "infantile neurosis" alone that the case report was designed to demonstrate; contemporary features of the patient's adjustment and relationship to the analyst received secondary consideration. Later teaching has not always emphasized the fact that Freud himself was not satisfied with the results and that almost immediately thereafter he proceeded to revise his therapeutic approach radically so as to give the present adjustment of the patient, and particularly his attitude toward the analyst, greater weight in the proceedings (Freud 1914, Kanzer 1966).

Harold P. Blum, whose paper on "The Borderline Childhood of the Wolf Man" (1974) opens our section on this case, challenges first the diagnosis of compulsive-obsessive neurosis which has always been associated with the patient, and suggests rather that his condition was "borderline" or even "paranoid." To establish a frame of reference consonant with a contemporary approach, he places the ample data which Freud gave us about the patient's childhood in a genetic perspective that permits a surprisingly modern "anamnesis" to be presented to us. It is within this context that he sets the individual incidents on which Freud laid great stress—traumata that were experienced—in phase-specific relationships to his family life that helped determine their impact on him. Preoedipal aspects receive greater due than were accorded them in Freud's evaluation: the oral significance of the danger posed by the wolves, for example, who made their terrifying appearance in his nightmare. Actually, the oral triad of Lewin, which the latter applied to this case (1950), is found to be very relevant. The phase in which the patient, as a child, had "two mothers," a peasant nursemaid and an aristocratic and ailing, often absent one, acquires great significance in predetermining conflicting lines of development within his personality.

Blum also re-assesses the period of treatment with Ruth Mack Brunswick when Freud had become critically ill and shows how much more it involved than a mere working through of residual transferences to Freud, as she assumed. Blum discerns a sister-transference to her that had not emerged during the treatment with Freud, as well as a "brother countertransference" which had its part in her insistence that he was not Freud's "favorite patient"; she herself was in analysis with Freud during a period when such incestuous arrangements were not regarded with any special misgivings. The role of the primal scene, on which both Freud and Brunswick laid so much stress, provokes Blum's scepticism. He would place more weight on such factors as malaria at the age of eighteen months, the hypochondriasis of the mother and the psychosis of the father as influences disposing the Wolf Man to a narcissistic line of development. We are led to wonder at the usual representation of the father in the case history as an incapacitated individual with a purely negative status and influence when we also learn that he was a leading liberal statesman of his generation. Blum sums up his viewpoint with the statement that "in the window of his nightmare, in looking and being looked at in the mirror, [the patient] attempted to face his conflicts, to find his narcissistic object and confirm his identity. The persecutory nightmare was repeated in the adult paranoia and followed by reparative efforts at ego mastery of the dread of borderline regression into narcissistic fusion."

In another article, "The Pathogenic Influence of the Primal Scene: A Re-evaluation," Blum points out that analysts have not yet fully resolved the problems of the primal scene. Analysts continue their search for full understanding of its influence. It is not yet certain whether primal scene experiences need be traumatic, disturbing or pathogenic. Their influence on mastery, maturity and sublimation skill requires study. Research on the role of primal scene observations in other cultures and the influence of such observations during different developmental stages must continue.

Robert J. Langs also offers several alternative and persuasive re-interpretations of the Wolf Man's analysis based on supplementing the infantile origins of transferences with a consideration of their current applications to Freud and to Brunswick. He points out, for example, a transference aspect to the dream of the wolves when, in the course of his associations, the patient described an experiment in which a follower of Pasteur inoculated the sheep on his father's estate whereupon the sheep died in droves. The Wolf Man apparently realized that more than therapy was involved in Freud's interest in him and drew a picture of the dream wolves that he turned over to Freud, whom he came to regard as a senior collaborator in an experiment. The essays in this section lead us to question whether he was altogether wrong.

Langs regards the experimental purposes to which the patient was put as a "misalliance," in contrast to a therapeutic alliance, and regards as "deviations" such coercive measures as setting a termination date for the treatment as well as Brunswick's insistence that he was not Freud's favorite patient. (To such "misalliances" might well be added the agreement at the beginning of treatment that the patient might hope to win over his girlfriend as a result and the temporary interruption of treatment to give him a chance to do so—developments not recounted in the official case history.)

Eugene Halpert casts light on a point in the analysis which is obscure in the recorded report but that is not without interest. After the death of his sister by suicide, the young man had stopped off at the grave of a noted poet who had been killed in a duel and gave vent to a great outburst of grief. Freud considered this a displacement from his feelings about the sister. He does not give the poet's name and Strachey surmises in the *Standard Edition* that it was Pushkin. Later however the Wolf Man revealed it to be Lermontov, whom he was said to resemble physically and in whose works he had been much interested. Halpert justifiably raises the question as to whether the mourning at his grave was for the sister or, narcissistically, for himself.

In "Freud's Search for a Primal Science," I underline the fact that Freud's determination to trace his patient's neurosis to an infantile neurosis concentrated more and more on the details of the primal scene he assumed to have occurred, on the age at which it was perceived and on whether or not it represented an actual memory or a fantasy. The circumstances in Freud's home as a child when he shared a room with his parents and younger siblings until the age of three would have been conducive to concern with dating the Wolf Man's primal scene at about the same age. (See also Schur 1972, p. 21.) He was so disturbed by his inability to come to a decision that he withheld publication of the case for four years and finally arrived at a remarkable conclusion: that even if the patient had not actually observed a primal scene, his racially inherited memories endowed him with one that would be instigated by related experiences in childhood (such as witnessing animals in copulation) and then would fill in the details for him.

I have noted the extraordinary weight that Freud placed upon verifying the reality of the primal scene and to opinions that no longer hold in psychoanalysis: "I must admit that this question is the most delicate in the whole domain of psychoanalysis. . . . No doubt has troubled me more decisively in holding back from publishing my case." He was able to comfort himself with the thought that "The description of such early phases and of such deep strata of mental life has been a task which has never before been attempted; and it is better to perform the task badly than to take flight before it" (1918, pp. 103–104). I suggest that these are the sentiments of a heroic investigator who feels that he has failed in his mission. By exploring the relevance of Freud's own early dream of his sleeping or dead mother borne by two Egyptian bird-headed gods, and quoting similar opinions by Eva Rosenfeld (1956), it seems that in pursuing the reality of the Wolf Man's primal scene, Freud was substitutively seeking to attain such a "final goal" for his own analysis. Two decades later, when Freud, in *Analysis Terminable and Interminable* (1937), acknowledged the unlikelihood that an analysis could be finally terminated, it was the Wolf Man that came to his mind: self-analysis was also interminable.

References

Arlow, J. and Brenner, C. (1964) *Psychoanalytic Concepts and the Structural Theory*. New York: International Universities Press.

Bell, A. (1961). Some observations on the role of the scrotal sac and testicles. *Journal of the American Psychoanalytic Association* 9: 261-286.

Blum, H. P. (1974) The borderline childhood of the Wolf Man Journal of the American Psychoanalytic Association 22:721–742. Part VI chapter 1 of this volume.

———— (1979). The pathogenic influence of the primal scene: A reevaluation. Part VI chapter 3 of this volume.

Breuer, J., and Freud, S. (1893-95). Studies on hysteria. *Standard Edition* 2.

Erikson, E.H. (1962). Reality and actuality. *Journal of the American Psychoanalytic Association* 10: 451-474.

Freud, S. (1900). The interpretation of dreams. *Standard Edition* 4 and 5.

———— (1909). Analysis of a phobia in a five-year-old boy. *Standard Edition* 10: 135-149.

———— (1914). On the history of the psycho-analytic movement. Standard Edition 14: 7-66.

Freud, S. (1918). From the history of an infantile neurosis. *Standard Edition* 17:7–122.

———— (1937). Analysis terminable interminable *Standard Edition*.23: 216-253.

———— (1954). *Origins of Psychoanalysis (1887-1902)*. New York: Basic Books

Gardiner, M. Editor (1971) *The Wolf Man by The Wolf Man*. New York: Basic BooksGill, M., and Muslim, H. (1976). Early interpretation of transference. *Journal of the American Psychoanalytic Association* 24: 779-794.

Greenson, R. R. (1965). The working alliance and the transference neurosis. *Psychoanalytic Quarterly* 34: 155-181.

Jones, E. (1955). *The Life and Works of Sigmund Freud,* vol. 2. New York: Basic Books.

Kanzer, M. (1966). The motor sphere of the transference. *Psychoanalytic Quarterly* 35: 522-539.

Kanzer, M. and Glenn, J., editors (1979). *Freud and His Self-Analysis.* New York: Jason Aronson.

Kris, E. (1951). Ego psychology and interpretation in psychoanalytic therapy. *Psychoanalytic Quarterly.* 20: 15-30.

Lewin, B.D. (1950). *The Psychoanalysis of Elation.* New York: Norton.

Kestenberg, J. (1966). Rhythm and organization in obsessive-compulsive development. *International Journal of Psycho-Analysis* 47: 151-159.

Major, R. (1974). The language of interpretation. *International Review of Psychoanalysis* 1: 425-436.

Nunberg, H. and Federn, E. (1962). *Minutes of the Vienna Psychoanalytic Society.* Vol. 1, 1906–1908.

Rosenfeld, E. (1956) Dream and Vision. *International Journal of Psycho-Analysis* 37:97–105.

Schur, M. (1966) Some additional "day residues" of the specimen dream of psychoanalysis. In *Psychoanalysis—A General Psychology.* Ed. R.M. Loewenstein, L. Newman, M. Schur, A.J. Solnit. pp. 45-85. New York: International Universities Press. Chapter 6, *Freud and His Self-Analysis,* volume 1 of the Downstate Twenty-fifth Anniversary Series.

———— (1972). *Freud: Living and Dying.* New York: International Universities Press.

———— (1971). More about rats and rat people. *International Journal of Psycho-Analysis* 52: 277-288. This volume, Part IV, Chapter 3.

Shengold, L. (1967). The effects of overstimulation: rat people. *International Journal of Psycho-Analysis* 48: 403-415.

Zetzel, E. (1956). Current concepts of transference. *International Journal of Psycho-Analysis* 37: 369-376.

———— (1966). The analytic situation. In *Psychoanalysis in the Americas,* Ed. R.E. Litman. New York: International Universities Press.

Chapter 2

CONCLUSION

MARK KANZER, M.D. and JULES GLENN, M.D.

In his paper on the Wolf Man, Harold Blum comments on the fidelity with which his instructors at Downstate reproduced without criticism Freud's case histories. Certainly it is not uncommon even today to find veneration vitiating the true legacy of Freud, which was to explore, innovate and decide for himself without awe of tradition or, for that matter, his own previous opinions. Blum, and so many other contributors to this volume whose education was at Downstate, seem to have imbibed the latter spirit, whatever the shortcomings of particular instructors. One of them recalls how futile it was to curb the spirit of inquiry among the students—a measure sometimes invoked to avoid embarassing displays of ignorance.

In contradistinction to the overidealization of the case histories is the feeling that they should be done away with, or at least reduced in significance, in favor of more modern and appropriate guidelines to current teachings in psychoanalysis. It seems as unlikely that this will occur as that the Greek plays or Shakespeare's works will be replaced by more contemporary productions. The timeless elements in Freud's case histories seem to derive from the fact that the inner workings of the patient's mind are bared for us so cogently and artfully that we ourselves are involved. This is sadly not always the case with the more technically and theoretically correct presentations of the present. Freud once remarked that *Oedipus Rex* unraveled like an analysis and we may say in turn that his analyses develop like great dramas that one never forgets.

429

The problem of correct teaching remains. Concepts and techniques have changed, often at Freud's own initiative, on the basis of the lessons to be learned from these very cases. The "Homosexual Woman," the last of Freud's cases to be published (1920), was compiled when Freud was on the eve of his theory of aggression and the structural framework of the mind. Child and adolescent analysis were in their infancy; Freud was to express amazement years later at the new discoveries about female psychology that were being made by women analysts. Nor did he leave psychoanalysis in such a petrified state at the time of his death in 1939 that it was incapable of further advances; it is advancing very rapidly today.

The very fascination of the cases, however, obscures the obsolescence of important segments both for students and teachers. The studies were frequently presented as fragments and designed to illustrate particular problems which have long been settled or seen in a different light. On the other hand, significance which Freud never saw in them has been adduced by modern observers and used to support contemporary arguments. An instructor is therefore called upon to take cognizance of these complexities. Can he do so without appearing to the students, or even to more conservative members of the faculty, as challenging Freud's authority and introducing elements of confusion? The fact is that the students themselves, particularly when, as is usual, they make their acquaintance with the cases early in training, often cannot appreciate the distinctions being made by the instructor and will resent his reservations about cases hallowed by tradition and stamped by authentic genius.

These problems are not lessened when the instructor, as is often the case, is a younger member of the faculty chosen on the assumption, which we find to be mistaken, that the cases "teach themselves." It follows from these considerations that candidates are most likely to be benefited when the cases are presented at a late stage of their training and by the most experienced and authoritative instructors.

Our volume necessarily places itself with the latter category. We have transposed the cases into modern frameworks, have provided supplementary material that has been culled over the years and have had the advantage of published follow-ups in some of them. The current disposition to see the analytic process as involving a two-person relationship has led us to focus upon Freud as well as the patient in the interchanges between them. His intuitive and pioneering interventions are part of the fascination that the cases hold and his choice of language and metaphors often indicates, on the basis of extensive self-analytic and biographical commentaries, the inner depths from which his conceptions arise and the suggestive influences that pass reciprocally between the patient and himself. In this sense, we regard ourselves as carrying forward an essential task of psychoanalysis that could rarely appear in Freud's published works: the alternations between the analysis of the patient and the self-analysis of the therapist.

Beyond the value of the cases in providing us with a history of analytic ideas, both theoretical and technical, as well as a valuable and unique approach to comprehending the genius of Freud, we find in them rare works of art and a record of the human mind in one of its most unparalleled works of scientific discovery. There is no illusion that we offer more than momentary and sometimes clouded glimpses of an odyssey, but we are encouraged by Freud's words that "It is better to perform the task badly than to take flight before it." A quarter of a century of teaching and study at one analytic institute offers a document that cannot be devoid of interest for psychoanalysts everywhere.

Appendix:

ABSTRACTS OF FREUD'S CASE HISTORIES

HARVEY BEZAHLER, M.D.

Summaries of Freud's analysis of Dora and his discussion of Schreber's Memoirs appear in "Freud's Adolescent Patients: Dora, Katharina and the 'Homosexual Woman' " (Part II, chapter 1) and "Teaching Freud's Case Histories: The Schreber Case" (Part III, chapter 4).

In this appendix the reader can find abstracts of the three remaining major case histories: Hans, the Rat Man and the Wolf Man. We do not intend these to be substitutes for the original articles or complete summaries. They will serve to refresh the reader's memory regarding the clinical course of the analyses, and will deal with theoretical issues only minimally.

Abstract of Analysis of a Phobia in a Five-Year-Old Boy (The Case of Little Hans)

In the introduction Freud presents the background material preceding the onset of the analysis of his "youthful patient." Hans was the son of a musicologist and his wife, a former patient of Freud's, both early adherents to psychoanalytic views. Following Freud's suggestion, Hans's father had made careful records of the child's development. Hans's early and continuing interest in his "widdler" (his penis) was in accordance with psychoanalytic constructions from adult analysis. Before he was three he observed a cow's udder and confused it with a penis. At that same age, when he asked his mother about her widdler, she deceptively informed him that she had one. Nevertheless, his curiosity persisted. The boy expended much effort to maintain his belief that both males and females have penises. He insisted that his little sister Hanna—born when he was three and a half—had one.

We learn of Hans's exuberant love life which involved many girls, male friends, and, of course, his parents. He revealed his awareness of pleasure in his genitals when he invited his mother to touch him following his bath; he was rebuked by her for doing this.

At age four and three-quarters Hans's neurosis appeared. In January, 1908, he had a bad dream in which he lost his "Mummy" and had no one to "coax with" (caress). Over the next several days concern about losing his mother (who would allow him into her bed to soothe him) continued, developing into a refusal to go on walks and culminating in his pronouncement: "I was afraid a horse would bite me." Freud dismissed his confessed masturbation as a source of the problem because it had existed for over a year. In fact Hans was presently trying to control it, a more likely factor in the generation of the anxiety. Freud advised the father, who had asked him for help, to inform Hans that the "business about horses was a piece of nonsense." Further, he suggested that the father tell Hans that he was fond of his mother and of being in her bed, and that his fear came from his interest in widdlers. Lastly, Freud recommended that father correct Hans's misconception concerning females; he was to tell him that they actually have no widdlers.

These directions were of minimal help. The symptoms ebbed but promptly returned after a bout of influenza followed by a tonsilectomy. The boy's father suggested that Hans's anxiety came from his masturbating and even placed Hans in a sleeping bag to aid in his control. The child then described a masturbatory fantasy: "I put my finger to my widdler just a very little. I saw Mummy quite naked in her chemise, and she let me see her widdler. I showed Grete, my Grete, what Mummy was doing, and showed her my widdler. Then I took my hand away from my widdler quick."

The sexual enlightenment fell on deaf ears. Instead of correcting a past error, Hans felt an intense need to reassure himself that his widdler was "fixed in." A former source of pleasure, the large animals in the park were now a source of anxiety, not just because of their size, but because he saw that his widdler was small in comparison.

Hans's father reported a fantasy which frightened Hans who then went to sleep in his parents' bed. A big giraffe called out because Hans took a crumpled giraffe away from it. When the big giraffe became quiet, Hans sat down on top of the crumpled one. This fantasy referred to the father's (big giraffe) unsuccessful attempts to keep Hans from going into his mother's (crumpled giraffe) bed each morning.

Freud met his little patient only once during his analysis. At that time he learned more details which enabled him to link father and horse. The black marks around the animal's mouth were like his father's mustache. In a bold interpretation, he told Hans that he is afraid of his father's anger over Hans's love of his mother, but that he need not be frightened. He could tell his father of his troubles with impunity. Some improvement followed, allowing Hans to venture out of his street door even when horses were passing. He expanded on the significance of his relationship to his father, attesting to his fondness for his father as well as his anger. He was afraid *of* his father who would retaliate in response to Hans's hostility, but he also feared *for* his father whom he loved as well as hated.

The complications and nuances of the phobia became more apparent. Hans focused on the comings and goings of wagons at a government warehouse across the street. He was especially upset about horses falling, carts starting to move, and horses moving quickly rather than slowly. Large horses provoked more fright than small ones. This was a typical extension of a phobia with links to chance events, wishes and feelings. Hans tried to deal with the phobia by pretending to be a horse and biting his father. Though he became freer in movement, even crossing the street, fear persisted and special preoccupations with black muzzles and making a row with one's feet intensified. Discussion of the foot noise resulted in Hans's revealing that he became angry when expected to go *lumf* (defecate) or urinate when he wanted to play. The subject of *lumf* led to his disclosing his pleasure when watching his mother on the toilet. Another source for the importance of horses was found in games Hans played in the summer when a child, acting as a horse, fell and cut his knee.

In the daily reports on Hans's analysis, the *lumf* theme became integrated with the other motifs and adumbrated an interest in pregnancy, in particular the birth of his sister Hanna who was equated with a bowel movement, a common infantile fantasy. The noise feces make in the toilet, the fear of heavy carts and a fear of a heavily-loaded abdomen all came into focus and appeared related. A fear of falling into the tub derived from a wish that his sister undergo such a fate.

Eventually Hans let his father know that he had been aware of his mother's pregnancy. The horses pulling wagons symbolized mother with her heavy abdomen. A series of fantasies depicted Hans's knowledge about his mother's pregnancy and the birth of his sister. His sister had been present, he correctly said, during their summer holiday before she was born. She had lived in the "stork box" and traveled to their vacation house in a special enclosure. Wishes to beat a horse reflected his infantile sexual desires toward his mother and antagonism toward his father, whom he wished to beat as a rival. Hans wanted to be rid of his father, whom he saw as "proud," like a horse, so that he could be alone with his mother when he came to her bed at night. Also, he wished his father would fall and cut himself, as the child who acted the horse had done.

Hans continued to struggle with the problem of pregnancy and birth as he thought of becoming a mother himself. Putting a knife into a doll's abdomen and then pulling it out of a hole between its legs, he symbolized the birth process. Seizing upon the fact that chickens produce eggs, he told of his wishes for a baby—he would lay an egg and out would come another Hanna. Hans's explorations always ended in confusion because he did not understand the difference between male and female genitals. Despite Freud's prodding, Hans's father only partially clarified the mysteries for Hans. He told him that mothers carry babies and undergo pain, like that felt during defecation, when they are being delivered. He did not tell Hans of the father's role. Despite these limitations in Hans's enlightenment, there was a substantial improvement in his behavior.

Their discussions led father to explore with Hans his desire to be rid of his father and to have his mother for himself. It was but a short step to his interest in having a baby with mother—the image of a loaded bus filled with people appeared here—but confusion as to the role of the man in having children interfered with its clear conceptualization. Almost his entire attention, as seen in his fantasies and games, centered on the pregnancy and birth theme as the analysis was coming to an end. As this increased there was almost complete loss of anxiety. Hans talked of having "his children" in bed with him, imagining having a baby when he made a *lumf*. He spent his time loading and unloading packing cases, simulating the activity in the courtyard opposite his house where he had been frightened of seeing loaded carts leave, a symbolic depiction of his mother being taken away from him at the time of confinement. In a master stroke, Hans told his father that he, Hans, would wed mother and have children while the father would be grandfather married to grandmother. Hans was cured, moving freely again without fear, even venturing back into the park. Hans revealed another reparative fantasy—a new version of an earlier one: "The plumber came; and first he took away my behind with a pair of pincers, and then gave me another, and then the same with my widdler." The father interpreted this: "He gave you a bigger widdler and a bigger behind."

Abstract of "Notes upon a case of Obsessional Neurosis" (The Case of the Rat Man)

A young man of university education presented himself to Freud complaining of obsessions dating from childhood which had become worse in the past four years. He feared injury to his father and a lady he admired, and suffered from impulses to cut his own throat with a razor. No prior treatment had helped, but when he engaged in sexual activity regularly he felt better. He described his sexual life as "stunted" and said that he first had intercourse at twenty-six. He had developed a peculiar obsession about rats which was to be associated with his name in Freudian literature.

The next meeting, the first analytic session, was reported in considerable detail. His initial statements that two men had reassured him of his ethical and intellectual qualities reflected a latent homosexual orientation. The first became his tutor when he was fourteen. The second man was a current friend in whom he confided. In the same session he said that after exploring the genitals of his governess, Frëulein Peter, when he was four or five years old, he was "left with a burning and tormenting curiosity to see the female body." Further sexual opportunities arose with a second governess and by six he "suffered from erections." He hesitated to turn to his parents, but had the idea that they knew his thoughts as if he had spoken them. He thought that he had to do "all sorts of things" to prevent the disastrous consequences of desiring to see girls naked.

From an early age he feared his father might die. His father had, in fact, been dead for several years when he first saw Freud, yet this fear had continued.

In the second session he told Freud of a related fear which plagued him. While on military maneuvers, he had learned from a captain, a man inclined to cruelty, of a particularly horrible punishment. Rats, enclosed in a pot, bore their way into the anus of the offender. He was suddenly struck by the idea that the rat torture was happening to someone dear to him—his father or his lady friend. Often he had to combat irrational obsessional ideas with other thoughts in order, he thought, to prevent a fantasy from coming true. For instance, when the captain gave him a package, a replacement for his lost pince-nez, and informed him that he had to pay the fee to a Lieutenant A., the patient immediately thought that he was *not* to give the money back; otherwise the rat punishment would materialize. A sanction—"You must pay the 3.8 *kronen* to Lieutenant A."—countered the previous thought. A confusing set of contradictory acts and plans followed, hinting at the unconscious motives at work. He tried to pay Lieutenant A. who refused the money, saying that the patient did not owe it to him. He planned to give the money to Lieutenant A. to hand over to Lieutenant B. to whom he now thought he owed the money. After deciding to visit his friend rather than find the lieutenants, he changed his mind and agonized over which station he should get off at in order to reach them. Eventually, he mailed the money to a young woman at the post office to whom the money was, in fact, owed. He had "known" throughout the time of his obsessional anguish that he owed the money to neither Lieutenant A. nor Lieutenant B., but to her.

Freud proceeded to detail the material of the fourth, fifth, sixth and seventh sessions. Nine years earlier, the patient's father had died in the Rat Man's absence. He knew that his sick father was in the midst of a medical crisis, but assumed erroneously that he would recover after the crisis and so went to sleep. Thereafter he thought and acted as if his father were still alive. Eighteen months later he started to feel tormented because he had not been present at his father's death.

In the ensuing sessions, Freud attempted to educate his patient about psychoanalysis. He told him that his feeling of guilt was justified but that the cause of the guilt was unconscious. He discussed the characteristics of the unconscious and the infantile sources of adult symptoms in relation to material his patient presented. The Rat Man, although skeptical, was taken with these ideas. He recalled "another self in childhood doing things." Ideas of his father's death had arisen from the unconscious mind several times in his life. When he was twelve he thought that such a misfortune would win the attention of a girl he liked. Shortly before his father died he thought that his father's demise would leave him wealthy and able to marry. He thus linked his inhibited sensual feeling and his father's death.

In the seventh session the patient described a "criminal act" he had committed before the age of eight against an ambivalently loved younger brother of whom he was intensely jealous. He pulled the trigger of a loaded toy gun as his brother looked down its barrel. Although he had wished to severely injure him, he merely hit his forehead. Freud suggested that the Rat Man must have harbored an earlier similar wish toward his father.

Freud stopped reporting individual sessions in detail and presented the themes that emerged as the analysis continued. (The "Original Record of the Case" comprising Freud's notes on the first four months of the analysis was published at a later date in the *Standard Edition,* volume 10, and has lent unique understanding of the actual interchange between Freud and this patient. It also amplifies our understanding of the Rat Man's neurosis.) He described the Rat Man's suicidal impulses in detail. A thought of cutting his own throat with a razor was a reaction to a wish to kill his lady's grandmother when his lady left him to nurse the elderly woman. The patient's intense reaction to jealousy and rage was further amplified when he imposed a vigorous weight-reducing regime on himself, a punishment for wanting to kill a man named Richard (Dick = fat) whom his lady admired. He also felt impelled to jump off a cliff, another self-punitive act. Other obsessions contained a wish to reassure himself of his lady's favor; to be sure that he understood her correctly, he repeatedly asked, "What did you say?" Ambivalent feelings toward her produced symptomatic acts of doing and undoing. He removed a rock from her path to protect her and then replaced it. The conflict, so typical of compulsive patients, between love and hate manifested itself in a dream expressing a fear that he would act impertinantly toward the analyst when condolence was appropriate.

At this point, Freud discovered the precipitating cause of the Rat Man's illness. The patient's mother had revealed a plan for him to marry a wealthy relative's daughter when his education was completed. The family plan placed the Rat Man in a conflictual situation. He had to choose between marriage for money and marriage for love to his poor lady. In fact, he found himself in a position similar to his father who had married his wealthy mother. A conflict between love for his father and his lady was thus exacerbated. By falling ill he avoided resolving the conflict. The patient became convinced of the reality of the dilemma through the transference. He imagined that Freud wanted him to marry his daughter for money—a fantasy that expressed itself in a dream in which patches of dung replaced her eyes.

The conflict with his father had its origin in childhood and appeared in his masturbation fantasies. The Rat Man's masturbatory practices were unusual in that especially fine or poetic moments associated with prohibition and defiance stimulated onanism. He also reported that, when a student, he would interrupt his studying shortly after midnight to open the front door as if to look for his dead father and then go back into the apartment and gaze at his penis in the hall mirror. The aim of this bizarre behavior was to please his father by his hard work and then defy him by his sexual activity.

Freud offered a construction to the effect that early in his life his father had chastised him for masturbation, causing the Rat Man to view him as a prohibiter of sexual pleasure. In response, the patient recounted a childhood tale that was told to him about an event that he did not actually recall. When he was three or four years of age he became furious after his father hit him as punishment for a forbidden act—biting someone, probably his nurse. Following this outburst he repressed his anger for fear of its murderous intensity.

Freud soon turned to unraveling the meanings of the patient's obsessive preoccupation with the army captain's rat story and the instructions to repay the money. Rats, particularly important to the patient, had many meanings. As a young man his father had been an ardent card player (a *spielratte* or play-rat) in the army. He had used group money to pay a gambling debt and was saved from legal difficulties by a friend who lent him money. The loan was probably never repaid. Owing the young postal service lady money led the Rat Man to identify with her father and also activated sexual feelings. In the patient's mind she was the rival of another young woman, the daughter of the inn keeper near the post office, again a situation reminiscent of his father's when he had to choose between two women. The patient's obsession regarding which of the two lieutenants he should pay also derived from this conflict.

The captain's description of the rat torture activated the patient's anal-erotism and evoked memories of the excitement he experienced when infected with intestinal worms in childhood. Rats (*ratten*) were anal symbols associated with money (installments = raten), particularly his payments to Freud and his father's legacy. The rat, in addition, stood for the penis which, like the rat, can transmit disease. Rats were equated with children; children, including the patient himself when he was young, bite, as do rats. In this regard, Freud noted that the Rat Man was fond of children and hence hesitated to marry his lady who was barren as a result of surgery.

After the rat language was mastered, the process by which the obsessional thoughts of the rat punishment were formed became obvious to Freud. He described the solution clearly:

When, at the afternoon halt (during which he had lost his pince-nez), the captain had told him about the rat punishment, the patient had only been struck at first by the combined cruelty and lasciviousness of the situation depicted. But immediately afterwards a connection had been set up with the scene from his childhood in which he himself had bitten someone. The captain—a man who could defend such punishments—had become a substitute for his father, and had thus drawn down upon himself a part of the reviving animosity which had burst out, on the original occasion, against his cruel father. The idea which came into his consciousness for a moment, to the effect that something of the sort might happen to some one he was fond of, is probably to be translated into a wish such as, "You ought to have the same thing done to you!," aimed at the teller of the story, but through him at his father. A day and a half later, when the captain had handed him the packet upon which the charges were due and had requested him to pay back the 3.80 *kronen* to Lieutenant A., he had already been aware that his "cruel superior" was making a mistake, and that the only person he owed anything to was the young lady at the post office. It might easily, therefore, have occurred to him to think of some derisive reply, such as, "Will I, though?" or "Pay your grandmother!" or "Yes! You bet I'll pay him back the money!"—answers which would have been subject to no compulsive force. But instead, out of the stirrings of his father-complex and out of his memory of the scene from his childhood, there formed in his mind some such answer as: "Yes! I'll pay back the money to A. when my father and the lady have children!" or "As sure as my father and the lady can have children, I'll pay him back the money!" In short, a derisive affirmation attached to an absurd condition which could never be fulfilled. pp. [217–218]

This was, for the patient, a crime against his father and his lady, and one which needed punishing; he was bound to an impossible obsessive task. The illness came upon him at a time of increased sexual tension and at a time of revolt against his dead father's authority as well as his attachment to his lady. The complicated interweaving of the obsession, once solved, allowed the rat delirium to disappear.

Abstract of "From the History of an Infantile Neurosis" (The Case of the Wolf Man)

Facing the defection of Adler and Jung, Freud returned to a primary source, a case study, to reaffirm the central importance of infantile sexuality in psychoanalytic theory. *From the History of an Infantile Neurosis,* taken from an extensive analytic treatment, deals largely with material focusing on early sexual stimuli and their continuing impact on the development of the patient. The history of the patient fell in two separate periods, an emotional illness precipitated at eighteen years of age after a gonorrheal infection which led him to analytic treatment, and a period from four to ten when he suffered first from anxiety hysteria with an animal phobia and then from religious obsessions. Freud concentrated on the early illness and offered relatively few comments about the adult illness. The paper contains comments directed at the "new" detractors of psychoanalysis, those who accept the method but dismiss essential aspects such as the existence of a sexual life in children.

This was a difficult and lengthy case for Freud. He made it clear that movement was very slow, the initial years yielding little for the effort. He evidences the degree of frustration he felt, tempered largely by his commitment to the method and belief in the validity of the concepts. He felt fortunate that circumstances eventually permitted him to pursue the intricacies of the patient's illness. Resistance, a seemingly intractable isolation, held sway. This very intelligent patient kept his analyst at a safe distance, "listened, understood and remained unapproachable" as he maintained an attitude of "obliging apathy." It was only through his positive attachment to Freud that the analyst could shift the balance and induce the patient to truly enter into the work. Finally, in a calculated manner, Freud set an irrevocable date for ending for the treatment, with the expectation that this would mobilize the patient. In a brief period of time, resistance lessened and a rush of material clarified the infantile neurosis.

His patient came from a wealthy Russian family. He had a sister two years his senior whom Freud characterized as "lively, gifted and precociously naughty." His parents were both ill, his mother with some form of gastrointestinal disorder, his father suffering from manic-depressive psychosis. The early years of his life were divided between two country estates and at about the age of five, a house in the city. At first his care rested with a "Nanya," but then briefly an English governess was involved. After the governess's first summer with him, his parents returned from a holiday to find him quite changed. He had become an irritable, violent, almost unmanageable child. They attributed the alteration either to the impact of the governess, discovered to be a drinker, or to battles between her and his beloved Nanya. For the patient that period of his life was at first obscure. He recalled intense disappointment about not receiving ample presents one Christmas, also his birthday, and therefore entitling him to a double share, and the onset of a strange animal phobia occurring sometime before he was five. The sight of a particular picture, a wolf standing upright, would lead to terror and screaming—a scene his sister delighted in precipitating. He once froze in fear while chasing a yellow striped butterfly. He remembered, in addition, a fear of beetles and caterpillars as well as a previous period in which he mutilated insects. Horses "gave him an uncanny feeling." He cried when he saw them beaten, but sometimes enjoyed beating them. The phase of anxiety was replaced by a period in which he was extremely and compulsively pious, given to long hours of praying and kissing holy pictures. Blasphemy existed side by side with religiosity. Thoughts, as "God-swine" or "God-shit," "three heaps of horse dung" signifying the Holy Trinity, marked this period. These early years also saw a shift from a close worshipful relation to his father to one of estrangement, disappointment and fear.

The Wolf Man's seduction by his sister at three and a quarter was crucial. Fantasies of his undressing his sister turned out to be reversals of memories of her playing with his penis and telling him tales of Nanya doing the same with others, like the gardener: "she used to stand him on his head and then take hold of his genitals." This sister, while an aggressive, intelligent child, developed severe symptoms in adulthood, and eventually committed suicide by ingesting poison. Her intellectual superiority plagued his early years, but at fourteen they became fast friends until he made a sexual overture which she rejected. He turned to a servant bearing the same name and thereafter sought women of inferior rank and intelligence as a lasting reproach to his sister. This, however, was but one source of his object-choices, as Freud later discovered.

Returning to the earlier history of his patient's childhood, Freud then discussed the consequences of the seduction. The Wolf Man soon turned from his sister to Nanya, masturbating in front of her, but was met with disapproval and warned that he would get a "wound." This diminished her in his eyes, but he continued to seek passive sexual satisfaction. In effect, the rejection as well as the activation of castration concern thwarted his genital activity and provoked an intense regression to the anal-sadistic phase. Cruelty to animals and his Nanya became his primary sexual outlet, and masturbation was suppressed. Masochistic as well as sadistic fantasies also arose at this time and served to expiate his guilt. He had fantasies of boys being beaten on the penis and of a young prince beaten in a dark narrow room. His father became a more important object, replacing Nanya, and he provoked him with naughty behavior to attain gratification.

This period of perversity dated from the seduction until he was four when anxiety entered the picture, ushered in by a key dream, a nightmare. The patient described the dream as follows:

> I dreamt that it was night and that I was lying in my bed. (My bed stood with its foot towards the window; in front of the window there was a row of old walnut trees. I know it was winter when I had the dream, and nighttime.) Suddenly the window opened of its own accord, and I was terrified to see that some white wolves were sitting on the big walnut tree . . . . There were six or seven of them. The wolves were quite white, and looked more like foxes or sheep dogs, for they had big tails like foxes and they had their ears pricked like dogs when they pay attention to something. In great terror, evidently of being eaten up by the wolves, I screamed and woke up. [p. 29]

Associations to this dream continued until the end of the analysis—and even beyond it. The initial associations given by Freud referred to the inactivity and intense staring in the dream; the history of the picture book wolf fear; white sheep that died; a story told by his grandfather of a tailor who cut the tail from a wolf only to meet him later in the woods where he saved himself by reminding the wolf of his missing tail; and another fairy tale, "The Wolf and the Seven Little Goats" in which a white-pawed wolf eats six goats, the seventh one escaping by hiding in a clock case. Actual work with this dream occupied Freud and his patient over several years. It led to the illumination of the infantile neurosis.

After focusing upon feelings for the father, represented by the wolf, we are directed to the use of transposition when the patient relates the opening of the windows to the opening of his eyes, as awakening, and the staring of the wolves to be *his* intense staring. Further, the idea of immobility is also a transposition. Motion, the opposite of stillness, characterizes what the child saw when he opened his eyes. Eventually, it was determined that the dream depicted, in a disguised form, a memory in which the Wolf Man awoke and opened his eyes to see his parents in intercourse.

Another memory fixed the dream to Christmas. A wish for satisfaction from his father activated castration anxiety which was expressed in the fear of being eaten by the wolf. Corroborating subsequent dreams, associations and memories led to the construction that at age one and a half the patient, after napping one afternoon at a time he suffered from malaria, awoke at about five o'clock to see his parents occupied in intercourse *a tergo,* that is, with penetration from the rear exposing both parents' genitals. This incident, which deeply impressed him, disappeared from consciousness but was worked on in his development and surfaced in organized form at the time of the dream. The position of his father was duplicated in the feared wolf picture which was traced to an illustration in the story "The Wolf and the Seven Little Goats." His mother's position in the primal scene determined his becoming sexually excited in his adult life when he saw a woman bending down with her buttocks facing him.

His religious preoccupations were filled with the ambivalent emotions typical of the obsessive: he kissed the holy pictures but also criticized God the Father for the existence of wickedness. Within the context of religion, many of his sexual preoccupations were further elaborated. He expressed anger with his father, homosexual wishes, and the idea that children could come from men or women. In addition he feared God, who had allowed his Son, born like the patient on Christmas day, to be killed.

A study of the patient's intestinal difficulties, in the adult neurosis manifested by constipation, brought together several more lines in the development of his sexual ideas. Significantly, there was an underlying identification with his mother and, through the cloacal theory, the belief in the anus as the female organ of sexual intercourse became more firm. In accordance with the laws of the unconscious, this belief existed simultaneously with the fear of castration which had also been activated by the primal scene. The castration anxiety of this man stemmed for his wish to be a woman; to become one required the loss of his genitals.

The Wolf Man's feminine identification persisted in the intestinal symptoms. Ultimately the associations led to the construction that the patient had interrupted the original primal scene by passing a stool and screaming.

With the announced intent to terminate the analysis, material flowed in a virtual torrent, clearing up many of the remaining mysteries. A particularly important series of associations centered around a fear of a butterfly with yellow striped wings which was linked to a pear of similar color called a "Grusha," which was also the name of an early nursemaid. It was with this maid, at age two and a half, that he urinated while watching her from behind as she washed the floor, and was admonished, probably in terms perceived as a castration threat. The view of Grusha revived the primal scene image of his mother. Urinating in Grusha's presence, a childlike seductive act, reflected his masculine identification. The emergence of the Grusha episode and its analysis explained his attraction to women of low rank—revenants of Grusha, who was in turn associated with his mother.

Another recollection cleared up one more aspect of the symptomatology: the feeling of seeing the world through a veil broken only at the moment of defecation after an enema. Associated with the information that he had been born in a caul came a superstitious conviction of invincibility which broke down when he acquired gonorrhea. According to Freud, who was attacking Jung's contention that rebirth fantasies were primary, the Wolf Man's wish to be reborn, achieved in fantasy when he felt as if the veil broke, was on a deeper level an expression of his desire to replace his mother and be sexually satisfied by his father. This was another aspect of his reactions to the primal scene which taught him not only the mysteries of sex but those of birth as well.

Once again, historical events, myths, fantasies and wishes weld together, leading to symptoms and character formation. Only through analysis of the individual history can the picture be fully understood.

In later years several relapses by the Wolf Man, and especially a period of treatment by Ruth Mack Brunswick (1928), added to the understanding of his mental disorder and problems of treatment associated with it.

References

Brunswick, R. M. (1928). A supplement to Freud's 'History of an infantile neurosis.' *International Journal of Psycho-Analysis* 9:439–476.

INDEX